Alina Szapocznikow
Sculpture Undone, 1955–1972

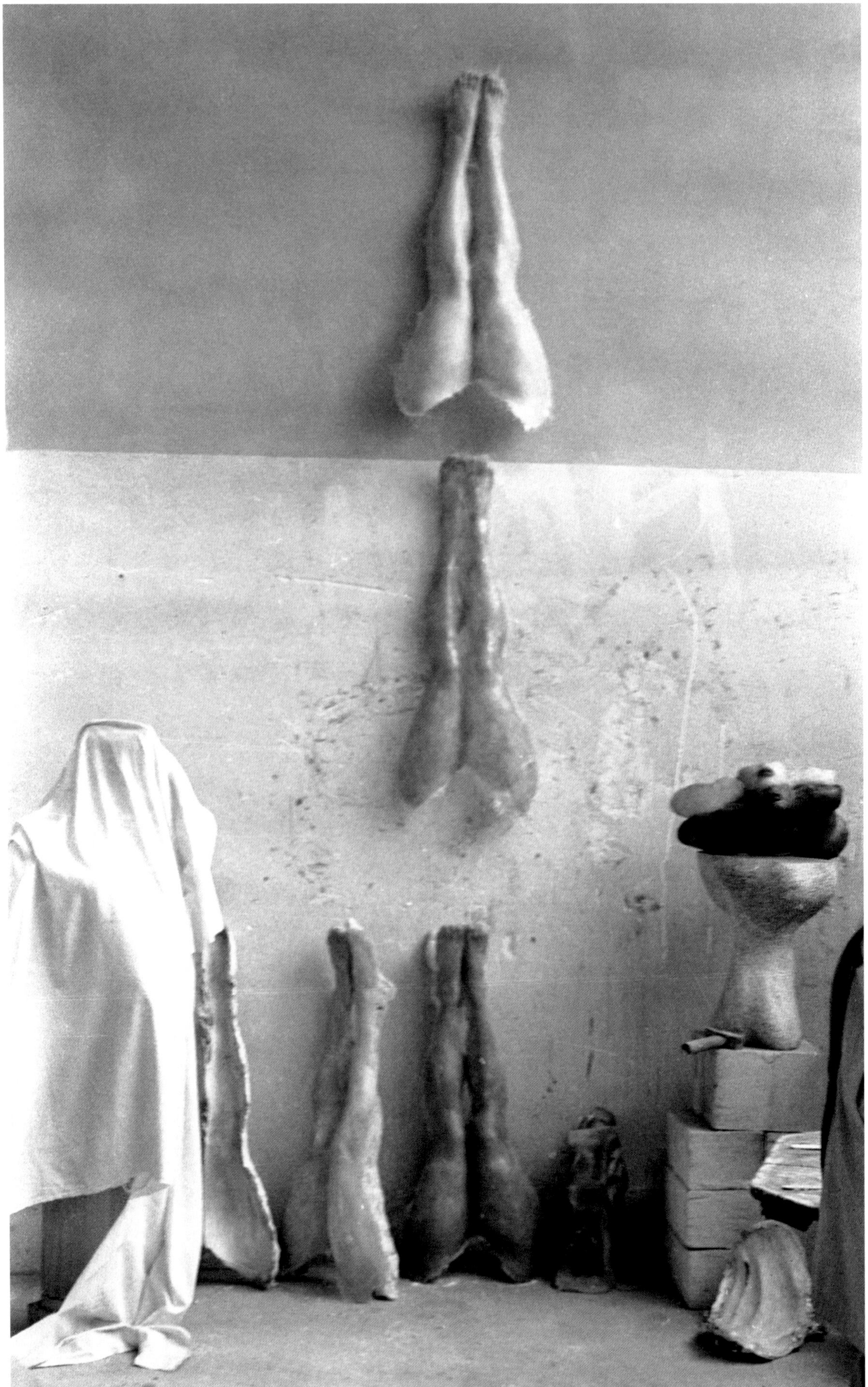

Alina Szapocznikow Sculpture Undone 1955–1972

Elena Filipovic and Joanna Mytkowska

Cornelia Butler
Jola Gola
Allegra Pesenti

The Museum of Modern Art, New York
and Mercatorfonds, Brussels

in collaboration with
WIELS Contemporary Art Centre, Brussels
Museum of Modern Art, Warsaw
Hammer Museum, Los Angeles

Published in conjunction with the exhibition *Alina Szapocznikow: Sculpture Undone, 1955–1972*, organized by WIELS Contemporary Art Centre, Brussels, and the Museum of Modern Art, Warsaw, in collaboration with The Museum of Modern Art, New York, and the Hammer Museum, Los Angeles.

Curated by Elena Filipovic and Joanna Mytkowska.

Tour of the exhibition:

WIELS Contemporary Art Centre, Brussels
September 10, 2011–January 8, 2012

Hammer Museum, Los Angeles
February 5, 2012–April 29, 2012

Wexner Center for the Arts, Columbus, Ohio
May 19, 2012–August 5, 2012

The Museum of Modern Art, New York
October 7, 2012–January 28, 2013

The initiation of this project was made possible through the key support of the Adam Mickiewicz Institute in the framework of I, CULTURE, the International Cultural Program of the Polish EU Presidency.

This exhibition and catalogue were generously supported by The Andy Warhol Foundation for the Visual Arts.

Additional support for the exhibition at WIELS in Brussels was provided by the Flemish Community, Brussels Regional Government, and the French Community, as well as the Polish Institute in Brussels and BNP Paribas Fortis.

Additional support for the exhibition at the Hammer Museum, Los Angeles, was provided by a major gift from Alice and Nahum Lainer. Generous support was also provided by Herta and Paul Amir, Alisa and Kevin Ratner, and The Audrey & Sydney Irmas Charitable Foundation.

Front cover: *Petit Dessert I* (Small Dessert I), 1970–71.
Back cover: The artist posing with body casts in her Malakoff studio, 1967.
Page 2: Studio view, including *Szkic I* (Sketch I, no longer extant), c. 1967.
Page 8–9: The artist in her Malakoff studio, 1967.

Produced by the Department of Publications,
The Museum of Modern Art, New York
11 West 53 Street
New York, NY 10019
www.moma.org

and

Mercatorfonds
rue du Midi 2
1000 Brussels, Belgium
www.mercatorfonds.be

Distributed in the United States and Canada
by ARTBOOK | D.A.P.
155 Sixth Avenue, 2nd floor, New York,
New York 10013
www.artbook.com

Distributed outside the United States
and Canada by Thames & Hudson Ltd.,
181 High Holborn, London WC1V 7QX,
United Kingdom
www.thamesandhudson.com

Edited by Lisa Gabrielle Mark
Proofread by Jane Hyun
English translations (pp. 28, 29, 108) by Elise Nussbaum
Designed by Luc Derycke
Layout by Studio Luc Derycke, Kristien Behets and Thomas Desmet
Production by Tijdsbeeld & Pièce Montée, Ghent, under the direction of Ronny Gobyn
Coordination by Hannelore Duflou, Tijdsbeeld & Pièce Montée
Color separations, printing, and binding by Die Keure, Bruges

This book is typeset in Minion and Pragmatica and printed on Condat Périgord 150g.

Copyright credits for certain illustrations are on page 215.

Library of Congress Control Number:
2011935487

ISBN 978-0-87070-824-4

Directors' Foreword

"Alina Szapocznikow: Sculpture Undone, 1955–1972" constitutes the first major assessment of the artist's experimental work outside of Poland and has been initiated by WIELS Contemporary Art Centre, Brussels, and the Museum of Modern Art, Warsaw. More than two years in the making, the exhibition reveals the utter contemporaneity of Szapocznikow's oeuvre. The artist's experimental practice and her unique way of grappling with such issues as memory, trauma, the Holocaust, and the human body in the world—as well as the way her work *undoes* rigid conformity to conventional forms or techniques—continues to inspire some of the most interesting and radical artists working today. Perhaps it is fitting that two fairly new institutions committed to contemporary art should galvanize a wider reassessment of Szapocznikow's complex oeuvre. The Museum of Modern Art, Warsaw, began this task with the exhibition "Awkward Objects" in 2009, which featured Szapocznikow in the context of other artists and was accompanied by an international conference and publication, all of which provided an important foundation for the research and development of this project. At the initiative of Curator Elena Filipovic, WIELS approached our colleagues in Warsaw to extend this effort by helping conceive the first major exhibition outside Szapocznikow's native country that would be uniquely devoted to her late experimental works, which remain little known. This project is the result of that combined effort and, we hope, will serve as a catalyst to articulate the artist's place in a new art history. The support and interest of the Hammer Museum, Los Angeles, and The Museum of Modern Art, New York, in presenting this exhibition after its presentation at WIELS helped us understand that there were institutions and publics similarly invested in finding a place for this important, yet nearly forgotten, figure. We are grateful for the participation of the Wexner Center for the Arts in the American tour of this exhibition and the commitment of Director Sherri Geldin.

This exhibition would be unimaginable without the support and cooperation of Piotr Stanisławski, the artist's son, who not only lent many of the pieces now held in the Estate of Alina Szapocznikow, but also offered his relentless encouragement and involvement every step of the way. We are similarly indebted to the Adam Mickiewicz Institute and its director, Pawel Potoroczyn, who understood the importance of making the artist's work better known and was instrumental in making the Brussels presentation possible in the context of the Polish Presidency of the European Union Council in addition to generously supporting the catalogue. The dedicated board of WIELS, led by President Herman Daled and Vice-President Pierre Iserbyt, as well as the many supportive members of the WIELS Club, have helped make ambitious projects like this a reality. Special thanks go to lenders, both private and public, who helped us bring together the most important examples of Szapocznikow's experimental late practice. Among those, we especially appreciate the following for collaborating to make large groups of works from their collections accessible (most never before shown outside Poland): Zofia Gołubiew, director of the National Museum in Kraków; Mariusz Hermansdorfer, director of the National Museum in Wrocław; Jarosław Suchan, director of Muzeum Sztuki, Łódź; and Wojciech Suchocki, director of the National Museum in Poznań. We warmly acknowledge Gisela Capitain, representative of the artist's estate, who provided generous assistance, and the Polish Institute in Brussels —including Director Beata Podgórska, Ambassador Slawomir Czarlewski, and Ambassador Jan Tombiński. We commend Elena Filipovic, co-curator of the exhibition, and Marta Dziewańska, curatorial collaborator on the project, for their impassioned commitment, and our gratitude also goes to Connie Butler and Allegra Pesenti at The Museum of Modern Art, New York, and the Hammer Museum, respectively, for their incredible enthusiasm and dedication to realizing this ambitious project with us.

Dirk Snauwaert
WIELS Contemporary Art Centre, Brussels

Joanna Mytkowska
Museum of Modern Art, Warsaw

Directors' Foreword

It is a remarkable privilege to collaborate with our European partners WIELS Contemporary Art Centre in Brussels and the Museum of Modern Art in Warsaw on the retrospective exhibition of the extraordinary work of Polish artist Alina Szapocznikow. We are honored to be hosting "Alina Szapocznikow: Sculpture Undone, 1955–1972," the artist's first museum exhibition in North America.

The Museum of Modern Art (MoMA) in New York and the Hammer Museum in Los Angeles partnered once before on another historic exhibition of an important late twentieth-century woman artist: "Lee Bontecou: A Retrospective" (2004) was co-organized by the Hammer Museum and the Museum of Contemporary Art, Chicago, and traveled to MoMA. That project brought back to public appreciation Bontecou's prolific and inspiring work. With the Szapocznikow retrospective, we present the work of an artist who emerged during the tumultuous postwar period—from her academic training in the Socialist Realist tradition and her early career designing monuments for the Communist regime—ultimately to create a body of sculpture that radically synthesizes Surrealism, Pop art, and conceptual practice in a short but surprisingly innovative career. This kind of scholarly curatorial reexamination is among the most valuable and rewarding work we do. The freshness and contemporary relevance of Szapocznikow's oeuvre argues for itself, and we are proud to be a part of recontextualizing it for a new generation of viewers.

We are grateful to our colleagues Dirk Snauwaert, director at WIELS, and Joanna Mytkowska, director at the Museum of Modern Art, Warsaw, for inviting our institutions to collaborate. We extend special appreciation to WIELS Curator Elena Filipovic who, together with Mytkowska, initiated the project and framed the artist's work through rigorous research and with acute curatorial intelligence. The Robert Lehman Foundation Chief Curator of Drawings Connie Butler at MoMA and Curator Allegra Pesenti of the Grunwald Center for the Graphic Arts at the Hammer Museum came together out of mutual enthusiasm for Szapocznikow's work and the belief that the time was right for greater exposure of this major artist in New York and Los Angeles.

We thank The Andy Warhol Foundation for the Visual Arts, especially Joel Wachs, president; Pamela Clapp, former program director; and James Bewley, program officer, for their early and generous support of this project. On behalf of MoMA, we thank Monika Fabijańska and the Polish Cultural Institute, New York, for providing early travel and research support when Anda Rottenberg, curator of Szapocznikow's 1998 retrospective at Zachęta Gallery of Art, Warsaw, solicited MoMA's participation in the important conference organized by the Museum of Modern Art in Warsaw in 2009. On behalf of the Hammer Museum, we would like to express our sincere gratitude to Alice and Nahum Lainer, Herta and Paul Amir, Alisa and Kevin Ratner, and The Audrey & Sydney Irmas Charitable Foundation for their support of the Los Angeles presentation of the exhibition.

We are grateful to the wonderful lenders who parted with extremely fragile works in recognition of the importance of this project. Our deepest appreciation goes to Piotr Stanisławski, the artist's son, not only for the loans of many precious works from both the estate and his personal collection but also for his commitment to this undertaking. It is because of his belief that his mother's art deserves broad and scholarly attention that this project came to fruition.

Glenn D. Lowry
The Museum of Modern Art, New York

Ann Philbin
Hammer Museum, Los Angeles

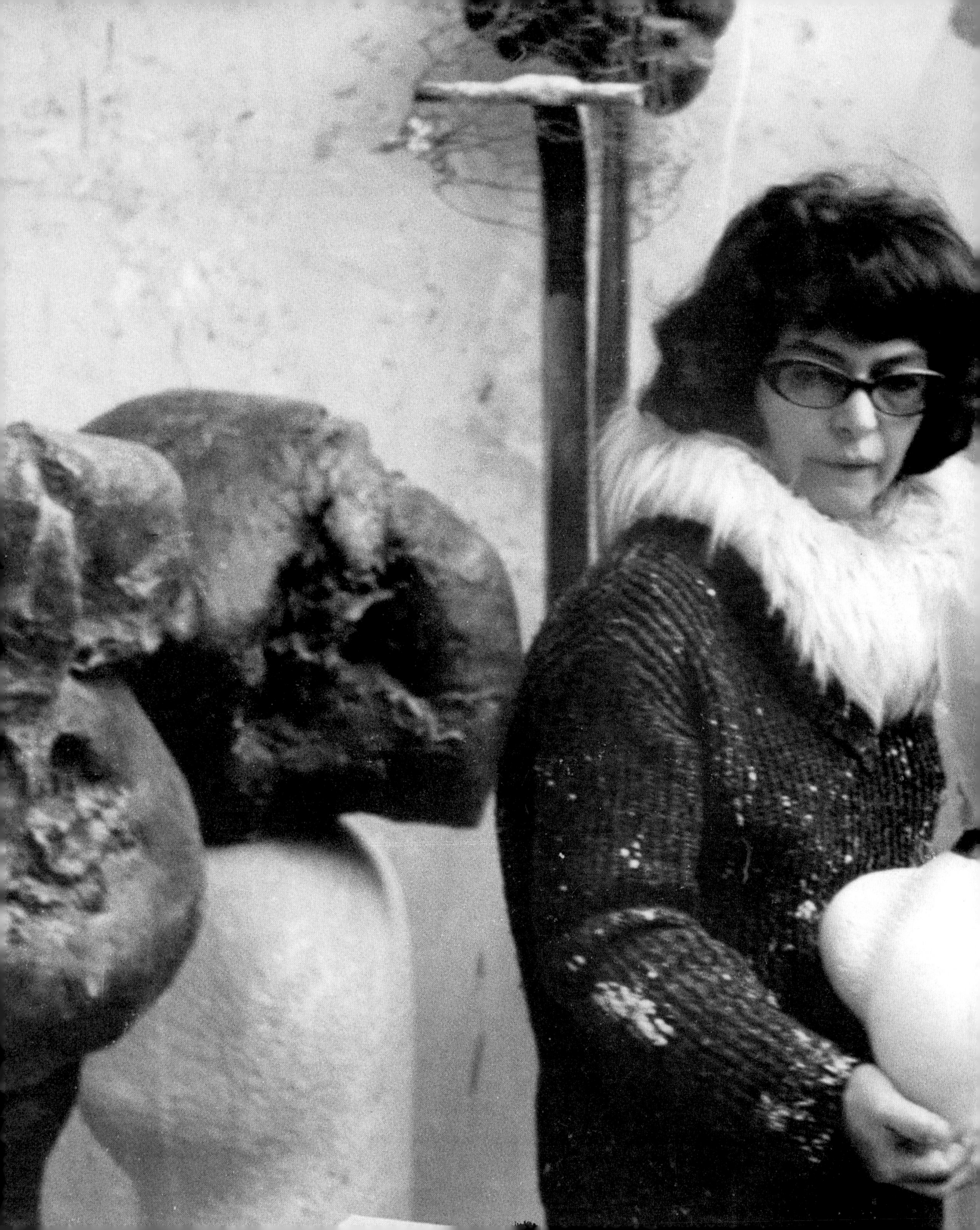

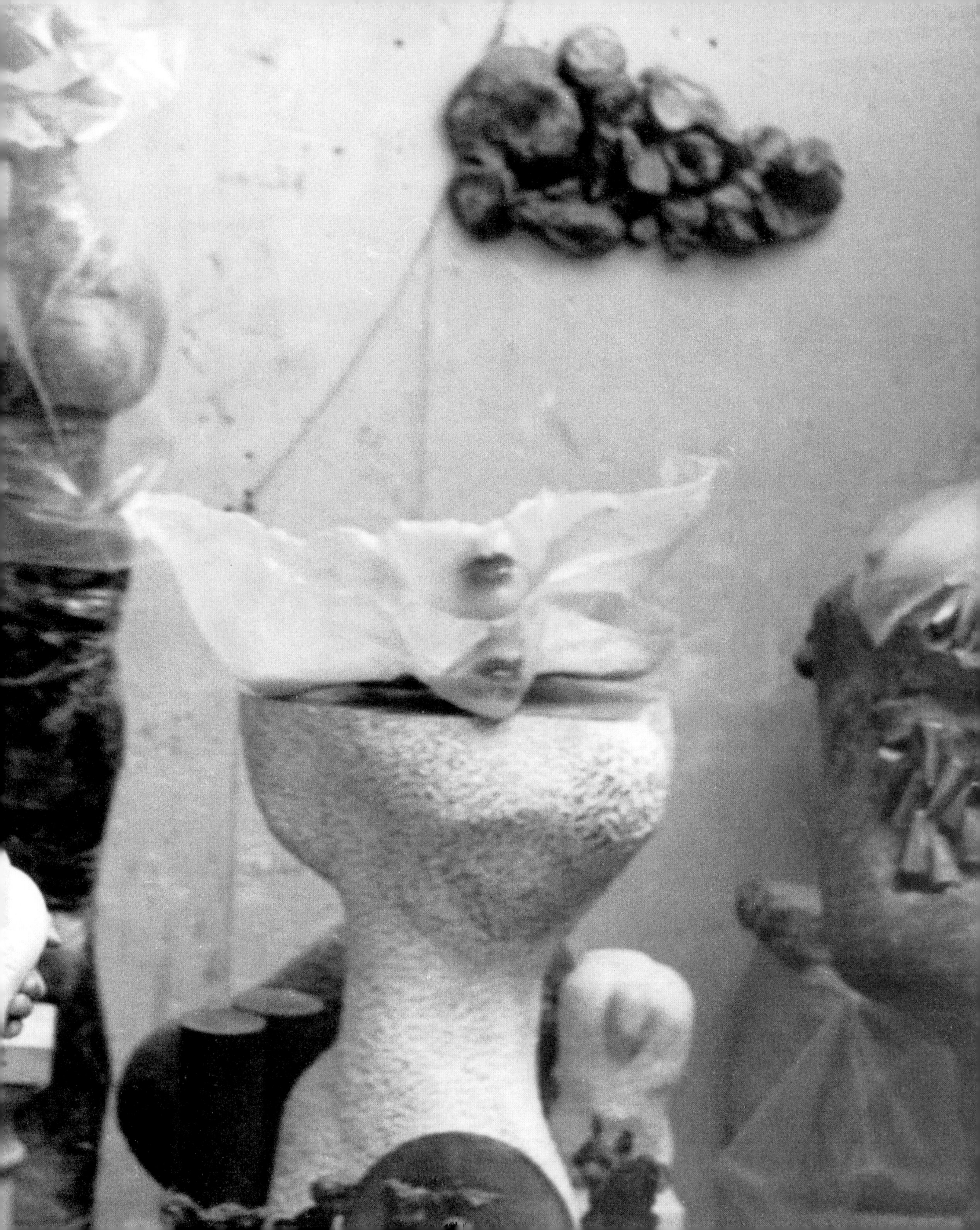

Introduction

Elena Filipovic and Joanna Mytkowska

Nearly forty years after her death, the restlessly experimental oeuvre of Alina Szapocznikow remains unfinished business—her place in the history of art not yet secured despite the radical innovation of her practice and the way her work continues to speak with urgency. This expansive solo exhibition, one of the first large-scale surveys of the artist's work outside Poland, encompasses the period from 1955 to just before her untimely death in 1973, at age forty-seven, concentrating in particular on the mid-1960s and early 70s. This experimental phase of the artist's oeuvre—which is the crux of this exhibition—marks her use of new and unorthodox materials, methods, and forms.

Born in 1926 to a Jewish intellectual family in Kalisz, Poland, at age sixteen Szapocznikow was sent to the camp of Bergen-Belsen via Auschwitz. She survived thanks to her mother's work as a doctor, as she served as her assistant. After the war, she did not return to Poland but instead went to Prague, where she studied sculpture, leaving in 1948 for Paris to study at the École des Beaux Arts. Summoned by the Polish government and suffering from tuberculosis, she returned to Poland in 1951, where interest in her work grew quickly. She was invited to take part in a number of public commissions and exhibitions—including, most notably, a solo show at the prestigious Zachęta National Gallery of Art in Warsaw in 1957 and the Venice Biennale in 1962, where she represented her country with two other artists. Having achieved success in Poland, in 1963 she left for Paris, where she was part of the intellectual and artistic milieu gathered around Pierre Restany and the Nouveaux Réalistes. There she produced feverishly, exhibited sporadically, and remained for the rest of her life.

Spanning one of the most rich and complex periods of the twentieth century, Szapocznikow's oeuvre responded to many of the ideological and artistic developments of her time. Still, as a sculptor who emerged during the postwar period working in a classical figurative manner, Szapocznikow's later conception of sculpture shifted considerably, leaving behind a legacy of provocative objects—at once sexualized, fragmented, vulnerable, humorous, and political—that sit uneasily between Surrealism, Nouveau Réalisme, and Pop art. While she has been well known and highly influential in Poland since early in

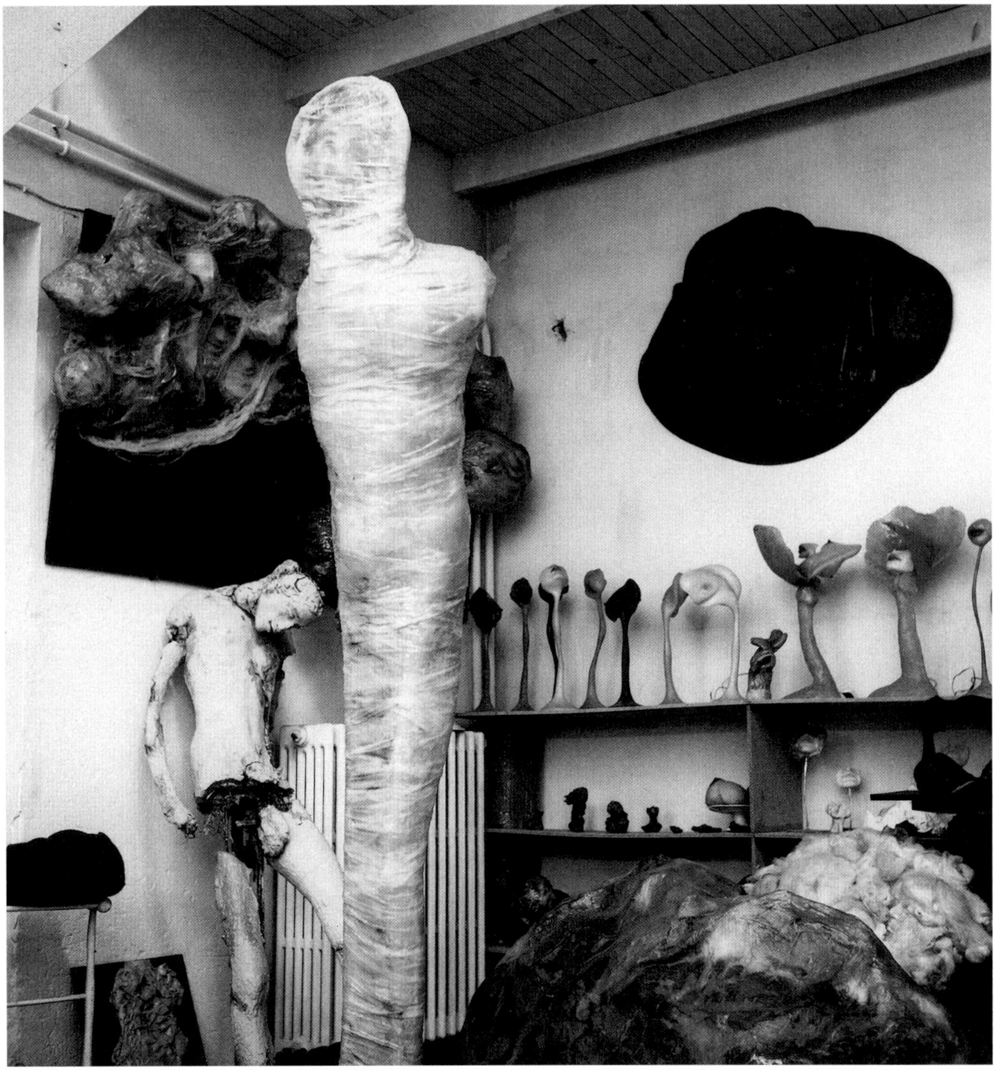

1. View of Malakoff studio, 1971.

her career, her work has remained more obscure internationally, and what little attention it has received has been largely infused with biographical determinism, disproportionately focused on the trauma of her concentration-camp experiences, recurrent ill health, and premature death. As a result, Szapocznikow's work has suffered posthumously from a foreclosure of meaning, its critical discourse becoming ossified despite the work's continued contemporaneity and dynamism—linking as it does Eastern and Western European influences, classical figuration and experimental body art, the theoretical model of the index and the practice of sculpture, and the auratic art object and the notion of commodity. To look at her body of work today [ill. 1] is thus to understand that Szapocznikow's oeuvre unquestionably merits a place in the history of contemporary art, alongside many artists—like Lynda Benglis, Eva Hesse, Paul Thek—who were working in the same period and whose exploration of new sculptural methods and materials, though belatedly considered, have helped to reimagine sculpture as it was traditionally understood.

Szapocznikow's thematic and stylistic range is impressive: one need only note the differences between works such as *Ekshumowany* (*Exhumed*, 1957) [ill. 2, plate 146], a truncated body whose abraded surface and haunting posture evoke corpses recovered from mass

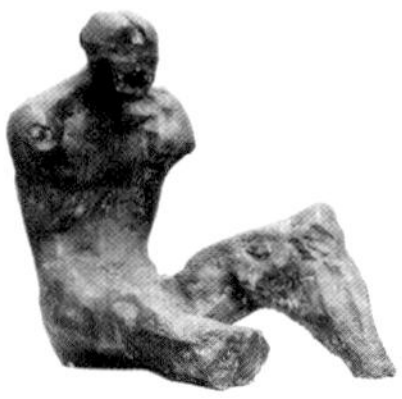

2.

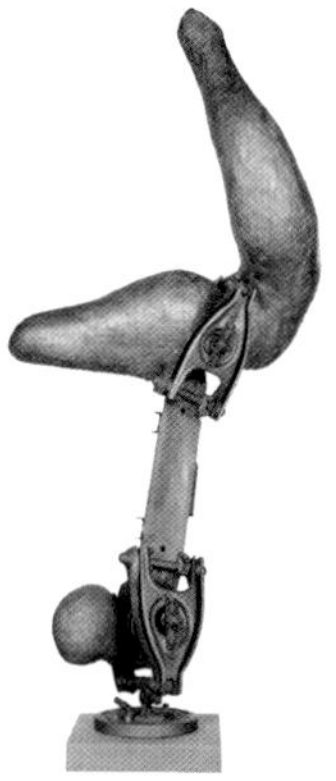

3.

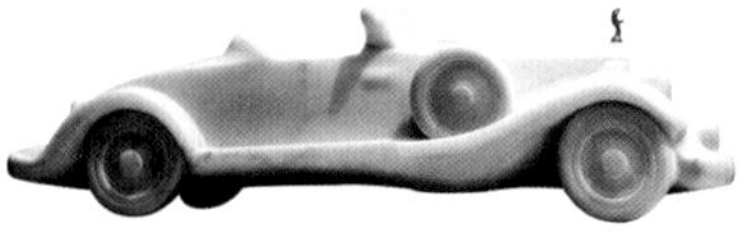

4.

graves; *Goldfinger* (1965) [ill. 3, plate 101], a shimmering display of two golden, cement, leg-like forms spread with a readymade car part in between, its title referring to the James Bond film of the same name; and *Rolls Royce II* (1971) [ill. 4, plate 35], a pink Portuguese marble model for an unrealized two-to-one-sized replica of the eponymous luxury car that she had intended to make. This range expanded over time as her experimentation with materials brought her to new and unusual substances, like polyester resin and polyurethane foam, used mainly by the commercial construction industry at the time. With these materials, Szapocznikow was able to extend her questioning of corporeal form and go beyond merely representing the body to casting directly from it.

Her experiments assumed many guises, including domestic and utilitarian objects from the mid-1960s, such as desk lamps featuring elongated stems topped with glowing casts of the artist's own lips made from polyester resin and cushions in soft polyurethane foam cast from a friend's voluptuous belly—both intentionally courting a space of ambiguity between art objects and prototypes for mass production. Her series Desserts (1970–71) [plates 20–22] tackled the commodity differently, combining readymade elements like dessert trays and glass bowls with cast body parts and oozing, brightly colored forms, creating a correlation between the fragmented body and indulgent foodstuff. These diminutive objects turned Pop's commentary on mass consumption into something carnal and uncanny, black-humored and biting, a combination that characterized so much of her work.

Starting in 1968, Szapocznikow's use of poured polyurethane, which congealed into something relatively rigid, opened up still more possibilities for rethinking conventional sculptural form and resulted in some of her darkest works (both literally and metaphorically), with cast body parts such as legs, bellies, and torsos becoming encrusted in spills of lavalike foam. These gave way to the Tumeur (Tumor, 1969) series [plate 60]—in which quickly drying polyester resin was coaxed into haunting, formless agglutinations, paralleling the development of her cancer and revealing the aplomb with which she managed to approach her own impending death—and the Fétiches (Fetishes, 1970–71) [plates 29–34], in which elements of her clothing or other memorabilia were covered in layers of the same polyester resin.

Around that time Szapocznikow began to actively incorporate photography into her work and, for the first time, direct references to the horrors of the Holocaust. During the last year of her life she also labored on two major works: *Piotr* (1972) [ill. 8, plate 6], a leaning life-size polyester cast of her son that summarized so many of her sculptural concerns, and the Herbier (Herbarium) series (1972) [plates 2–4], in which thin layers of polyester taken from casts of her son's face or body were flattened and attached to wooden panels before they had solidified into hardened forms. Hung on the wall like paintings but engaging all the peculiar materiality and spatial problems of sculpture, the strangely arresting skin-like forms literalize Szapocznikow's long-standing quest to create imprints or traces of the human body *as* sculpture. This also points back to the drawings and monotypes that consistently accompanied her process, allowing her to think through and about the body and its objectification. To look closely at the artist's prints and drawings is also to witness how she struggled with and attempted to reimagine sculptural form.

Haunting, visceral, playful, strange, sensual, unsettling, devastatingly critical, endlessly uncanny—these words hardly begin to describe fully Szapocznikow's output of lips,

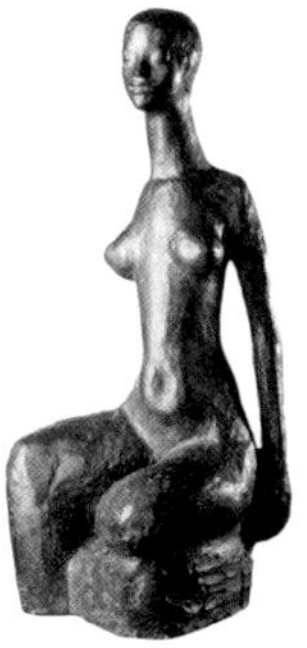
5.

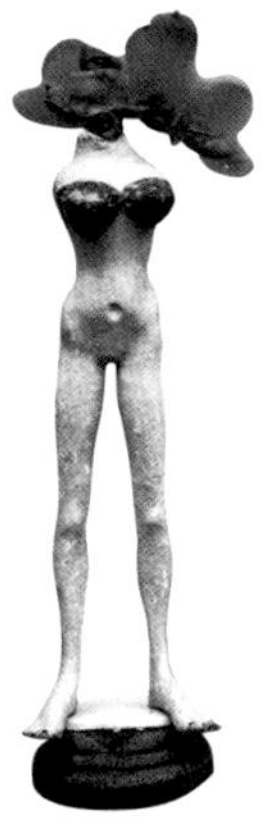
6.

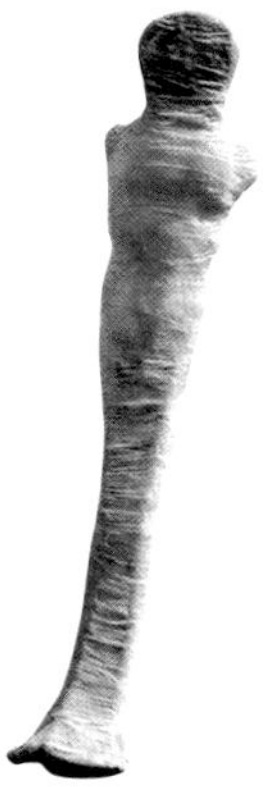
7.

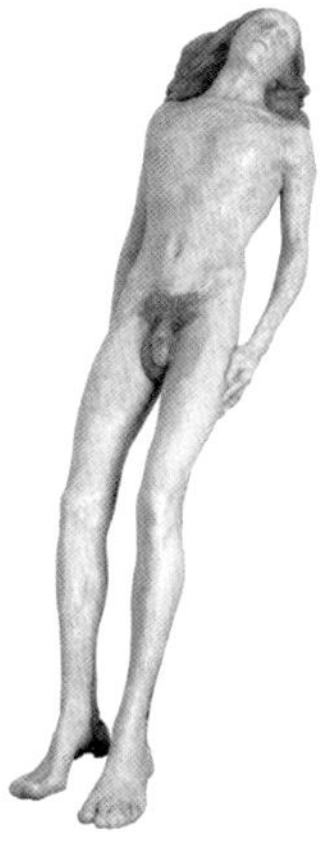
8.

breasts, bellies, lugubrious forms, and accretions of matter. Her focus remained fixed on the body—its experiences and limitations—but also the vulnerability at the heart of the human condition. As Pierre Cabanne noted the year of her death, "In the catalogue of Alina's fetishes, eroticism becomes transformed into exorcism; one never knows precisely whether the breasts or thighs emerge from a bed which is ravished by embraces, or else by the mud of Hiroshima. One never knows whether they reveal love or death."[1] Indeed her work maintained a willful ambiguity between anguish and ecstasy, Eros and Thanatos, humor and self-degradation, but also, at times, between sculpture and something less defined, more evanescent. The result, as Griselda Pollock astutely observed, "[is] not expanded sculpture so much as dissolving… Szapocznikow's work reformulated modes for confronting the body, embodiment, carnality, sexuality and, always, death."[2]

Szapocznikow's is a story of sculpture's undoing—in which, through the act of making, the category of sculpture is undone from within. Over the course of her life and evident particularly in her late work, her heretical approach to sculpture and its materials constantly questioned and redefined her own practice in order to destabilize the idea of what constitutes sculpture. In Szapocznikow's view, she was engaged in making nothing more than "awkward objects," a self-conscious response to what she considered "the failure of a thwarted vocation."[3] In her hands, sculpture thus became a conglomeration of fragments, multiples, formless things, and quotidian objects. And if, materially, her works often suggest tentativeness or fragility, many works also indicate how much formal disequilibrium was also part of her radical thinking. Even some of her earliest sculptures have elements that are strangely attenuated: the extended necks in *Pierwsza miłość* (*First Love*, 1954) [ill. 5, plate 147] and *Trudny wiek* (*Difficult Age*, 1956) [plate 149], or the strangely elongated legs of *Femme illuminée* (*Illuminated Woman*, 1966–67) [ill. 6, plate 91]. These are figures whose centers of gravity have shifted, whose heads or legs might not indeed be consistent with the rest of their bodies. These attenuations presage the way later works flirt with precariousness, which, too, became a form of sculptural undoing.

Some of Szapocznikow's sculptures are hopelessly fragile, already broken or requiring support, as if their undoing and destruction *inheres* in the work itself. Throughout her oeuvre, there is a willed instability and a persistent play with gravity; many are top heavy, ungainly, not able to support their own weight, including *Caprice – Monstre* (*Caprice – Monster*) [plate 92], *L'Apesanteur (Hommage à Komarow)* (*Weightlessness [Homage to Komarov]*) [ill. 7, plate 90], and *Le Voyage* (*Journey*) [plate 89], all from 1967, as well as *Piotr* and the Fiancée folle (Mad fiancée) sculptures (1971) [plates 7–10]—not to mention lamps on which glowing lips hover atop elongated stems, including *Lampe – bouche* (*Illuminated Lips*, 1966) [plate 17]. They court what could be called a vertigo of form, refusing the stable ground upon which so much traditional sculpture stands. Laboring at the margins of classical sculpture, Szapocznikow veered towards making objects that perform their very recalcitrance to erectness and stability; they stand precariously between uprightness and toppling destruction.

It is fitting, then, that when asked to contribute to Pierre Restany's conceptual exhibition project "Operazione Vesuvio" (1972), to be held near Mount Vesuvius, Szapocznikow imagined filling the volcano's crater with ice, making it a massive ice-skating rink, complete with radio contact and the wafting sounds of a waltz.[4] She noted cheekily that if the volcano spontaneously erupted, the ice skaters would be forever

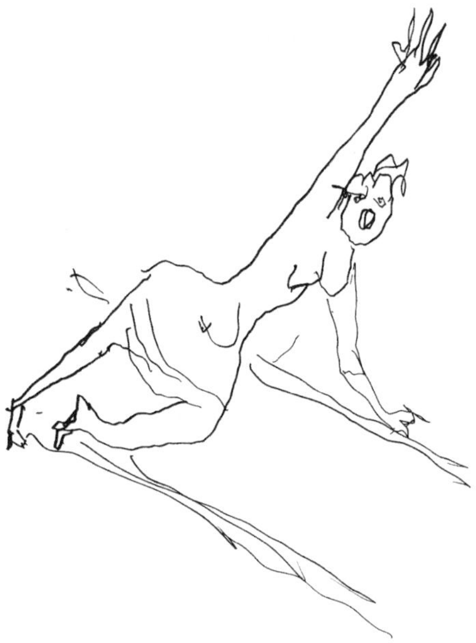

9. Untitled (The Last Drawing from the Hospital), 1973. Felt-tip pen on paper, 8 3/16 x 5 3/16" (20.7 x 13.2 cm). Location unknown.

embalmed by the molten lava. Not only does the volcano become an oversized version of her wildly organic forms, but the act of skating—that is, sliding forward on two thin blades of metal seemingly in defiance of gravity—is indicative of the tenuous balance that her work maintains. This idea is echoed in Untitled (The Last Drawing from the Hospital) [ill. 9], dated the year of her death, in which the artist depicted herself waving, thrust forward and balanced uneasily on a treacherous incline. Szapocznikow's work can thus be read as a metaphor for the fate and functioning of the body itself, that "most vulnerable" of all "manifestations of the ephemeral," as she would say.[5] She seems to suggest that if the body is impermanent, vulnerable, and under constant threat—and if our existence is transient—sculpture should be, too.

"Alina Szapocznikow: Sculpture Undone, 1955–1972" and this accompanying catalogue pay homage to the fearlessness that is at the heart of the artist's oeuvre. Featuring roughly one hundred artworks, as well as archival documents and other preparatory and documentary materials, the exhibition shows the array of materials and processes with which Szapocznikow was engaged and suggests the roles played by photography and drawing in relation to her primary practices of sculpture and object-making. The exhibition itself is loosely arranged according to chronology from 1955 onward. Starting with the end of Stalinism in Poland and the rise of state-sanctioned artistic freedom, which was coincident with her own formal experimentation, and concluding with her very last works, the exhibition is arranged according to her different series and themes. However, it is important to note that there is little that is easy or neat in the progression of Szapocznikow's work. Instead, one finds it full of returns and lateral, experimental moves, simultaneously edging towards and away from history, trauma, memory, and solidity—the sole constant being, perhaps, the fragmented body. It tells the story of one artist's attempt at undoing, not only the classical integrity and equilibrium through which the body—and indeed sculpture itself—is traditionally represented, but also art's myths of mastery and the art-historical narratives from which Szapocznikow was otherwise excluded. Attempting to decisively claim her place in the history of art, this exhibition is a testament to her remarkable oeuvre, its prescience, inventiveness, criticality, sensuousness, and humor—full of purposefully precarious and awkward objects that show us what it can mean to create a body of work that both advances and undoes sculpture from within.

Notes

1. Pierre Cabanne, "Alina: Against All Odds" (1972), reprinted in *Alina Szapocznikow. Zatrzymać życie. Rysunki i rzeżby (Capturing Life. Drawings and Sculptures)*, ed. Józef Grabski (Kraków and Warsaw: IRSA, 2004), 126.
2. Griselda Pollock, "Too Early and Too Late: Melting Solids and Traumatic Encryption in the Sculptural Dissolutions of Alina Szapocznikow," in Agata Jakubowska, ed., *Alina Szapocznikow. Awkward Objects* (Warsaw: Museum of Modern Art, 2011), 99.
3. Szapocznikow, statement, March 1972, "Mon oeuvre puise ses racines…," signed typescript. See page 28, elsewhere in this volume.
4. Szapocznikow, statement, March 1972, "Patinoire dans le cratère du Vésuve," typescript. See page 29, elsewhere in this volume, as well as Anke Kempkes, "Black Drips and Dark Matter, The Luxury Gap, Concept Individual, Quarry Dessert: The Incommensurable Contemporaneity of Alina Szapocznikow," in *Alina Szapocznikow* (2011), 170.
5. Szapocznikow, statement, March 1972, "Mon oeuvre puise ses racines…," signed typescript. See page 28, elsewhere in this volume.

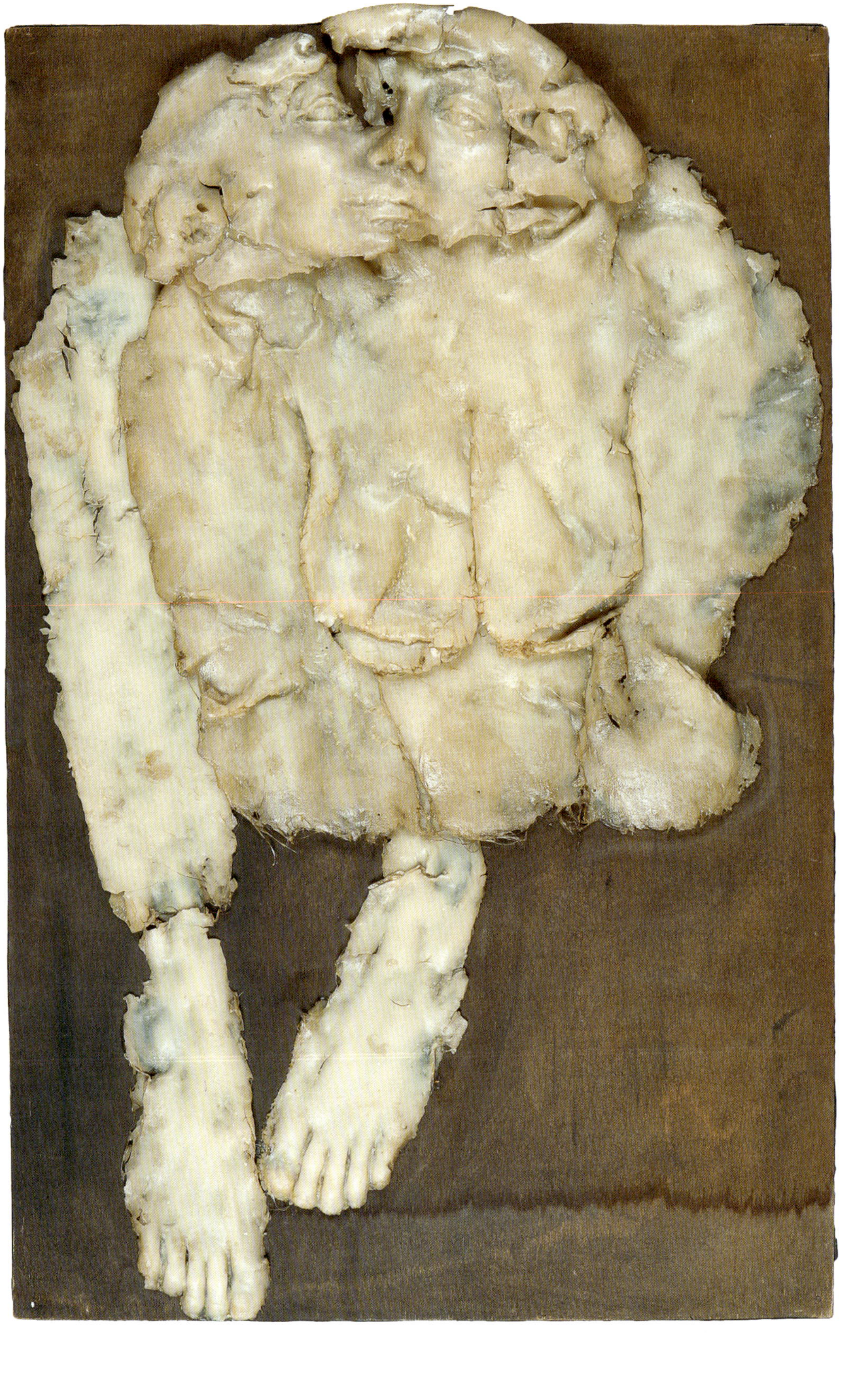

Plate 1

Autoportrait – Herbier (Self-portrait – Herbarium), 1971
Polyester and polychrome wood
31 7/8 x 20 1/2 x 2" (81 x 52 x 5 cm)

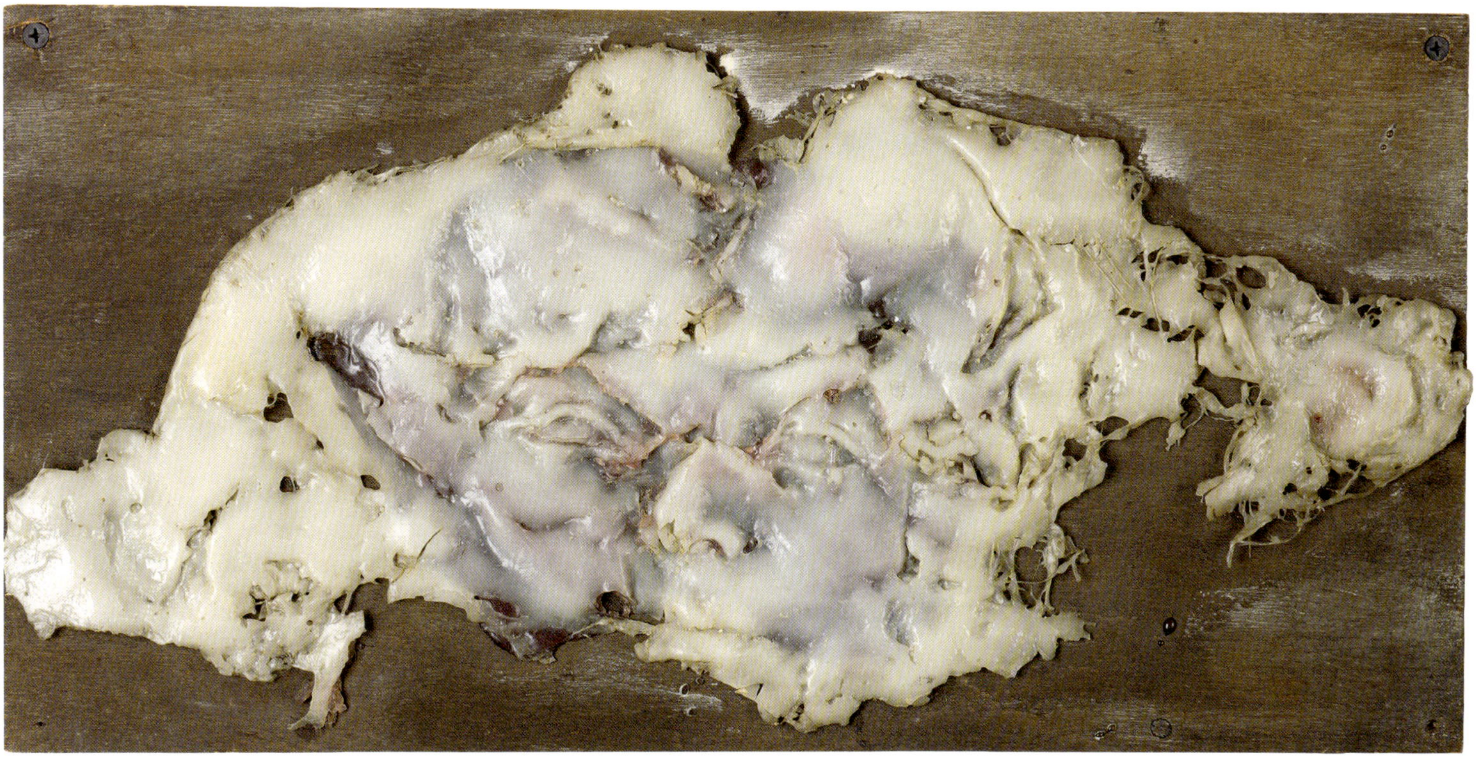

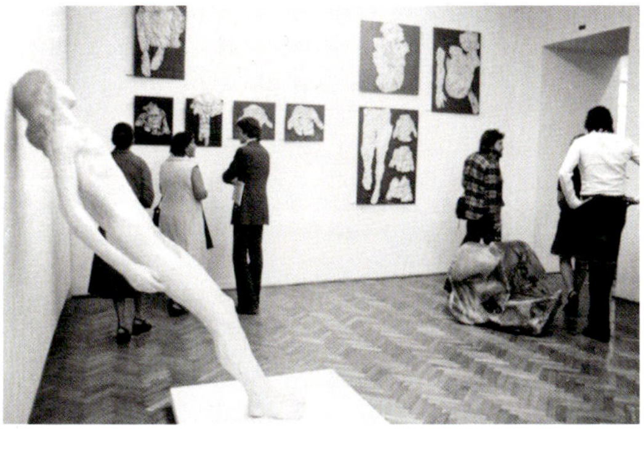

Muzeum Sztuki, Łódź, 1975.

Plate 2

Herbier XI (Herbarium XI), 1972
Polyester resin and polychrome wood
9 7/16 x 15" (24 x 38 cm)

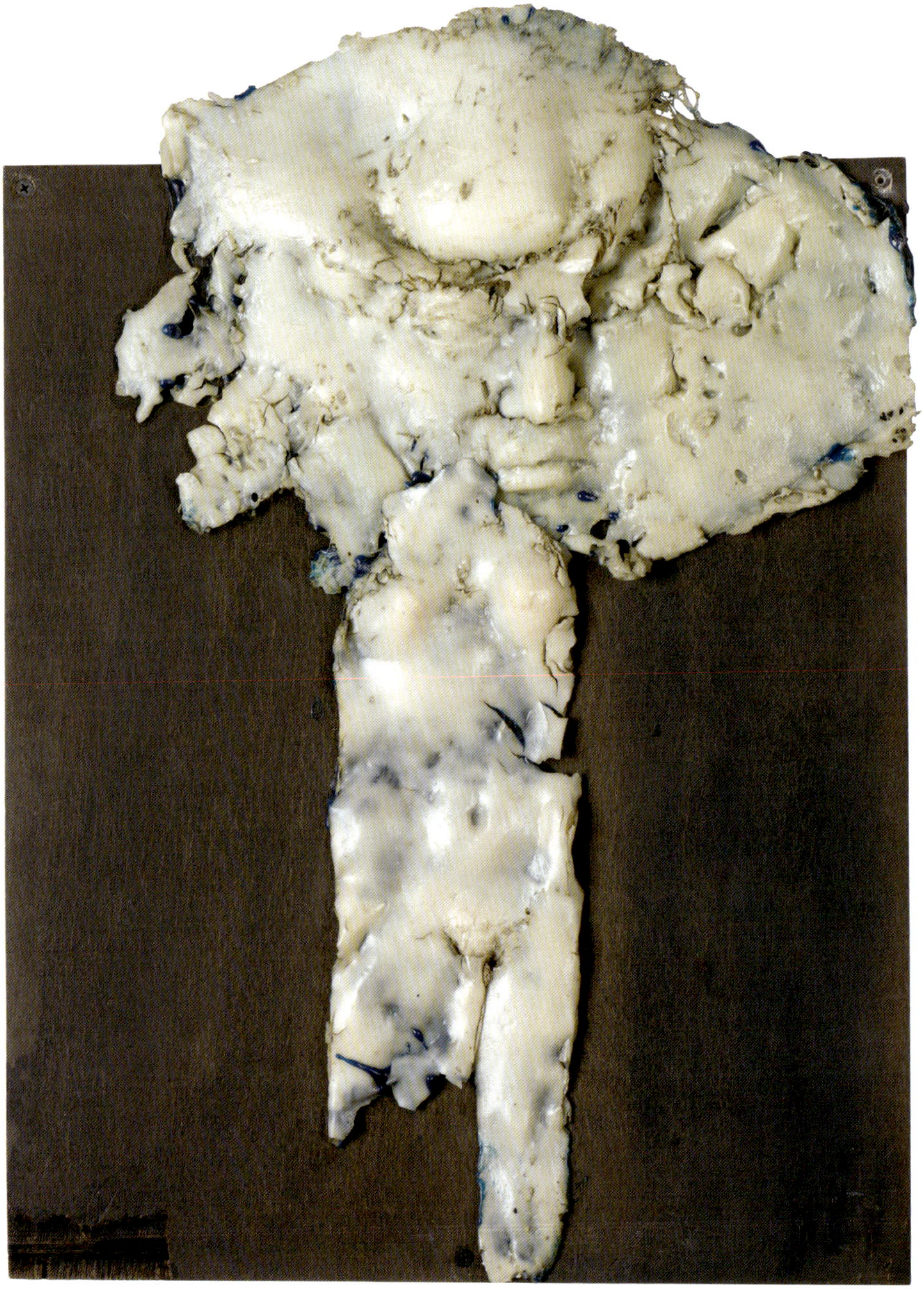

Plate 3

Herbier VIII (Herbarium VIII), 1972
Polyester resin and polychrome wood
21 1/4 x 15 3/4" (54 x 40 cm)

opposite
Plate 4

Herbier XIII (Herbarium XIII), 1972
Polyester resin and polychrome wood
43 5/16 x 31 1/2" (110 x 80 cm)

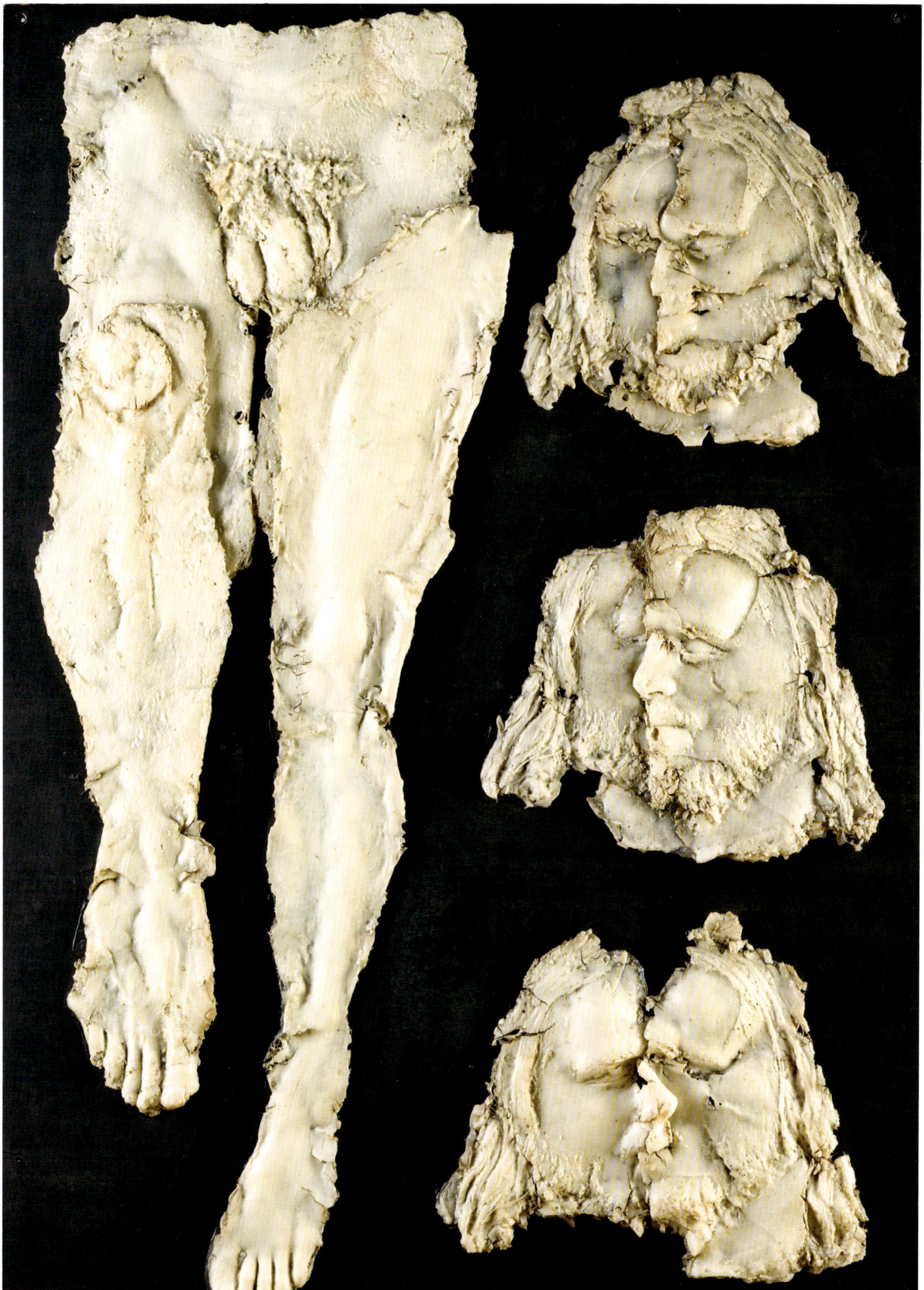

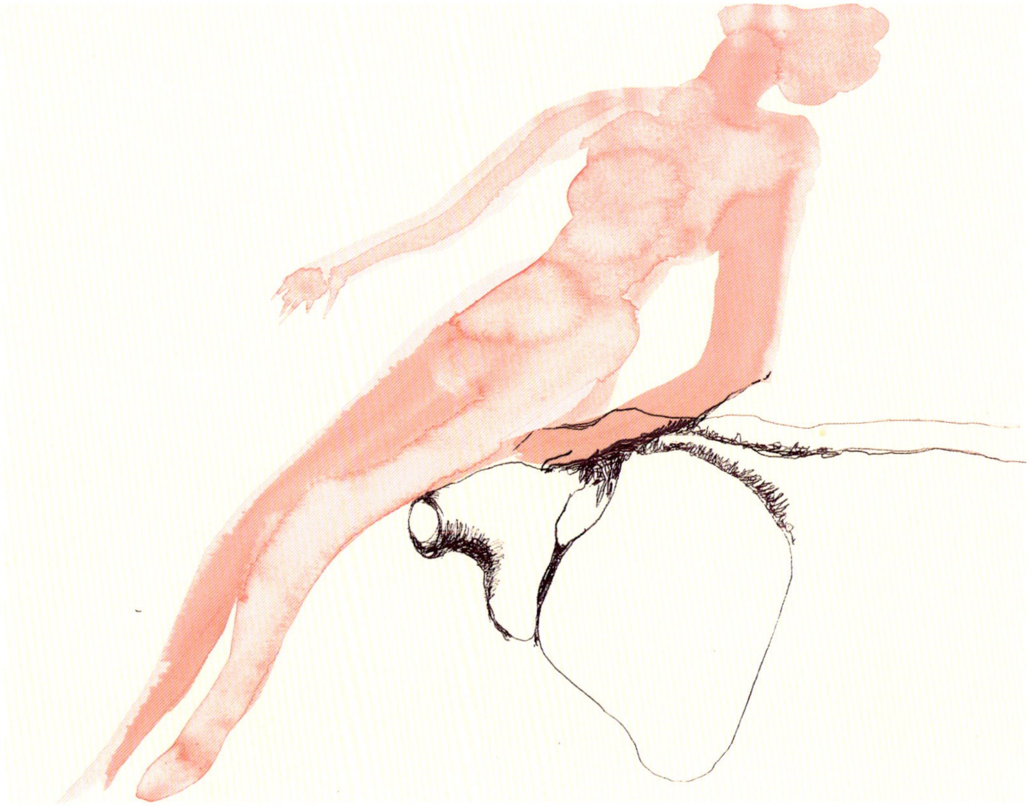

Plate 5

Untitled (From the series Paysage humain [Human Landscape]), c. 1971–72
Watercolor and felt-tip pen on paper
9 7/16 x 12 5/8" (24 x 32 cm)
Location unknown

opposite
Plate 6

Piotr, 1972
Polyester resin
80 3/4 x 17 11/16 x 13" (205 x 45 x 33 cm)

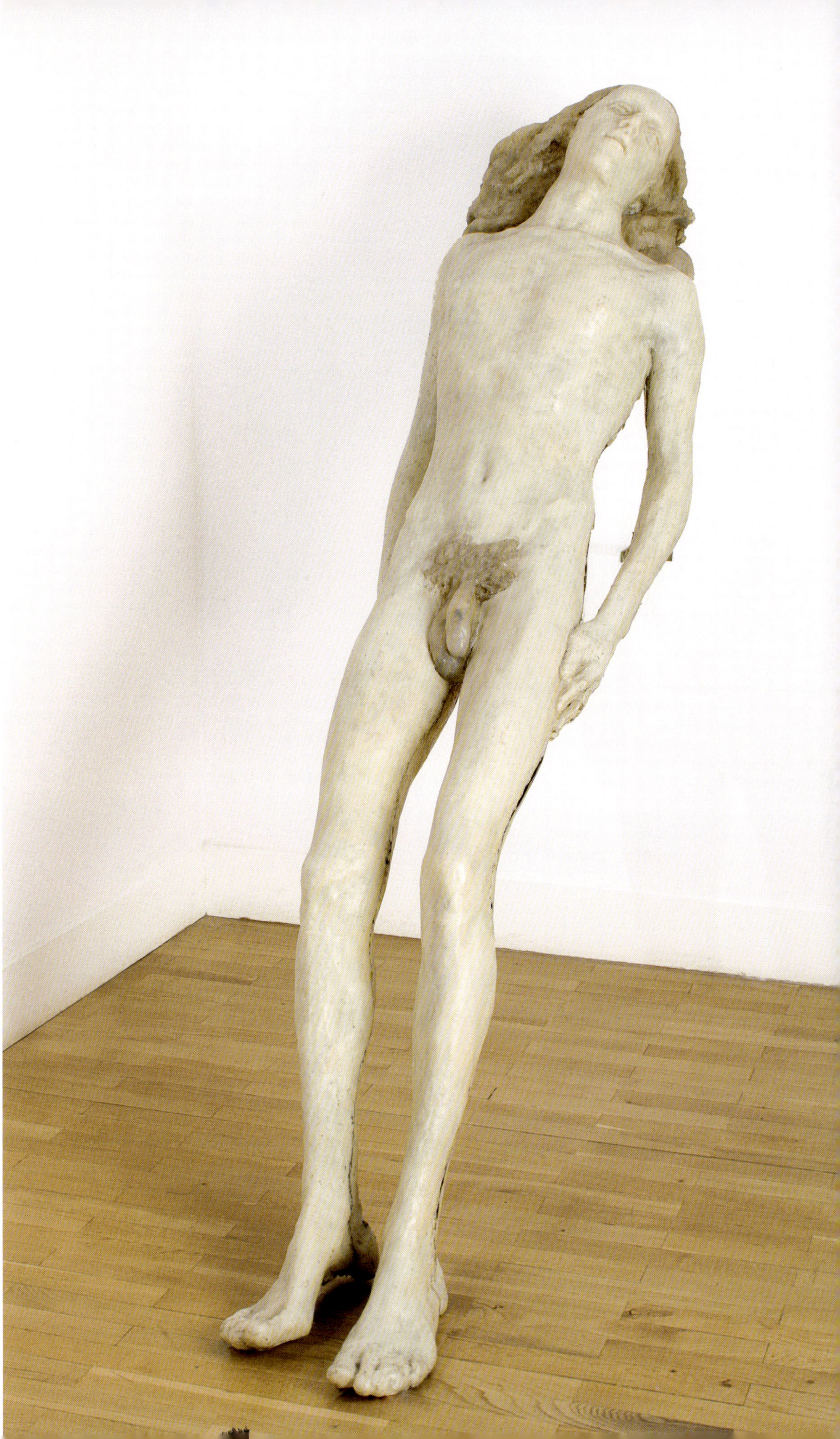

22

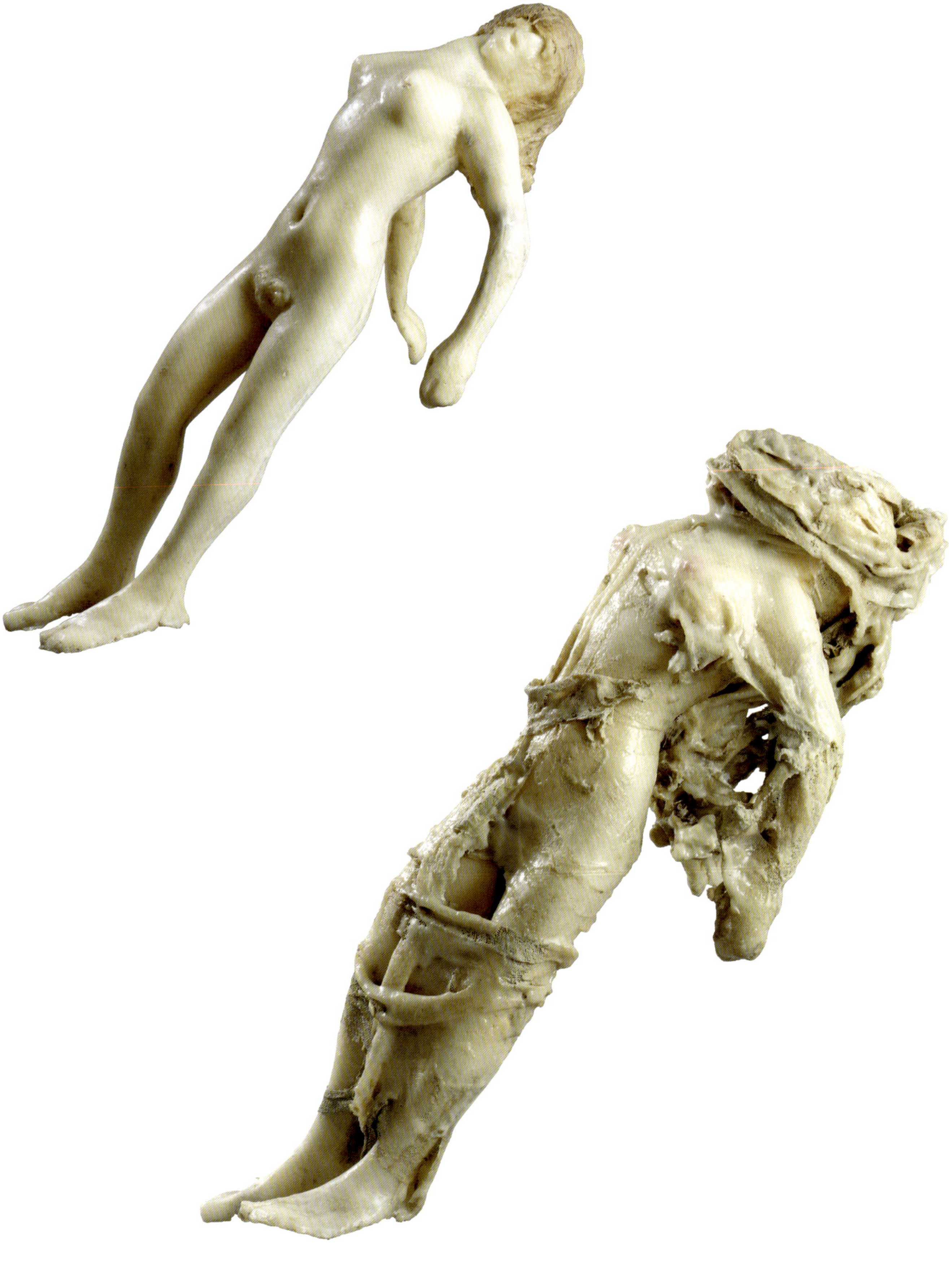

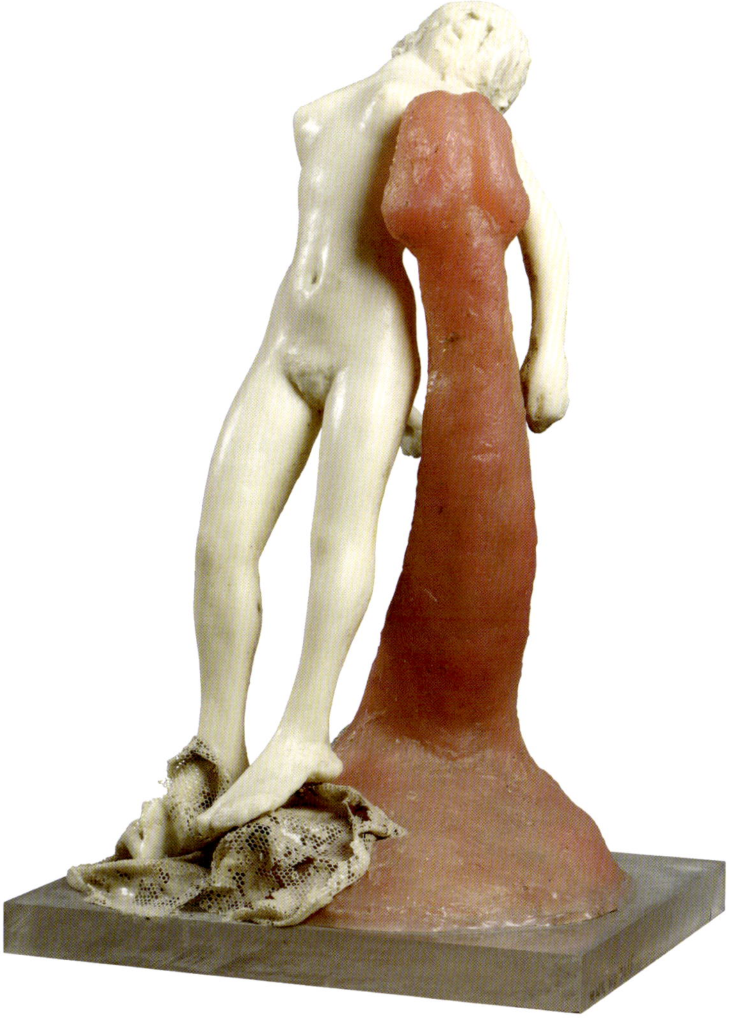

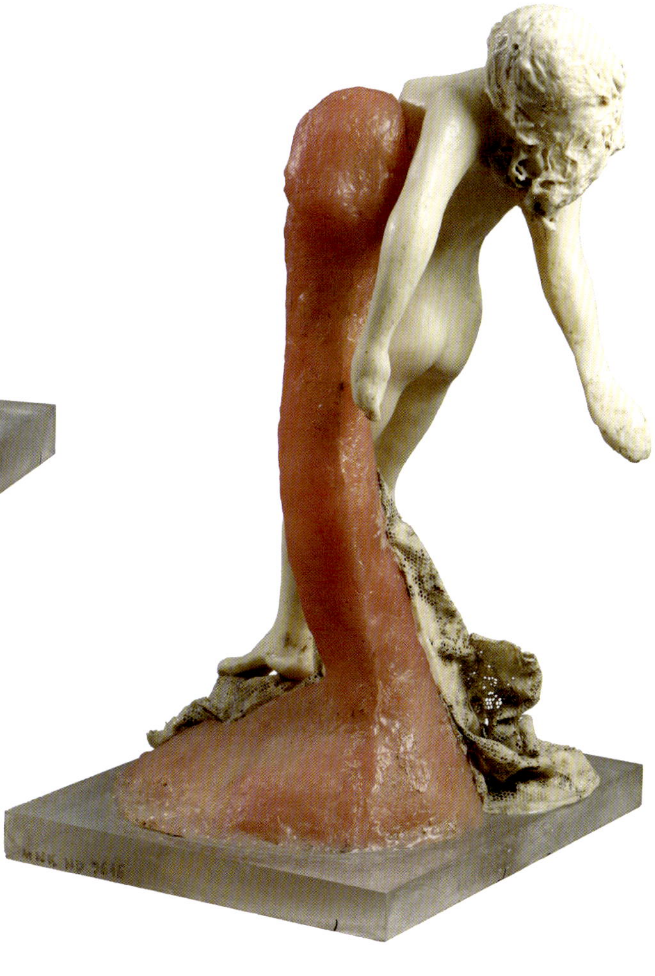

opposite top

Plate 7

Fiancée folle (Mad fiancée), 1971
Polyester resin
6 7/8 x 18 15/16 x 16 5/16" (17.5 x 48 x 16 cm)

opposite bottom

Plate 8

Fiancée folle mariée (Mad married fiancée), 1971
Polyester resin, gauze, newspaper
8 1/4 x 18 15/16 x 7 1/8" (21 x 48 x 18 cm)

above

Plates 9–10

Fiancée folle blanche (Mad white fiancée), 1971
Polyester resin and fabric
18 1/8 x 11 13/16 x 11 13/16" (46 x 30 x 30 cm)

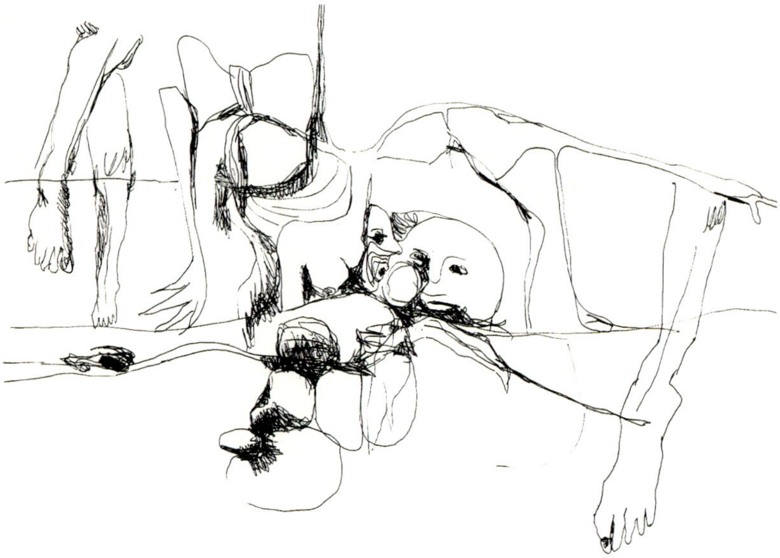

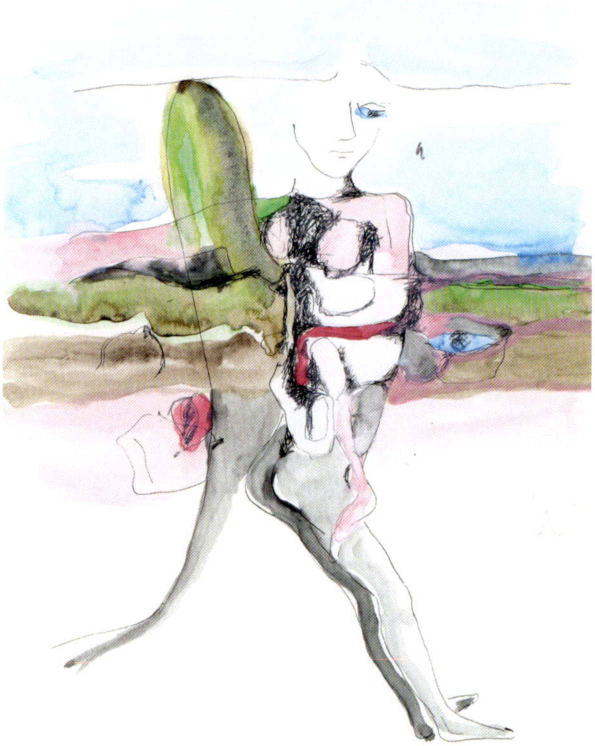

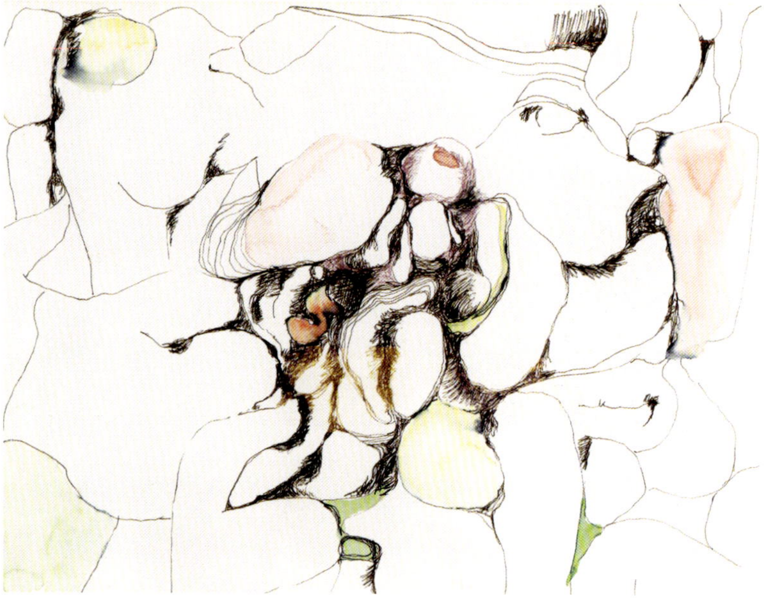

clockwise from top left

Plate 11

Untitled (From the series Paysage humain [Human Landscape]), c. 1971–72
Ballpoint pen on paper
8 1/4 x 11 7/16" (21 x 29 cm)
Location unknown

Plate 12

Untitled (From the series Paysage humain [Human Landscape]), c. 1971–72
Watercolor and felt-tip pen on paper
11 9/16 x 8 1/8" (29.3 x 20.6 cm)

Plate 13

Paysage humain III (Human Landscape III), 1971
Ink, watercolor, and felt-tip pen on paper mounted on paper
9 7/16 x 12 5/8" (24 x 32 cm)

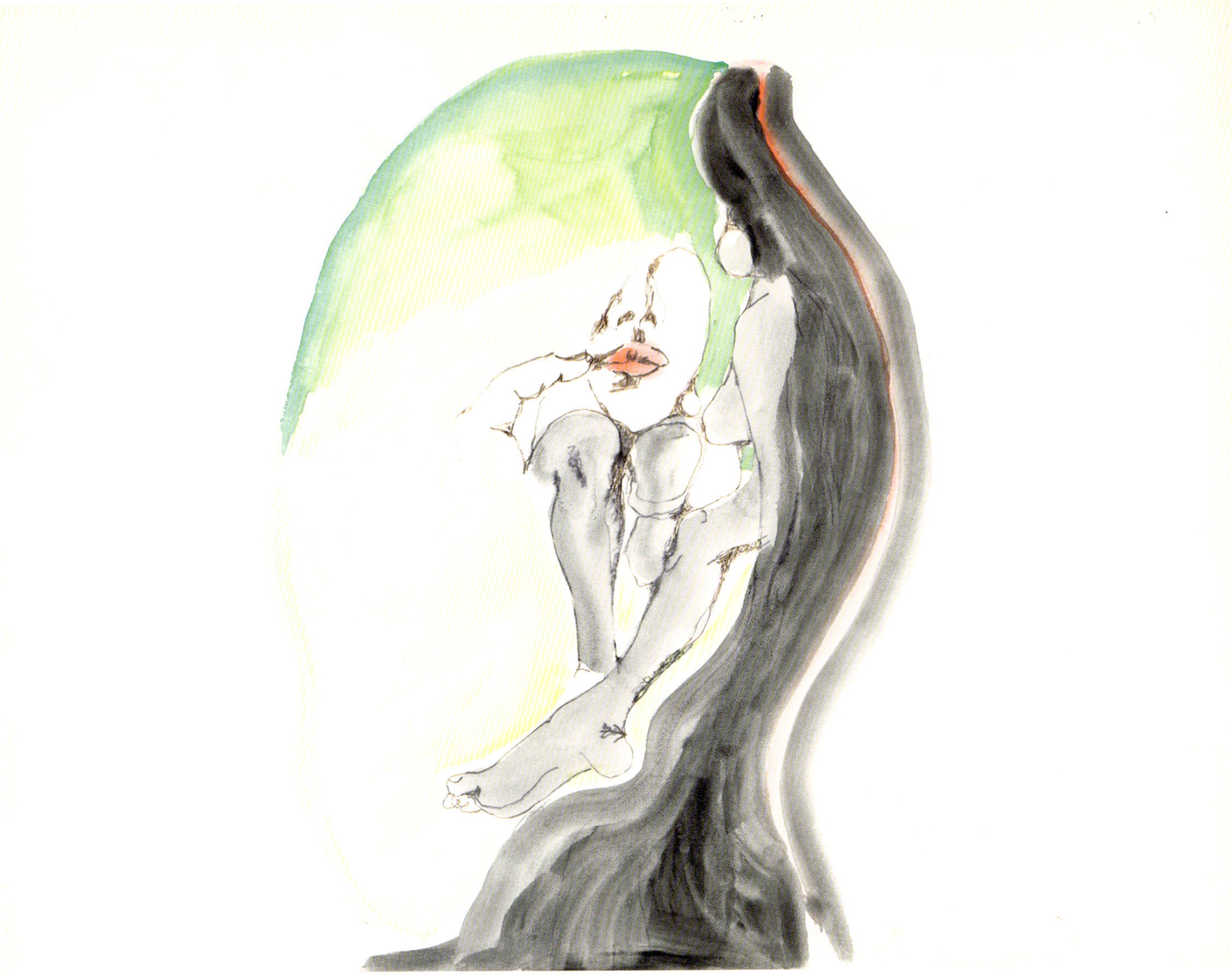

Plate 14

Untitled (From the series Paysage humain [Human Landscape]), c. 1971–72
Watercolor and felt-tip pen on cardboard
19 9/16 x 25 1/2" (49.7 x 64.7 cm)

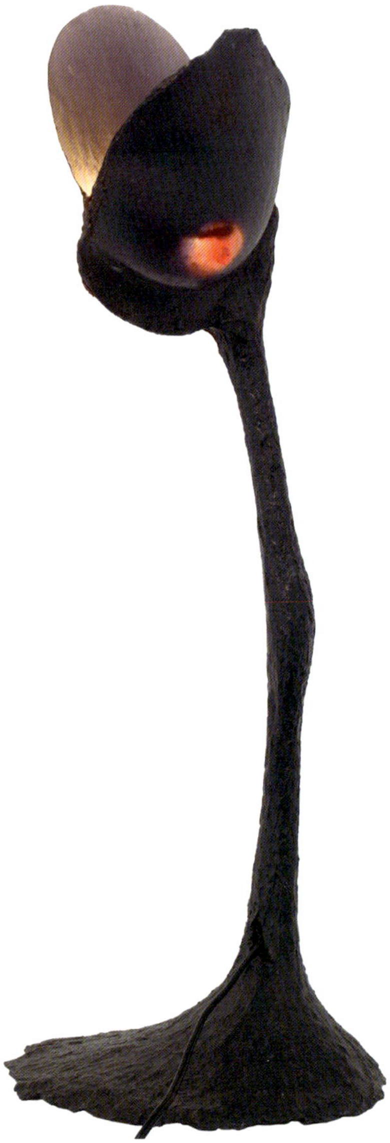

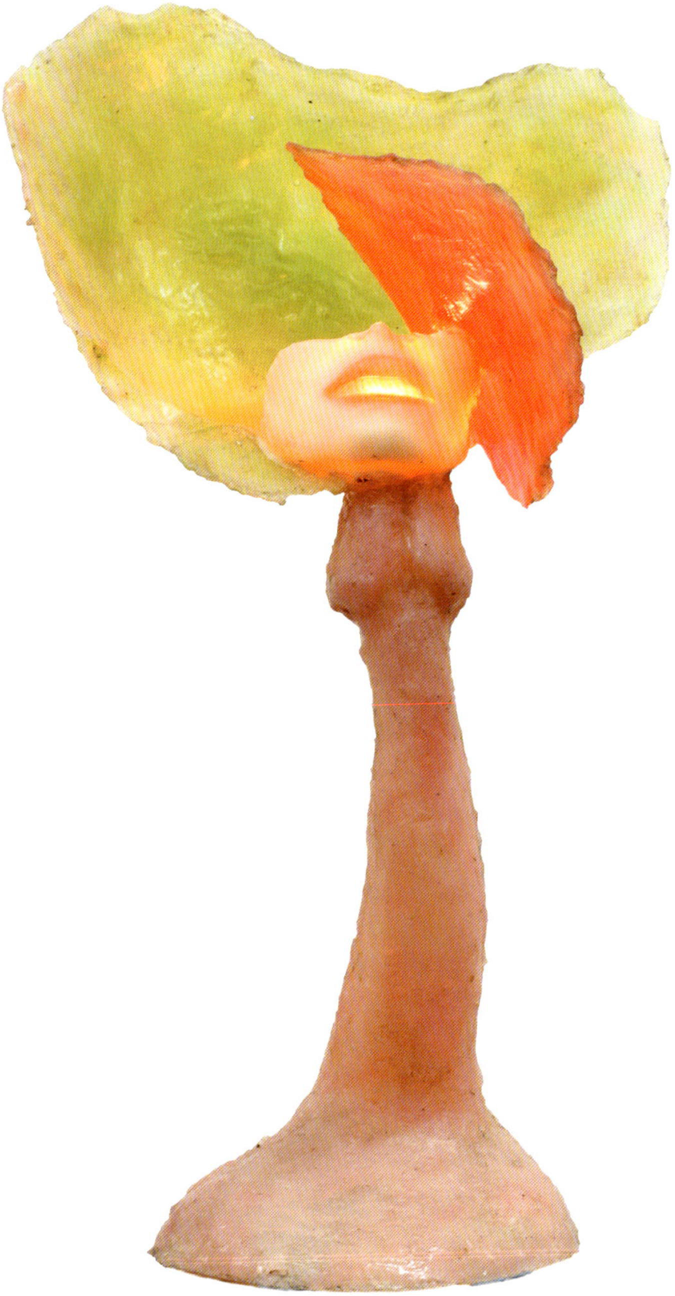

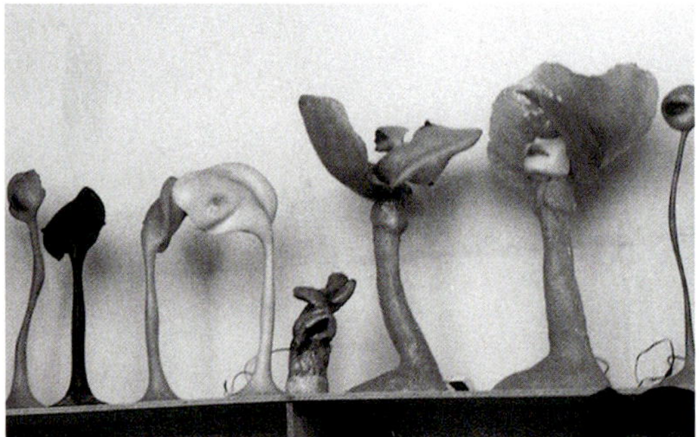

The artist's Malakoff studio, 1971.

left

Plate 15

Buste étincelant I (Glowing Bust), 1967
Colored polyester resin and electrical wiring
22 7/8 x 8 1/4 x 7 7/8" (58 x 21 x 20 cm)

right

Plate 16

Sculpture – Lampe IV (Sculpture – Lamp IV), 1970
Colored polyester resin and electrical wiring
24 13/16 x 14 3/16 x 12 3/16" (63 x 36 x 31 cm)

opposite

Plate 17

Lampe – bouche (Illuminated Lips), 1966
Colored polyester resin, metal, electrical wiring
Ranging from 11 1/4" (28.5 cm) to 17 15/16" (45.5 cm) high

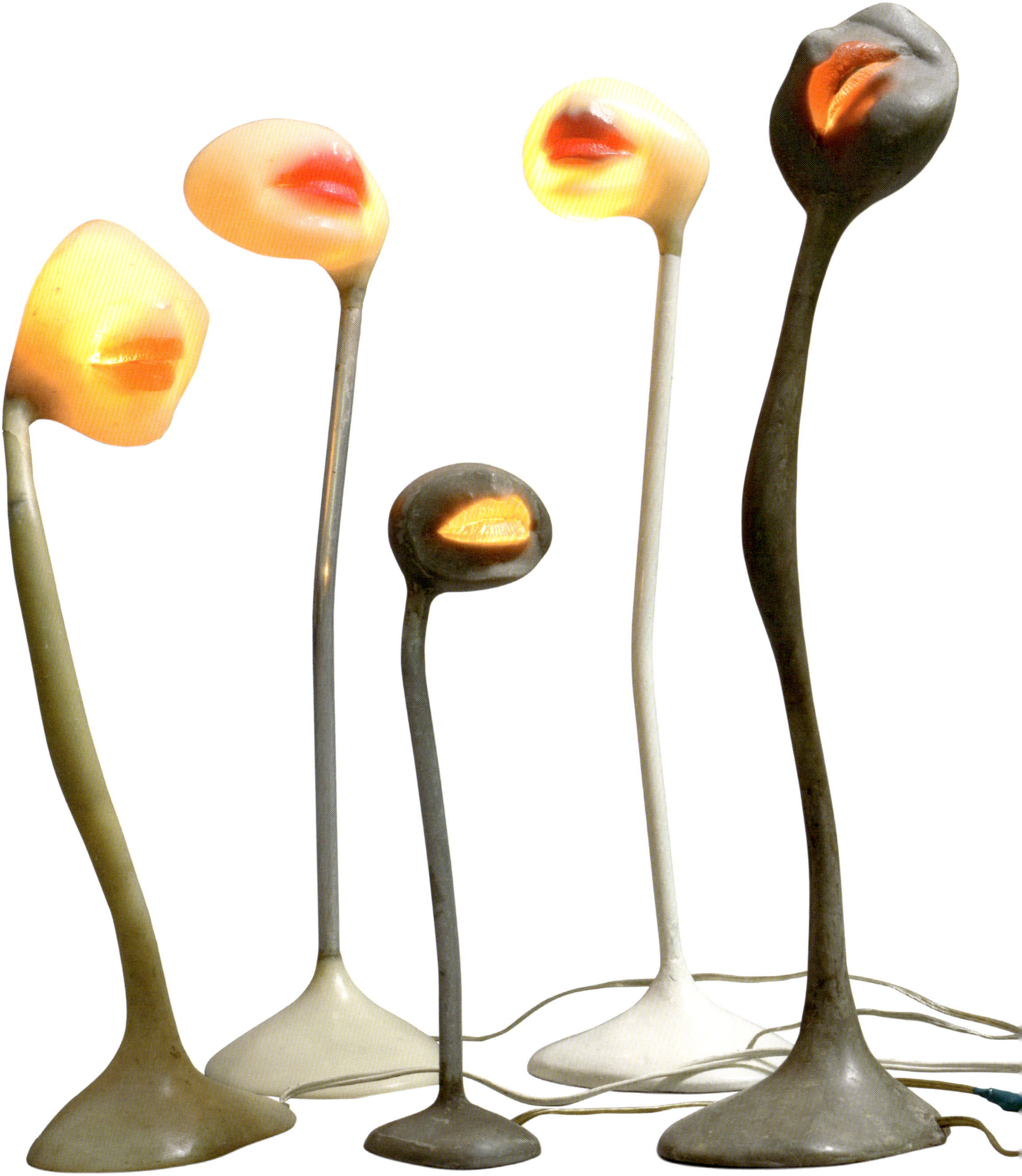

[handwritten] I was educated as a classical sculptor

My work has its roots in sculpture. For years I threw myself into studying problems of balance, volume, space, shadow and light. All in order to arrive at what I am today: nothing other than a sculptor who has experienced the failure of a thwarted vocation. I took stock of the awareness of our time. I used my knowledge of the craft, my intuition and my intelligence, to note with increased clarity the poverty of my methods in comparison to modern techniques. I have been conquered by the hero-miracle of our age, the machine. To it belong beauty, revelations, testimonies, the recording of history. To it belong, in the end, truthful dreams and public demand.

As for me, I produce awkward objects. This absurd and convulsive mania proves the existence of an unknown, secret gland, necessary for life. Yes, this mania can be reduced to a single gesture, within the reach of us all. But this gesture is sufficient unto itself, it is the confirmation of our human presence.

My gesture is addressed to the human body, "that complete erogenous zone," to its most vague and ephemeral sensations. I want to exalt the ephemeral in the folds of our body, in the traces of our passage.

Through casts of the body I try to fix the fleeting moments of life, its paradoxes and absurdity, in transparent polyester. My work is difficult, as sensation that is felt in a very immediate and diffuse way is often resistant to identification. Often everything is all mixed up, the situation is ambiguous, and sensory limits are erased.

Despite everything, I persist in trying to fix in resin the traces of our body: I am convinced that of all the manifestations of the ephemeral the human body is the most vulnerable, the only source of all joy, all suffering and all truth, because of its essential nudity, [handwritten: is] as inevitable as it is inadmissible on any conscious level.

Alina Szapocznikow
March 1972
92 Malakoff

[handwritten] April 1972
Nothing is definitive in my work, if not the immediate pleasure of feeling the material, of touching and palpating [inserted: the distinct material of] the mud as children [inserted: do] on a riverbank.

[handwritten] Alina!
Here is your text, which is beautiful. I'm sending it back with some French "sauce," a little late. Don't hate me.
Love,

P.R. [Pierre Restany]
March 27, 1972

"Mon oeuvre puise ses racines ...," 1972

j'ai reçu la formation de sculpteur classique

Mon oeuvre puise ses racines dans le métier de la sculpture. Pendant des années je me suis livrée à fond à l'étude des problèmes d'équilibre, de volume, d'espace, d'ombre et de lumière. Pour en arriver à ce que je suis aujour'hui: rien d'autre qu'un sculpteur qui assiste à la faillite d'une vocation contrariée. Car j'ai assumé la prise de conscience de notre temps. J'ai fait appel à mes connaissances du métier, à mon intuition et à mon intelligence pour constater avec une lucidité accrue la misère de mes moyens par rapport à la technique moderne. J'ai été vaincue par le héros-miracle de notre époque, la machine. A elle la beauté, les révélations, les témoignages, l'enregistrement de l'histoire. A elle enfin les rêves vrais et la demande du public.

Moi je produis des objets maladroits. Cette manie absurde et convulsive prouve l'existence d'une glande inconnue et secrète, nécessaire à notre vie. D'accord, cette manie peut se réduire à un seul geste, à la portée de nous tous. Mais ce geste se suffit à lui-même, il est la confirmation de notre présence humaine.

Mon geste s'adresse au corps humain, "cette zone érogène totale", à ses sensations les plus vagues et les plus éphémères. Exalter l'éphémère, dans les replis de notre corps, dans les traces de notre passage.

A travers les empreintes du corps j'essaie de fixer dans le polyester transparent les moments fugitifs de la vie, ses paradoxes et son absurde. Mon travail est difficile, la sensation éprouvée de façon immédiate et diffuse étant souvent rebelle à l'identification. Souvent tout est embrouillé, la situation est ambiguë, les limites ~~sensorielles~~ sont effacées.

Malgré tout je persiste à tenter de fixer dans la résine les empreintes de notre corps: ~~je suis convaincue que~~ de toutes les manifestations de l'éphémère le corps humain est la plus vulnérable, l'unique source de toute joie, de toute souffrance et de toute vérité, à cause de son essentiel dénûment, est aussi inéluctable qu'inadmissible au niveau de la conscience.

Alina SZAPOCZNIKOW
mars 1972
92 MALAKOFF

avril 1972

Rien n'est irrévocable dans mon travail, si ce n'est le plaisir immédiat de ~~sentir la matière~~, de toucher et de palper ~~la~~ la matière cette boue comme font les enfants au bord de la rivière.

Alina!
Voilà ton texte, qui est beau. Je te le rends accommodé à la sauce française, avec un peu de retard. Tu ne m'en voudras pas. Je t'embrasse
P. R.
27 mars 1972

ICE RINK IN THE CRATER OF VESUVIUS

Designing and producing an artificial ice skating rink, like an eye at the bottom of a volcanic crater, seems to me like a capital idea, from two perspectives:

1) This human gesture, by posing a challenge to nature, tames and bewitches it, bending it to our whim.
2) The futility and playfulness of the gesture belie its great importance.

The paradoxical absurdity of the project must be emphasized by a party atmosphere, music appropriate for the place (recording and playing Russian waltzes such as "The Hills of Manchuria" on a cassette player, illumination (paper lanterns) and coloring (artificial snow) of the ski slopes that will lead from the upper station of the cable car down to the skating rink.

Man will come to play where the earth recently spilled out infernal fire, spurting it from its open entrails: a challenge and a blasphemy.
Challenge up to a certain point; an icy surface at the bottom of a crater has an immediate symbolic signification (like Barnett Newman's inverted obelisk) and, though its playfulness is opposed to all transcendentality, this supreme challenge is also a manifestation of reverence before nature.

If one day during a figure skating competition, the Peggy Fleming of the moment performs her moves in the field in the iced-over crater, and if we, spectators awed by her prodigious and trivial pirouettes, are swept away by a sudden eruption of lava, fixed for eternity like the Pompeiians—then the triumph of the instant, of the transitory, will be complete.

A fleeting instant, a trivial instant, such is the only symbol of our terrestrial passage.

Alina Szapocznikow
April 1972

N.B. The audiovisual information about the rink can be delegated to many different artists.

PATINOIRE DANS LE CRATERE DU VESUVE

Concevoir et réaliser une patinoire artificielle, comme un oeil au fond du cratére volcanique, me semble une idée capitale à deux points de vue:

I) Ce geste humain, en jetant un défi à la nature, l'aprivoise et l'envoûte selon son caprice.
2) La futilité et l'aspect ludique de ce geste revêtent une grande importance.

La côté paradoxal et absurde doit en être souligné par une ambiance de fête, une musique approprié à ces lieux (enregistrement et diffusion par magnétophone des airs de valses russes tels que "Sur les monts de Mandchurie", l'illumination (lampions) et la colorations (neige artificielle) des pistes de ski qui méneront de la station supérieure du téléphérique à la patinoire.

L'homme vient jouer là où jadis la terre a répandu le feu infernal jaillissant de ses entrailles ouvertes: un defi et un blasphémeI
Défi jusqu'a un certain point; une surface de glace au fond du cratére a une signification symbolique immédiate (comme l'obelisque renversé d'un Barnett Newman) et, si elle s'oppose à toute transcendantalité par son côté ludique, ce défi suprême est aussi une manifestation de recueilement devant la nature.

Si un jour pendant les compétitions de patinage artistique la Peggy Fleming du moment exécutera ses figures libres dans le cratére gelé et si nous, spectateurs ébahis de ses pirouettes prodigieuses et futiles nous sommes pris par une brusque éruption de lave et figés pour l'éternité comme les pompé-pompéiens, alors le triomphe de l'instant et du fugitif sera complet.

Un instant fugitif, un instant futile, tel est le seul symbole de notre passage terestre.

Alina SZAPOCZNIKOW
Avril I972

N.B. L'information audio-visuelle sur la patinoire peut être confiée à une pléiade d'artistes.

"Patinoire dans le cratère du Vésuve," 1972

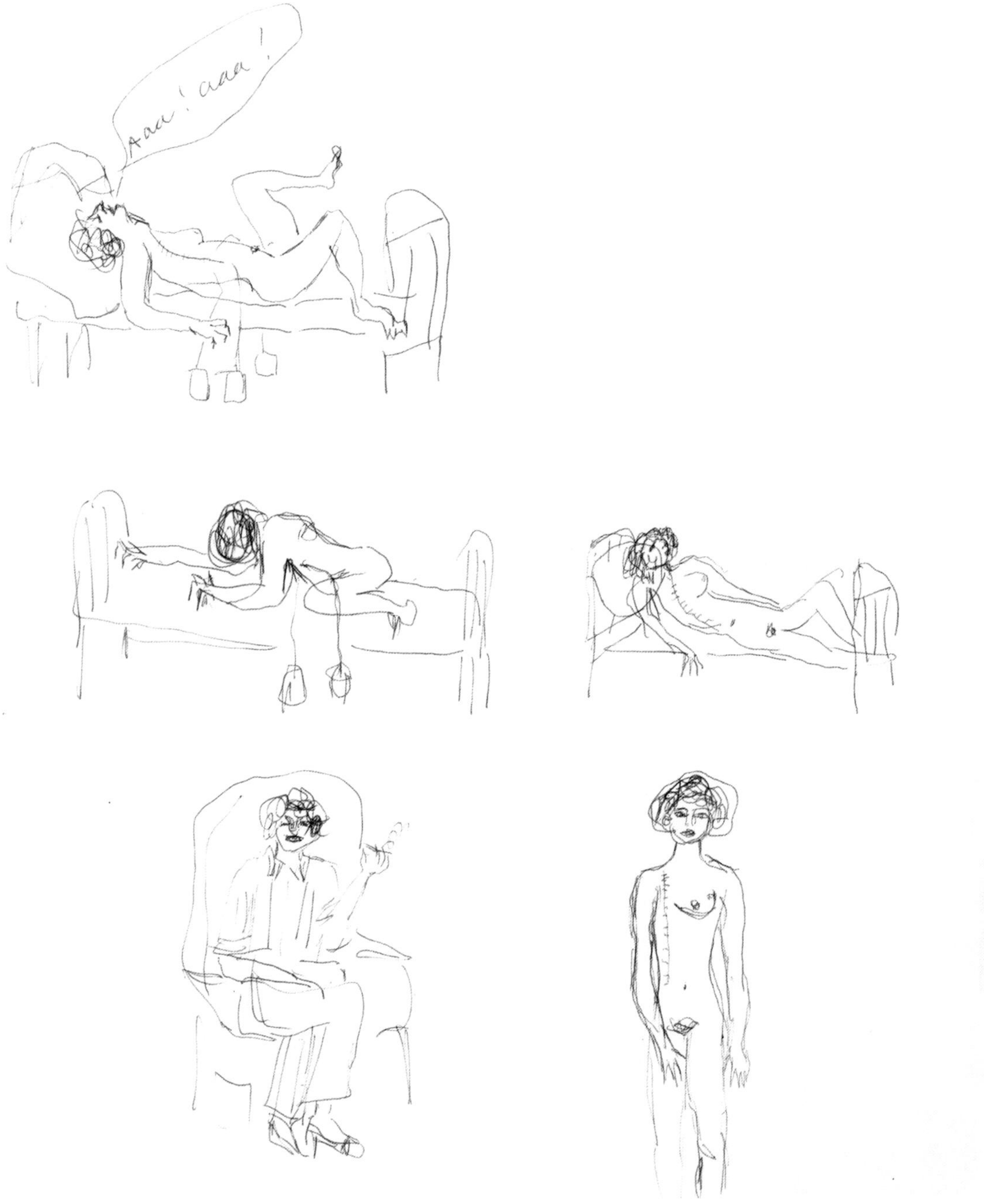

Plate 18

Untitled, c. 1971–72
Ballpoint pen on paper
11 5/8 x 8 1/4" (29.5 x 21 cm)

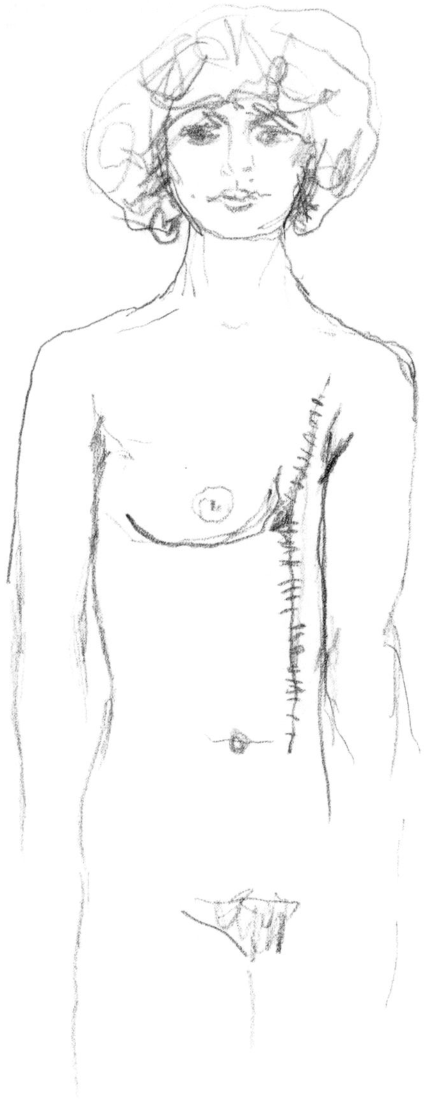

Plate 19

Untitled, c. 1971–72
Pencil on paper
11 5/8 x 8 1/4" (29.5 x 21 cm)

Soft Body/Soft Sculpture: The Gendered Surrealism of Alina Szapocznikow

Cornelia Butler

Art is always self-parading, I think. Always was, always will be.
Is there something wrong with the self? I parade as much as I can.

—Paul Thek[1]

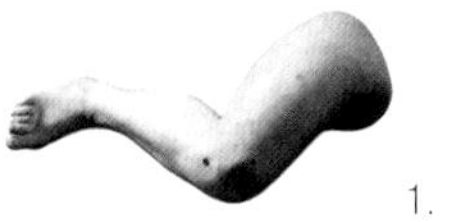

1.

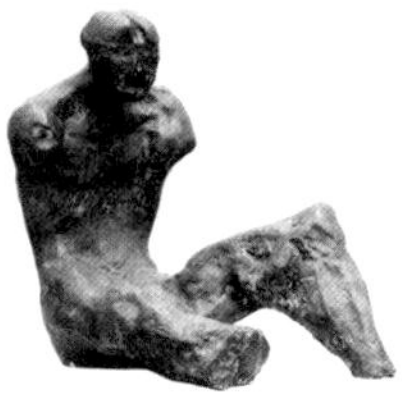

2.

In 1962 Alina Szapocznikow made a plaster cast of her right leg. A slight and poetic fragment, *Noga* (*Leg*, 1962) [ill. 1, plate 129] starts at the upper thigh and extends to the foot; it rests delicately, almost tentatively, facing down, as if the body it belongs to is at rest. Nothing in the artist's oeuvre or prior studio practice anticipated this move, though her struggles to represent the partial body and the body in transformation are visible in small studies from the mid- to late 1950s, such as *Ekshumowany* (*Exhumed*, 1957) [ill. 2, plate 146]. Other figure studies in bronze, lead, and stone are restless, enervated attempts at metamorphosis in sculptural form. In a letter written in 1966, Szapocznikow reflected back on *Leg*, expressing surprise at the implications of casting her own body:

> Haunted by the increasingly academic nature of abstract art, and at the same time, partly out of my spirit of contradiction and partly perhaps out of some artistic exhibitionism, I made a cast of my own leg and an assemblage of casts of my face… Fortunately we believe that in art everything has been already, so nothing has been yet.[2]

Leg was made in 1962, just prior to the artist's relocation to Paris from Warsaw. She had been living there since 1951, following a period spent in Prague after being released from a World War II concentration camp and time spent in Paris attending art school and, later, convalescing from near-fatal tuberculosis. *Leg* anticipates much of her later work, which made use of casting through a variety of experimental materials, including polyester resin, polyurethane, plastic cement, and cement. On the threshold of transition—between Warsaw and Paris and between more traditional carved stone sculptures and cast imprints of the body, part of her relentless material experimentation—it is striking that she described the casting process as exhibitionist. Making public or visible her own body, Szapocznikow would transform the anonymous model of modernist sculpture into a particularized double of her own body.

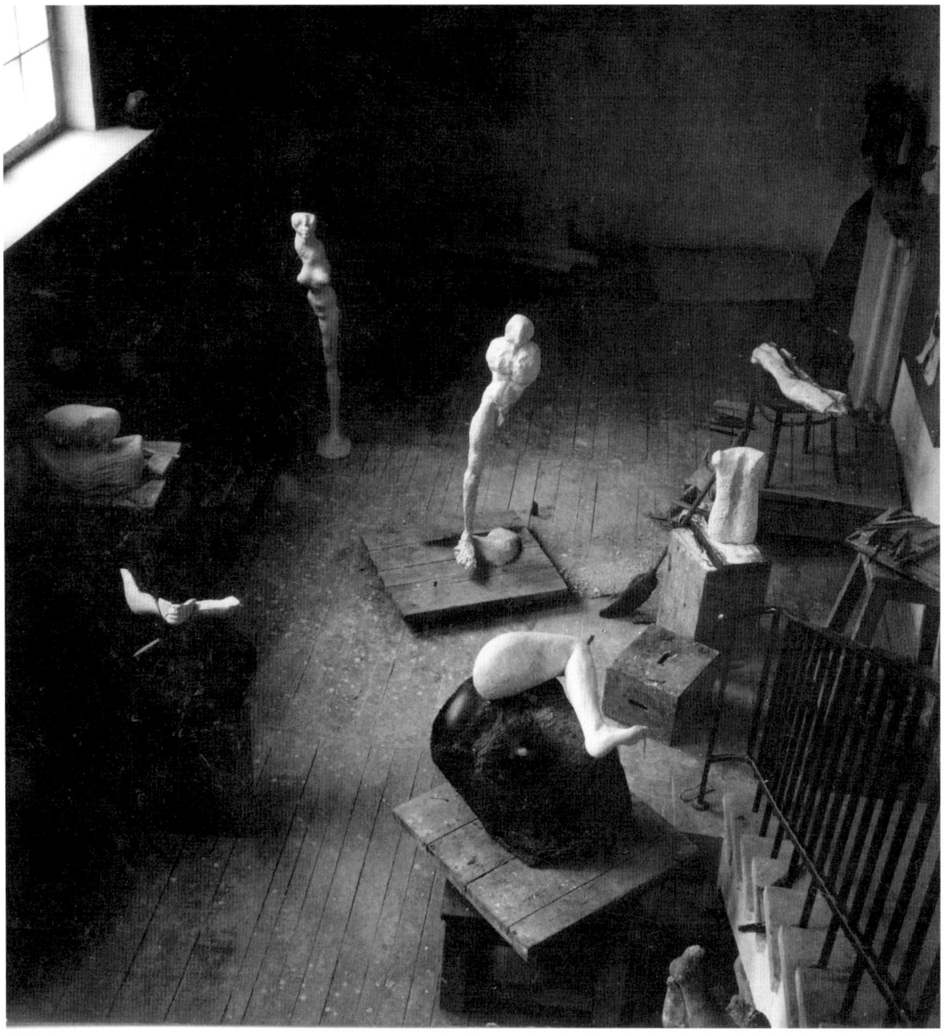

3. The artist's Warsaw studio, 1965. *Noga* (Leg), her 1962 sculpture newly placed on a piece of granite, is visible in the foreground.

Paris

Later in the same letter, Szapocznikow remarked on another bodily form visible in international art circles at that time: the aggressive and very vertical sculpture *Thumb* (1965) by César, an artist associated with Nouveau Réalisme, the proto-Pop movement originated in 1960 by a group of primarily French artists who embraced Yves Klein's *Leap into the Void* (1960) as their founding gesture. The short-lived movement produced a manifesto signed by Arman, François Dufrêne, Raymond Hains, Klein, Martial Raysse, Daniel Spoerri, Jean Tinguely, and Jacques Villeglé. The only woman in the group, Niki de Saint Phalle, was invited to join on the basis of her Tirs, often referred to as her "shooting paintings." César's sixteen-and-a-quarter-inch rendition of his own thumb in shiny bronze can be read as a phallus, a synecdoche for the artist's hand, or as indicative of the widely understood gesture "thumbs up." The fact that César's aggressively confident *Thumb* followed Szapocznikow's tentative and poetic *Leg* by an interval of just three years was not lost on the Polish artist, who seemed to take her competition in stride. Upon moving to Paris in 1963, Szapocznikow maintained an informal connection with Nouveau Réalisme through her most visible and loyal champion at the time, Pierre Restany, the critic and curator who named and theorized the movement and curated several parallel exhibitions of Szapocznikow's work in Paris.

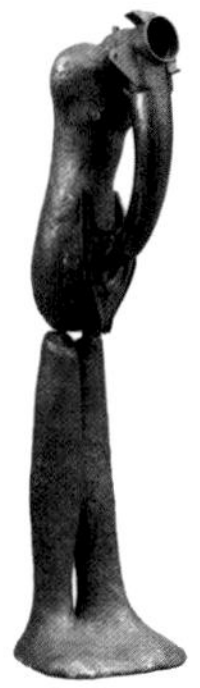

4.

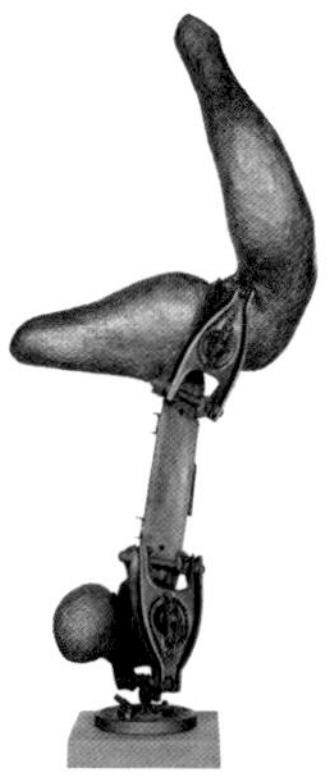

5.

The same year that *Thumb* appeared, Szapocznikow evolved *Leg* by combining the plaster cast leg with a partially worked chunk of black granite [ill. 3]. In 1967, she made a bronze cast of her leg, which she combined with the black granite chunk, transforming the sculpture into something more finished, less tentative and experimental. During the mid-1960s, a period of rapid innovation for Szapocznikow, she began to combine body casts of a leg, or a mouth, or a closed eye. (Incidentally, Jasper Johns's *Target with Plaster Casts* [1955]—which contained a bas-relief element featuring faces and body parts running along its top edge—was in circulation in Paris as part of "L'Exposition Internationale du Surréalisme: 1959–1960," organized by Marcel Duchamp and André Breton.[3]) For Szapocznikow the cast of the leg initiated a new exploration in which proliferating lips, breasts, and bellies were mashed up with industrially made car parts in such important works as *Człowiek z instrumentem* (*Man with Instrument*) [ill. 4, plate 99], *Femme de ménage* (*Cleaning Lady*), and *Goldfinger* [ill. 5, plate 101], all from 1965. An untitled series of Głowa (Heads) with industrial shards embedded in them can be seen in studio photographs that document this experimental conflation of body and material. This formal conjunction enabled Szapocznikow to reassemble the body, as if from the inside out. Most elegantly expressed in a series of spindly lamps, each titled *Lampe – bouche* (*Illuminated Lips*, 1966) [ill. 6, plate 17], the machine aesthetic exhausted by male contemporaries like César and Arman is given new life by Szapocznikow. Lips teeter on tentacles of electricity, blossoming like flowers on gold-colored stalks and perched as if to kiss or exhale. The polychromy of these is both visceral and kitsch; they are both dead and alive. *Bouches en Marche* (*Marching Lips*, c. 1966) [ill. 7, plate 95] features lips captured in a frozen arabesque. In strange and lovely sculptures like the Illuminated Lips and the Desserts [ill. 8, plates 20–22], utilitarian household objects are charged with something forbidden and powerful.

Szapocznikow's proto-Pop combinations of industrial and bodily form, deeply influenced by her traumatic experiences during World War II, suggest parallels with the work of de Saint Phalle. Like Arman, César, and the other Nouveaux Réalistes, de Saint Phalle incorporated mechanical, often menacing, industrially made objects and fragments into her early assemblages. In the mid-1960s, she began to focus on monumental forms based on the female figure. Her Nanas took the form of voluptuous bodies, symbols of a ferocious fecundity and eroticism. In 1966 de Saint Phalle created the monumental *Hon*, or "she" in Swedish, a reclining female form that occupied an entire gallery of the Moderna Museet in Stockholm [ill. 9]. (Two years later Szapocznikow would create *Grands Ventres* [1968], casts of a friend's belly enlarged to the point of abstraction.) The works for which de Saint Phalle received the greatest acclaim during her lifetime, however, were the actions-cum-paintings known as Tirs, made between 1961 and 1963, likely because of their direct association with painting—and no doubt because of the erotic charge of the beautiful artist aiming a gun at her own work. For her own part, de Saint Phalle viewed these as the outward expression of violence and aggression:

> As a child I could not identify with my mother or my grandmother, my aunts or my mother's friends. They seemed to be a pretty unhappy lot… I didn't want to become like them, guardians of the hearth; I wanted the world, and the world then belonged to MEN… I wanted the outside world to be mine also. Very early I got the message that MEN HAD POWER AND I WANTED IT.[4]

Neither Szapocznikow's nor de Saint Phalle's work has been properly integrated into the critical discourses of art history and feminism, and the contribution of women

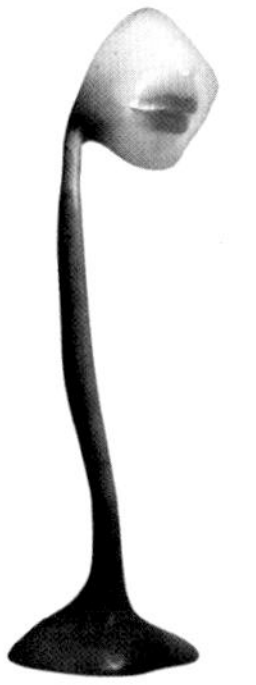
6.

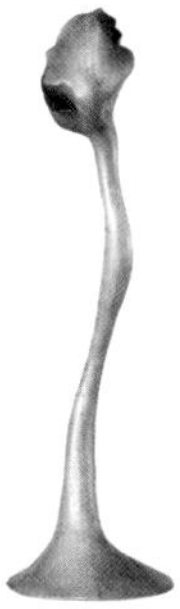
7.

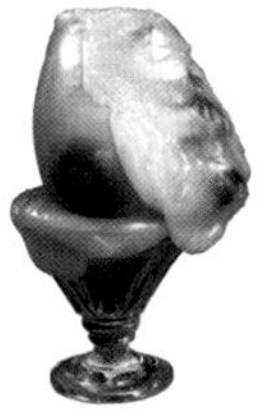
8.

to the history of Pop art is virtually unwritten. Despite their involvement from its inception, the work of women artists was always seen as somehow "not Pop enough."[5] Like Szapocznikow's, de Saint Phalle's work—with its increasing scale and its over the top exaggeration of the female form, both grotesque and celebratory—remains problematic within an institutional feminist history that prefers its women artists Minimal or Conceptual. The same might be said for Nancy Spero, who lived in Paris between 1959 and 1964, leaving just a year after Szapocznikow settled there. The thick, dark paintings of primal themes such as death, birth, sex, romantic love, and yearning that Spero made in Paris are almost essentialist in their depictions of bodies imprinted by life.

The coincidence of César's *Thumb* notwithstanding, it is worth exploring the very different use that Szapocznikow, like de Saint Phalle, made of the conjunction of her bodily forms and casts with fragments of cars and other machines. Rather than read *Leg* as a relic of violence done to the body, one can read the fragility and abject horizontality of the form as an example of the fragment as fetish, connecting the work back to Surrealism's affront to sexual orthodoxies of the 1960s.[6] What seems clear is that the collective unconscious of women like de Saint Phalle; French artist ORLAN, who beginning in 1964 made photographs of her own body in Hans Bellmeresque sculptural configurations with a mannequin [ill. 14]; and Annette Messager, whom Szapocznikow knew in Paris—as well as Lynda Benglis, Louise Bourgeois, Hannah Wilke, and others in the United States—provided a kind of underground and unarticulated discourse of the erotic. Contextualizing Bourgeois's use of the phallus as fragment in sculptures such as *Fillette* (1968), Mignon Nixon wrote:

> In historical terms, the fate of the part-object in postwar art is bound up with the complex historical receptions of Surrealism and Marcel Duchamp . . . Surrealism and Duchamp represented a disclaimed subhistory of modernism; today, in the reversal of these positions, it is the aesthetic autonomy of high modernism that is disavowed. One explanation, then, for the reiteration of the part-object in so much recent artistic production might be that it is redeemed as a marker of Surrealist and Duchampian representations of the body-in-pieces, and in repudiation of the modernist gestalt.[7]

One begins, then, to concoct a lineage of such part-objects, a history of repurposed and missing parts, that includes Matthew Barney, Benglis, Robert Gober, Yayoi Kusama, Gabriel Orozco, Thek [ill. 10], and Wilke, bearing in mind the haptic relationship so central to sculptural practice.[8] Often pictured inhabiting or otherwise performing their sculptural works, naked in proximity to them, these artists create situations where architecture and the body are tested together as performative sites.

With *Cleaning Lady*, *Man with Instrument,* and *Goldfinger*, Szapocznikow executed an extraordinary group of sculptures in which found car parts are embedded in cement or plastic cement. This group is both humorous and deeply disturbing. In each case, a vertical element structures the assemblage, either impressed deeply into a malleable substance—appearing to have morphed out of a molten state, then hardened—or in the form of a rod or metal strut between and around which hand-formed elements are glommed as if clamped and cinched at pressure points.

The representation of women's bodies coupled with the image of the automobile is a hallmark of both twentieth-century male fantasy and consumer culture. The mod-

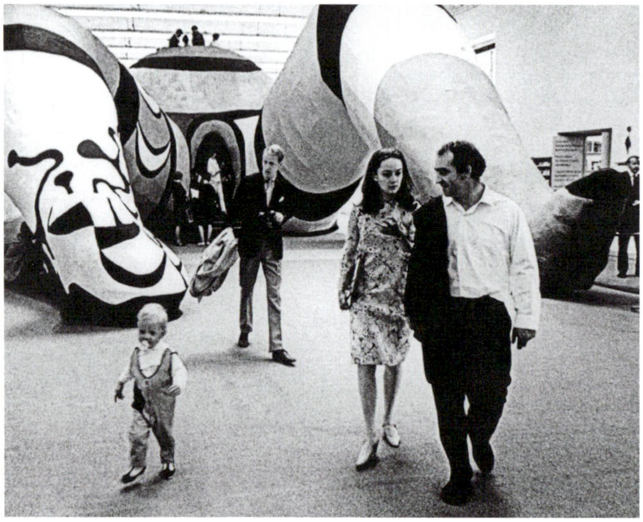

9. Jean Tinguely and Niki de Saint Phalle at the opening of *Hon*, Moderna Museet, Stockholm, 1966.

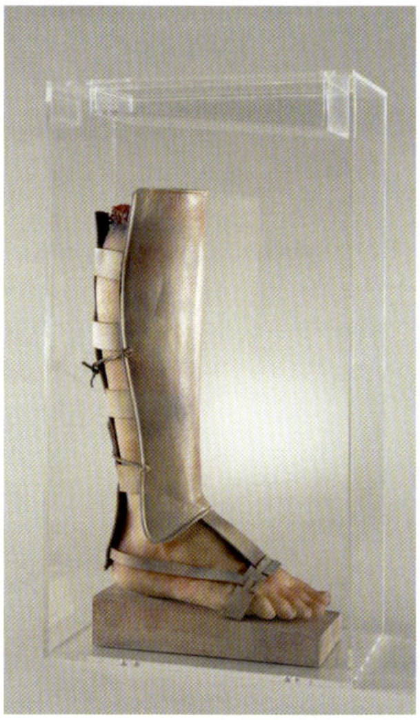

10. Paul Thek (American, 1933–1988), *Warrior's Leg*, 1966–67. Wax, metal, leather, and paint, 21 1/2 x 2 1/8 x 7" (54.5 x 30.7 x 17.7 cm). In artist's vitrine: 26 1/4 x 8 1/4 x 14 1/2" (66.7 x 21 x 36.8 cm). Hirshhorn Museum and Sculpture Garden, Smithsonian Institution, Joseph H. Hirshhorn Bequest Fund, 1990.

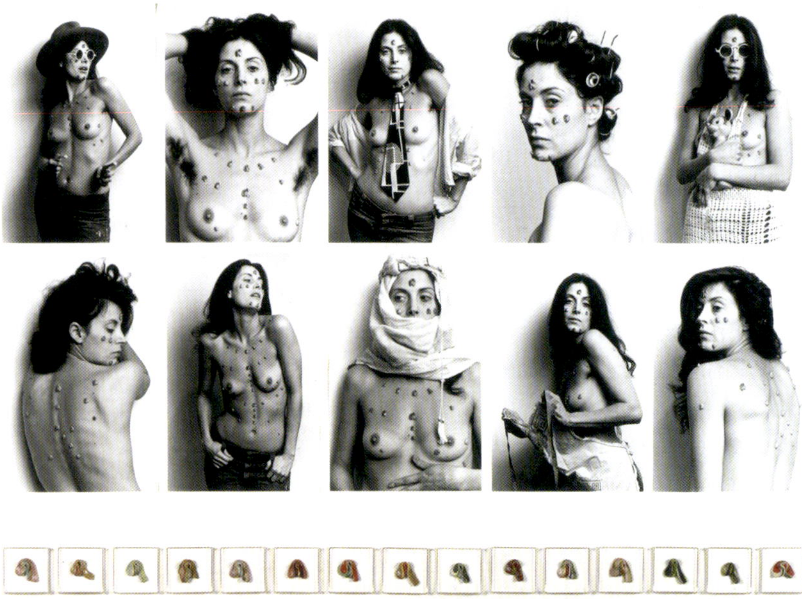

11. Hannah Wilke (American, 1940–1993), *S.O.S. – Starification Object Series*, 1974–82. Gelatin silver prints with chewing gum sculptures, 40 x 58 1/2 x 2 1/4" (101.6 x 148.6 x 5.7 cm). The Museum of Modern Art, New York. Purchase.

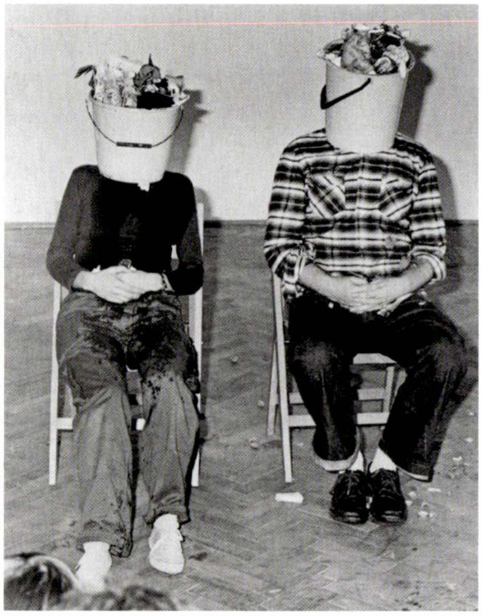

12. KwieKulik (Zofia Kulik, Polish, born 1947; and Przemysław Kwiek, Polish, born 1945), *Działanie na głowę (trzy odsłony)* (Activities with the Head [3 parts]). 1978. Performance view.

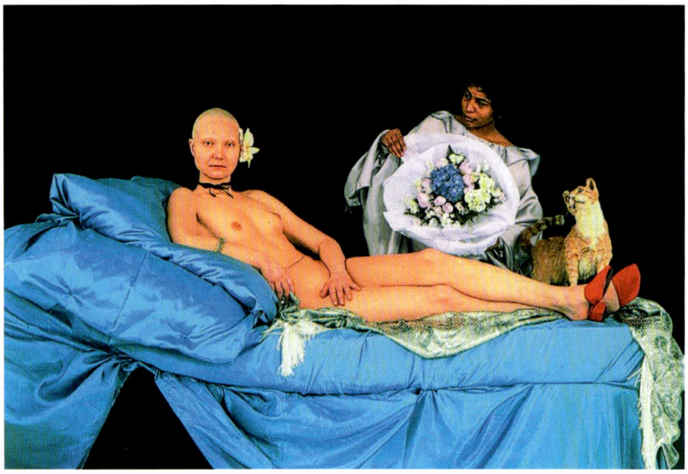

13. Katarzyna Kozyra (Polish, born 1963), detail of *Olympia*, 1996. Installation with three color photographs, 70 7/8 x 90 9/16" (180 x 230 cm) each, and single-channel video, color, sound, 12 min. Private collection.

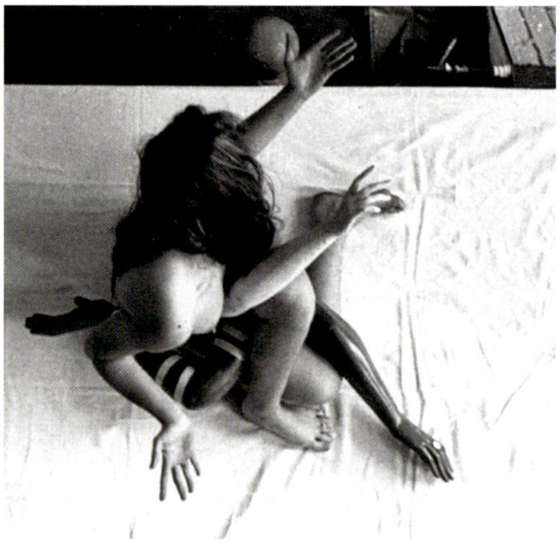

14. ORLAN (French, born 1947), *Corps-sculpture No. 3 dit Shiva ou tentacules de bras multiples* (Body-sculpture No. 3 called "Shiva, or many-armed tentacles"), 1964. Black-and-white photograph, 3 9/16 x 3 15/16" (9 x 10 cm), 31 7/8 x 29 15/16" (81 x 76 cm) framed. Courtesy Galerie Michel Rein, Paris.

ernist association between the abstracted female form and symbols of speed and the future has its roots early in the century, not only in Futurism but also in the writings of Georges Bataille, who is often invoked in reference to Szapocznikow. In *Cleaning Lady*, the undulating form becomes female when crowned with a plaster cast of the artist's lips. Szapocznikow's figure is sightless, with two holes from some automotive hardware where the eyes would be, ensnared by what appears to be a twisted and blackened abstraction of form. She both emerges from and is subsumed by the mass that frames her mouth. *Goldfinger* is at once all limbs and barely a body at all. Made of cement and an automobile shock absorber with a luminous gold surface, the sculpture evokes the 1964 James Bond film whose title sequence features scenes from the movie (including the requisite car chase and various beautiful women) projected onto the body of a woman seemingly painted gold. Like the statue-like body of the golden woman, the sculpture cannot breathe, its orifices coated with the residue of modern excess. What first appears to be a double phallus is actually a crimped pair of thighs, clamped just at the juncture where the crotch would be. Once deciphered, these are undeniably the truncated thighs of *Étant donnés* (1946–66), Duchamp's *chef d'oeuvre*, twenty years in development. Duchamp himself sat on the jury for the Copley Prize, which Szapocznikow won in 1966, after a studio visit with the artist the previous year during which he was apparently impressed with *Goldfinger*, among other works.

The Surrealist trope of scrambling the body's hierarchy, of purposefully disorienting the viewer's kinesthetic response to the object and image of the body, would have been familiar territory for Szapocznikow, having been exposed to such work in Paris during the late 1950s and then again upon her permanent return in 1963. Her Polish colleague Zofia Rydet's photocollages with mannequin imagery exist as a proto-feminist critique of gender, as do the early erotic drawings of Czech artist Toyen (Marie Cerminova), who was in Prague when Szapocznikow arrived after the war and lived in Paris between 1946 and 1967 and whose work circulated in major European exhibitions of Dada and Surrealism. (Incidentally, she referred to herself in the masculine.) The Surrealist disintegration of the body presaged images of the Holocaust that would be seared into memory as a result of World War II. The semi-abstract language of a kind of corporeal obliteration was associated with art that embodied this trauma—literally giving form to the unrepresentable. Following on the heels of World War I, whose devastation was not as widely recorded through the medium of photography, the Surrealist reorganization of the body tended to revolve around the notion of the fetish. As many artists associated with "degenerate" movements like Surrealism were forced to flee Europe during the war—with Duchamp famously relocating to New York—their influence dissipated, to be picked up later by a generation after Abstract Expressionism, many of whom were women whose works engaged the representation of the body, shuttling between abstraction and figuration. As Edouard Roditi explained: "It is the sexual content of Surrealist art and its unique dependence upon the human body… that has performed this miracle of raising Surrealism from the dead to triumph like an avenging archangel over the routed hordes of the abstract movement."[9] Artists including Evelyne Axell, Lee Bontecou, Bourgeois, Eva Hesse, Ketty La Rocca, Messager, Carol Rama, de Saint Phalle, and Wilke [ill. 11] brought a uniquely gendered and even nascent feminist perspective to the discourse of the body inherited from the Surrealists.

Perfection is on everybody's lips. Personally, I have a taste for defects or blemishes which, when skillfully accumulated, may acquire their special power. With my permission and in compliance with my will, they add the picture its character.

—Teresa Pągowska[10]

Despite the associations with feminism shared by many of the women artists with whom Szapocznikow's work shares an affinity, her work was not and never intended to be associated with political feminism or feminist content as it was understood in Poland. Indeed, western notions of feminism are virtually useless when applied to Eastern Europe.[11] According to art historian Agata Jakubowska, who has written extensively about Szapocznikow and Polish women artists, western feminist discourse understands socialism as a model of equality for men and women and therefore confuses the role of the Church, for example, in reenforcing traditional models of the passive female, whose place was in the home and with the family.[12] Government-enforced notions of privacy and public space dictated that artwork depicting the body was not permitted under the Communist regime. Body art, a productive mode for so many male and female artists in Western Europe during the 1960s and advanced by critics such as Lea Vergine in Italy and the artist VALIE EXPORT in Austria, was not a viable term or practice in Poland until after 1970, when artists such as KwieKulik (the collaborative duo of Zofia Kulik and Przemysław Kwiek) [ill. 12] were active.[13] Through video and collaborative performances that dealt with their domestic and artistic partnership, which KwieKulik referred to as "Soc art," they engaged the Socialist framework from which their work emerged but attempted to enact a politically engaged social realism in sharp contrast to the failed Socialist Realism of government-sponsored painting and sculpture.[14] Feminism as an organized movement did not exist in Poland during Szapocznikow's life and only recently has a younger generation of artists, including Katarzyna Kozyra [ill. 13], Paulina Ołowska, and Artur Żmijewski—choosing to remain there after Communism's fall in 1989—adopted post-feminism in the absence of a first-generation feminist history.[15] For many of these artists, Szapocznikow is the bridge. Despite living in Paris for the last decade of her life, she remains tremendously influential in Poland and can now be understood as the through-line between a history of radical abstraction and a gendered expression of the body through the *informe*.

Szapocznikow extracted herself from the Polish context first between 1949 and 1951 and then again after 1963, when she moved permanently to Paris. Many important women artists whose work did touch on gender—including Ewa Partum, Natalia Lach-Lachowicz, and Maria Pinińska-Bereś—chose to remain in Poland. Szapocznikow would have known some, while others she would likely have encountered during one of her many trips there to exhibit her work. In addition to her counterparts elsewhere in Europe and the United States, these women artists suggest a network of practices against which Szapocznikow's might productively be read. While there was no organized feminist movement in art during the late 1960s in Poland, there was an avant-garde organized around conceptual strategies and performance related to the legacy of artists such as Tadeusz Kantor, Edward Krasiński, and Władysław Strzemiński. Geometric abstraction, which dominated radical art practice there before World War II, included the work of Russian-born artist Katarzyna Kobro, who along with Strzemiński advanced an approach to abstraction called "Unism" [ill. 19]. A well-documented artist who spent her career in Poland and whose work is foundational to the collection at the Muzeum Sztuki, Łódź, Kobro's spatial compositions from the 1930s have recently been paired with the mid-1960s relational objects of Brazilian artist Lygia Clark.[16] Szapocznikow was intimately familiar with the history of Polish avant-garde art, and it is interesting to compare Kobro's abstraction, which evolved from a geometric and spatial model of vertical and horizontal elements describing space, with Szapocznikow's embodied model of sculpture in which the abstraction and representation of organic forms never moved away from the body but from its exterior to its interior.

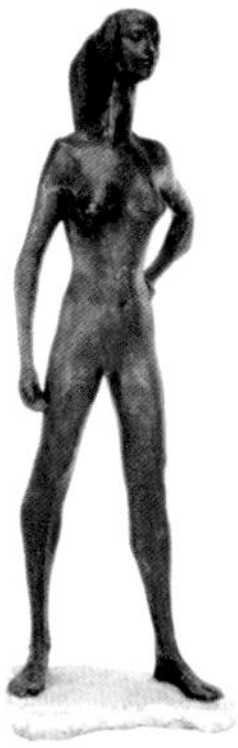

15.

Art historian and curator Izabela Kowalczyk, writing in the recent catalogue for the groundbreaking exhibition "Gender Check: Femininity and Masculinity in the Art of Eastern Europe," describes the received model for women in Communist Poland in the following:

> Traditionally women were represented as the "pathetic" figure of the *Polish mother* who looked after the Polish home and was the guardian of national values ... The cultural myth of the Polish mother is connected with the country's struggle for independence ... The Polish mother was responsible for the continuity of faith, language, and culture ... Even in the late twentieth century women were depicted in this traditional and national context as Polonia, Polish mothers, and mourning women.[17]

The Socialist-Realist painting *Postaci* (Figures, 1950) [ill. 20] by Szapocznikow's contemporary Wojciech Fangor represents the evolution of two social classes in postwar Poland: the modern woman on the left represents the politically active class involved in the reconstruction of Poland, among which Szapocznikow would have counted herself, and on the right, looking at her with some suspicion, is the peasant woman, the traditional Polish woman, worker, and mother.

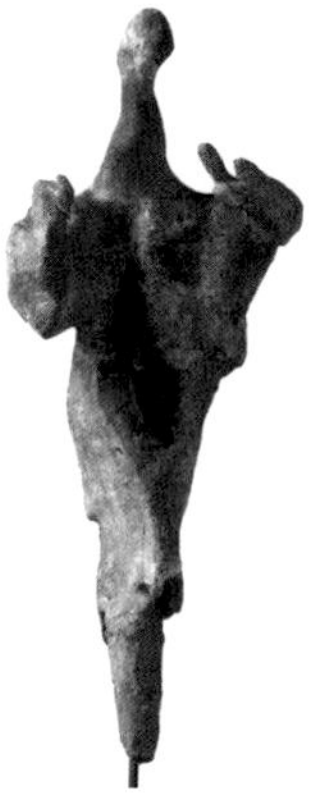

16.

In several public commissions that were executed under the Communist regime, Szapocznikow could be seen in subtle ways to grapple with these engrained female identities and to question the authority of Socialist Realism as a sculptural and representational tradition. Among her early works, cited by Kowalczyk and others as a challenge to Communist notions of privacy and the female body, is *Trudny wiek* (*Difficult Age*, 1956) [ill. 15, plate 149]. Compared to the modesty and narrative character of a work like *Rybaczka II* (*Fisherwoman II*, 1947), the aggressive verticality and confident sexuality of *Difficult Age* would have been striking at a moment when heroic sculpture almost exclusively honored the military dominance of male figures in service to Communism. In other works such as *Maria Magdalena* (*Mary Magdalene*, 1957–58) [ill. 16, plate 143], Szapocznikow introduced abstraction as a way of prying apart traditional representations of the body from within. By opening up the art-historically encoded body of the virgin/whore, she reduced Magdalene's used and repentant body to a humble bony remnant of itself. In a lineage that includes Donatello's haunting *Mary Magdalene* (1454–55), the sculpture is a poignant and extremely vulnerable expression of depletion and a body expended. The brutal nakedness and human scale of *Naga* (*Naked*, 1961) [ill. 17, plate 132], with its bulging lumps and anthropomorphic suggestions of a body barely held together in its skin, anticipates Szapocznikow's later Tu-

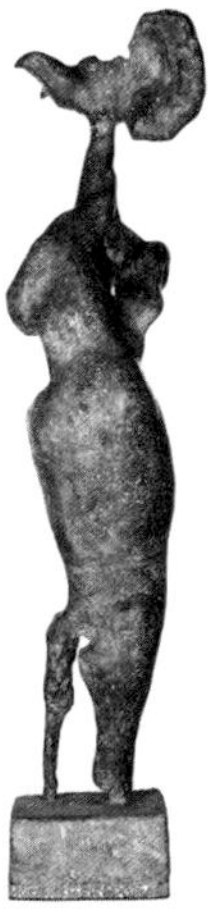

17.

meur (Tumor) sculptures from 1969 on and her *Souvenirs* (1967) [ill. 18, plate 56], in which form is completely abstracted by its own transformation.

If Szapocznikow moved quickly from conventional representations of "woman" in the late 1950s to a kind of embodied abstraction that began to reflect Surrealism reanimated by an exploration of sexuality and eroticism in the early 1960s, Polish contemporaries like Magdalena Abakanowicz and Teresa Pągowska were also working prior to a feminist language or discourse, but clearly interrogating how the integrity of the modernist body might be undone. Trained as a weaver but employing off-loom sculptural techniques to make fiber-based installations, Abakanowicz created large woven structures she called Abakans [ill. 21]—a term derived from her own name—that inhabited space with an erotic charge created through rich color and suggestive form.[18] Her early monumental, soft, and often vaginal forms gave way to a more descriptive representation of the human figure, but the Abakans can be seen as related to Szapocznikow's Tumor sculptures, which share an interiority and presence that is clearly of the artist's own body.

Pągowska, a painter whose work was included in the 1961 exhibition "15 Polish Painters" at The Museum of Modern Art in New York, was with Szapocznikow when the latter showed a group of ten sculptures in the Polish pavilion at the 1962 Venice Biennale.[19] Like Abakanowicz, Pągowska struggled to allow a kind of abstract language to invade the representation of the human, often female, body. Her careful composition of painted forms and areas of exposed raw canvas yielded a strangely surrealistic merging of flatness and figuration [ill. 22]. Pągowska achieved in two dimensions a hybrid image of the body in flux that was akin to Szapocznikow's, which represented the pull of abstraction on the figurative imagery she had been negotiating for several years. Each oeuvre embodied a combination of organic form and a mangled, poignant ugliness that was often remarked upon in the critical response to their work—in Szapocznikow's case representing the persistence of form in the face of the relentless and inevitable cycle of life and death. This semi-abstract language of a corporeal obliteration was associated with Western European painting—in particular, Jean Fautrier's tactile working of malleable concrete into the painted surface, the visceral line of Jean Dubuffet's 1950 series of works titled Corps de Dame [ill. 23], and the burned plastic masses of Alberto Burri, all of which embodied the devastation of postwar Europe and its population, bodies literally undone by the experience of unrepresentable trauma.

Obliteration

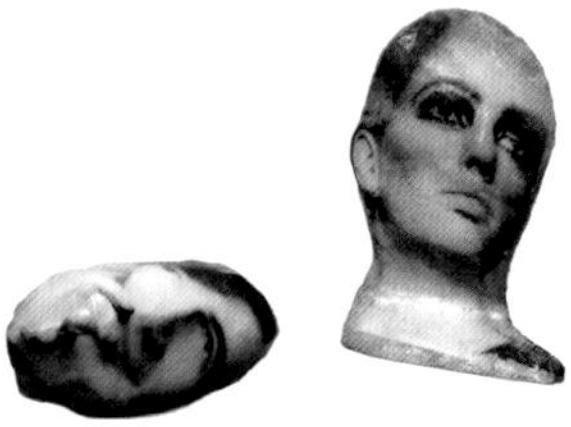

18.

> The modernist notion of fragment as microcosm has given way in current artworks to a willingness to let fragment be fragment, to allow partiality to exist … Art is creation in response to lack. The art object is a kind of fetish, a replacement for some real thing that is missing, as differentiated from a stand-in for the archetype which must be there, somewhere.
>
> —Mike Kelley[20]

Ultimately it is the restless instability of Szapocznikow's body of work that makes it contemporary and potentially deeply feminist ahead of its time. Her cancer, suspected in 1968 and finally diagnosed in 1969, played a role in her conceiving of the form and image of partiality, literally a body in fragments. In many ways, the last part of her career is

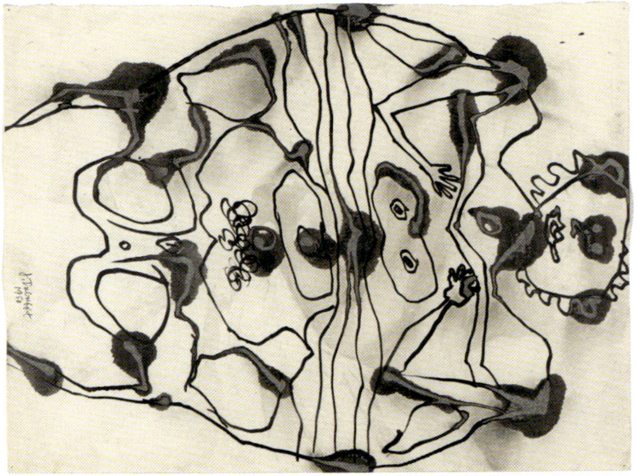

23. Jean Dubuffet (French, 1901–1985), *Corps de Dame*, 1950. Ink on paper, 12 3/4 x 9 7/8" (32.4 x 25.1 cm). The Museum of Modern Art, New York. The Joan and Lester Avnet Collection.

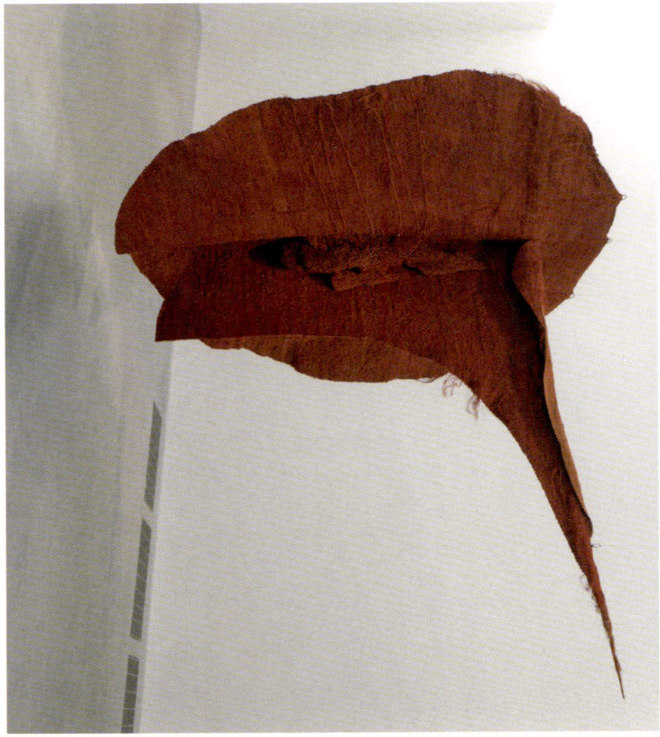

21. Magdalena Abakanowicz (Polish, born 1930), *Abakan Red*, 1969. Sisal and metal, 118 1/8 x 118 1/8 x 137 3/4" (300 x 300 x 350 cm). Tate, London. Presented anonymously, 2009.

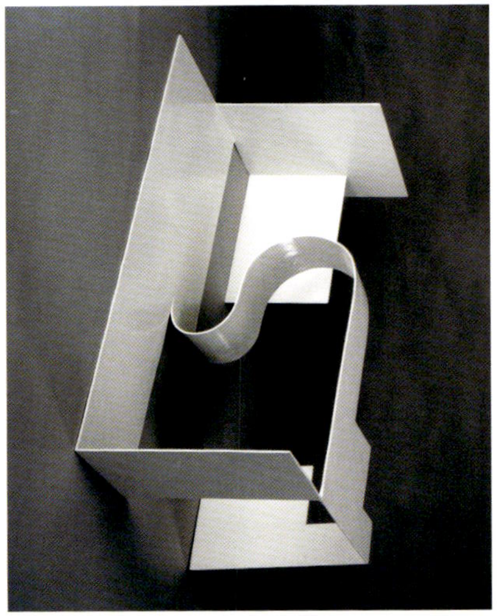

19. Katarzyna Kobro (Russian, 1898–1951), *Kompozycja przestrzenna (5)* (Spatial Composition [5]), 1929. Painted steel, 9 7/8 x 25 3/16 x 15 3/4" (25 x 64 x 40 cm). Muzeum Sztuki, Łódź.

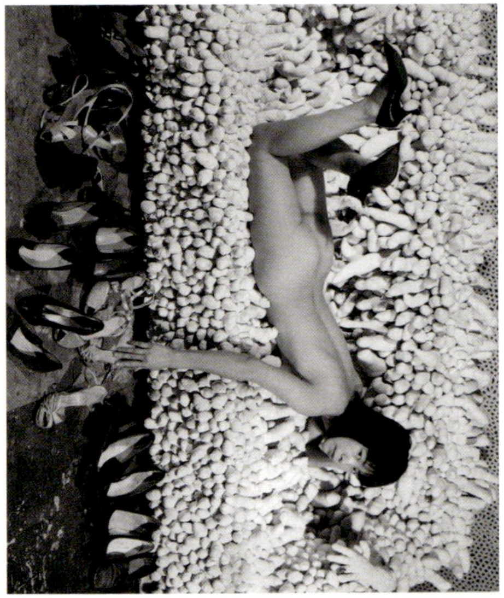

24. Yayoi Kusama (Japanese, born 1929) with her work, New York, 1964.

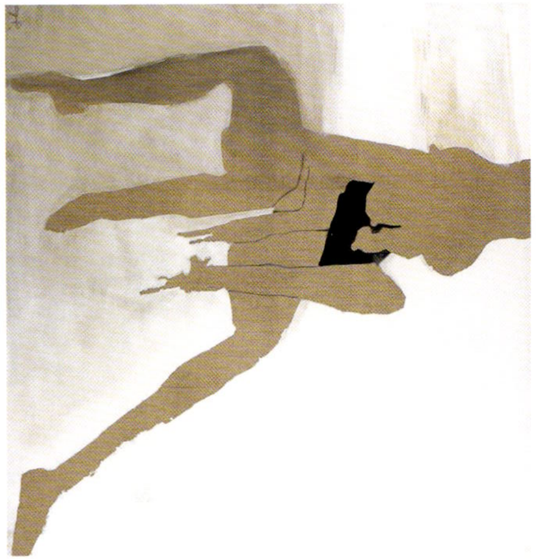

22. Teresa Pągowska (Polish, 1926–2007), *Monochromat XXXXC (5)* (Monochrome XXXXC [5]), 1975. Tempera and acrylic on canvas, 47 1/4 x 51 3/16" (120 x 130 cm). Courtesy Galeria aTAK, Warsaw.

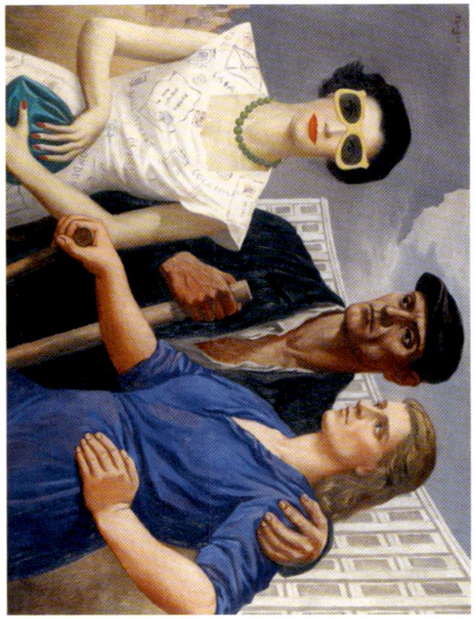

20. Wojciech Fangor (Polish, born 1922), *Postaci* (Figures), 1950. Oil on canvas, 39 3/8 x 49 1/4" (100 x 125 cm). Muzeum Sztuki, Łódź.

her most radical. Eerily, just prior to her illness, *Souvenirs* appears as a haunting swarm of fragments distinguished by the incorporation of photography but whose sculptural *informe* is also equally compelling.[21] Bearing the photographic portraits of Christian Boltanski, an artist-friend who would later become known for his enduring images of the Holocaust; Sophia Loren, a filmic icon of exaggerated female sexuality; screen star Monica Vitti; surrealist novelist and poet Fernando Arrabal, and two anonymous figures, Szapocznikow's three-dimensional works—in which images are frozen in shards of resin, bent, cracked, and scattered on the ground—can only be understood as accumulations of fragments. Paralleling other sculptural accumulations, such as those of Bourgeois, Kusama, or Wilke, *Souvenirs* is a serial accretion of form. Writing about Kusama's *Accumulation II* (1966), Helen Molesworth describes the artist's desire for full-body contact with her sculpture [ill. 24]:

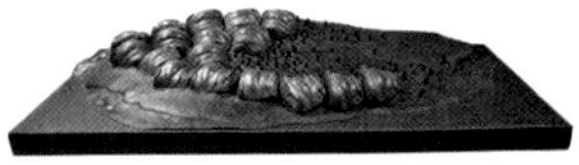

25.

> [O]ne of the effects of the swarming tactility of Kusama's encrusted objects is that of obliteration—an intensely radical dismissal not only of the boundaries between the world of objects and sculptures but also of persons and things . . . the boundaries between bodies and objects and bodies and space are dissolved.[22]

Echoing Kusama, Szapocznikow is seen in archival photographs posing playfully with the sculptures and "wearing" them close to her body [ill. 29]. While one can read *Souvenirs* as voraciously multiplying cancerous forms, they can also surely be understood as remnants, insistent evidence of the enduring force of the body, remembrances of a life.

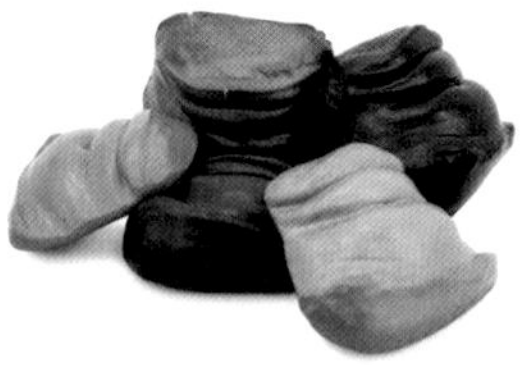

26.

In sculptural clusters of bellies, such as *Grande Plage* (*Big Beach*, 1968) [ill. 25, plate 76] and *Ventres - coussins* (*Belly Cushions*, 1968) [ill. 26, plate 75]; breasts, such as those in *Krużlowa (Macierzyństwo)* (*Madonna of Krużlowa [Motherhood]*, 1969) [plate 63] and the Fétiche (Fetish) series of 1970–71 and Dessert arrangements of 1970–71; and tumors, including *L'Enterrement d'Alina* (*Alina's Funeral*, 1970) [ill. 27, plate 66], *Envahissement des Tumeurs* (*Invasion of Tumors*, 1970), and *Tumeurs personnifiées* (*Tumors personified*, 1971) [plate 64], one senses an artist desperate to create, or indeed procreate, form by deploying her own body in the face of its inevitable and rapid decline. In 1971, following the incorporation of her "death mask" in *Tumors personified*, Szapocznikow moved radically back to a figuration reworked through the merging of the body with the form and material of her sculptures. Pressing the body into material before it set—in some ways analogous to the indexical nature of the photograph—she created excruciating and fragile images of herself and her son Piotr that appear in the sculptures of the Herbier (Herbarium) series. Functioning as a phantasmagoria of the maternal body, these works are the most literal and vulnerable artistic statements of her career.

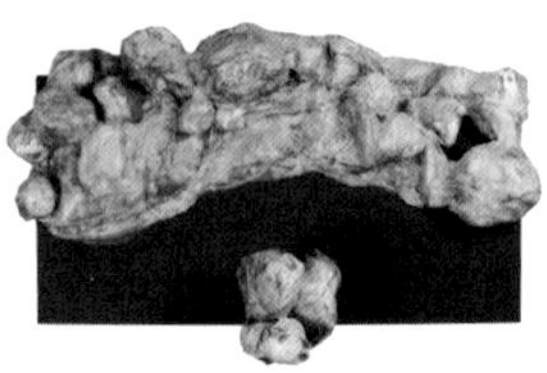

27.

During the last year of her life, Szapocznikow agreed to participate in "Labyrinths/Women and the Arts: Multi Media," a multimedia festival at the Roundhouse in London. The exhibition was postponed to May 1973, and she died a few months before it opened. This was the first and only instance during her life when her sculpture would have been included in an all-woman context—with a fascinating list of artists including Bontecou, Chryssa, Barbara Hepworth, Marisol, Louise Nevelson, and de Saint Phalle, as well as actors, poets, and nonfiction writers Simone de Beauvoir, Eva Figes, Betty Freidan, and Germaine Greer.[23] While scholarship connecting Szapocznikow to the issue of gender is relatively new, it is also emerging that her work is part of a reconception of Surrealism that occurred throughout the 1960s, in which artists—many of them women—radically reimagined the erotics of the sculptural body.

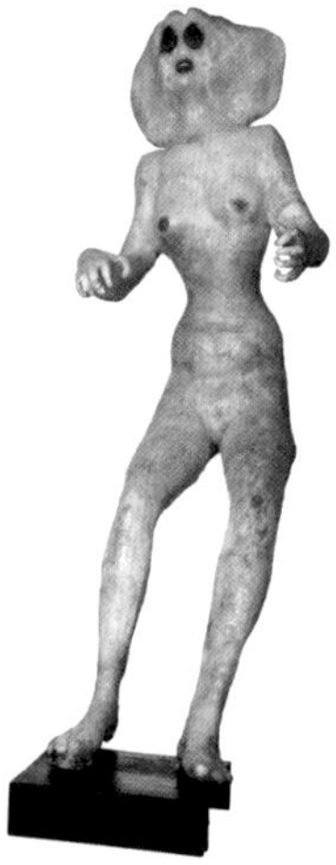

28.

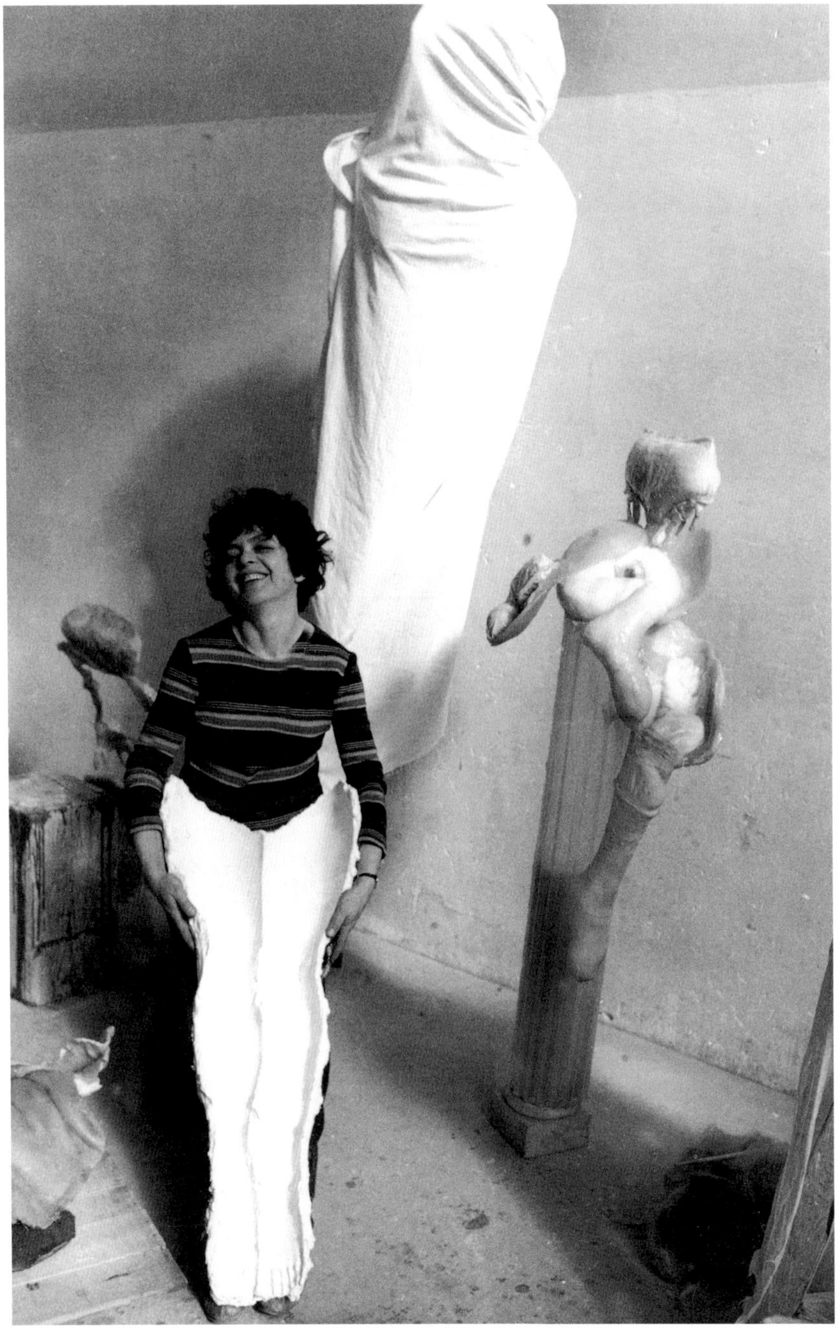

29. The artist in her Malakoff studio, 1967.

Postscript

In the 1976 film *Ślad (Trace)*, made three years after the artist's death, the strange specter of the artist's sculpture *Le Voyage* (*Journey*, 1967) [ill. 28, plate 89] is seen making its way through the still rough streets of Poland's industrial capital, Łódź.[24] Hovering just above the street, tilted slightly off its center of gravity, arms raised as if reaching for some unseen force, the blind creature looks up at the sky or towards the future. The figure is androgynous, without sex or beyond it—its nipples and lips lit up in red, its coiffed headdress fanning out as if it were in drag, and its eyes like black orbs. The film captures the spirit and larger-than-life ambition of the artist for her awkward and compelling forms. Szapocznikow represented in three dimensions a vertiginous in-betweenness that is virtually unprecedented in the history of twentieth-century sculpture—between the vertical and the horizontal, the coherent and the *informe*, the beginning and the end.

Notes

1. Paul Thek, postcard to Robert Pincus-Witten, Amsterdam, 1969, quoted in *Paul Thek: Tales the Tortoise Taught Us*, ed. Margrit Brehm, Axel Heil, and Roberto Ohrt (Cologne: Verlag der Buchhandlung Walther König, 2008), 66.
2. Alina Szapocznikow, letter to Jerzy Stajuda, later published as "Z Paryża pisze Alina Szapocznikow [o Giacomettim]," *Współczesność*, no. 5 (1966), quoted in *Alina Szapocznikow* (Warsaw: Institute for the Promotion of Art Foundation, Galeria Zachęta, 1998), 128. For further analysis of this sculpture see Agata Jakubowska, "Alina Szapocznikow's *Leg* and *Goldfinger*: Between Reality and Illusion," in *Alina Szapocznikow. Awkward Objects*, ed. Jakubowska (Warsaw: Museum of Modern Art, 2011), 123–31.
3. "L'Exposition Internationale du Surréalisme: 1959–1960," organized by Marcel Duchamp and André Breton, Galerie Daniel Cordier, Paris, December 15, 1959 – February 14, 1960. The work appears in the catalogue as both *Vaste construction-cible* and *Large Target Construction*. See *Exposition Internationale du Surréalisme* (Paris: Galerie Daniel Cordier, 1959), 26.
4. Niki de Saint Phalle, quoted in Uta Grosenick, "Niki de Saint Phalle's Letters – An Introduction," *Niki de Saint Phalle*, ed. Pontus Hulten (Bonn, Germany: Kunst- und Ausstellungshalle der Bundesrepublik Deutschland; and Stuttgart: Verlag Gerd Hatje, 1992), 147–48.
5. Two recent exhibitions have begun to redress this situation: "Seductive Subversion: Women Pop Artists, 1958–1968," University of the Arts, Philadelphia, January 22 – March 15, 2010; and "POWER UP – Female Pop Art," Kunsthalle Wien, November 5, 2010 – February 20, 2011. See Kalliopi Minioudaki, "Other(s') Pop: The Return of the Repressed of Two Discourses," in *POWER UP – Female Pop Art* (Vienna: Kunsthalle Wien; and Cologne, Germany: DuMont Buchverlag, 2010). The cultural contexts from which Pop art emerged internationally differed widely and in Poland in particular, where the Socialist economy regulated consumption.
6. See Scott Rothkopf, "Paul Thek and the Sixties Surreal," in *Paul Thek: Diver, A Retrospective* (New York: Whitney Museum of American Art; and Pittsburgh: Carnegie Museum of Art, 2010), 51.
7. Mignon Nixon, "Posing the Phallus," *October*, no. 92 (Spring 2000): 104.
8. Hal Foster and Helen Molesworth in the spring 2000 issue of *October* discuss the work of Robert Gober; see Foster, "An Art of Missing Parts," *October*, no. 92: 128–56; and Molesworth, "House Work and Art Work," ibid.: 71–97.
9. Edouard Roditi, "Letter from Paris: Surrealism Resurrected," *Apollo*, 83 no. 5 (May 1966): 380, quoted in Rothkopf, "Paul Thek and the Sixties Surreal," 52.
10. Teresa Pągowska, statement, March 25, 1994, in *Teresa Pągowska*, ed. Bożena Grochala, trans. Ewa Krasińska (Warsaw: Wydawnictwa Artystyczne i Filmowe Sp. z o.o., 1996), 6.
11. See Nanette Funk, "Fifteen Years of the East – West Women's Dialogue," in *Living Gender After Communism*, ed. Janet Elise Johnson and Jean C. Robinson (Bloomington: Indiana University Press, 2007), 203–27. See also Martina Pachmanová, "In? Out? In Between? Some Notes on the Invisibility of a Nascent Eastern European Feminist and Gender Discourse in Contemporary Art Theory," in *Gender Check: Femininity and Masculinity in the Art of Eastern Europe*, ed. Bojana Pejić (Vienna: Museum Moderner Kunst Stiftung Ludwig; and Cologne, Germany: Verlag der Buchhandlung Walther König, 2009), 241–48.
12. For a brief overview of women and the Church in Poland, see Izabela Kowalczyk, "Poland: Izabela Kowalczyk," *Gender Check*, 362.
13. Zofia Kulik, conversation with the author, October 2004. The partnership lasted from 1971 to 1987. Kulik is now widely regarded as one of Poland's leading female artists. She recalls having no intention to incorporate feminist content but now acknowledges it in her early work and collaborative practice as KwieKulik. For more on Body art in Poland, see Jakubowska, "Body Art in Poland," in *Body and the East: From the 1960s to the Present* (Ljubljana: Moderna galerija, 1998), 125.
14. See Łukasz Ronduda, "Soc-Art; or an Attempt at Politicizing Aesthetics," in *Polish Art of the 70s* (Warsaw: Center for Contemporary Art – Ujazdowski Castle, 2009), 222–42. Ronduda also organized "The Films of Polish Women Artists in the 1970s and 1980s – From the Archive of Polish Experimental Film," presented at the Kitchen, New York, April 28, 2003. See program notes, available at http://www.artmargins.com/index.php/6-film-a-video/216-the-films-of-polish-women-artists-in-the-1970s-and-1980s-from-the-archive-of-polish-experimental-film-; and Archive of Polish Experimental Film website, http://www.csw.art.pl/archfilm.

15. Aneta Szyłak, ed., *Architectures of Gender: Contemporary Women's Art in Poland* (Warsaw: National Museum in Warsaw, 2003). This was one of the first exhibitions to highlight this history.
16. "Katarzyna Kobro/Lygia Clark," Muzeum Sztuki, Łódź, Poland, November 21, 2008 – March 1, 2009. Ryszard Stanisławski, Szapocznikow's first husband, was director of the Muzeum Sztuki from 1965 to 1990. The museum was a center of intellectual activity in the 1960s and remains the repository of the most important collection of Polish avant-garde art, including major holdings of work by Kobro.
17. Kowalczyk, "Poland: Izabela Kowalczyk," 362. See also Ewa Grigar on the *Matka Polka* (Mother Pole) in "The Gendered Body as Raw Material for Women Artists of Central Eastern Europe after Communism," in *Living Gender after Communism*, 84.
18. Abakanowicz and Szapocznikow had solo exhibitions at Warsaw's Zachęta National Gallery of Art in 1965 and 1967, respectively, and participated in exhibitions at the same venues in Poland throughout the early 1960s. They would have known each other's work throughout the 1960s.
19. In MoMA's archives there is evidence of a correspondence between Szapocznikow, Chief Curator of Painting and Sculpture Peter Selz, and Curator of Photography Peter Bunnell. Between 1963 and 1970, she and Selz write about the possibility of showing her work at MoMA or elsewhere in New York. In a letter dated 24 May 1964, Selz facilitates Szapocznikow's introduction to Marcel Duchamp. See Chronology elsewhere in this volume.
20. Mike Kelley, introduction to *The Uncanny* (Arnhem, Netherlands: Sonsbeek, 1993), 15–16. Kelley's contribution to the international exhibition "Sonsbeek 93" comprised, among others things, a small book featuring a selection of fragmentary works and objects, including Thek's *Warrior's Leg* (1966–67).
21. Griselda Pollock has analyzed the residue of trauma in Szapocznikow's work in her forthcoming essay "Traumatic Encryption in the Sculptural Dissolutions of Alina Szapocznikow," in *After-affect/Afterimage: Trauma and Aesthetic Inscription in the Virtual Feminist Museum* (Manchester, England: Manchester University Press, 2012). I am enormously grateful to Pollock for introducing me to Szapocznikow's work long before I was ready to understand it. This text has benefited immensely from her groundbreaking work.
22. Molesworth, *Part Object Part Sculpture* (Columbus, Ohio: Wexner Center for the Arts, Ohio State University; and University Park, Pennsylvania: Pennsylvania State University Press, 2005), 167. It is impossible to discuss women artists' relation to the notion of the erotic object without citing Molesworth's important exhibition.
23. Correspondence in Alina Szapocznikow Archive/ Piotr Stanisławski/National Museum in Kraków. A synopsis of the exhibition is available online at http://www.artmuseum.pl/archiwa.php?l=1&a=1&skrot=0&id=1512&id=1512.
24. *Ślad (Trace)*, a color film directed by Helena Włodarczyk from the series "Polska Plastyka Współczesna," produced by Film Polski, 1976. Włodarczyk, a student at the time, made this little-known film after the artist's death with the cooperation of Stanisławski, then-director of the museum in Łódź, who released the sculpture to the filmmaker and allowed it to be paraded in the street.

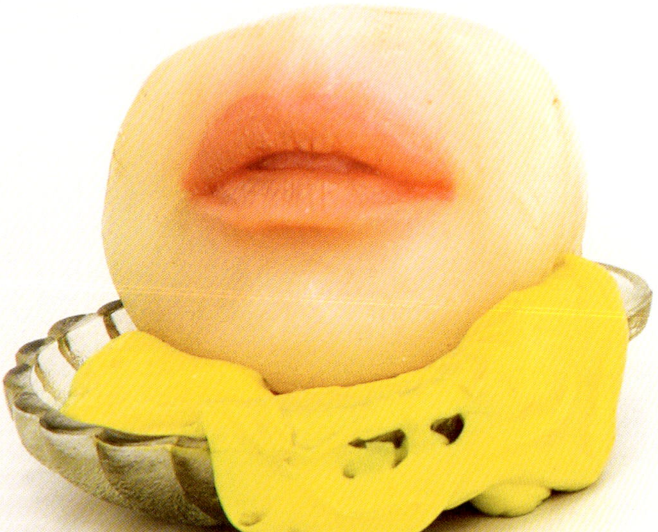

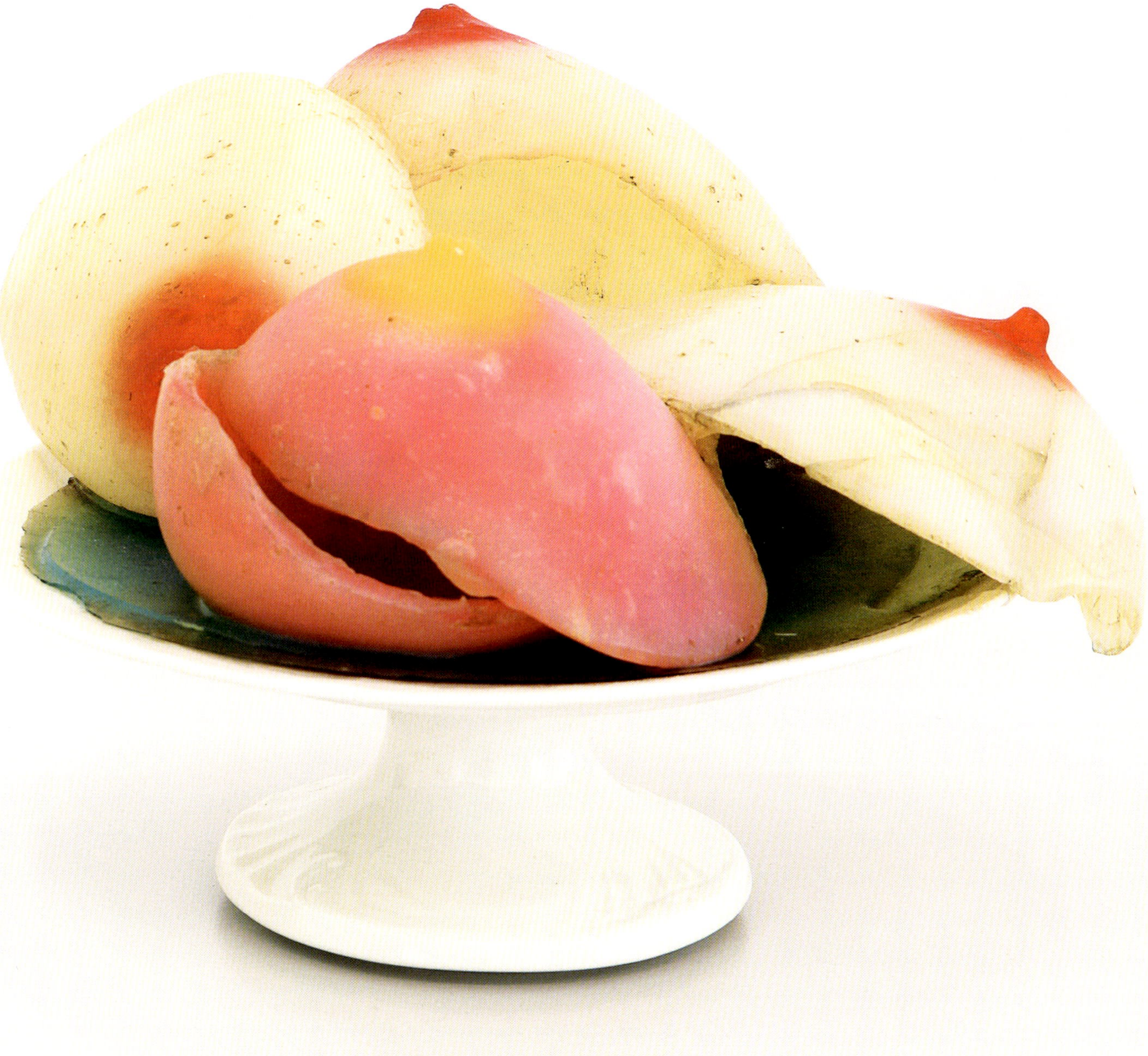

Plate 20 a, b

left

Petit Dessert I (Small Dessert I), 1970–71
Colored polyester resin and glass
3 3/16 x 4 5/16 x 5 1/8" (8 x 11 x 13 cm)

right

Dessert III, 1971
Colored polyester resin and porcelain base
7 1/8 x 9 7/16 x 9 7/8" (18 x 24 x 25 cm)

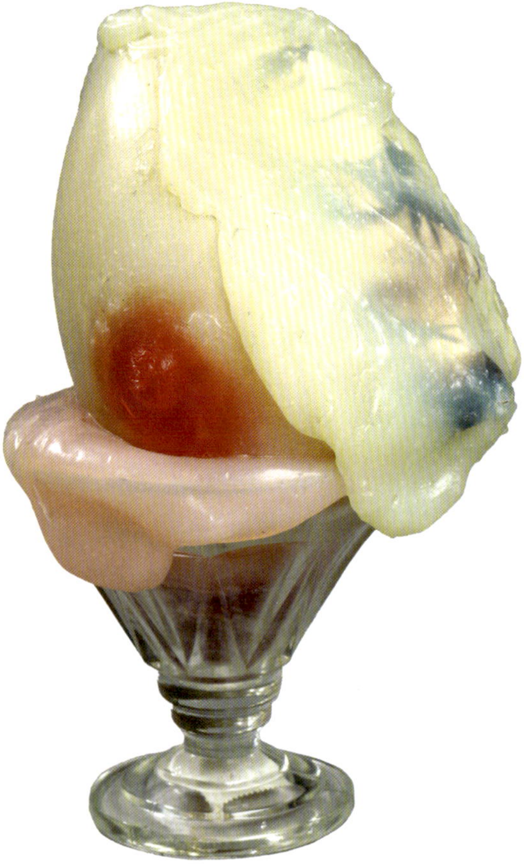

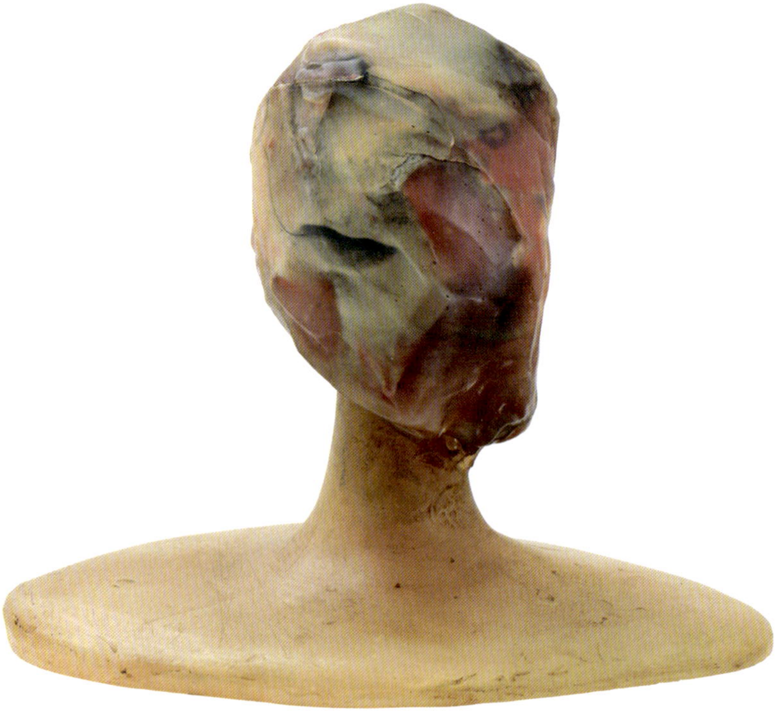

left

Plate 21

Dessert II, 1970–71
Polyester resin, glass, photographs
7 1/2 x 5 1/8 x 5 1/8" (19 x 13 x 13 cm)

right

Plate 22

Dessert V, 1971
Colored polyester resin and photographs
9 1/16 x 6 5/16 x 7 1/2" (23 x 16 x 19 cm)

opposite

Plate 23

Fajrant (End of Day's Work), 1971
Polyester resin, rubber glove, brush
10 1/4 x 6 5/16 x 4 5/16" (26 x 16 x 11 cm)

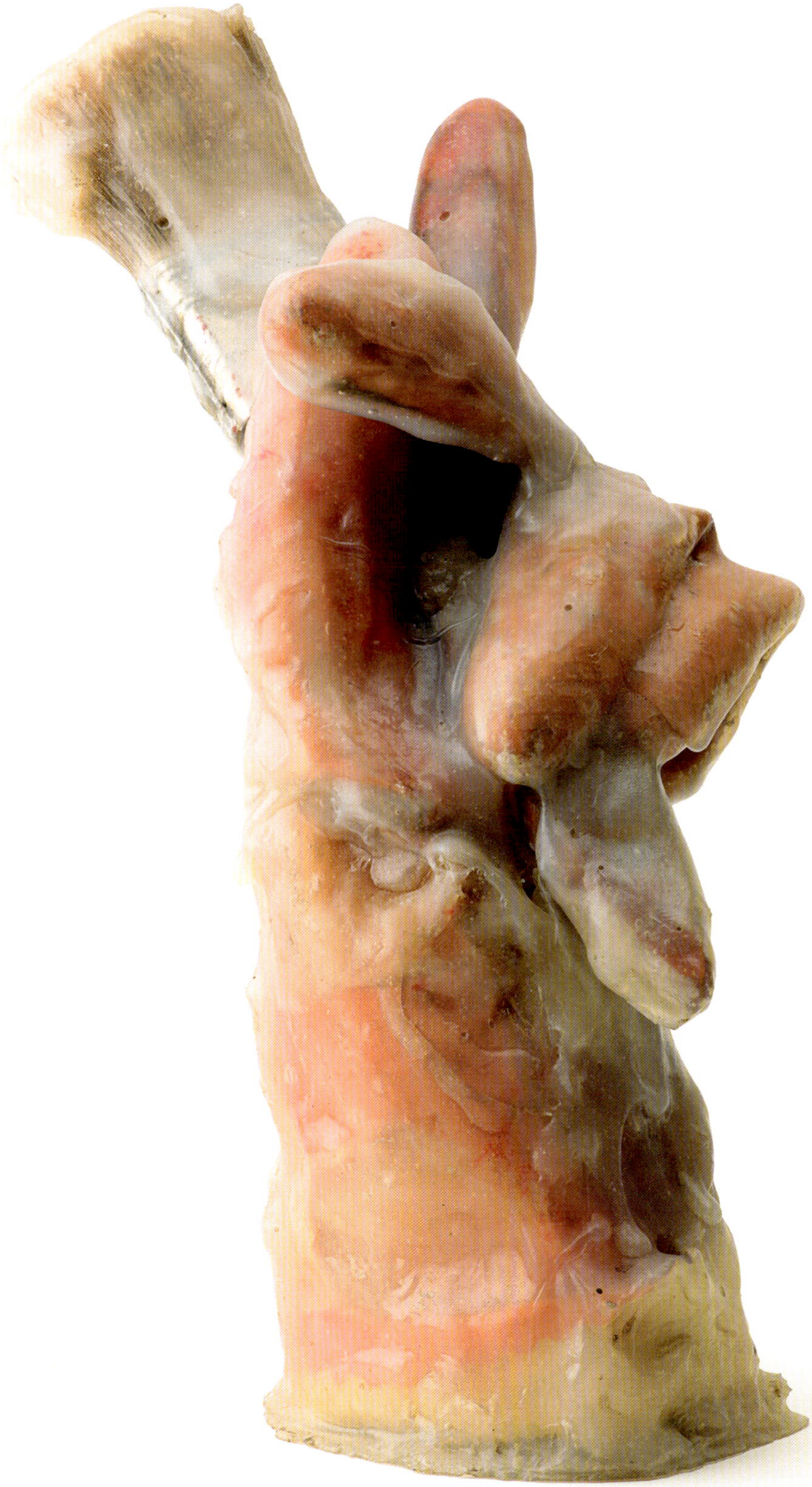

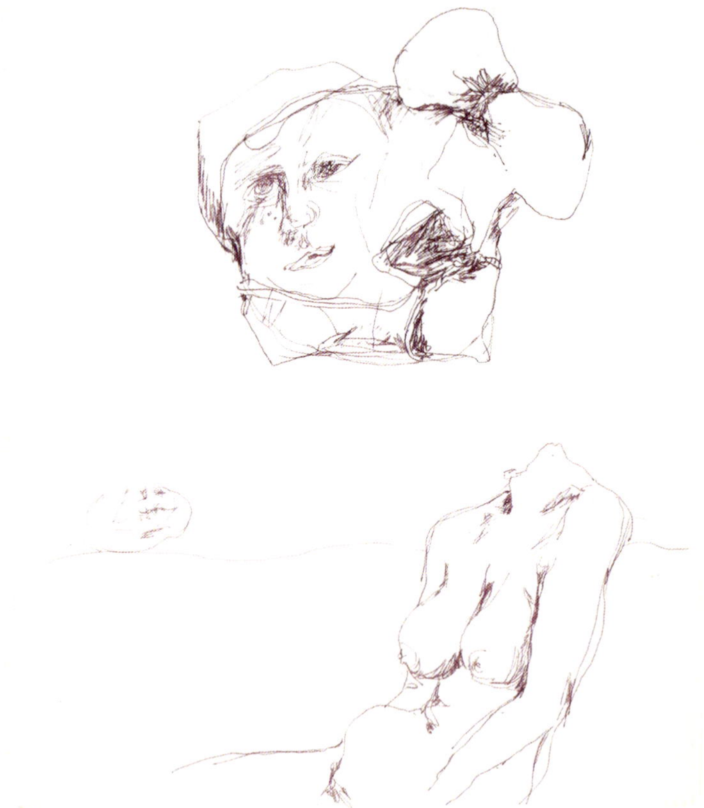

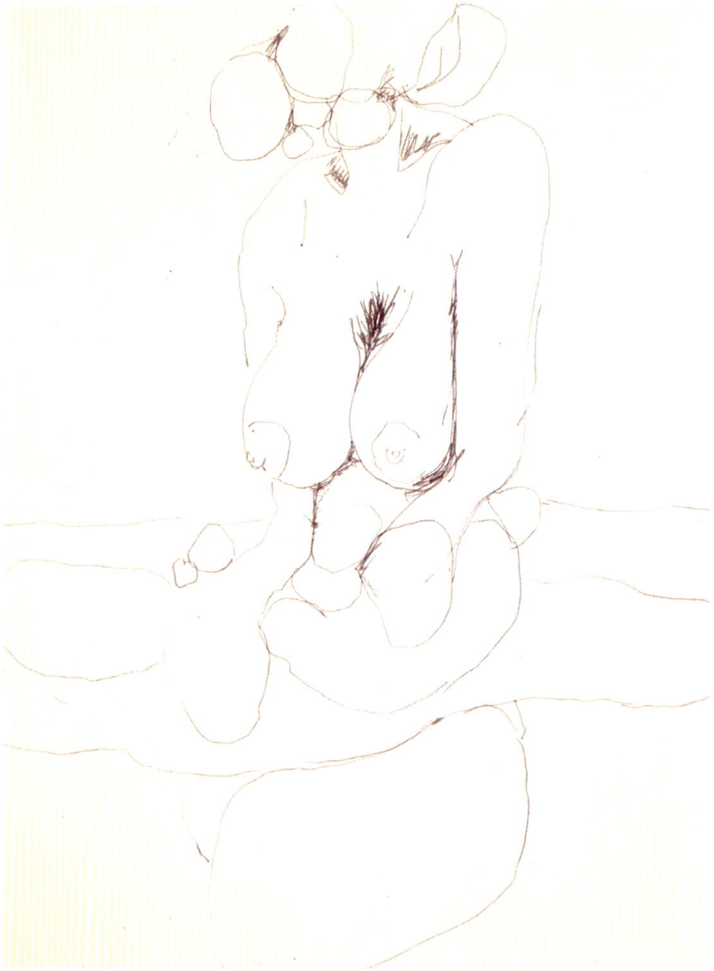

left

Plate 24

Untitled (Bust-Length Figure of a Woman, Headless 1), c. 1971
Felt-tip pen on paper
13 3/8 x 10 1/2" (34 x 26.7 cm)

right

Plate 25

Untitled (Bust-Length Figure of a Woman, Headless 2), c. 1971
Felt-tip pen on paper
12 5/8 x 9 1/4" (32 x 23.4 cm)
Private collection

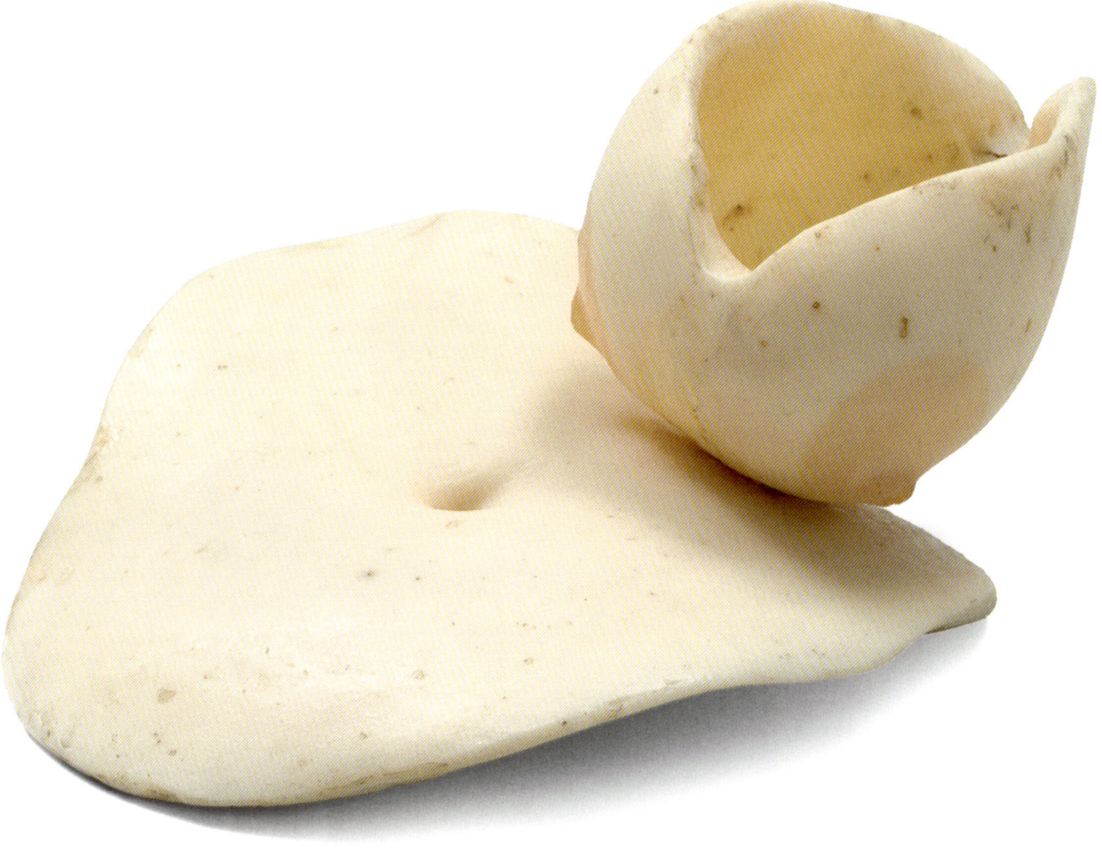

Plate 26

Cendrier de Célibataire II (The Bachelor's Ashtray II), 1972
Polyester resin
5 1/8 x 10 5/8 x 7 1/8" (13 x 27 x 18 cm)

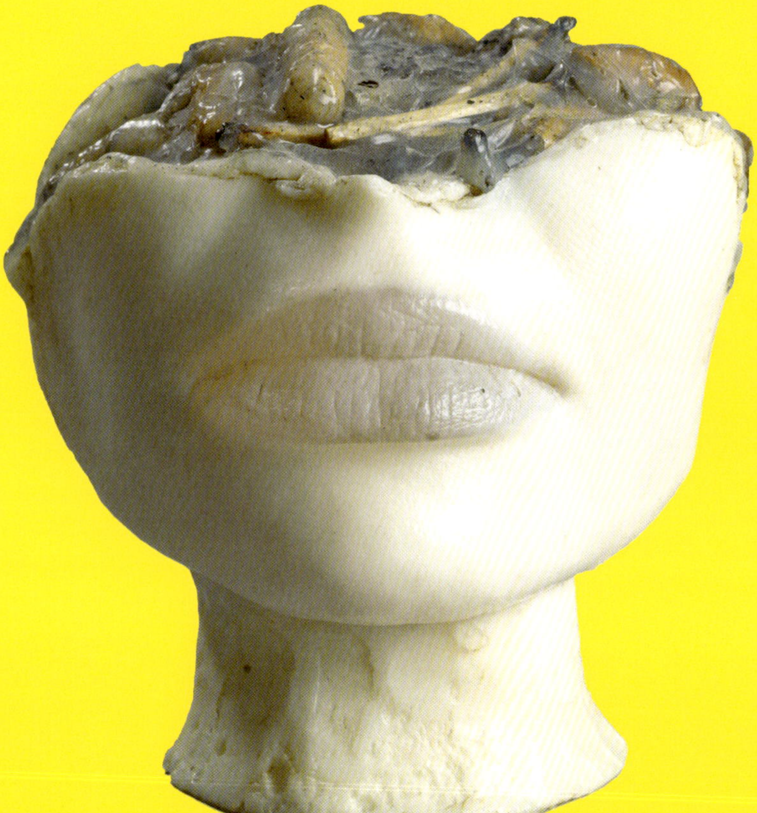

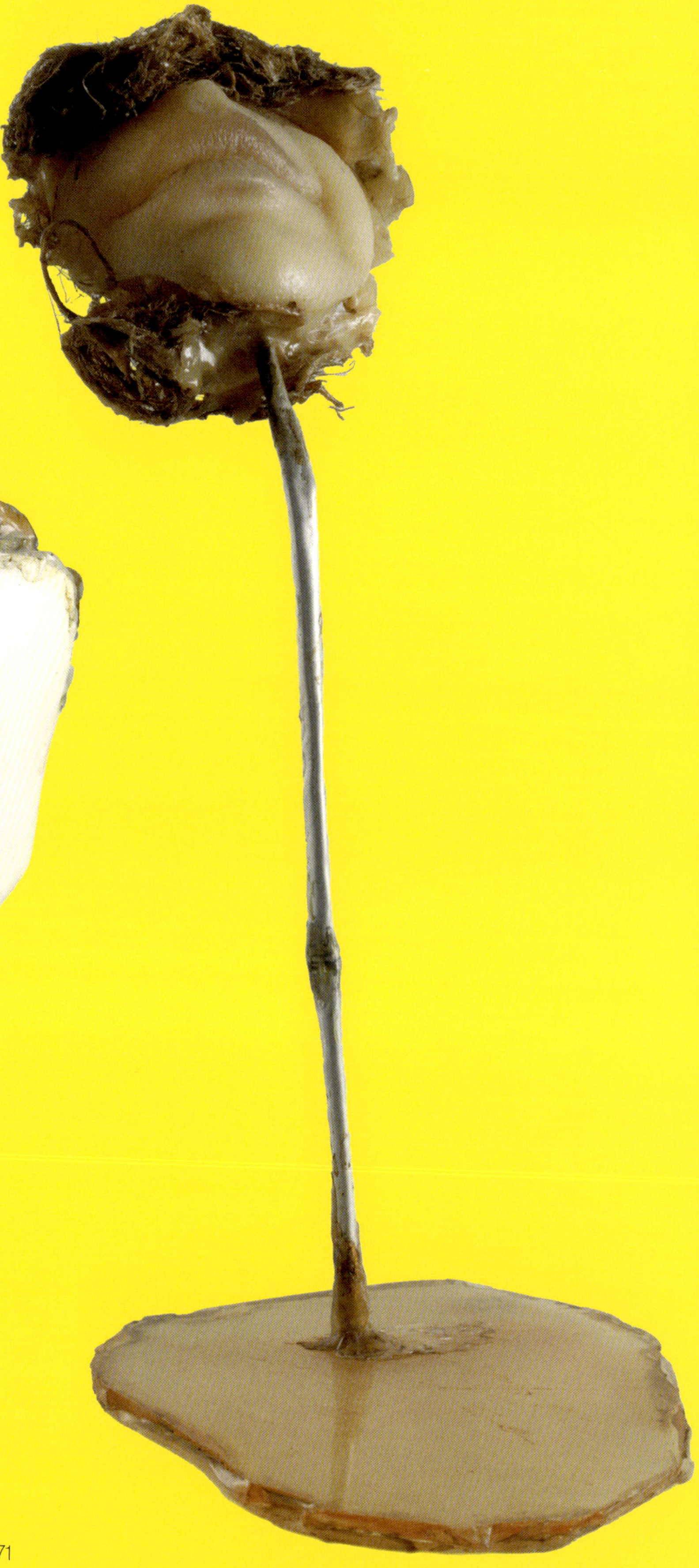

left
Plate 27

Cendrier de Célibataire I
(The Bachelor's Ashtray I), 1972
Colored polyester resin and cigarette butts
4 9/16 x 4 15/16 x 4 5/16" (11.5 x 12.5 x 11 cm)

right
Plate 28

Bouche sur tige (Lips on a Stem), 1971
Polyester resin, hemp, aluminum wire
13" (33 cm) high

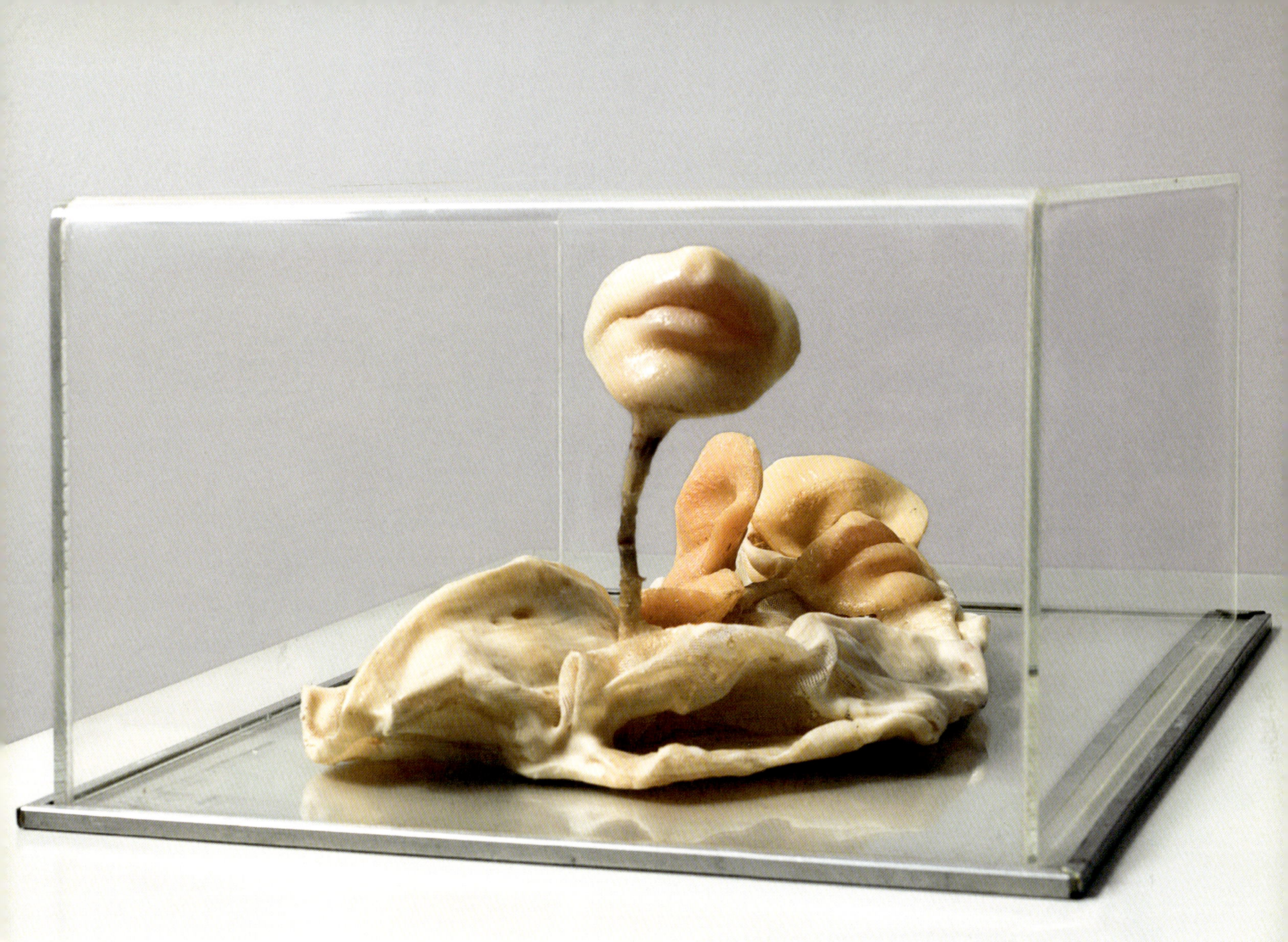

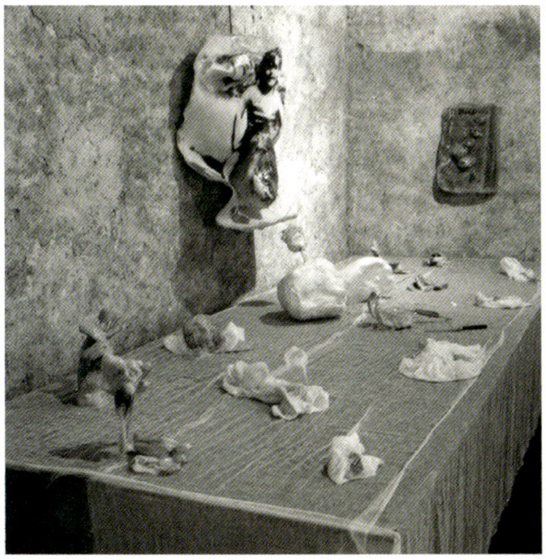

Aurora Gallery, Geneva, 1971.

Plate 29

Bouche en marche (Fétiche III) (Marching lips [Fetish III]), 1970
Polyester resin, plastic lace, Plexiglas vitrine
7 1/8 x 14 9/16 x 9 7/16" (18 x 37 x 24 cm)

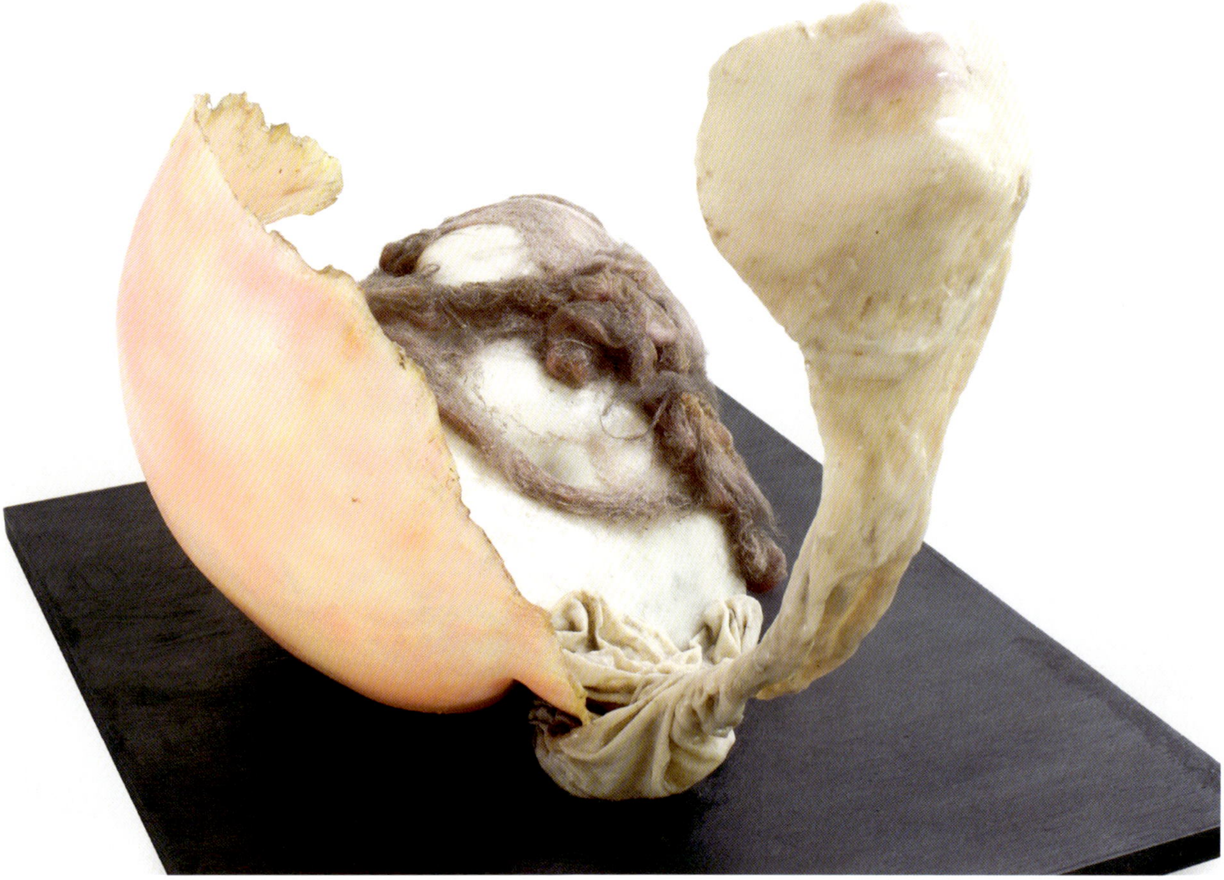

Plate 30

Untitled (*Fétiche VII*) (Fetish VII), 1971
Polyester resin, nylon tights, wool
13 13/16 x 19 11/16 x 15 3/4" (35 x 50 x 40 cm)

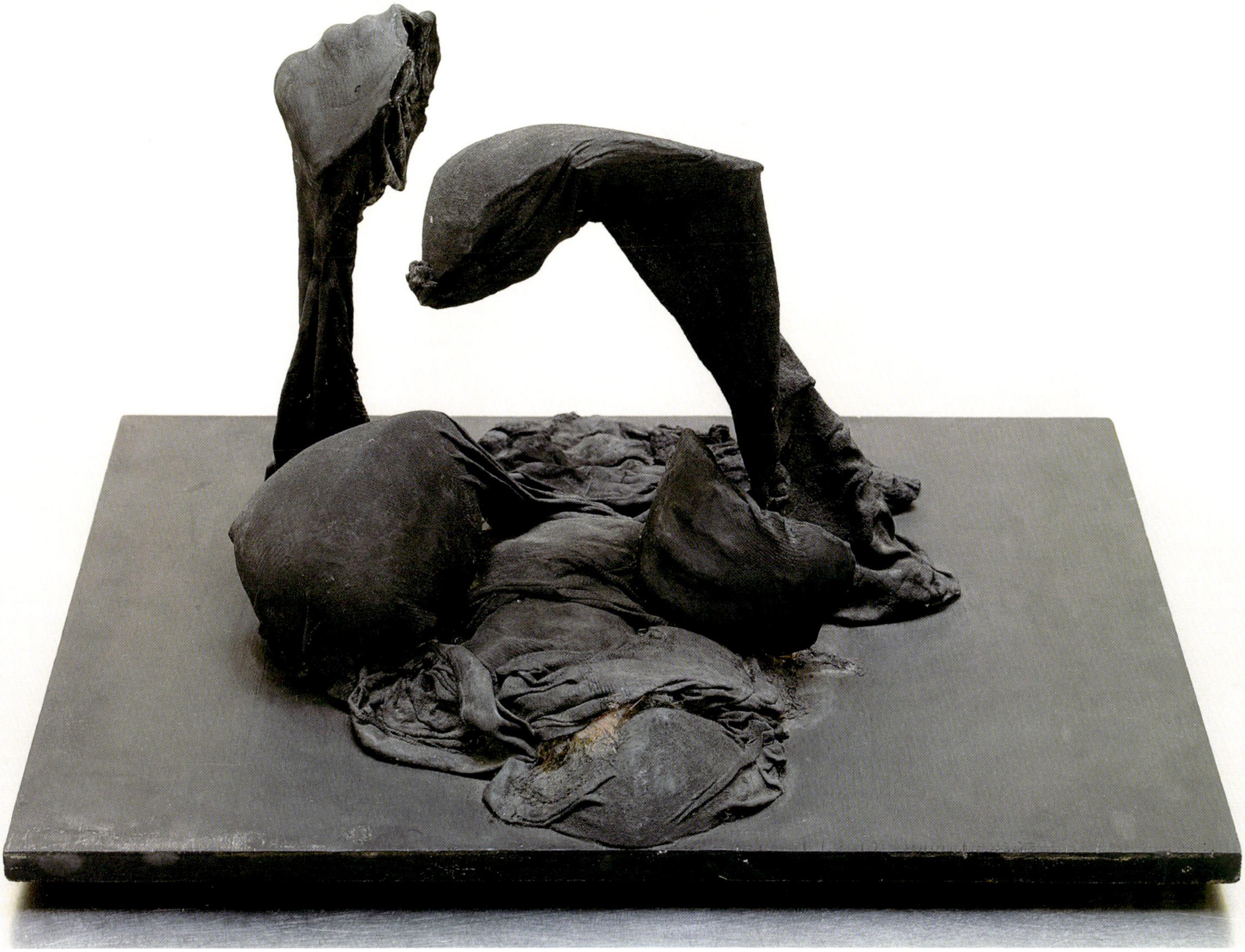

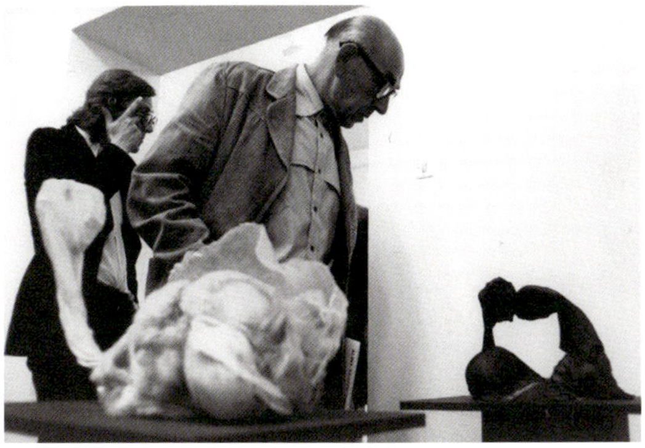

Muzeum Sztuki, Łódź, 1975.

Plate 31

Sculpture (Fétiche IV) (Sculpture [Fetish IV]), 1971
Polyester resin, stockings, wood, lingerie
10 1/4 x 13 3/8 x 15 9/16" (26 x 34 x 39.5 cm)

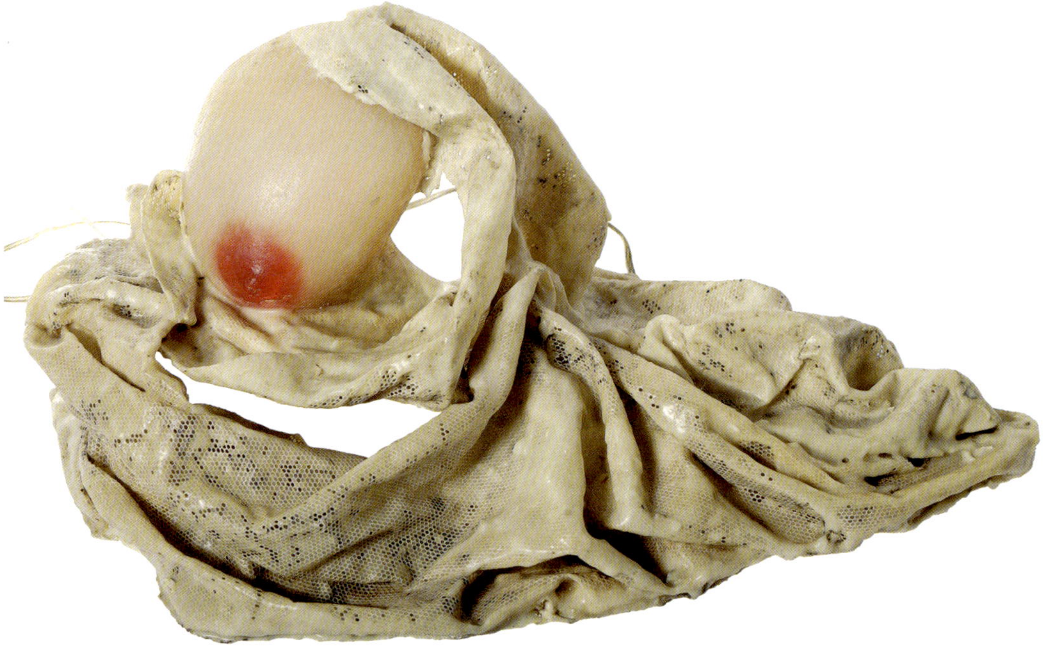

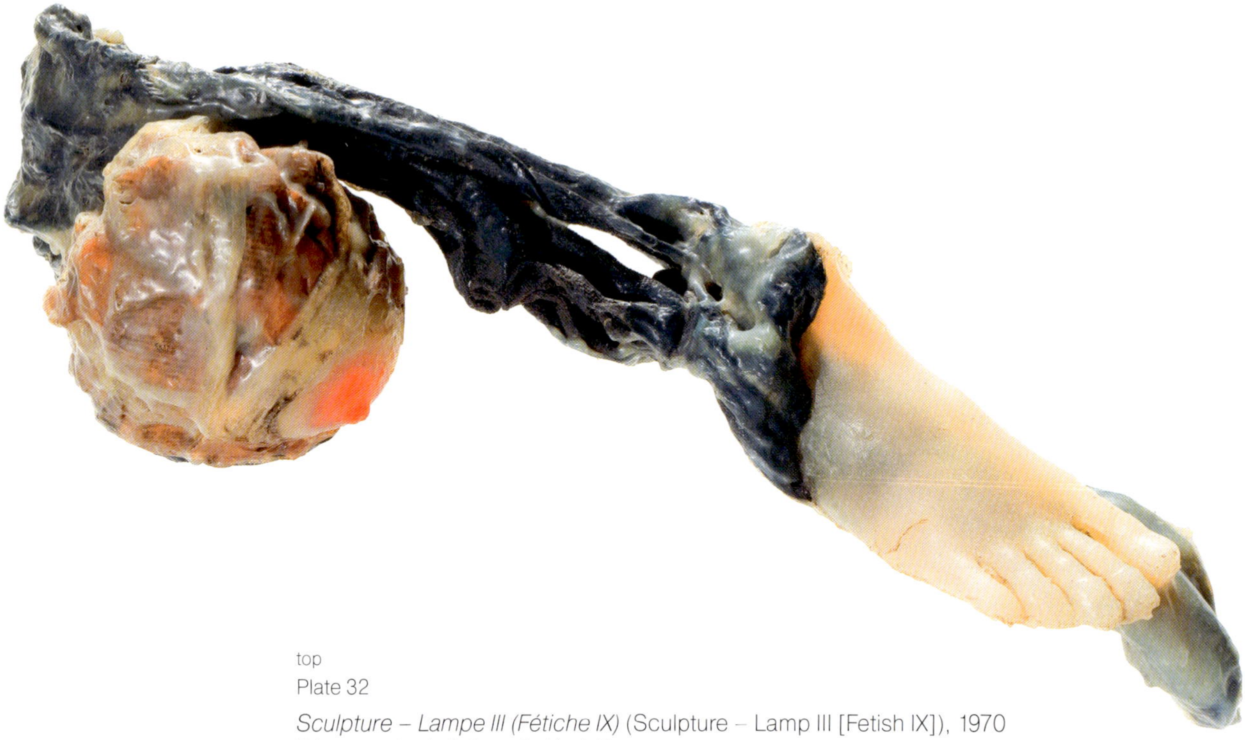

top
Plate 32

Sculpture – Lampe III (Fétiche IX) (Sculpture – Lamp III [Fetish IX]), 1970
Polyester resin, plastic lace, electrical wiring
7 7/8 x 17 11/16 x 9 7/8" (20 x 45 x 25 cm)

bottom
Plate 33

Le pied (Fétiche V) (Foot [Fetish V]), 1971
Colored polyester resin, newspaper, nylon stockings, glass wool, Plexiglas
9 7/8 x 21 11/16 x 14 3/16" (25 x 55 x 36 cm)

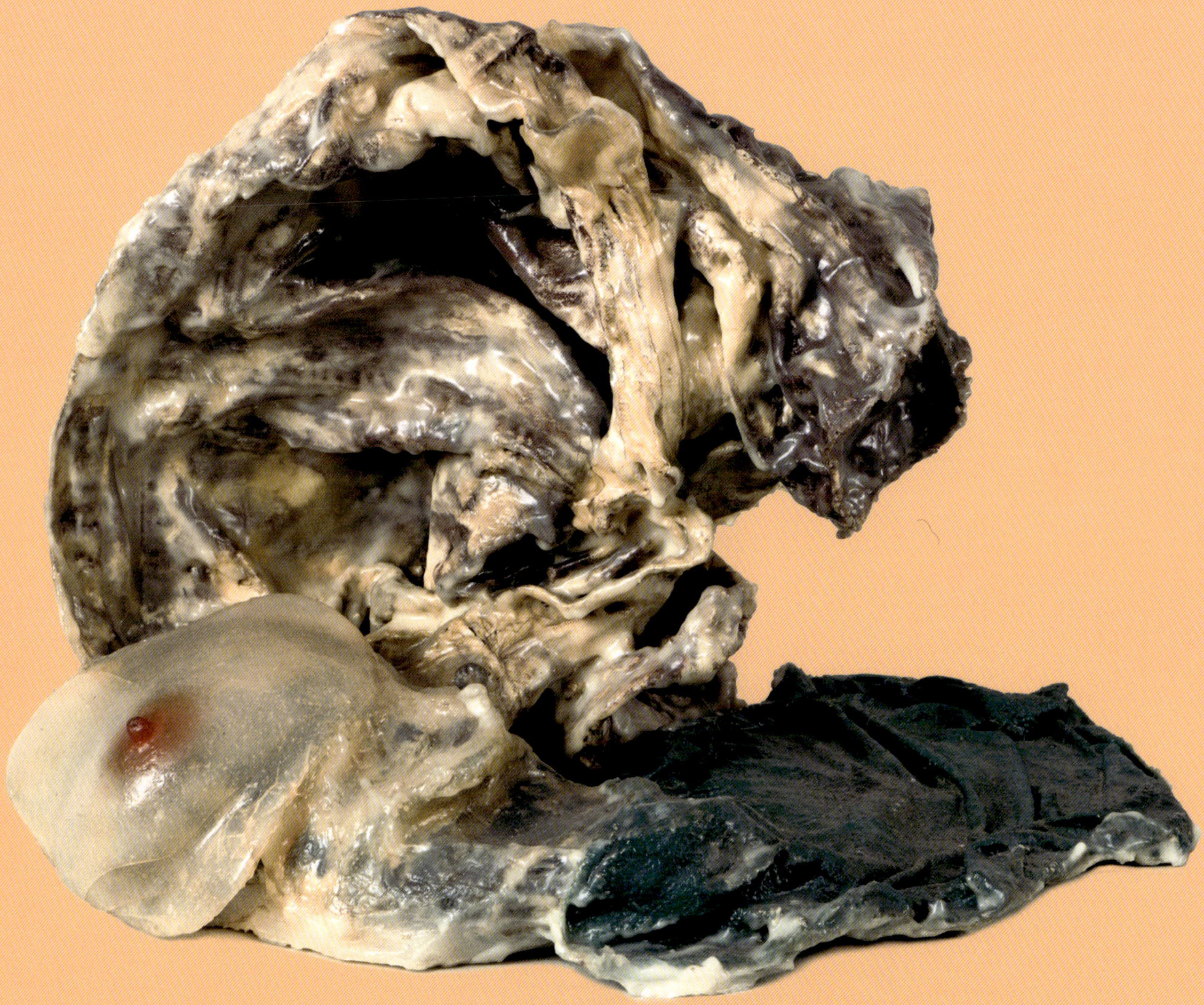

Plate 34

Sein en chiffon vert (Fétiche II) (Breast in a Green Cloth [Fetish II]), 1970–71

Jacket, leather shoe, polyester resin, paint

14 3/16 x 19 11/16 x 12 3/16" (36 x 50 x 31 cm)

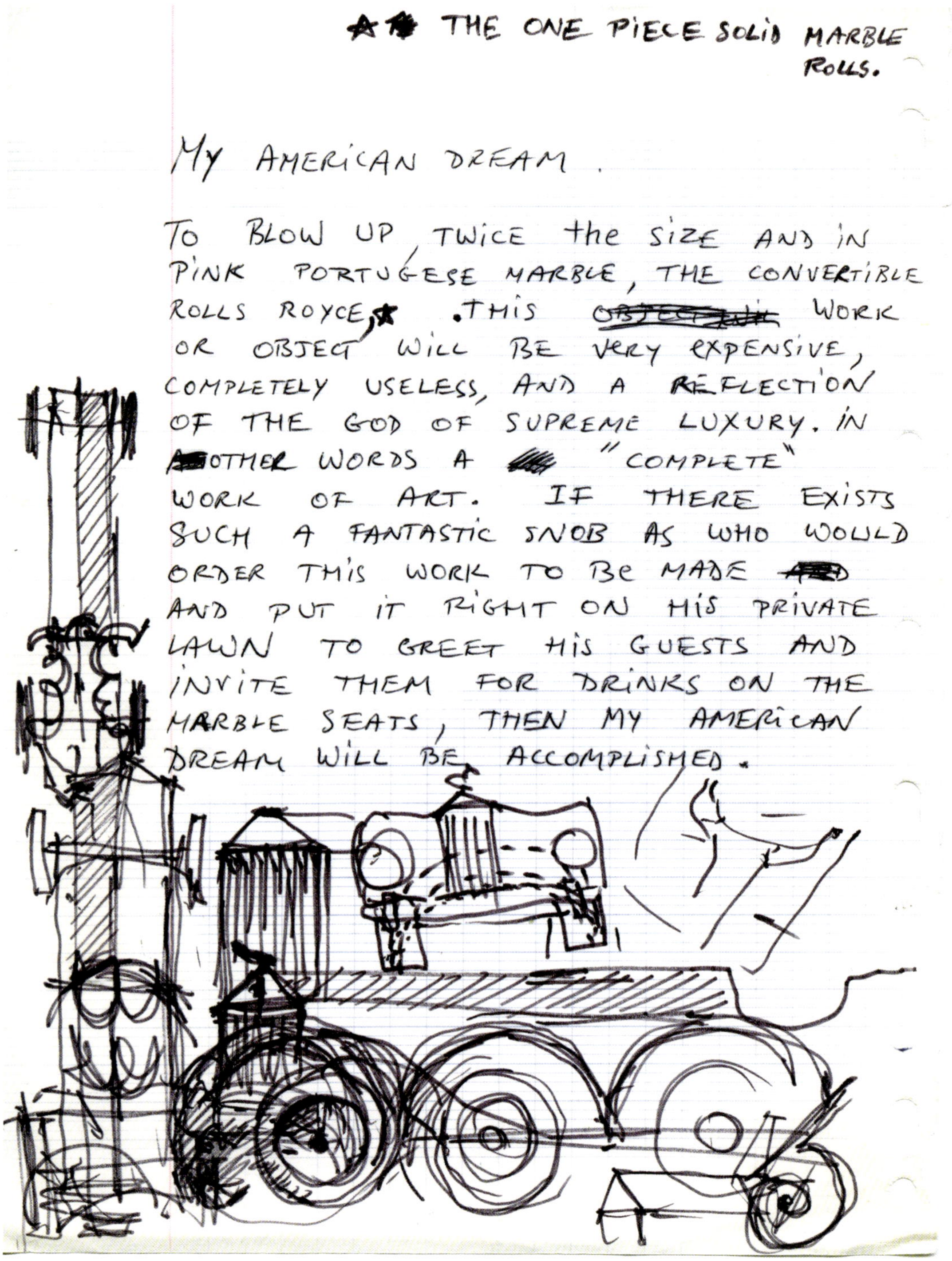

★ THE ONE PIECE SOLID MARBLE ROLLS.

MY AMERICAN DREAM.

TO BLOW UP, TWICE THE SIZE AND IN PINK PORTUGESE MARBLE, THE CONVERTIBLE ROLLS ROYCE,★ . THIS ~~OBJECT~~ WORK OR OBJECT WILL BE VERY EXPENSIVE, COMPLETELY USELESS, AND A REFLECTION OF THE GOD OF SUPREME LUXURY. IN ANOTHER WORDS A "COMPLETE" WORK OF ART. IF THERE EXISTS SUCH A FANTASTIC SNOB AS WHO WOULD ORDER THIS WORK TO BE MADE ~~AND~~ AND PUT IT RIGHT ON HIS PRIVATE LAWN TO GREET HIS GUESTS AND INVITE THEM FOR DRINKS ON THE MARBLE SEATS, THEN MY AMERICAN DREAM WILL BE ACCOMPLISHED.

"My American Dream," 1970

opposite

Plate 35

Rolls Royce II, 1971

Pink Portuguese marble and hood ornament

7 7/8 x 25 3/16 x 8 1/4" (20 x 64 x 21 cm)

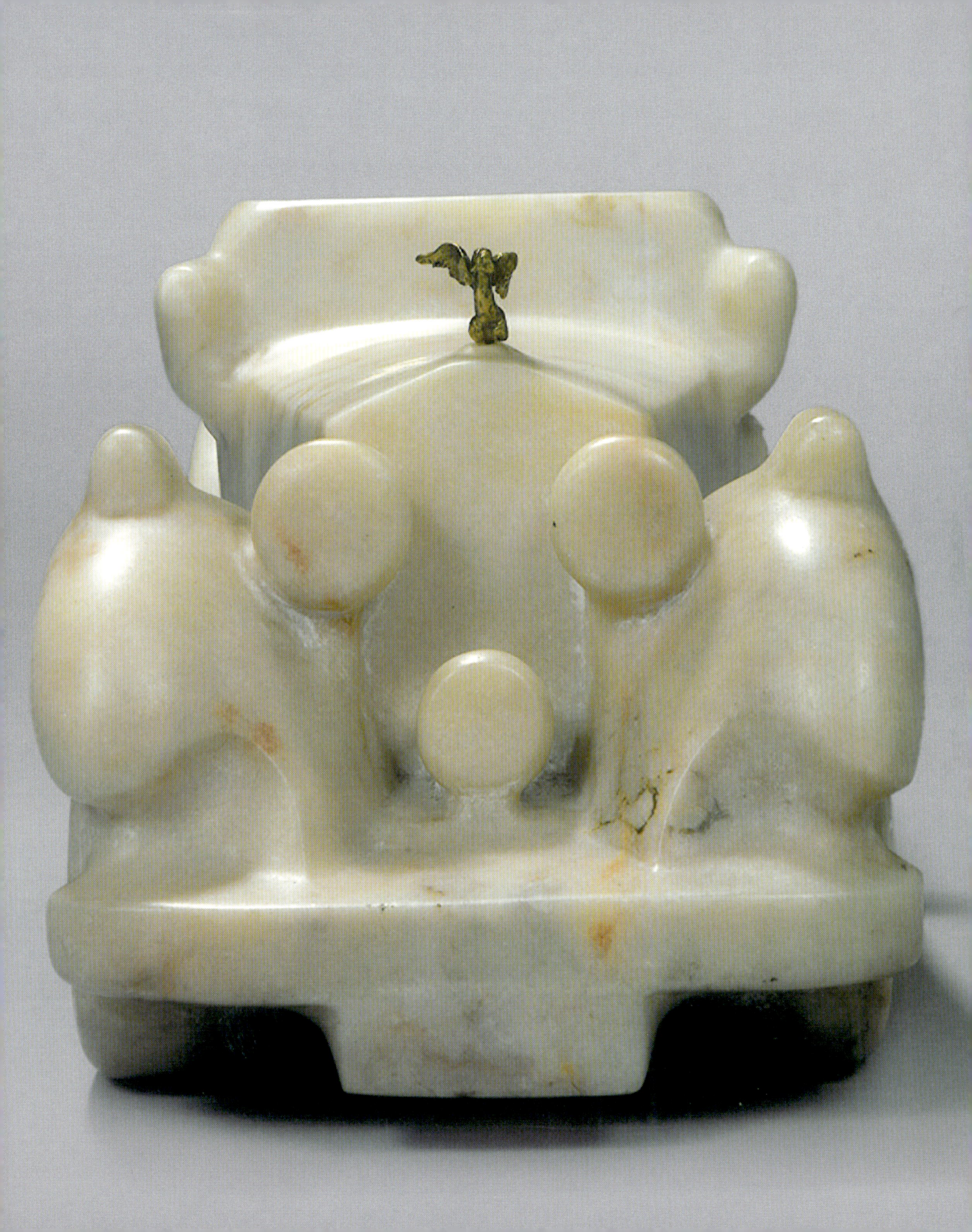

The other day, Saturday, tired from having spent hours polishing my Rolls-Royce in pink Portuguese marble, I sat in the sun and day-dreamed as I mechanically chewed a bit of gum.

In shaping with my mouth odd-looking and bizarre forms, I suddenly realized what an extraordinary collection of abstract sculptures was moving between my teeth.

One has only to photograph and enlarge my masticated creations in order to achieve a sculptural presence.

Chew well then. Look around you. Creation lies just between dreams and daily work.

92 Malakoff, 22 June 1971
Alina Szapocznikow

"The other day, Saturday ...," 1971

pages 61–63
Plates 36–55

Fotorzeźby (Photosculptures), 1971/2007
Twenty gelatin silver prints
Original dimensions: 7 1/16 x 9 7/16" (18 x 24 cm)
and 9 7/16 x 7 1/16" (24 x 18 cm)

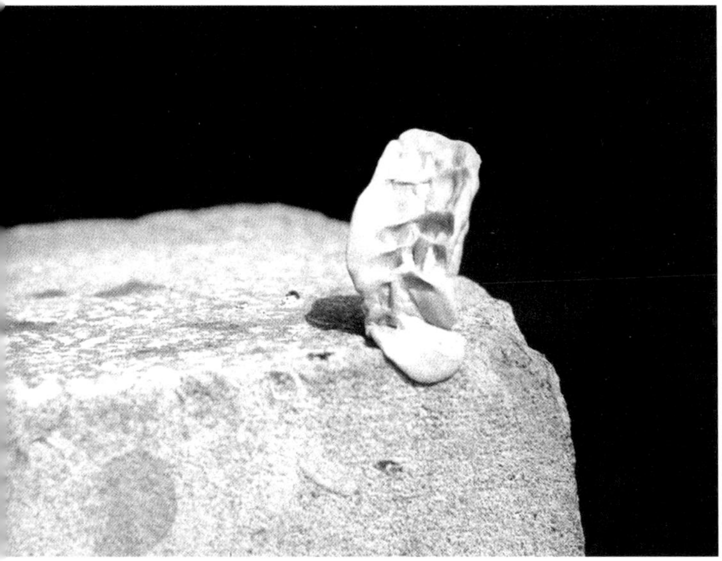
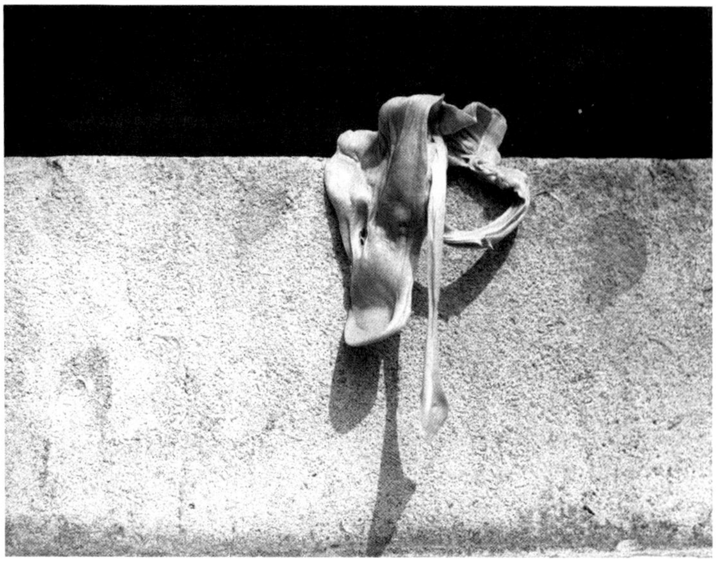
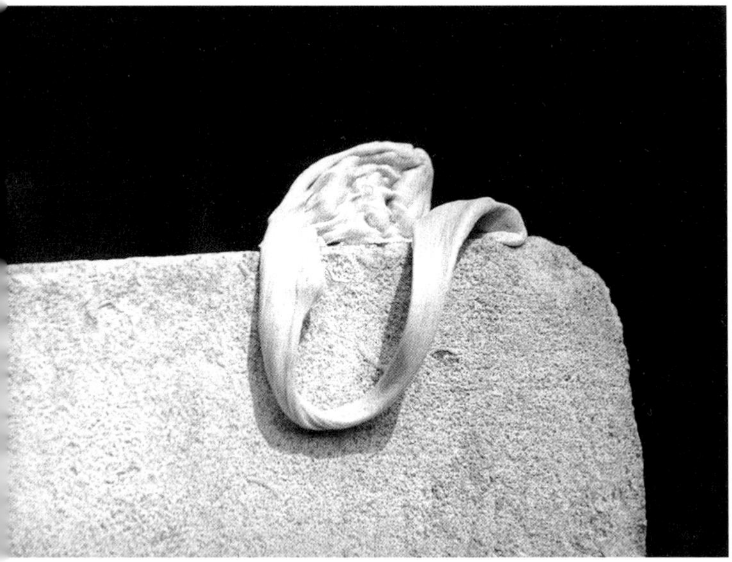
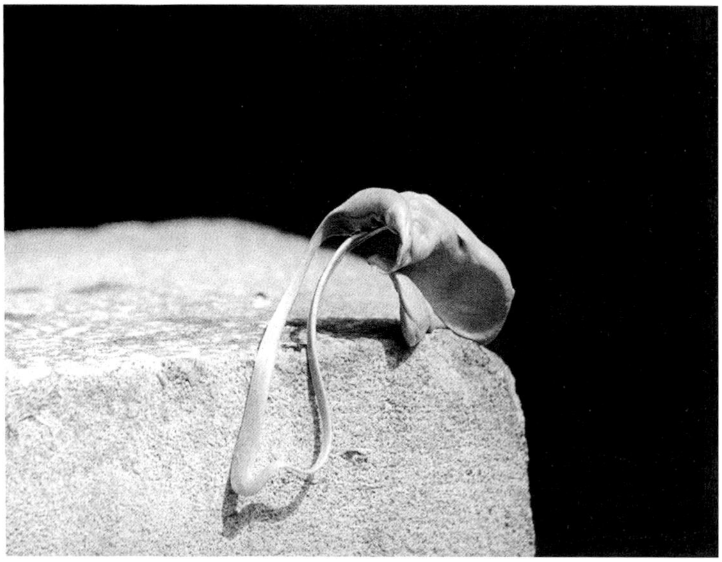
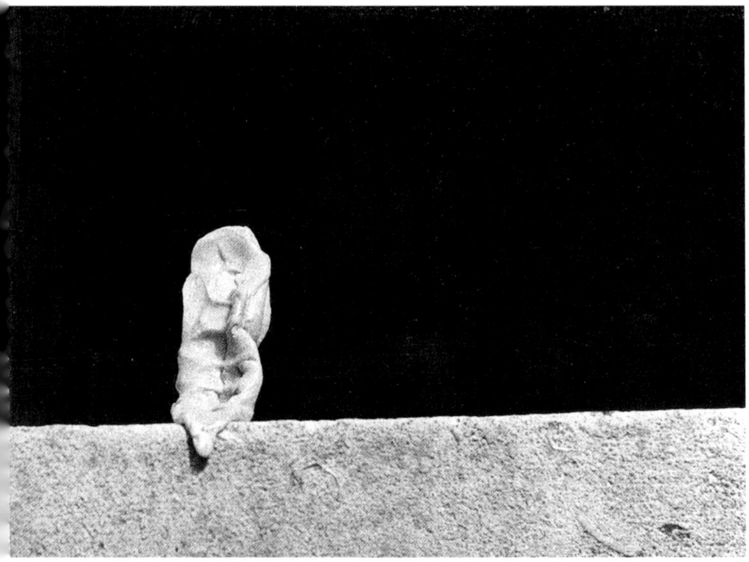
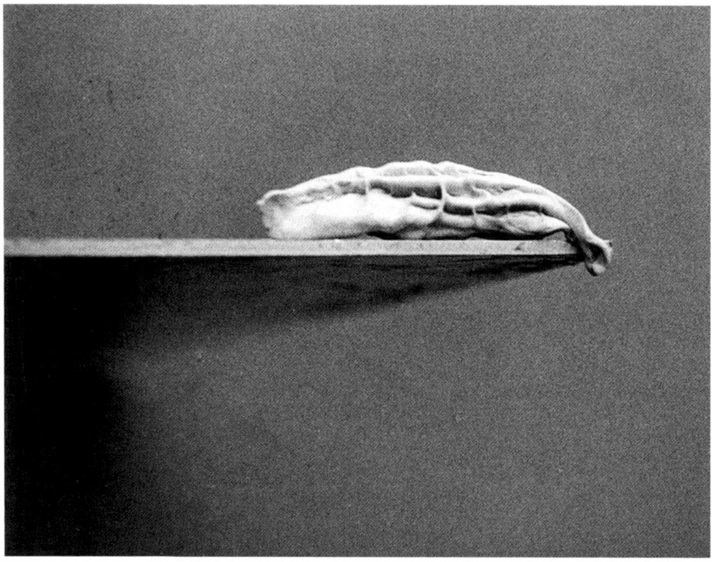

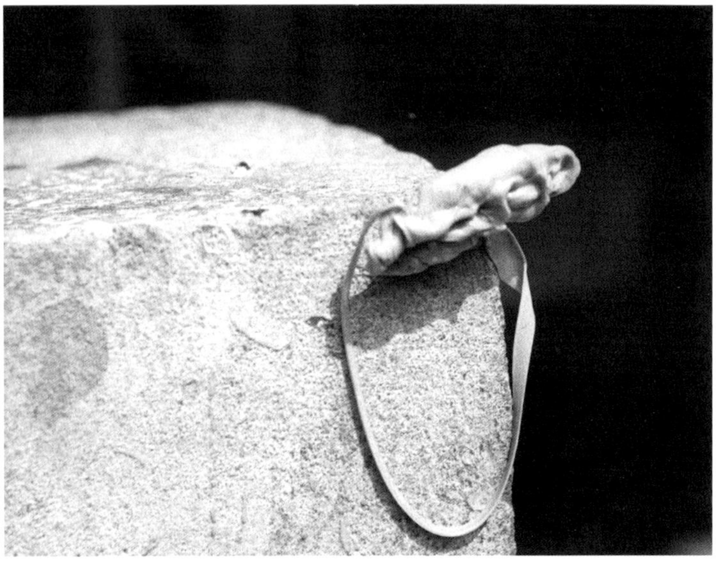
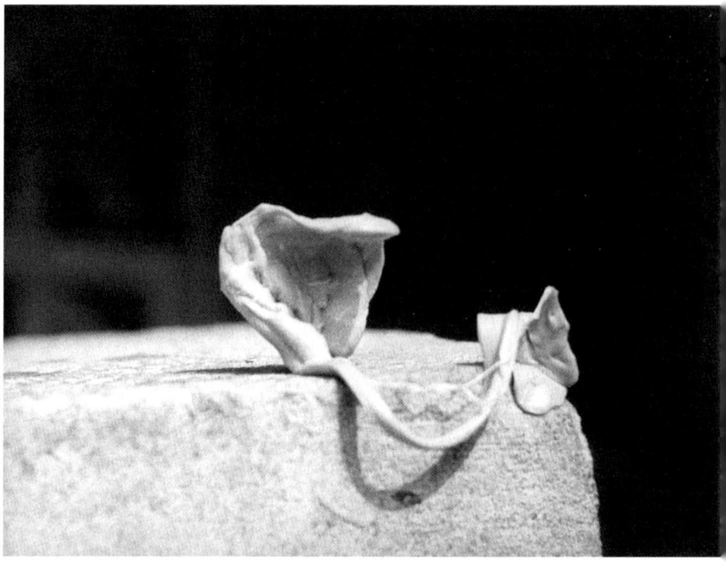
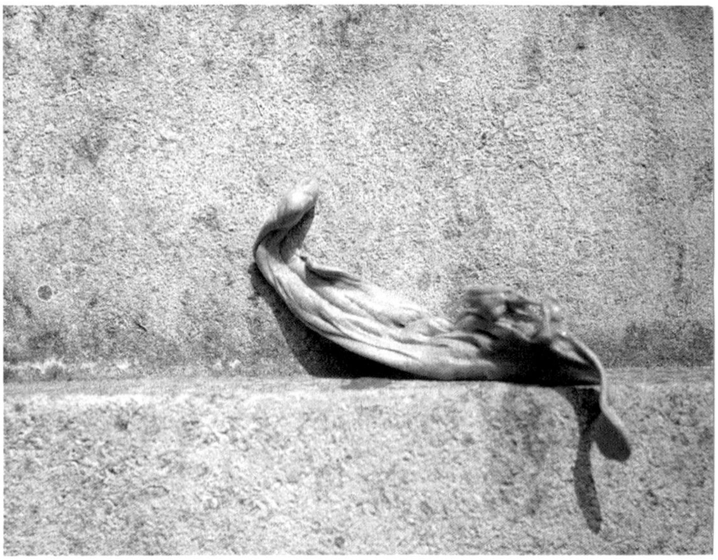
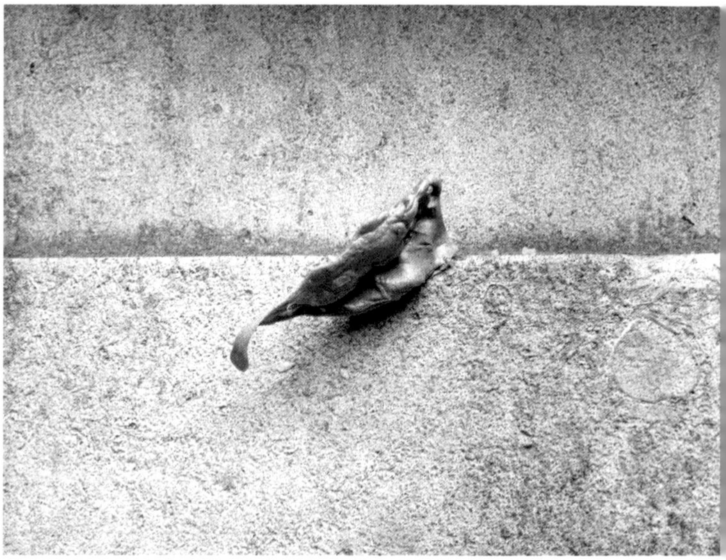
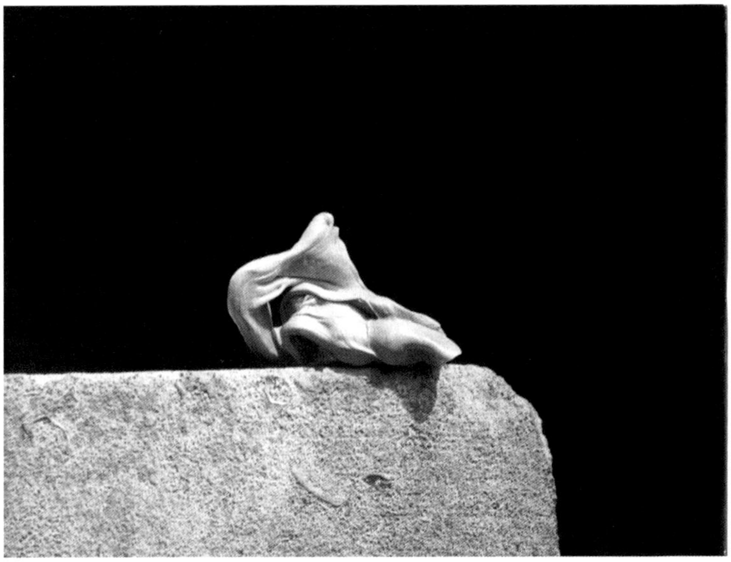
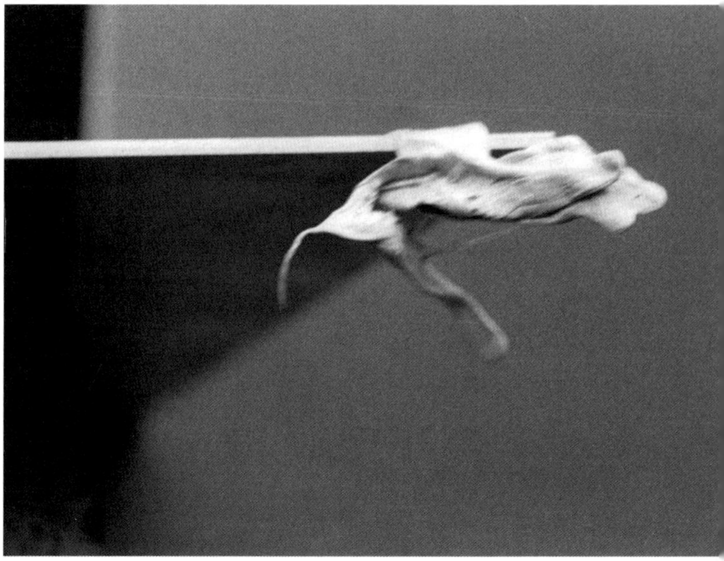

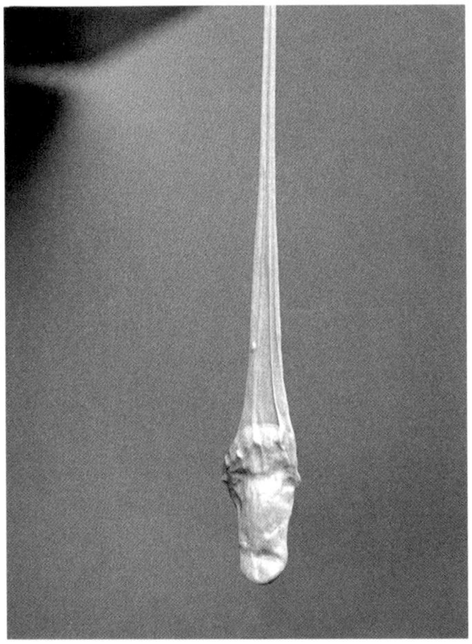
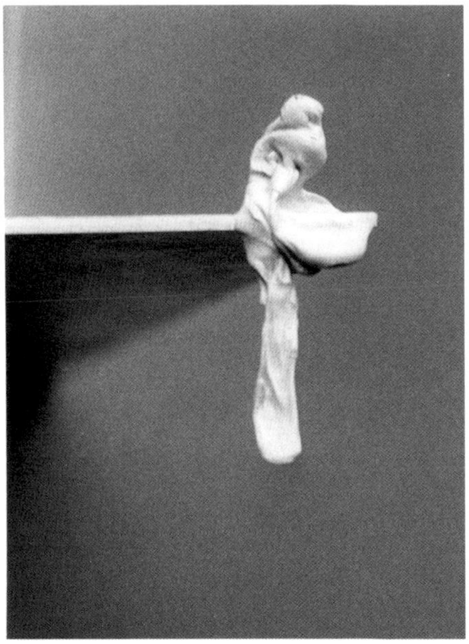
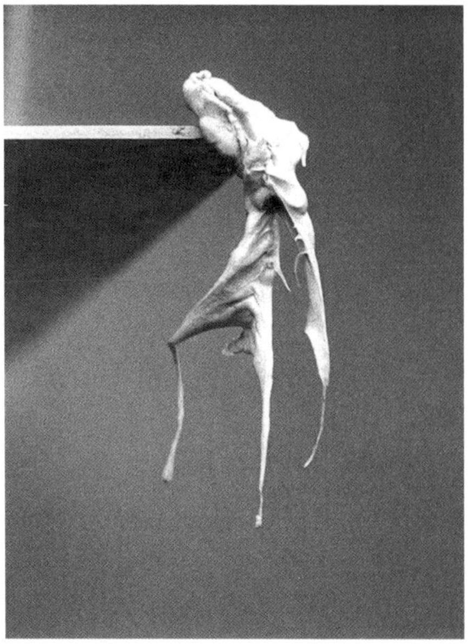
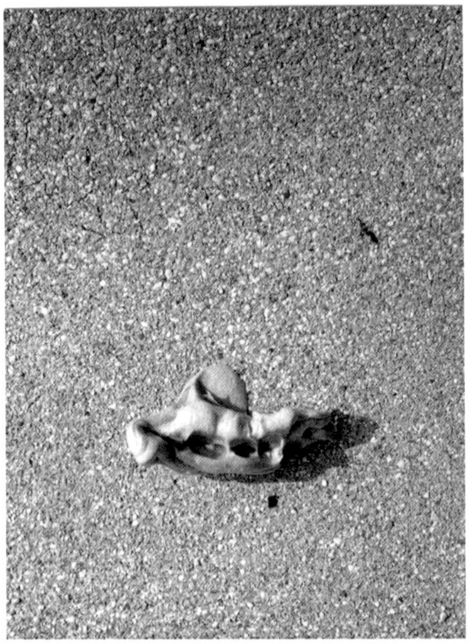
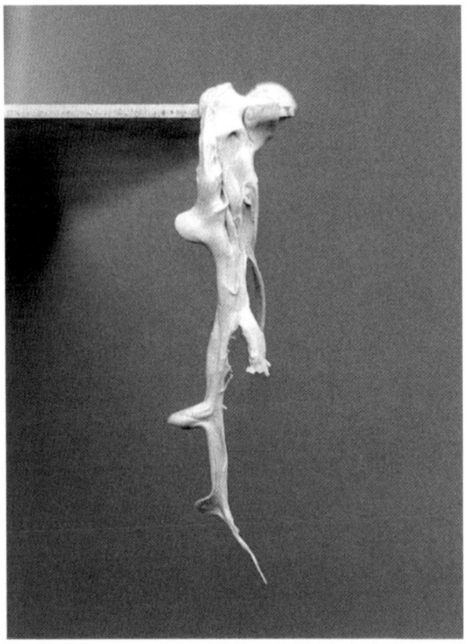
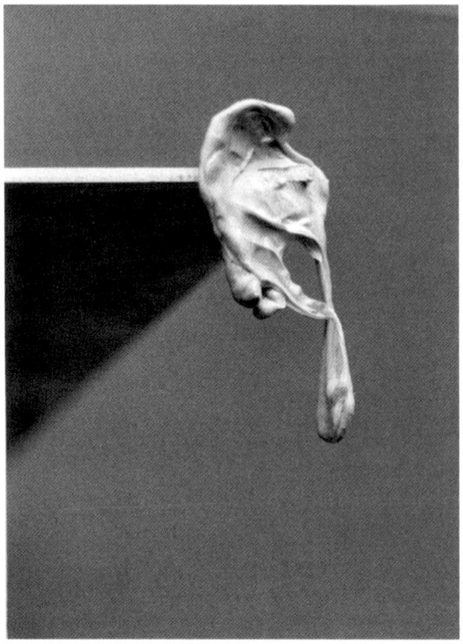
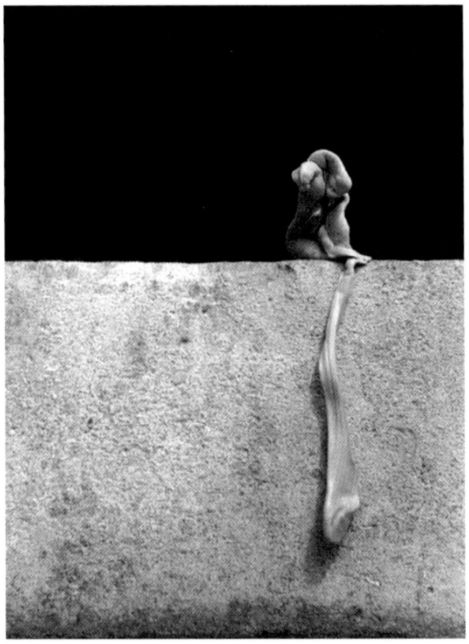
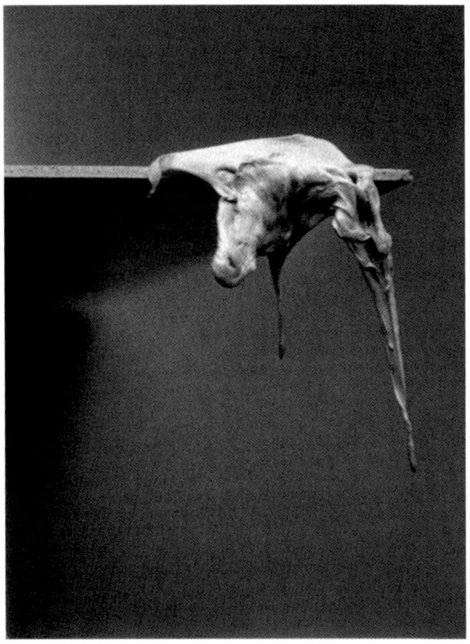

Photosculptural: Alina Szapocznikow's Index of the Body

Elena Filipovic

As an index, every [photographic] image is an emanation of a body from the past that, disappearing and no longer here, has left behind a fragment of itself.

— Eduardo Cadava and Paola Cortés-Rocca[1]

In 1971, Alina Szapocznikow had twenty photographs made of different permutations of chewing gum that she had pulled from her mouth and placed on a stone ledge, the sticky drooping specimens stretched and distended like the most malleable of sculptural materials. She called the work *Fotorzeźby* (*Photosculptures*) [ill. 1, plates 36–55] and accompanied it with a text that suggested the tension between a result both immanent (in a sculptural sense) and impermanent: "One has only to photograph and enlarge my masticated creations in order to achieve a sculptural presence."[2] Although one senses that a conceptual art practice was not a primary concern for Szapocznikow, aesthetically the piece looked much like the photo-conceptual work being made at the time: the typewritten text and the stark close-ups in black and white of individually framed "sculptures" could be seen as a riposte to Bernd and Hilla Becher's photographs of water towers and other "anonymous sculpture" from the mid-1960s and 70s or Richard Serra's film *Hand Catching Lead* (1968), and even anticipating such projects as Eleanor Antin's *Carving: A Traditional Sculpture* (1972) or Mary Kelly's *Post-Partum Document* (1973–79). This fact is hardly incidental; Szapocznikow was, after all, keenly aware of developments in art during her own time. However, connections between the *Photosculptures* and the artist's larger sculptural practice reach much deeper: formally, the stretched chewing gum recalled Szapocznikow's biomorphic sculptures of the 1950s, while operationally, the idea of sculpture being molded by the body itself is consistent with much of her late work. As the only photographic series she would consider an artwork in its own right, *Photosculptures* is seemingly an exception within her oeuvre.

The truth is, Szapocznikow was, above all, a sculptor, and one might assume that she was not much interested in photography as such. Such assumptions arise at least in part because sculpture is conventionally thought to be concerned with materiality, solidity, and space, while photography—a fleeting moment imprinted on a light-sensitive surface—seems its diametrical opposite.[3] Szapocznikow professed no explicit interest in photography and, aside from the casual snapshot, she barely touched a camera. Unlike Constantin Brancusi, she took none of the countless photographs of her own sculp-

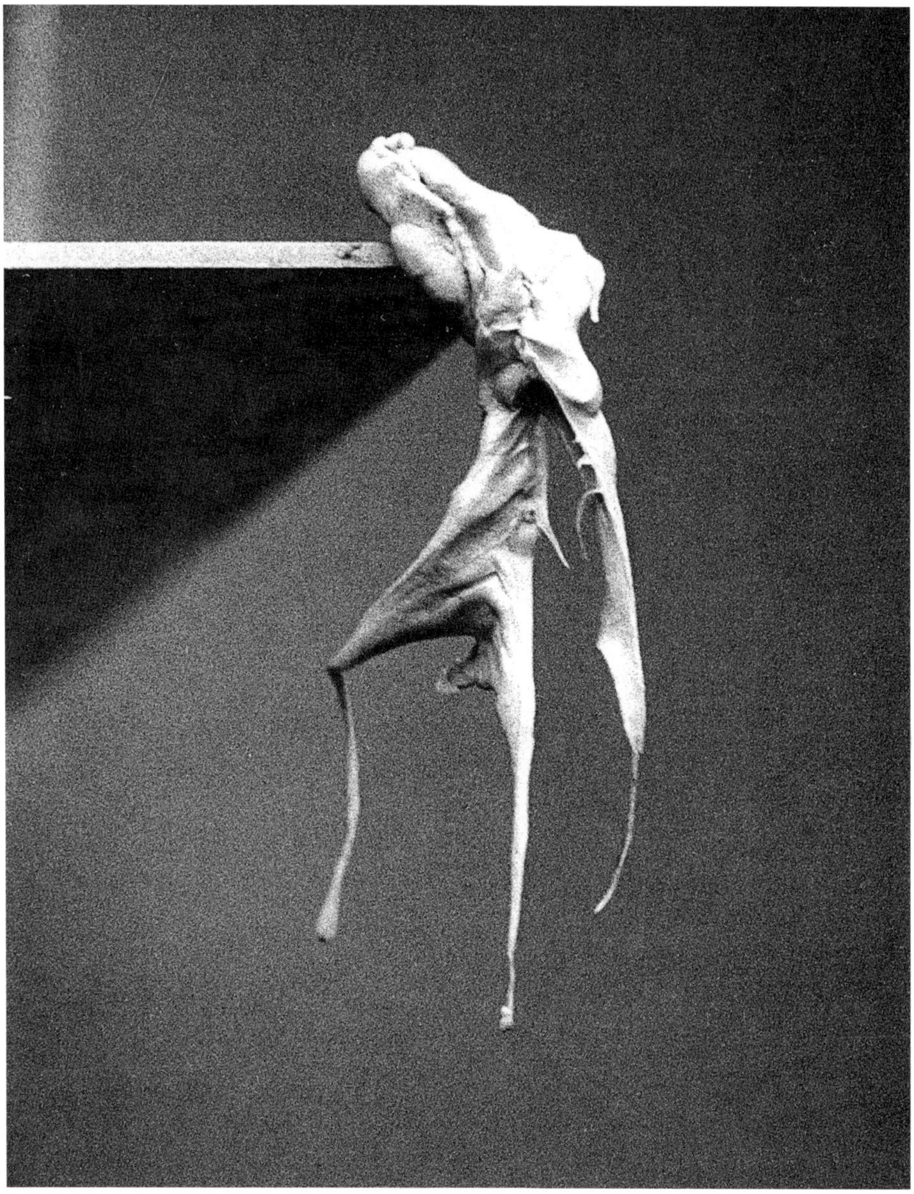

1. Image from *Fotorzeźby* (Photosculptures), 1971.

tures or studio that are currently in her archive. There is no consistent aesthetic to these photos, no widespread dissemination of them as opposed to, for instance, those of Auguste Rodin, who, it has been claimed, was "the first artist to realize the potential of the commodity form of the studio itself."[4] There is even no sense that she very deliberately staged or controlled the images of her work as Brancusi had (to such an extreme that at a certain point he refused all photographs except those he took).[5] Yet, astonishingly, Szapocznikow's archive is filled with thousands of photographs (possibly more than seven thousand), a fact that undeniably attests to a relationship with photography, however unarticulated. She called again and again on the services of photographers (friends, lovers, colleagues passing by the studio),[6] resulting in a substantive visual record of her individual artworks and studios, as well as her art practice, hardly equaled in terms of quantity among her colleagues at the time. These images have contributed to conveying a picture of the artist as beautiful, independent, and unabashedly in control of her

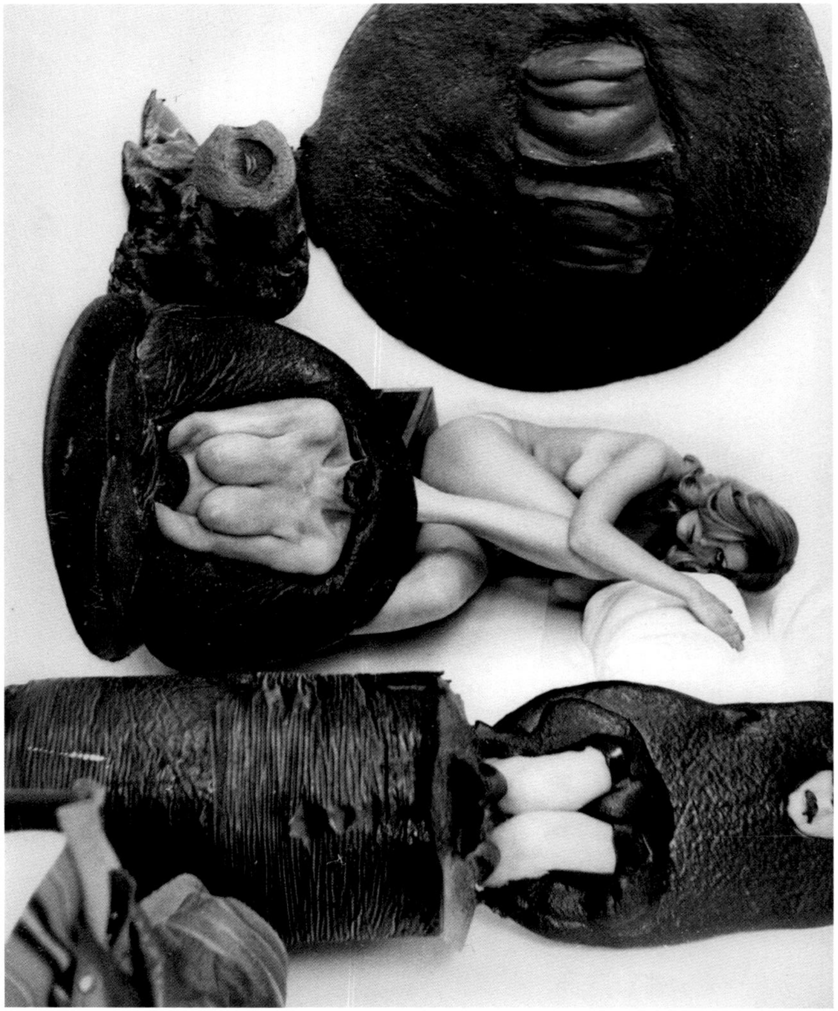

4. Model Anna Karin posing with various polyurethane sculptures in Szapocznikow's Malakoff studio, 1968.

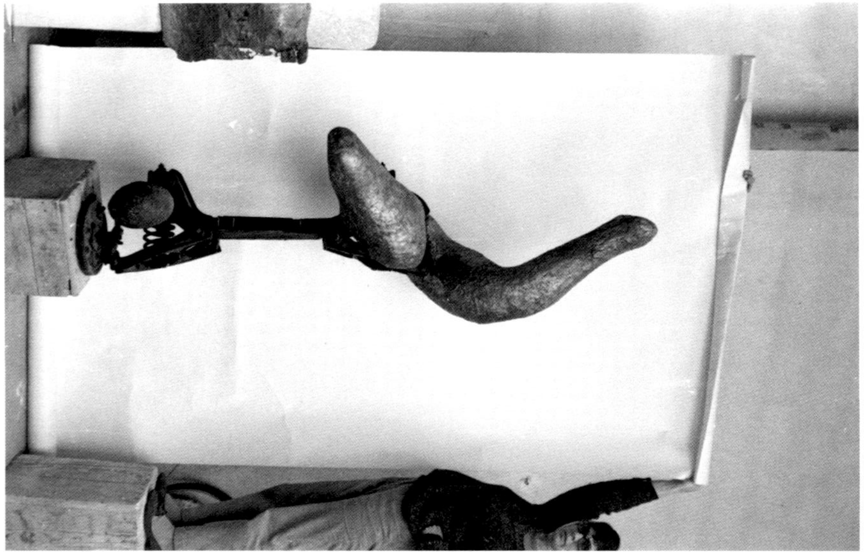

2. The artist in her Malakoff studio with *Goldfinger*, c. 1965.

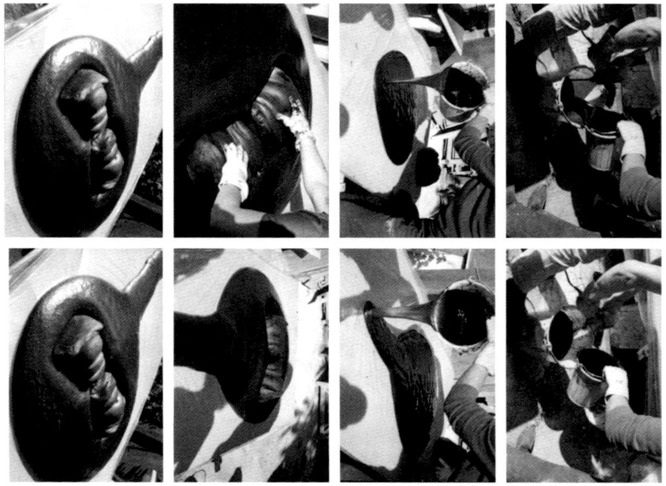

3. The artist with assistants outside her Malakoff studio making polyurethane sculptures, 1968.

medium. And while her voracious desire to document her work and herself working reveals a concern with posterity—also suggesting she might have used photography to anticipate reception of her work (seeing objects as viewers might)—this is not the only aspect of photography about which I wish to speak here. The various ways in which Szapocznikow repeatedly used photography expose much about her larger practice and ultimately what could be called—following her lead—a photosculptural impulse.

Photography as Document

There is an image in Szapocznikow's archives that shows the white backdrop against which one of her sculptures is being photographed [ill. 2]. While not elaborately staged, it nevertheless reveals a clear desire for the photograph to record something well. What though? The artist herself can be seen at the edge of the image, holding up the ad hoc paper backdrop behind *Goldfinger* (1965) [plate 101], one of a number of her "mechanical" works that incorporated car or other machine parts as readymade elements in the sculpture, inspired, it seems, by Marcel Duchamp. (Szapocznikow made a sculpture [no longer extant] titled *Ready Made* in 1964, the precise year Duchamp made editions of his previously little-known store-bought objects from the 1910s.[7]) The photo in question was likely meant to be cropped, as both the artist and the "behind-the-scenes" view were seemingly not meant to be visible. Still, the result suggests the degree to which nearly all Szapocznikow's sculptures were directly or indirectly modeled on the human body—most often her own. *Goldfinger* almost seems made to her scale, reproducing her proportions. One senses that even if the artist was, at the moment of the photograph, only beginning to become preoccupied with the direct body casting that would propel so much later work, the idea of sculpture as a reflection of her own body was already vividly present. Most of all, though, the photograph reveals Szapocznikow's decided interest and active role in leaving behind photographic traces of her production.

Another series of photographs, from 1968, capture frame-by-frame (almost like stop-motion animation) the various stages of producing new sculptures using an entirely experimental material [ill. 3]. Having worked in bronze, marble, terracotta, plaster, and other traditional sculptural materials, for which a sculptor shapes and controls the ultimate form, Szapocznikow now turned towards the unstable and dynamic liquefaction of polyurethane foam. This is perhaps surprising because polyurethane, largely used in building construction in order to seal quickly and easily the space in between two building joints, would hardly have seemed like a natural choice for a sculptor at that time. But the material's agglutination, like blistering lava that hardens into the image of its own temporary flux, attracted the sculptor, whose use of experimental materials during the mid-1960s marked a decisive turning point in her practice. In this new process, the "accident" became a resource (she even titled a series thus [plate 87]), since the resulting sculptural forms were not only unforeseen but also unforeseeable, with gravity acting as an agent. Puddles of polyurethane excrescence slid and then hardened to emerge like fecal- or mud-colored conglomerates thickened into volumes. Some months later, for a magazine photo shoot, she choreographed the poses of a naked model in her studio amongst the same polyurethane sculptures, emphasizing connections between their bodily shapes [ill. 4]. Szapocznikow's own body need not have appeared in the photographs for them to announce it was *the* body and not just *a* body at stake—indeed, that doubling might have been redundant. But if those disarmingly direct shots emphasized the femininity of the cast elements and undulant organic forms, the process photographs that preceded them documented not just finished objects for posterity but also the volatile procedural action of the objects' making.

Szapocznikow's archive is also filled with photographs of no longer extant works. Some of these, one imagines, were simply lost, broken, or discarded along the way, but in other cases, it seems the artist might have made fugitive configurations (experimenting, testing) that she wanted photographed and rendered somehow present through their documentation. She might have relinquished their claim to permanence even as (perhaps because) they could be personally kept—immortalized—through photography. Many of her archive photographs document objects that had no further existence, except as temporary experimentations of form whose elements would in some cases get recycled into something else. One can see, for example, how the life-sized plaster figure of *Panna* (*Unmarried*, 1962–63) [ill. 7] would get wrapped, mummy-like, and transformed to become *Bouquet II* (1966) [ill. 5, plate 97], or how *Ça coule en rouge* (*Leaking Red*, 1967; no longer extant) formally recalls other more permanent but equally top heavy and precariously balanced forms in her practice [ill. 8]. These images suggest how a sculpture or element was reused in another and how a research of forms might have led a particular object to become the basis for thinking about others.

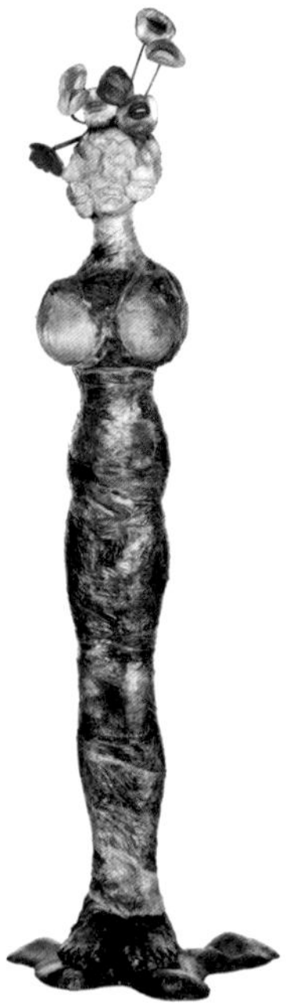

5.

The photographs *Cendrier de Célibataire III* and *IV* (*The Bachelor's Ashtray III* and *IV*, both 1972) are perhaps the most salient examples of how the artist used photography conceptually [ills. 9 and 10]. The sculpture *The Bachelor's Ashtray I* (1972) [ill. 6, plate 27] is a polyester vessel or "ashtray" cast from the artist's own mouth, chin, and neck (each doubled), into which are embedded real cigarette butts. The related photographs do not depict the sculpture, but show used cigarette butts pressed into a stick of butter, deforming and slightly melting the perfect geometry of the butter on contact. Photography here plays a vital role—not so much as evidence of a lost "object," but as a model for an experimental piece that the artist imagined making, each time anew, from comestible substances. That different staged photographs exist suggests the artist's interest in the project was more than negligible. Shortly after they were made, Szapocznikow had to be hospitalized, but she sent instructions to her friend and colleague Annette Messager that the photographs were to serve as the model through which to realize the piece for a show in Paris later that year. Photography here served Szapocznikow as both conceptual document and schematic for an artwork that emphatically courts its own evanescence.

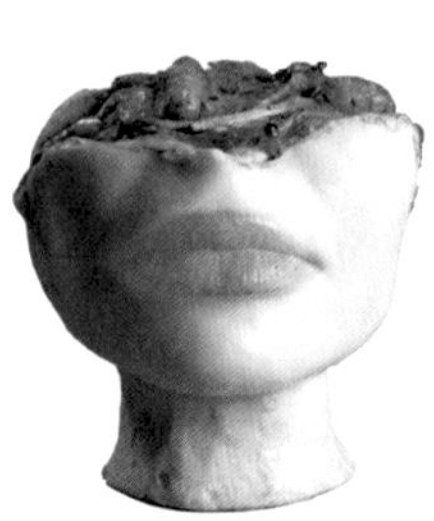

6.

One senses that Szapocznikow's endeavor to record things photographically was motivated by the desire to register the ephemeral existence of things. French cinema theorist André Bazin eloquently theorized this aspect of photography in a 1960 essay:

> The objective nature of photography confers on it a credibility absent from all other picture-making. In spite of any objections our critical spirit may offer, we are forced to accept as real the existence of the object reproduced, actually *re*-presented, set before us, that is to say, in time and space.[8]

Echoing Bazin, Roland Barthes later contended, "Photography never lies; or rather, it can lie as to the meaning of the thing… never as to its existence."[9] Szapocznikow, so haunted by the fragility of the body and life, could not have been untouched by this potential of the photograph, its ability to certify what Barthes called the "having-been-there" of the thing photographed.[10]

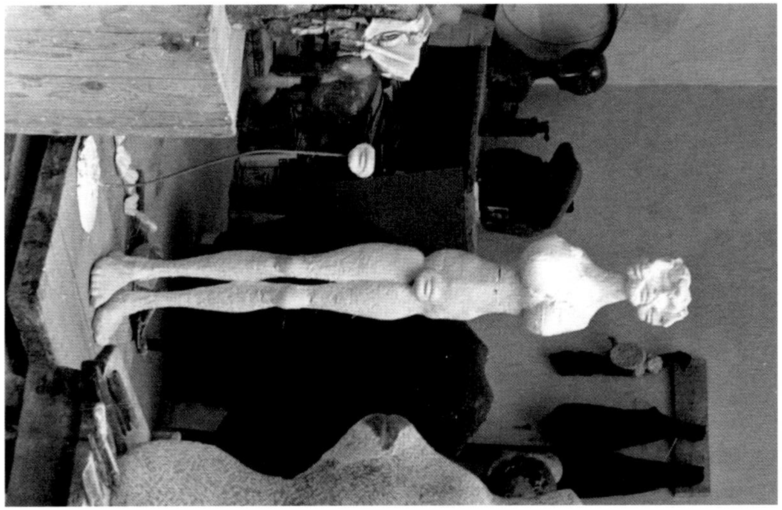

7. *Panna* (Unmarried), 1962–63 [no longer extant], in the artist's studio, c. 1965.

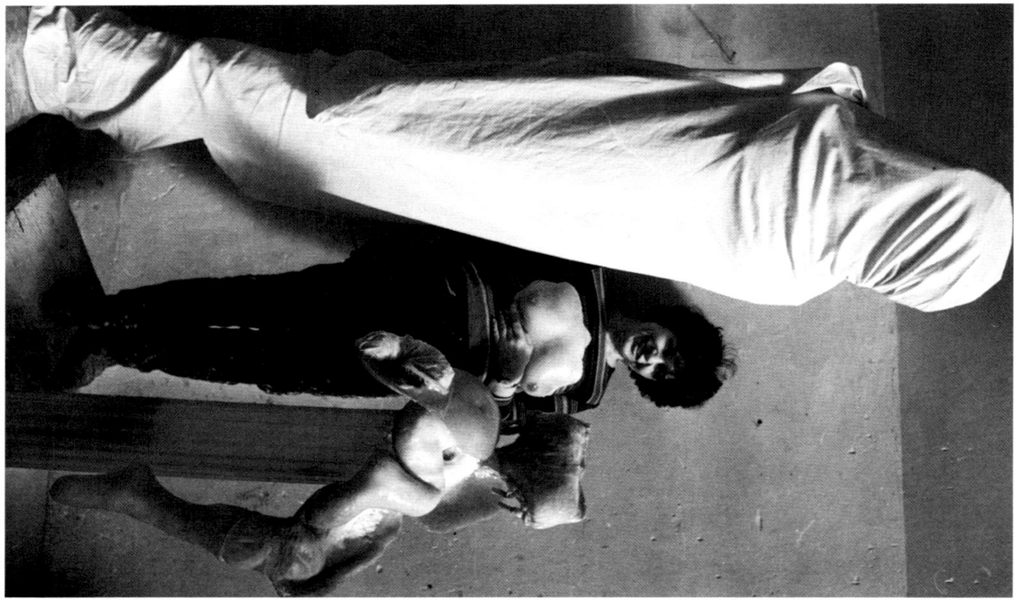

8. The artist posing amidst her work in her Malakoff studio, 1967, with *Ça coule en rouge* (Leaking Red), 1967 [no longer extant], in the foreground.

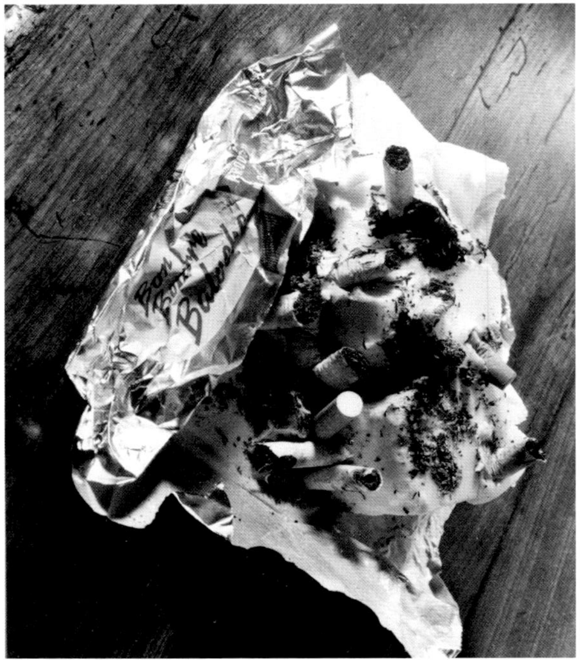

9. *Cendrier de Célibataire III* (The Bachelor's Ashtray III), also called *Cendrier d'Ambiance III* (Ambiance Ashtray III), 1972.

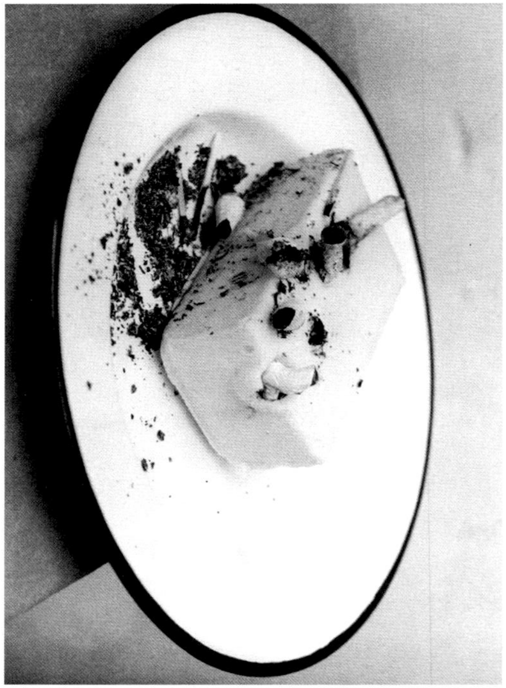

10. *Cendrier de Célibataire IV* (The Bachelor's Ashtray IV), also called *Cendrier d'Ambiance IV* (Ambiance Ashtray IV), 1972.

Photography as Index

The particular and irreducible condition of the analogue photograph, as many have pointed out, is its indexical quality.[11] By dint of its being made by the passage of light from its subject to a light-sensitive surface, it retains a physical relation to its referent, like a fingerprint or footprint. Thus, as Bazin theorized, there is an implicit connection between the thing and its photographic index: "No matter how fuzzy, disoriented, or discolored, no matter how lacking in documentary value the image may be, it shares, by virtue of the very process of its becoming, the being of the model of which it is the reproduction; it *is* the model."[12]

The cast is similarly indexical. Like the photograph, it testifies undeniably that the thing from which it is cast *has been*. Made from the contact imprint of mold meeting matter, a cast is a direct registration of the real, such that Bazin's argument about the specificity of photography can be effectively extended to casting: it, too, *is* the model of what it reproduces. From a single matrix or mold, an infinite number of casts can be made. This capacity had discredited it as an art form at precisely the time that Szapocznikow turned to it. As Helen Molesworth explained, "Under the aesthetic regime of modernism, casting came to be denigrated because it was presumed to offer the repetition of an existing form, or to enable the production of identical forms—both of which were seen to be antithetical to the privileging of the sculptural object as unique."[13] In defiance of precisely that hierarchy, Szapocznikow began to deploy the technique in her practice in the early 1960s and thereafter used it to develop a new syntax—the multiplication of an identical cast form—that would animate much of work her from that point forward.

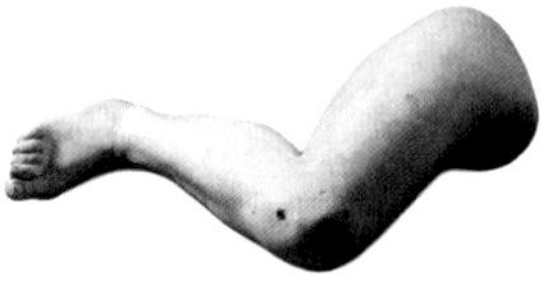

11.

For Szapocznikow, the cast was never just about the potential for endless replication or the result of surface contact with *some* thing; above all, *bodily* contact was at stake. She turned immediately to her own body, casting it in pieces—a single leg came first (*Noga* [*Leg*], 1962) [ill. 11, plate 129]. Reminiscent of a fragment of classical sculpture, the plaster (and later, bronze) leg sat resolutely on its marble base. Rodin had been perhaps the first to make the partial body acceptable as a total entity, followed by Brancusi, making it a venerable tradition. However, whereas their broken torsos and disembodied heads belonged to a tradition that was no doubt indebted to the unearthing of ancient artifacts, broken by time, Szapocznikow's insistent preoccupation with fragmentation would reveal itself as driven by an altogether different impulse. For her, the part was not necessarily a metonym for the whole; instead, she sought the sublime in the lowest states and, perhaps above all, in the leftover.

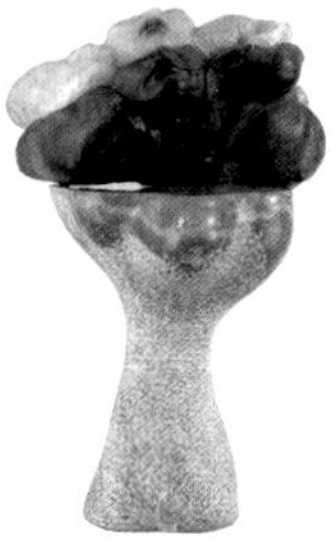

12.

Szapocznikow made *Portret wielokrotny (dwukrotny)* (*Multiple Portrait [Double]*, 1967) [ill. 12, plate 106] by superimposing two casts of the lower part of her face and inverting casts of her shoulders on a granite base. Her desire to push the possibilities of casting inspired her use of new and experimental materials such as polyester resin and poured polyurethane and led to casting more body parts (lips, breasts, legs, torsos, feet), but also to combining multiple repeated parts in a single sculpture. The result was a willfully uneasy reciprocity between the actual body and the cast body, between origin and replication.

Szapocznikow's turn to casting—a method of imprinting in which the body itself is the primary generator of the sculptural form—was based on a radical idea of sculpture's role and potential. It announced, implicitly, that conventional approaches to sculptural figuration could not always adequately or authentically represent the body. The viscous,

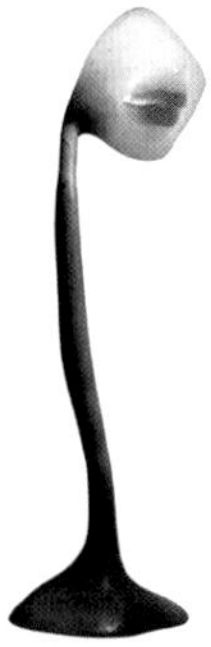
13.

quick-drying, and experimental materials she used—like polyester resin, a newly available material used commercially—could retain an eerily fleshlike luminescence as well as a tentativeness and fragility that more traditional sculptural materials could not. The forms Szapocznikow made with these new materials were not the result of an attempt to *re*present what the sculptor saw or imagined, but the result of casting's direct duplication; this contact between a matrix and formless matter produces a replica that is determined neither abstractly, ideally, or inventively, but *corporeally* [ill. 17].[14]

The endless multiplication possible through casting would lead Szapocznikow to reimagine sculpture (as well as the body) in other, more utilitarian ways. For instance, she made dozens of fully functional lamps, each a variant of her *Lampe-bouche I* (*Illuminated Lips I*, 1966) [ill. 13, plate 17], from a polyester resin cast of her mouth (a few including lips and breasts or breasts alone) with an integrated light bulb and held aloft by an elongated stem. Alternatively, her *Ventres-coussins* (*Belly cushions*, 1968) [ill. 14, plate 75], for which she planned to make one hundred cast copies from a friend's voluptuous belly, offered foam folds of flesh in place of comfy sofa cushions. What could be a more subversive end for sculpture than to refuse to allow it to sit quietly as an unambiguous and auratic art object? Instead these objects announce unabashedly an approach to sculpture straddling the quotidian and the uncanny, at once useful and unsettling. While for Baudelaire in the nineteenth century the problem was "the potential confusion between modern sculpture and luxury commodity"[15] and for Brancusi in the 1920s the need to defend his sculptures against claims that they might be nothing more than utilitarian objects, Szapocznikow *wanted* her artworks to be commodities.

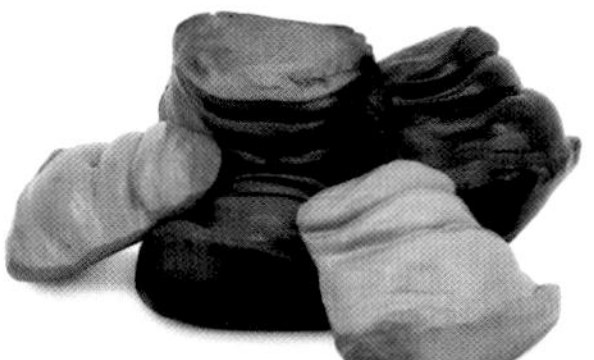
14.

The process shots of her 1968 experiments with polyurethane expose that their imprint is the result of the uncontrollable movement of liquefied material in relation to the tabletop, floor, or corner against which they were poured. Like Robert Smithson's *Asphalt Rundown* or *Glue Pour* (both 1969) or Serra's *Casting* (1969) made from molten metal repeatedly slung where floor meets wall, Szapocznikow's polyurethane sculptures reveal not only the movement of their materials but also the surfaces they touched in the process of becoming. Although not pictured in the process shots, *Siège-Piège* (*Seat-Trap*, 1968) [ill. 15, plate 85] renders the capacity of polyurethane to imprint perhaps most literally. Szapocznikow added liquefied polyurethane atop a Minimal cube of foam and sat on it, so that the final sculpture would forever bear the indentation caused by her buttocks. The result is a cube topped with the undulating waves of poured blackened polyurethane, adding a corporeal dimension to a platonic form. Most of Szapocznikow's polyurethane works were augmented before hardening with cast elements of the body made from either polyester resin or polyurethane (such as bellies, legs, lips, and torsos), doubling their indexicality.

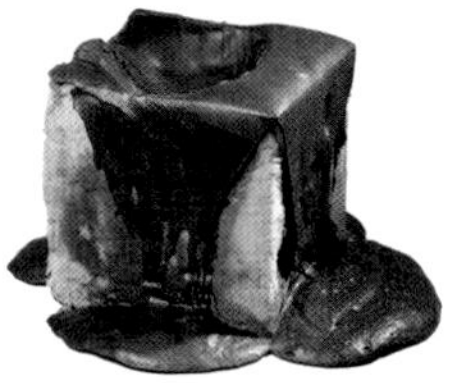
15.

During the last year of her life, Szapocznikow repeated numerous casting sessions with her adolescent son Piotr, who posed for long, painful stretches of time in order to create his full body cast. From these sessions emerged the eerie sculpture *Piotr* (1972) [ill. 16, plate 6], a one-to-one replica in luminescent polyester resin leaning back precariously like Christ in a *pietà,* but without a mother figure to support or stabilize him. It represents the apotheosis of a particular and insistent instability characteristic of much of Szapocznikow's oeuvre. The casting sessions also resulted in one of her most unsettling bodies of work, the Herbier (Herbarium) series from 1972 [plates 2–4], in which flayed skin-like layers of the polyester resin cast from her son's different body parts are flattened and

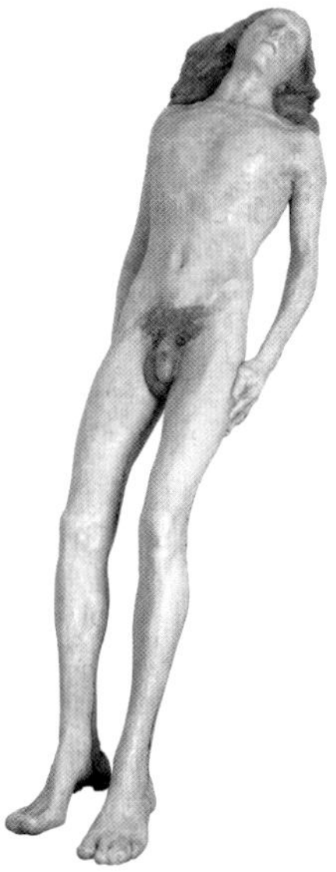
16.

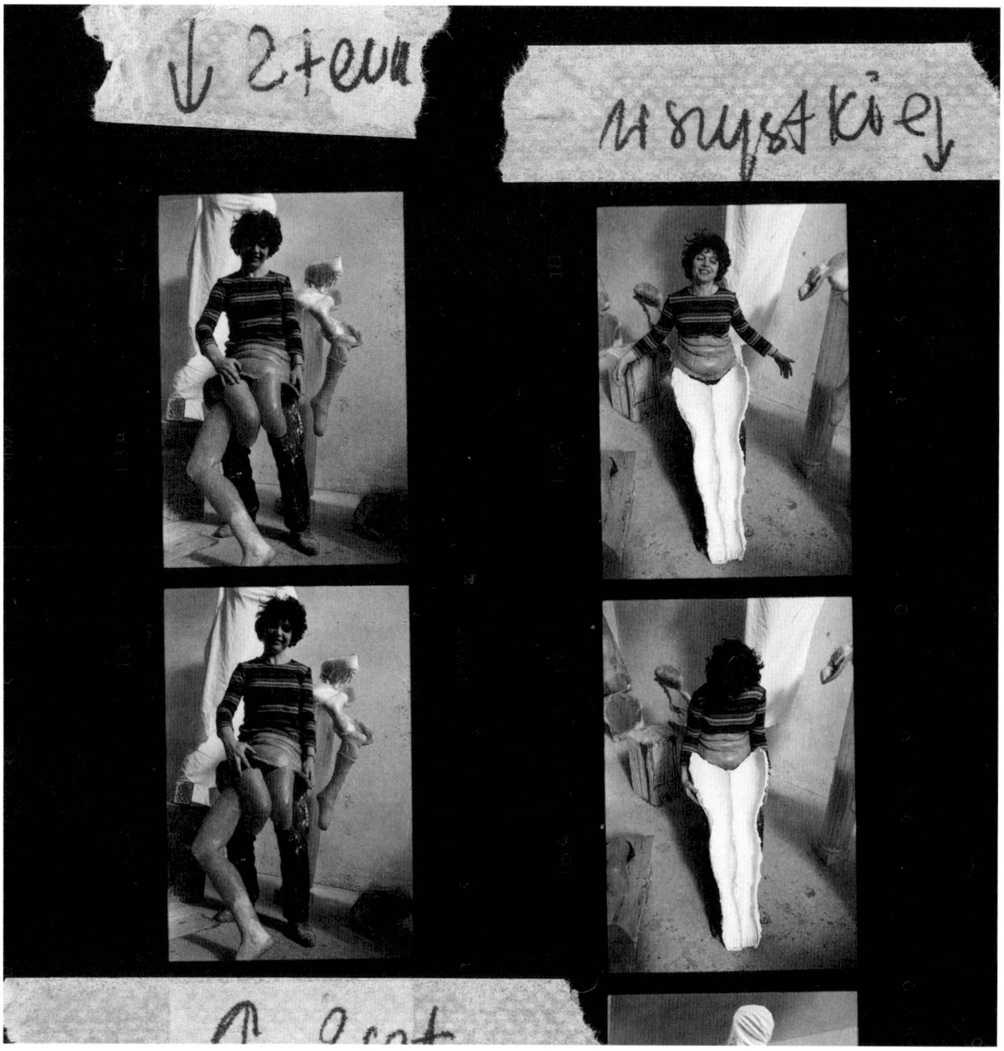

17. Contact-sheet images of the artist posing with various body casts, c. 1967.

attached to polychromed wooden panels. Though the series title draws a connection to flowers pressed between the pages of a book, Szapocznikow's pressed forms hardly look like flowers, nor do they provide the easy comfort looking at beautiful things. Instead, each *Herbarium* looks more like a ghostly burial shroud, some recalling the imprint of Christ's face on the famous Shroud of Turin. What to make of the series's uncanny resemblance to something that is, if nothing else, a primordial example of the index: Christ's mythic contact with the cloth leaving behind a stain imprint of his features?[16] *Piotr* and the related Herbarium series are the culmination of Szapocznikow's desire to cast the real body and, in the process, redefine notions of originality and sculptural form.

To insist on the index, however, is not to suggest that the resulting form was in any way given or automatic. Both casting and photography could potentially be driven by the same logic as mass production, in which the resultant object is identical to the other copies and its original "model." But looking at the casts of Szapocznikow's lips or legs, each is clearly *of* the artist while also a copy, infinitely repeatable; yet no two seem the same. Despite talk of mass marketing her lamps, her forms resemble handcrafted sculpture rather than assembly-line production—no matter that she theorized what she called the *Module répété* (Repeated module) and claimed inspiration in the industrial.[17] Translating the logic of Carl Andre's bricks or Donald Judd's stacked boxes, she created an intimately personal version in which her own body—fragile, traumatized, ill, effervescent, conflicted, sensual—was her most often-used matrix.

It should not be forgotten that at this time, avant-gardism seemed to imply a removal of the artist's hand; from Andy Warhol's *Brillo Boxes* (1964) to Minimalism's cool, geometric objects of the mid-1960s to early 70s, these works were anything but personal or emotional. Szapocznikow rejected inviolable stability, the cold authority of geometry, and the sheen of industry in favor of something more unsettled and unsettling. Like Paul Thek's "technological reliquaries" or Eva Hesse's contingent, accumulated matter,[18] her materials appeared tentative, her surfaces vulnerable. And while Duchamp's readymades have been credited with the removal of the hand in art, his odd little handmade cast objects of the 1950s, like *Female Fig Leaf* (1950–51), may have been more important than we know to the aesthetics of artists like Szapocznikow, who were at that moment forging an alternative to high modernity's cult of perfection and transcendence.[19]

Photography as Catastrophe

Some years after Szapocznikow's passing and without knowledge of her work, Rosalind Krauss penned the 1977 essay "Notes on the Index," which argues for "indexicality" as the model through which many artists were working during the 1970s. She asserted that the operative logic of photography, which Duchamp was the first to apply, gave way to an array of works that were not specifically photo-based, including earthworks, body art, and video.[20] Even if Szapocznikow's aesthetics might not seem aligned with the art Krauss discussed, her essay resonates deeply with the artist's late work—to the degree even that Krauss wrote of "the overwhelming presence of the original object, fixed in this trace of the cast."[21] Yet, if one can speak of Szapocznikow's indexicality or a photosculptural impulse in her work, these stem as much from an interest in seriality, the notion of the multiple, and the strange equivalency of the index about which Krauss wrote, as from something else entirely: the "catastrophe" that Barthes located as the very epicenter of how the photograph functions.

The catastrophe of the photograph was, for Barthes, its indissoluble connection to death—both of the moment and the subject pictured in the photograph, a connection inextricable from the way the photograph signifies and how it can, over time, speak to those that come upon it. "Death," as Barthes wrote, is the *eidos* of the photograph.[22] When the author looked at a photograph of his own mother as a child, an image that would propel what would become one of the most vital theorizations of photography written, he concluded: "I tell myself: she is going to die; I shudder [...] *over a catastrophe which has already occurred*. Whether or not the subject is already dead, every photograph is this catastrophe."[23] One could say the same of the cast: its physical and indivisible bond with its subject testifies to the (inevitable) end of the subject.

Catastrophe, it must be said, was something with which Szapocznikow was all too familiar. Hers was a life punctuated by war, ghettos, concentration camps, death, homelessness, near-fatal tuberculosis, and returning bouts of cancer. While much has been made of her biography, to the point of often overshadowing her radical and innovative practice, one senses that for Szapocznikow, traditional sculpture—with its auratic claims and representation of a self-contained, whole human body—was unable to account for what she called the "paradoxes and absurdities" of the human condition. Classical sculpture had, in historian Alex Potts's description, "become the reification of a fixed subjective

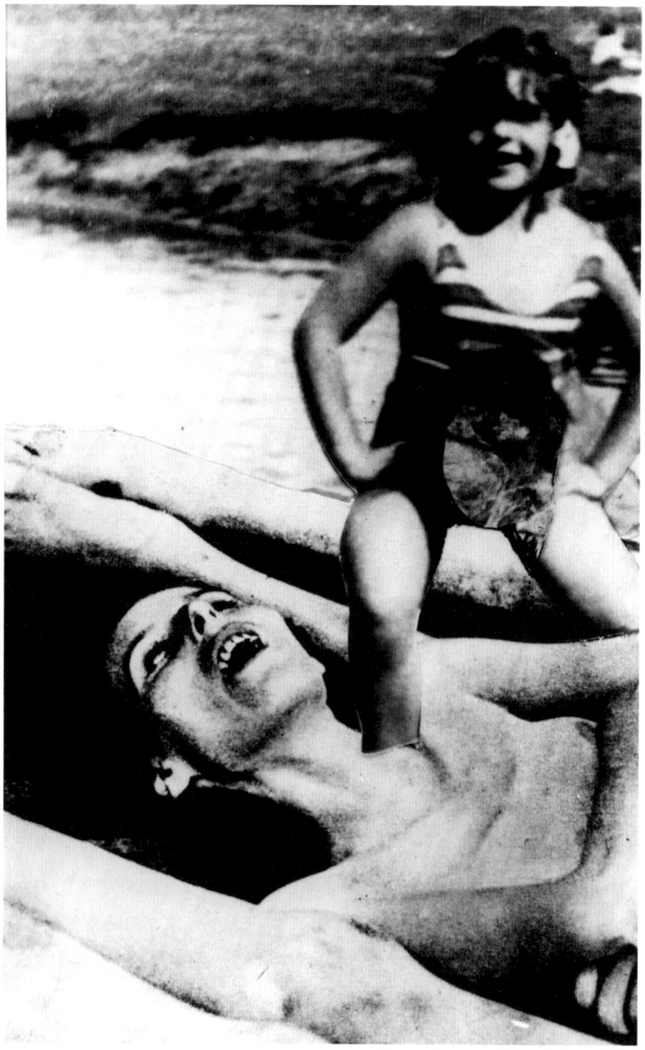

18. Photocollage of an image of the artist as a young girl and of a Holocaust concentration-camp victim, used in preparation for *Souvenir I*, 1971.

ideal, rather than a stimulus to think subjectivity anew."[24] It was *this* ideal of sculpture—occupied with projecting "a familiar and gratifying image of the self"[25]—that Szapocznikow resisted: "[I am] nothing other than a sculptor who has experienced the failure of a thwarted vocation,"[26] she wrote less than a year before she would die. In rejecting the cult of originality that would disregard the validity of casting and the classical sculptural model of internal formal integrity, she offered instead the disconcerting proposition of the body in pieces, repeated, copied, unstable, offering itself as a witness to humanity's own vulnerability: "Despite everything," Szapocznikow wrote, "I persist in trying to fix in resin the traces of our body: I am convinced that of all the manifestations of the ephemeral the human body is the most vulnerable, the only source of all joy, all suffering and all truth."[27]

The photograph as imprint—and as such, testament to catastrophe—would be no more explicitly literalized than in the photographic images of death camps that circulated in the media during the 1960s, prompted by both Adolf Eichmann's trial in 1961 and the Frankfurt Auschwitz trial in 1964.[28] Szapocznikow had a photograph made of one of the images in circulation, made multiple prints from it, and by the late 1960s began to collage them with other images and embed them into the formless layers of her polyester sculpture [ill. 18].[29] What had seeing those shocking photographs—the indexical traces of an experience she knew from memory—incited in her? We might

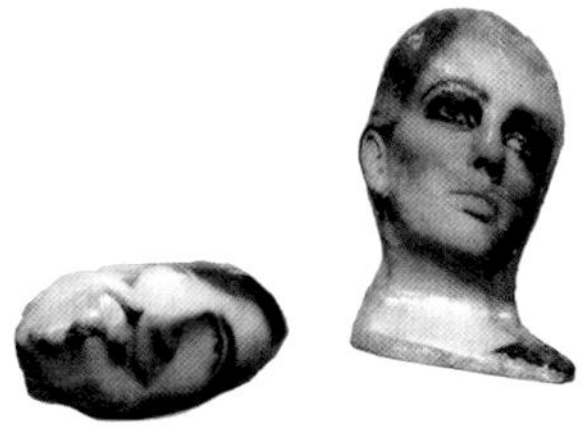

19.

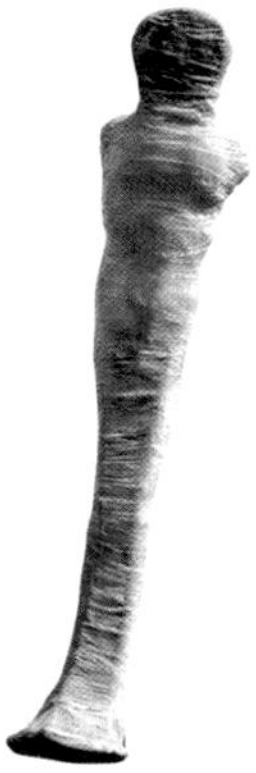

20.

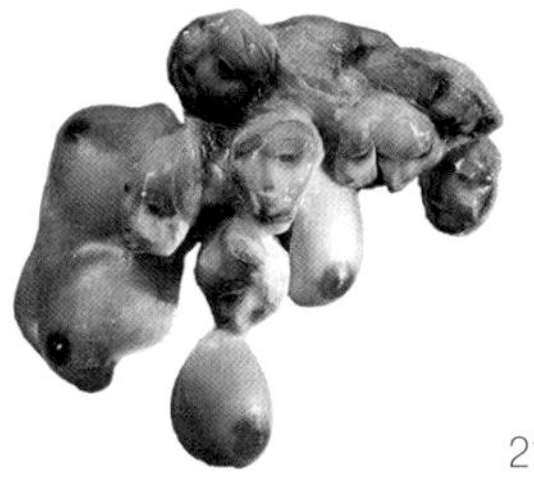

21.

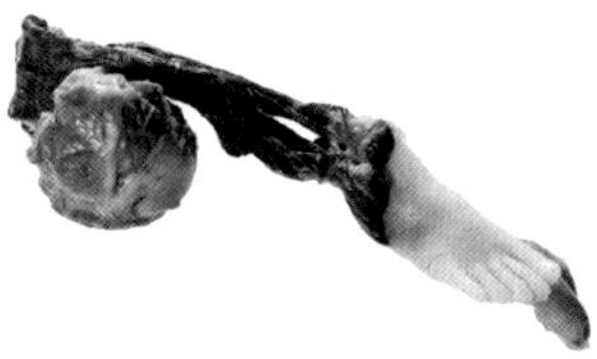

22.

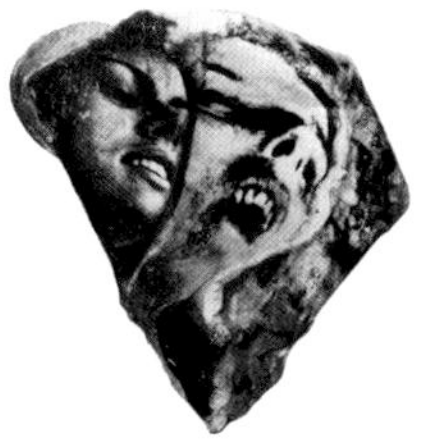

23.

wonder in hindsight if Szapocznikow's integration of not only those photographs, but indeed *all* photography into her sculpture might be traced to the same origins: the forced recognition of photography's undeniably "testimonial" function.

Photography had all along accompanied Szapocznikow's practice, alternately documentary and generative, but by 1966 photography had found its way into her sculptures literally—beginning with photo booth images, dozens of black-and-white, palm-sized representations of the artist's face, the epitome of some indexical guarantee of identity (think of their use in passports and official documents). She attached them to matchboxes and built a small towering structure, like a house of cards, and embalmed them in layers of polyester resin. *Photomaton* (1966) marks the beginning of the direct use of photographs in her work. Perhaps fittingly (or ironically), the sculpture is known only through documentary photographs. Did she prefer it not exist, destroying it after the photo was taken? Did she give it away, never to be found again? Was it accidentally destroyed? We cannot know for certain. What is certain, however, is that *Photomaton* heralded the integration of photographs into her work.

One cannot easily imagine today how strange and singular Szapocznikow's use of photography in her sculptures would appear at the time. Photography as a medium was only just becoming accepted as a fine art form, and it was rarely used in relation to sculpture. After *Photomaton*, Szapocznikow began to appropriate other images, using them to create several innovative series of sculptural works, including what she called her Souvenirs [ill. 19, plate 56] and Tumeurs (Tumors) [plate 60]. She used media images—of a cosmonaut, an artwork, and cinema stars—as well as portraits of herself, fellow artists, or friends, embedding them into semi-translucent layers of polyester or, in the case of *L'Apesanteur (Hommage à Komarow)* (*Weightlessness [Homage to Komarov]*, 1967) [ill. 20, plate 90], in layers of plastic foil so that they became both part of the surface (visible through it) and wholly integrated into it. In a curious twist imbricating photography and sculpture, *Krużlowa (Macierzyństwo)* (*Madonna of Krużlowa [Motherhood]*, 1969) [ill. 21, plate 63] combined cast body parts (several pendulous breasts) with identical reproductions of a fifteenth-century sculpture of Poland's Madonna of Krużlowa. *L'Enterrement d'Alina* (*Alina's Funeral*, 1970) [plate 66] combines bits of clothing (striped swatches recalling a prisoner's or concentration-camp detainee's uniform) with photographs of the artist, friends, and colleagues enveloped by drooping, lumpy forms (evoking the tumors that were invading her body) in a devastating meditation on the fragility of life, literally her own. Here photography announces and accompanies death. Serving as a fragment of the real, it connects to what she called her Fétiches (Fetishes, 1970–71) [ill. 22, plates 29–34], a series of sculptures incorporating actual clothing (underwear, stockings, work clothes) and other "real" objects. Photography became another example of the real suspended in the very materials she used, offering a riposte to classical sculpture's mimetic *representation* of the world.

Soon, other more disturbing images emerged. Lest one forget, a photograph *bears witness* not only to the existence of something or someone (and thus its inevitable end), but also to the fact that something ineffable might be revealed or *speak* in the image, pricking you like Barthes's *punctum*.[30] During the last years of her life, her most experimental phase, photography bore witness to the catastrophe of which she rarely spoke. *Grande Tumeur I* and *II* (*Big Tumor I* and *II*, both 1969) [ill. 23, plate 60] include an image of one of the female victims taken from Nazi death camps, blown up to grand proportions and embalmed within the sculpture's fleshlike formlessness; it is provocatively juxtaposed with the face of actress Emmanuelle Riva in Alain Renais's *Hiroshima Mon Amour* (1959), head thrown back and mouth parted in apparent ecstasy. *Souvenir I* (1971) [ill. 24, plate 57] has embedded within it an image of the artist as a young girl in her bathing suit, cut from a family holiday snapshot in which the artist was perched on her father's shoulders, a happy time *before*—before the trauma and loss, as Griselda Pollock has described it.[31] Individual experience (memories of her own childhood) and collective history (the horrors of the Holocaust) meet for first time in *Souvenir I*: encrusted beneath its layers, hovering around the figure of the little girl and in the bulbous form between her legs (where her father's face appeared in the snapshot), are images of the same female death-camp victim that appeared in *Big Tumor I* and *II*, as well as several other pieces in the Souvenir and Tumor series. Szapocznikow turned repeatedly to that single image, featuring the face—mouth ajar and eyes hollowed—of a female corpse seemingly frozen in the throes of suffering, the emaciated legs of other victims lying on either side of her. The photograph is irrefutable evidence of the camps, a ghastly, horrific indexical trace; it was Szapocznikow's *punctum*, evoking the history she seldom spoke of or represented in her art, but which emerged via photography towards the end of her life.

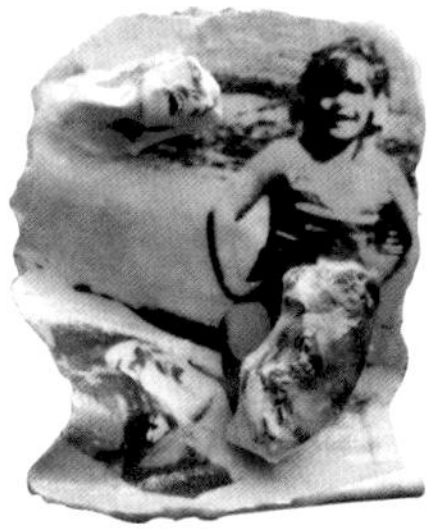
24.

Photography appeared throughout Szapocznikow's oeuvre in many guises. As document, conceptual record, model, material, and testament to unspeakable horrors, it served as a powerful tool to help her shift and invade traditional ideas of sculpture. Looking at her oeuvre in relation to photography—and its indexical twin, casting—tells us something about the ways she grappled with sculpture as a kind of imprint—of herself, of memory, and of history. To do so meant that her late oeuvre refused one of the most stalwart pillars of sculptural convention: rather than perpetuating the long-standing faith in mimetic representation, Szapocznikow offered cast copies of the real instead—as if the body as a vessel of joy, trauma, or eroticism could not be adequately represented, but instead only cast from life. Indeed, it is arguable that although it constitutes the only photographic series within her sculptural oeuvre, in depicting what is formed in the inner recesses of the body, *Photosculptures* offers a telling allegory for the whole of Szapocznikow's work—imprinting that which is otherwise *unrepresentable*. Her insistent and repetitive casting of the body was her attempt to figure the reality of human vulnerability, struggling to present the body as unique and irreducible (i.e., utterly unreproducible) and its experiences as collectively shared (i.e., infinitely reproducible). Her work obstinately sits in this breach between the two, where photography played its ultimate role.

Notes

1. Eduardo Cadava and Paola Cortés-Rocca, "Notes on Love and Photography," in *Photography Degree Zero: Reflections on Roland Barthes's* Camera Lucida, ed. Geoffrey Batchen (Cambridge, Massachusetts: MIT Press, 2009), 121.
2. Alina Szapocznikow, statement, 22 June 1971. For full text, see page 60, elsewhere in this volume.
3. As we now know, the development of sculpture in modernity cannot so easily be separated from its reification through photography. See Roxana Marcoci, ed., *The Original Copy: Photography of Sculpture, 1839 to Today* (New York: The Museum of Modern Art, 2010), for further consideration of this issue.
4. Briony Fer, *Eva Hesse: Studiowork* (Edinburgh: Fruitmarket Gallery; and New Haven, Connecticut: Yale University Press, 2010), 33.
5. See Paul Paret, "Sculpture and its Negative: The Photographs of Constantin Brancusi," in Geraldine A. Johnson, ed., *Sculpture and Photography: Envisioning the Third Dimension* (Cambridge, England: Cambridge University Press, 1998).
6. Ryszard Stanisławski, Wojciech Zamecznik,

Tadeusz Rolke, Jan Kosiński, Jerzy Langda, Ewa Kozłowska Tomczyk, Witalis Wolny, and Krystyna Zakrzewska in Poland and Władysław Slawny, Antoni Miralda, Eustachy Kossakowski, and Roman Cieślewicz in France were just some of the many photographers involved in documenting Szapocznikow's work. The bulk of these records currently constitute the Alina Szapocznikow Estate Archive, on long-term loan to the National Museum in Kraków. I thank Jola Gola for indicating the names of the photographers.

7. In choosing this title, Szapocznikow could not have overlooked Duchamp's neologism.
8. André Bazin, "The Ontology of the Photographic Image," *Film Quarterly* 13, no. 4 (Summer 1960): 7–8.
9. Roland Barthes, *Camera Lucida* (New York: Hill and Wang, 1981), 87.
10. Barthes, "The Rhetoric of the Image," in *Image, Music, Text*, trans. Stephen Heath (New York: Hill and Wang, 1977), 44.
11. Batchen and many of the contributors to *Photography Degree Zero* also posit the special relationship between a thing and its indexical trace as the essence of photography.
12. Bazin, "The Ontology of the Photographic Image," 8. Cited in Rosalind Krauss, "Notes on the Index: Seventies Art in America," *October*, no. 3 (Spring 1977): 75.
13. Helen Molesworth, ed., *Part Object Part Sculpture* (Columbus, Ohio: Wexner Center for the Arts, 2005), 211.
14. Georges Didi-Huberman has written about what he calls "resemblance by contact," the direct physical transference of a form from one surface or material to another in such diverse objects as archaeological remains, the Shroud of Turin, death masks, Rodin's casts of body parts, and Duchamp's *Female Fig Leaf*. See in particular his exhibition catalogue *L'Empreinte* (Paris: Centre Georges Pompidou, 1997). See also Marta Dziewańska's evocative study based on Didi-Huberman, "Awkward Objects: Creative Barbarity – on Awkward Beginnings," in Agata Jakubowska, ed., *Alina Szapocznikow. Awkward Objects* (Warsaw: Museum of Modern Art, 2011).
15. Charles Baudelaire, "Le Salon de 1846," reprinted in his *Oeuvres complètes* (Paris: Gallimard, 1961), 943.
16. See Didi-Huberman on the relationship between photography, indexicality, figuration, and the shroud: "The Index of the Absent Wound (Monograph on a Stain)," trans. Thomas Repensek, *October*, no. 29 (Summer 1984): 63–81.
17. Szapocznikow, "Les materiaux plastiques," typescript, 1968. See page 108, elsewhere in this volume.
18. See Lynn Zelevansky and Elisabeth Sussman, eds., *Paul Thek: Diver, a Retrospective* (New York: Whitney Museum of American Art, 2010); and Fer, *Eva Hesse*.
19. This notion of *another* thread of modern sculpture is brilliantly analyzed and catalogued by Molesworth in *Part Object Part Sculpture*, where she argues that Duchamp's cast erotic objects made way for the production of readymades that emerged in 1964, which were, as it happens, "handmade." His *Female Fig Leaf* also emerges as a central figure in Didi-Huberman's discussion of the cast in *L'Empreinte*. Before Szapocznikow was awarded the Copley Foundation prize in 1966, for which Duchamp was a member of the jury, he visited her studio in 1965, just as his "handmade" replicas of readymades were beginning to circulate.
20. Krauss, "Notes on the Index: Seventies Art in America," 68–81; and "Notes on the Index: Seventies Art in America. Part 2," *October*, no. 4 (Autumn 1977): 58–67. Krauss's two-part essay was one of the first attempts at theorizing logician Charles Sanders Peirce's notion of the index in relation to the visual arts. See his "Logic as Semiotic: The Theory of Signs," in *Philosophical Writings of Peirce* (New York: Dover Publications, 1955).
21. Those words refer specifically to David Askevold's *The Ambit* (1975), in which there appear a thumbprint and shadows of the artist's outstretched arm. Krauss, 80.
22. Barthes, *Camera Lucida*, 15.
23. Ibid., 96.
24. Alex Potts, *The Sculptural Imagination: Figurative, Modernist, Minimalist* (New Haven, Connecticut: Yale University Press, 2000), 17.
25. Ibid.
26. Szapocznikow, "Mon oeuvre puise ses racines . . . ," signed typescript, March 1972. See page 28, elsewhere in this volume.
27. Ibid.
28. Images of the death camps, including a few graphic photographs of victims, were first released by the Allied Forces upon liberation of the camps in 1945 and visible in Soviet newsreels in the postwar period, as well as, for instance, in Alain Renais's highly discussed *Nuit et Brouillard* (1955). The complicated reception, signification, and status of these photographs, however, shifted dramatically in the 1960s, when the media began to circulate them again, this time less in light of the celebration of Allied heroism but instead with an emphasis on the victims, suggesting a different meaning and way of reading the photographs. See Janina Struk, *Photographing the Holocaust: Interpretations of the Evidence* (London: I. B. Tauris, 2004).
29. A negative of the startling visage of a female concentration-camp victim's face—and it is telling that Szapocznikow chose to repeatedly reproduce only that one image—remains in the artist's archives, evidence of her work on the series that feature it. Its published source is unknown, but likely it was a book rather than a magazine (since she would have clipped it as she regularly did with other magazine images); perhaps it is the publication that her son remembers her having in the late 1960s and looking at in secret. Piotr Stanisławski, in conversation with the author.
30. See Barthes, *Camera Lucida*.
31. Griselda Pollock, "Too Early and Too Late: Melting Solids and Traumatic Encryption in the Sculptural Dissolutions of Alina Szapocznikow," in Jakubowska, ed., *Alina Szapocznikow. Awkward Objects*, 85.

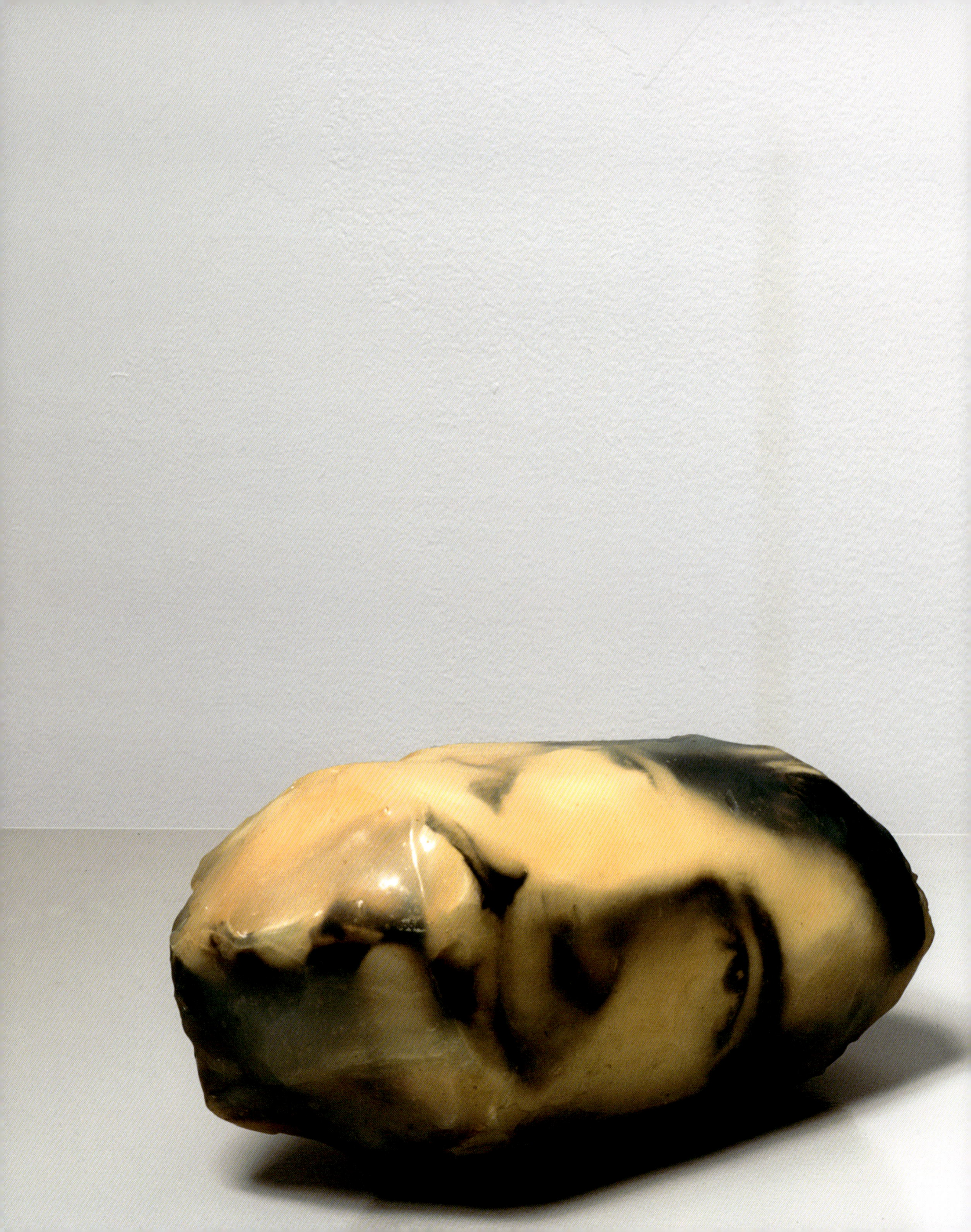

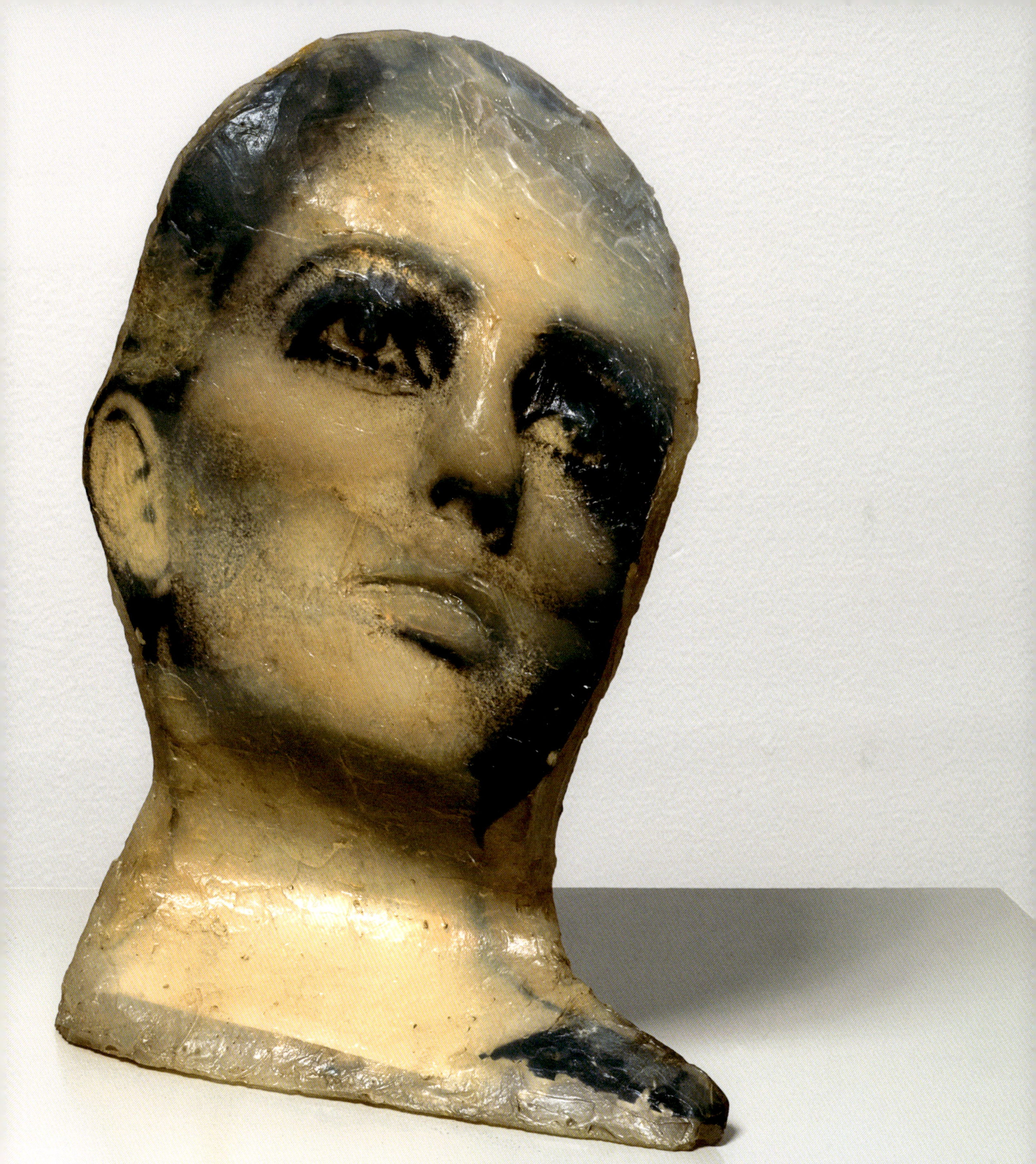

Plate 56

Souvenirs, 1967
Polyester resin and photographs
Left: 4 1/2 x 1 3/8 x 2 3/4" (11.5 x 3.5 x 7 cm); right: 11 13/16 x 8 5/8 x 3 9/16" (30 x 22 x 9 cm)

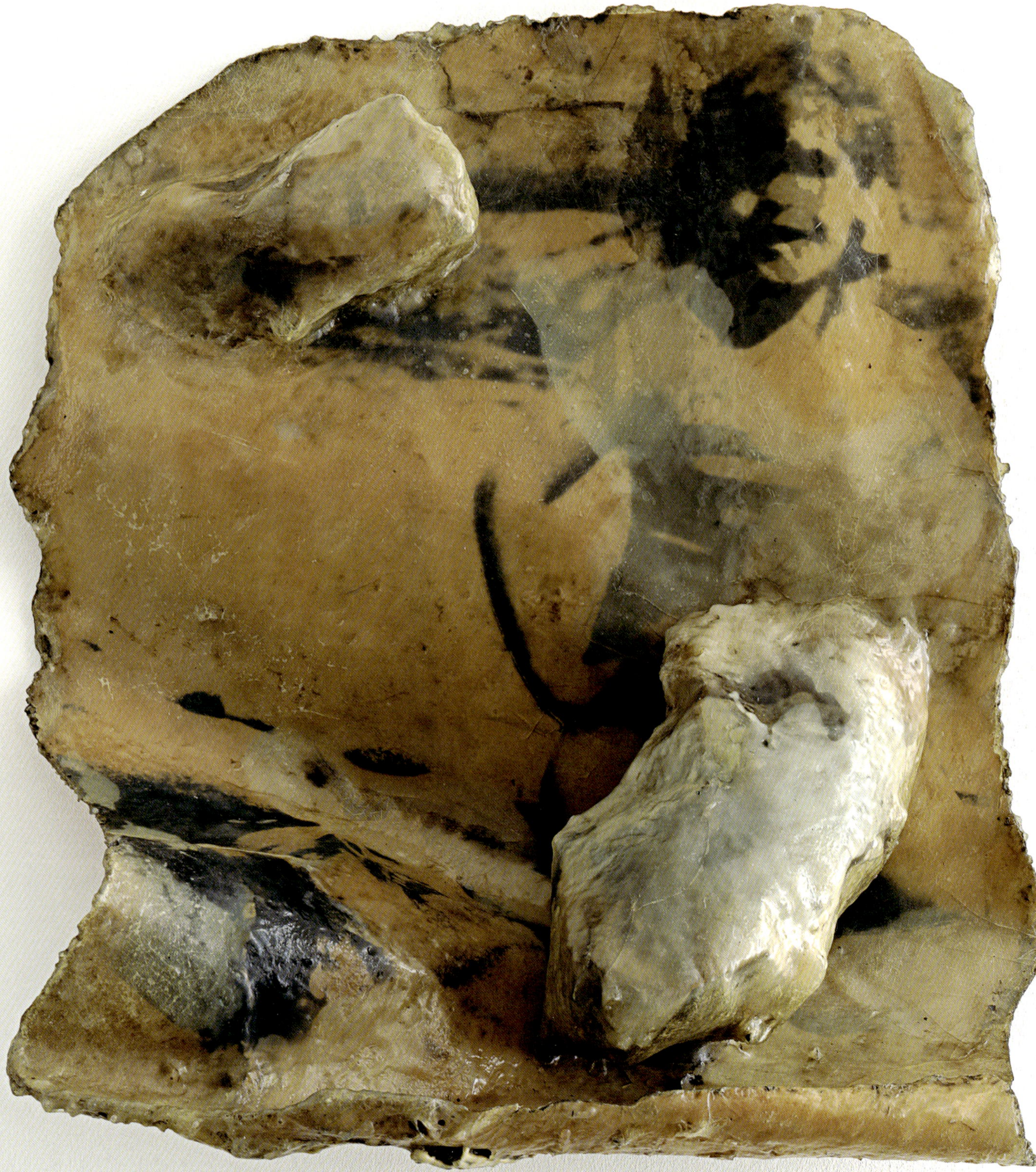

Plate 57

Souvenir I, 1971
Polyester resin, glass, wool, photographs
29 9/16 x 27 9/16 x 13" (75 x 70 x 33 cm)

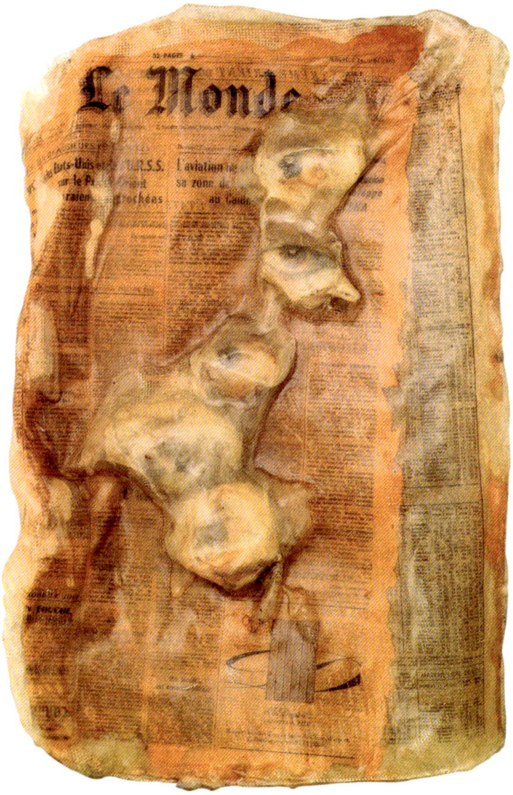

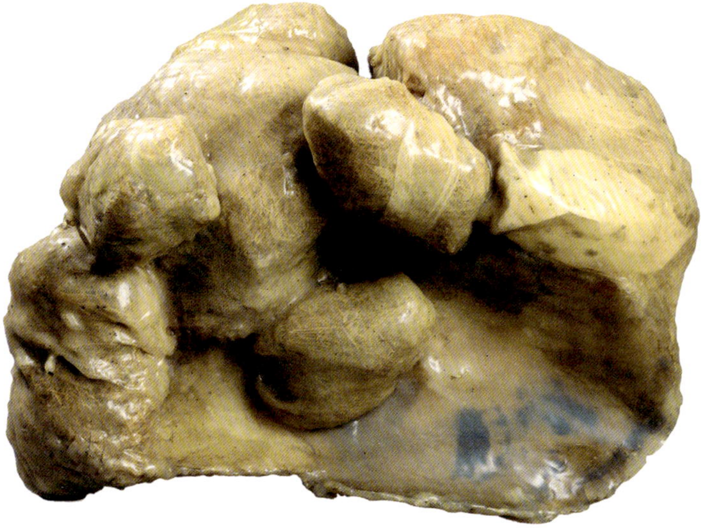

top

Plate 58

Le Monde, 1971
Polyester resin and *Le Monde* newspaper
19 7/8 x 13 3/8 x 3 9/16" (50.5 x 34 x 9 cm)

bottom

Plate 59

Souvenir II, 1971
Polyester resin and photograph
15 x 20 7/8 x 9 7/16" (38 x 53 x 24 cm)

pages 82–83

Plate 60

Grande Tumeur I (Big Tumor I), 1969
Polyester resin and photograph
28 3/4 x 36 5/8" (73 x 93 x 97 cm)
The National Museum in Wrocław

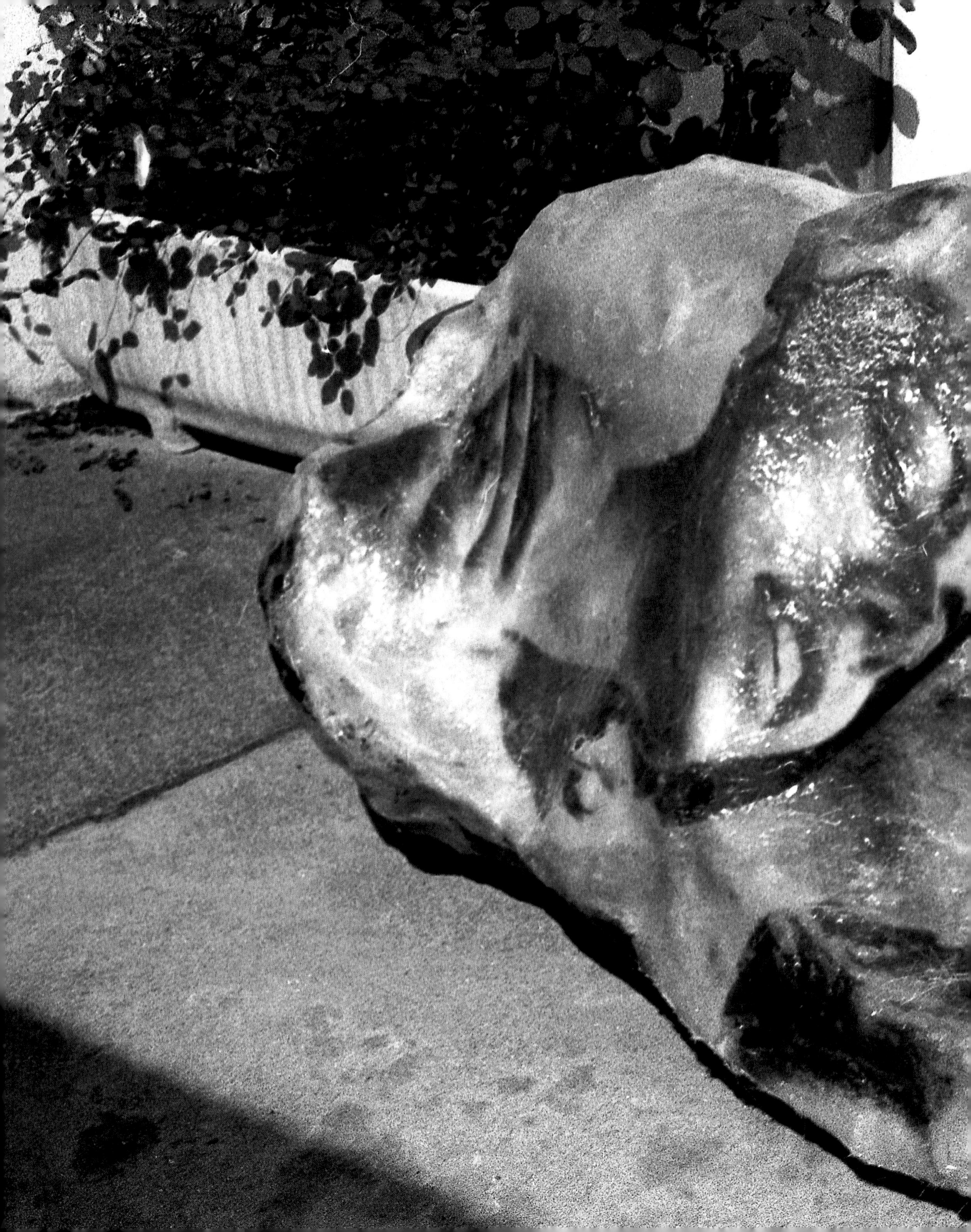

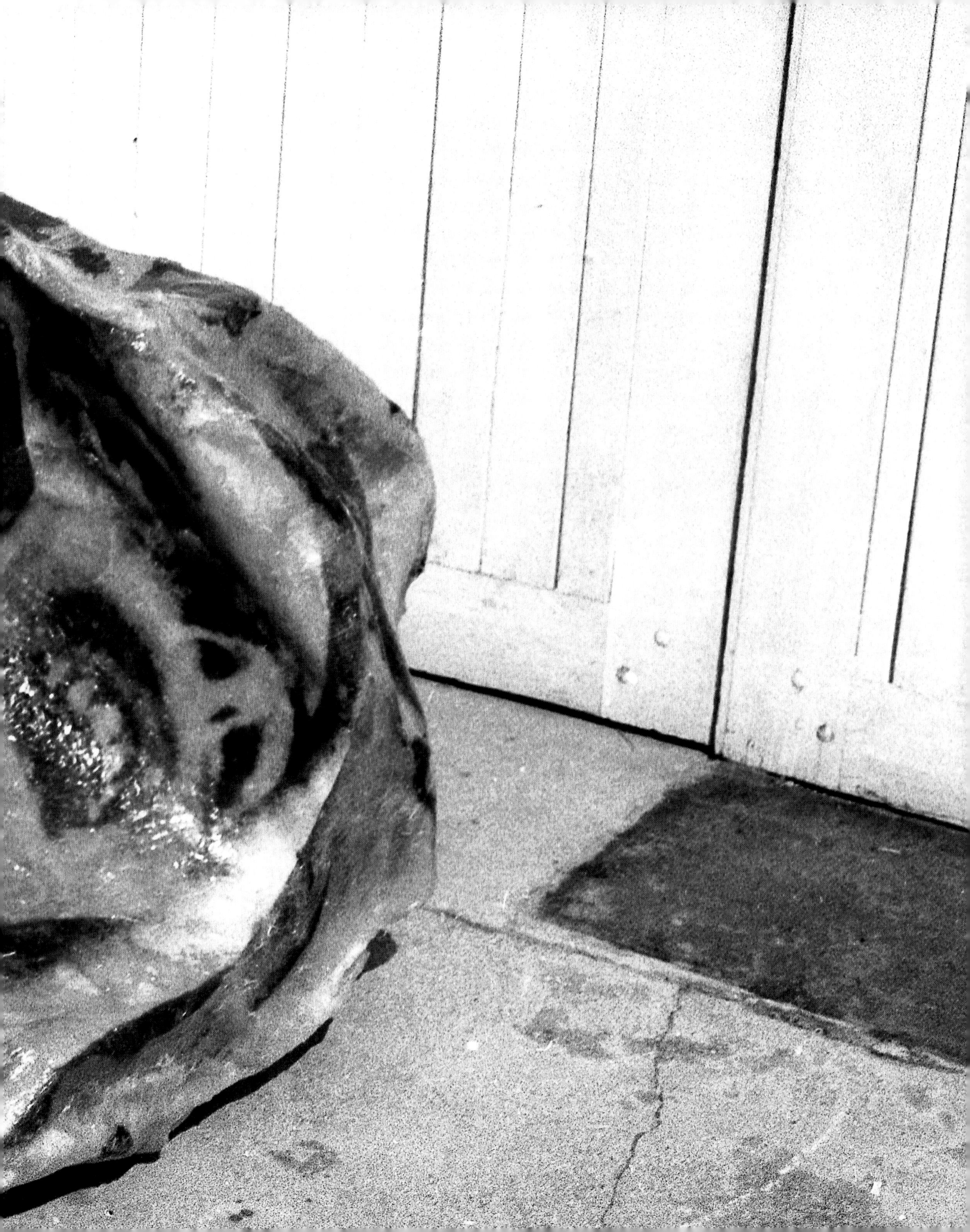

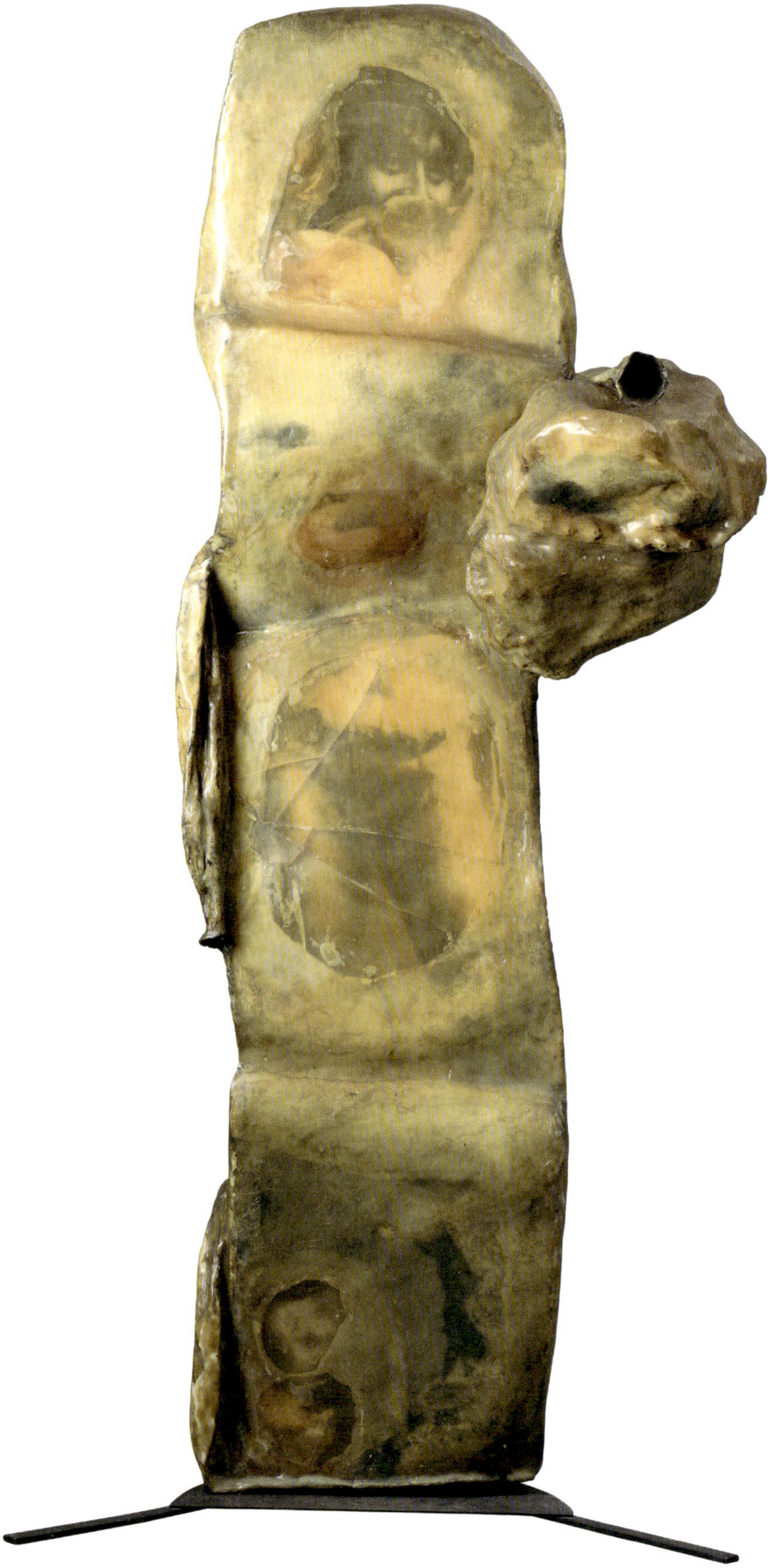

Plate 61

Alex, 1970
Polyester resin, photographs, clothing
68 1/2 x 26 3/8 x 19 11/16" (174 x 67 x 50 cm)

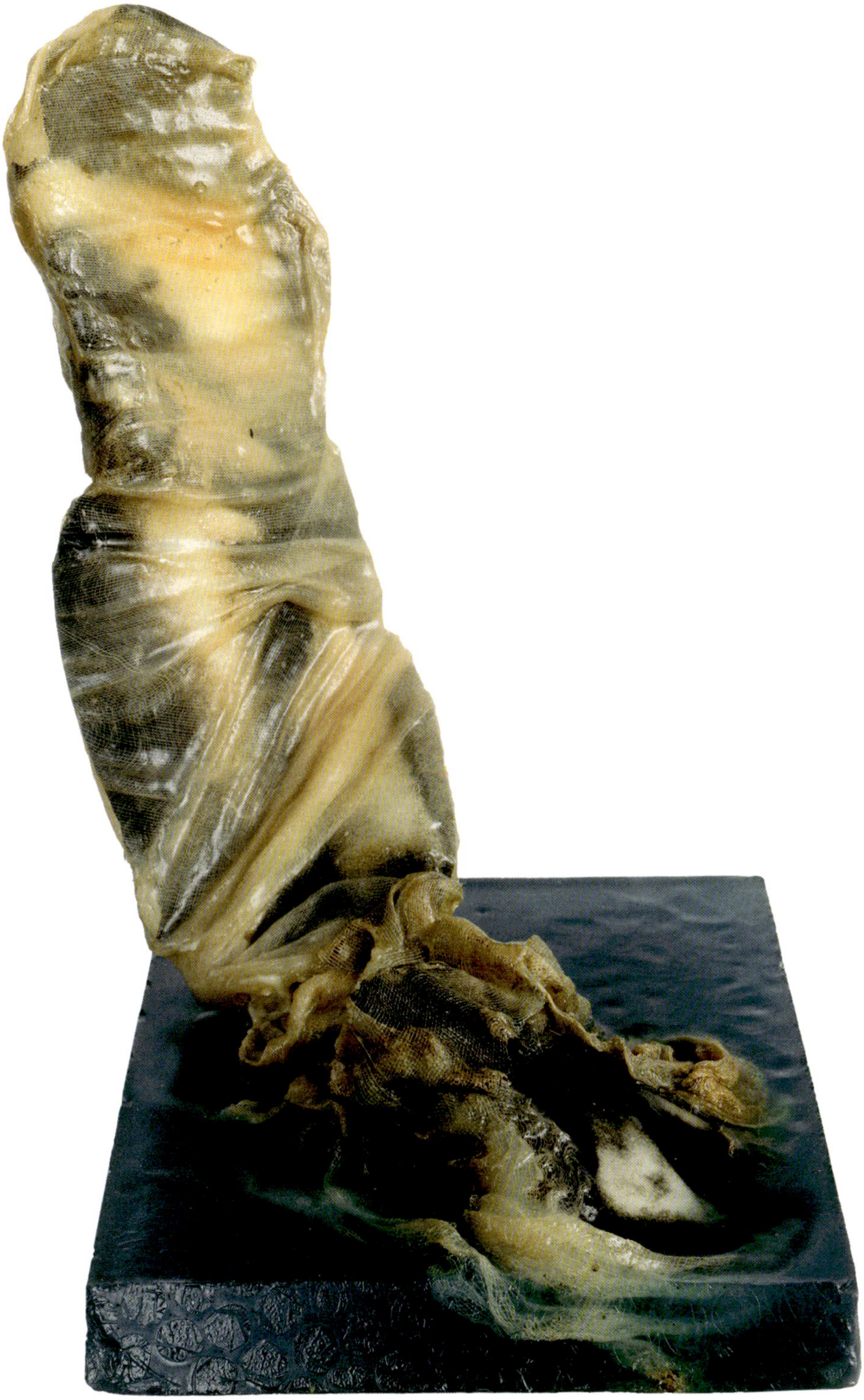

Plate 62

Petit Alex (Small Alex), 1970
Colored polyester resin, photographs, gauze
9 7/8 x 11 1/16 x 9 1/16" (25 x 28 x 23 cm)

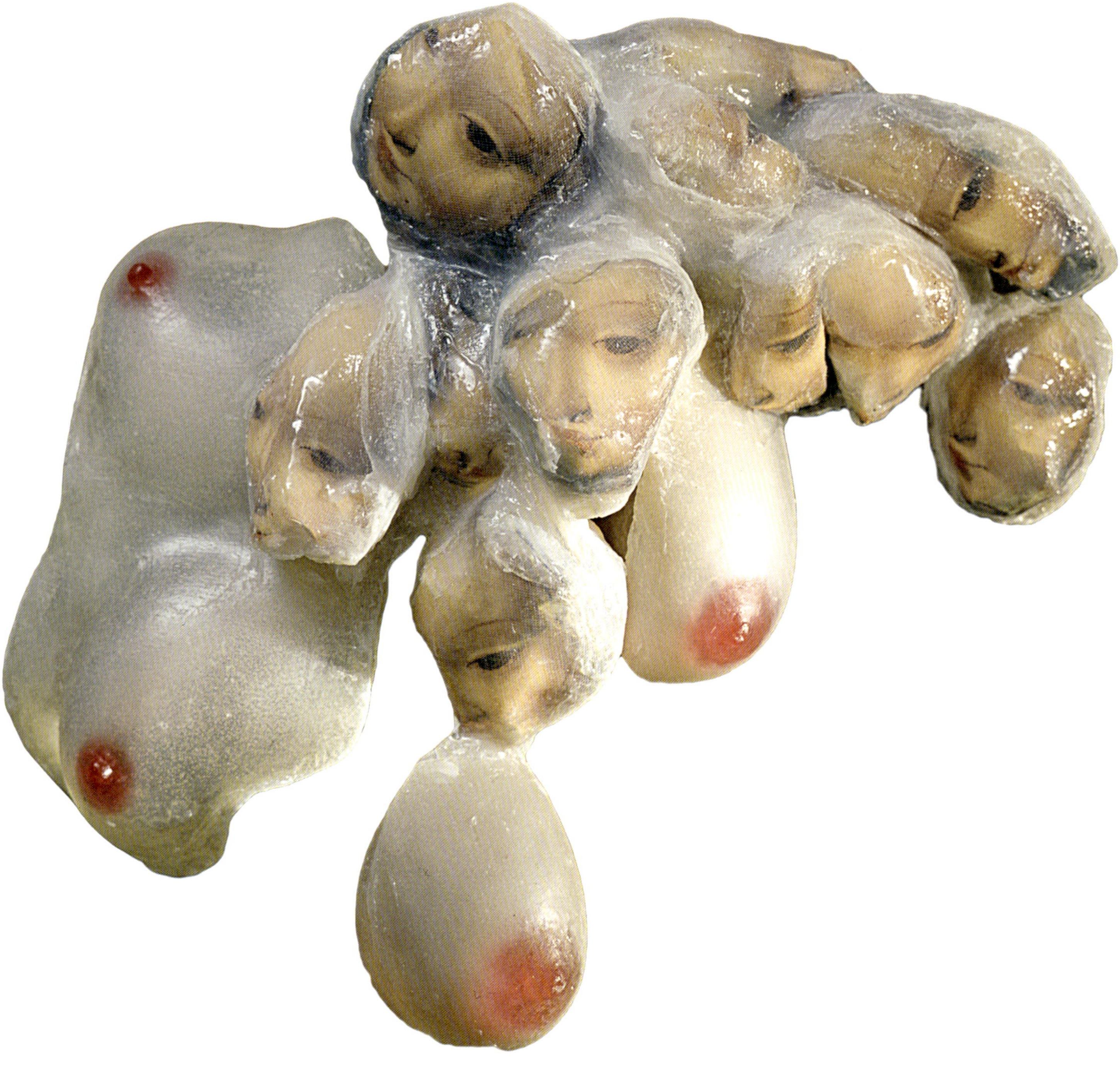

Plate 63

Krużlowa (Macierzyństwo) (Madonna of Krużlowa [Motherhood]), 1969
Colored polyester resin, photographs, gauze
16 9/16 x 20 1/2 x 7 1/8" (42 x 52 x 18 cm)

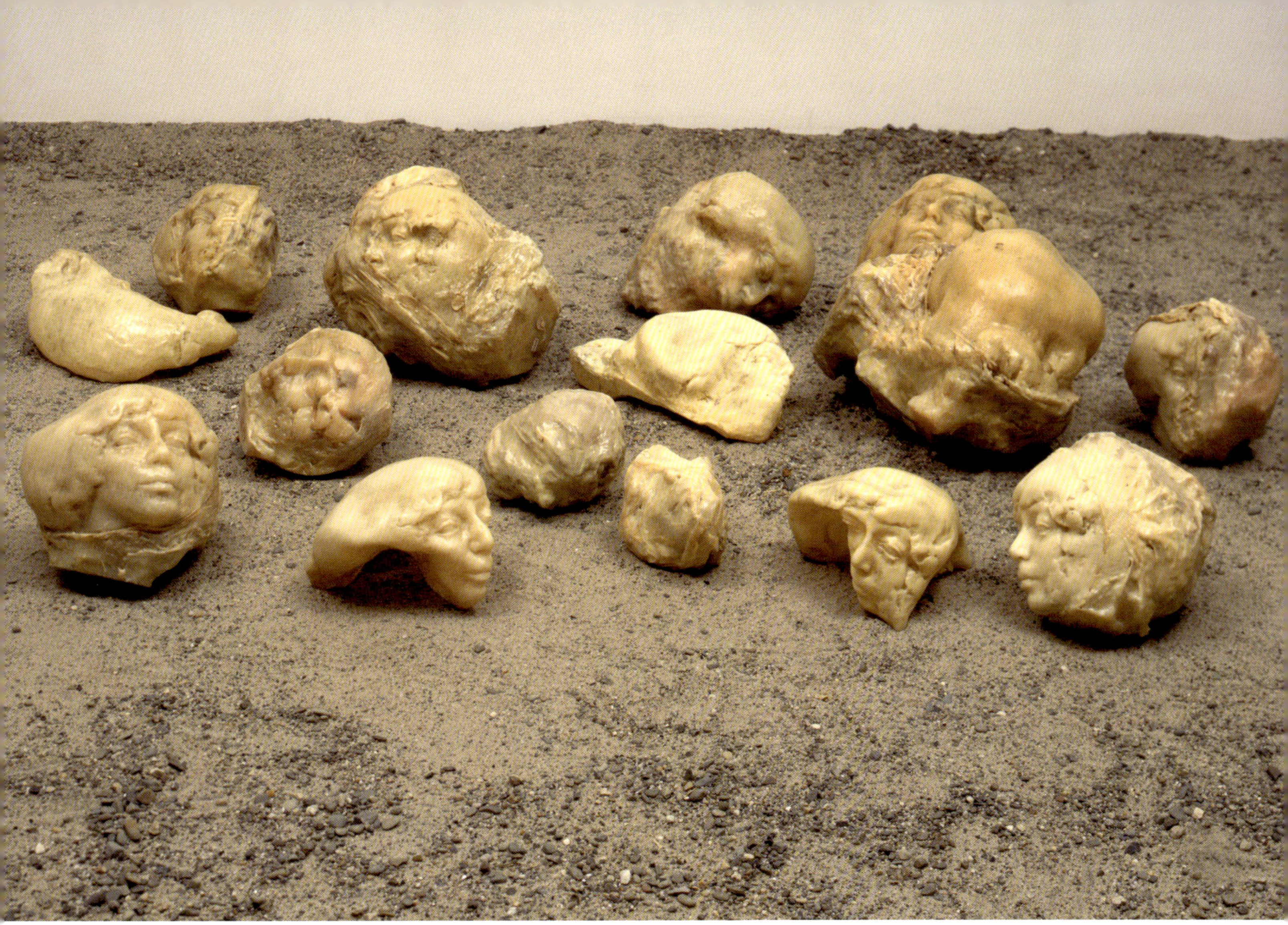

Plate 64

Tumeurs personnifiées (Tumors personified), 1971
Polyester resin, fiberglass, paper, gauze
Ranging from 13 x 22 1/16 x 13 3/8" (33 x 56 x 34 cm) to 5 15/16 x 9 1/16 x 6 5/16" (15 x 23 x 16 cm)

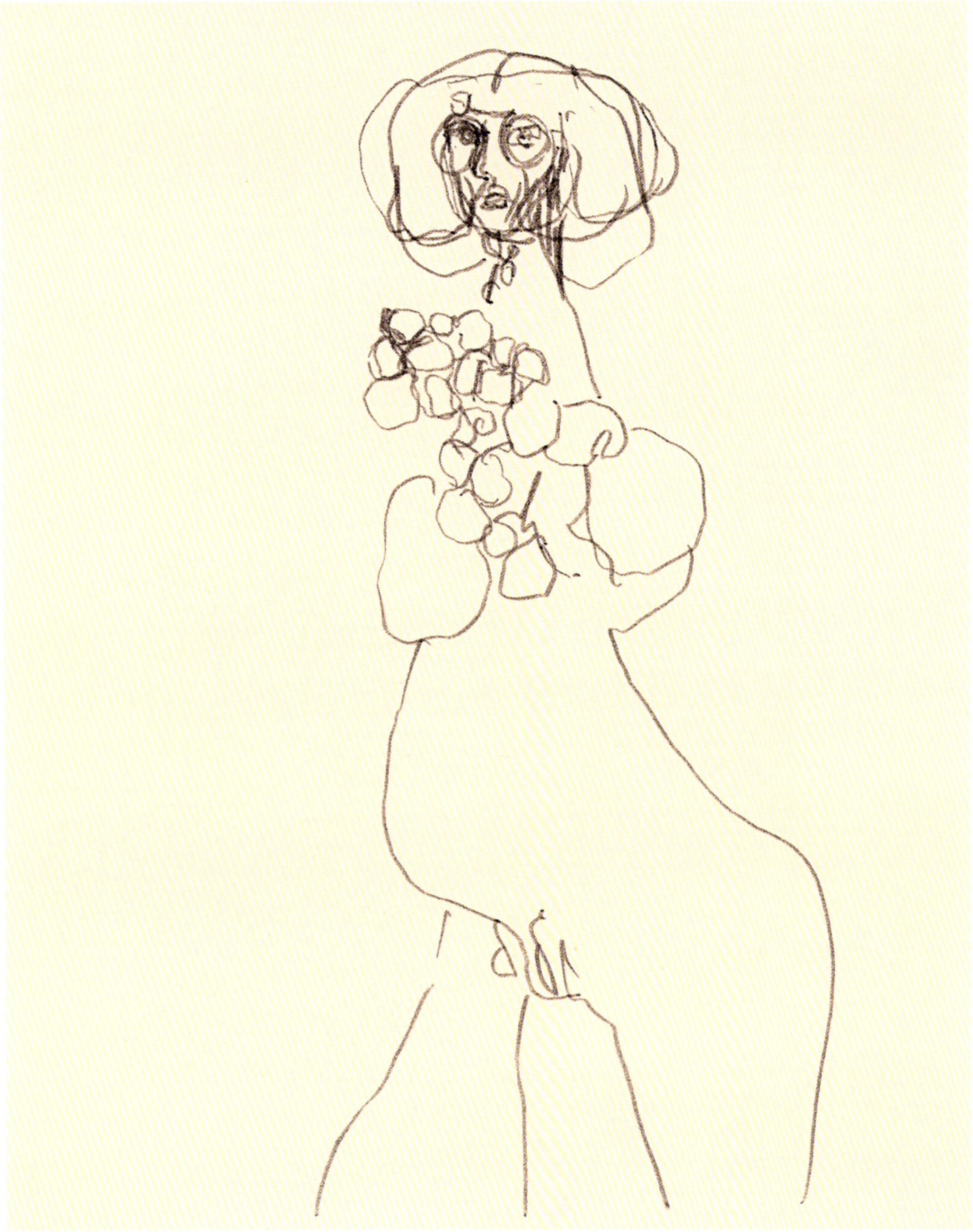

Plate 65

Untitled (Sketch of *Le Voyage* [Journey] with Growths 2), c. 1970
Felt-tip pen on paper
8 1/4 x 6 11/16" (21 x 17 cm)

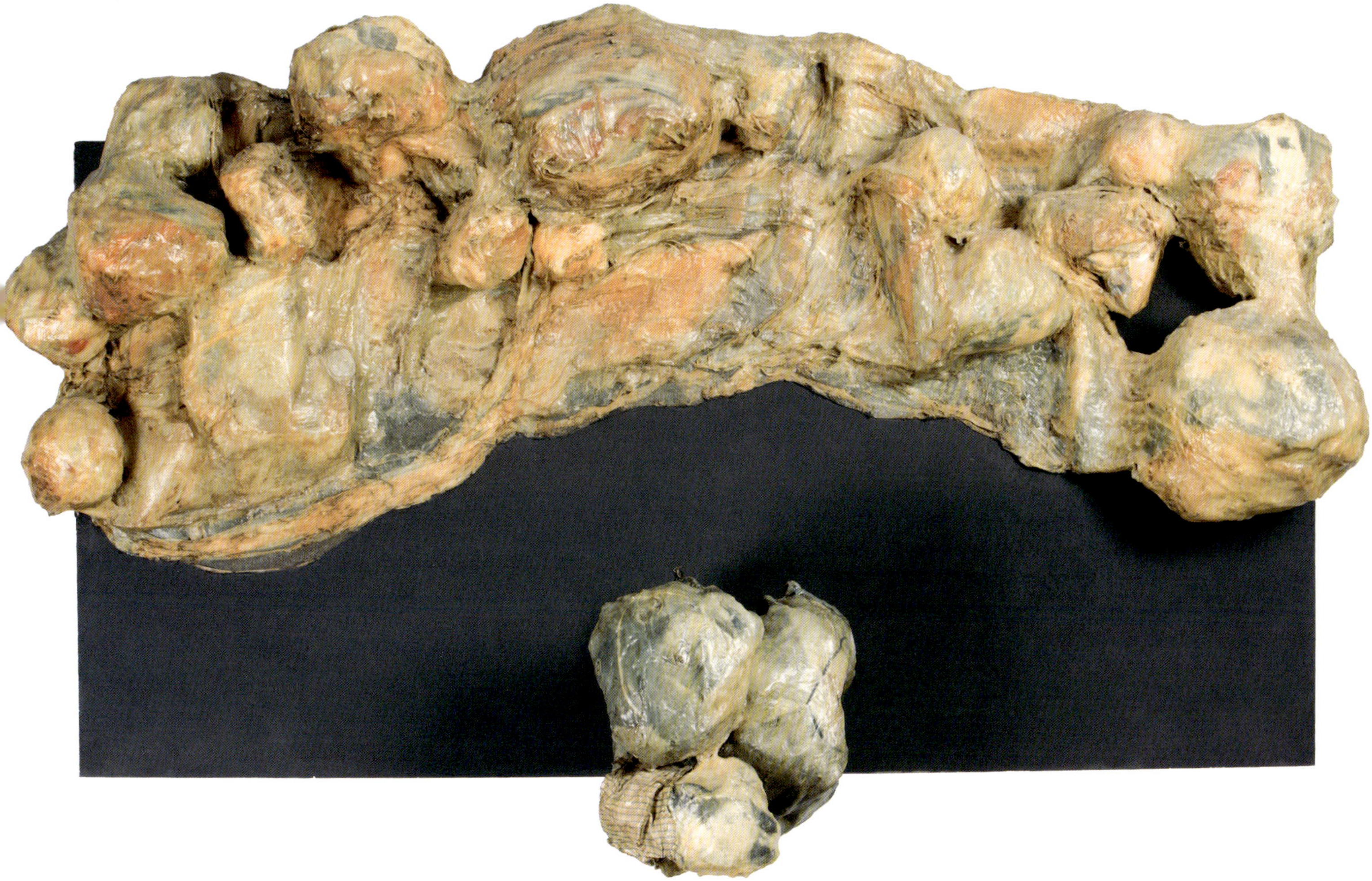

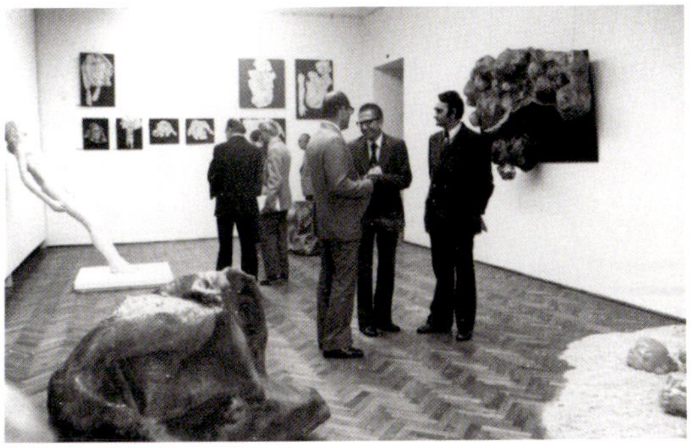

Muzeum Sztuki, Łódź, 1975.

Plate 66

L'Enterrement d'Alina (Alina's Funeral), 1970
Polyester resin, glass wool, photographs, wood, gauze, artist's clothing
53 3/16 x 82 11/16 x 19 11/16" (135 x 210 x 50 cm)

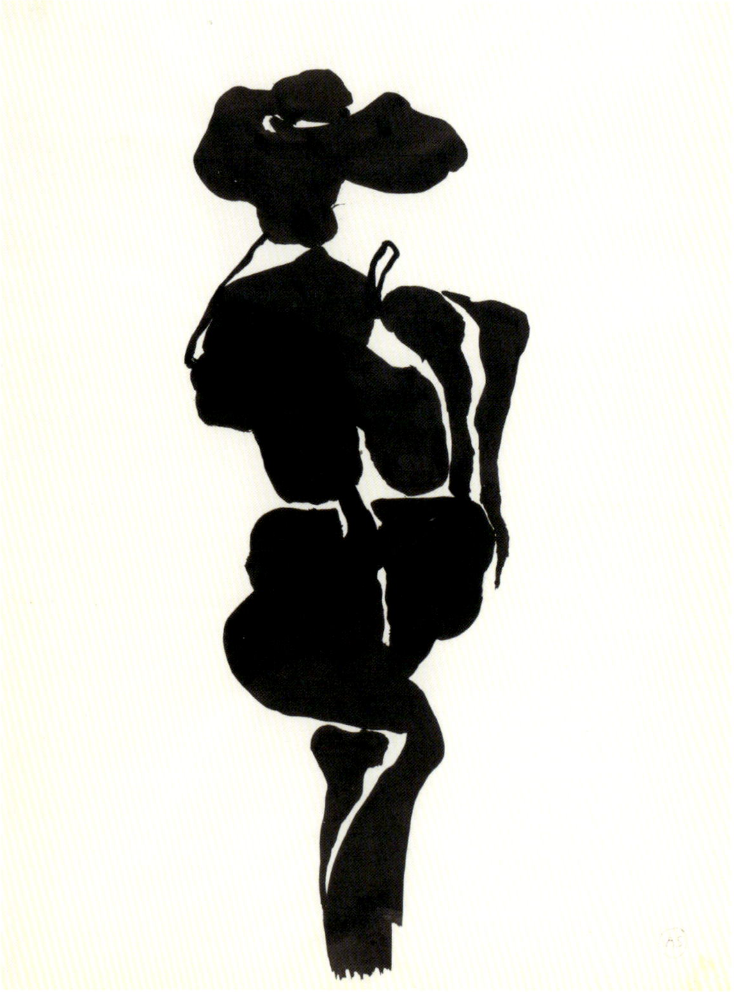

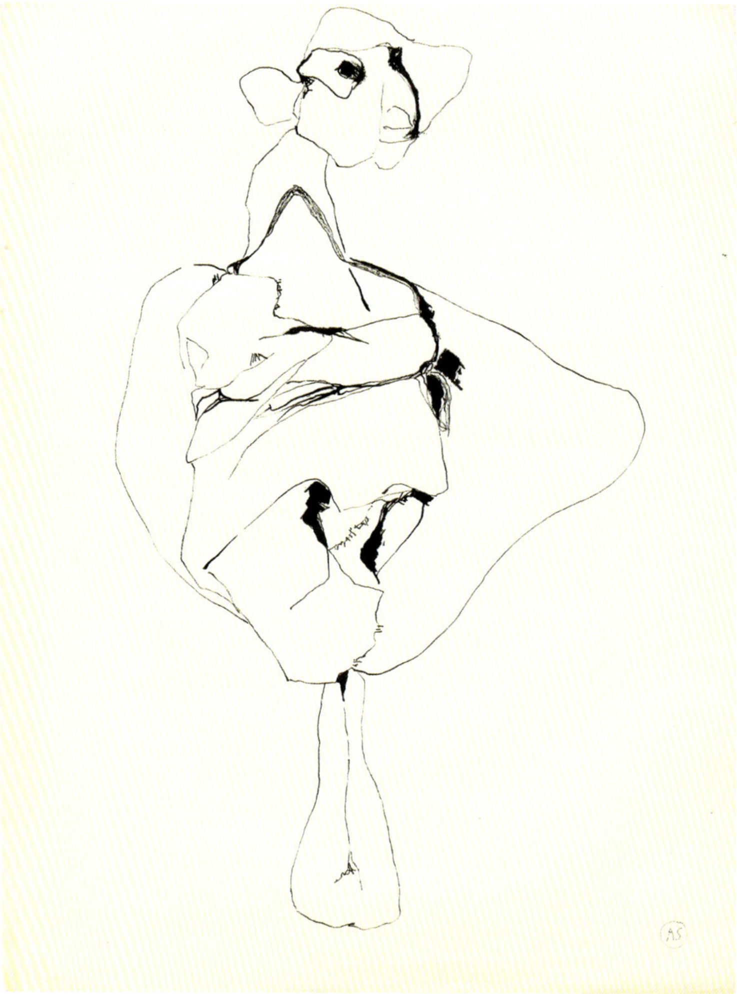

left

Plate 67

Untitled, c. 1970–71

Ink on paper

25 5/8 x 19 11/16" (65 x 50 cm)

right

Plate 68

Untitled, c. 1970–71

Ink on paper

28 1/4 x 22 1/4" (71.8 x 56.5 cm)

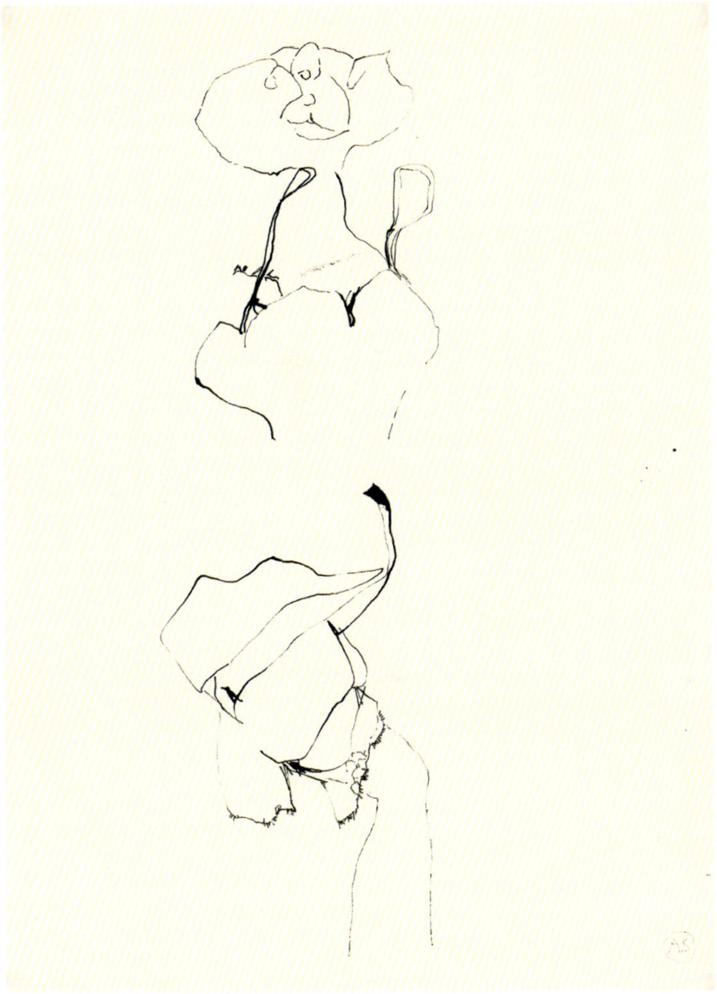

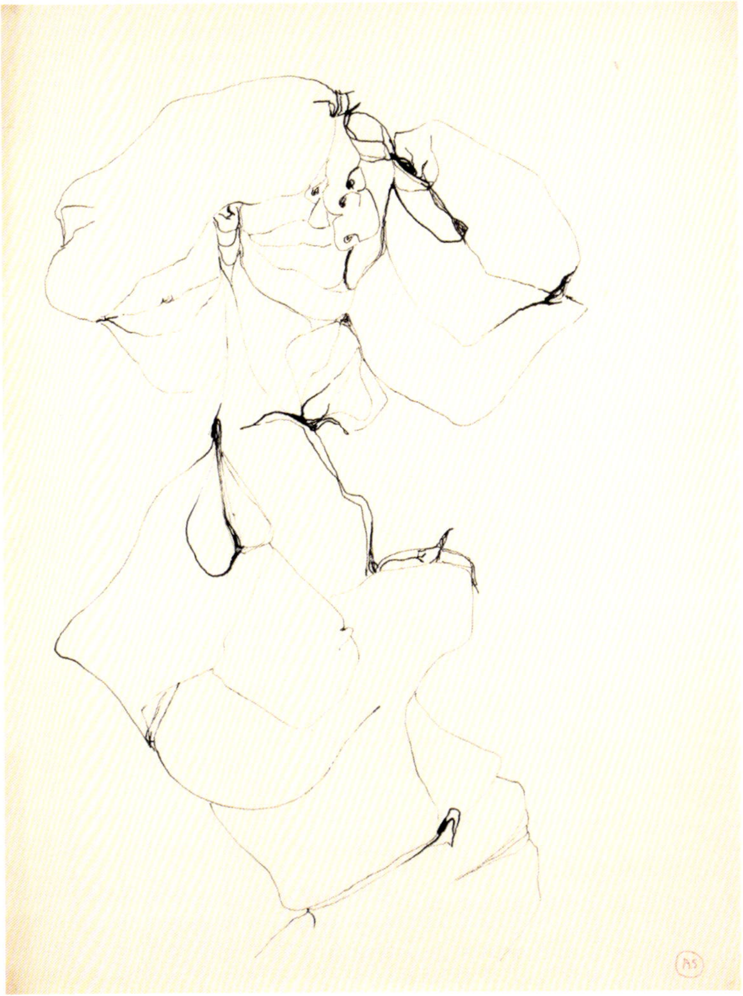

left
Plate 69
Untitled, c. 1970–71
Ink on paper
24 15/16 x 18 15/16" (63.3 x 48.1 cm)

right
Plate 70
Untitled, c. 1970–71
Ink on paper
24 13/16 x 18 15/16" (63 x 48 cm)

Traces of Passage: The Drawings of Alina Szapocznikow

Allegra Pesenti

Alina Szapocznikow considered herself first and foremost a sculptor, but her work on paper was a fundamental part of her sculptural practice.[1] The integration of both media within the artist's creative process is suggested in a photograph taken in her Paris studio in 1964 [ill. 1]. Propped up on a shelf among a group of Szapocznikow's sculptures and some tools in a carefully staged still life is a drawing; it is not a preparatory sketch for any of the objects displayed nearby, but it echoes their fluctuating extensions and textured surfaces. Over six hundred drawings and monotypes by Szapocznikow survive, and most, like this one, can be considered alongside the sculptures as parallel but independent expressions of form. Many are monogrammed and dated by the artist, as she intended her works on paper to be seen and exhibited them sporadically during the course of her career.[2]

Szapocznikow's works on paper are imbued with allusions to the human figure—in particular, her own body—which is at the epicenter of her art. "You say nothing about yourself, but you expose yourself," Jean-Marie Drot commented to her during the 1966 recording of his documentary film on Polish artists.[3] His remark followed her refusal to discuss the atrocities she endured as a Jewish prisoner in Nazi concentration camps during World War II.[4] By the time this interview aired in France in 1969, Szapocznikow had been diagnosed with cancer, the disease that ultimately caused her death at age forty-seven in 1973. Her response to his questioning was characteristically evasive and humorous, as she posed above two overlapping casts of the lower part of her face, thus physically completing the sculpture [ill. 2]. Beneath this layer of irony, in her work's poignant evocations of the transience of human life and the ephemeral nature of the body, lies the answer.

Szapocznikow sought to establish herself as an independent artist in Warsaw and Paris, through both precarious health conditions and tempestuous political events. Upon release from her incarceration in 1945, she did not return to Poland but forged her identity as a Czech citizen in order to study in Prague. In 1949, following her move to Paris, she was diagnosed with a potentially fatal case of tuberculosis. In 1951, with her husband Ryszard Stanisławski, she relocated to Warsaw, where she won a succession of

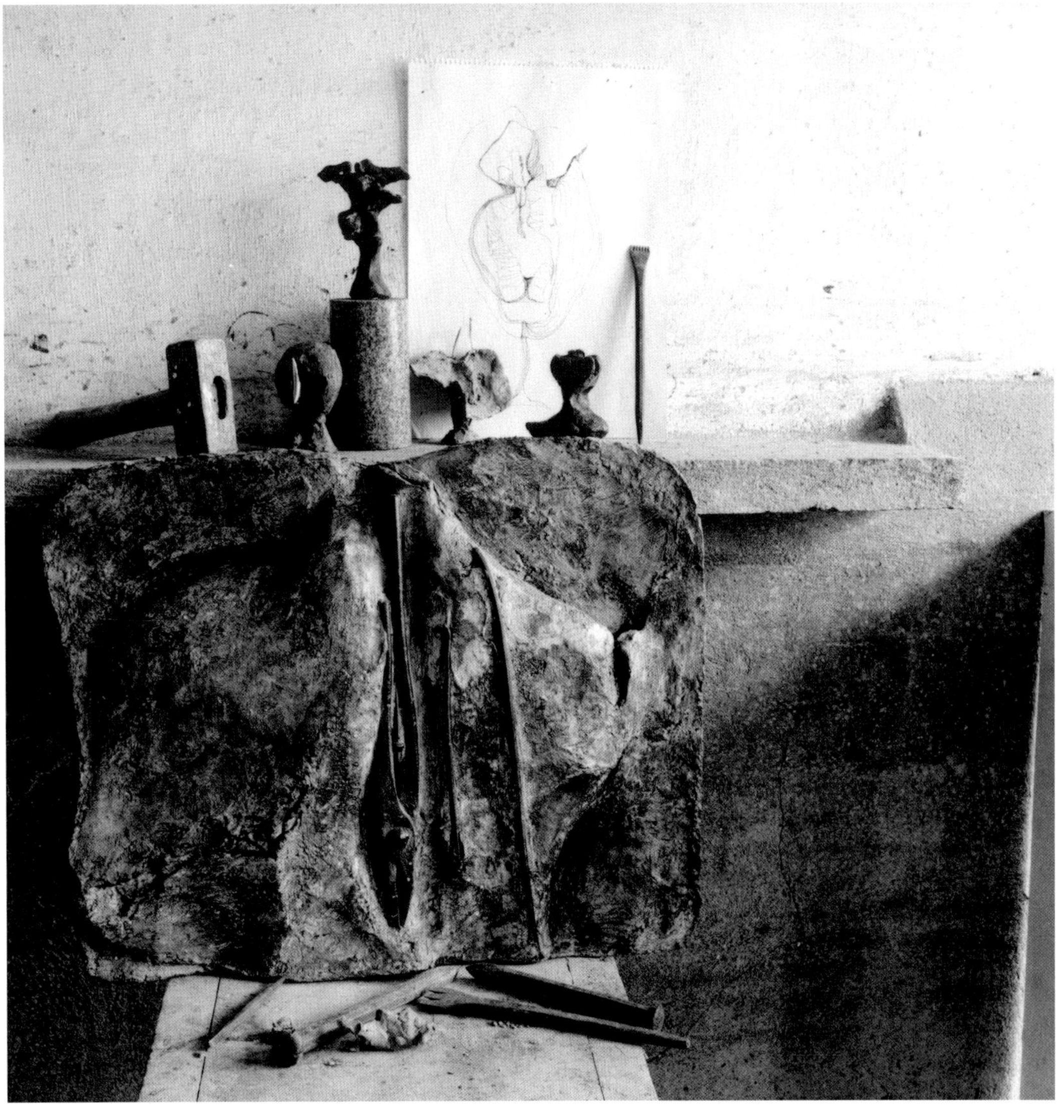

1. The artist's studio in Paris, 1964.

competitions and received acclaim from the local artistic community. Poland, ravaged by German bombings, was now under Stalinist Communism and marred by social unrest and economic depression. In 1963, she moved back to Paris with her son, Piotr Stanisławski, and second husband Roman Cieślewicz. By that time, France too had undergone its own upheavals with the bloody Algerian War (1954–62) and would soon experience the strikes and student riots of 1968. Despite cancer and socio-political turbulence, Szapocznikow remained staunchly committed to her work until the last days of her life.

An analysis of her drawings and monotypes reveals four main stylistic phases, each one marked by a gradual transformation of the figure from a whole and integral entity through to an elated presence. The first period is marked by academic study and rigorous observation of the human body, which provided a foundation for Szapocznikow's practice. Around 1955, as political pressure began to lift and the demand for Socialist Realism began to wane, her outlines loosened and expanded, allowing her figures to metamorphose into an array of anthropomorphic subjects. This "disarticulation of

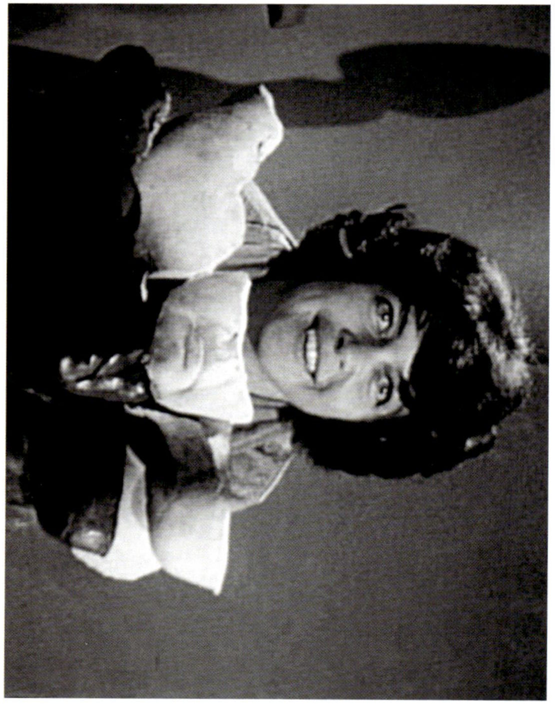

2. Still from a segment of Jean-Marie Drot's television program *Journal de Voyage en Pologne*, filmed in the artist's Warsaw studio, 1966.

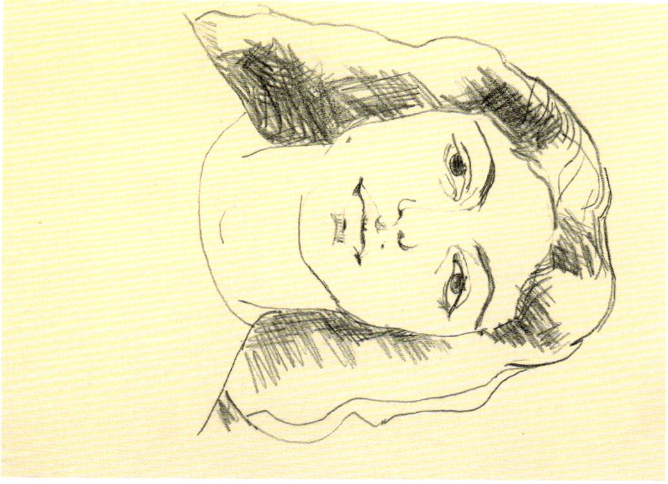

3. Untitled (Self-Portrait with Long Hair), c. 1946–48. Pencil on paper, 11 1/16 x

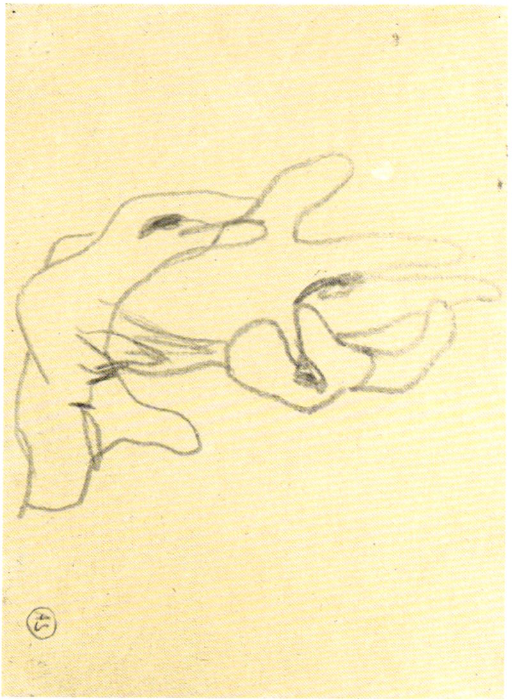

4. Untitled (Study of Hands for the Auschwitz Monument I), c. 1958. Pencil on paper, 8 3/16 x 11 13/16" (20.7 x 30 cm). The Estate of Alina Szapocznikow/Piotr Stanisławski.

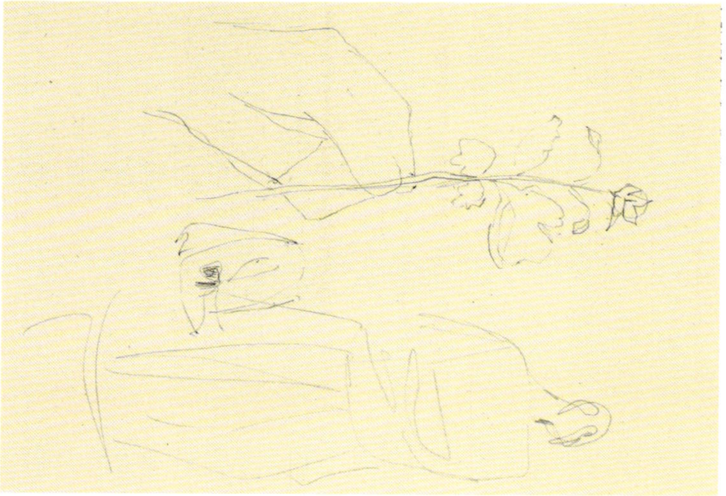

5. Untitled (Studies of a Flower and a Figure), c. 1959. Pencil on paper, 11 7/16 x 8 3/16" (29 x 20.8 cm). The Estate of Alina Szapocznikow/Piotr Stanisławski.

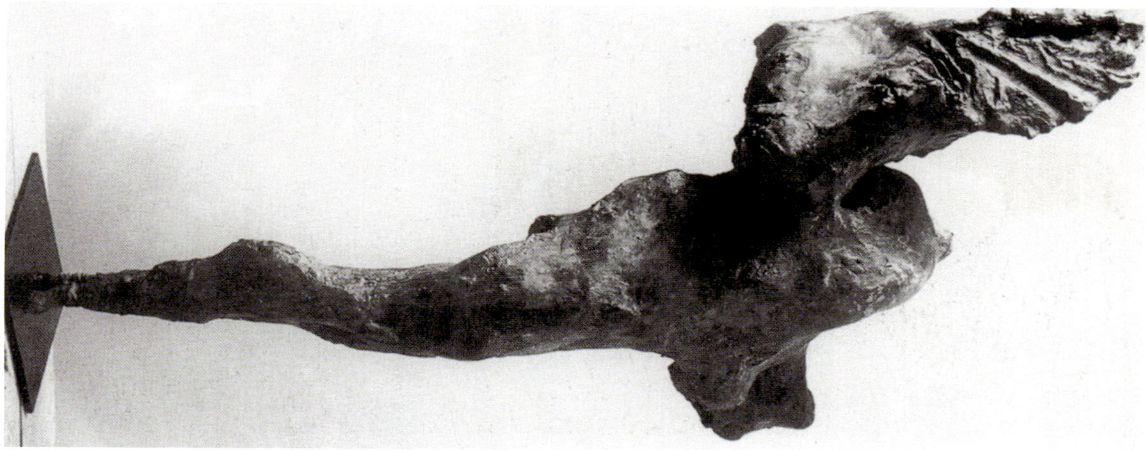

6. *Kwiato-ptak* (Flower-Bird), 1959–60 [no longer extant]. Patinated plaster, 57 1/2" (146 cm) high.

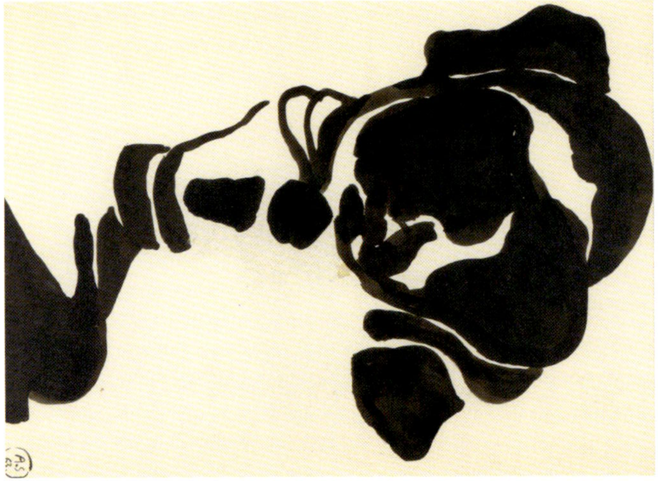

9. Untitled, 1963. Ink on cardboard, 14 3/16 x 11 1/16" (36 x 28 cm). The Estate of Alina Szapocznikow/Piotr Stanisławski.

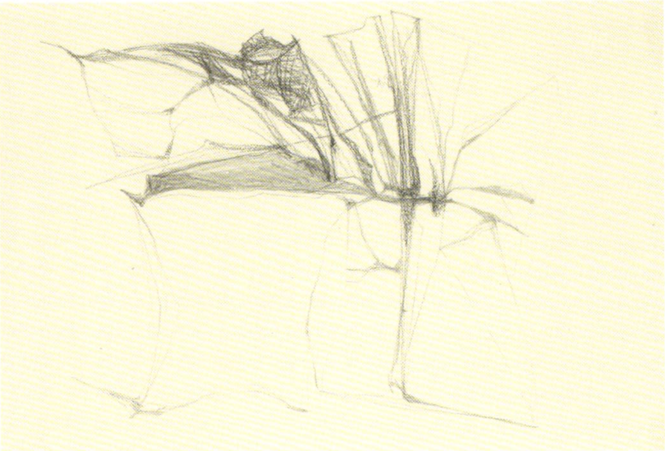

7. Untitled (Sketch for the Sculpture *Rozłupany* [Shattered] 2), c. 1960–61. Pencil on paper, 11 5/8 x 8 1/4" (29.5 x 21 cm). The Estate of Alina Szapocznikow/Piotr Stanisławski.

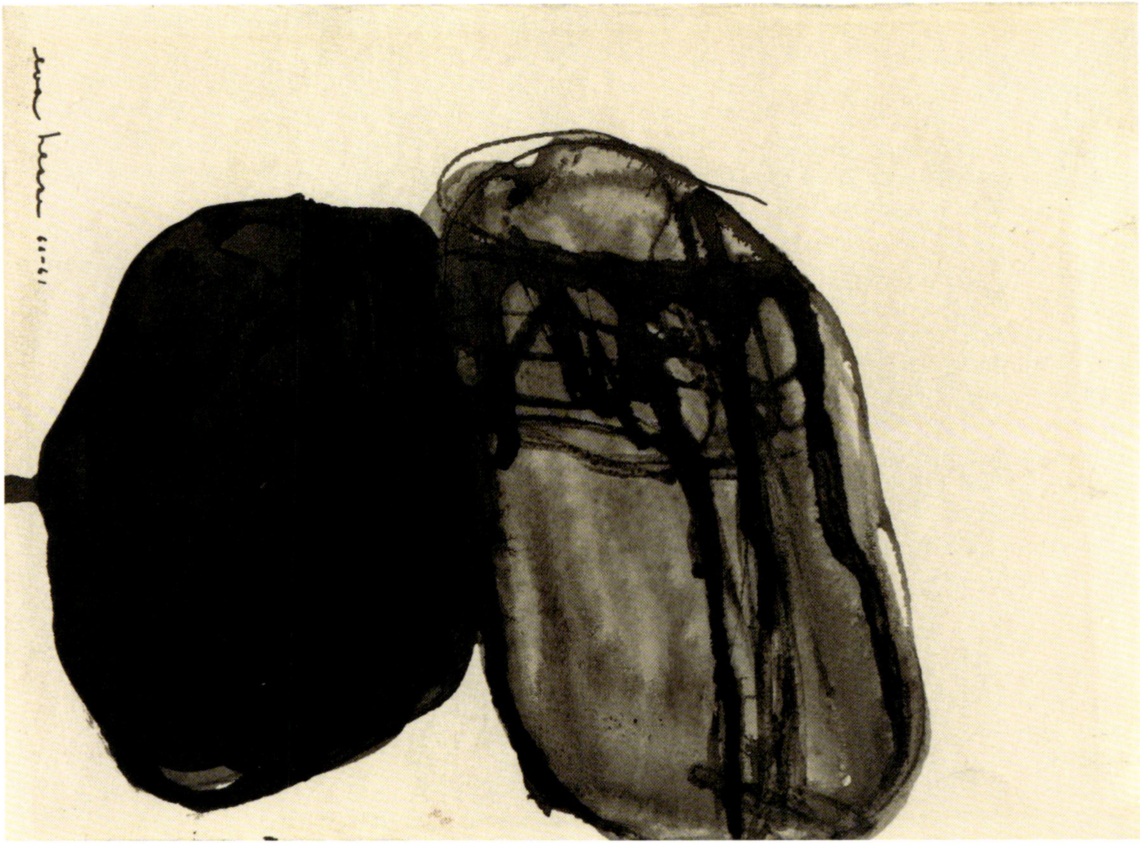

10. Eva Hesse (American, born Germany; 1936–1970), No title, 1960–61. Gouache and ink on paper, 6 x 4 1/2" (15.2 x 11.4 cm). The Museum of Modern Art, New York. Gift of Tony Ganz in memory of Sally Ganz and her friendship with Robert Storr.

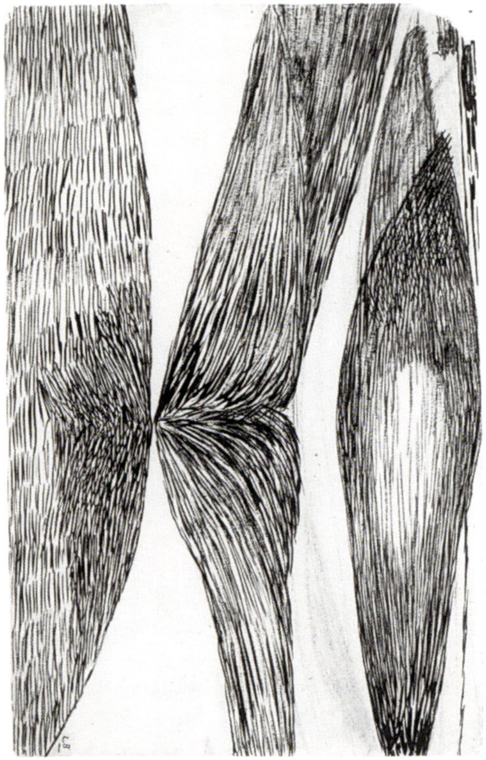

8. Louise Bourgeois (American, born France; 1911–2010), *Point of Contact*, 1950. Ink and pencil on paper, 9 1/2 x 15 3/8" (24.1 x 39.1 cm). Hammer Museum, Los Angeles. Gift of Sally and Wynn Kramarsky in honor of Ann Philbin.

form,"[5] as Pierre Restany described it, shifted to a decomposition of form in 1962, when Szapocznikow started to make casts of individual parts of her own body. The final phase is marked by transparency and weightlessness, as Szapocznikow introduced sparse washes of watercolor to her images and allowed her strange and disproportioned characters to collide in a dreamlike state.

Roots (1945–55)

My work has its roots in sculpture.
For years I threw myself into studying problems of balance, volume, space, shadow and light.

—Alina Szapocznikow[6]

In the opening of her artist 1972 statement, Szapocznikow situated her work within a classical tradition of sculpture. Interested in stone as a medium from the outset, she committed herself avidly to the study of carving during her formative years in Prague and Paris. Undaunted by its physical challenges, she fully engaged herself with the material as she learned to shape it. Drawing assisted her during this period of education and would remain a fundamental part of her practice throughout her artistic career.

Draftmanship has for centuries been at the foundation of sculpture, and Szapocznikow's studies align her with generations of sculptors from Michelangelo Buonarroti, Gianlorenzo Bernini, and Antonio Canova to Henry Moore and Barbara Hepworth—all of whom worked with stone, which allows few mistakes. Historical stone sculptures particularly captured her imagination, including the haunting scenes carved directly into sandstone grottoes by the Baroque master Matthias Bernhard Braun, near the village of Kuks in the former Czechoslovakia,[7] and the medieval biblical narratives she sketched in and around the churches of Brittany in 1950.[8] Szapocznikow related to the carved stones, which have endured the ravages of time, as representative of permanence and eternal memory, like the marble tombstones she encountered in the Père Lachaise cemetery in Paris in 1949.

Her early studies are attentive observations of the proportions and volumes of the body. She scrutinized the figure in an extensive group of sketches after nude female models and a series of anatomical drawings traced from a book.[9] The tangible presence of the figure is felt in pencil drawings such as Untitled (Study of a Seated Woman. Self-Portrait, c. 1948–54) [plate 151], in which bold rendering emphasizes the slump of the sitter's body as she leans her head languidly onto her hand. In Untitled (Study of a Man Standing with Raised Arms, Seen from Behind, c. 1951–54) [plate 152], Szapocznikow's focus is on the physical structure of the body, examining the way her model's clothes gravitate to the ground even as he reaches up. The sturdy features of her figures are reiterated in the commemorative sculptures she produced in Warsaw around the same time, like her *Pomnik Przyjaźni Polsko-Radzieckiej* (*Monument to Polish-Soviet Friendship*, 1954).

While her public work assumed a Socialist-Realist vocabulary, she developed a more personal artistic vocabulary in her works on paper. Her earliest surviving drawings are self-portraits, including Untitled (Self-Portrait with Long Hair, c. 1946–48), in which the artist's face is depicted frontally [ill. 3], her features briskly summarized and assertive. As a group, Szapocznikow's early drawings announce the self-referential and corporeal character of her art.

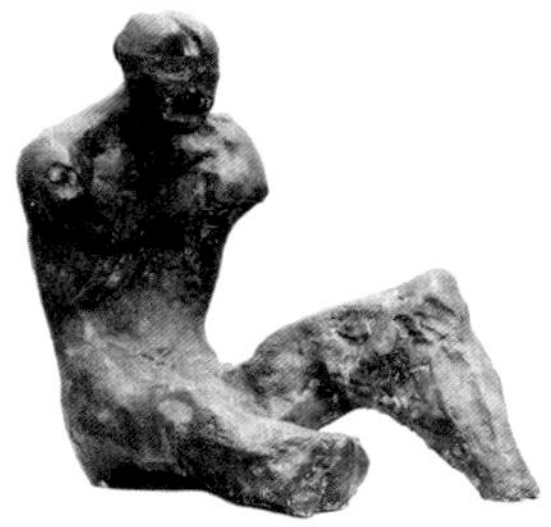

11.

Your death repeated in the hearts of men
Shall re-enact my grief and my lament.
But now your blood shall change into a flower.

—Ovid[10]

Once, I drew attention to a beautiful bouquet of roses in a vase.
I was interested above all in a curved, cracked rose. A few years later,
I came across these drawings and I made the sculpture *Woman-Rose*.

—Alina Szapocznikow[11]

Having mastered the proportions of the body, Szapocznikow began to distort them, a shift that is first apparent in the 1955 iteration of the sculpture *Ekshumowany* (*Exhumed*, 1957) [ill. 11, plate 146]. A rebuke to Stalinism, it was made in honor of Hungarian activist László Rajk, who was murdered in 1949. By using cement over an iron structure in this earlier version rather than the less versatile and subtractive technique of carving, she could mold the figure's limbs and extend its forms, emulating unearthed and disfigured cadavers. A similar malleability of form occurs on paper: in Untitled (Study of a Nude, c. 1959), the outlines of a female figure are slackened, as if reflected in water [plate 140]. Elastic contours describe the contorted hands in Untitled (Study of Hands for the Auschwitz Monument 1, c. 1958) [ill. 4].[12] Szapocznikow attempted to liberate her forms from their earthly connections. She elongated them and allowed them to hover above the ground; some dance or perform balletic poses[13] in drawings such as Untitled (c. 1960) [plate 139]. In both her sculptures and drawings of this period, the human body morphs into a compendium of hybrid characters.

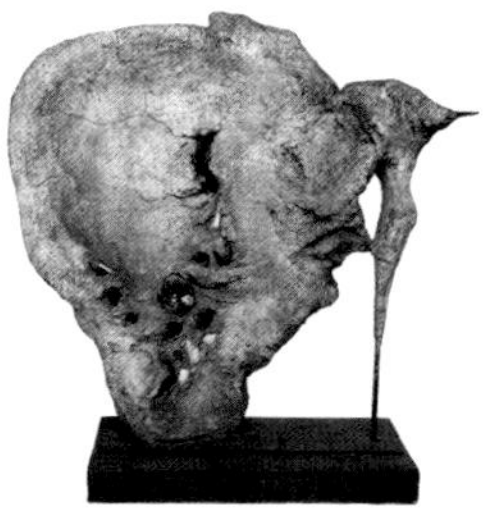

12.

Kwiato-ptak (*Flower-Bird*, 1959–60) [ill. 6] pirouettes into space from a precariously slim base,[14] while a drawing in blue ink, Untitled (Study for *Kwiato-ptak* [Flower-Bird] 2, c. 1959–60) [plate 138]—among her first uses of color on paper—shares the same twists and contractions of form, possessing the elusive quality that characterizes Szapocznikow's work at this time. A wave that extends from a knotted form might refer to a beak or perhaps a wing or petal. The relationship between the drawing and the sculpture is tentative—one of interpretation rather than preparation. A loose connection can also be made between the drawing in colored crayon Untitled (Sketch 1, c. 1959–60) [plate 137] and the sculpture *Małża* (*Mollusc*, 1960) [ill. 12, plate 135]. The use of color in both these examples is independent of the sculptures, which assume instead the neutral tones of their materials.

While she often chose animal and natural subjects, Szapocznikow's point of departure was almost always the human figure, usually a female body. The direct correlation is emphasized in the spontaneous Untitled (Studies of a Flower and a Figure, c. 1959) [ill. 5]. Though it belongs to a consecutive group of drawings of flowers, the rapidly jotted figure here is particularly revealing of the artist's thought process. The theme of woman-flower has another incarnation in the vagina-like sketches Untitled (Study for *Kobieta-róża* [Woman-Rose]) [plate 141] and Untitled (Studies of Some Organic Forms) [plate 142] (both c. 1959). Perhaps unintentionally, these drawings echo the erotic inventions of Hans Bellmer and the deconstructed figures in the Dadaist photomontages of Hannah Hoch. Another conflation of forms appears in Untitled (Sketch for the Sculpture *Przemiany* [Metamorphoses] 2, c. 1961) [plate 130], where studies of winged shapes refer to female

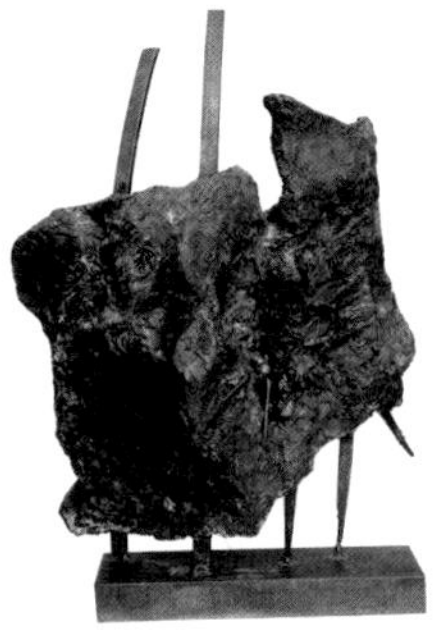

13.

genitalia and also lips, evoking the suppleness and curvaceous structure of a sandstone sculpture now known only through photographs. Beyond the transient and erotic nature of these works, however, is a more brutal aspect of Szapocznikow's metaphorical creations, apparent in the fierceness of the claws that extend from the mutilated surface of *Rozłupany* (*Shattered*, 1960) [ill. 13, plate 136], for example. A related drawing, Untitled (Sketch for the Sculpture *Rozłupany* [Shattered] 2, c. 1960–61) [ill. 7], is softer in detail but possesses the same sense of anguish in the tension of its lines.

Another series of drawings from this period is distinguished by abstract elaborations of organic form; shapes mutate in a range of biomorphic compositions. In Untitled (c. 1960–61) [plate 115], the main "body" is rendered in seeping black ink with finer filaments extending in and around it. The speckled texture visible at center suggests the artist modeled her image over a monotype base and passed a wide dry brush across the surface of the sheet as a final step. The intuitive and painterly character of this drawing recalls Eva Hesse's small black sketches of around the same time [ill. 10].[15] Both artists exploited the intensity of their mediums and created dramatic contrasts between their dark pools of ink (or watercolor, in Hesse's case) and the blankness of the page. Manipulating the spatial boundaries of their surfaces, they pushed their forms off center and beyond the edges of the sheet. Hesse's drawing was made shortly before she transitioned from painting to sculpture; however, there is a sense that her composition, like those of Szapocznikow, could also exist in space. Hesse and Szapocznikow may never have met, but there are many similarities in their practices. Both victims of Nazi persecution, they searched for themselves in art amid greater existential questions. Particularly in their drawings, they affirmed presence through the pictorial trace of gesture.

Two other contemporary sculptors-cum-draftspeople whose works relate to that of Szapocznikow are Lee Bontecou and Louise Bourgeois. Bontecou's haunting drawings in soot from around 1958 assume a much larger scale, but also evoke the engulfing depths of the biomorphic.[16] Bourgeois similarly explored organic form[17]—at once botanical and anatomical—in works on paper such as *Point of Contact* (1950) [ill. 8]. These intensely prolific artists produced drawings that exist independently of their sculptures but also fulfilled a desire for direct expression. As Bourgeois commented vis-à-vis her own practice, "The abstract drawings come from a deep need to achieve peace, rest, and sleep. They relate to unconscious memories… [In contrast, the realistic drawings represent the] overcoming of negative memory, the need to erase and get rid of it."[18]

Szapocznikow's ability to experiment with any readily available material led to some of her most original works on paper. Around 1960, she began to practice a form of printmaking often referred to as monotype. Technically, a monotype is a unique print, produced by printing a single impression from a smooth unmarked surface such as glass or metal. Most likely, however, Szapocznikow applied stencils directly onto a smooth sheet of paper—a process that provided immediate results and allowed the artist to work without using assistants or a printing press. The stencils were variously inked or colored with a greasy black crayon or oil stick, then imprinted onto the paper. Their powdery texture suggests they were made out of porous cardboard, but they may also have been made of wood,[19] which would explain the grainy texture in the background of a series made between 1963 and 1965 [plates 112–113].

At first glance, Untitled (c. 1963–65) [plate 113] seems like a complex puzzle of organic shapes, the threaded gaps between the forms creating what appear to be streams of liquid in the composition. A closer look reveals Szapocznikow's printing process: the same stencil with a pointed beaklike edge was applied twice to the sheet, along its upper and lower edges, overlapped with a lung-shaped form that was printed from another stencil. These stencils were used variously for other prints in the same series. Szapocznikow regulated the tones, a range of blacks and greys, through pressure and different amounts of pigment applied to each stencil. She used colored stencils and a brush to enhance her forms in yet another group of monotypes, in which patches of blue, pink, red, yellow, and brown accompany the black base [plates 133–134]. Her largest works on paper are the series of untitled monotypes she worked on around 1961, each one measuring approximately twenty-five by nineteen inches [plate 118]. The familiar wing-shaped form observed in her drawings is reinterpreted here and applied to different colored papers. Though it was not uncommon for artists to make monotypes in Poland at this time, Szapocznikow's particular technique may well have been self-taught and conceived to suit her purposes. Her amorphous cells allude to dissected human and organic matter, bridging the so-called disarticulation and decomposition stages of her work. While her drawings and sculptures delineate physiques, the monotypes lead instead to the interior of the body, to its fluids, muscle, and tissue. These imprints are, furthermore, an evocative precedent to the artist's casts of body parts during the next phase of her career.

Fragmentation (1962–71)

To scrutinize means to search: I am searching the other's body, as if I wanted to see what was inside it, as if the mechanical cause of my desire were in the adverse body (I am like those children who take a clock apart in order to find out what time it is) . . . It is obvious that I am in the process of fetishizing a corpse.

—Roland Barthes[20]

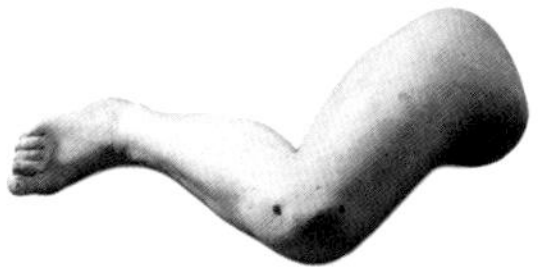

14.

In the Drot interview, Szapocznikow described a bronze sculpture of a female leg, rounded at the hip, folded at the knee, and placed horizontally on a granite plinth like a sacrificial offering: "Part of it is cast from my leg, and part of it is molded."[21] The origin of this object is a plaster cast she made in 1962, a year before moving to Paris [ill. 14, plate 129]. Her attention thereafter shifted to using her own body as the principle matrix of her art. As she immersed herself in casting isolated parts of her body, a simultaneous decomposition of the figure occurs in her drawings whereby she undoes the figure and reconfigures its parts into singular organisms of her own imagination. In an untitled sheet of 1963, a conflagration of limbs and joints is shaped into a peculiar anthropomorphic form with vacuous eyes [plate 127]. It is drawn with a thick, black felt-tip pen, the technique most recurrent in her drawings of this period, and a finer pen for speckles crowning the "face." Another sheet demonstrates Szapocznikow's emboldened line and her shift towards tighter, more condensed compositions. Here three airy loops are conjoined around a sinewy knot.

The year 1963 was one of Szapocznikow's most prolific in terms of draftsmanship, due perhaps to the accessibility of the medium during her relocation from Warsaw to Paris, but also to the many directions her work was taking at this time. A range of styles characterizes the over one hundred drawings and monotypes dated that year. Some are defined by a puzzle of forms, densely depicted with the brush and black ink [ill. 9], while

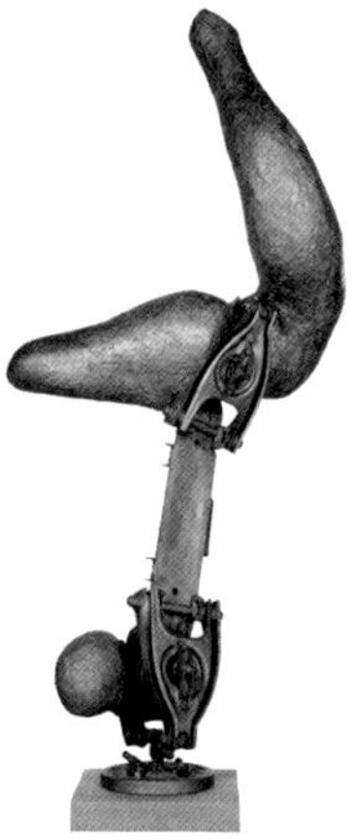

15.

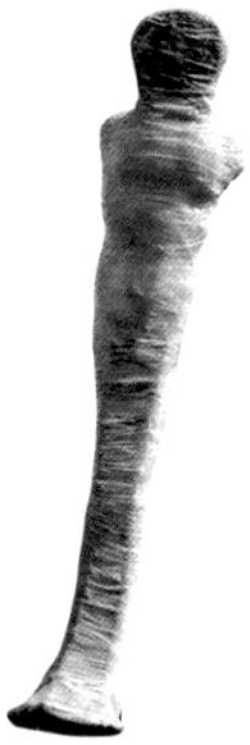

16.

others echo her works in chiseled stone. The drawings that relate to her carved sculptures are more finely described, like the rounded form rendered in ballpoint pen on an untitled sheet from 1963 [plate 117]. All share an underlying sensuality, many including references to male and female sexual organs.

The fluid linearity of these drawings contrasted with the brutal intensity of Szapocznikow's three-dimensional work during the early 1960s. A further and fundamental change in her sculptures began in 1963 with the incorporation of found objects, such as weapons implanted in cement, that recall the horrors of World War II. A more technical type of preparatory drawing accompanied this increasingly complex sculptural technique. In Untitled (Sketch of a Sculpture with "Industrial" Elements, 1963) [plate 103], she works out the construction of a piece with an engine-like device. The separate segments are carefully laid out on squared school paper. Although no related sculpture survives, the specificity of this drawing suggests its potential role in the conception and realization of a work. The making of the 1965 sculpture *Goldfinger* [ill. 15, plate 101] necessitated similar constructive studies [plate 100]. In one of her most extraordinary contraptions, using both manipulated form and found object, Szapocznikow positioned two female legs molded out of cement over an automobile shock absorber. This work won her a nomination for the Copley Foundation prize and the attention of Marcel Duchamp, who was on the jury. Her drawings for *Goldfinger* focus on the verticality of the object—with its uncomfortable and sexually explicit contortion—and on the placement of the shock absorber between the legs. The structure was first delineated with a ballpoint pen, then reinforced with a thicker felt-tip pen. Although these preparatory drawings were executed with particular sculptures in mind, their three-dimensionality is only vaguely suggested. They are studies of contour and content—not, as with many sculptors' drawings, representations of the object in space.

Around 1965, Szapocznikow began to connect her sculptures more seamlessly to the floor, while at the same time attempting to project them into a dimension beyond. *Filozof* (*Philosopher*, 1965) [ill. 17], for instance, precariously balances on a single foot, as the rest of the body shoots up. An outstretched limb and triangular-shaped foot appear in the drawing of a spinning figure from around the same time [ill. 18]. Physical lightness and loss of gravity define the sculpture *L'Apesanteur (Hommage à Komarow)* (*Weightlessness [Homage to Komarov]*, 1967) [ill. 16, plate 90]. Her studies for this tribute to the Russian cosmonaut suggest the upward thrust of the body, but also the structural need to fix it to the floor [ill. 20]. They show the artist considering different bases for the sculpture, which she eventually attached to an unobtrusive and almost invisible flat support.

With Szapocznikow's cancer diagnosis in 1969 (it was suspected as early as 1968), the subject of death became more vivid in her work—as did the tragic reality of the human condition. In the series Tumeurs (Tumors, 1969), the body is reduced to pure matter in the form of photographic images crumpled within bundles of polyester resin [plate 60]. Related drawings display lumpy cumuli either mounted into piles or dispersed across the sheet [plates 71–72], rendering the multiplication of alien accretions; the bodies that she once drew whole now seemed to melt like butter. Similarly, Hannah Wilke used her body in her art and also portrayed the transformative effects of her own cancer. Her *Intra-Venus Hand* (1991) [ill. 19] is bluntly rendered in primary

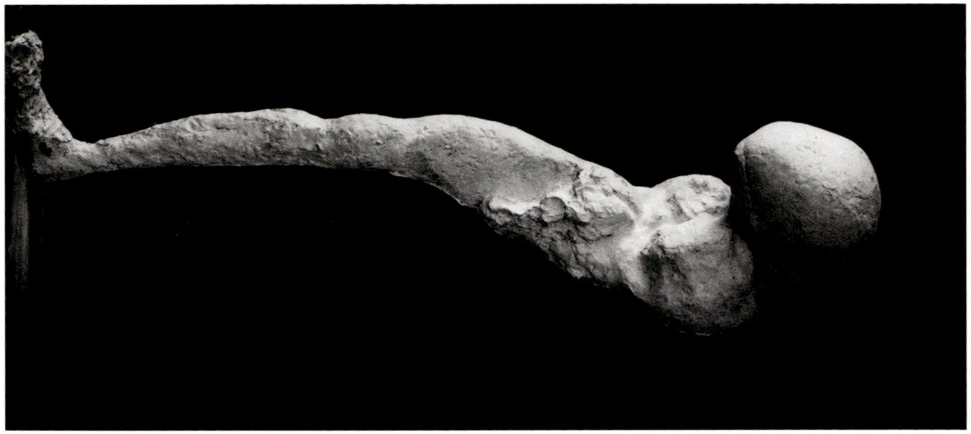

17. *Filozof* (Philosopher), 1965. Plaster, 53 15/16 x 9 7/8 x 12 3/16" (137 x 25 x 31 cm). The Estate of Alina Szapocznikow/Piotr Stanisławski.

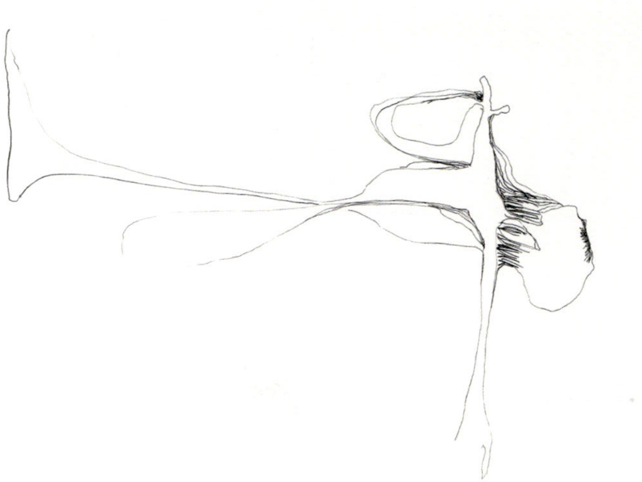

18. Untitled, c. 1963–68. Ink on paper, 10 5/8 x 8 1/4" (27 x 21 cm). The Estate of Alina Szapocznikow/Piotr Stanisławski.

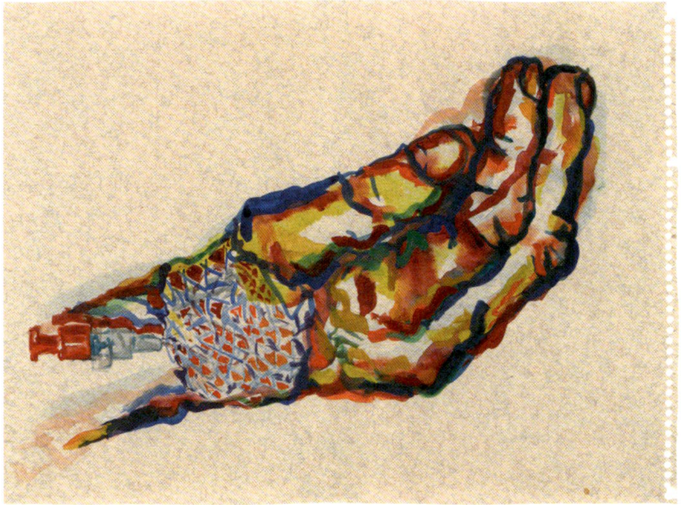

19. Hannah Wilke (American, 1940–1993), *Intra-Venus Hand No. 9. October 1991*, 1991. Gouache and watercolor on notebook paper, 12 1/2 x 9 1/2" (31.8 x 24.1 cm). The Museum of Modern Art, New York. The Judith Rothschild Foundation Contemporary Drawings Collection Gift.

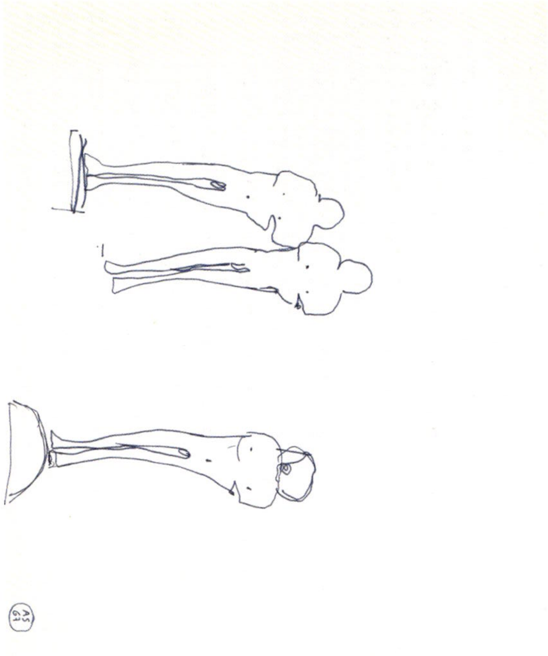

20. Untitled (Sketches for *L'Apesanteur [Hommage à Komarow]*) [Weightlessness (Homage to Komarov)] 1), 1967. Felt-tip pen on paper, 8 1/4 x 10 1/2" (21 x 26.6 cm). The Estate of Alina Szapocznikow/Piotr Stanisławski.

colors.[22] A portrait of a hand, it is limp and detached yet alive through the vigorous strokes and the intensity of the watercolor.

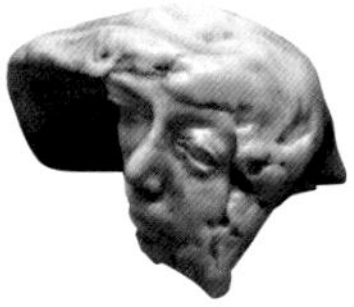

21.

Cancerous growths infiltrated Szapocznikow's drawings, either as attachments to the body or as part of her reconfigurations of the figure. A sense of irony comes through in caricatured drawings such as Untitled (Sketch of *Le Voyage* [Journey] with Growths 2, c. 1970) [plate 65]. A particularly striking drawing, Untitled (Bust-Length Figure of a Woman, Headless 1, c. 1971) [plate 24], evokes the disembodied heads cast from the artist's face in its sculptural counterpart, *Tumeurs personnifiées* (*Tumors personified*, 1971) [ill. 21 (detail), plate 64]. Here, the accretion extends from a disfigured self-portrait; it shares the sheet with a headless female nude, laid along the lower edge of the paper, and a lone lip that sits on a horizon line in the distance. The realism of the nude's features contrasts with the absurdity of its condition within this incoherent landscape and announces Szapocznikow's final phase of draftsmanship.

Human Landscapes (1971–72)

> ... withered Adonises, bald-faced dandies, glassy corpses,
> Lovelaces in decline, the universal shimmy of the *danse macabre*
> carries you away into unknown regions.
>
> —Charles Baudelaire[23]

Szapocznikow's intention to raise her objects physically and metaphorically above the floor is evident throughout her oeuvre. Until the last years of her life, she emphasized verticality in her drawings, but in her final cycle of works, that verticality is dramatically surrendered to flatness and, ultimately, to the transcendental essence of weightlessness.[24] In a drawing from the series Paysage humain (Human Landscape, 1971) [plate 13], the composition stretches across the surface of the sheet, her title indicating the expansive scope of this new direction.[25] In previous years, she had described her biological forms and disjointed figures on paper; now she appeared to be creating scenes for them—the incongruous settings of Salvador Dalí come to mind, as do the organic pastiches of Arshile Gorky. Szapocznikow enhanced the dreamy realm of the Human Landscape drawings with heavily diluted washes of green, pink, grey, and blue watercolor that are more Pop than Surrealist, recalling the loose washes in Claes Oldenburg's drawings of the 1960s.[26] While Szapocznikow's use of color had previously been largely descriptive, her images were now bathed in it.

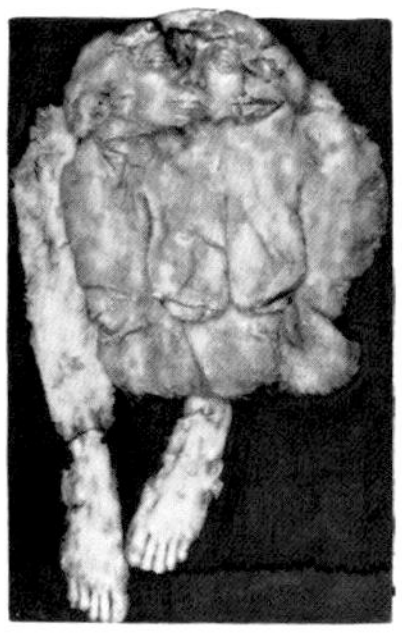

22.

Szapocznikow's full repertory of forms appears in this series, rearranged and conflated into a fantastical cast: lumps converge with vaginas, lips rest on disjointed legs, eyes peer through the horizon, a female figure drifts onto a phallus. At times, the erotic tension is condensed in the vividness of the medium, like the patches of pale pink in a number of untitled drawings from the Human Landscape series [plates 12–14]; the palpability of flesh is instantly felt. She might have looked at Auguste Rodin's watercolors of female nudes on one of her frequent visits to the Musée Rodin. In drawings like *Reclining Woman* (1900–06) [ill. 23], Rodin exploited the transparency and allusive quality of the washes, his figures afloat on the sheet. Confronting her impending death, Szapocznikow created her own transporting scenes, like intimate passages into the afterlife.

Szapocznikow's final sculptures can also be considered "human" landscapes. In the Herbarium series (1971–72), casts taken from her own body and that of her son were

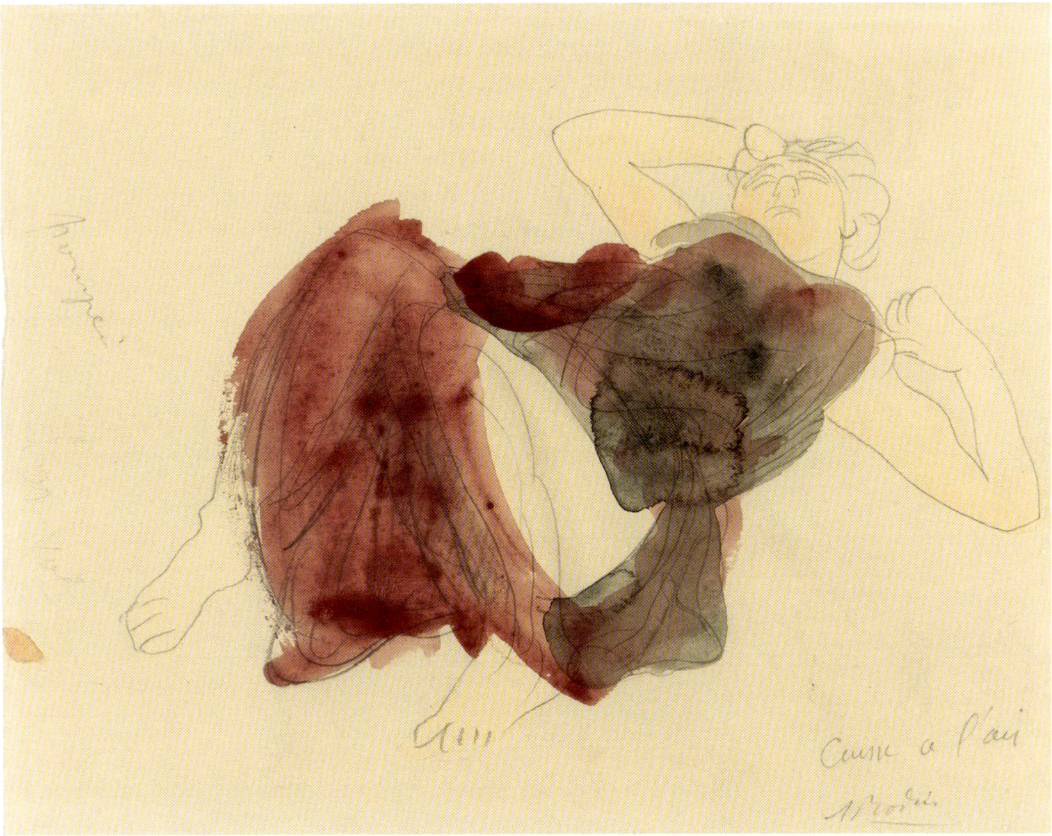

23. Auguste Rodin (French, 1840–1917), *Reclining Woman*, c. 1900–06. Watercolor and pencil on paper, 9 7/8 x 12 13/16" (25 x 32.5 cm). The Museum of Modern Art, New York. Bequest of Mina Turner.

crushed and laid flat like flayed skins in what was the artist's most visceral attempt to make the impermanent permanent [ill. 22, plates 1–4]. The title refers to the tradition of preserving plant specimens by pressing them in books. Szapocznikow's imprinted layers of polyester resin certainly allude to death, yet flattening the casts somehow makes them more lifelike than death masks.[27] They beg the question, asked by Georges Didi-Huberman, "Does the process of imprinting induce contact with the origin or loss of the origin?"[28] Do they invoke the presence or the absence of the subject? The Herbarium cycle is an eerie evocation of both. As Szapocznikow's *memento mori*, they, along with the Human Landscape series, are material reminders of the evanescence of the human body. Her stated aim was ultimately "to exalt the ephemeral in the folds of our body, in the traces of our passage."[29]

Draftsmanship served as an immediate and primal mode of artistic production for Szapocznikow. She drew on any available surface, as her son Piotr later recalled, even on a packet of cigarettes.[30] Ideas born on paper were reconfigured in consecutive compositions; endless possibilities evolved from a single theme. Some developed into three-dimensional form, while others existed purely on the two-dimensional picture plane. Occasionally, a drawing took its cue from a sculpture, but all affirmed the artist's presence within the trace of her gesture. The calligraphic marks of her hand in the drawings correspond to the casts she took of her body. They reflect Szapocznikow's need to exist through her work, like the "absurd and convulsive mania [that] proves the existence of an unknown, secret gland, necessary for life" she refers to in her 1972 credo.[31]

The entire scope of Szapocznikow's draftsmanship is presented for the first time in this exhibition, more than thirty-eight years after her death, revealing the mastery of her touch and the tremendous range of her compositions. This work bears witness to one of the most original minds of the twentieth century and, in particular, to the intensity of her passage through life.

Notes

1. I am deeply indebted to Jola Gola's extensive research on the drawings of Alina Szapocznikow. See her "Catalogue of Drawings by Alina Szapocznikow," in *Alina Szapocznikow. Zatrzymać życie. Rysunki i rzeźby (Capturing Life. Drawings and Sculptures)*, ed. Józef Grabski (Kraków and Warsaw: IRSA, 2004). I am extremely grateful to Piotr Stanisławski for allowing me to view his drawings and monotypes in Paris, and to Joanna Mytkowska and Marta Dziewańska for their assistance in the archive in Warsaw. I also thank Cynthia Burlingham, Gaia Colombati, and Diana Widmaier Picasso for their generous suggestions during the writing of this essay.
2. In 1960, a group of drawings was shown at the Galleria Falsetti in Prato, Italy, and a selection of monotypes was part of the exhibition "Confrontations 1960" at the Galeria Krzywe Koło in Warsaw. Drawings were included in "Rzeźba Aliny Szapocznikow," BWA Sopot, Poland, 1960 (see brochure in Alina Szapocznikow Archives, Museum of Modern Art, Warsaw). Drawings were also presented at the exhibition "Instants et Choses" at the Aurora Gallery in Geneva in 1971.
3. "Tu ne dis rien de toi mais tu te montres." Jean-Marie Drot in *Journal de Voyage en Pologne*, filmed in 1966 and aired in 1969. Documentary film. See Gola, "Chronology of Alina Szapocznikow's Life and Work," elsewhere in this volume.
4. Szapocznikow included her imprisonment in the handwritten curriculum vitae she sent to the Copley Foundation as part of her submission for the prize she was nominated for in 1965: "1940–1945 Emprisonnée au camps concentration Allemagne (Auschwitz, etc.) libérée en Tchécoslovaquie et séjour à l'École des Arts à Prague 1945–1947." Getty Research Institute, Special Collections, Los Angeles.
5. Pierre Restany, in *Alina Szapocznikow* (Warsaw: Institute for the Promotion of Art Foundation, Galeria Zachęta, 1998), 26.
6. Szapocznikow, statement, March 1972, "Mon oeuvre puise ses racines . . . ," signed typescript. Original reads: "Mon oeuvre puise ses racines dans le métier de la sculpture. Pendant des années je me suis livrée à fond à l'étude des problèmes d'équilibre, de volume, d'espace, d'ombre et de lumière." See page 28, elsewhere in this volume.
7. See Urszula Czartoryska, in *Alina Szapocznikow*, 12. On Matthias Bernhard Braun, see Jan Lukas, *Kuks: A Shrine of Baroque Sculpture* (Prague: Artia, 1950); and Albrecht Schindler, *Das Kukusbad in Böhmen: Annäherung an einen Ort der Heilung in Texten und Bildern (1967)* (Schalksmühle, Germany: Pomaska, 2003).
8. Illustrated in Anna Żakiewicz, "On Alina Szapocznikow's Drawings," in *Alina Szapocznikow. Zatrzymać życie (Capturing Life)*, 42. For a series of sketches after the sculptures in Saint-Jean-du-Doigt in Brittany, see Gola, "Catalogue of Drawings by Alina Szapocznikow," cat. nos. 27–30, 208.
9. Ibid., cat. nos. 102–74 and 57–68, 218–27, 212–13.
10. Ovid, *Metamorphoses*, translated by A.D. Melville (Oxford, England: Oxford University Press, 1986), Book X (Atalanta), lines 716–39, 248.
11. Szapocznikow, cited by Żakiewicz in "On Alina Szapocznikow's Drawings," 39.
12. A similar composition was used for *Dłoń. Projekt Pomnika Bohaterów Warszawy II* (*Hand. Monument to the Heroes of Warsaw*, 1957). See ibid., cat. nos. 183–87, 228–29.
13. See for example *Błazen* (*Jester*) (1959–60) and *Derwisz* (*Dervish*) (1960) in Gola, *Katalog rzeźb Aliny Szapocznikow* (Kraków: Muzeum Naradowe w Krakowie, 2001), cat. nos. 177.2 and 186, 99, and 101. For the drawing, see Gola, "Catalogue of Drawings by Alina Szapocznikow," cat. no. 258, 239. According to Gola, this drawing relates to the sculpture *Naga* (*Naked*) (1961).
14. This sculpture is no longer extant. See Gola, *Katalog rzeźb*, cat. no. 173, 97. (Note that the illustration is incorrectly published as cat. no. 172.)
15. See Catherine de Zegher, ed., *Eva Hesse Drawing*, exh. cat. (New York: Drawing Center; and New Haven, Connecticut: Yale University Press, 2006), figs. 16–19, 26–29.
16. See *Lee Bontecou: A Retrospective*, ed. Elizabeth A. T. Smith and Ann Philbin, exh. cat. (Chicago: Museum of Contemporary Art; and Los Angeles: UCLA Hammer Museum, 2003), pls. 6–7, 22–23, 224.
17. See Louise Bourgeois with Lawrence Rinder, *Louise Bourgeois: Drawings and Observations*, exh. cat. (Berkeley: University Art Museum and Pacific Film Archive; and Boston: Bullfinch Press, 1995), 112, 188.
18. Cited in Frances Morris, ed., *Louise Bourgeois*, exh. cat. (London: Tate Publications, 2007), 104. Original citation from Paulo Herkenhoff and Angélica de Moraes, *Louise Bourgeois: desenhos/drawings*, exh. cat. (Rio de Janeiro, Brazil: Centro Cultural Light, 1997), 29.
19. I would like to thank artist James Welling and my colleague Cynthia Burlingham for their insightful

comments on Szapocznikow's monotype technique. Welling suggested the stencils may have been made of wood (conversation with author, 9 May 2011). Szapocznikow probably used a crayon with a square nib and rubbed it vigorously over the stencils, as traces of her scribbles are occasionally transferred to the sheet.

20. Roland Barthes, *A Lover's Discourse: Fragments*, trans. Richard Howard (New York: Hill and Wang, 1978), 71.
21. The sculpture is dated 1967. Drot, *Journal de Voyage en Pologne*.
22. See Nancy Princenthal, *Hannah Wilke* (Munich: Prestel, 2010), 134, illus. 140.
23. Charles Baudelaire, "XCVII: Danse Macabre," in *The Flowers of Evil*, trans. Keith Waldrop (Middletown, Connecticut: Wesleyan University Press, 2006), 128.
24. In 1972, drawings from the series Human Landscape were juried by Pierre Alechinsky, Alexander Calder, Joan Miró, and Antoni Tàpies, and won her a prize at the III International Drawing Exhibition at the Moderna Galeria in Rijeka, Yugoslavia. See Żakiewicz in "On Alina Szapocznikow's Drawings," 35.
25. Szapocznikow had titled another drawing Human Landscape in 1970. See ibid., cat. no. 552, 274.
26. See Janie C. Lee, *Claes Oldenburg Drawings, 1959–1977/Claes Oldenburg with Coosje van Bruggen Drawings, 1992–1998*, exh. cat. (New York: Whitney Museum of American Art, 2002). Szapocznikow visited an exhibition of works by Oldenburg at the Musée Rodin in 1964. See Dagmara Budzbon, "Alina Szapocznikow: The Ecstatic Carnival of Forms" (M.A. report, Courtauld Institute of Art, London, 2008).
27. Szapocznikow made death masks of her friends Tadeusz Trepkowski (1954) and Jan Lebestein (1969).
28. Original reads: "Le processus d'empreinte est-il contact de l'origine ou bien perte de l'origine?" See Georges Didi-Huberman, *L'Empreinte*, exh. cat. (Paris: Centre Georges Pompidou, 1997), 19. Translated by the author.
29. Szapocznikow, statement, March 1972. Original reads: "Exalter l'éphémère, dans les replis de notre corps, dans les traces de notre passage." See page 28, elsewhere in this volume.
30. Cited in Krystyna Czerni, "The Second Wing or Alina Szapocznikow's Dream about Flying," in Gola, "Catalogue of Drawings by Alina Szapocznikow," 13.
31. Szapocznikow, statement, March 1972. Original reads: "Cette manie absurde et convulsive prouve l'existence d'une glande inconnue et secrète, nécessaire à notre vie." Translated by the author. See page 28, elsewhere in this volume.

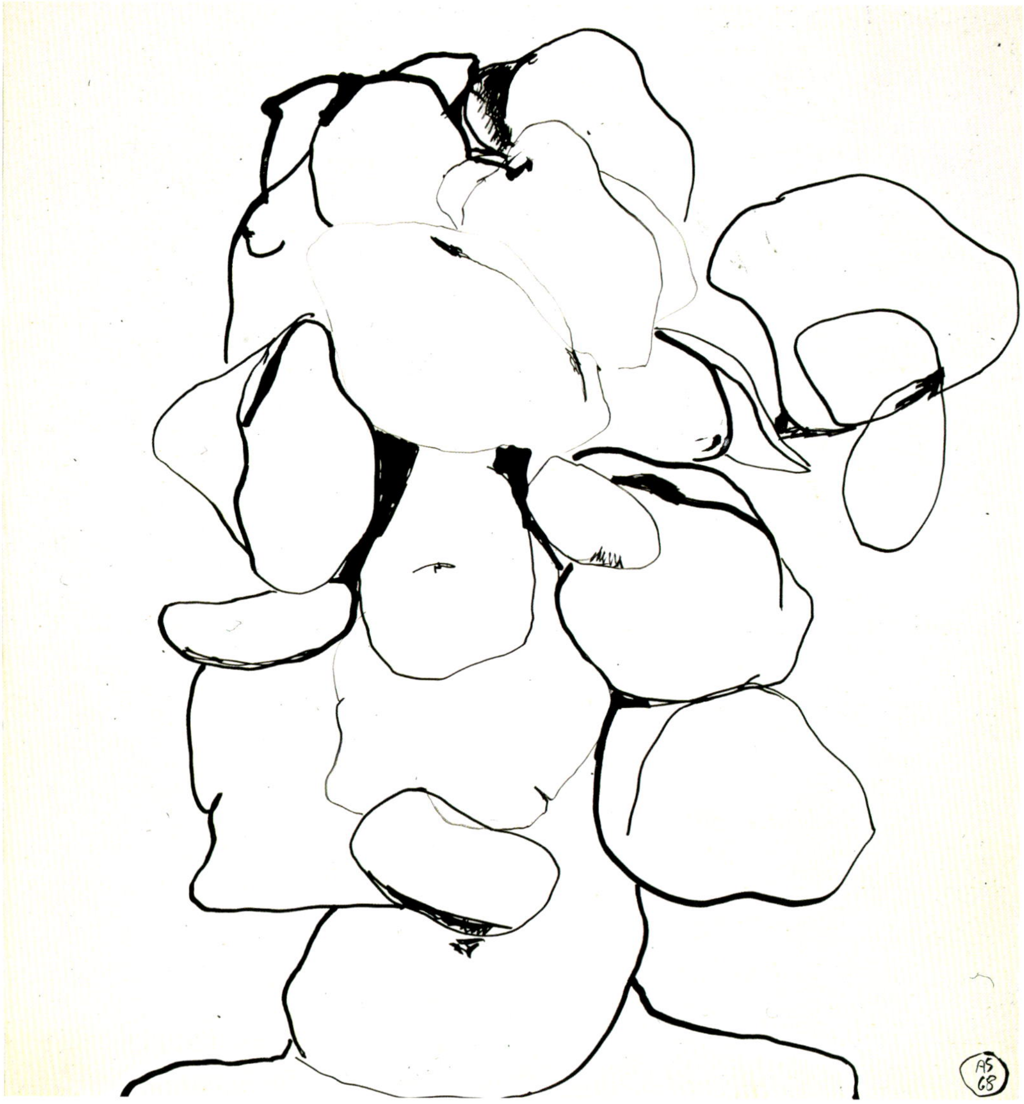

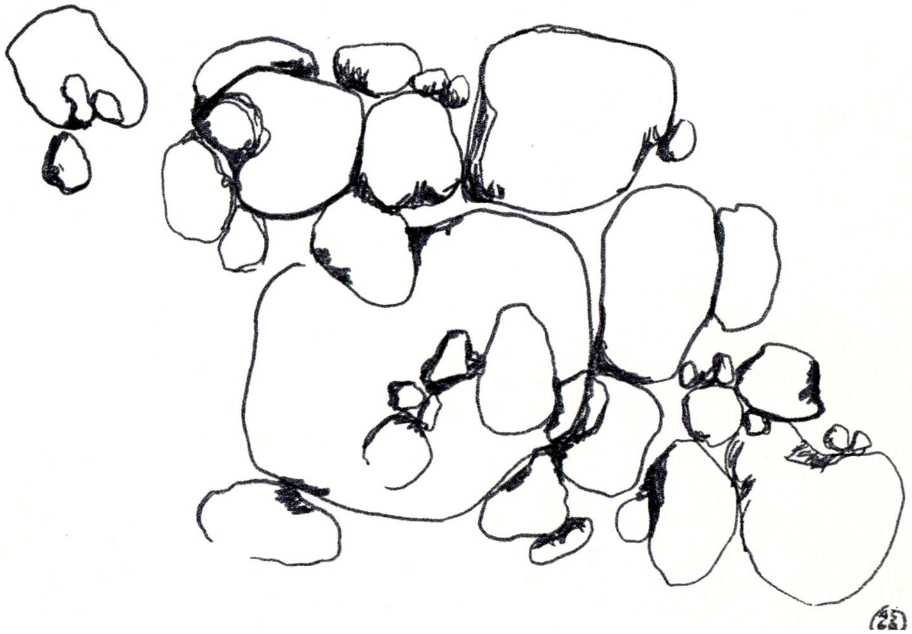

top
Plate 71

Untitled, 1968
Ink on cardboard
17 5/16 x 16 9/16" (44 x 42 cm)

bottom
Plate 72

Untitled, 1969
Felt-tip pen on paper
4 3/4 x 7 1/8" (12 x 18 cm)

opposite top
Plate 73

Untitled (Sketch of Growths on a Leg 1), 1970
Felt-tip pen on paper
13 3/8 x 10 1/2" (33.9 x 26.7 cm)

opposite bottom
Plate 74

Untitled, 1968
Felt-tip pen on cardboard
17 1/2 x 17 1/2" (44.5 x 44.5 cm)

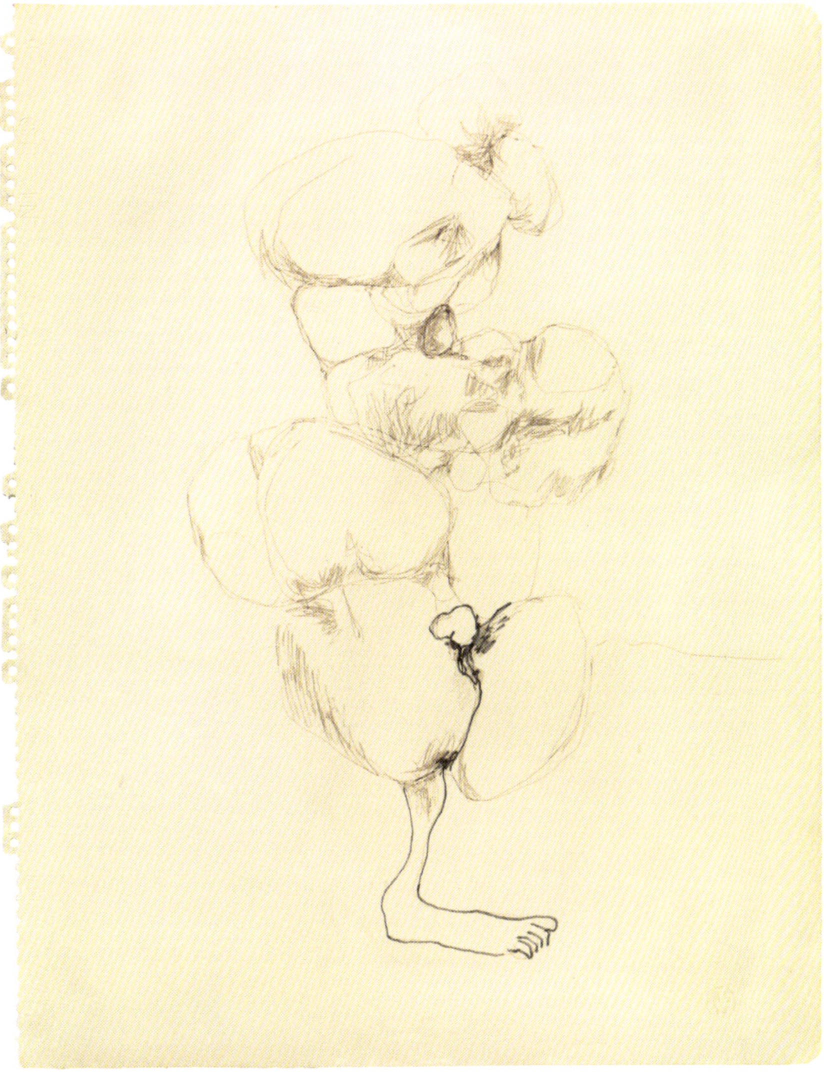

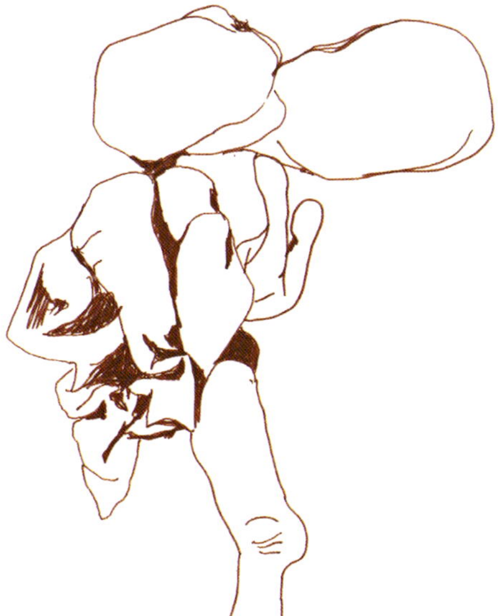

Paris March 7, 1968

Plastic materials, which I have used for 10 years in my studio pieces, seem perfect to me for attempts to express and capture our age because of their repetitive possibilities, their lightness, their colors, their transparency, their inexpensiveness.
The age of modular multiplication, of swift mass consumption, of automatic repetition. These symptoms that are so characteristic, so superficially gay and so sadly monotone and moving.

I hope to be able to explore deeply the problem of the repeated module, in direct contact with the module's industrial production.

Alina Szapocznikow

Paris le 7 mars I968

Le materiaux plastiques, que j'utilise depuis IO ans dans me travaux d'atelier, par leur possibilites de repetition, leur légerté, leurs couleurs, leur transparance, leur bonne marchè, me semblent parfait ~~ax~~ pour les tentatives d'exprimer et saissir notre epoque.

Le temps de multiplication de la module, de consomation vite et en masse de répetition automatique. Ces simptomes qui sont si caracteristiques, si superfitielment gaies et si tristement monotonnes et empoignant.

J'espere de poivoir approfondir le probleme de la module repétè, en contact direct avec la production industrielle de la module.

Alina Szapocznikow

"Le materiaux plastiques ...," 1968

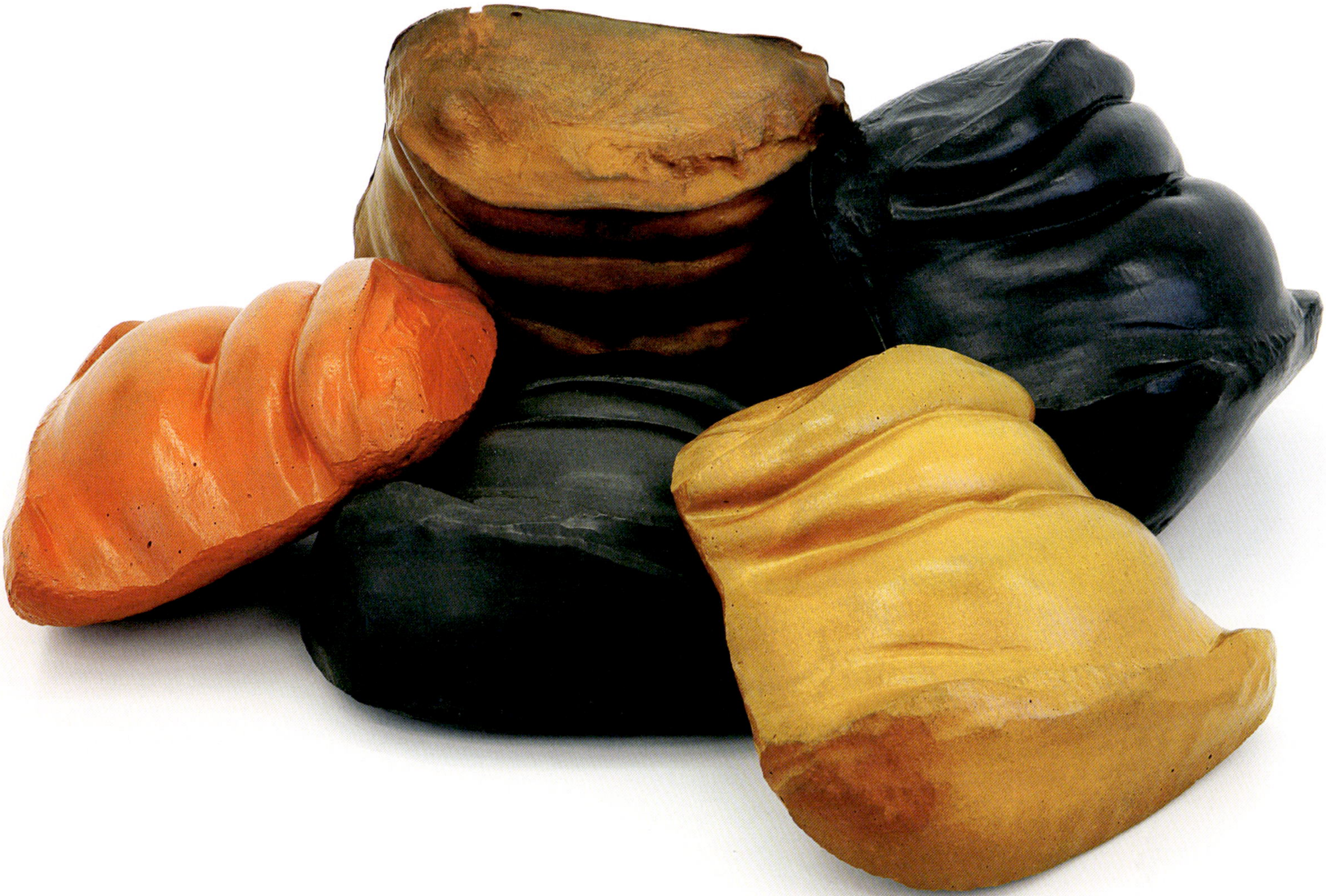

Plate 75

Ventres – coussins (Belly cushions), 1968
Polyurethane foam
Five pieces, each 5 1/8 – 7 x 11 13/16 x 13 3/8" (13 – 17.8 x 30 x 34 cm)

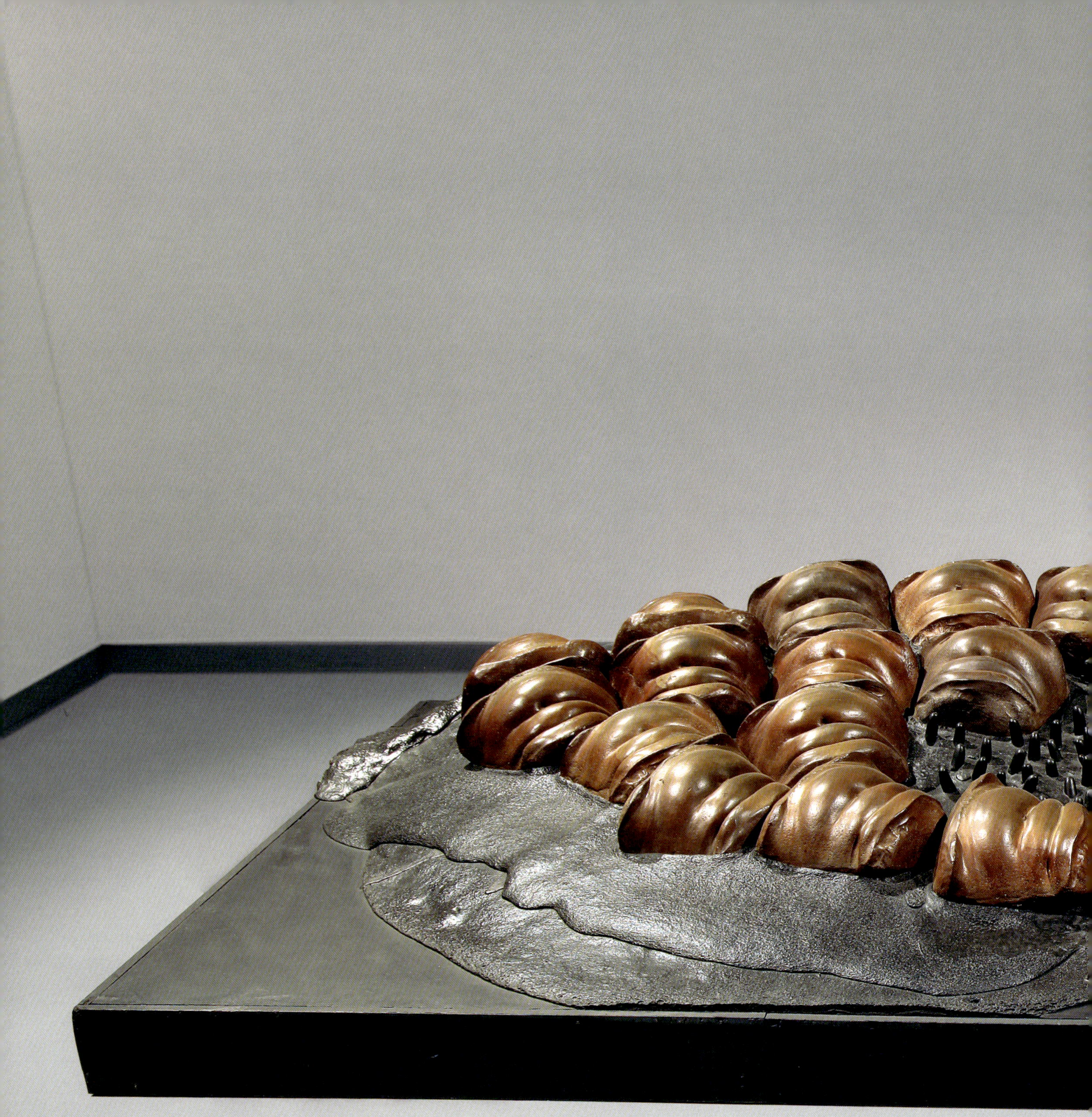

Plate 76

Grande Plage (Big Beach), 1968
Polyester resin, colored polyurethane foam, wood
22 7/16 x 133 7/8 x 65" (57 x 340 x 165 cm)

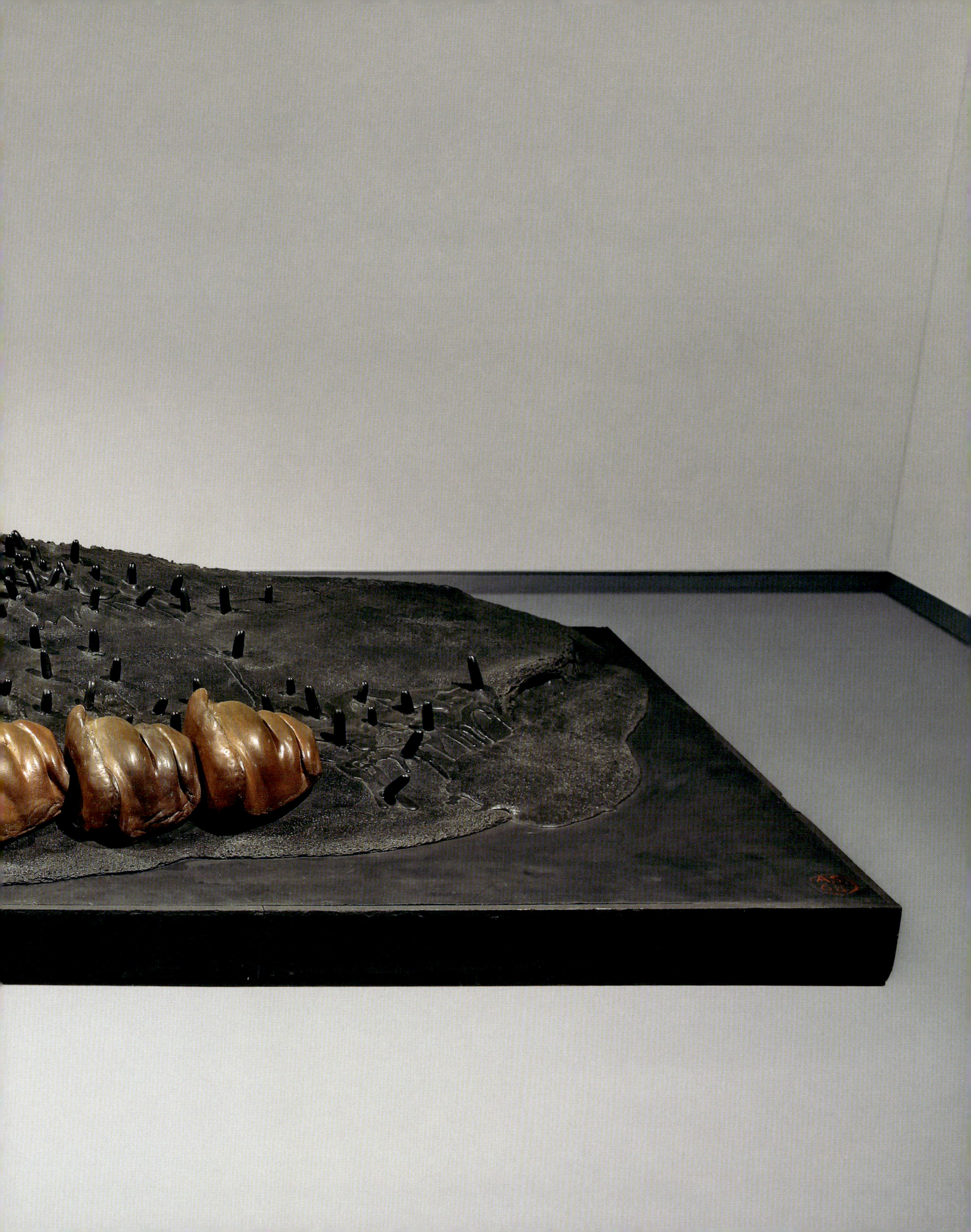

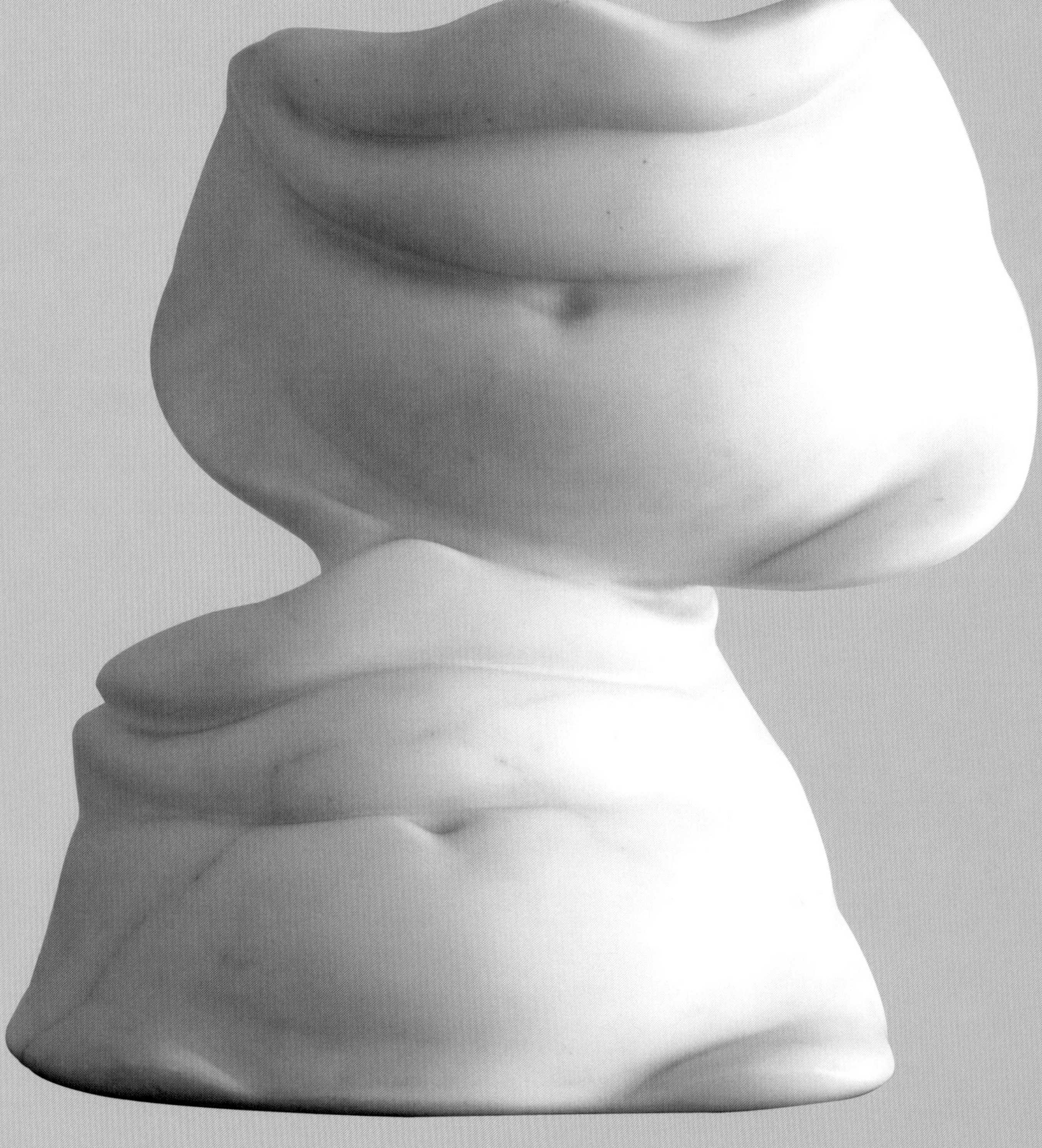

Plate 77

Petits ventres (Small Bellies), 1968
Carrara marble
11 13/16 x 11 7/16 x 5 1/2" (30 x 29 x 14 cm)

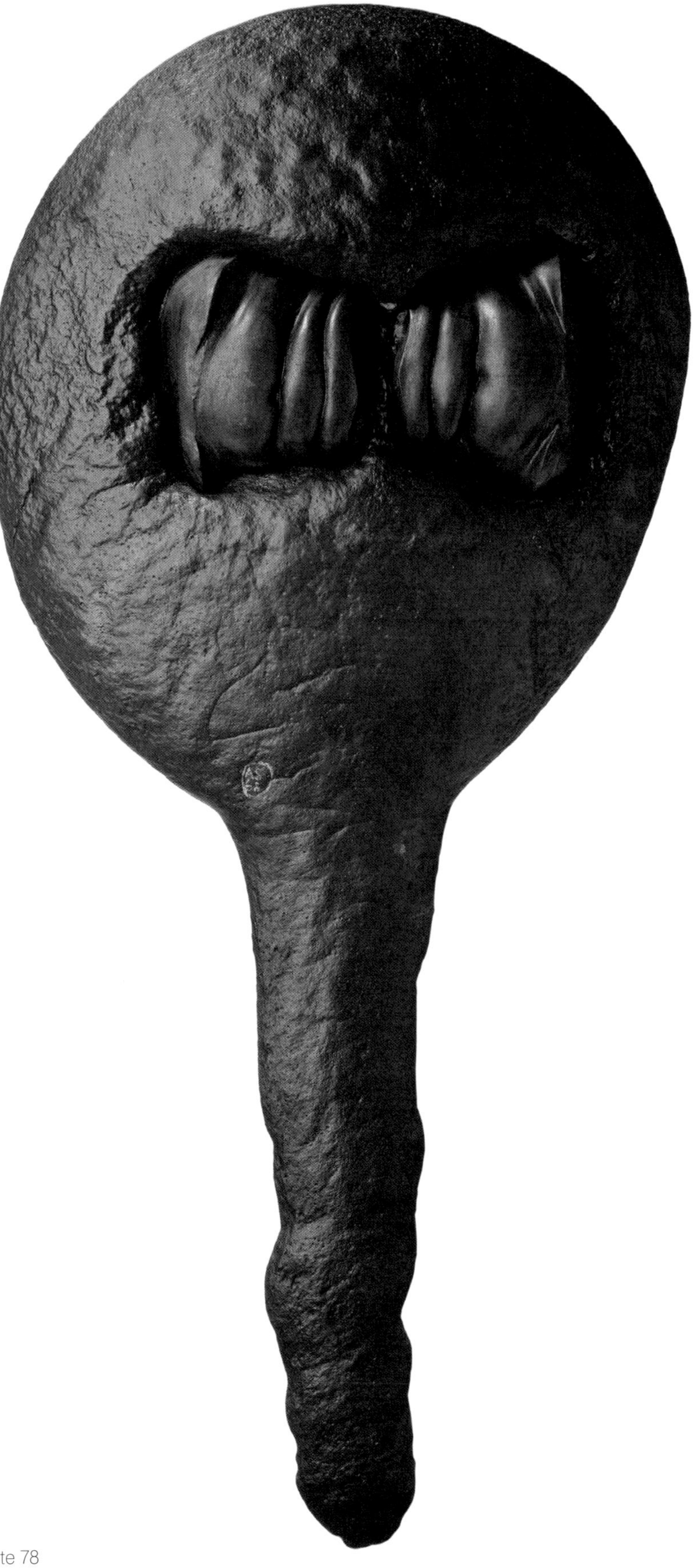

Plate 78

Janus, 1968
Polyurethane foam
82 11/16 x 39 3/8 x 7 1/8" (210 x 100 x 18 cm)

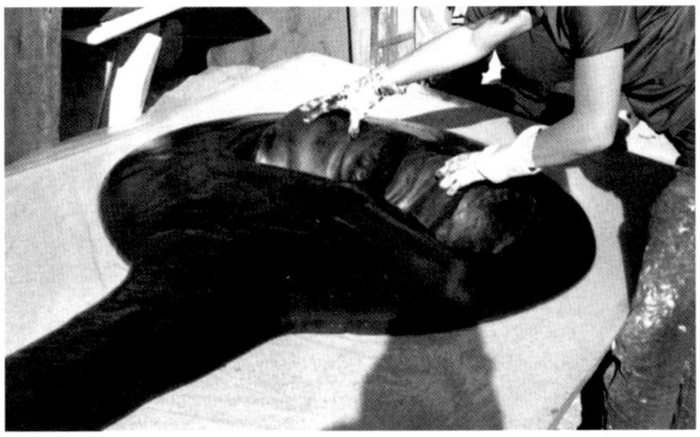

Outside the artist's studio, Malakoff, 1968.

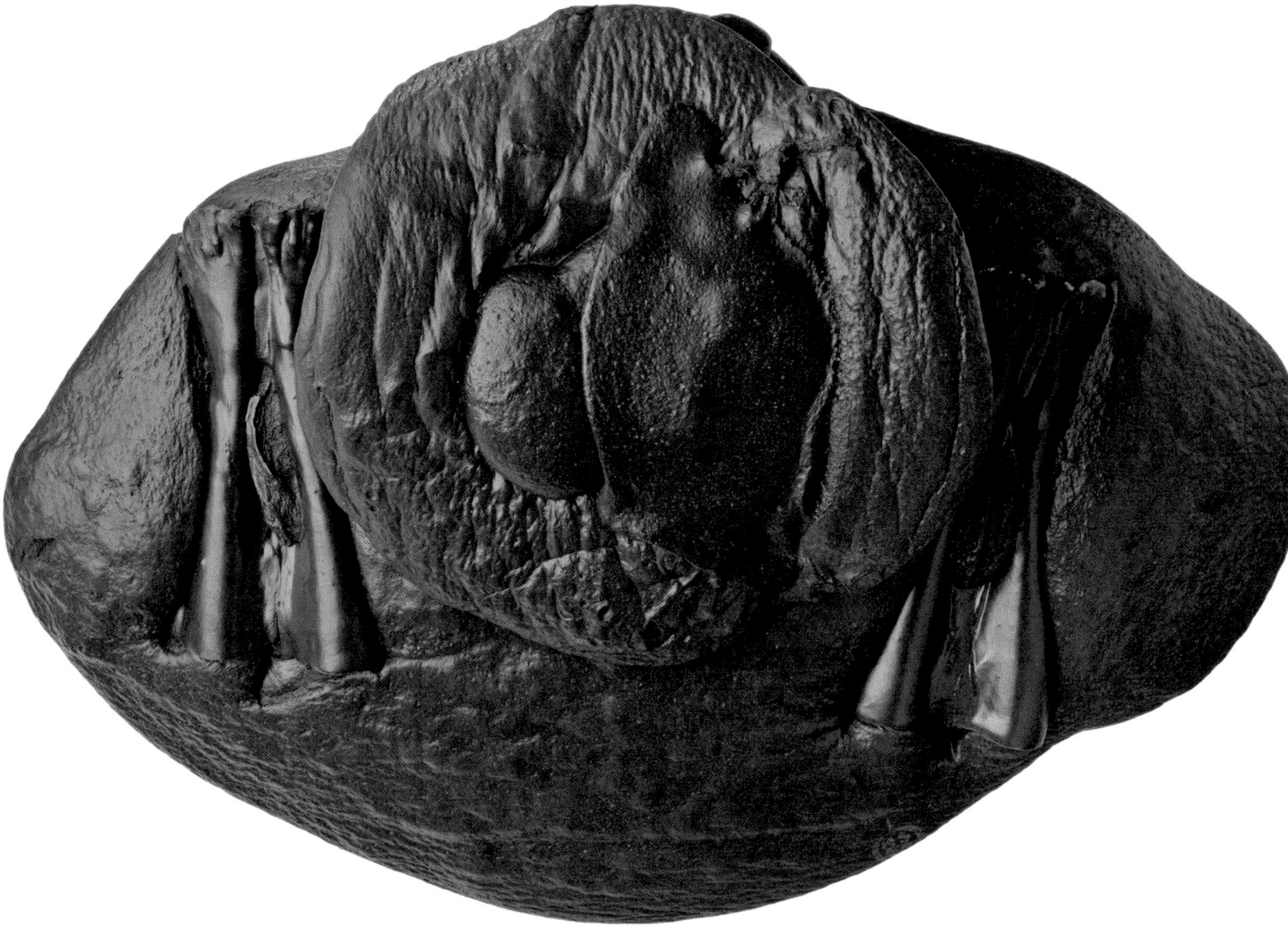

Plate 79

Centrale (Central), 1968

Polyester resin and polyurethane foam

35 7/16 x 48 1/16 x 9 7/8" (90 x 122 x 25 cm)

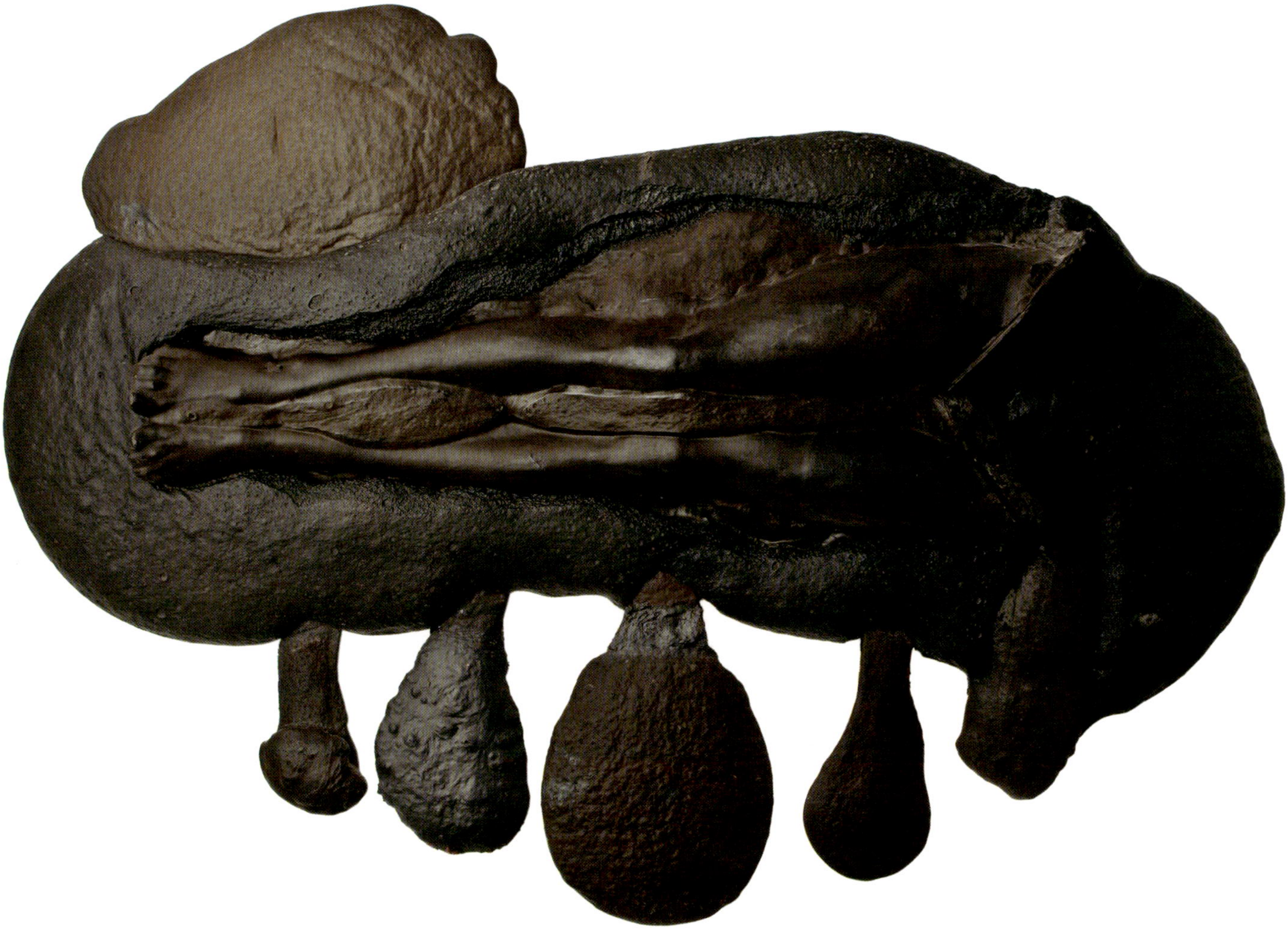

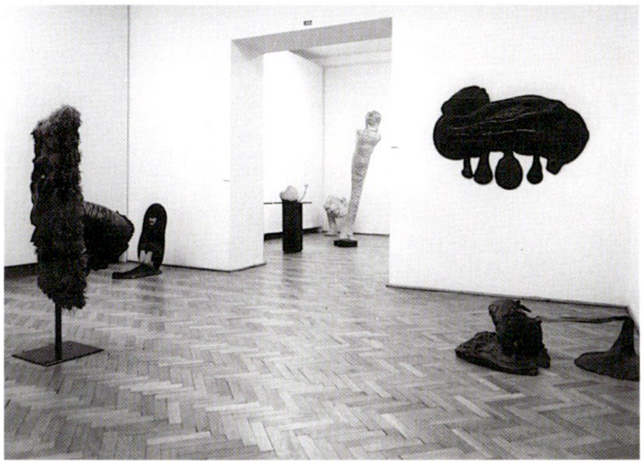

Muzeum Sztuki, Łódź, 1975.

Plate 80

Les capuchons, Jambes noyées (Drips, Embedded Legs), 1968
Polyester resin and polyurethane foam
37 13/16 x 54 3/4 x 5 15/16" (96 x 139 x 15 cm)

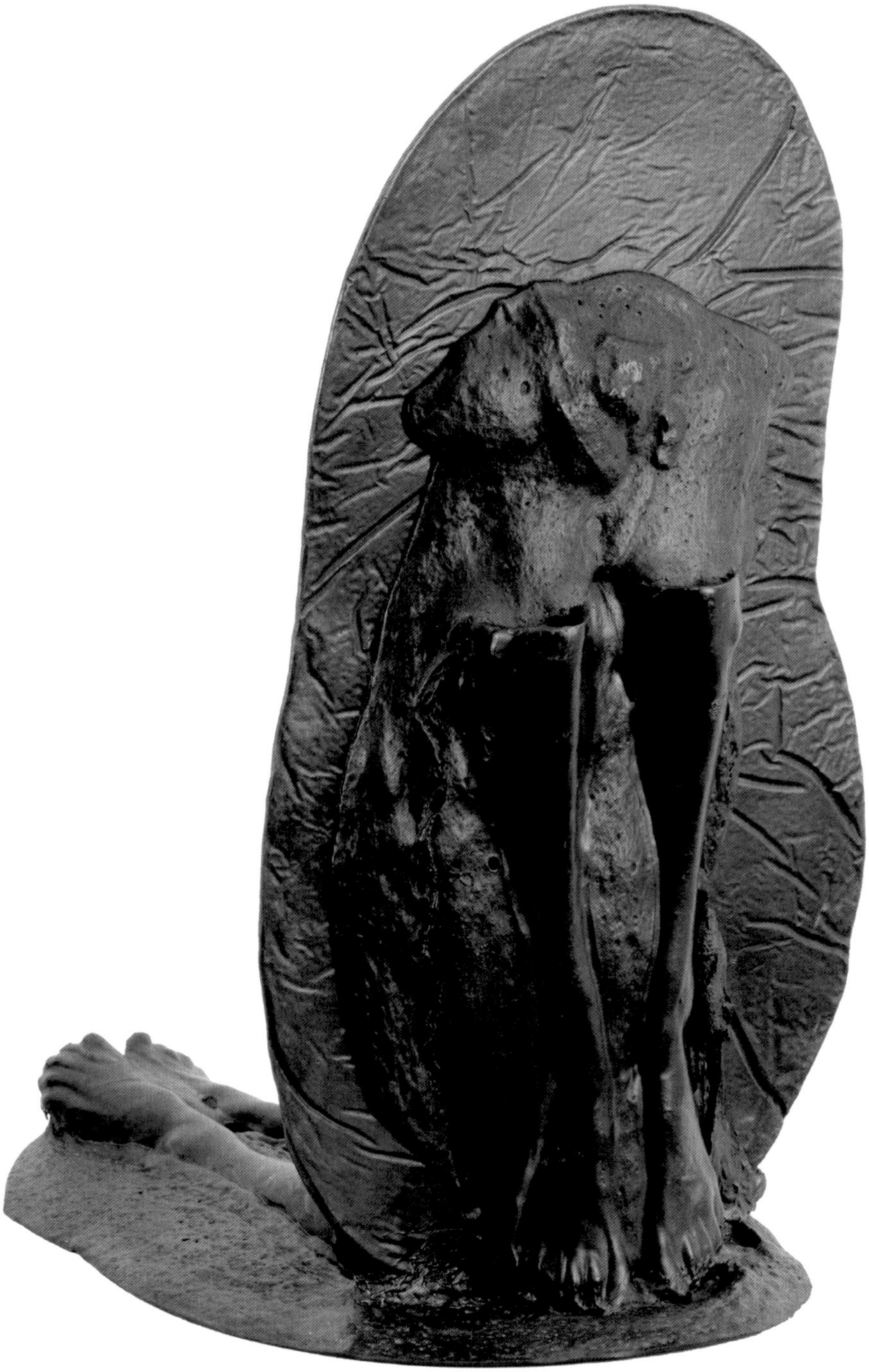

Plates 81–82

Stèle (Stele), 1968 (back and front views)
Polyester resin and polyurethane foam
31 1/16 x 18 1/8 x 27 3/16" (79 x 46 x 69 cm)

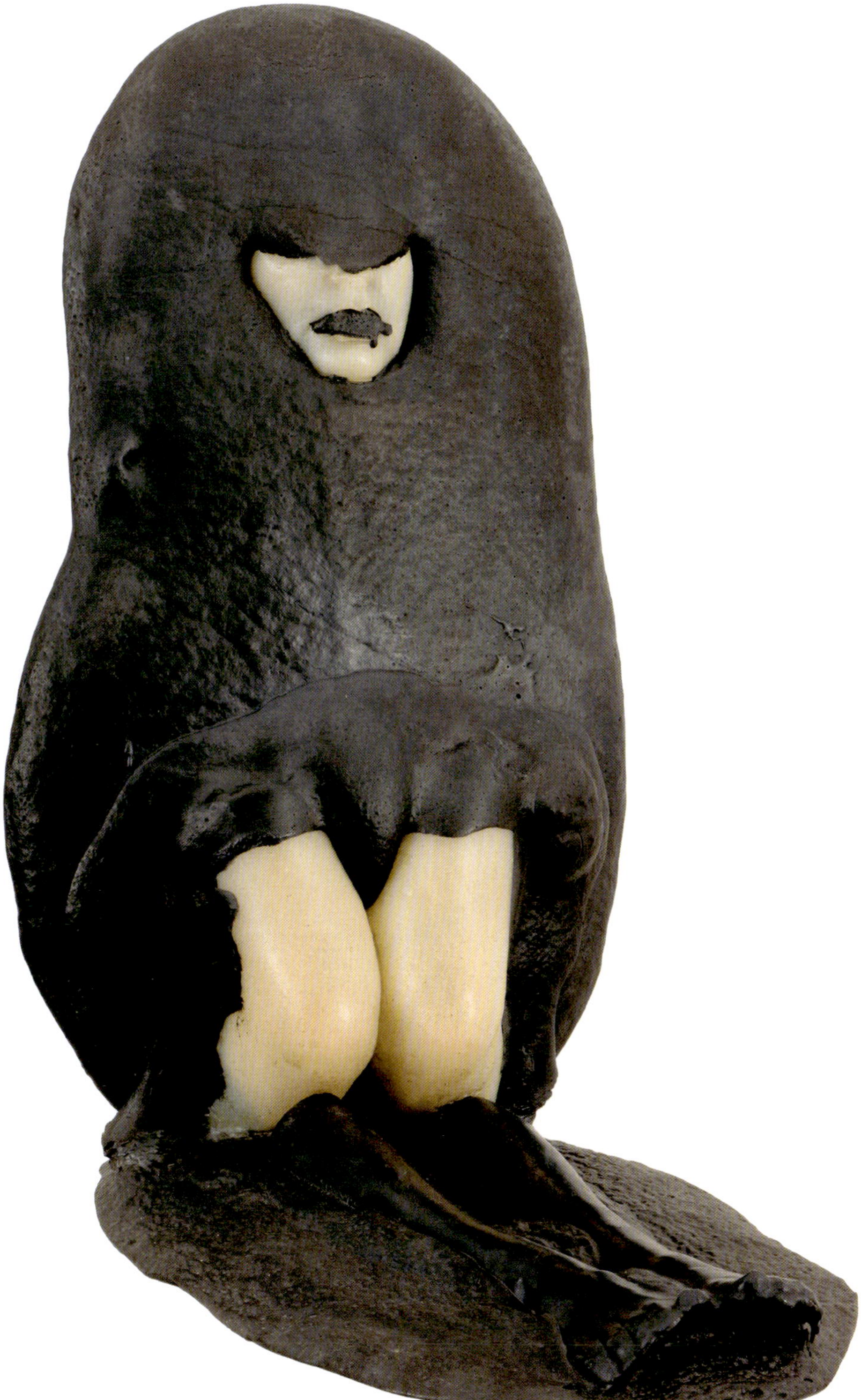

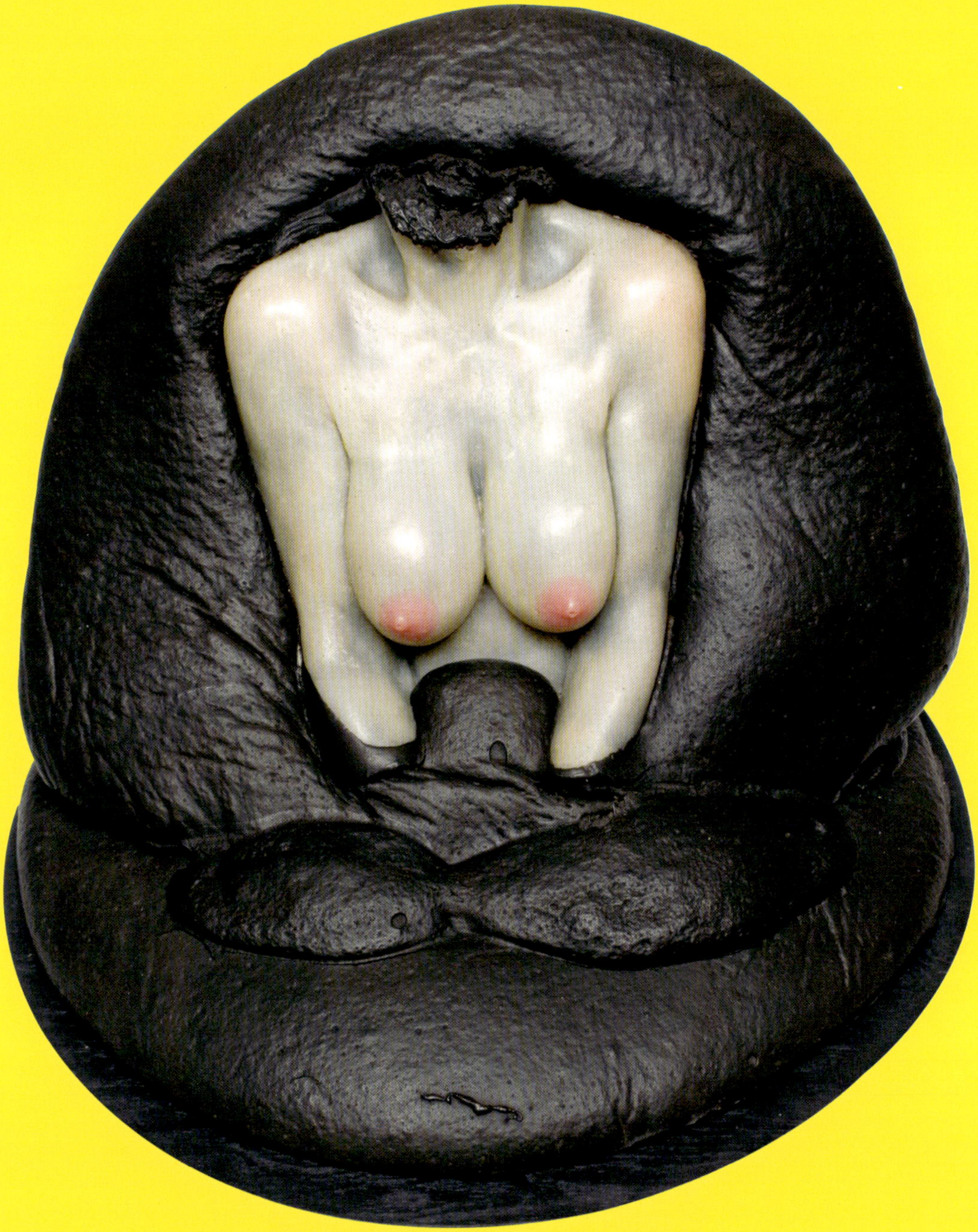

Plate 83

Torse noyé (Headless Torso), 1968
Polyester resin and polyurethane foam
18 1/8 x 25 3/16 x 28 3/4" (46 x 64 x 73 cm)

opposite top
Plate 84

Sous la coupole (Under the Cupola), 1970
Polyurethane foam and nylon tights
14 3/16 x 28 3/4 x 39 3/8" (36 x 73 x 100 cm)

opposite bottom
Plate 85

Siège-Piège (Seat-Trap), 1968
Sponge and polyurethane foam
13 3/8 x 26 3/4 x 24 13/16" (34 x 68 x 63 cm)

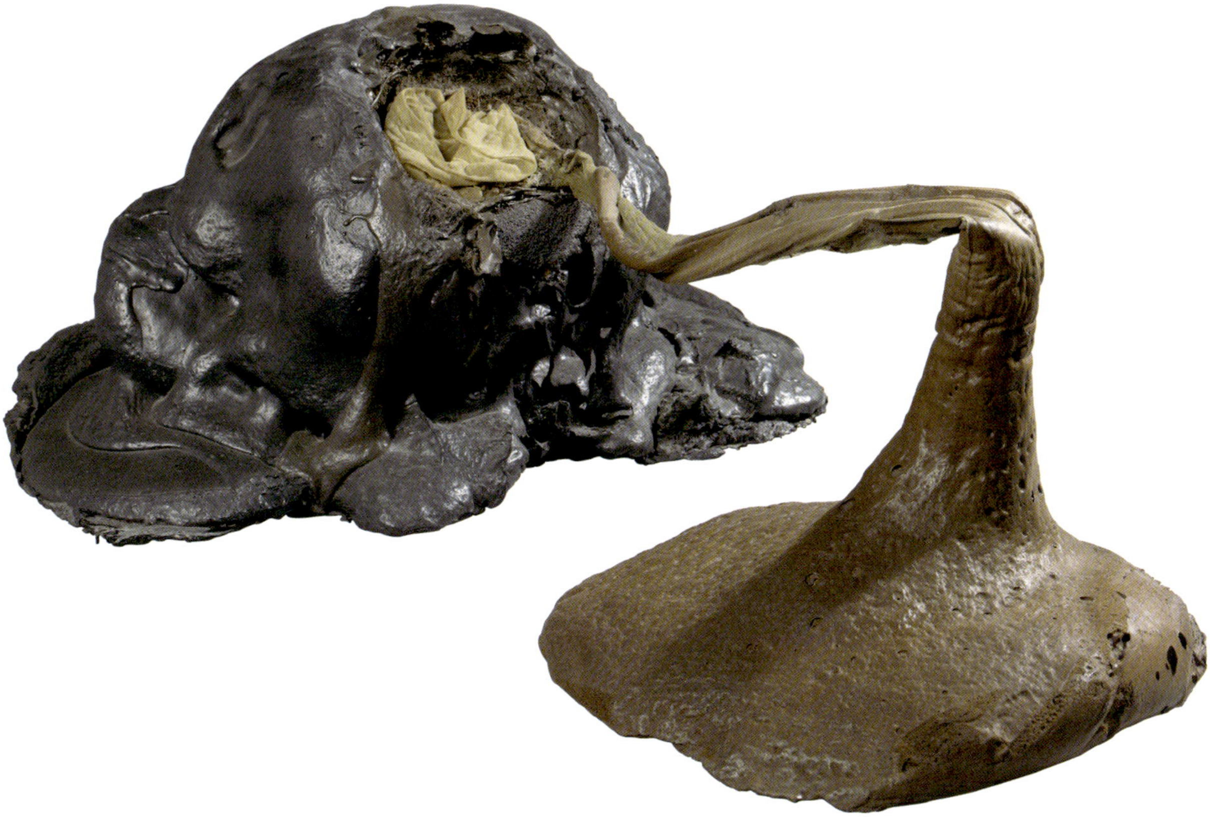

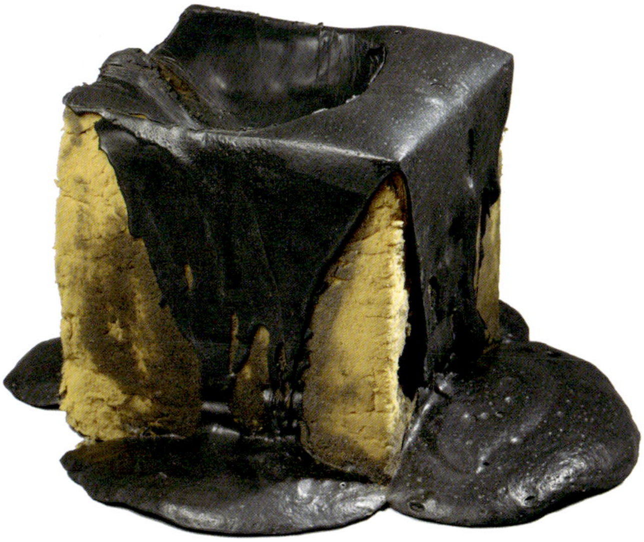

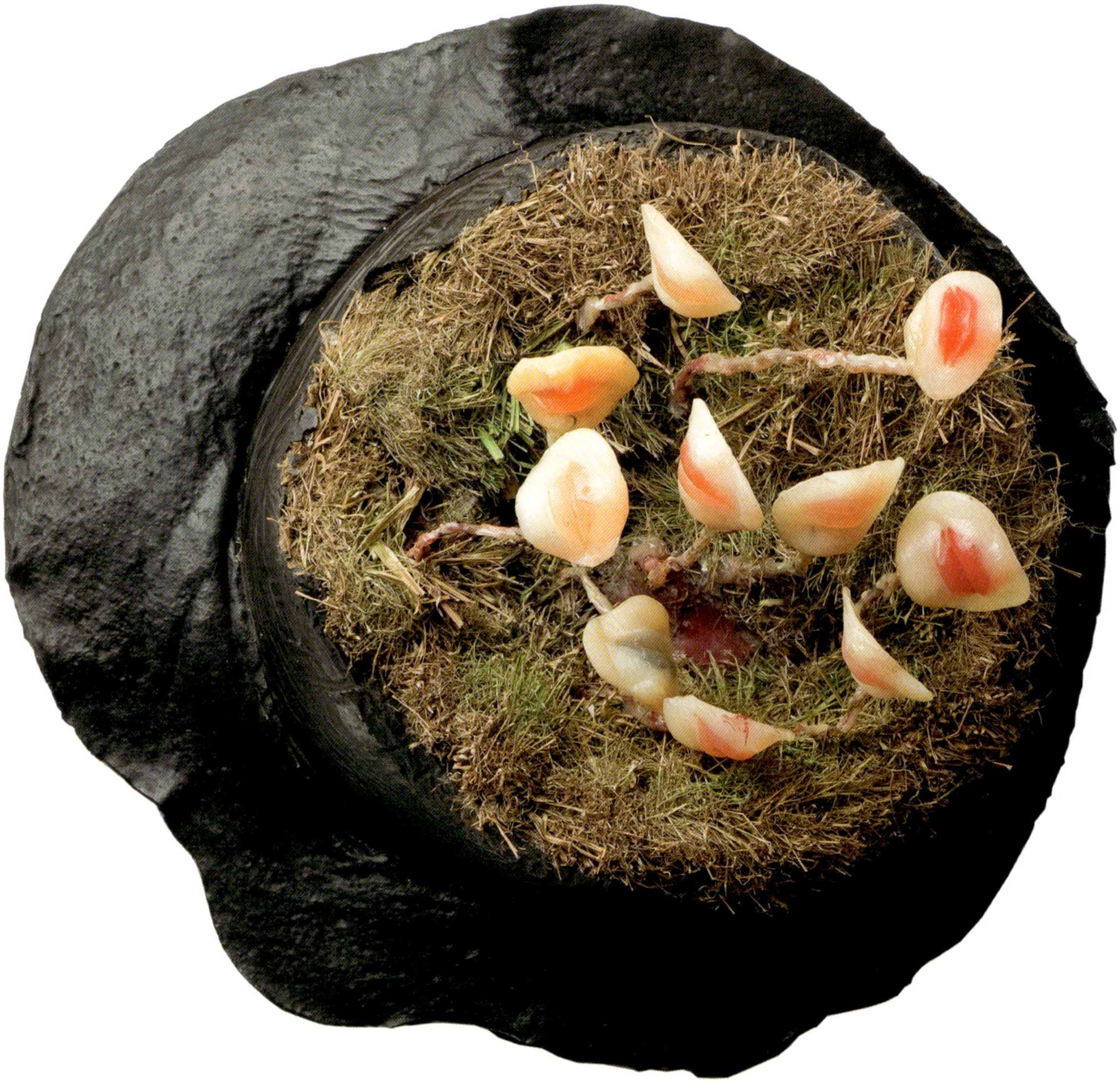

Plate 86

La Couronne de la Mariée (Bride's Wreath), 1968
Polyurethane foam, polyester resin, grass, metal
25 5/8 x 23 5/8 x 11 13/16" (65 x 60 x 30 cm)

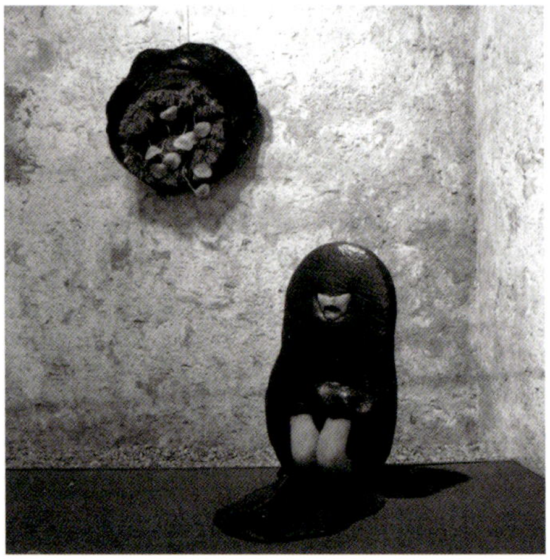

Aurora Gallery, Geneva, 1971.

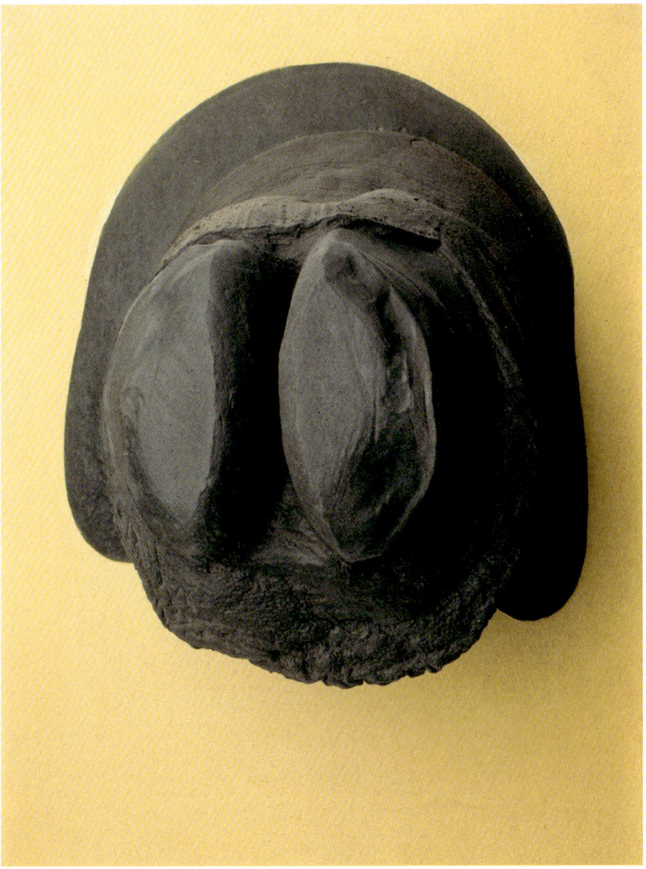

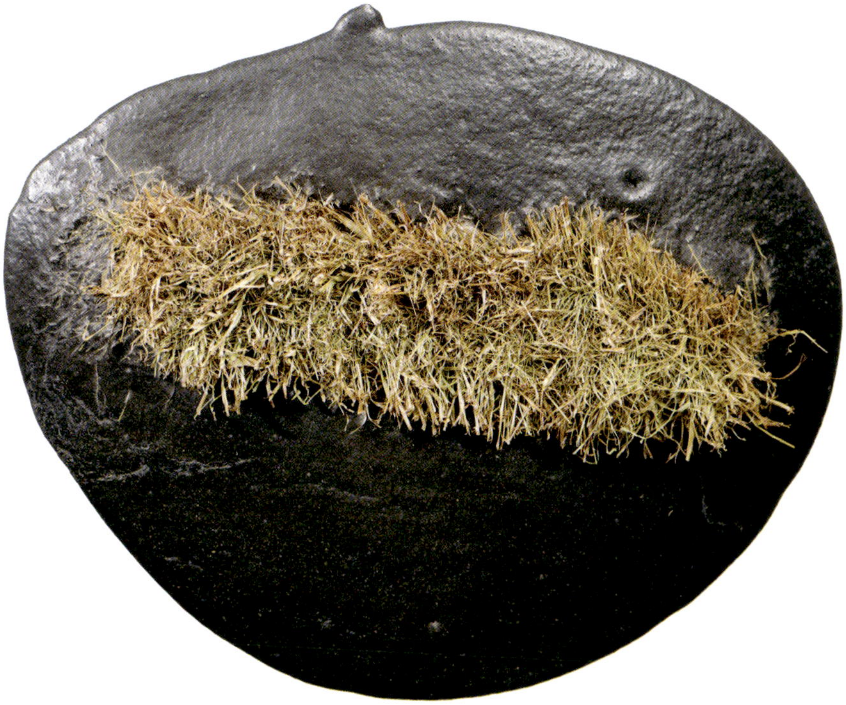

top
Plate 87

Accident III, 1968
Polyurethane foam and polychrome wood
39 3/8 x 28 3/16 x 18 1/8" (100 x 71.5 x 46 cm)

bottom
Plate 88

Pollution II, 1968
Polyurethane foam, metal, grass
15 3/4 x 18 1/2 x 2 3/4" (40 x 47 x 7 cm)

From Sculptures to Awkward Objects: A Short History of the Changing Reception of the Work of Alina Szapocznikow

Joanna Mytkowska

In Poland, where she was born on May 16, 1926, Alina Szapocznikow is above all a legend—highly regarded and one of few twentieth-century Polish women artists whose work enjoys significant renown. However, in writing a catalogue essay for what will be the first major presentation of her oeuvre outside Poland, I am faced with introducing Szapocznikow to an audience that, for the most part, is encountering her for the first time. This predicament reflects the history of the artist's reception both during her lifetime and since her death in 1973 and is perhaps also related to the demanding and risk-taking nature of her work, which evades easy definition. Although exhibited widely in Poland and in certain places quite revered, her work remained known and unknown, available and unavailable, simultaneously concealing and revealing meaning. After Szapocznikow's death in 1973, her work disappeared from view, present only within the history of Polish art despite the fact that the artist had spent most of her last decade in Paris, where she was in contact with many important art-world figures and was conversant with key international trends.

Szapocznikow's elusive status also resulted in a general lack of understanding about her position and her work; much of the interpretation was misguided or reductive. Moreover, a legend grew up around her, fuelled by the dramatic facts of her life, which ossified the reception of her work. I have, therefore, decided to use this space to survey her oeuvre through the filter of its reception, to trace the history of misunderstandings and omissions, traps and clichés, reductions and evasions that have accompanied its interpretation—that is, until the recent awakening of international interest. In this way I hope to disarm the legend that has obscured Szapocznikow's artistic legacy and to reveal what this legend may have concealed of her multifaceted work.

Certain artists' lives are indelibly marked by history. However, though it may be problematic to interpret an artist's work through a biographical lens, in some cases we simply cannot separate the work from the life and the life from the history—this is exactly the case with Szapocznikow. Due to the wealth of documentary photographs in her archive, a first encounter with the sculptor's work is often accompanied by images of a beautiful vivacious woman, whose life was nonetheless marked by several profound tragedies [ill. 1].

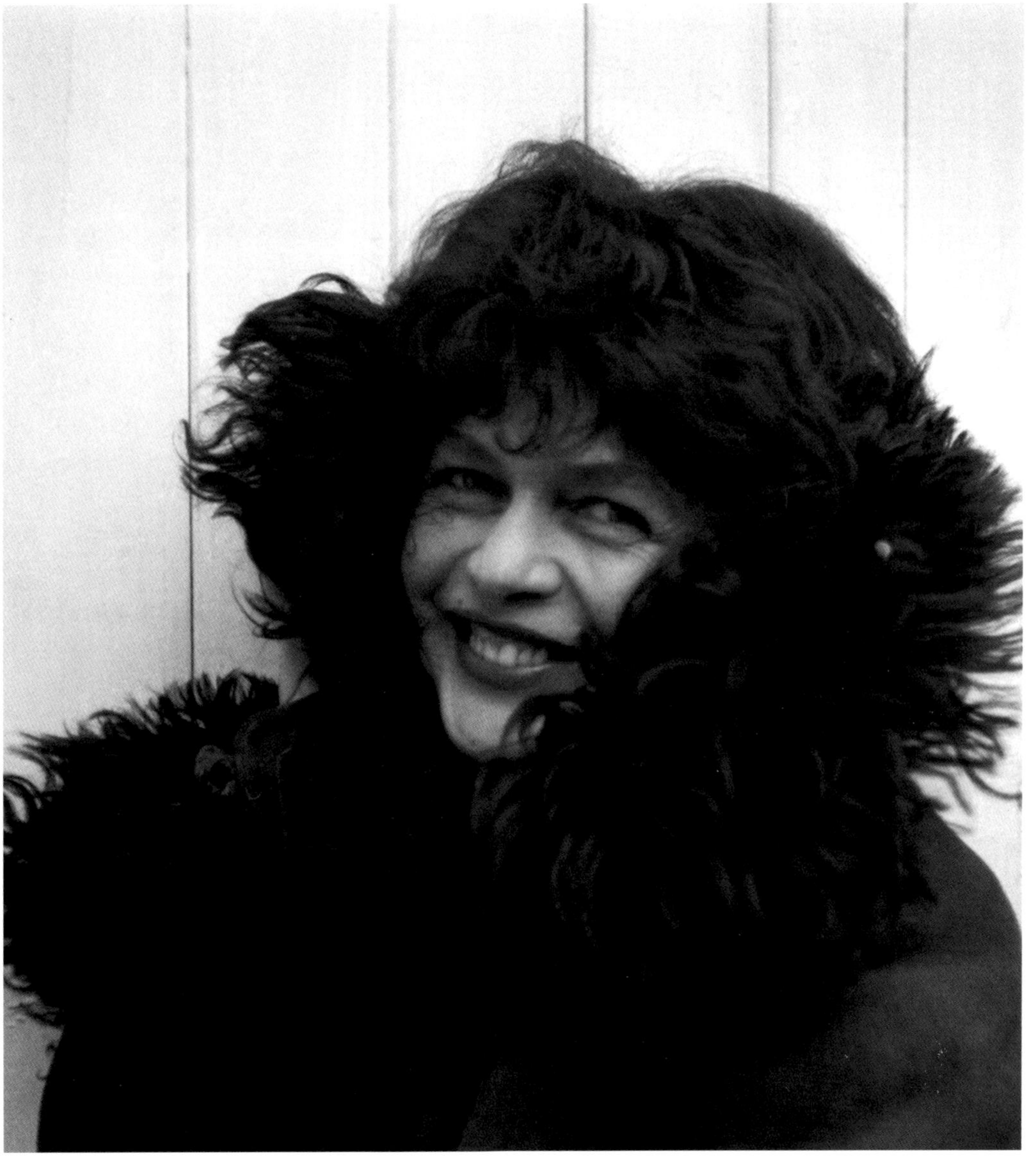

1. The artist at home in Malakoff, near Paris, 1967.

Three major events must be taken into consideration when discussing Szapocznikow's work. Most powerfully we should reflect on what the artist herself called "the baptism of despair": between 1939 and 1945 she survived incarceration in two ghettoes in Pabianice and Łódź and in a series of concentration camps including Auschwitz, Bergen-Belsen, and Terezín.[1] Szapocznikow very rarely mentioned these experiences[2]; yet, even if she did not often address her experiences of the Holocaust explicitly, she did join the public memorialization by participating in the competition for the monument to the Heroes of the Warsaw Ghetto [ill. 2, plate 145] and was part of a team entering the competition for the monument in Auschwitz, submitting *Kobieta w chuście* (*Woman in a Head Scarf*, 1949). Later she used a photograph from the Holocaust in works such as *Grande Tumeur I* (*Big Tumor I*, 1969) [plate 60] and *Souvenir I* (1971) [plate 57], possibly as an act of individual remembering. Only recently has a serious analysis of her Holocaust experience been used as a central element in interpreting her work, allowing for a different reading of her entire oeuvre.

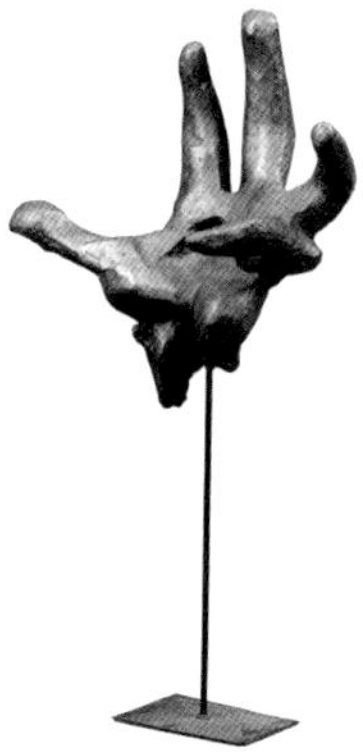

2.

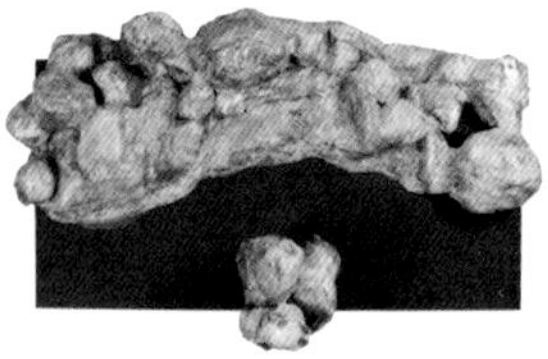

3.

The second crucial aspect of her biography is her experience of illness. In 1949–50, Szapocznikow almost died from peritoneal tuberculosis; though she was cured through the experimental use of antibiotics, the treatment resulted in loss of fertility. In January 1969, she was diagnosed with breast cancer, ultimately succumbing to it in 1973. While these experiences are the obvious interpretive foundation for some of her later works—especially the Tumeurs (Tumors) series of 1969 [plate 60] and *L'Enterrement d'Alina* (*Alina's Funeral*, 1970) [ill. 3, plate 66]—a consideration of her history of illnesses prompts us to reexamine all of her works, even earlier ones, bearing in mind her repeated confrontations with death [ill. 4].

The third biographical aspect is her position as Other—as a Jew, an outsider, and a woman. Though she suffered as a Jew during the Holocaust, she also had to negotiate being Jewish in postwar Communist Poland. She was an outsider in Prague and Paris but also in Warsaw, where she arrived for the first time as a mature artist in 1951 [ill. 5]. Any sense of alienation arising from these two factors would have only been compounded by the fact of being a woman artist in Paris during the 1960s [ill. 6]. But if this lack of belonging meant she was a stranger everywhere, she was also potentially at home everywhere, easily abandoning one place or position for another and demonstrating a cosmopolitan talent for adaptation. Numerous critics have praised her for her defiance of convention, her courage and independence, and the resulting uniqueness of her work.

Photographs have played an important role in the formation of Szapocznikow's public image. Numerous portraits were created throughout her life—she liked to be photographed and often appears laughing or charming the camera, with or without her sculptures, in her studio, at work, at exhibitions, in private and public situations. These pictures, encountered alongside her work, convey the image of an intriguing artist, vibrant and successful but at the same time mysteriously unfulfilled. They have blended with the reception of her work, influencing its interpretation. Thus apocryphal stories—occasionally the recollections of friends and acquaintances—circulate about her impetuousness, her *joie de vivre*, and her lively temperament, as well as her affairs and flirtations. These anecdotes reinforce the image of a seductive woman whose eroticism seems so evident in her works of the 1960s; yet this characterization stands in contrast to the darker aspects of her Holocaust experiences and her battles with disease. A paradoxical coupling of life and death thus emerges as a factor in the study of her work.

Let me take a closer look at the public reception of Szapocznikow's work from her emergence as an artist in the late 1940s. Relatively little documentation exists from the period between 1948 and 1951, when she first left Prague (where she trained) and was studying and participating in artistic life in Paris. Through Polish artists—emigrants and those visiting on fellowships—she was introduced to the Polish community in Paris and met Ryszard Stanisławski, her first husband, who later became a preeminent art historian and museum director. In 1951, she returned to Poland and accepted numerous commissions from the government—among them one for the prestigious sculpture decorating the main entrance to the Palace of Culture and Science, called *Pomnik Przyjaźni Polsko-Radzieckiej* (*Monument to Polish-Soviet Friendship*, 1954)[3]—quickly gaining recognition as a public artist. Although the character of Szapocznikow's work changed around 1955 in response to the

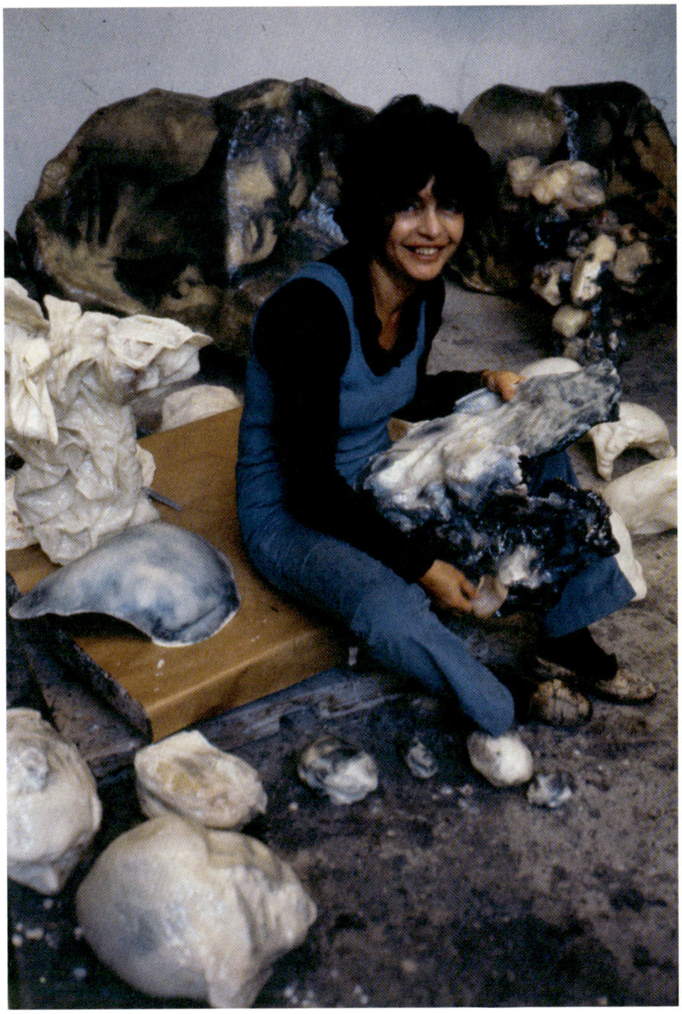

4. The artist in her studio in Malakoff, near Paris, 1971.

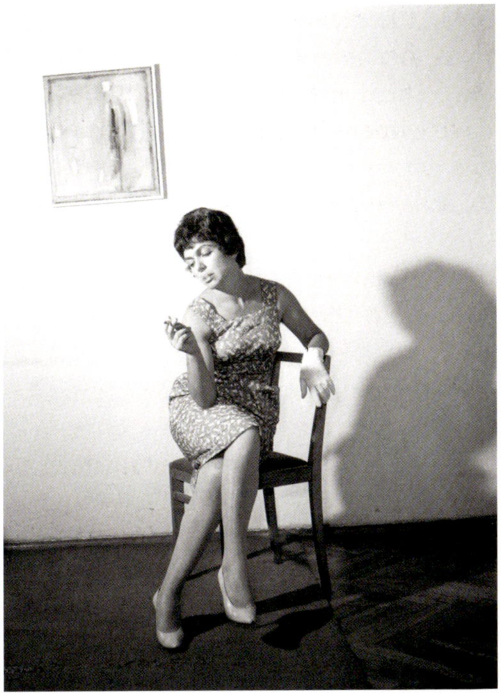

5. Szapocznikow, 1950s.

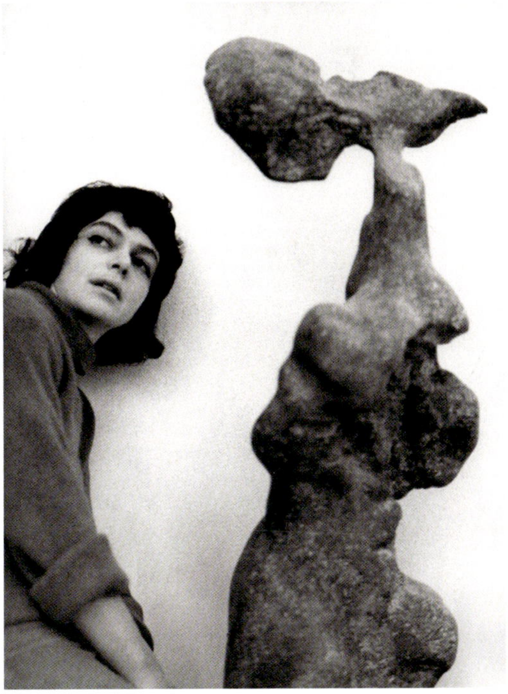

6. The artist with her work *Naga* (Naked), 1961.

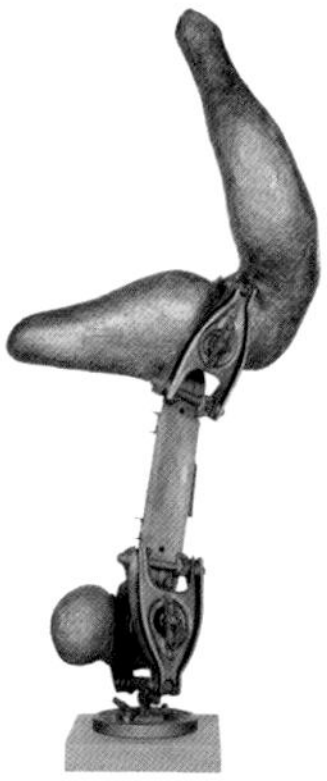

7.

so-called Polish thaw following the death of Stalin in 1953,[4] which allowed for the public display of individual artistic expression, interest in her work and artistic career remained consistent, and her artistic activity during the Stalinist/Socialist Realist period did not negatively impact her career. This phase is, however, usually ignored in the literature on her work.

Most regard Szapocznikow's mature period as beginning in 1955. For the next several years, she had shows in major Polish galleries—including a joint exhibition with Jerzy Tchórzewski at Warsaw's most prestigious gallery for modern art, Zachęta, in 1957 and a solo exhibition there in 1967. After meeting her in Poland in 1960, French critic Pierre Restany described her as "rightly recognized in her country, Poland, where she stands as a national celebrity figure."[5] In 1963, however, Szapocznikow immigrated to Paris with Roman Cieślewicz, who in 1967 became her second husband. There she became immersed in new concepts and movements such as Nouveau Réalisme, which is often considered the French version of Pop art but in fact was often critical of its American counterpart. Works such as *Goldfinger* (1965) [ill. 7, plate 101], whose title was taken from the James Bond movie (released in 1964), were the product of these encounters. Her social circle included members of Panique, a group created by Roland Topor, among others, whose focus was black humor and the grotesque. During this period, she began to use new industrial materials such as polyester to make body casts of lips, breasts, and abdomens, which were then made into objects and sculptures sometimes illuminated by electric light. Her highly individual interpretation of Pop art through various personal motifs kept her on the fringes of the movement—engagement with popular and commodity culture was of limited importance to her. As Restany described her relationship to Nouveau Réalisme:

> The artist seemed to escape the long torment of her life, the horror of her past of war and camps: she slowly woke up to a new objective consciousness of the world. [...] It will still take a long time for Alina to rip apart the anguish-ridden sails of her inner world. But the trigger has been pulled, and nothing will ever hinder this process.[6]

During the latter part of the 1960s—a period critical to the recent interpretation of her oeuvre—numerous works related to memory begin to emerge. Using poured polyurethane foam, she embedded fragmented body casts into sculptures as if sunk in asphalt. The process of their creation, and consequently the processual character of Szapocznikow's work, was emphasized in the catalogue designed by Cieślewicz for her 1968 exhibition in Cogeime Gallery, Brussels, organized by Restany and Giuseppe Marchiori. Formally, her sculptures became more and more fragmentary, like remnants, with the body casts assuming the quality of fetishes. During these intensely active years, Szapocznikow took part in many exhibitions in private galleries, the most important of which was "Instants et Choses" (1971) at the Aurora Gallery, Geneva, where she displayed a large group of works that appeared as a veritable manifesto on the disintegration of the coherent sculptural body. However, it does not seem as if her statement—so out of tune with the minimalist and conceptual trends of the time—was truly recognized. Although he did not fully appreciate Szapocznikow's position on the artistic scene, Restany invited her to participate in two shows: "Art Concepts from Europe" (1970) at Bonino Gallery, New York, and "Operazione Vesuvio" (1972) in Galleria Il Centro, Naples, and Centro Domus, Milan. These exhibitions gave

Szapocznikow an opportunity for exposure within an art community other than Paris and for experimentation with a conceptual mode that she appears to have embraced with her typical wit and dark humor. For these two projects, Szapocznikow produced two interesting works-cum-concepts. In a text titled “My American Dream” (1971), she proposed carving a double-life-sized Rolls Royce in pink marble as a commentary on useless luxury and consumption, and for the Italian project she proposed building a skating rink inside the crater of Vesuvius, near Pompeii, leading to the possible transformation of skaters into lava-encased mummies should the volcano erupt again.

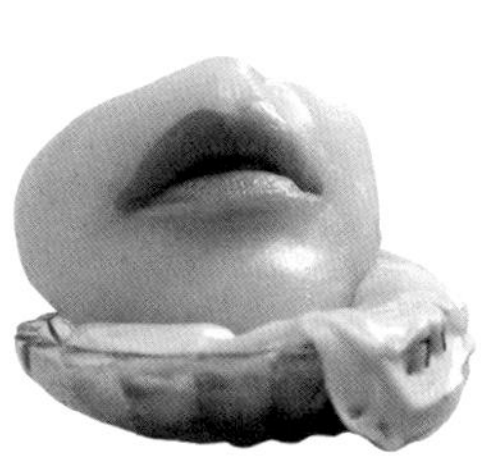

8.

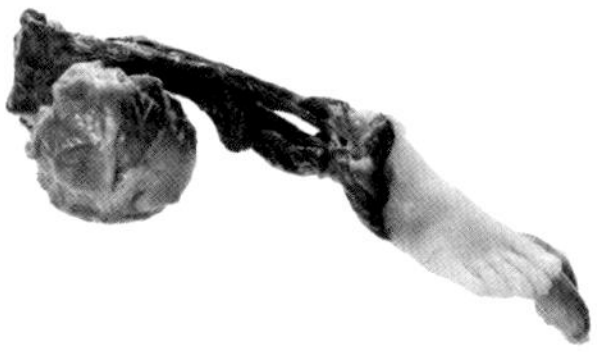

9.

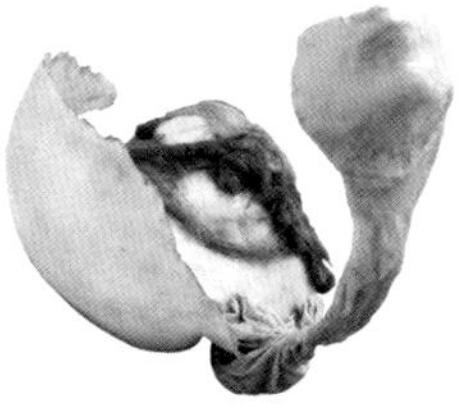

10.

Szapocznikow died on March 2, 1973, and in May of that year, Restany organized an exhibition called “Alina Szapocznikow. Tumeurs, herbier” (Alina Szapocznikow. Tumors, Herbarium) at the Musée d’Art Moderne de la Ville de Paris and designed the installation in collaboration with Cieślewicz, then a well-known graphic artist working for the Centre Pompidou, *Elle*, and *Opus International*. Unlike the suggestive arrangement at the Aurora Gallery, this show tended to classicize Szapocznikow’s work, essentially missing the spirit of the times and failing to address the Paris art community whose recognition she might have hoped to win. The show was hardly noticed.[7] In 1975, a retrospective was organized in Poland by Szapocznikow’s first husband, Stanisławski, then-director of the renowned Muzeum Sztuki, Łódź. “Alina Szapocznikow. 1926–1973” was presented in nine cities in Poland and Sweden. Quite comprehensive, with works from all periods of her career, the exhibition consolidated her reputation in Poland as an important figure in postwar European sculpture. From that moment on, her work was part of every important survey of national art and many thematic shows in Poland. Yet, even as her work remained visible, its interpretation grew stale, calcified. She became immobilized by adulation as “the great artist.” Appearing in anthologies and museum collections and on the covers of art publications, she existed more in the collective unconscious—her work neither provoking controversy nor inspiring reflection.

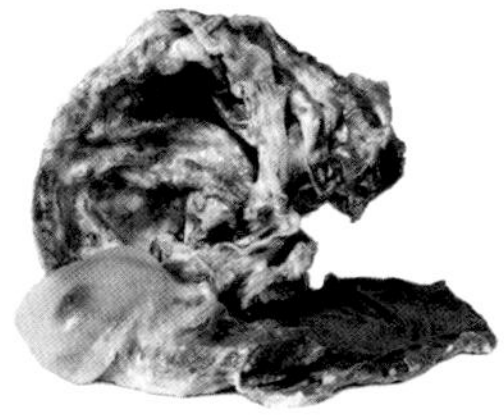

11.

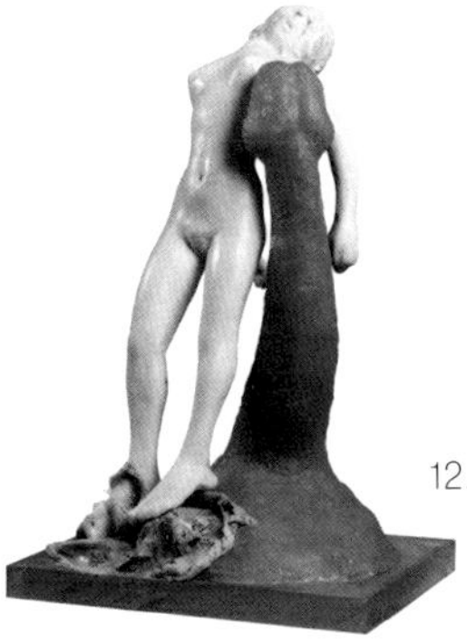

12.

A 1998 exhibition (with the same title as that from 1975, “Alina Szapocznikow. 1926–1973”) was organized by Anda Rottenberg for Zachęta National Gallery of Art in Warsaw to mark the twenty-fifth anniversary of the artist’s death. With this show came a breakthrough in Szapocznikow’s reception. The understanding of art history had undergone a radical revision in Poland after 1989,[8] when the corrupt official institutionalized language was rejected and the search began for a more authentic one. New modes of analysis were critically deployed, and it became clear in retrospect that her work, especially that from the 1960s, could be fruitfully addressed through feminist analyses of gender and the body.[9] Rottenberg’s exhibition drew attention to the significance of certain key biographical aspects in reading the later work. The arrangement in the gallery’s largest room—presenting the last period of the artist’s life through works such as Desserts [ill. 8, plates 20–22], Fétiches (Fetishes) [ills. 9–11, plates 29–34], and *Fiancée folle blanche* (*Mad white fiancée*) [ill. 12, plates 9–10]—remains unforgettable for those who saw the installation. For division and elevation, Rottenberg used white hospital screens and metal furniture, specifically connecting these works to Szapocznikow’s long and ultimately hopeless struggle against cancer [ill. 14].

At the time, this presentation caused very strong emotional reactions and incited much controversy. However, I believe I understand the intentions of Rottenberg, who above all wanted to raise the temperature around Szapocznikow’s work, to confront the legend of the artist's intensely lived but recurrently troubled life and to overcome the anodyne reiteration of biographical details without any real understanding of those events. In her essay "Personalizations," written many years later, Rottenberg attempted to redefine the interpenetration of Szapocznikow's life and work using contemporary theoretical terms such as "embodiment," "incorporation," and "personalization." Writing about *Tumeurs personnifiées* (*Tumors Personified*, 1971) [ill. 13 (detail), plate 64], Rottenberg observed:

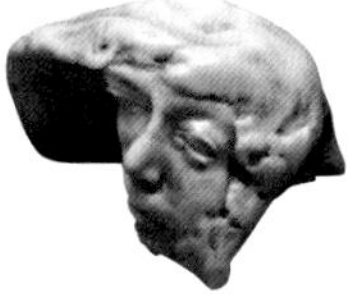

13.

> [T]he parallel of life and creation, previously seen in terms of disintegration, changed in this last phase into a process of concentration, the absorption of one by the other, unification. A process of personalization of art took place, in which the artistic subject "I" was converted into its object: her "self."[10]

This deep personal engagement, as well as the occasional tendency to identify with the artist, is a hallmark of Szapocznikow's posthumous curators and pioneering commentators, whose role has been to use new perspectives to reanimate the understanding and appreciation of this complex and powerful body of work. (Notably, the artist's two husbands were involved in organizing the first retrospectives after her death.) Rottenberg in particular has demonstrated a personal commitment to the task of restoring the "real" Szapocznikow for the benefit of her audience, revealing her own private reasons for her shocking frankness about illness and death in preparing the exhibition.[11] In addition, Jola Gola has been the most diligent scholar of Szapocznikow's career. For almost twenty years she has painstakingly reconstructed it, building up a massive amount of factual information on the artist. The deep commitment the work has inspired in those who study it suggests that its particular entanglement with the artist's life seems to demand personal investment by its most attentive scholars. The author of the only monographic study on Szapocznikow (still only available in Polish), Agata Jakubowska, theorized this stance in the light of feminist theories of situated knowledge and critical reflexivity:

> Szapocznikow's art is most often read as a confession, but I read it as a challenge. And I understand the encounter with the living presence of the face—or, to generalize, with a work—as an experience in which I accept the challenge and stand face-to-face with art. Such an interpretation is an activity in which the privileged position of the art historian, acquired through the use of the authority of objective knowledge, is revealed as inadequate. An attempt to understand her work is a process of dialogue in which not only the artist, but also the critic is revealed as an embodied and situated subject.[12]

Rottenberg's exhibition at Zachęta National Gallery of Art toured to almost all the large Polish museums, if in a more conventional form, and initiated a dramatic growth in new research and reinterpretation of Szapocznikow's work. Various studies were crowned with the publication of a catalogue raisonné of both sculpture and drawing, compiled by Gola.[13] The only disappointment was the continuing lack of interest outside Poland and the artist's persistent marginalization in the West, not only as a woman but also as one associated with the former Eastern Europe. Her exclusion from the mainstream of Western art history at that time was the fate of a number of other women artists, including Louise Bourgeois and Eva Hesse, who were both recognized late; however, that in combination with her exclusion on the basis of nationality is worthy of examination. Szapocznikow's case is complex. In Communist Poland, gender was not really an obstacle to one's artistic career; it was only after she went to

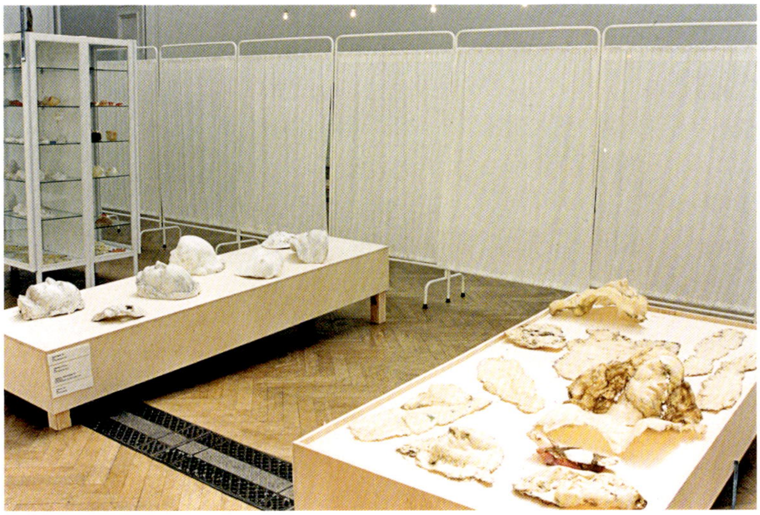

14. Installation view of the exhibition "Alina Szapocznikow. 1926–1973" at Zachęta National Gallery of Art, Warsaw, 1998, showing works from the Herbier (Herbarium) series, 1971–72.

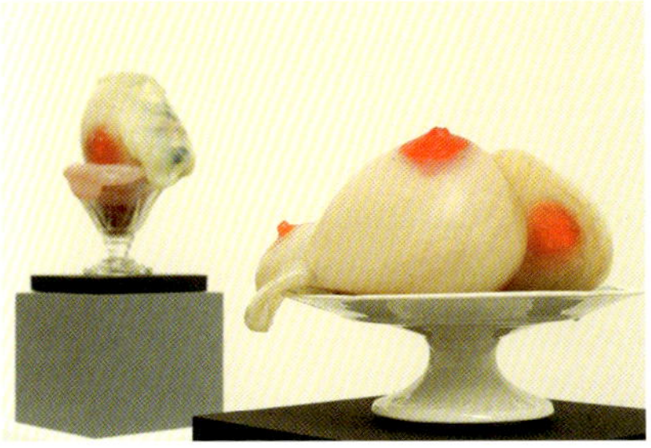

15. Installation view of the exhibition "Flesh at War with Enigma" at Kunsthalle Basel, 2004, showing *Dessert II*, 1970–71, and *Dessert III*, 1971.

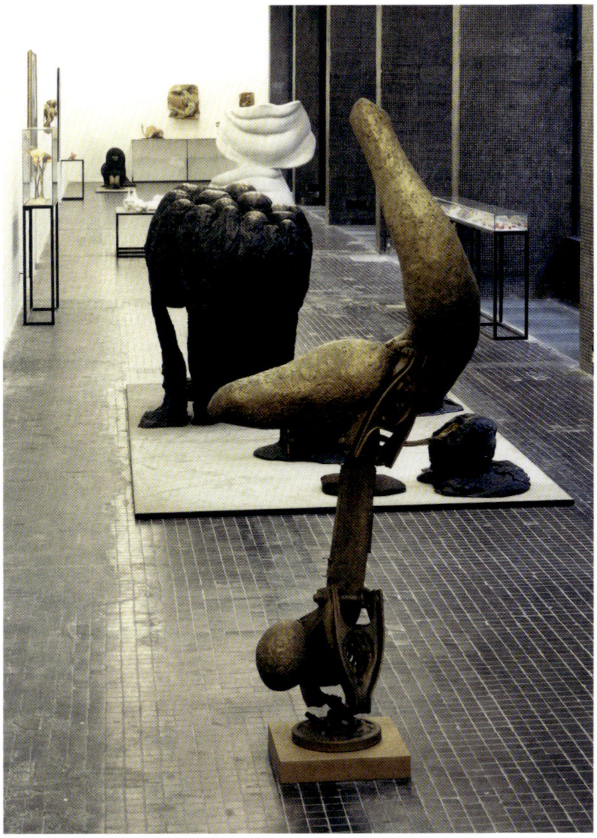

16. Installation view of the exhibition "Awkward Objects. Alina Szapocznikow, Maria Bartuszova, Pauline Boty, Louise Bourgeois, Eva Hesse and Paulina Ołowska" at the Museum of Modern Art, Warsaw, 2009. At front, Szapocznikow's *Goldfinger*, 1965.

Paris that she experienced marginalization based on gender. Hence, she continued to be recognized in Poland and unknown in the West. Since 1989, the challenge of introducing her into Western art discourse has been taken up by a few. I focus here on the history of her reception—by necessity, mostly Polish—to demonstrate the ways in which her complex and unique work has been repeatedly forcing her critics to reevaluate it, using the latest interpretative tools.

Significant changes in the reception of Szapocznikow's work came with its recontextualization in the realm of contemporary art. Two shows—"PRYM" at the BWA (Biuro Wystaw Artystycznych) in Zielona Góra, Poland, and "Flesh at War with Enigma" at the Kunsthalle Basel [ill. 15] (both 2004)[14]—juxtaposed Szapocznikow's works with those of contemporary artists, thus regaining for them an autonomous power of expression outside their immediate historical context. This triggered the interest of the art market[15] and led to museum purchases, the first of which was made in 2007 by the Centre Georges Pompidou, Paris, which acquired one of her most experimental works, *Fotorzeźby* (*Photosculptures*, 1971) [plates 36–55]. Simultaneously, her work was shown at Documenta 12 in Kassel, Germany, an ambitious exhibition aiming to rewrite art history and to expand its geography, particularly in the realms of conceptual and experimental art.

A couple of years later, after I assumed directorship of the newly established Museum of Modern Art in Warsaw, I assembled a team that included Jakubowska as guest curator and was committed to recapitulating Szapocznikow's recent reception and broadening the understanding of her work. In 2009 we began preparations for another major exhibition with the intention of sidestepping direct references to her biography. We decided to read her work comparatively, juxtaposing it with other artists' work of the same period in order to provide an international context [ills. 16, 17]. Since personal details so often threatened to undermine more nuanced or objective readings of Szapocznikow's work, we decided on a risky tactic: we would exhibit her work beside that of artists with whom she had no personal contact, nor experienced any type of artistic exchange. This inspired a discussion of various issues independent of her biography, placing emphasis on the work itself and indicating new lines of interpretation.[16]

The title of the exhibition, "Awkward Objects," was a quotation from the artist's most important programmatic text from 1972,[17] in which she expressed her conscious decision to be guided by intuition, rather than tradition or trends. This required her to adhere to the truth of lived experience. The most productive way to achieve that was by registering the complexity of the human body through radical experimentation, even if it meant destroying the structure of the sculptural object. We decided to focus on the Paris period only (1963 to 1973) and to begin with the first body casts, with their fragmentation of the body and their new materials. Juxtaposing these with drawings by Hesse showed that a struggle with the post-Bellmerian concept of the body-as-machine might lie at the foundation of many of Szapocznikow's formal experiments. A comparison with sculptures by Bourgeois highlighted the aspect of the *informe*, revealing Szapocznikow's proclivity for incompleteness, as well as her openness to material and processual accident. Peter Moore's photographic documentation of Bourgeois's performance *A Banquet/A Fashion Show of Body Parts* (1978) elicited discussion of artists' fetishization of women's body parts, intended to scandalize and liberate the body from unambiguous meaning.

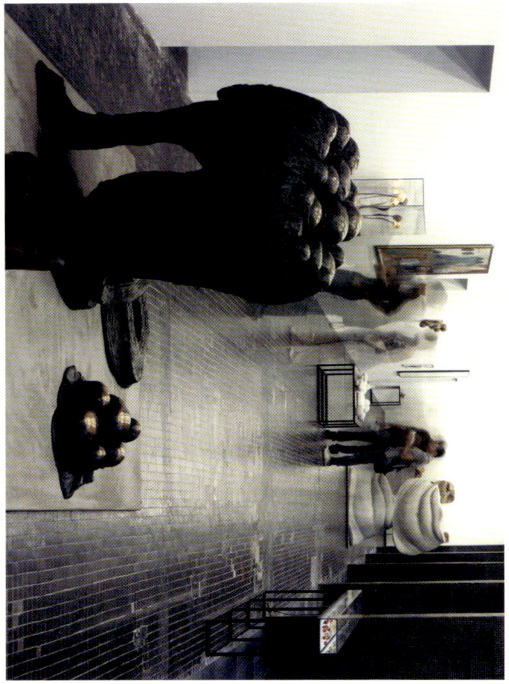

17. Installation view of the exhibition "Awkward Objects." At front, Louise Bourgeois's *Avenza Revisited II*, 1968–69, and *Unconscious Landscape*, 1967–68; at the back, Szapocznikow's *Grands Ventres* (Big Bellies), 1968.

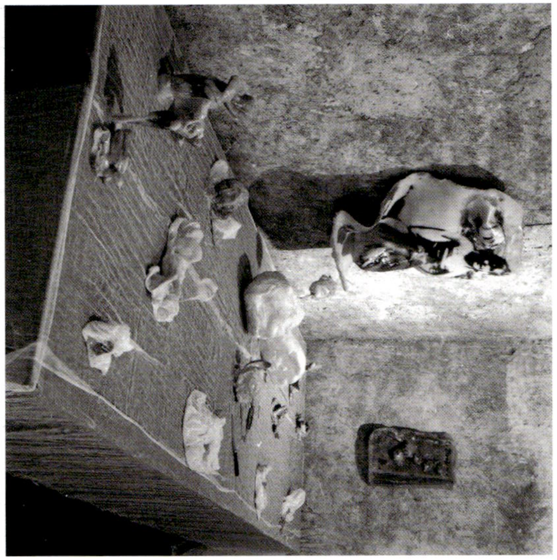

18. Szapocznikow, *Souvenir de la table de noce d'une femme heureuse* (Souvenir from the Wedding Table of a Happy Woman), 1971, on view in the exhibition "Instants et Choses" at Aurora Gallery, Geneva, 1971.

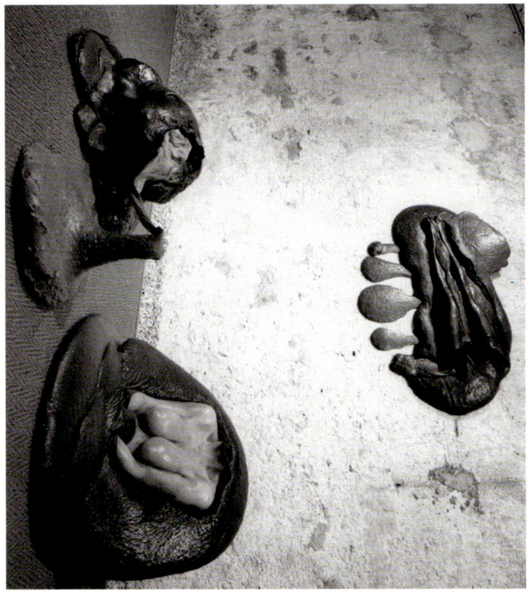

19. The exhibition "Instants et Choses" at Aurora Gallery Geneva, 1971. From left to right, works by Szapocznikow: *Sous la coupole* (Under the Cupola), 1970; *Les capuchons, Jambes noyées* (Drips, Embedded Legs), 1968; and *Stèle* (Stele), 1968.

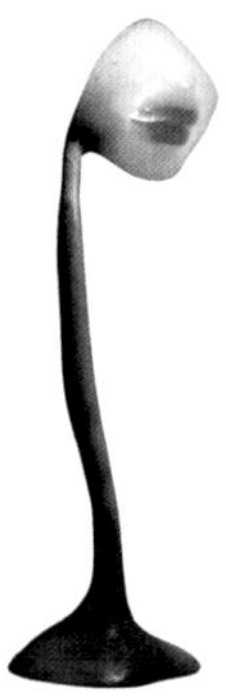
20.

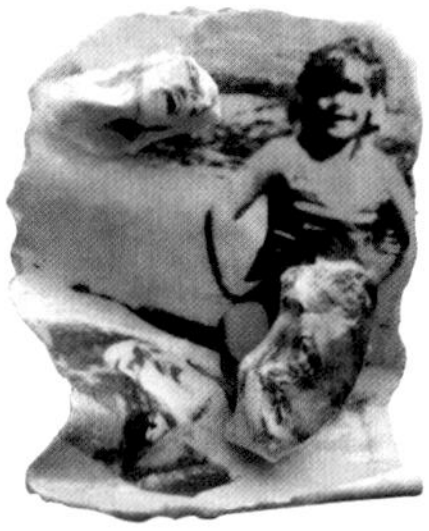
21.

Szapocznikow's strategy of multiplication, in which she turned sculptures into gadgets—her *Lampe-bouche* (*Illuminated Lips*, 1966) [ill. 20, plate 17] is a case in point—demonstrated her intentional degradation of sculpture. She deployed degradation as a conceptual strategy aimed at establishing the ambiguous status of the erotic object (in this case, lips), destabilizing the objective value of the art object, and highlighting the problematic presence of the fetish. Work by Pauline Boty, a British artist active in the London Pop art scene, prompted comparison with Szapocznikow's reexamination of images of women's bodies, while the work of a young artist, Paulina Ołowska, who often alludes to Szapocznikow, was a reminder of her continued relevance and the liberating effect of placing her in a contemporary art context. *Grands Ventres* (*Big Bellies*, 1968) suggested the variety of scales she worked with, while lending the whole exhibition an aura of surreality and the grotesque, qualities much appreciated by Szapocznikow. Works such as *Souvenir I* (1971) [ill. 21, plate 57] also brought to the surface the question of memory, which we reinforced by reproducing the historical arrangement of *Souvenir I* and other works from the Aurora Gallery exhibition [ill. 19], including *Souvenir de la table de noce d'une femme heureuse* (*Souvenir from the Wedding Table of a Happy Woman*, 1971), a work that may be read as a remembrance of sculpture as an autonomous object [ill. 18]. The Fetishes, intimate items of clothing sunk in polyester, emphasized the proto-feminist character of Szapocznikow's work particularly effectively. In addition to devoting significant space to ephemeral projects and documents, the exhibition was dominated by the body casts, contextualized in relation to Georges Didi-Huberman's theory of the imprint—involving both the indexicality of the body in its imprint [ill. 22] and the function of the imprint as testimony to the body's disappearance.

On the one hand, "Awkward Objects" aimed to make Szapocznikow more accessible by establishing connections between her experimental works and the discourses and tropes that were shared between several of the most radical women artists of that decade whose work centered around the body, found images, and/or new materials. On the other hand, we wished to emphasize the pioneering character of her work, especially as it was undertaken outside of New York or London, as well as to highlight her capacity to take artistic risks that led her to solutions entirely in accord with her contemporaries. The exhibition followed the transformation of an artist who began by using the classical language of sculpture into an artist who was apparently willing to destroy her own medium for the sake of finding an individual vocabulary of forms, materials, and processes that were at once entirely contemporary and suited to her particular aims.

This overview is intended neither to arrive at the most effective formula for interpretation nor to define the best method for exhibiting the work; for neither exist. Instead our intention has been to plot out the process that led to the deconstruction of dominant and limiting representations of Szapocznikow and her oeuvre. The initial difficulties her work presented to critics and its posthumous marginalization, despite achieving almost heroic status in Poland, now seems comprehensible in light of what we now appreciate as the artist's daring departure into the unknown, which took her beyond familiar forms, definitions, and artistic positions. Tracing the reception of her work teaches us that a strategy so individual and so distinct merits a different kind of attention, so as not to resolve contradictions that she actively sought to create and not to produce a false construct in an effort to have her conform to what is already known.

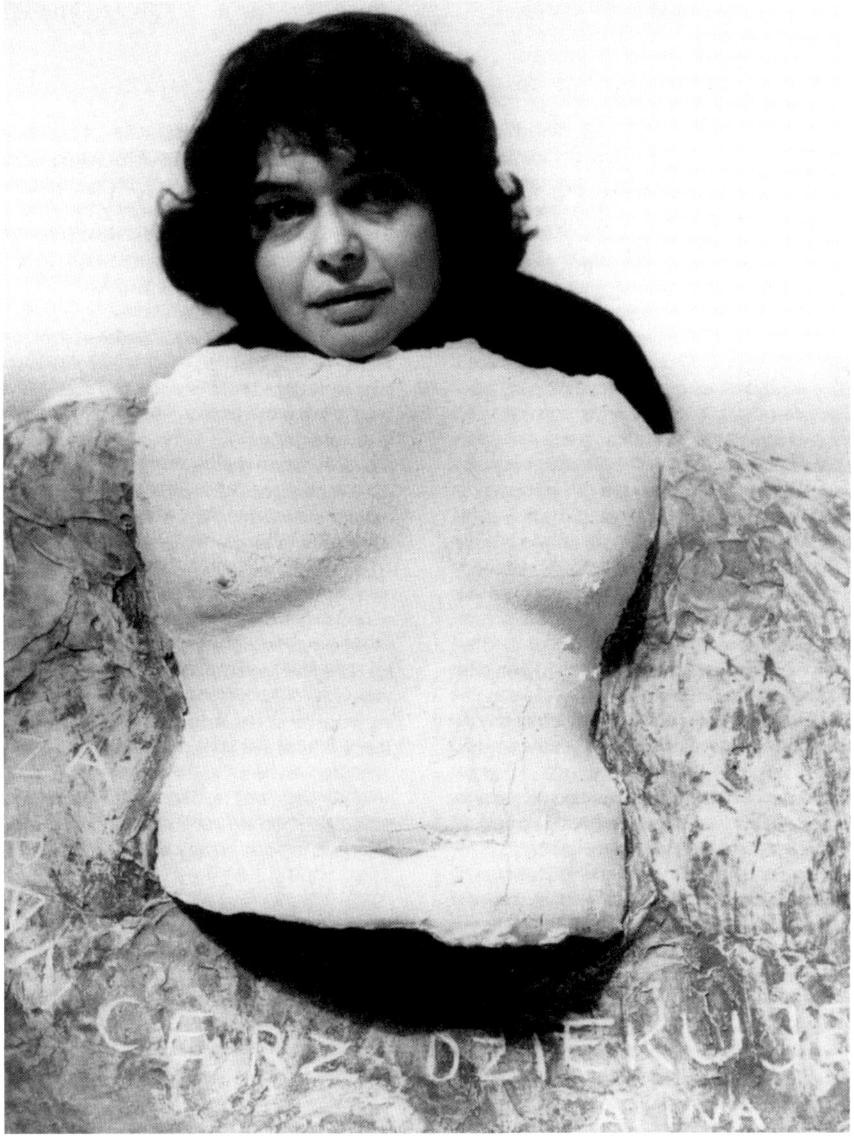

22. The artist with a body cast, 1966. Inscription on the photograph: "Thank you for the armature."

Perhaps ironically, during the conference accompanying "Awkward Objects" the biographical trope, transformed by more rigorous theorization, proved to be among the most effective.[18] Griselda Pollock's careful reading of Szapocznikow's oeuvre through the prism of trauma—the recollection of which led to the gradual entropy of sculptural forms—is one of the boldest and most admirable efforts at a total interpretation of the artist's work.[19] In no way contradicting the thesis of the exhibition, which argued that the deconstruction or degradation of sculpture was necessary in order to approach contemporary reality, Pollock merely emphasized a different aspect, saw different reasons for the same process. The multiplicity of possible interpretations generated through the conference brought back life and fullness to Szapocznikow's work and promoted interest internationally in articulating her position within art history.

The field of interpretation for Szapocznikow's work has broadened over time as its contradictions have emerged and as we have consented both to its absurdity and uneasy fit with dominant narratives and to its continual transformation. A long and convoluted process of reception is understandable (and common) for pioneering work, founded as it is on the imperative to express existential contradictions and a commitment to the work's continued relevance. Therefore analyses and interpretations of her works can be expected to stratify and complement each other, illuminating matters from different perspectives and offering various routes for approaching an understanding of her oeuvre.

Translated from the Polish by Krystyna Mazur.

Notes

1. Szapocznikow's presence at Terezín is not confirmed by camp documents and therefore remains uncertain. See Tomáš Pospíszyl, "Alina Szapocznikow in Prague," in Agata Jakubowska, ed., *Alina Szapocznikow. Awkward Objects* (Warsaw: Museum of Modern Art, 2011), 235.
2. We know only two fragments of letters in which Szapocznikow refers to her war experiences—and then only in passing. In a letter to Ryszard Stanisławski from January 1949, she wrote:

   > It is simply that you still look at some things in such a nice, polite, gracious manner, perhaps they way one should, and maybe I'm even sometimes jealous of that. But the difference is that in the process of your formation in the last 10 years you have not gone through that baptism of despair, all these things, everything didn't end for you irretrievably several times, as it did for me in the ghettos and the camps. I'm sorry, Rys, I'm embarrassed. You know how much I hate, how ashamed I am for those people who go on or "brag" about the years of torment they have lived through. But you have to understand me. I've told you before, maybe I will be able to tell you everything about those times, and in our case that is very important. Because you experienced a lot in those times, you lived, for better or worse, you loved and married, wanted to have a family (or not). But your terms have not changed radically as they did for me, so that now what remains for me of "nice, polite, gracious" is "beautiful, human, real to the bone." Maybe we can talk some time.

   In a letter to Stanisławski, from Paul-Brousse Hospital, Villejuif, in November 1949, she wrote:

   > But I want to live so much! I never knew it is so hard to die. In the camp people perished like flies. They didn't have the time for long dying. A woman from the opposite end of this room struggled all night to die. In fact it probably wasn't really her any more, because the terrible sounds and howls became inhuman and in the darkness awoke all my (it seemed forgotten) worst nightmares of the camps and of inhuman war misery. And around me these women, strangers (how inhumanly strange) indifferent (!) spoke about her with complete indifference, in a completely ordinary manner. They coughed, complained of the colic, threw up, and complained that they can't sleep because of the noise. Out of the horror-filled darkness came broken words of live people, but there was no one human soul. But in the camp, there were human souls who allowed you to survive and have faith.

   Both letters were translated by Krystyna Mazur and are contained in the archives at the Museum of Modern Art, Warsaw. Alternative translations are available in "Fragments of Alina Szapocznikow's Correspondence with Ryszard Stanisławski (1948–1959)," in *Alina Szapocznikow*, trans. Marzena Beata Guzowska, (Warsaw: Institute for the Promotion of Art Foundation and Galeria Zachęta, 1998), 143–44.
3. Agata Jakubowska discusses the circumstances of Szapocznikow's political commitment; her membership in the Communist Party in Prague; the idealized perception of Communism she acquired in Paris during the late 1940s; her dedication and desire to do large public projects in Poland; and finally the disenchantment with the limitations of dogmatic Socialist Realism. See "Zaangażowana" (Engaged), in *Portret wielokrotny dzieła Aliny Szapocznikow* (Poznań, Poland: Wydawnictwo Naukowe UAM, 2008). Ewa Toniak talks about the ambiguous position of women artists declaring women's emancipation in the Communist state in *Olbrzymki: kobiety i socrealizm* (Kraków, Poland: Korporacja Ha!art, 2008).
4. "The thaw" is a common term for the liberalization of the absolutist regime in the United Soviet Socialist Republic after Joseph Stalin's death in 1953 and the related changes, especially after Nikita Khrushchev's "Secret Speech" (1956) on "The Cult of the Individual" report was made public, in which Khrushchev revealed Stalin's crimes. The thaw spread to other Communist states: in Poland, the change in domestic politics, combined with the replacement of the top authorities and the liberalization of the political system, began in mid-1956 and culminated in the events of October that year.
5. Pierre Restany, *Alina Szapocznikow* (Paris: Galerie Florence Houston Brown, 1967). Quoted in English in Anke Kempkes, "Black Drips and

Dark Matter – The Luxury Gap – Concept *individuel* – Quarry Desert. The Incommensurable Contemporaneity of Alina Szapocznikow," in *Alina Szapocznikow. Awkward Objects*, 163.

6. Restany, ibid.
7. According to accounts by Anka Ptaszkowska, a gallerist and art critic living in Paris at the time.
8. In Poland, a change in the political system happened in 1989 as a result of the agreement of the so-called "Round Table" (a discussion of the authorities with representatives of the political opposition, Solidarity, and the Church, which took place during the first half of 1989) and of the first free parliamentary elections since 1945 (which took place June 4, 1989). For the rest of the so-called Eastern block, the fall of the Berlin Wall in November 1989 marked the beginning of such transformations.
9. At the conference accompanying the exhibition, as many as three papers interpreted Szapocznikow's works using the tools of feminist theory, including papers delivered by Jakubowska, Izabela Kowalczyk, and Magdalena Ujma. The catalogue from the exhibition contained a new comprehensive interpretation of Szapocznikow's work by Urszula Czartoryska. See "Okrutna Jasność" (Cruel Brightness), in *Alina Szapocznikow, 1926–1973* (Warsaw: Galeria Sztuki Wspólczesnej Zachęta, 1998), 12–23.
10. Anda Rottenberg, "Personalizations," in *Alina Szapocznikow. Awkward Objects*, 103–04.
11. "I was putting together a narrative for the exhibition which, in its hidden, entirely private layer was my way of saying goodbye to my friend Irena [Kolat-Ways]. In 1975 Irena organized the first posthumous exhibition of Alina Szapocznikow in the Łódź Museum and Hanka [Włodarczyk], my other friend, made a film based on it [called *Ślad* (*Trace*)]. Less than twenty years later Irena threw herself from the balcony of her eighth-floor Łódź apartment... Working on the exhibition about one sick woman I could not keep myself from remembering the other." Rottenberg, *Prosze bardzo* (Warsaw: W.A.B., 2009), 297.
12. Jakubowska, *Portret wielokrotny dzieła Aliny Szapocznikow*, 8. Translated by Krystyna Mazur.
13. Jola Gola, *Katalog rzeźb Aliny Szapocznikow* (Kraków: Muzeum Narodowe w Krakowie, 2001).
14. For additional information, see Gola, "Chronology of Alina Szapocznikow's Life and Work," elsewhere in this volume.
15. Solo exhibitions were organized by Galerie Gisela Capitain, Cologne, Germany (2007), and BROADWAY 1602, New York (2007/08 and 2010).
16. The exhibition owes many of its interpretive clues to Jakubowska's *Portret wielokrotny dzieła Aliny Szapocznikow*.
17. Szapocznikow, statement, March 1972, "Mon oeuvre puise ses racines...," signed typescript. See page 28, elsewhere in this volume.
18. "Alina Szapocznikow. Dokumenty. Prace. Interpretacje." (Alina Szapocznikow. Documents. Works. Interpretations.), an international conference at Museum of Modern Art, Warsaw, May 15–16, 2009. Transcribed texts are published in *Alina Szapocznikow. Awkward Objects*.
19. Griselda Pollock, "Too Early and Too Late: Melting Solids and Traumatic Encryption in the Sculptural Dissolutions of Alina Szapocznikow," in *Alina Szapocznikow. Awkward Objects*, 71–101.

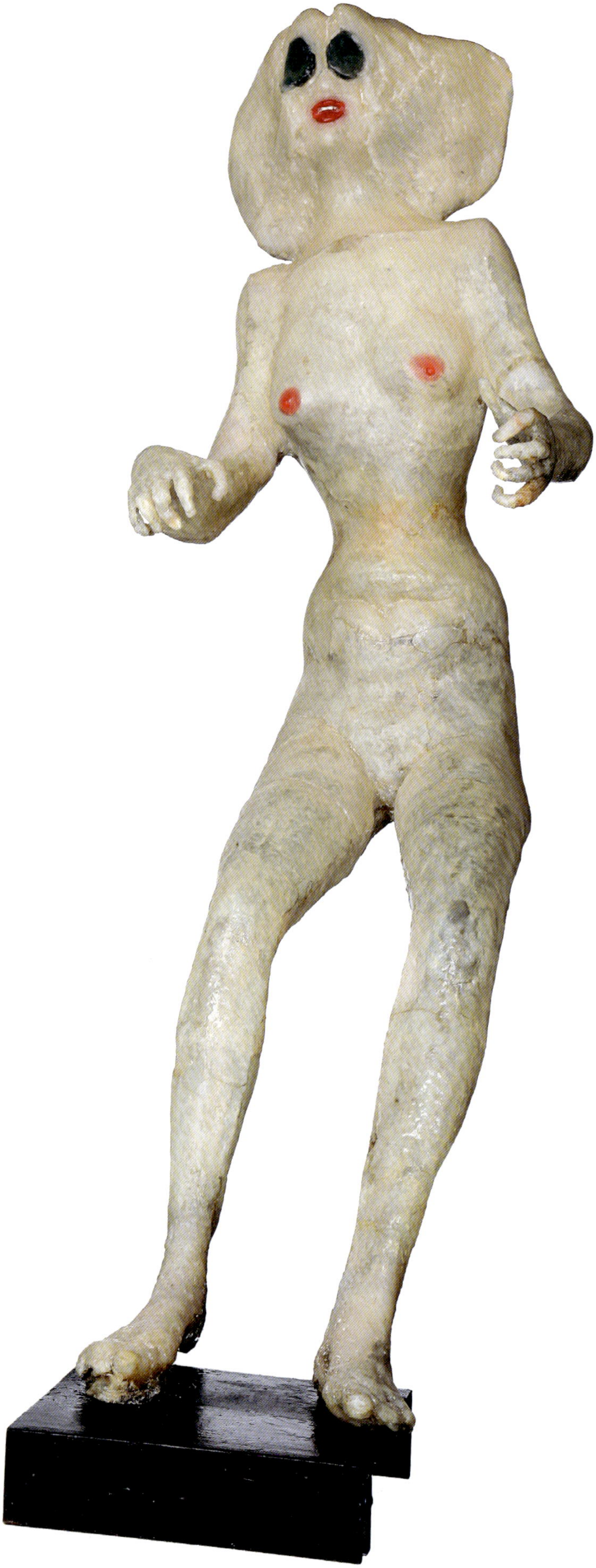

Plate 89

Le Voyage (Journey), 1967
Fiberglass and polyester resin and metal structure
70 7/8 x 43 5/16 x 23 5/8" (180 x 110 x 60 cm)
Muzeum Sztuki, Łódź

opposite
Plate 90

L'Apesanteur (Hommage à Komarow)
(Weightlessness [Homage to Komarov]), 1967
Polyester resin, gauze, metal, photograph
92 1/2 x 27 9/16 x 15 3/4" (235 x 70 x 40 cm)
The National Museum in Wrocław

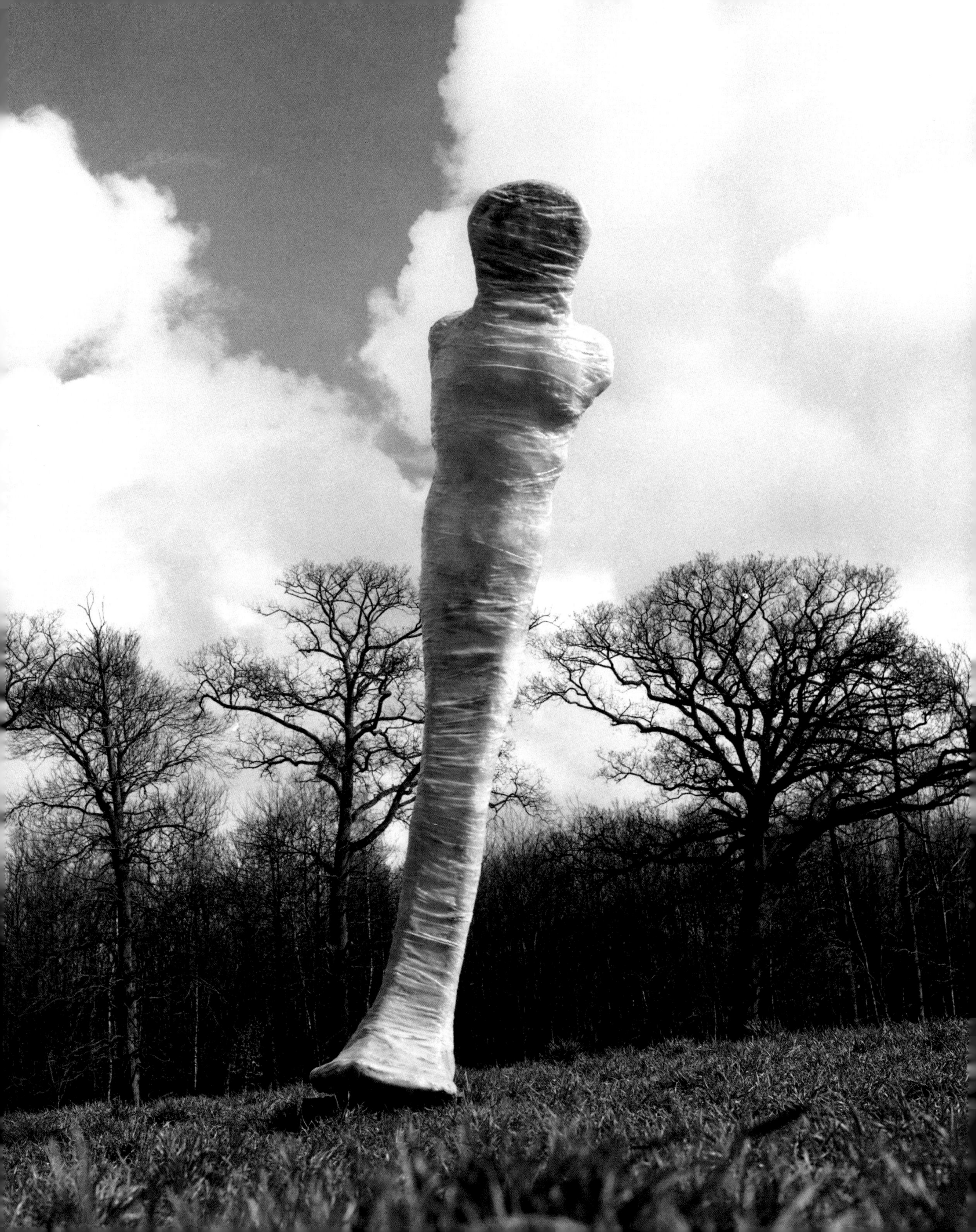

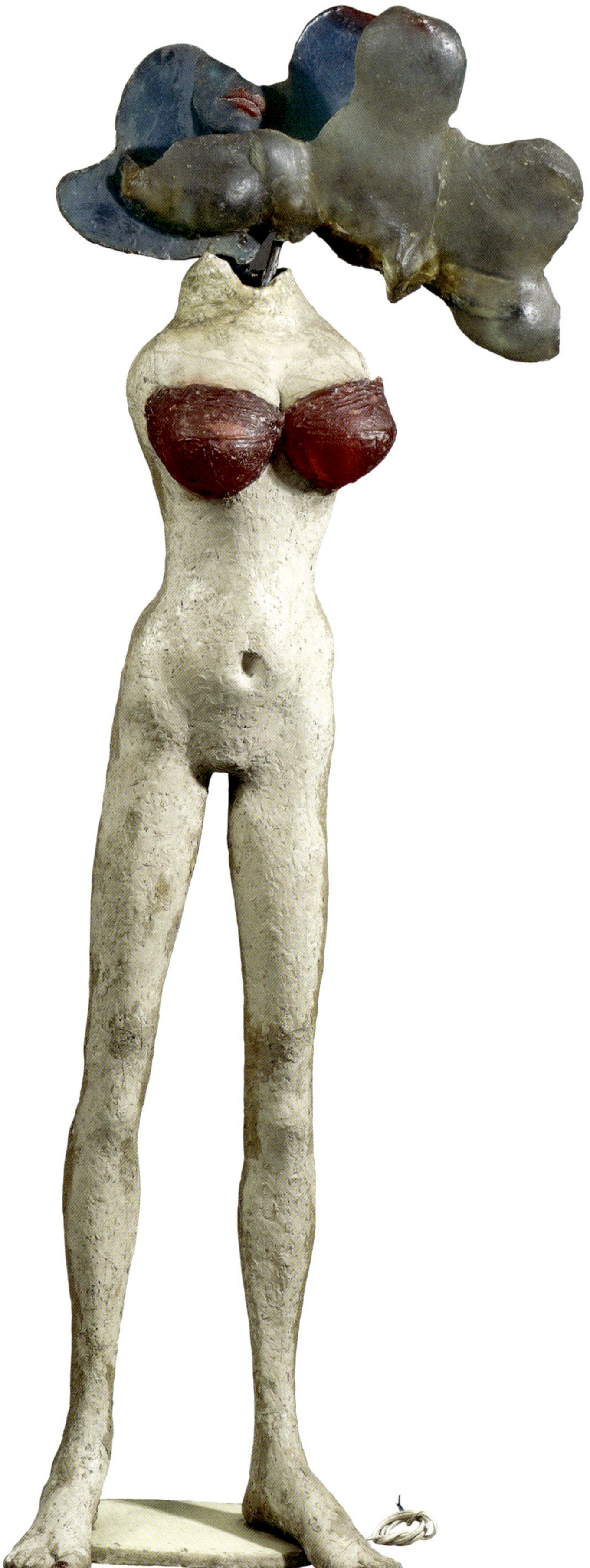

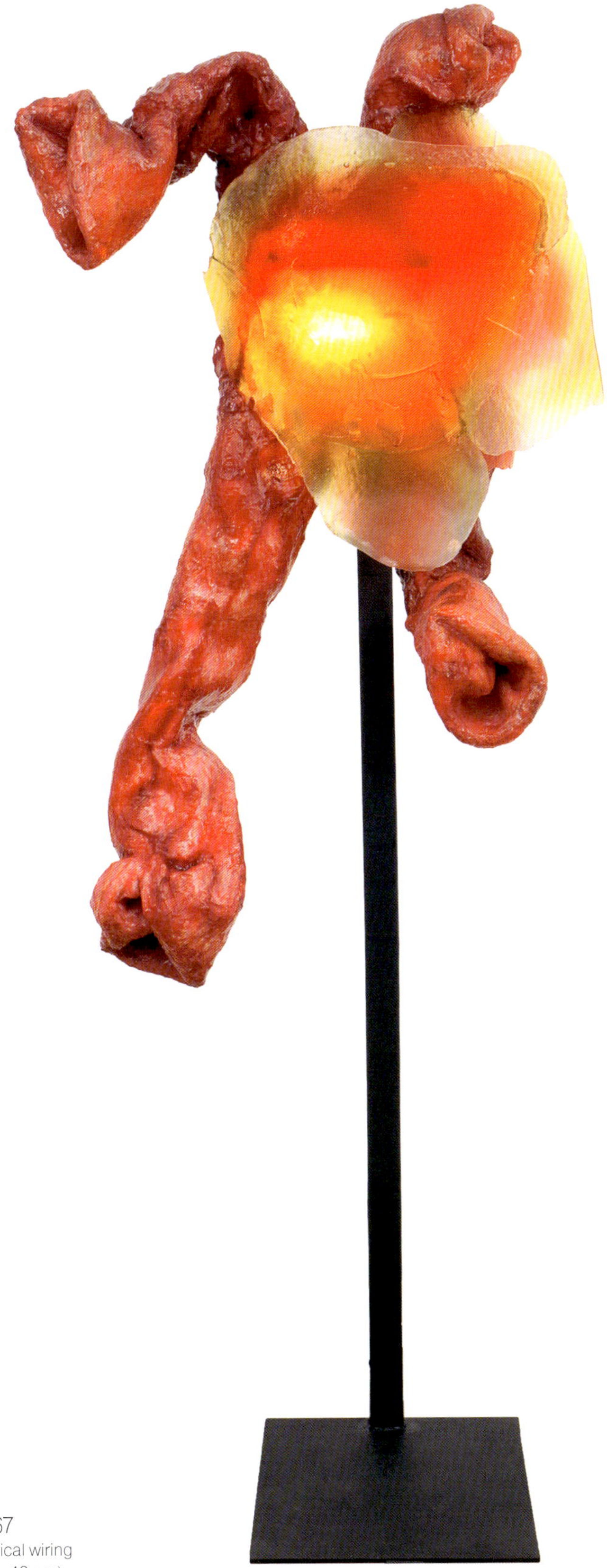

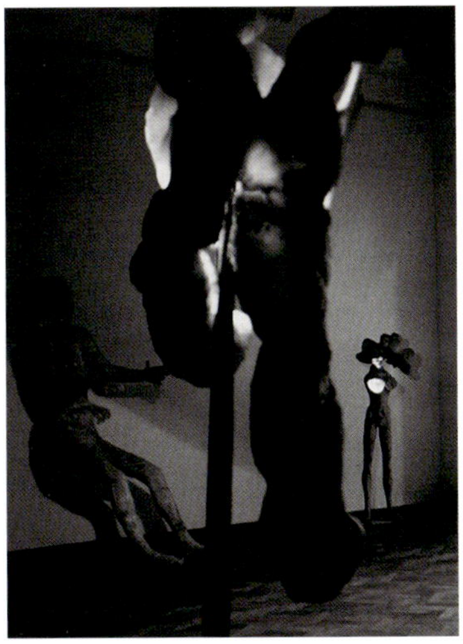

Muzeum Sztuki, Łódź, 1975.

opposite
Plate 91

Femme illuminée
(Illuminated Woman), 1966–67
Plaster, colored polyester resin, electrical wiring
61 1/16 x 22 7/16 x 15 3/4" (155 x 57 x 40 cm)

above
Plate 92

Caprice – Monstre (Caprice – Monster), 1967
Sponge, polyester resin, metal, electrical wiring
78 3/4" (200 cm) high

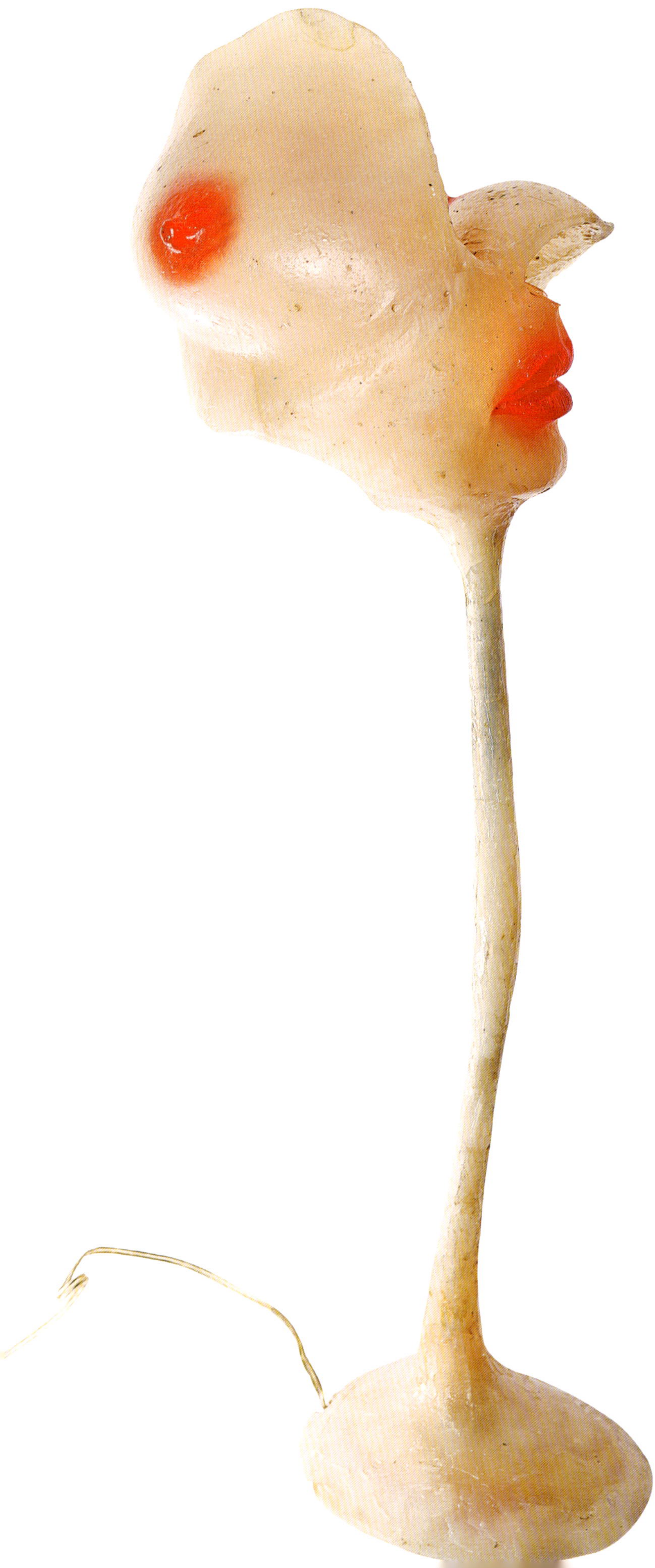

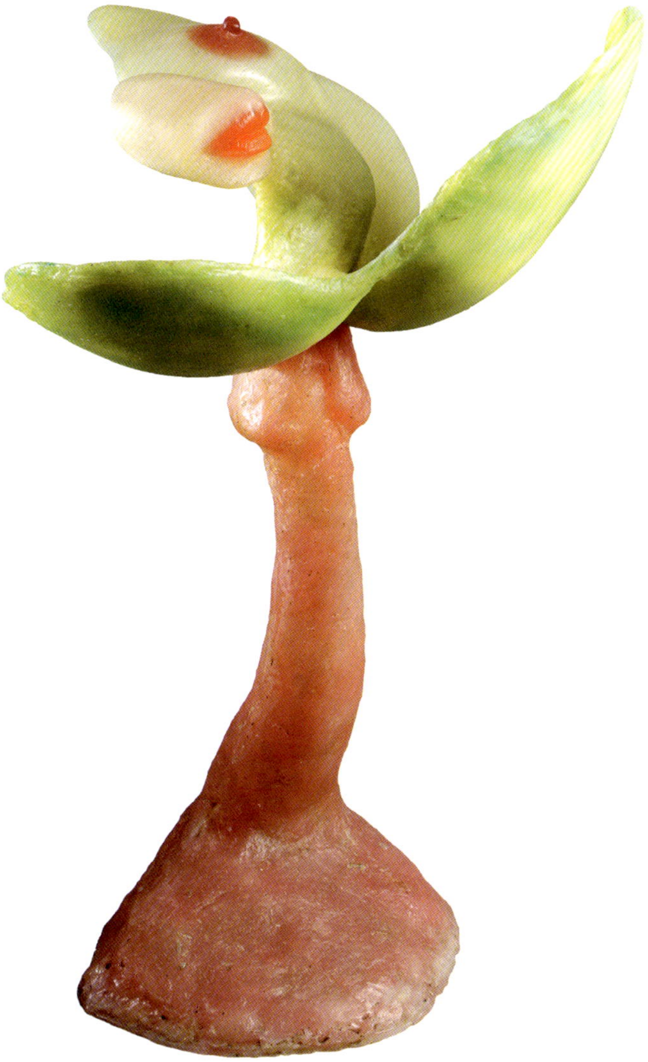

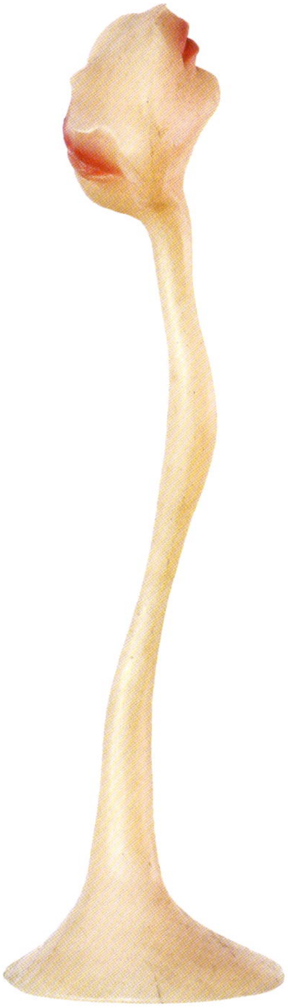

opposite

Plate 93

Sein illuminé (Illuminated Breast), 1966
Colored polyester resin and electrical wiring
22 1/16 x 6 7/8 x 6 5/16" (56 x 17.5 x 16 cm)

above left

Plate 94

Sculpture – Lampe VI (Sculpture – Lamp VI), 1970
Colored polyester resin and electrical wiring
22 1/16 x 12 5/8 x 13 13/16" (56 x 32 x 35 cm)

above right

Plate 95

Bouches en Marche (Marching Lips), c. 1966
Polyester resin
20 7/8" (53 cm) high

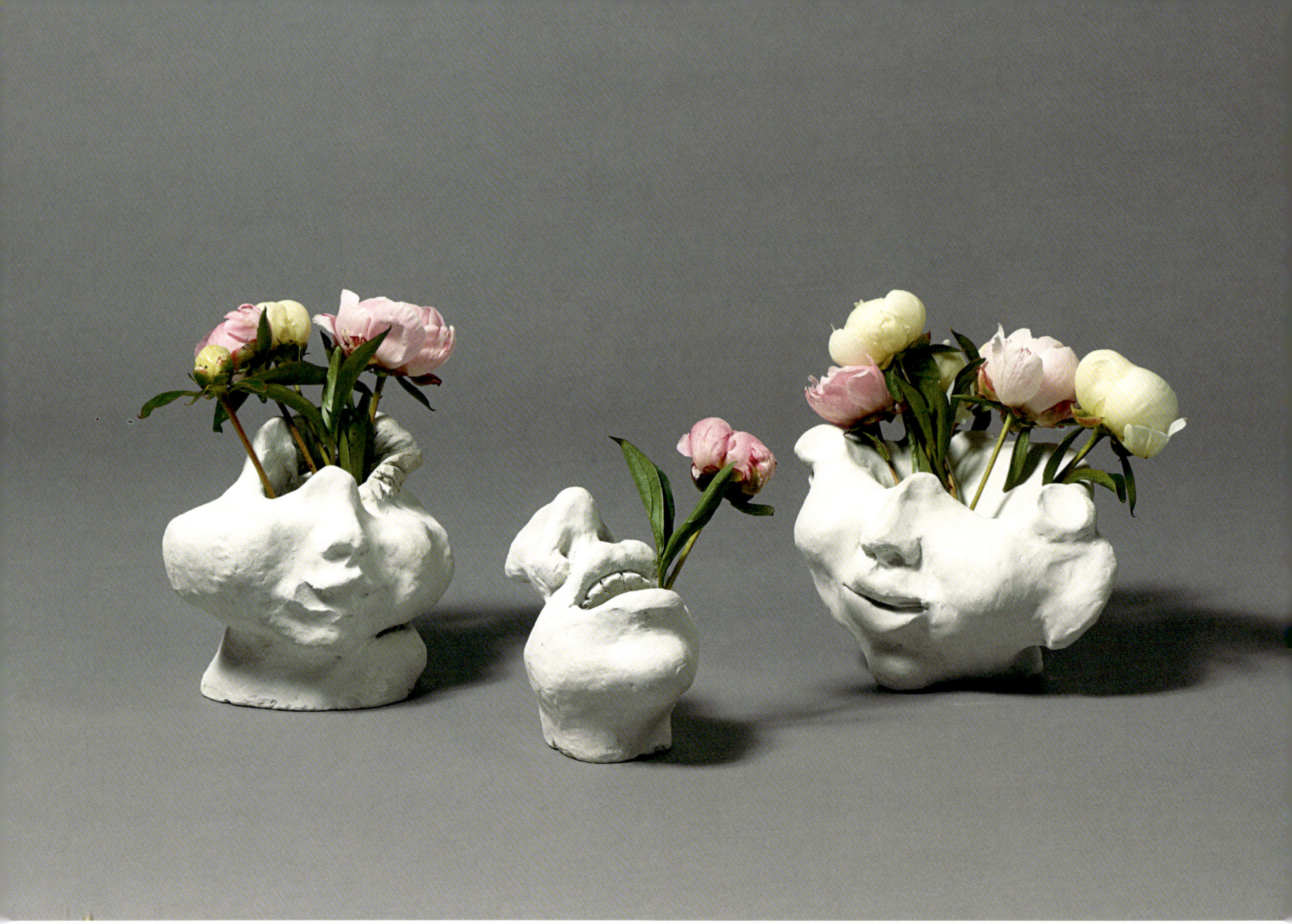

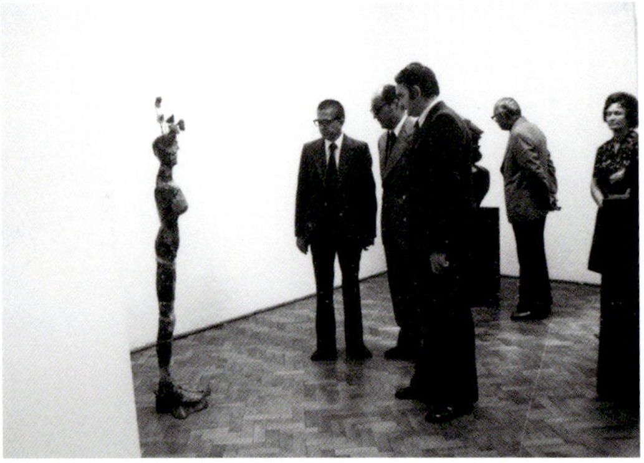

Muzeum Sztuki, Łódź, 1975.

Plate 96 a, b, c

From left to right

Ceramika II (Ceramic II), *Ceramika I* (Ceramic I), and *Ceramika III* (Ceramic III), all 1965

Terracotta

6 11/16 x 7 7/8 x 5 15/16" (17 x 20 x 15 cm),
5 3/4 x 3 15/16 x 6 11/16" (14.5 x 10 x 17 cm),
and 5 1/2 x 9 1/16 x 6 11/16" (14 x 23 x 17 cm)

opposite

Plate 97

Bouquet II, 1966

Plaster, plastic foil, colored polyester resin, metal

65 x 19 11/16 x 14 3/16" (165 x 50 x 36 cm)

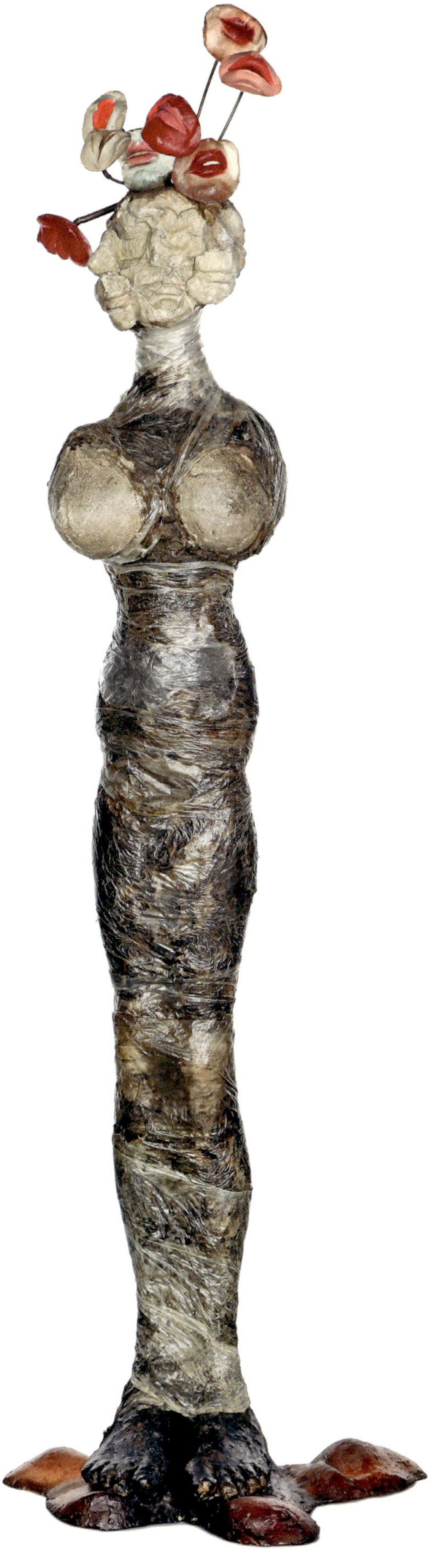

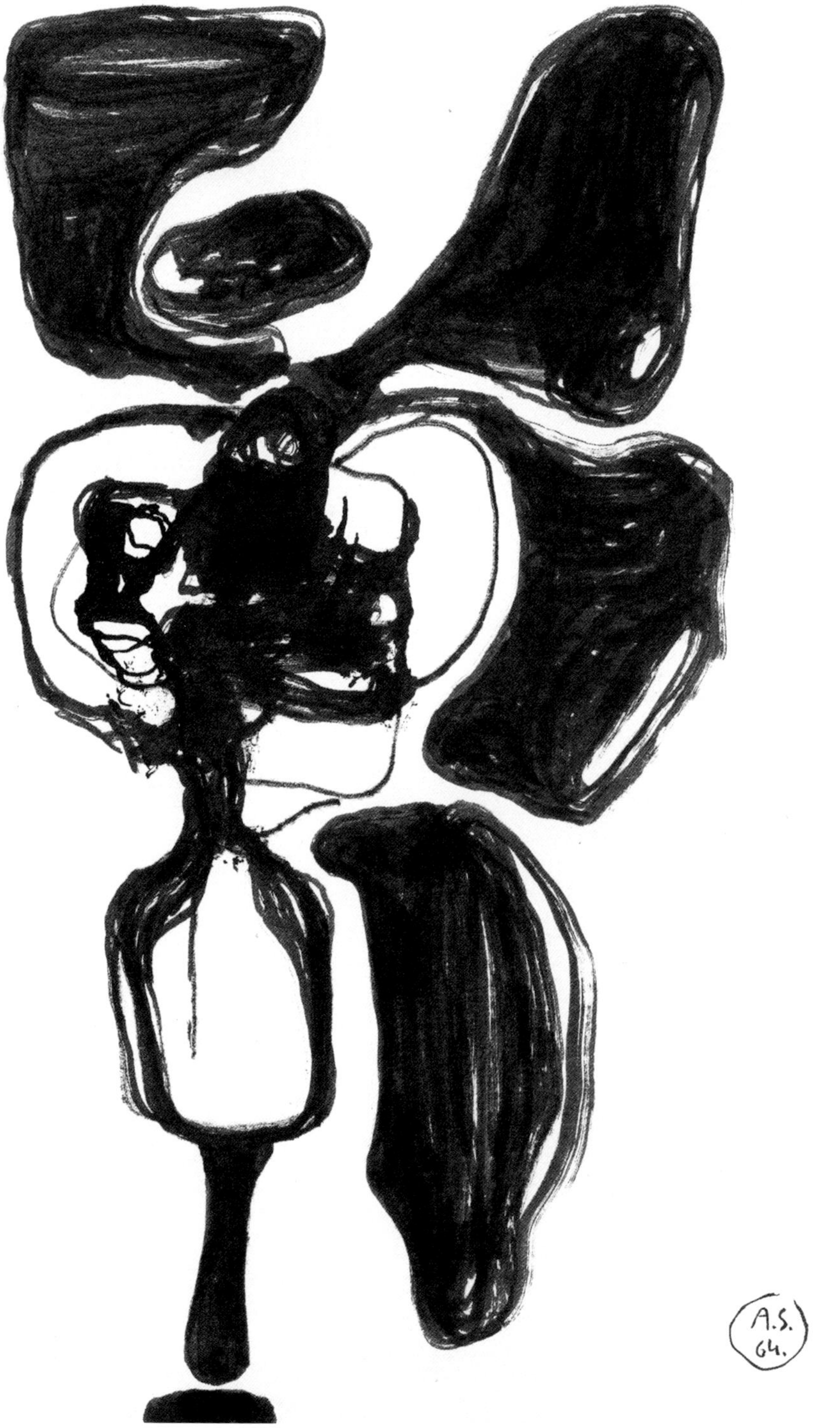

Plate 98

Untitled (Study of Forms with Elements of Industrial Origin 4), 1964
Ink and felt-tip pen on paper
12 5/16 x 9 1/4" (31.2 x 23.4 cm)

opposite
Plate 99

Człowiek z instrumentem (Man with Instrument), 1965
Cement, car part, black patina
58 1/4 x 15 3/4 x 13 13/16" (148 x 40 x 35 cm)

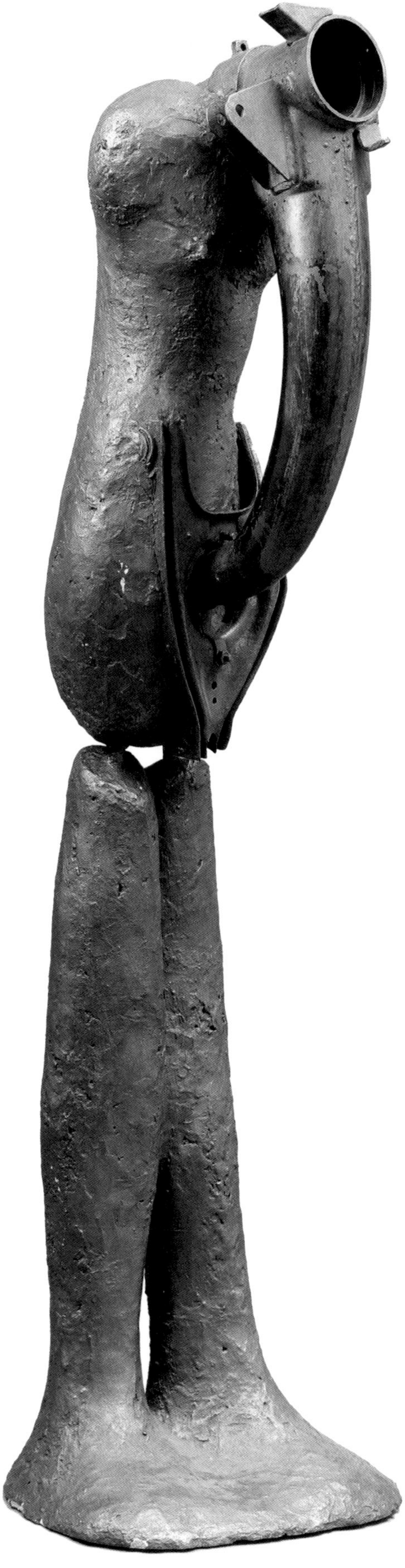

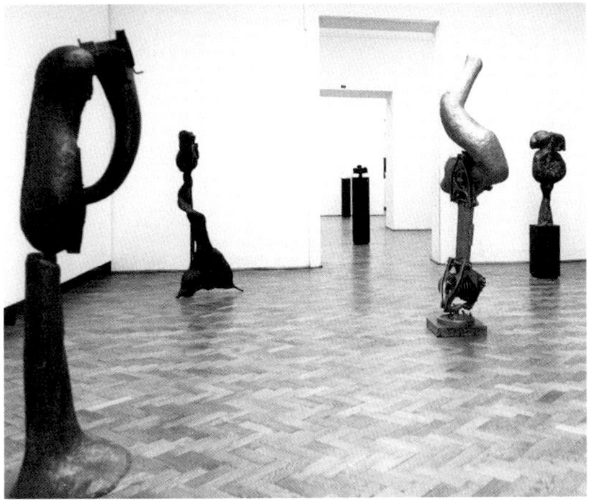

Muzeum Sztuki, Łódź, 1975.

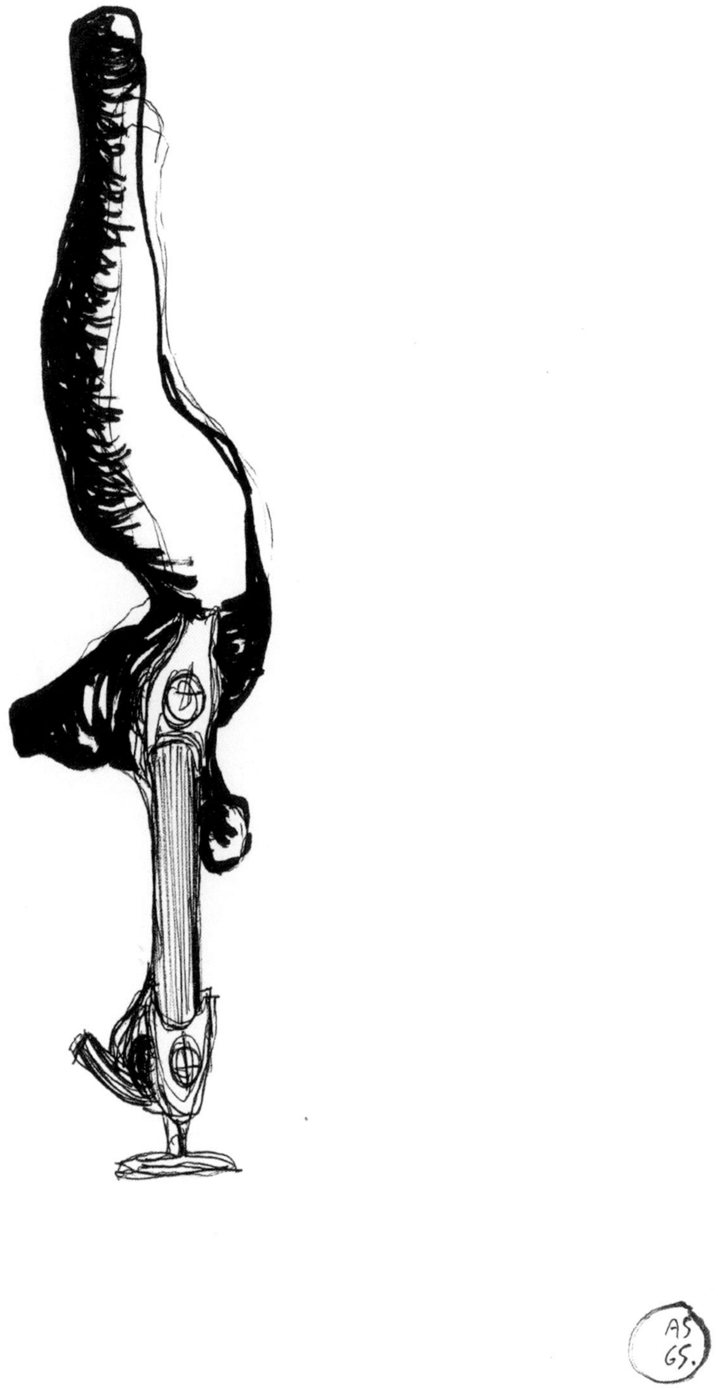

Plate 100

Untitled (Sketch for *Goldfinger* 1), 1965
Ballpoint pen and felt-tip pen on paper
10 5/8 x 7 11/16" (27 x 19.5 cm)

opposite
Plate 101

Goldfinger, 1965
Gold patinated cement and car part
72 1/16 x 29 15/16 x 22 7/16" (183 x 76 x 57 cm)

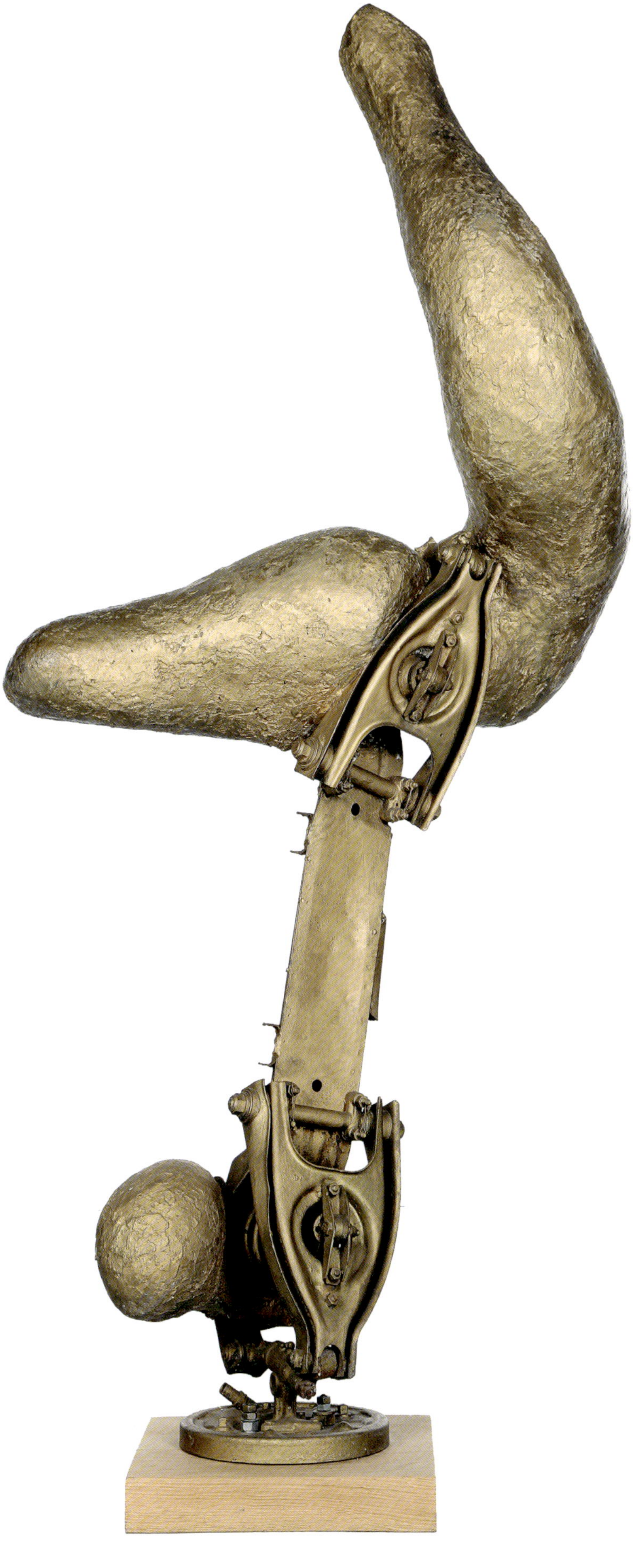

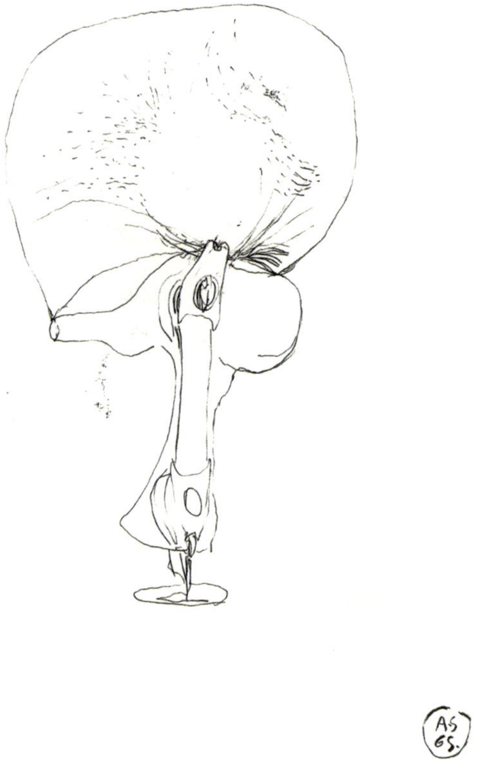

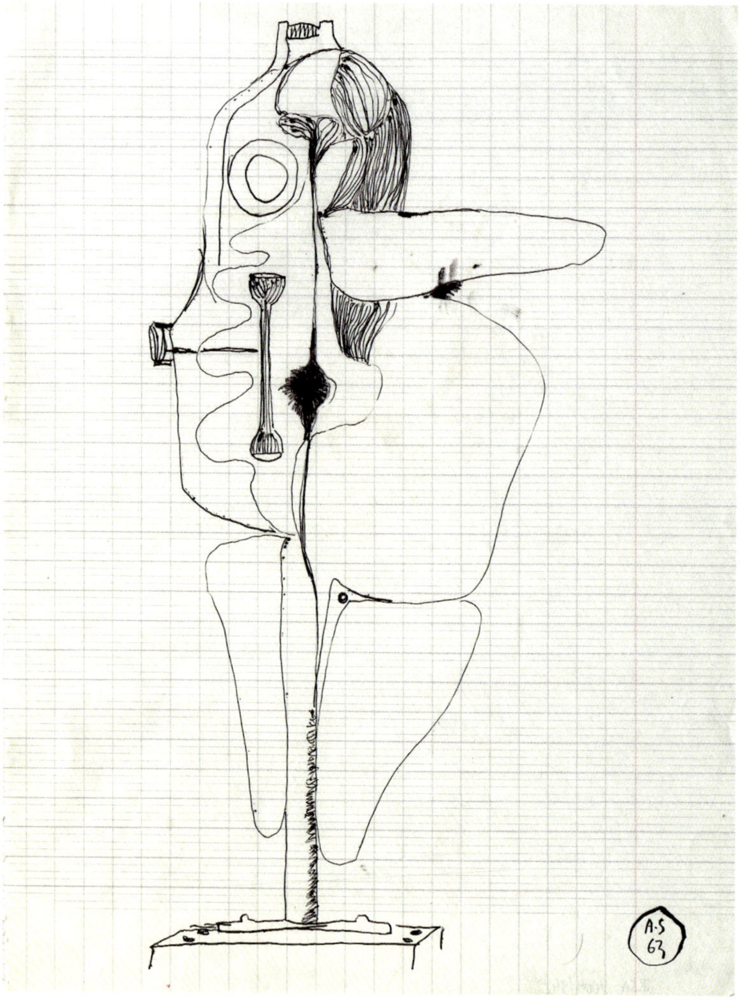

left

Plate 102

Untitled (Sketch of a Sculpture with Car Shock Absorber), 1965

Ballpoint pen on paper

10 5/8 x 8 3/16" (26.9 x 20.8 cm)

right

Plate 103

Untitled (Sketch of a Sculpture with “Industrial” Elements), 1963

Ballpoint pen on graph paper

10 5/8 x 8 3/16" (27 x 20.8 cm)

Location unknown

opposite

Plate 104

Dwuczęściowa (In Two Parts), 1965

Plastic cement and car part

16 15/16 x 19 11/16 x 11 1/16" (43 x 50 x 28 cm)

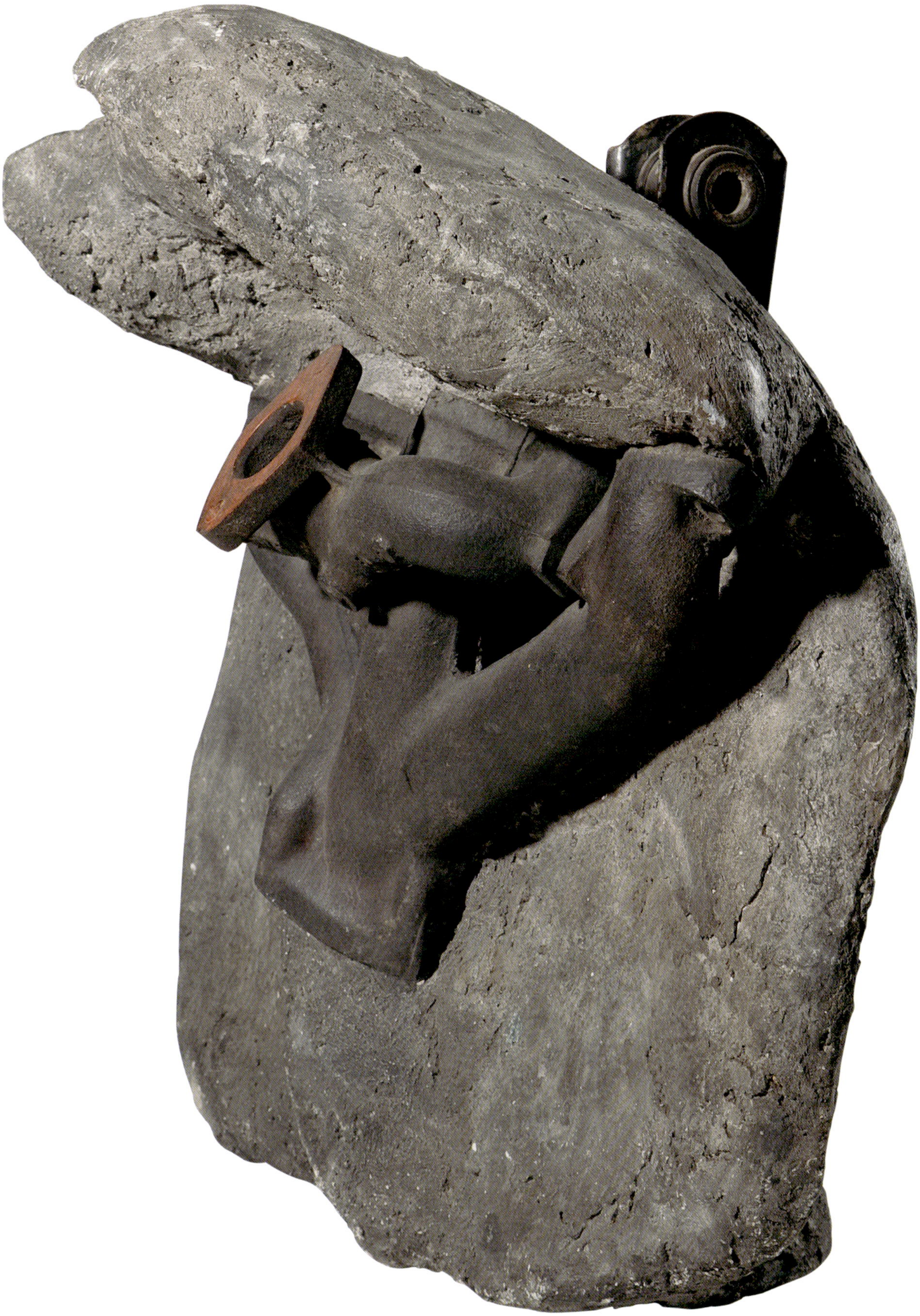

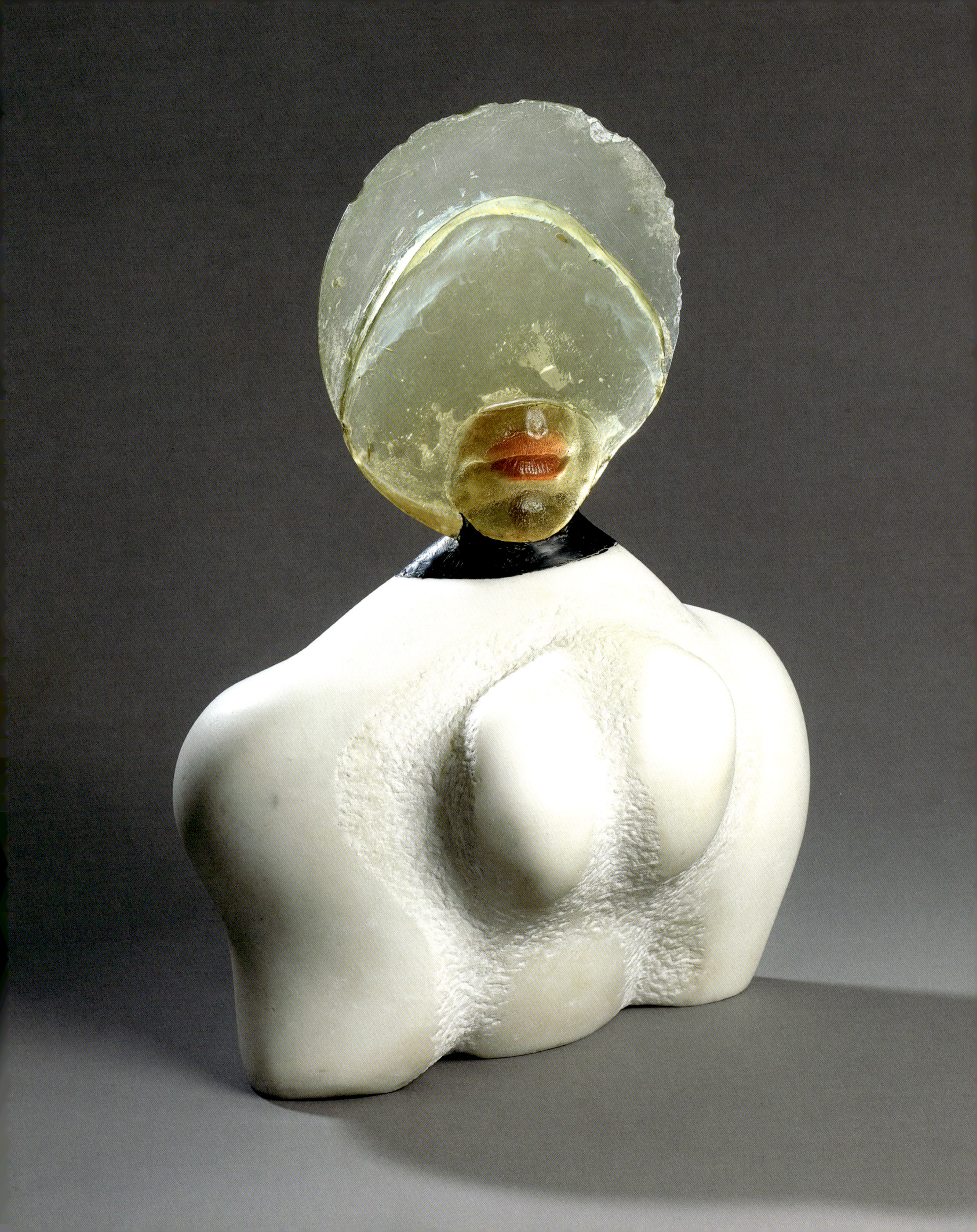

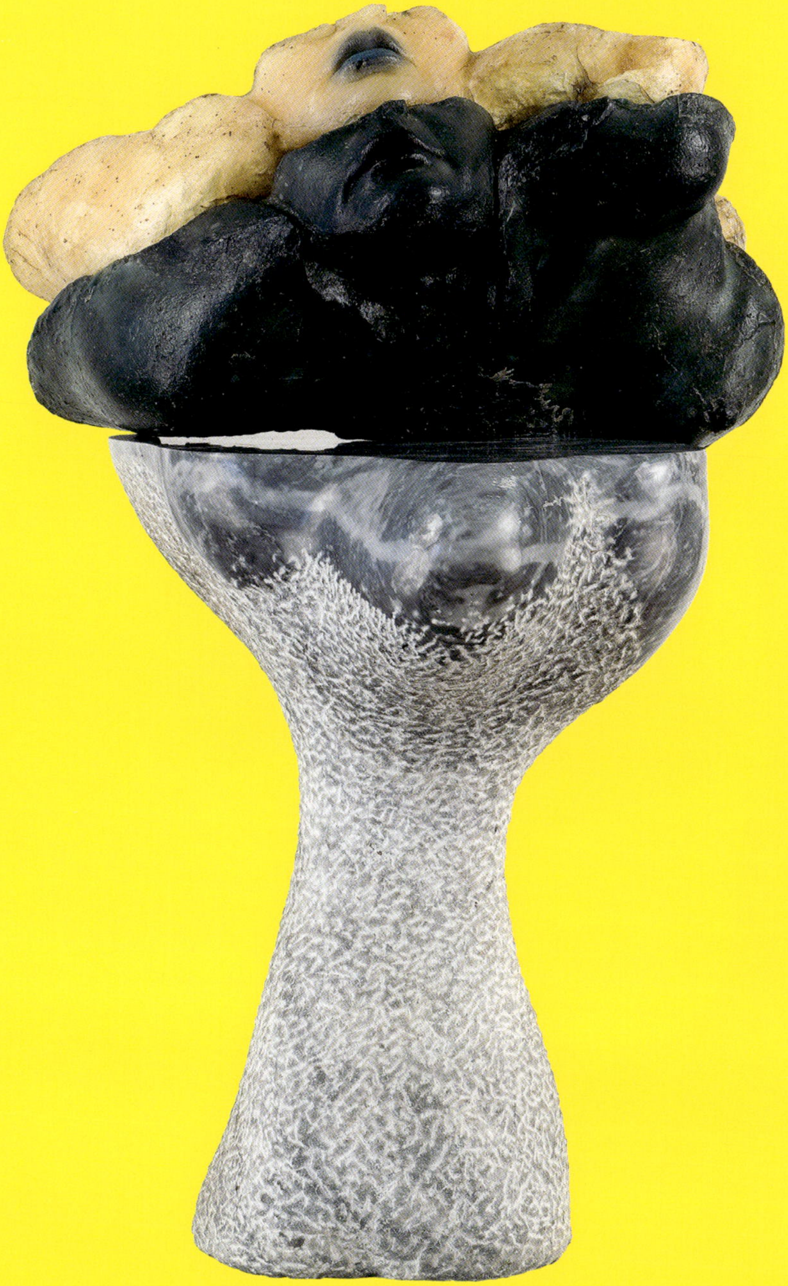

opposite
Plate 105

Autoportret I (Self-Portrait I), 1966
Marble and polyester resin
16 1/8 x 11 13/16 x 7 7/8" (41 x 30 x 20 cm)

above
Plate 106

Portret wielokrotny (dwukrotny) (Multiple Portrait [Double]), 1967
Colored polyester resin and granite
29 x 19 x 17" (73.7 x 48.3 x 43.2 cm)

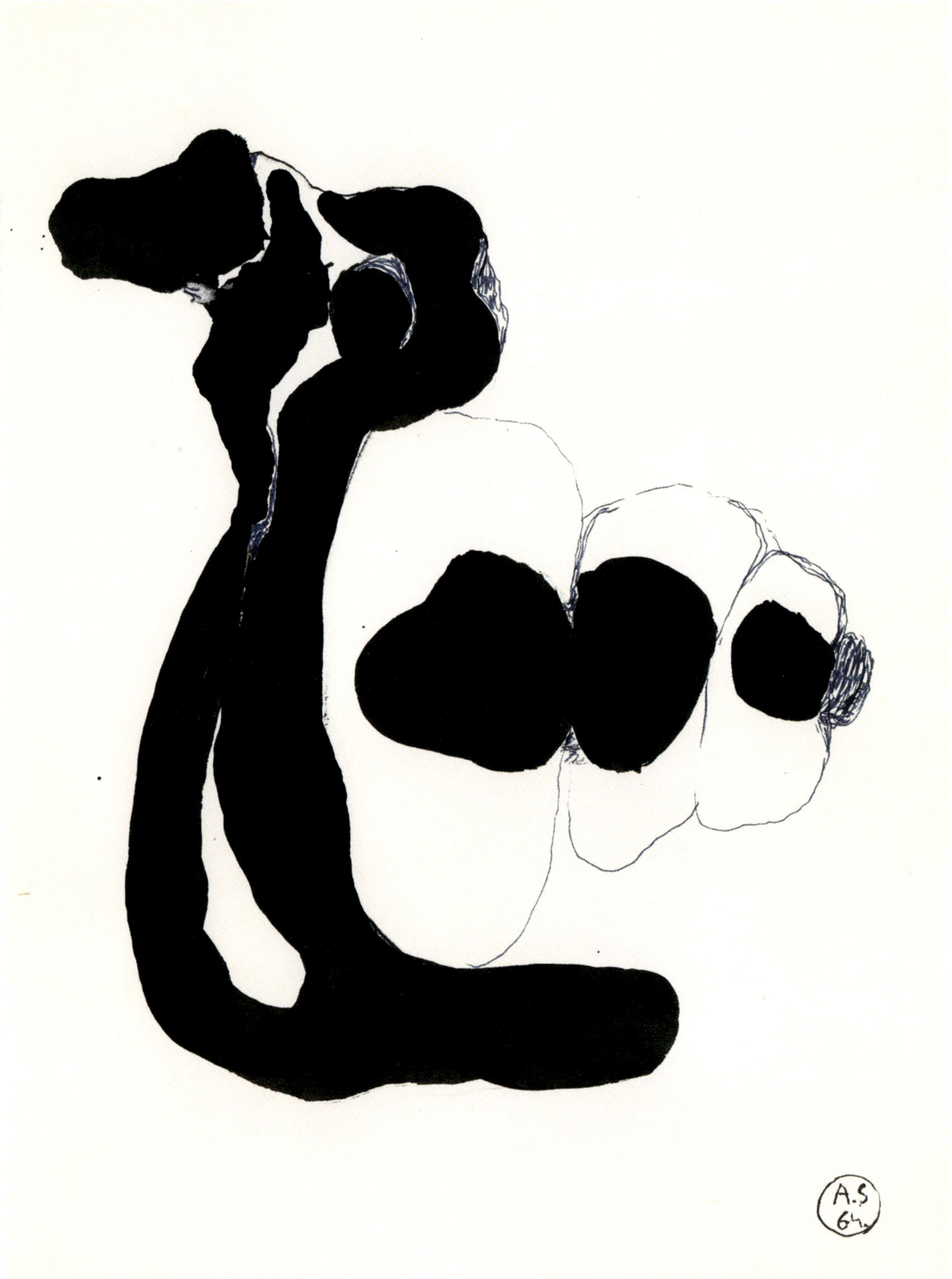

Plate 107

Untitled, 1964

Ink and blue ink on paper

12 5/16 x 9 5/16" (31.3 x 23.6 cm)

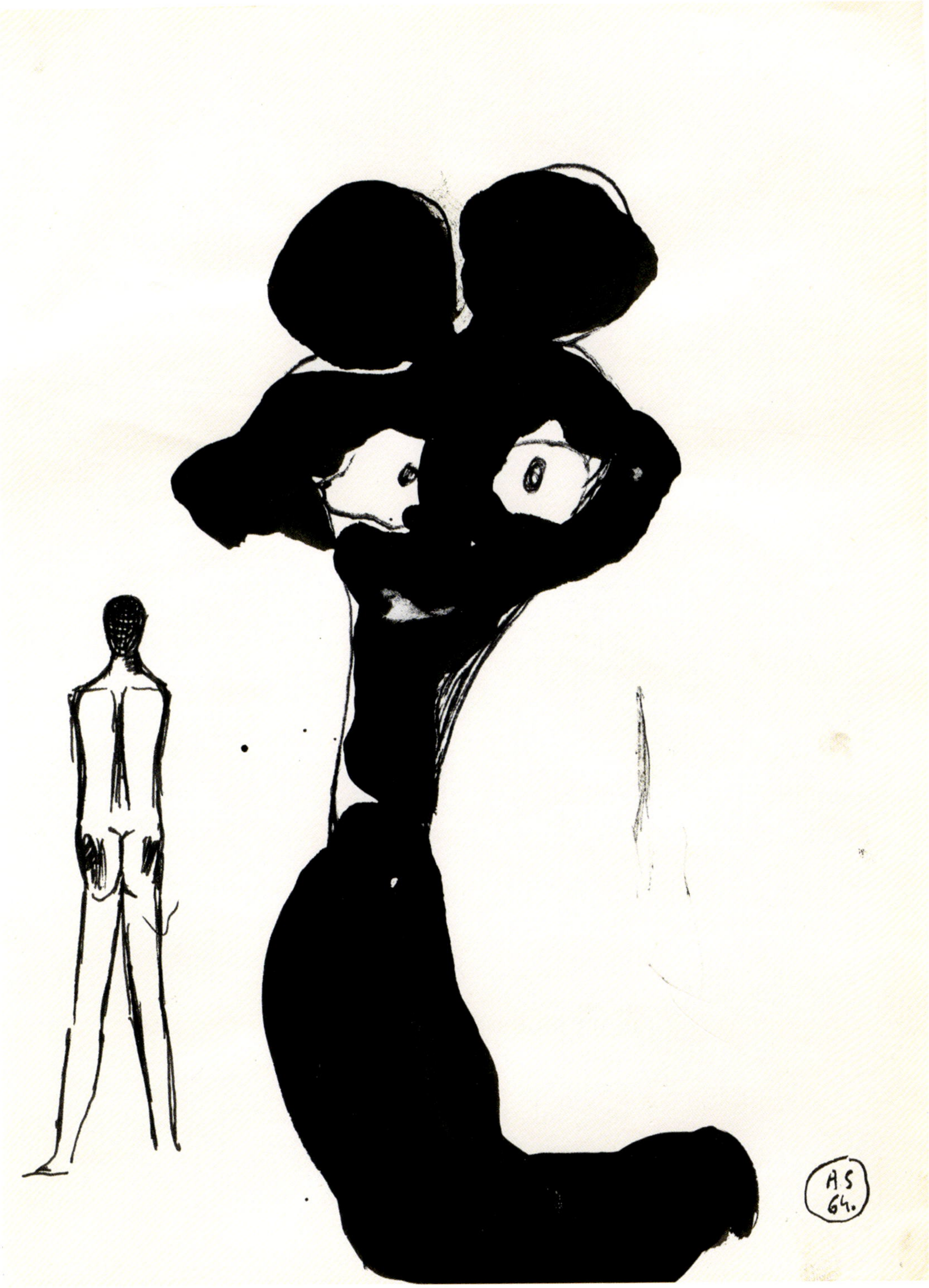

Plate 108

Untitled, 1964
Ink and felt-tip pen on paper
12 3/8 x 9 1/4" (31.4 x 23.4 cm)

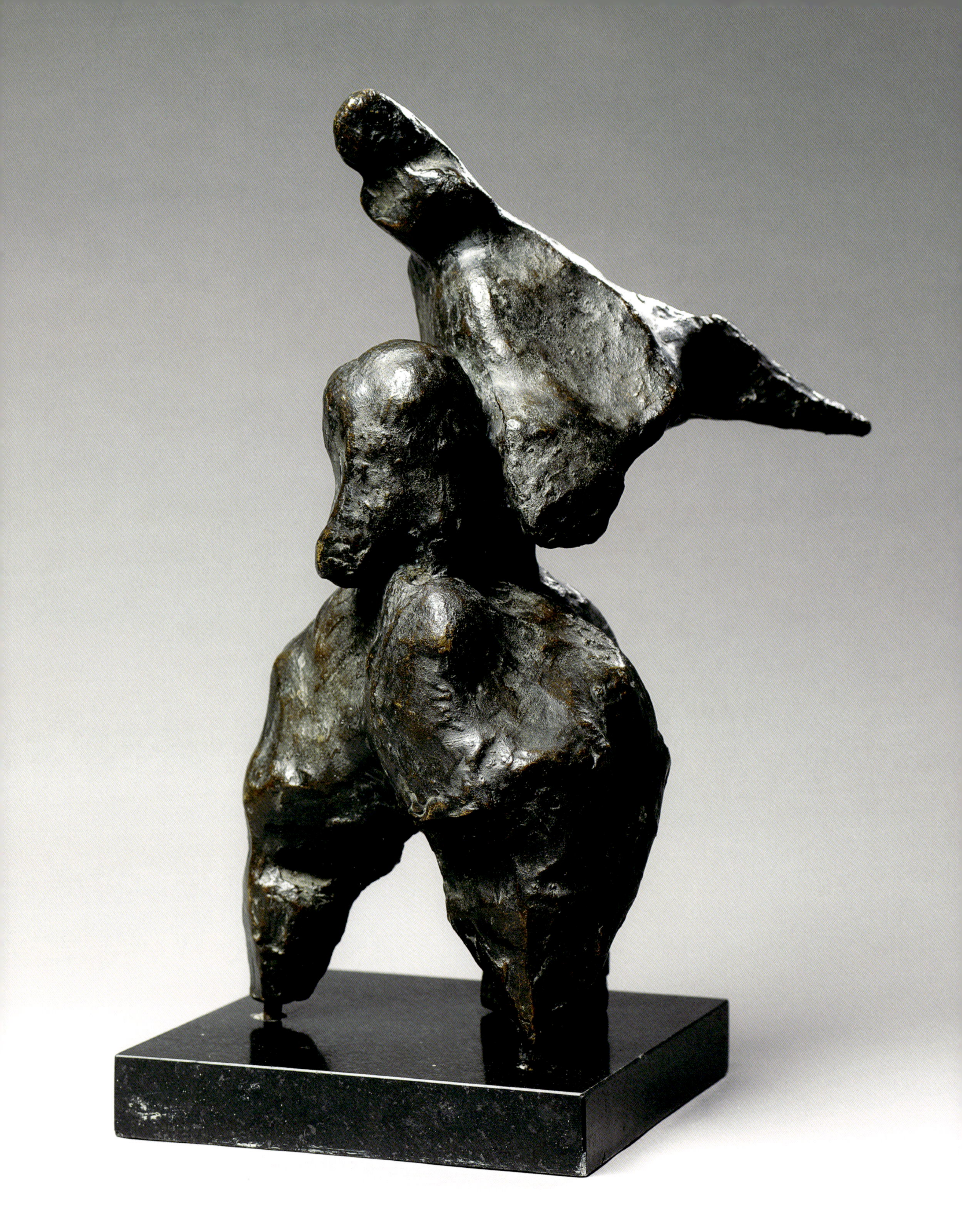

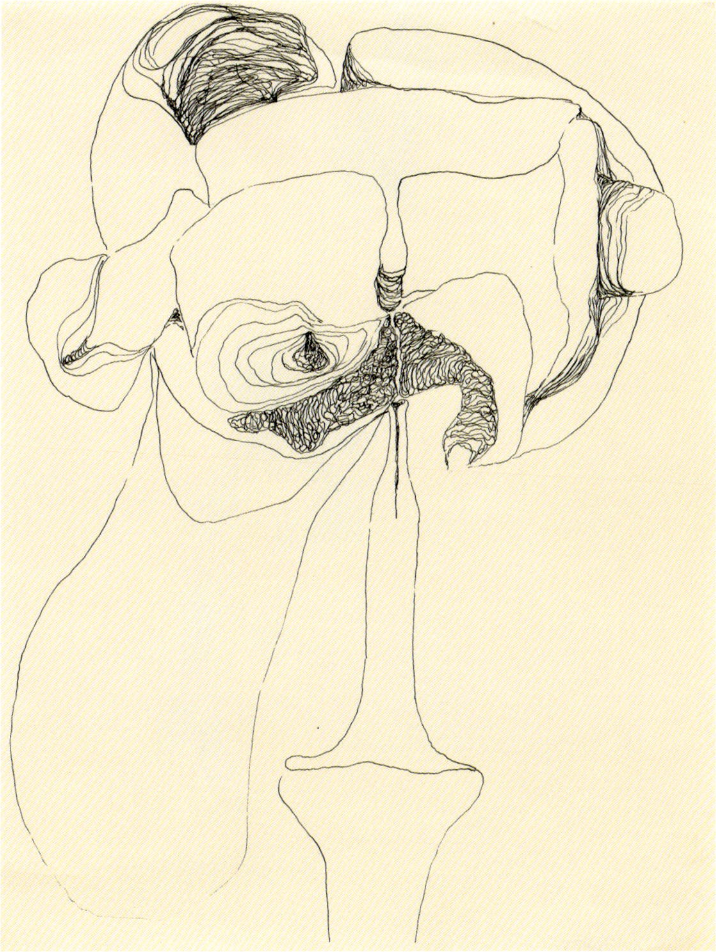

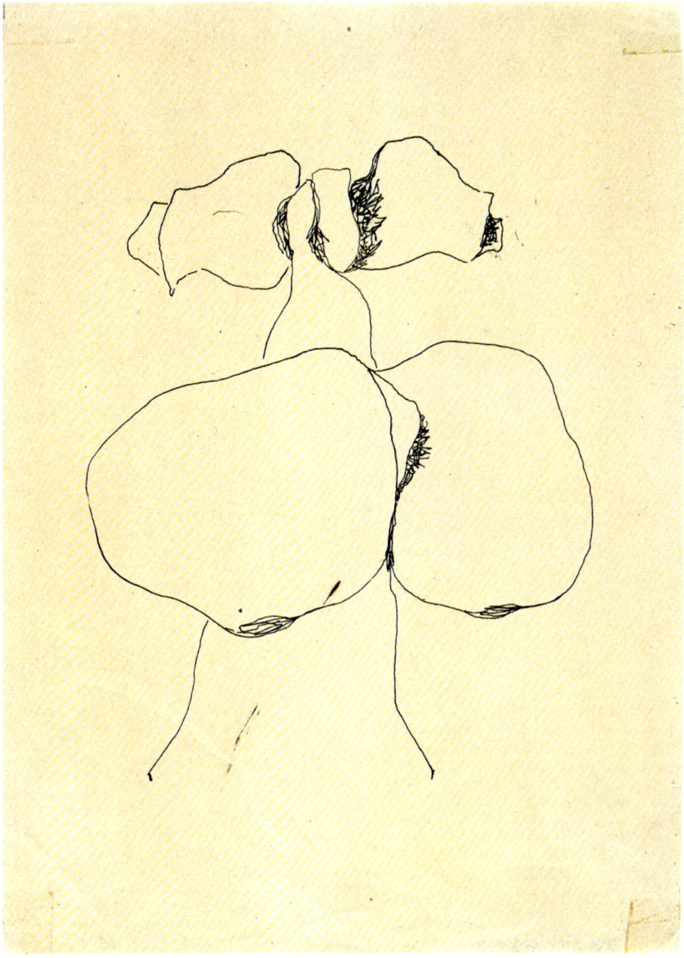

opposite
Plate 109

Balet (Ballet), 1958
Bronze
15 9/16 x 11 13/16 x 8 1/4" (39.5 x 30 x 21 cm)

above left
Plate 110

Untitled, c. 1963–68
Ink on copy paper
10 9/16 x 8 3/16" (26.8 x 20.8 cm)

above right
Plate 111

Untitled, c. 1963–68
Ink on paper
10 5/8 x 7 3/4" (27 x 19.6 cm)

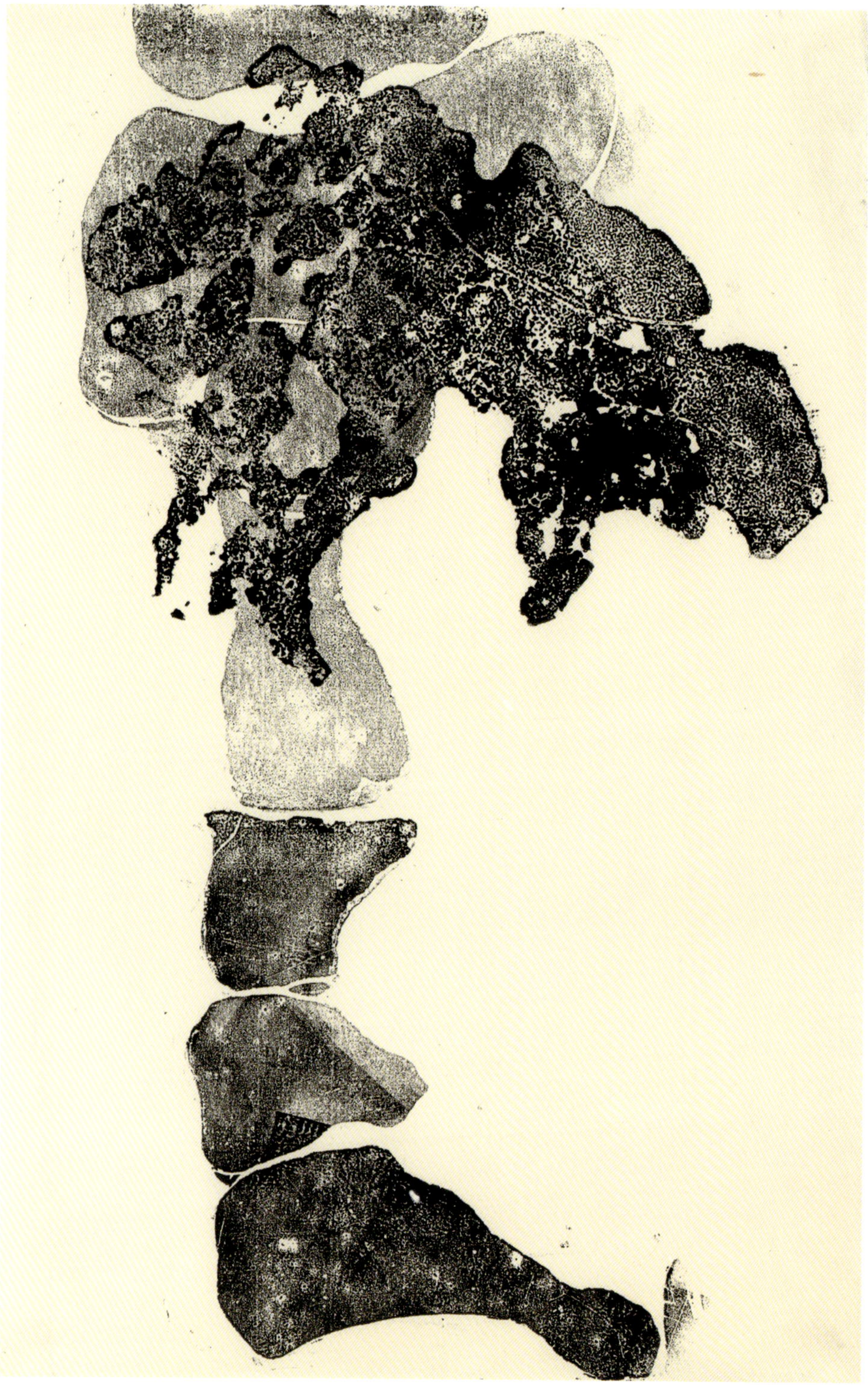

Plate 112

Untitled, c. 1963–65

Monotype and ink on paper

18 11/16 x 12 5/16" (47.5 x 31.2 cm)

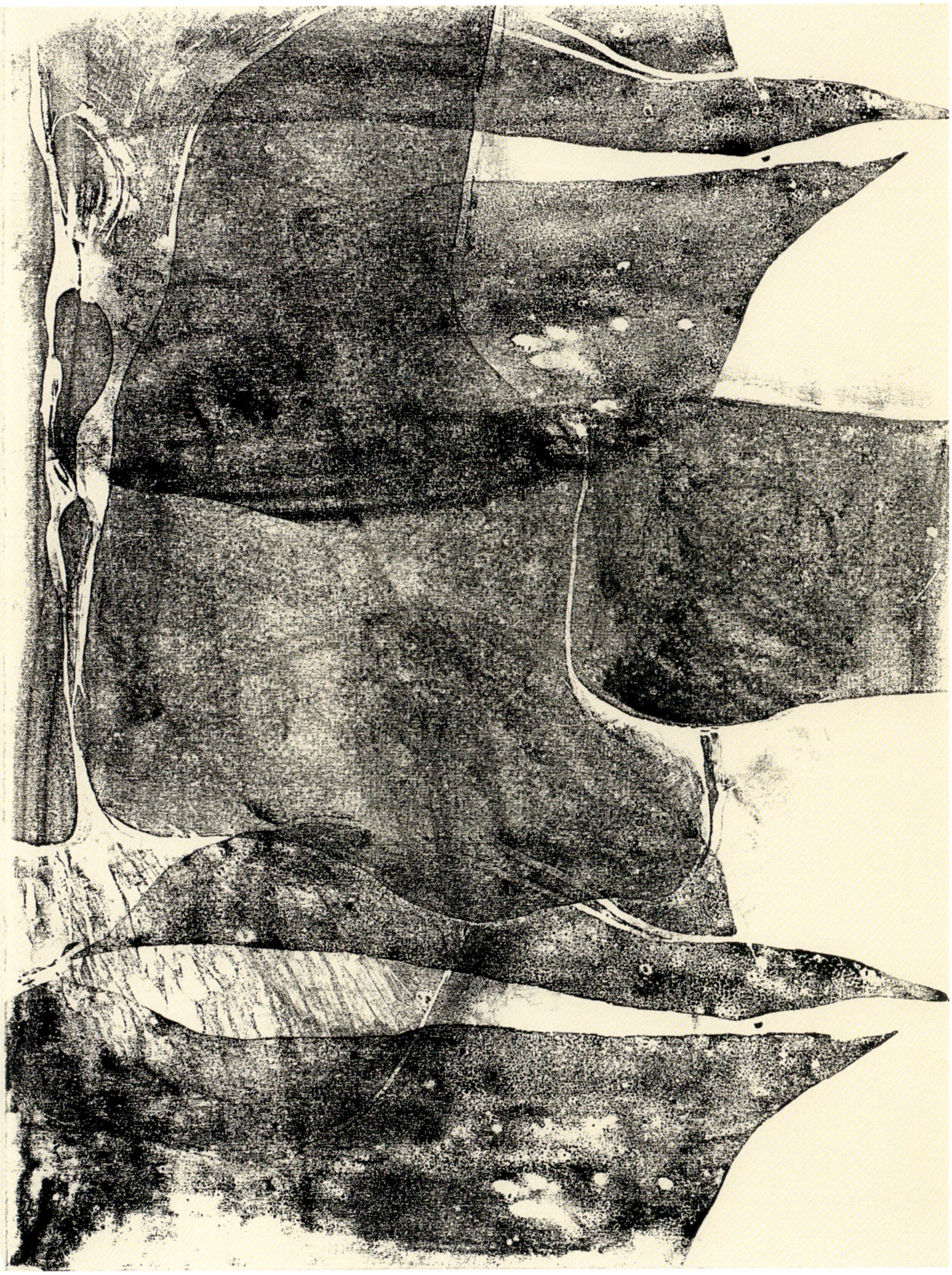

Plate 113

Untitled, c. 1963–65
Monotype and ink on paper
12 5/8 x 9 7/8" (32 x 25 cm)

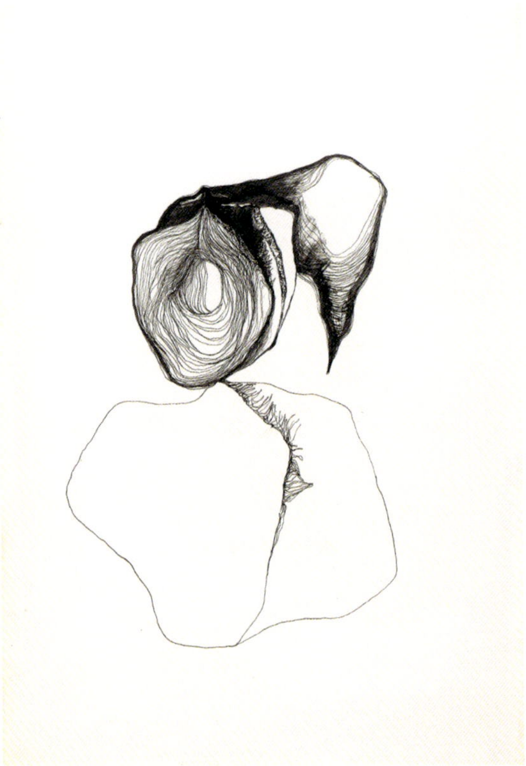

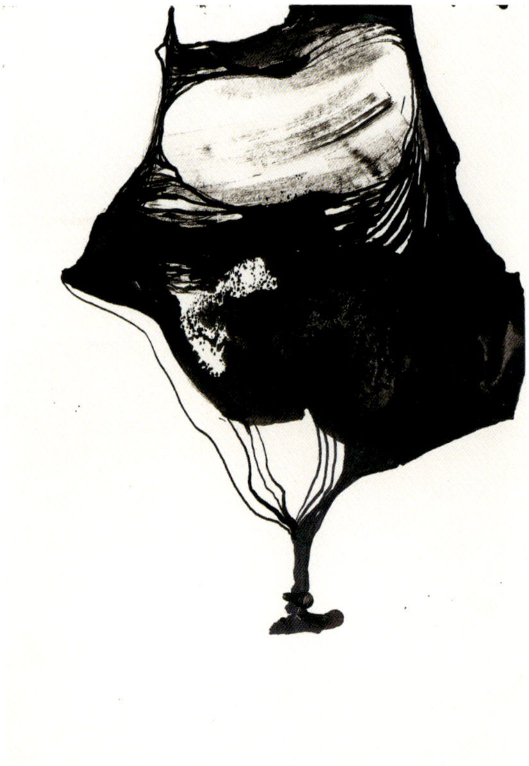

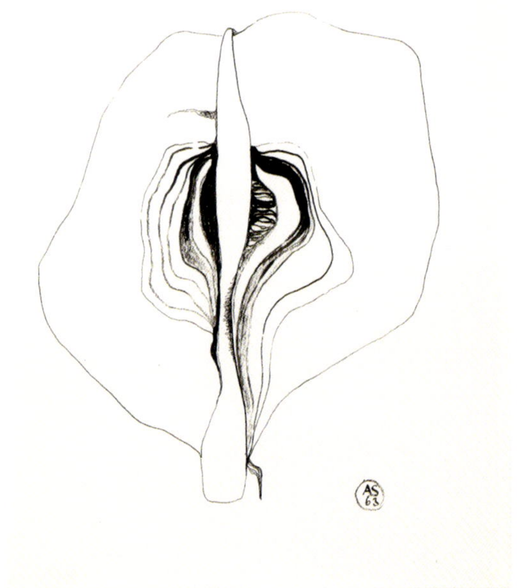

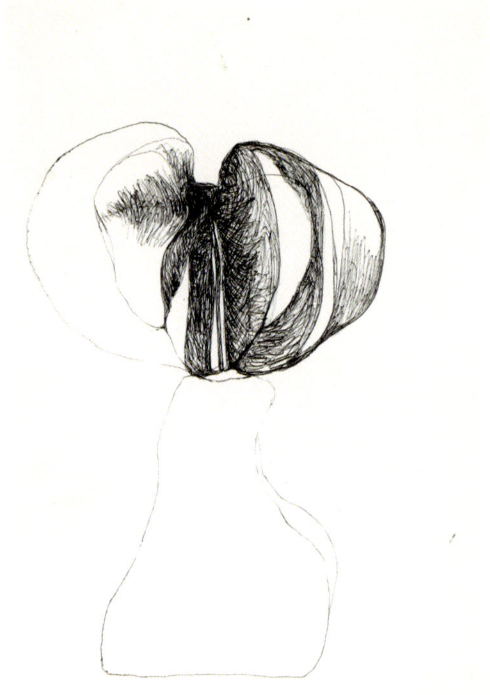

top left
Plate 114
Untitled (Study for a Sculpture 5), c. 1963
Ink on paper
16 9/16 x 11" (42 x 27.9 cm)

top right
Plate 115
Untitled, c. 1960–61
Ink on paper
12 x 8 1/4" (30.4 x 20.9 cm)

bottom left
Plate 116
Untitled, 1963
Felt-tip pen and ink on paper
14 1/8 x 10 9/16" (35.9 x 26.8 cm)

bottom right
Plate 117
Untitled, c. 1963
Ballpoint pen on paper
14 9/16 x 10 9/16" (37 x 26.8 cm)

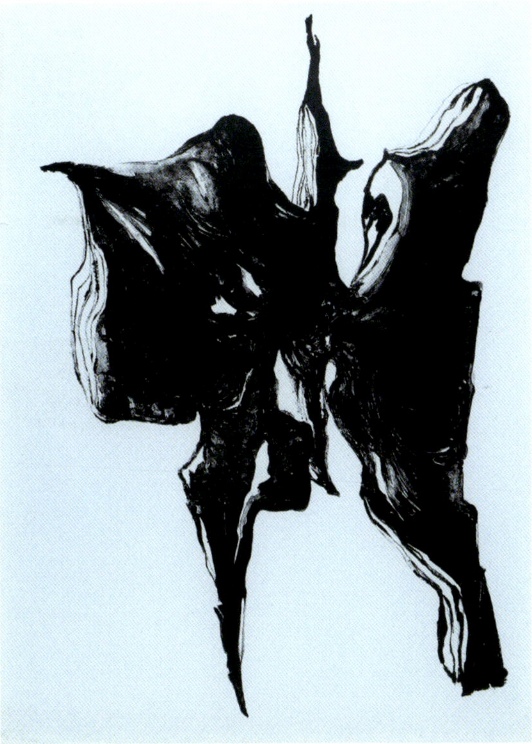

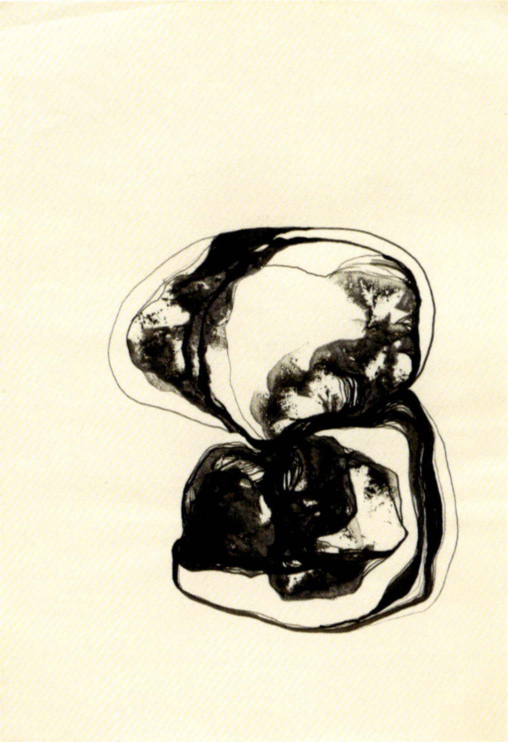

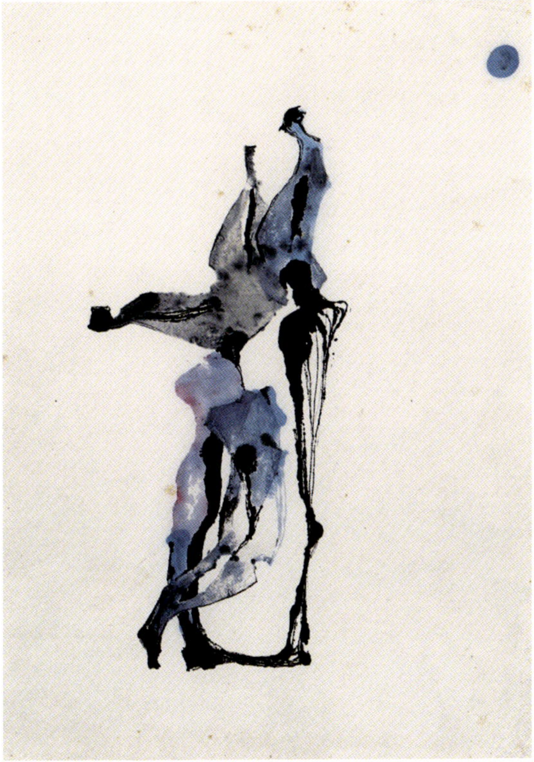

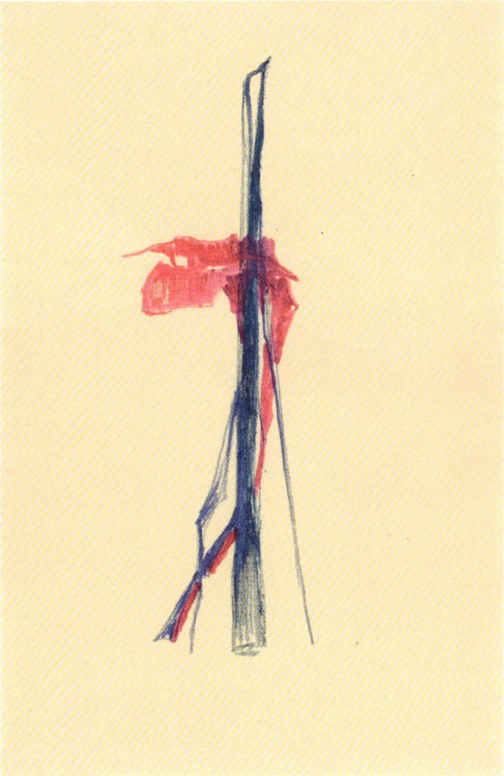

top left
Plate 118
Untitled, c. 1961
Monotype and ink on blue paper
25 13/16 x 18 15/16" (64.6 x 48 cm)

top right
Plate 119
Untitled (Study for a Sculpture 4), c. 1963
Monotype and ink on paper
16 7/16 x 15 9/16" (41.8 x 39.5 cm)

bottom left
Plate 120
Untitled, c. 1960
Ink on blotting paper
13 1/4 x 9 5/8" (33.7 x 24.4 cm)

bottom right
Plate 121
Untitled (Sketches of a Design for a Monument 1), c. 1958–61
Ink, crayon, and felt-tip pen on paper
11 3/4 x 7 7/8" (29.8 x 20 cm)

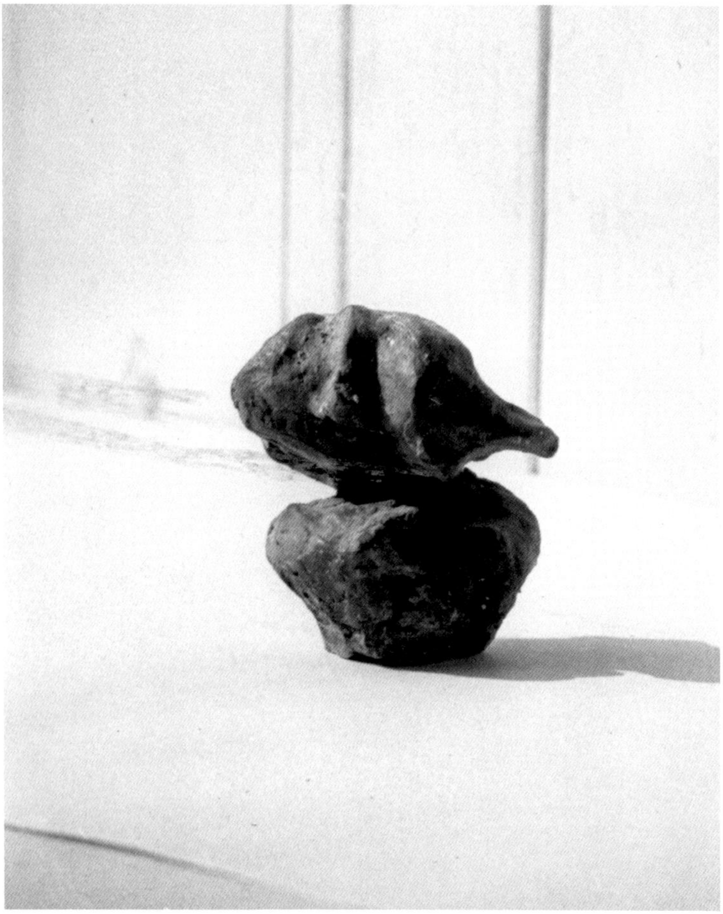
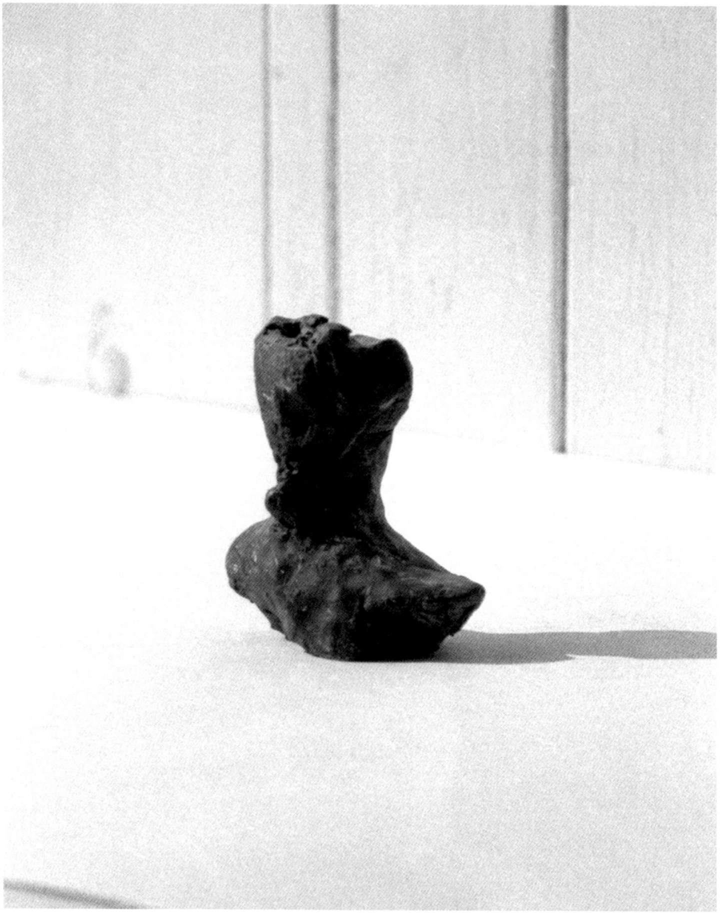
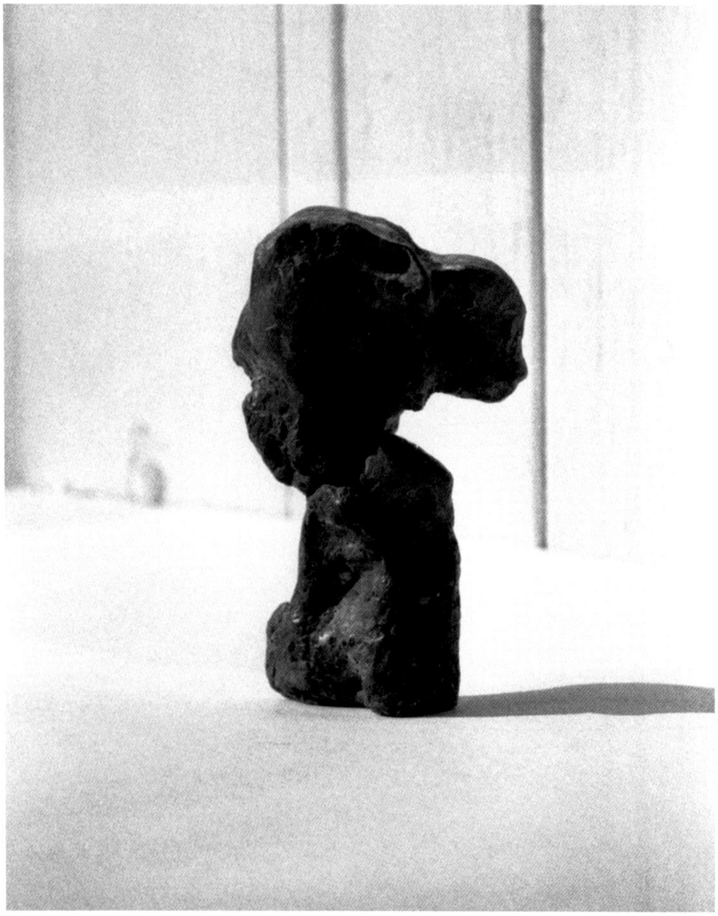
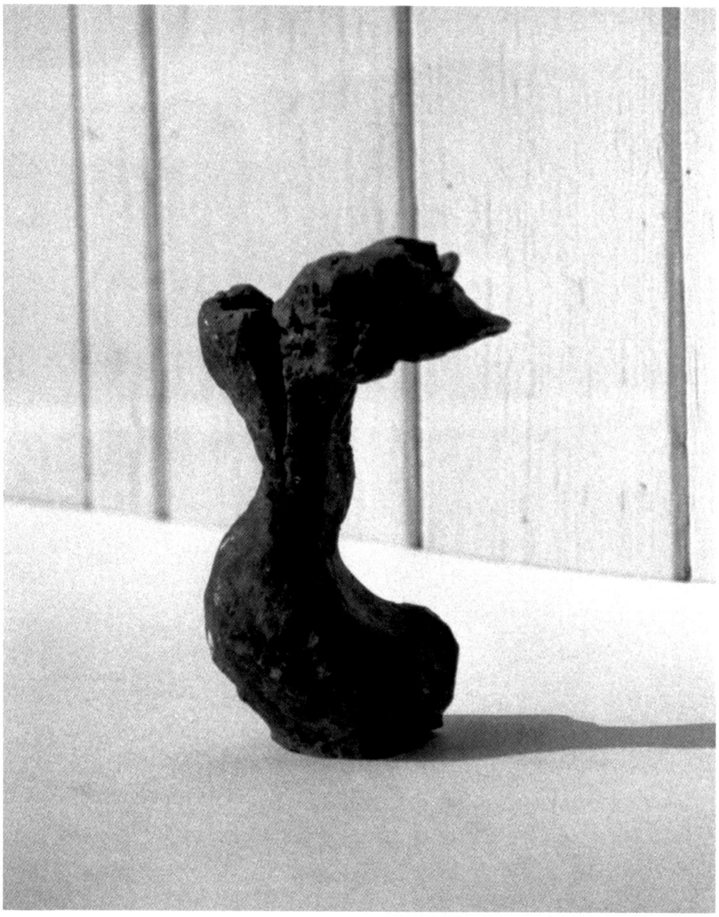

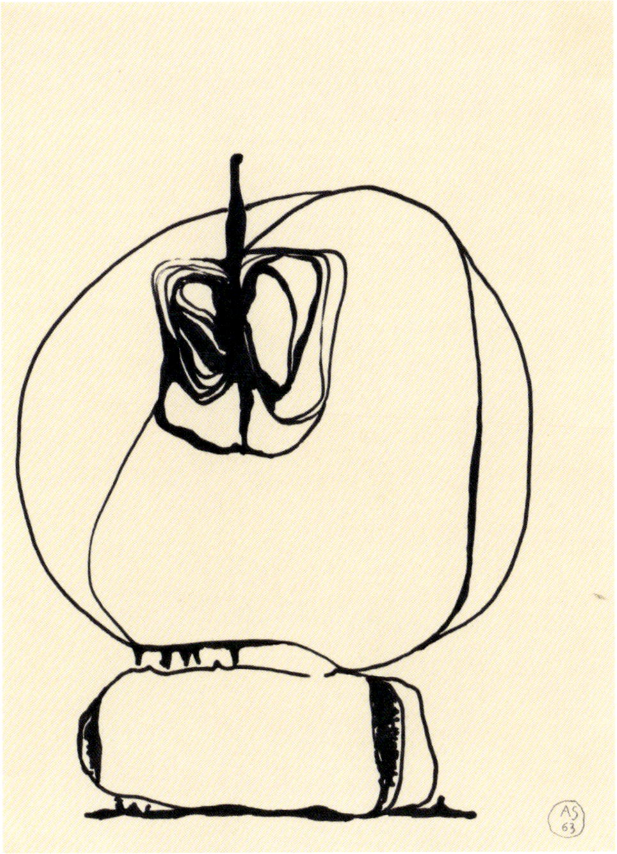

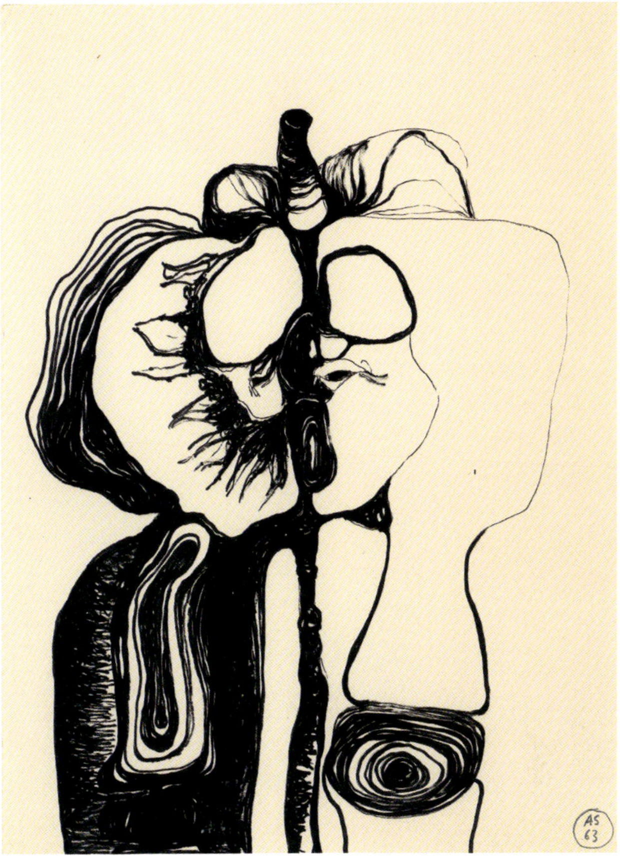

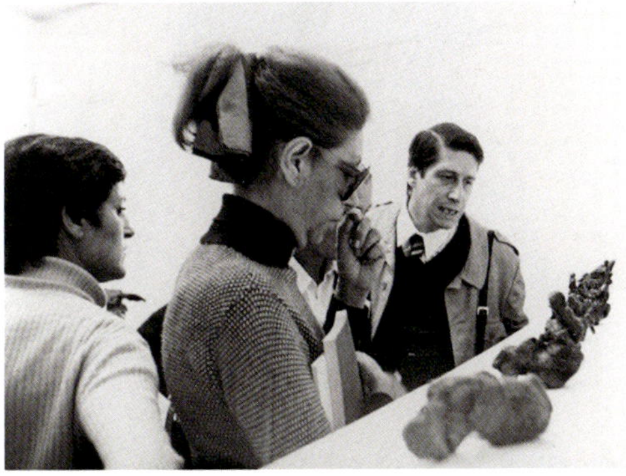

Muzeum Sztuki, Łódź, 1975.

opposite, clockwise from top left

Plate 122

Ołów I (Lead I), 1964
Lead
4 5/16 x 4 1/8 x 3 9/16" (11 x 10.5 x 9 cm)
The Estate of Alina Szapocznikow/Piotr Stanisławski

Plate 123

Ołów II (Lead II), 1964
Lead
3 9/16 x 3 3/16 x 2" (9 x 8 x 5 cm)

Plate 124

Ołów V (Lead V), 1964
Lead
5 1/8 x 2 15/16 x 3 3/16" (13 x 7.5 x 8 cm)

Plate 125

Ołów III (Lead III), 1964
Lead
6 1/8 x 3 3/4 x 2 3/8" (15.5 x 9.5 x 6 cm)
The Estate of Alina Szapocznikow/Piotr Stanisławski

above left

Plate 126

Untitled, 1963
Felt-tip pen on paper
14 1/8 x 10 9/16" (35.9 x 26.8 cm)

above right

Plate 127

Untitled, 1963
Felt-tip pen and ink on paper
12 1/16 x 9" (30.6 x 22.8 cm)

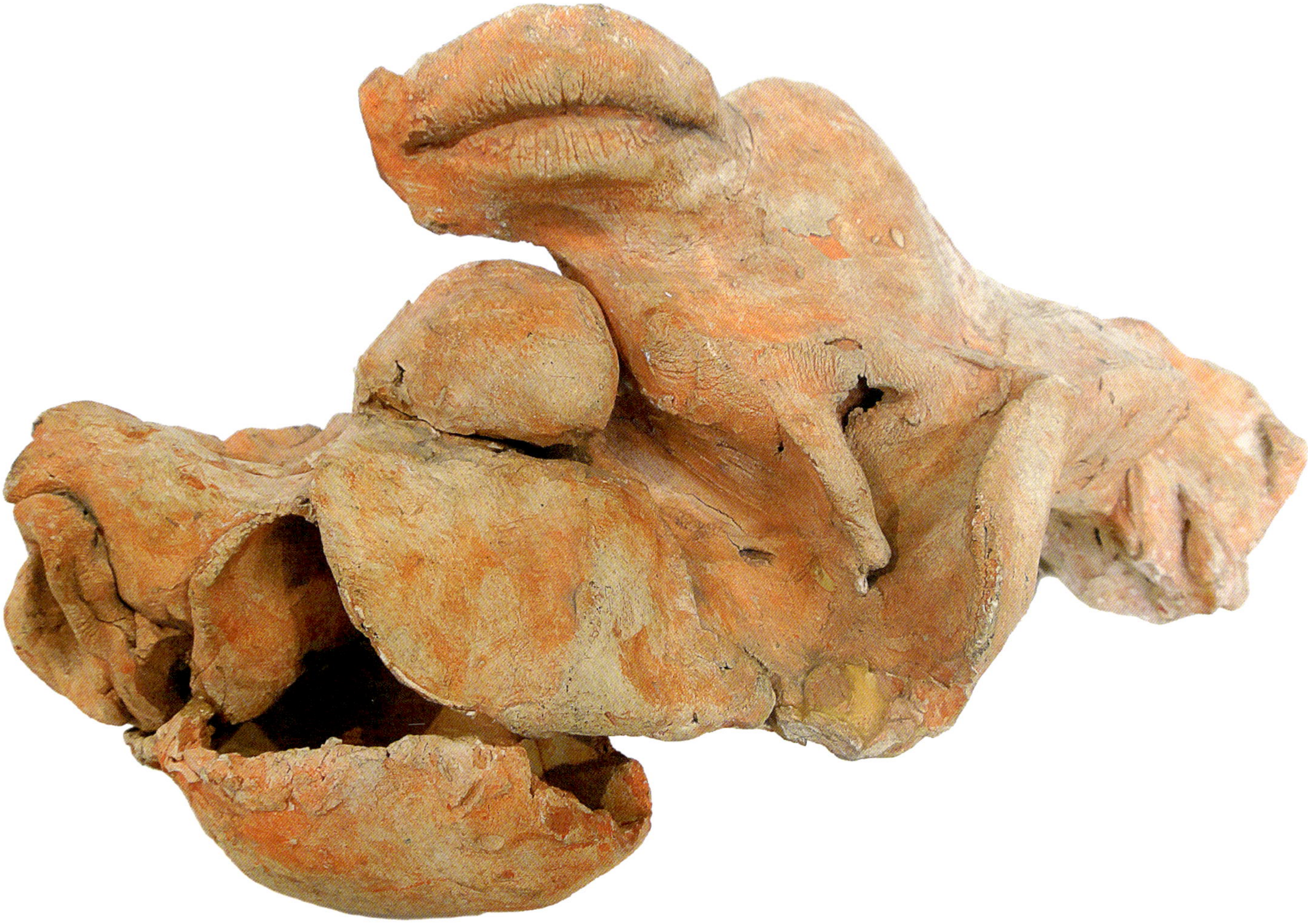

Plate 128

Forma II (Form II), 1964–65
Unfired pink terracotta
4 1/2 x 7 11/16 x 5 1/8" (11.5 x 19.5 x 13 cm)

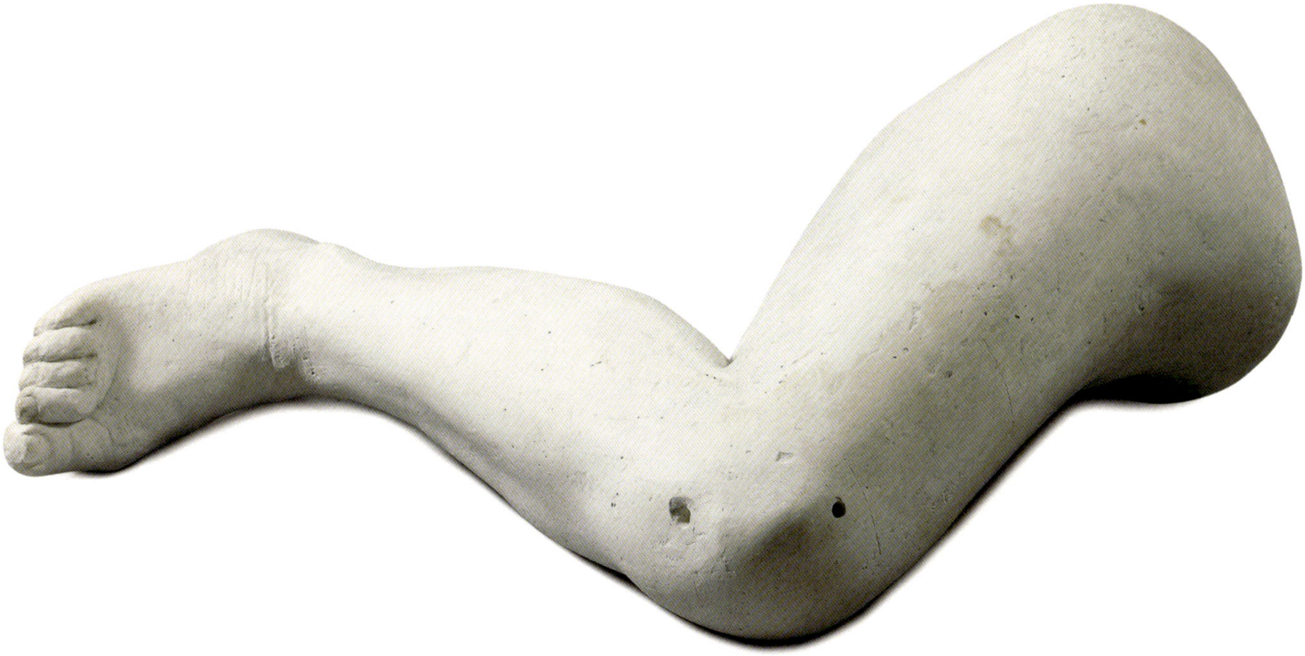

Plate 129

Noga (Leg), 1962
Plaster
7 7/8 x 19 11/16 x 19 11/16" (20 x 50 x 50 cm)

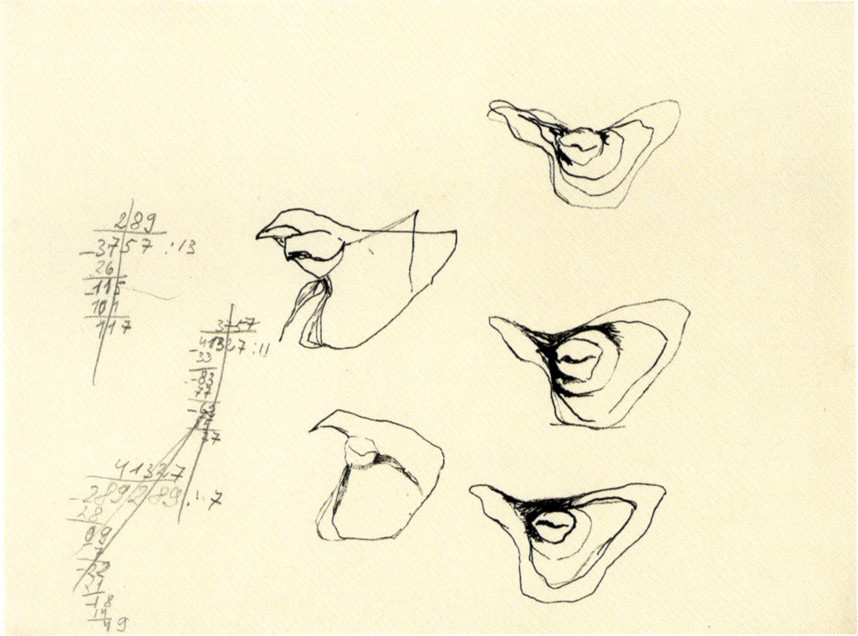

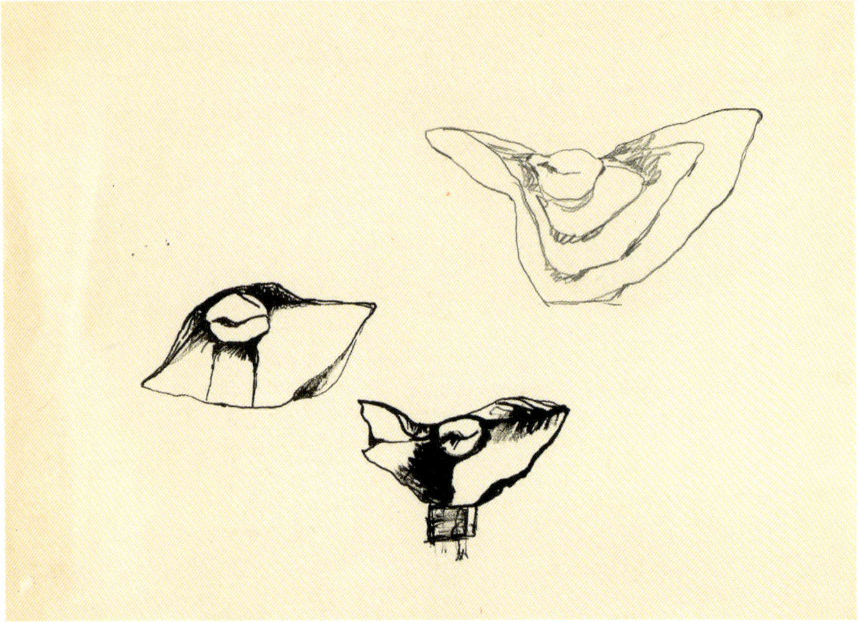

top

Plate 130

Untitled (Sketch for the Sculpture *Przemiany* [Metamorphoses] 2), c. 1961

Ink and pencil on paper

11 9/16 x 16 9/16" (29.3 x 42 cm)

bottom

Plate 131

Untitled (Sketch for the Sculpture *Przemiany* [Metamorphoses] 1), c. 1961

Ink and pencil on paper

11 5/8 x 16 3/8" (29.5 x 41.5 cm)

opposite

Plate 132

Naga (Naked), 1961

Terrazzo

63 x 15 3/4 x 13 13/16" (160 x 40 x 35 cm)

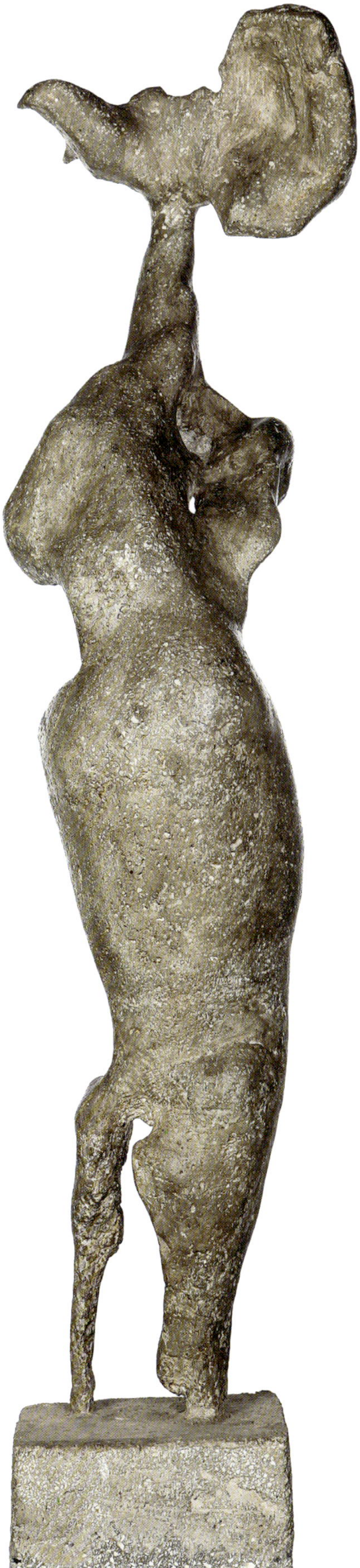

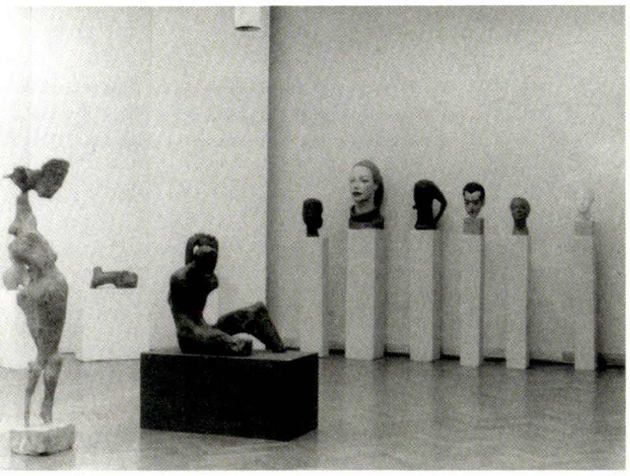

BWA Salon, Bydgoszcz, 1976.

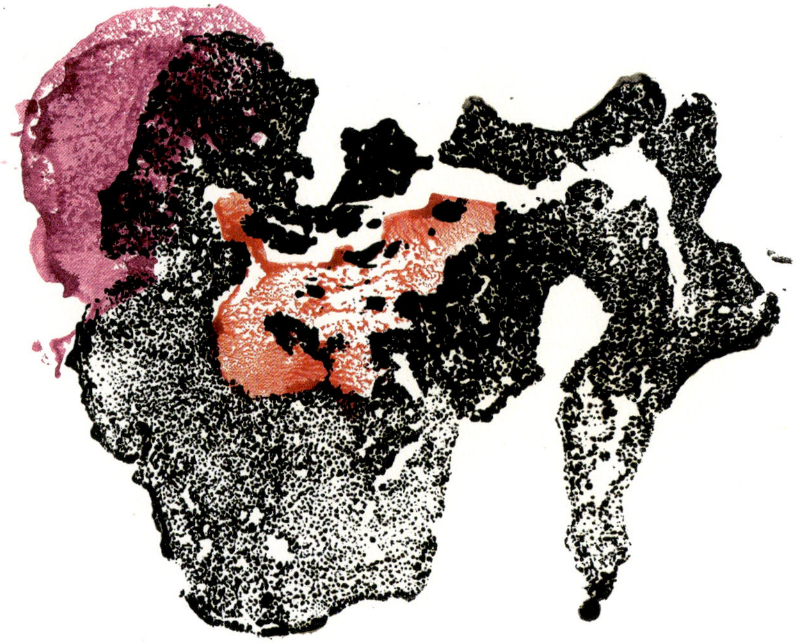

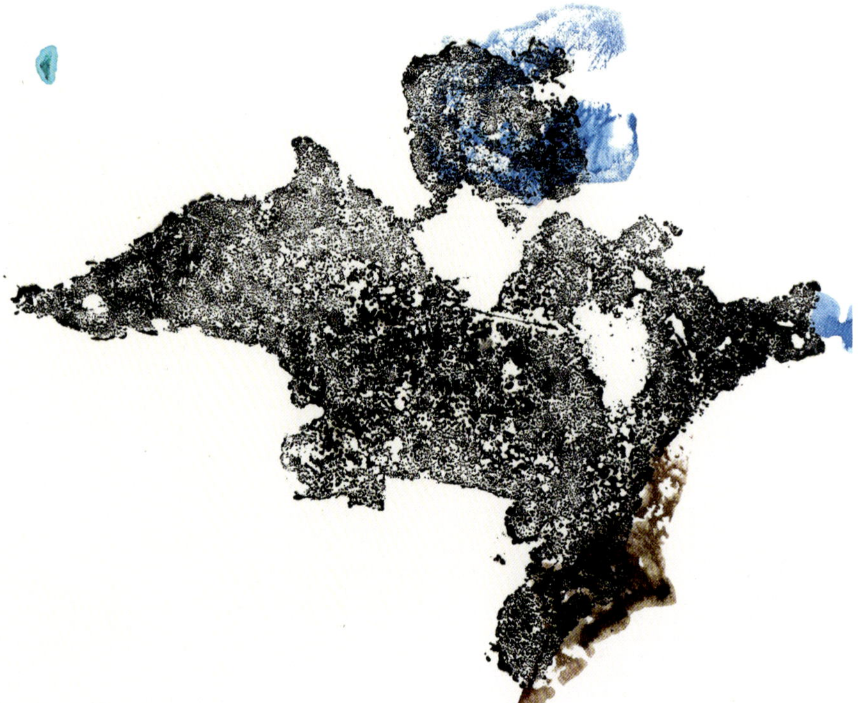

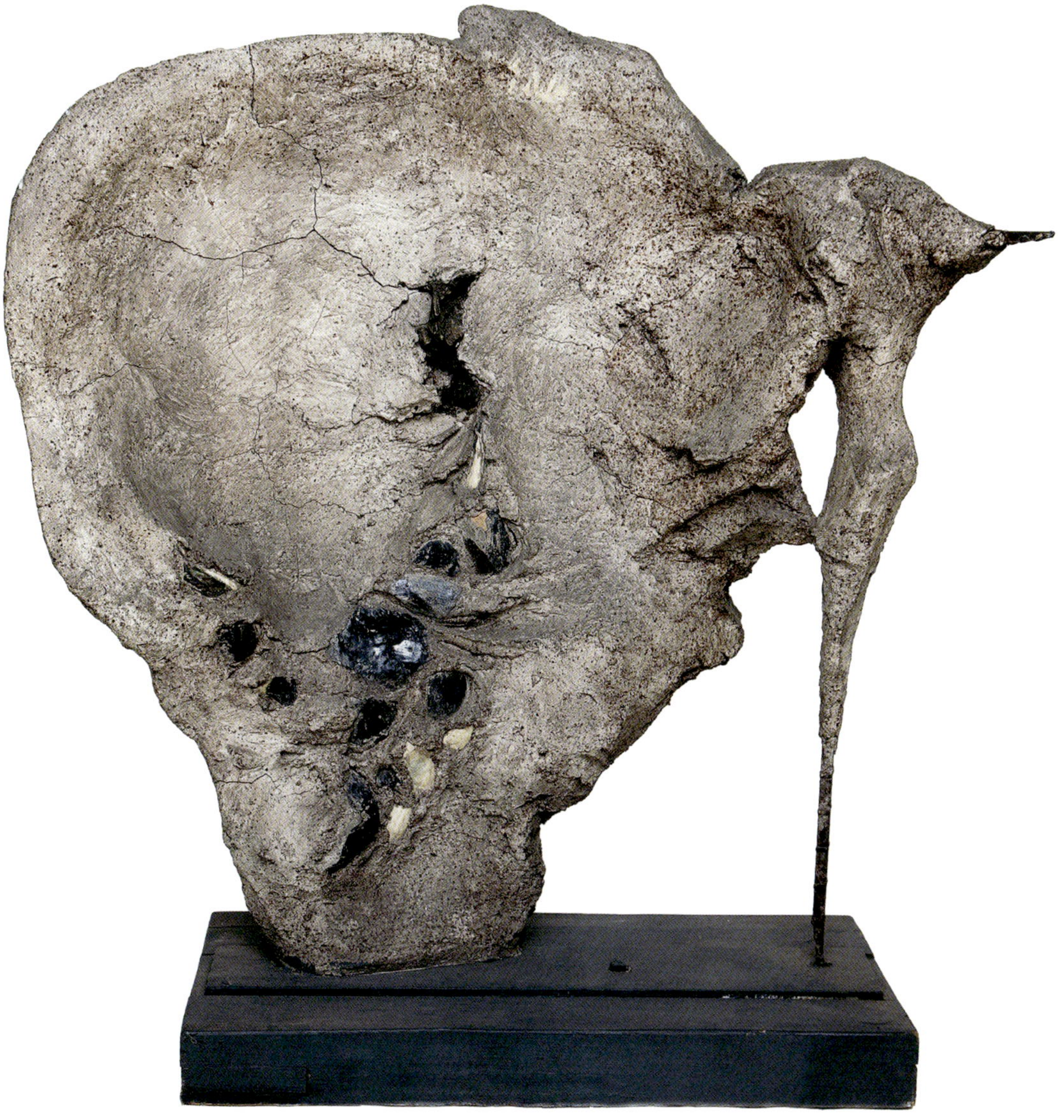

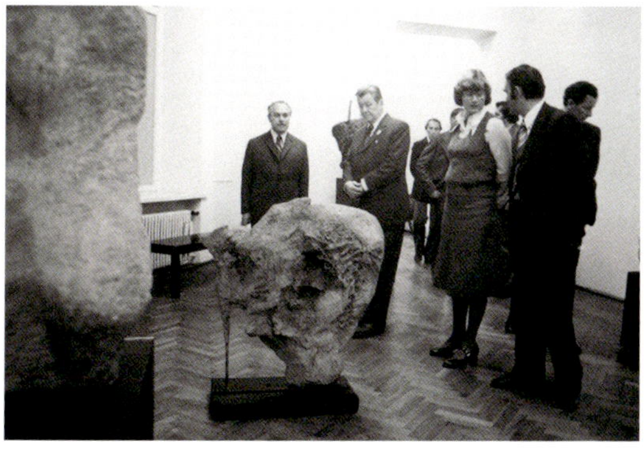

BWA Salon, Bydgoszcz, 1976.

opposite top

Plate 133

Untitled, c. 1960

Monotype and ink on paper

8 3/16 x 8 3/16" (20.8 x 20.7 cm)

opposite bottom

Plate 134

Untitled, c. 1960

Monotype and ink on paper

8 1/4 x 8 3/16" (21 x 20.7 cm)

above

Plate 135

Małża (Mollusc), 1960

Plastic cement, inlaid stone, ceramic, metal

40 9/16 x 38 3/16 x 13 13/16" (103 x 97 x 35 cm)

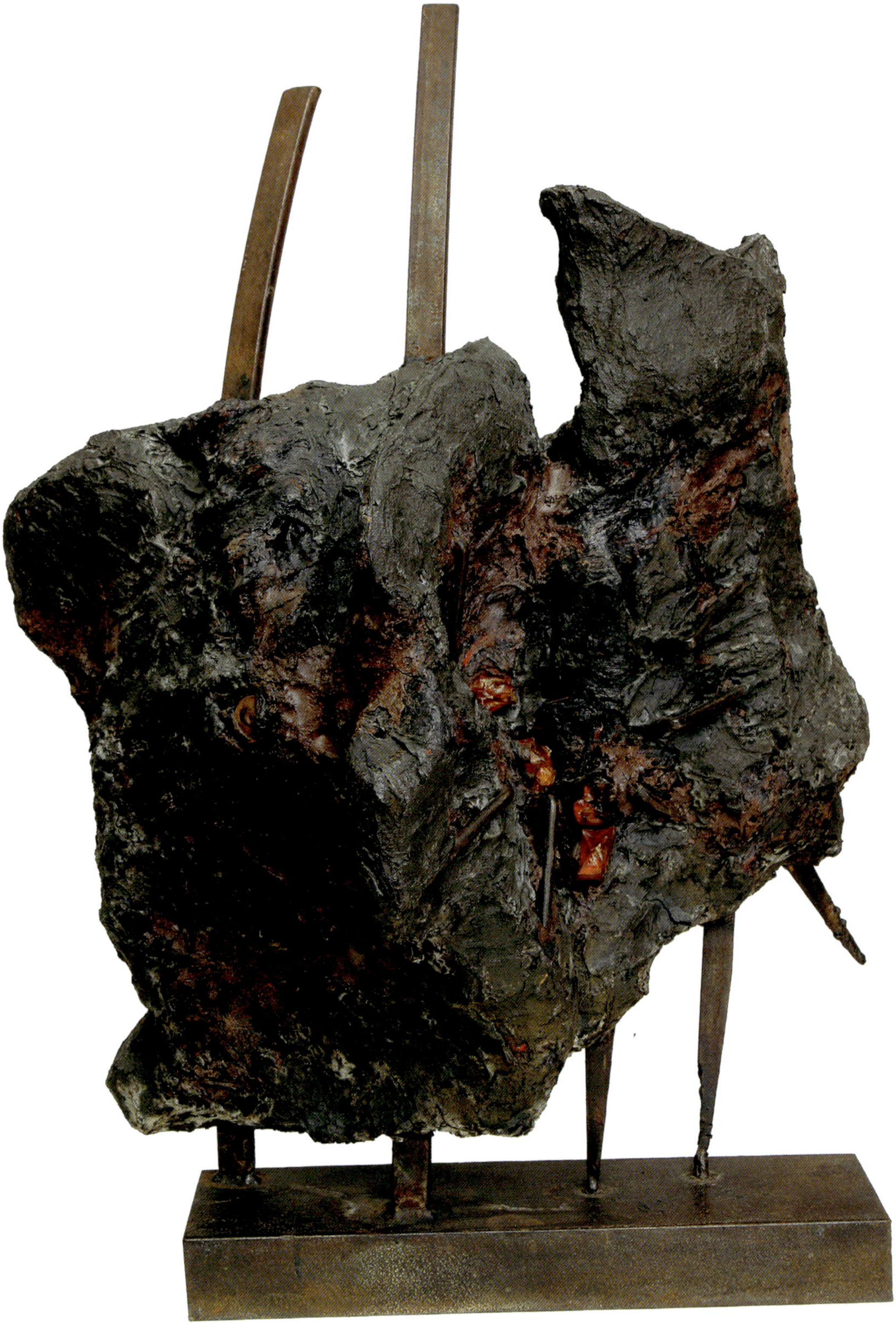

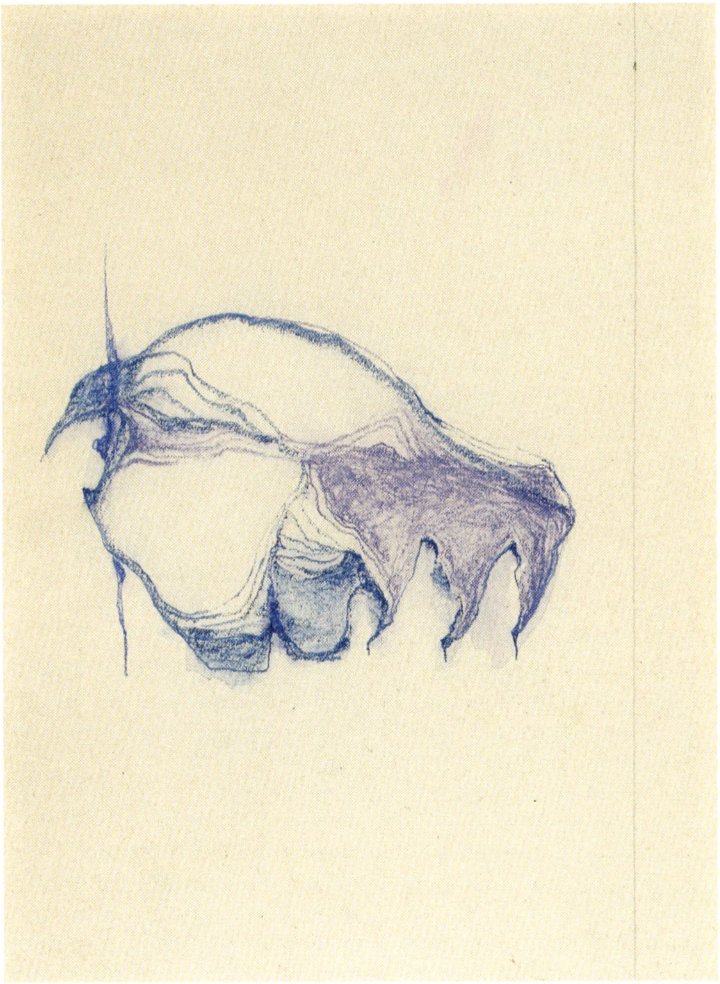

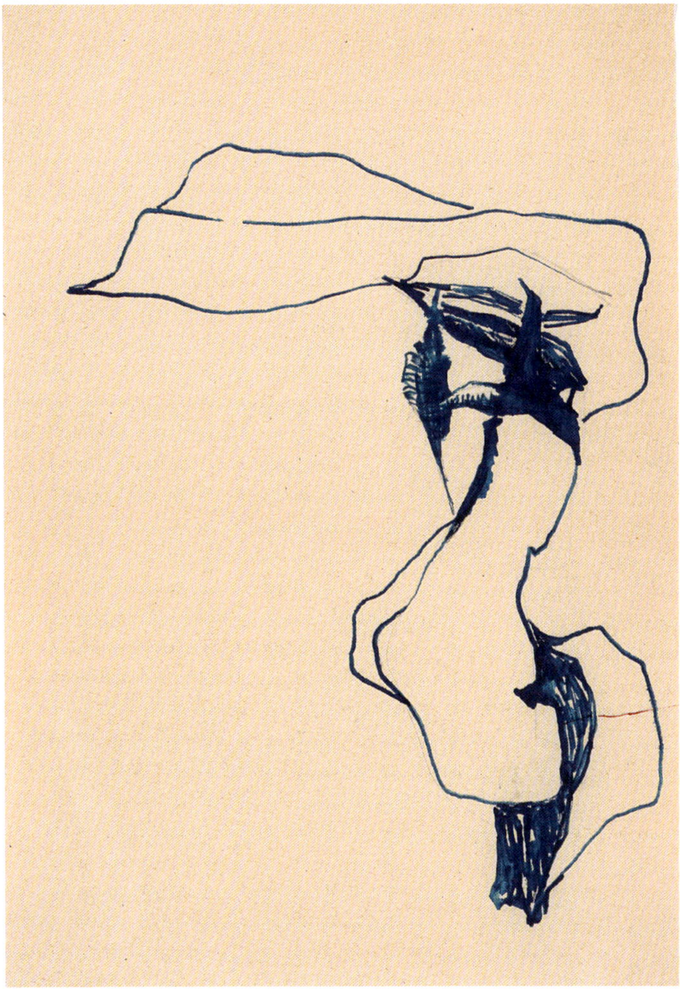

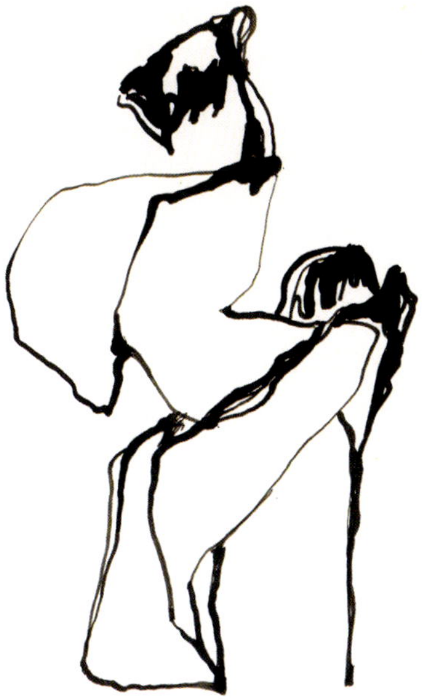

opposite
Plate 136

Rozłupany (Shattered), 1960
Polyester resin and metal bars
32 11/16 x 22 7/8 x 15" (83 x 58 x 38 cm)

above, clockwise from top left
Plate 137

Untitled (Sketch 1), c. 1959–60
Crayon on paper
12 7/16 x 9 3/16" (31.5 x 23.3 cm)

Plate 138

Untitled (Study for *Kwiato-ptak* [Flower-Bird] 2), c. 1959–60
Ink on paper
11 3/4 x 8 1/4" (29.8 x 21 cm)

Plate 139

Untitled, c. 1960
Ink on paper
11 9/16 x 8 3/16" (29.4 x 20.7 cm)

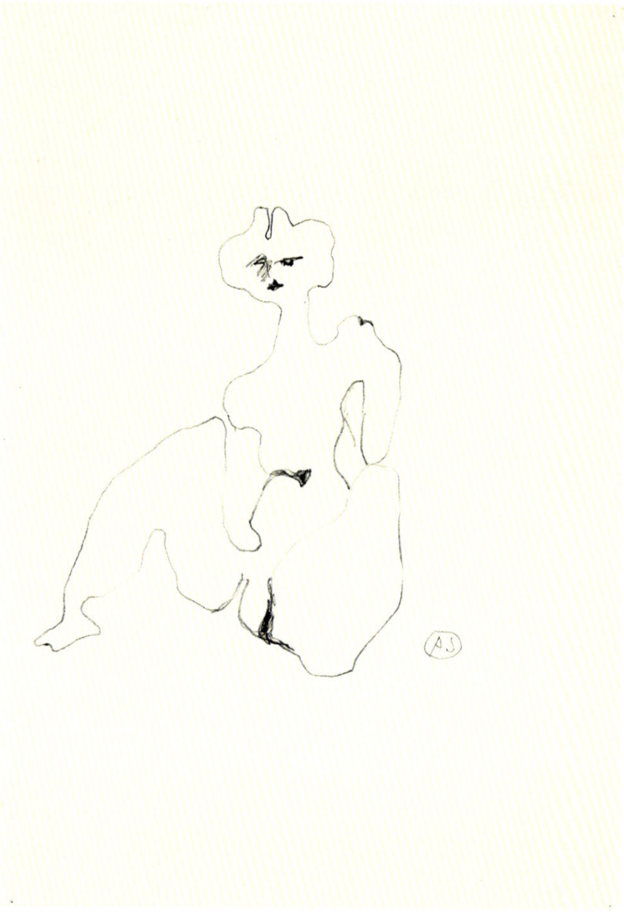

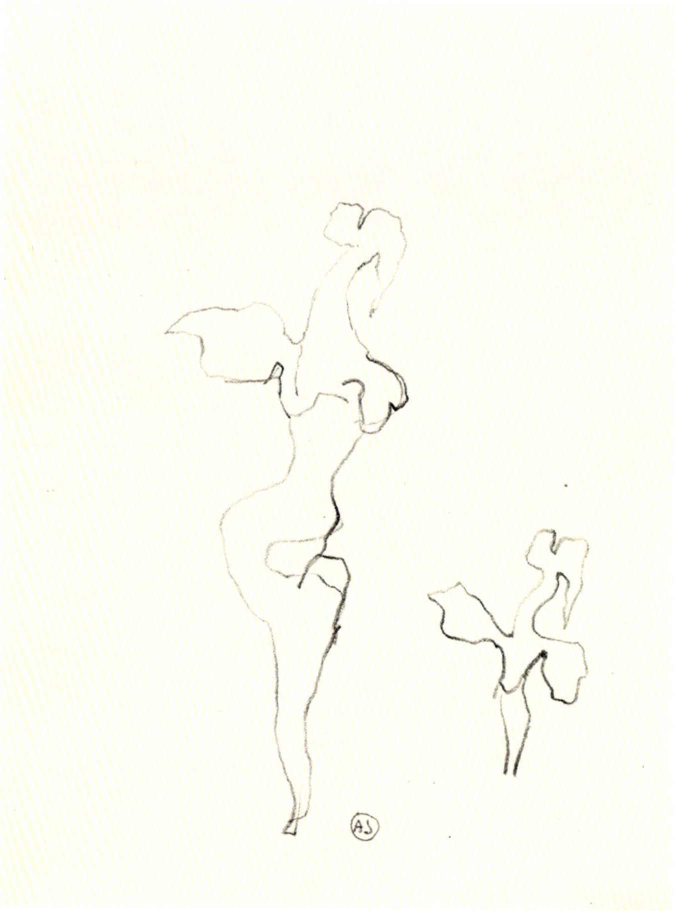

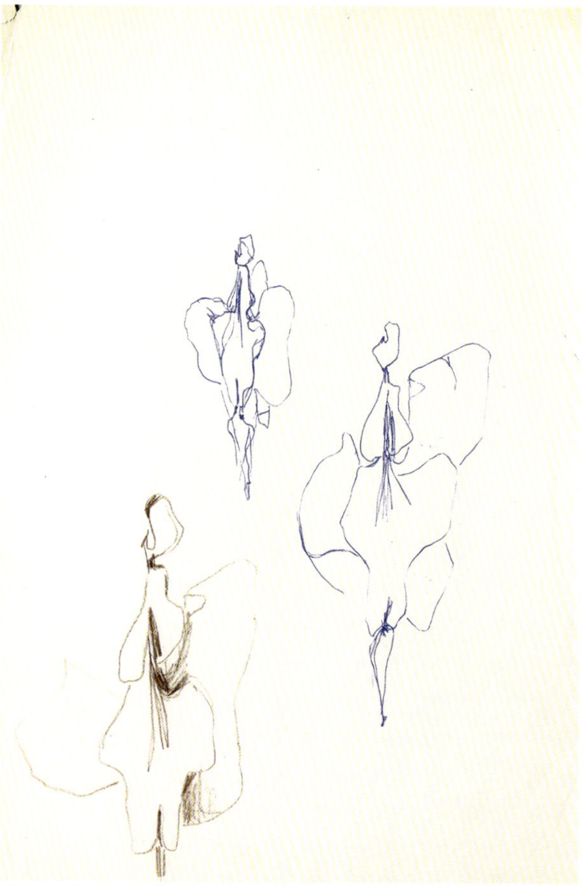

clockwise from top left

Plate 140

Untitled (Study of a Nude), c. 1959
Pencil on paper
11 13/16 x 8 5/8" (30 x 22 cm)

Plate 141

Untitled (Study for *Kobieta-róża*
[Woman-Rose]), c. 1959
Pencil on paper
10 15/16 x 8 3/16" (27.8 x 20.8 cm)

Plate 142

Untitled (Studies of Some Organic Forms), c. 1959
Crayon and ballpoint pen on paper
16 3/8 x 11 11/16" (41.5 x 29.7 cm)

opposite

Plate 143

Maria Magdalena (Mary Magdalene), 1957–58
Plaster and iron filings
68 15/16 x 22 7/8 x 18 1/8" (175 x 58 x 46 cm)

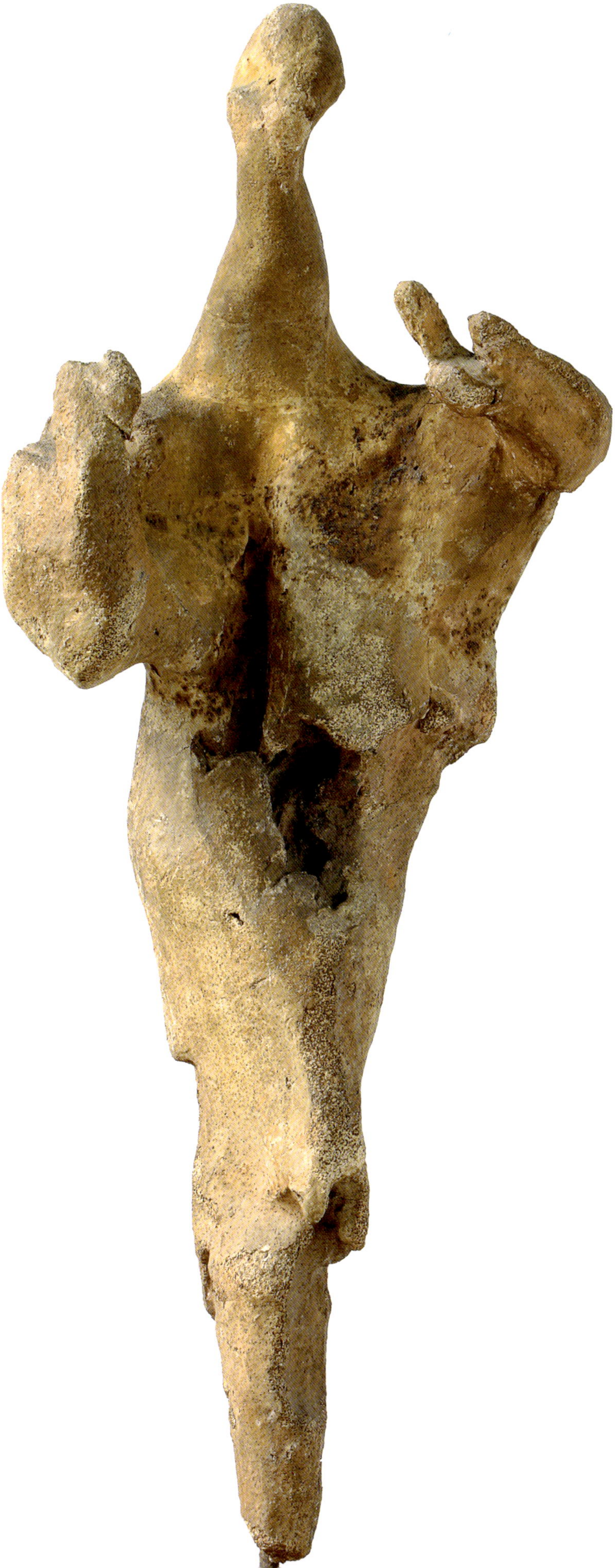

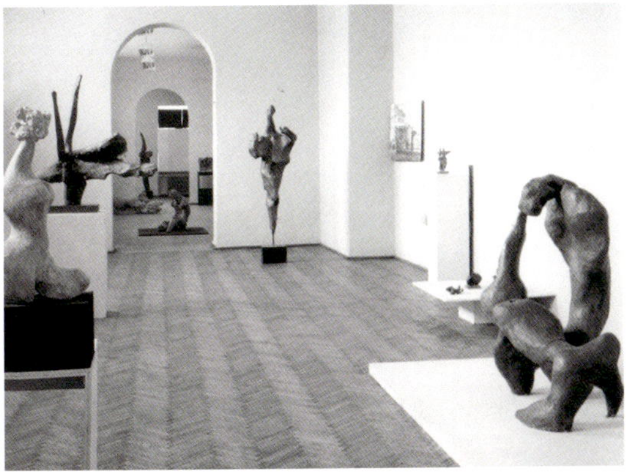

BWA "Arsenał," Poznań, 1960.

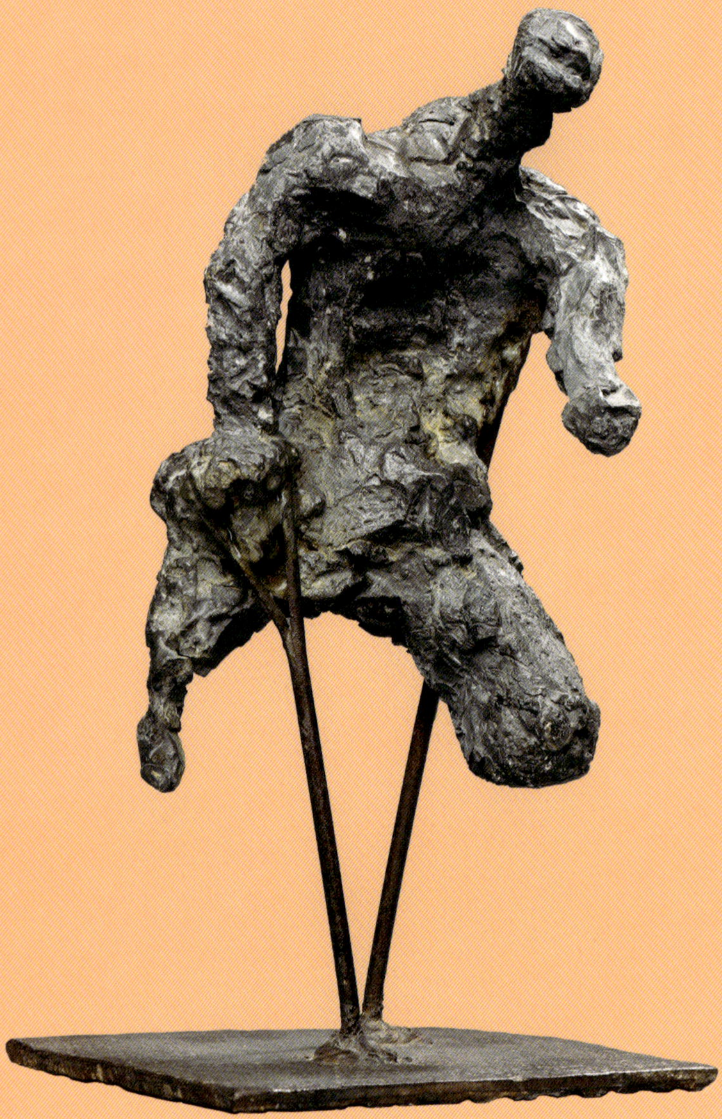
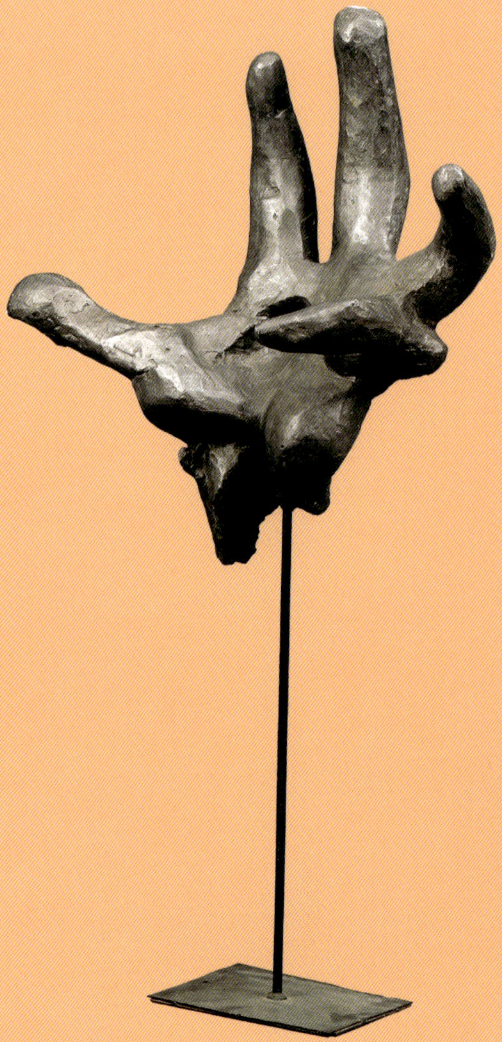

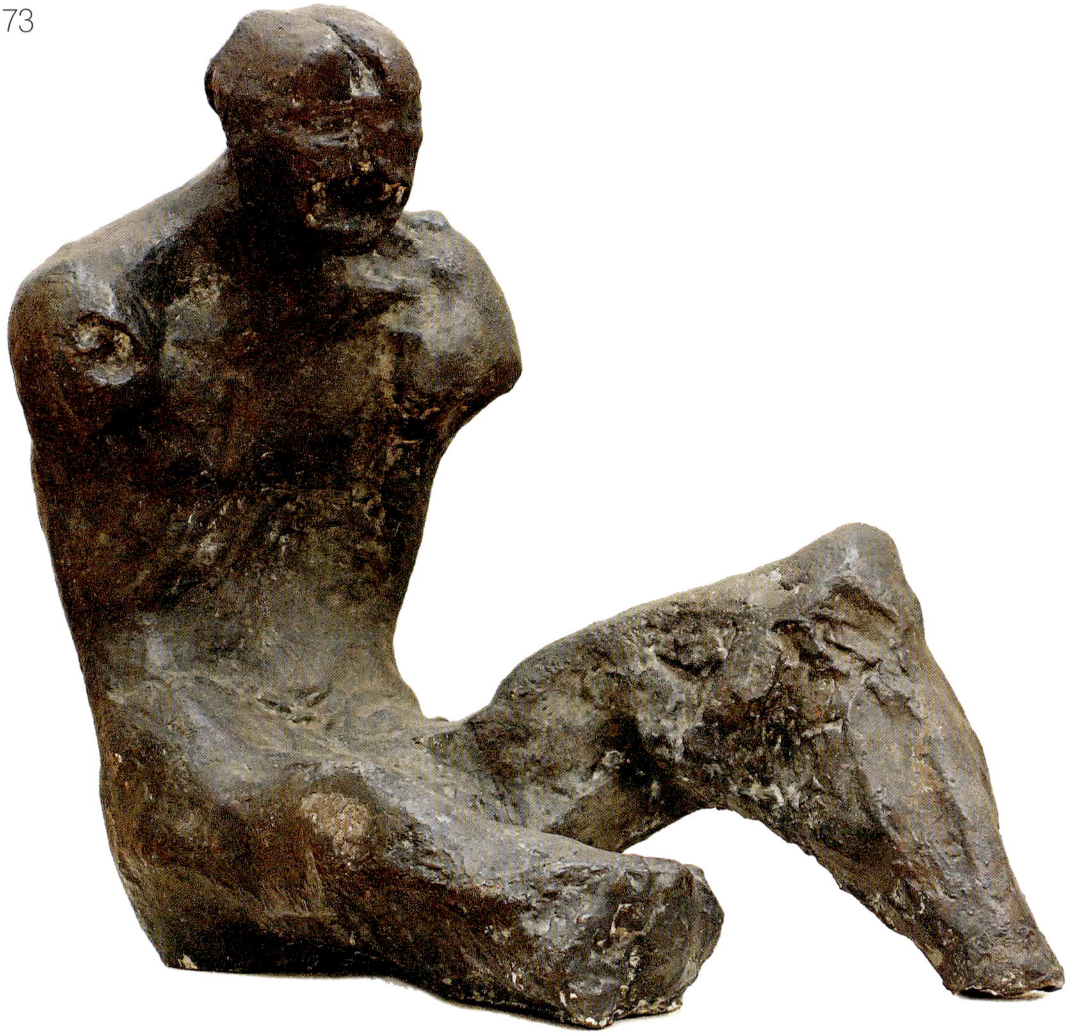

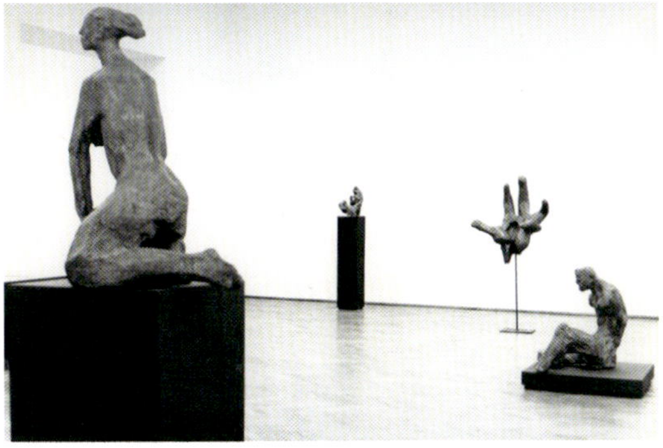

Muzeum Sztuki, Łódź, 1975.

opposite left
Plate 144

Monstrum II (Monster II), 1957
Lead and metal construction
10 5/8 x 5 1/2 x 5 1/2" (27 x 14 x 14 cm)

opposite right
Plate 145

Dłoń. Projekt Pomnika Bohaterów Warszawy II
(Hand. Monument to the Heroes of the Warsaw Ghetto), 1957
Patinated plaster, iron filings
56 7/8 x 28 3/4 x 16 9/16" (144.5 x 73 x 42 cm)

above
Plate 146

Ekshumowany (Exhumed), 1957
Bronze
25 3/16 x 16 9/16 x 11 13/16" (64 x 42 x 30 cm)

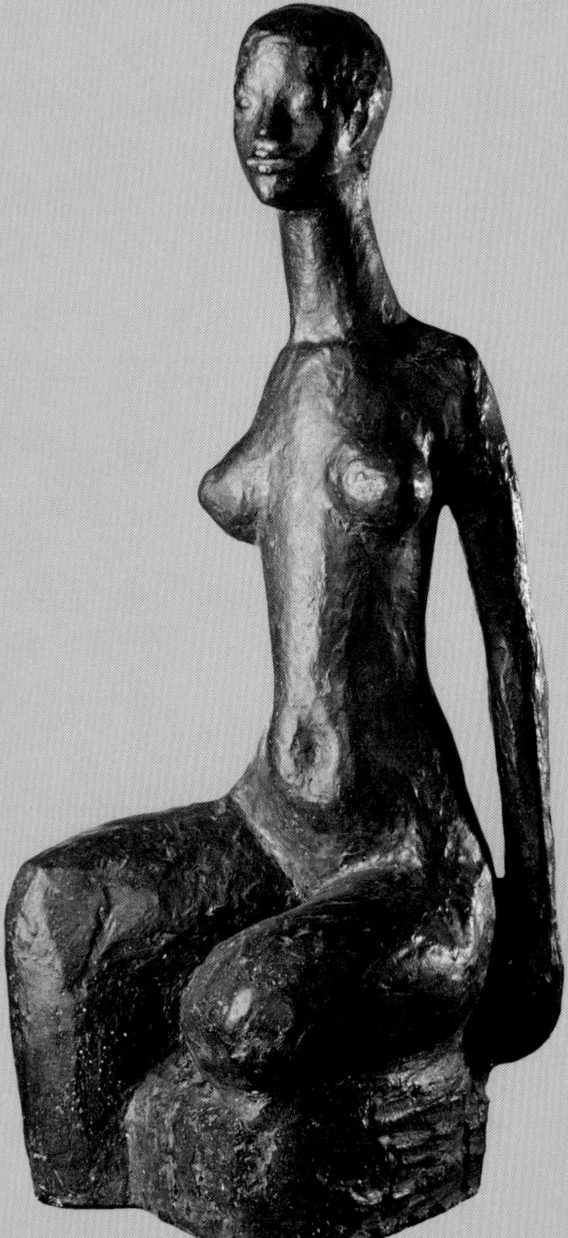

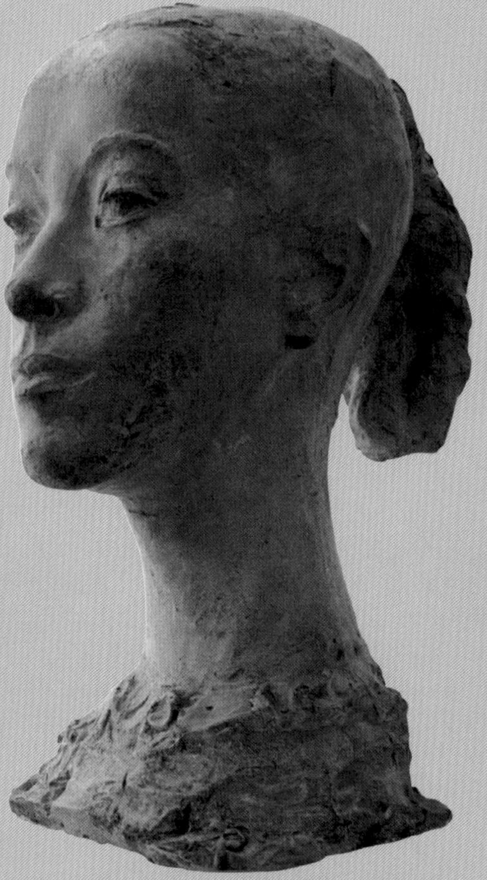

left
Plate 147
Pierwsza miłość (First Love), 1954
Encrusted plastic cement
35 7/16" (90 cm) high

right
Plate 148
Koński ogon – Portret Meksykanki
(A Pony Tail – Portrait of a Mexican Woman), 1955–56
Plaster
17 11/16 x 7 7/8 x 15" (45 x 20 x 38 cm)

opposite
Plate 149
Trudny wiek (Difficult Age), 1956
Bronze
74 7/16 x 23 1/4 x 15" (189 x 59 x 38 cm)

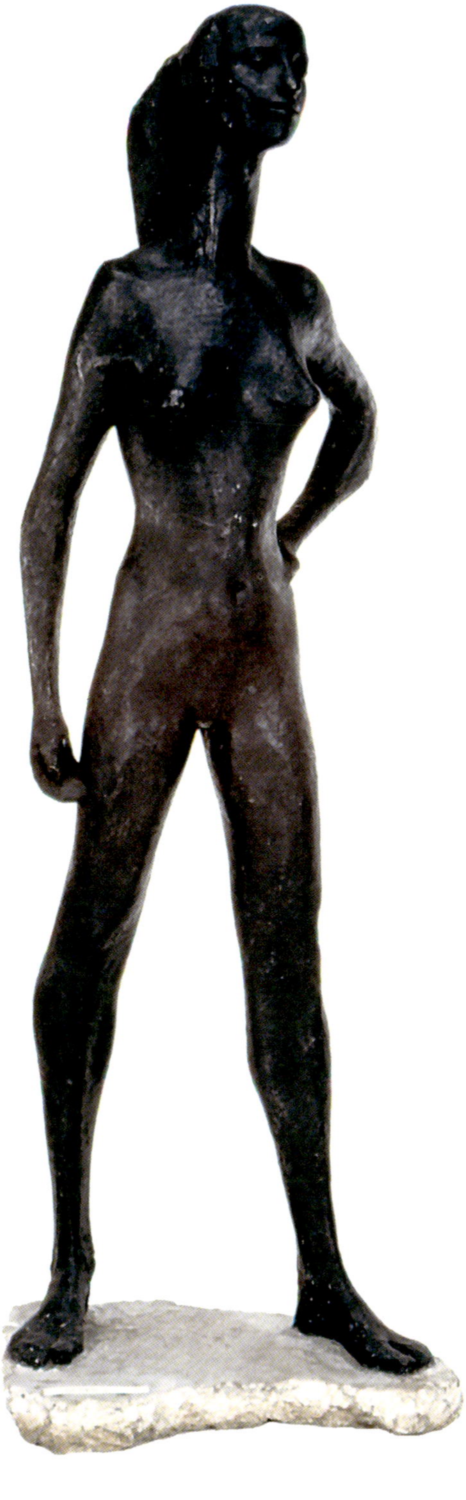

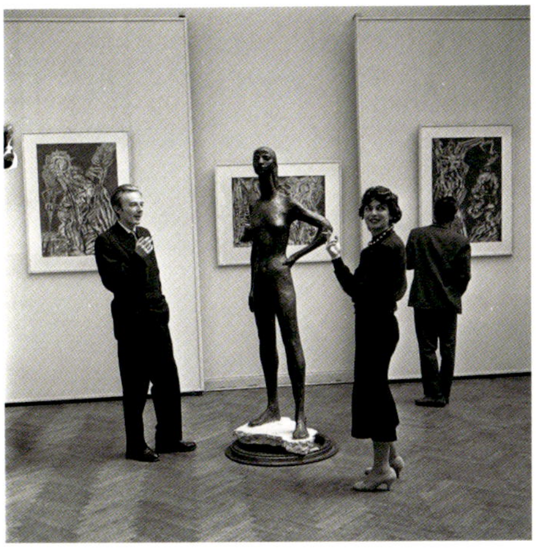

Zachęta National Gallery of Art, Warsaw, 1957.

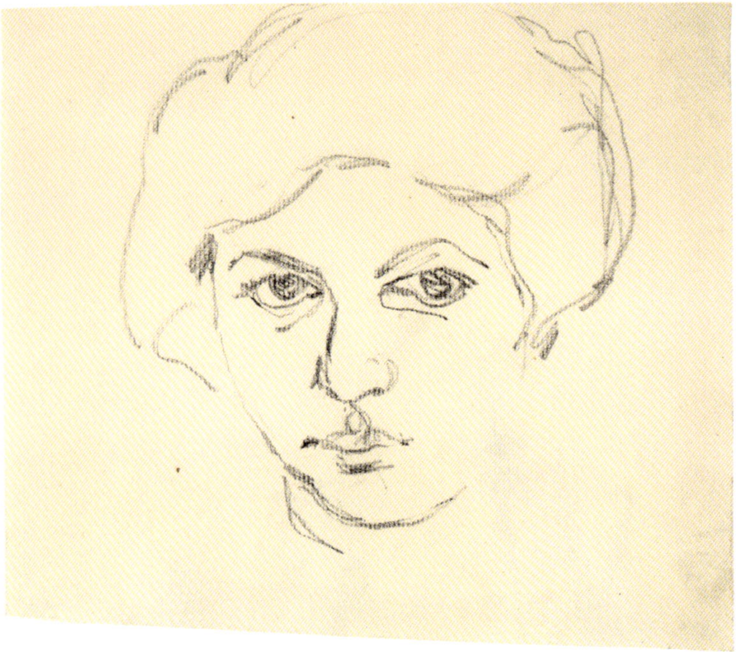

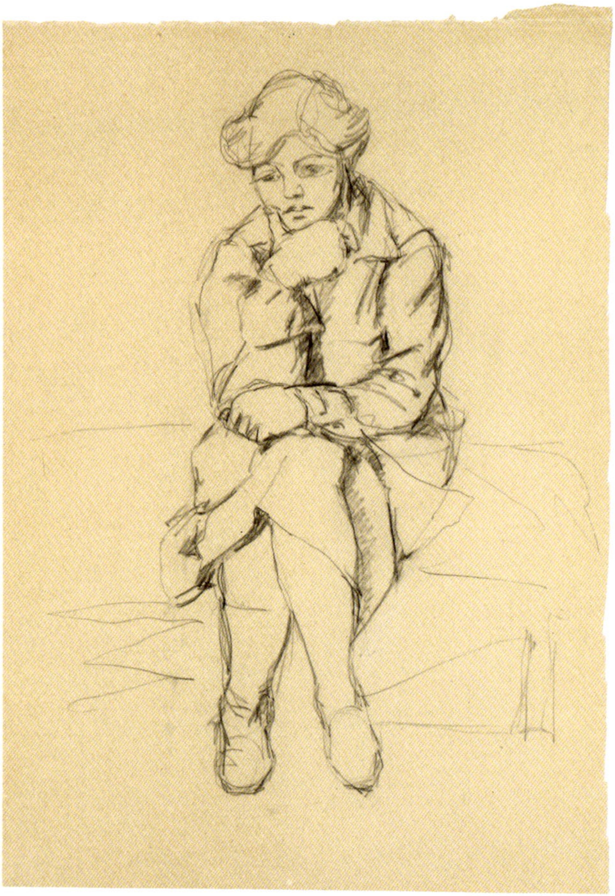

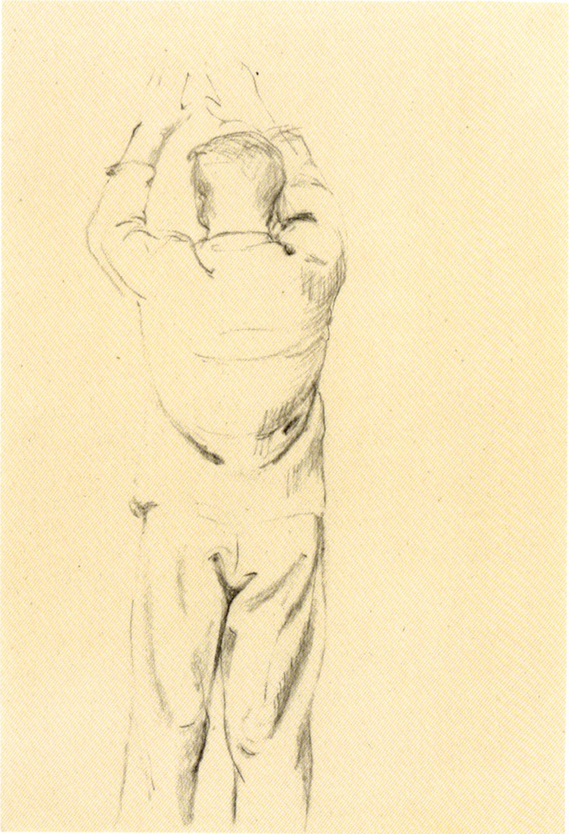

clockwise from top left

Plate 150

Untitled (Self-Portrait), c. 1948–56
Pencil on paper
7 1/2 x 8 3/4" (19 x 22.2 cm)

Plate 151

Untitled (Study of a Seated Woman. Self-Portrait), c. 1948–54
Pencil on paper
17 3/16 x 12 15/16" (43.7 x 32.8 cm)
The Estate of Alina Szapocznikow/Piotr Stanisławski

Plate 152

Untitled (Study of a Man Standing with Raised Arms, Seen from Behind), c. 1951–54
Pencil on paper
11 13/16 x 8 3/8" (30 x 20.2 cm)
The Estate of Alina Szapocznikow/Piotr Stanisławski

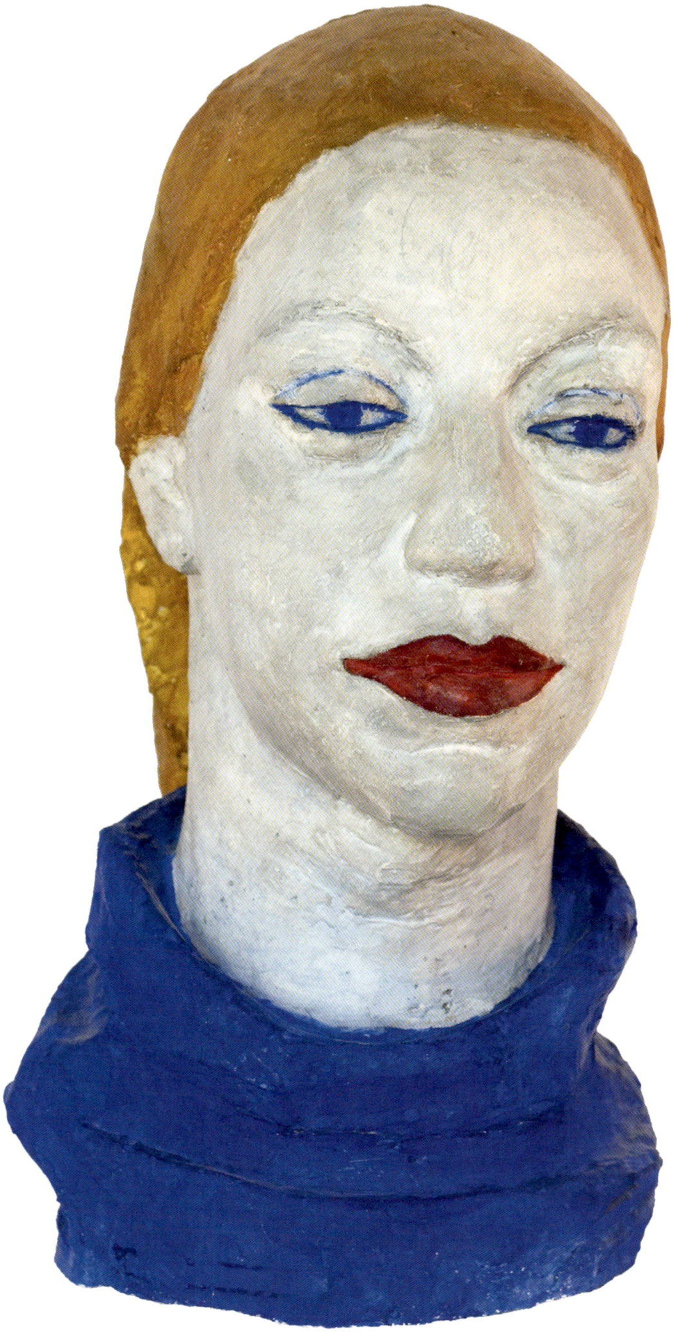

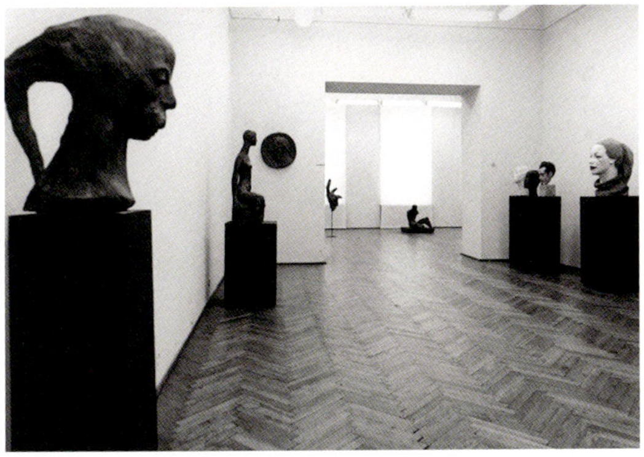

Muzeum Sztuki, Łódź, 1975.

Plate 153

Portret Barbary Kusak (Portrait of Barbara Kusak), 1955
Polychromed plaster
25 3/16 x 13 13/16 x 25 3/16" (64 x 35 x 60 cm)
Private collection, Germany

Chronology of Alina Szapocznikow's Life and Work

Compiled and written by Jola Gola

1926

Alina Szapocznikow is born on May 16 in Kalisz, Poland. For unknown reasons, her birth certificate states May 15, 1927, until November 1937, just before her father's death, when the date is adjusted to May 16, 1926, after a court decision. Szapocznikow's parents are non-practicing Jews; her father, Jakub, is a dentist, and her mother, Ryfka (née Auerbach), is a pediatrician.

1926–38

Szapocznikow lives with her family—including her younger brother, Mirosław—in Pabianice, near Łódź, where she attends a Polish grade school with her friend Rita (later Hilton), whose parents are also doctors of Jewish descent. Both families live in Pabianice's New Town, where the Polish intelligentsia often settled. Alina and Rita attend the St. Hedwig State Middle School on Puławskiego Street, to which only two girls of Jewish descent are accepted each year. Szapocznikow's brother Mirosław goes to a Jewish middle school in Łódź. Shortly before the war, in 1938, her father dies of tuberculosis.

1939–45

In February 1940, after the outbreak of World War II, Szapocznikow's family is interned in the Pabianice ghetto. With her mother, she works as a nurse in a ghetto hospital. After the Pabianice ghetto is liquidated in May 1942, the family is transferred to the Łódź ghetto.

According to an account by Rita Hilton, the Szapocznikow family was transported via Auschwitz to Bergen-Belsen, where they stayed for about ten months. Both mother and daughter worked at a camp hospital, but they became separated in the autumn of 1944. Szapocznikow's experiences during the final months of the war are unknown. She heads to Prague with a group of prisoners while her mother returns to Łódź. She stays in Prague most likely as a result of friendships she has established with some Czech Jews (including Sonja Bullaty, with whom she would remain in contact for many years). In order to gain Czech citizenship, Szapocznikow lists the Czech side of Cieszyn, a Polish/Czech border town, as her birthplace. She is given her papers, on which her name appears as Šapočniková. At that time, she is most probably convinced that all her family members are dead—in fact, her brother died on January 15, 1945, in Terezín, Czechoslovakia—and, according to accounts by her Czech acquaintances, is shocked when her mother tracks her down in Prague. In late 1945, she is given permission to go to Poland and visits her mother in January 1946, on the anniversary of her brother's death.

1945–47

Among the people she meets in Prague is the sculptor Stefan Bedřich, with whom she eventually lives and would maintain contact for many years. She works and learns the craft of stonemasonry at the studio of Otokar Velinsky. Later, in October 1945, she joins the studio of Josef Wagner at the Higher School of Arts and Industry. She would keep in touch with the Czech artistic community for many years, helping to organize exhibitions for her Czech colleagues in Poland and France. She leaves Prague in November 1947 for Paris.

> For us, her first classmates, her work was from the very beginning worthy of respect, if not admiration or envy. This was especially true of the girls in Wagner's studio, as none of them could be as brave as Alina in confounding the professor. Her works, both the good and the not-so-good sculptures, the questions with which she would bombard him—all this was necessary for her to make progress, to earn praise or reprimand, to discover what is next, how to proceed, and so on.

Miloš Chlupáč, unpublished text prepared for *Alina Szapocznikow. 1926 – 1973* (Łódź, Poland: Muzeum Sztuki, 1975). Translated by Szymon Włoch.

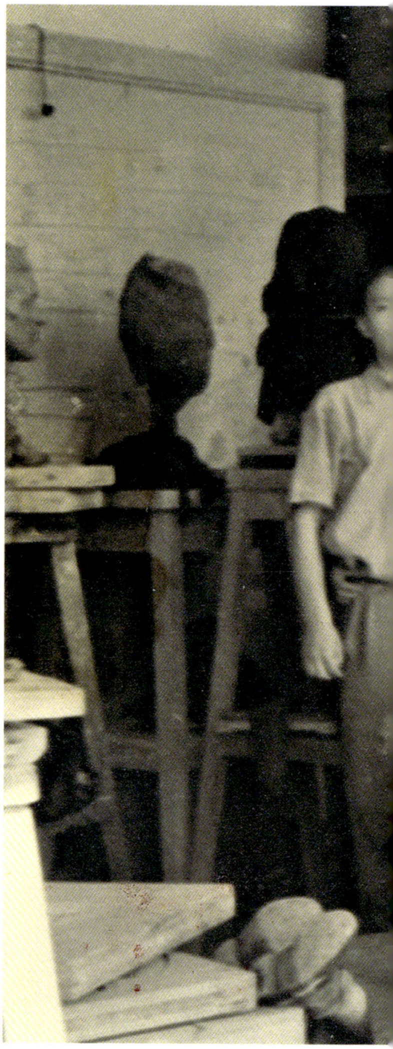

1948

Early in the year, Szapocznikow begins studying at the École Nationale Supérieure des Beaux-Arts in Paris, attending classes by Paul Niclausse as an auditing student for two years. She lives on rue d'Alesia. By then, she has already met César.

In the spring, she meets Ryszard Stanisławski, a student of mathematics at the Sorbonne who would soon begin studying art history at the École du Louvre. Stanisławski introduces Szapocznikow to his group of Polish friends, including

Mieczysław Szabliński; Lech Zahorski and his wife, Michelle; Szapocznikow's soon-to-be employers, the siblings Simone and Gaston Lerendu, owners of a stoneworking studio on avenue du Père-Lachaise; as well as Helena and Julien Lustre, distant relatives of Szapocznikow.

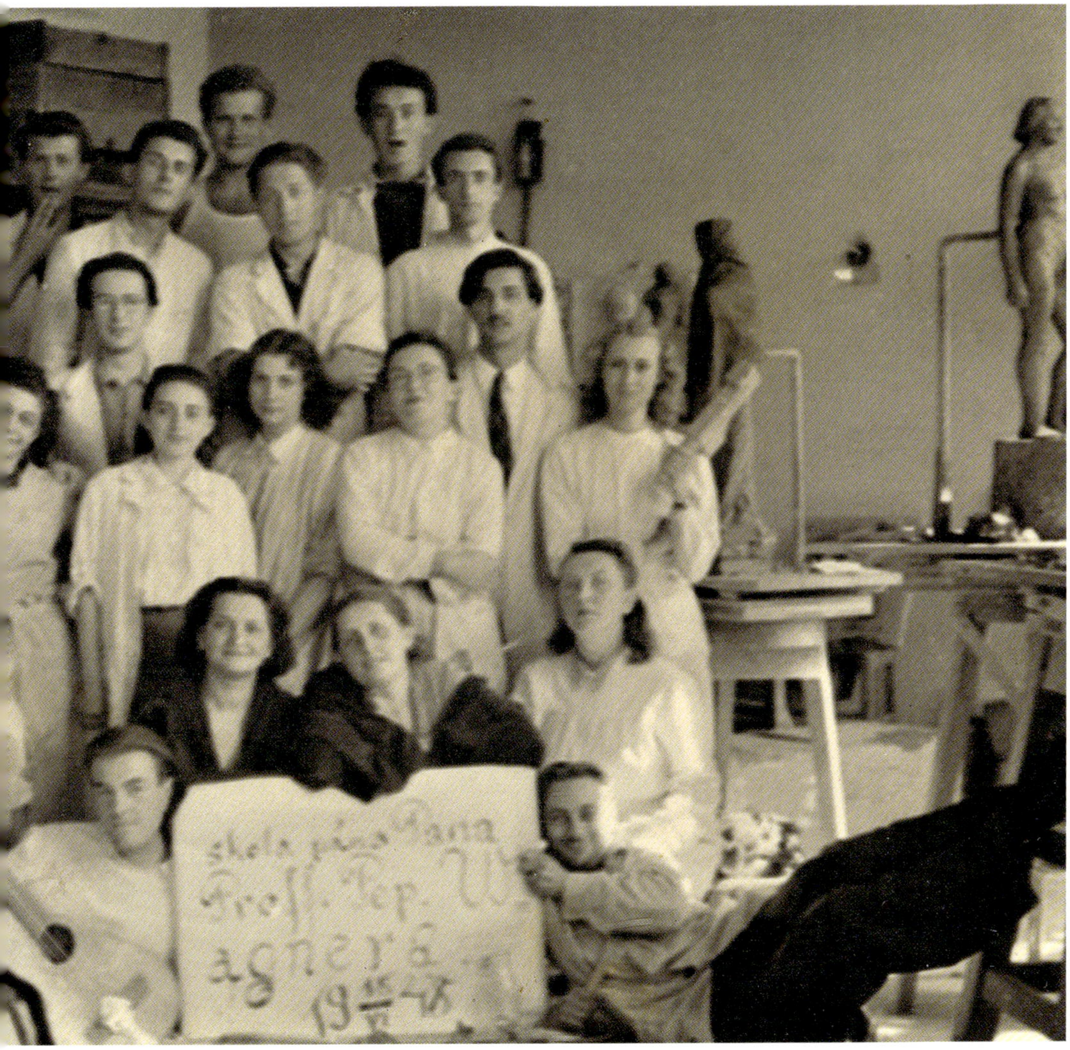

Josef Wagner's studio, Higher School of Arts and Industry in Prague, 1947. Szapocznikow is in the second row from the bottom, second from the left.

In December Szapocznikow goes to Prague, then continues on to Poland. She visits her mother in Łódź, spends two weeks in the mountain resort town of Zakopane, and frequents art exhibitions, including a retrospective of the sculptor Xawery Dunikowski at the National Museum in Warsaw. Her letters suggest a growing desire to return to Poland.

1949

In the early days of February, Szapocznikow returns to Paris, again via Prague, and lives with Stanisławski. In 1949–50, almost daily gatherings and discussions take place in the so-called "Polish room" of a restaurant at 3, rue Racine (in the heart of the Latin Quarter), where Polish expatriates are treated to free meals by the Polish embassy. In addition to the aforementioned group of Polish friends, these gatherings also include visitors from the home country, such as writers Jan Kott and Adam Ważyk, literary historian and critic Stefan Żółkiewski, art historians Jan Białostocki and Mieczysław Porębski, and artists Tadeusz Kantor and Eryk Lipiński.

Szapocznikow begins working in the J. Lerendu stoneworking studio near the Père-Lachaise cemetery. She also rents a small space next to the studio from Gaston Lerendu to use as her own private atelier.

In September, Szapocznikow is afflicted with a sudden illness. At Tenon hospital she is diagnosed with peritoneal tuberculosis, untreatable at the time. She is referred to the specialized hospital Paul-Brousse in Villejuif near Paris.

1950

On the recommendation of Dr. Monsaingeon, Szapocznikow goes with Stanisławski to Sirod in the Jura Mountains that spring, but her stay is interrupted by a sudden relapse. She goes to a private hospital in Champagnole, where she is successfully treated with antibiotics (Streptomycin), which were then being used experimentally at patients' own risk.

After returning to Paris, she goes back to work at the J. Lerendu studio. She makes portraits of the Lerendus, a reproduction of a Renaissance portrait of François I by Girolamo della Robbia for the castle in Chambord, and a sepulchral medallion (commissioned by Air France) of the violinist Ginette Neveu, who died in a tragic air catastrophe.

While in Paris, Szapocznikow had been continuing to use her Polish citizenship and the Polish version of her surname in addition to the Czech documentation obtained in Prague using a false birthplace. Her dual identity is noted in France, and proceedings for her deportation are initiated. Illness and financial troubles force Szapocznikow to abandon her studies.
Her 1950 diploma work *Nu (Grande Figure)* (*Large Nude*) is selected for the first-place medal, but she is not able to complete her defense for the diploma.

In May, Szapocznikow travels to Poland due to health and inheritance matters, spending the summer at the seaside with her mother. In her letters to Stanisławski, she expresses fascination with the possibilities in her native country. She visits the stoneworking studios of Warsaw's Old Town and the Powązki cemetery and tours the rebuilt city. Upon returning to Paris in late July, she creates a sketch of a male figure

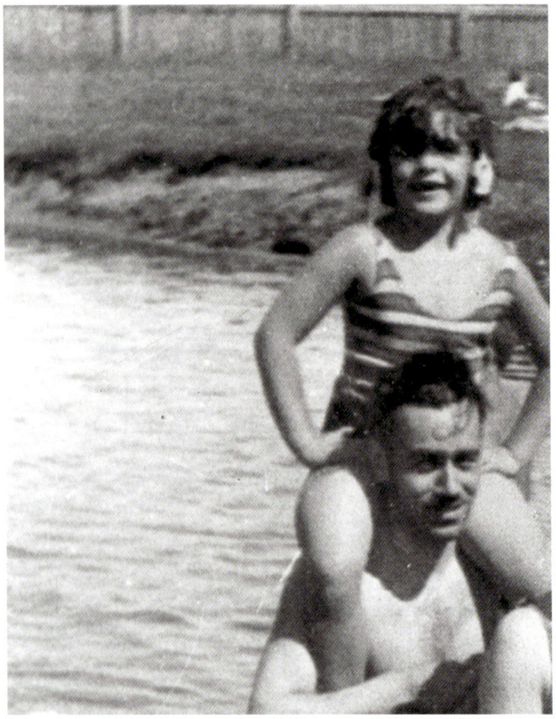
The artist with her father, on vacation at the seaside, mid-1930s. This image was used in her 1971 sculpture *Souvenir I*.

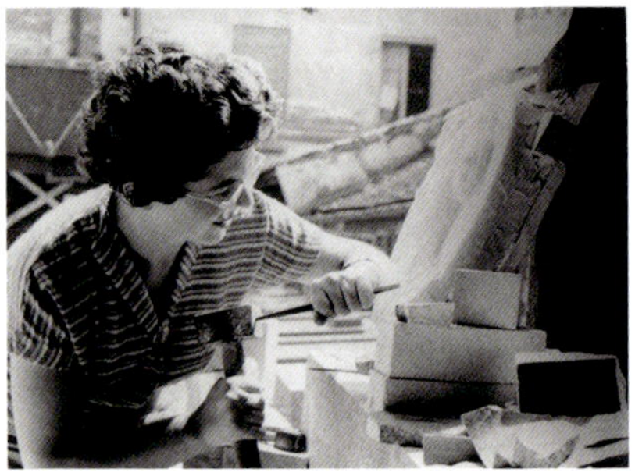
The artist working on a sepulchral medallion for the violinist Ginette Neveu, J. Lerendu studio, Paris, 1950.

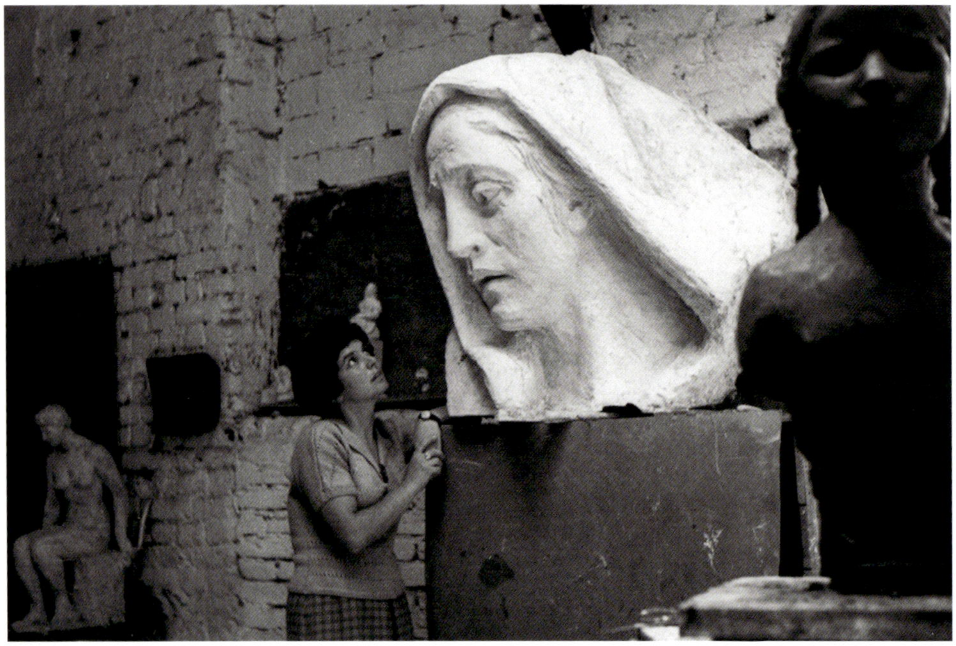
The artist in her Królewska Street studio in Warsaw, 1952.

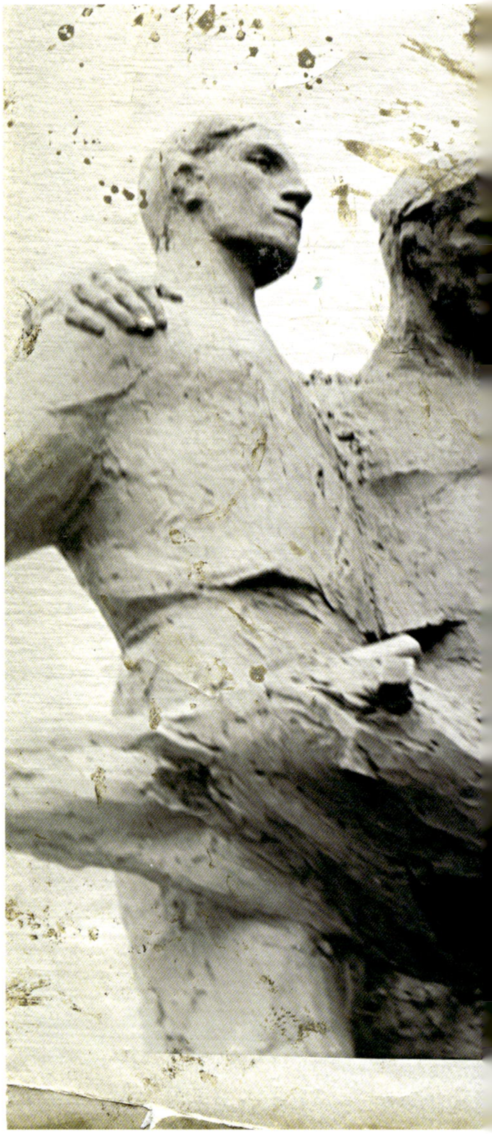

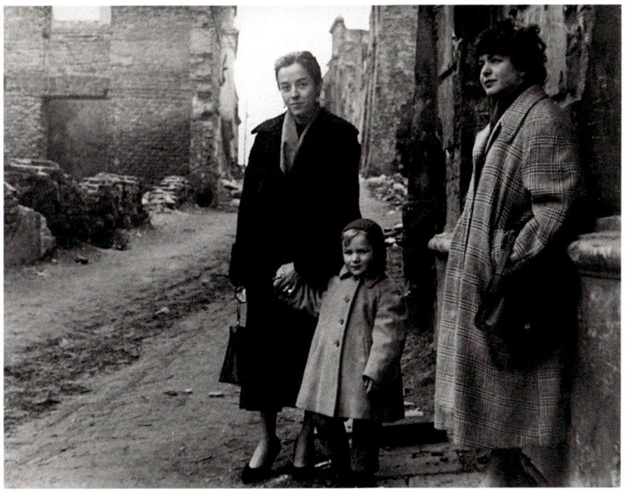

Naya Marquez-Rodilez, Piotr, and the artist amid the ruins of Warsaw, 1956.

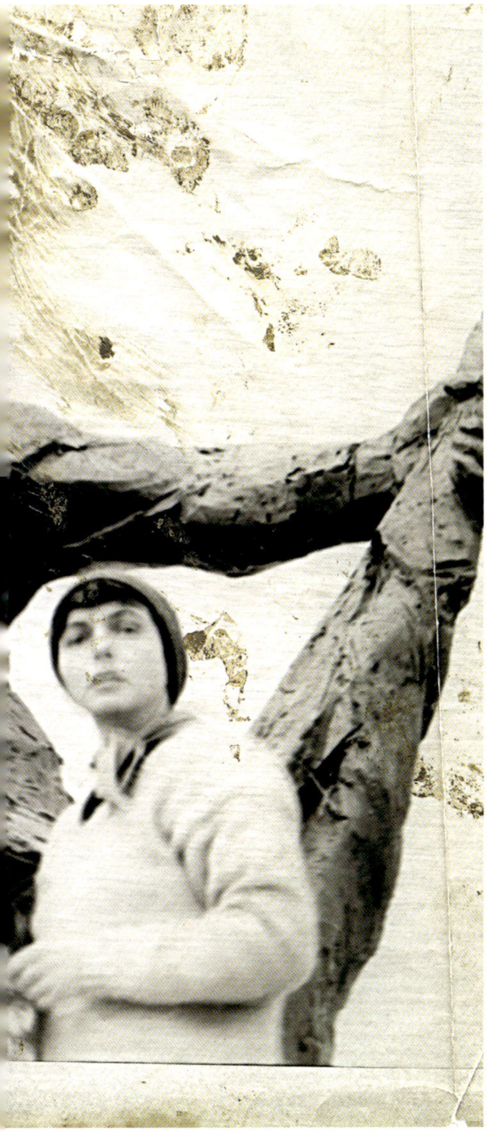

The artist with her work *Pomnik Przyjaźni Polsko-Radzieckiej* (Monument to Polish-Soviet Friendship), c. 1954.

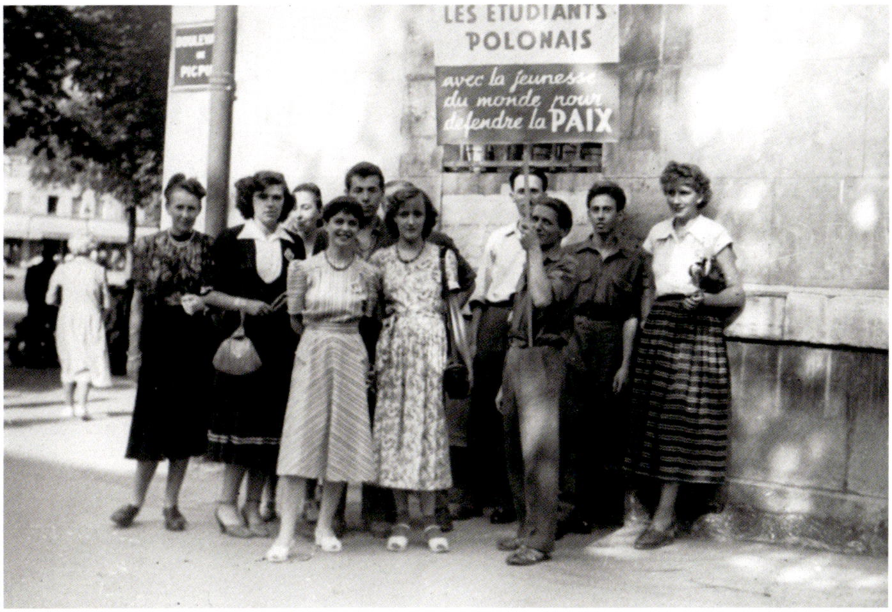

Polish students demonstrating in Paris, 1949. Szapocznikow is third from the left, in a striped dress.

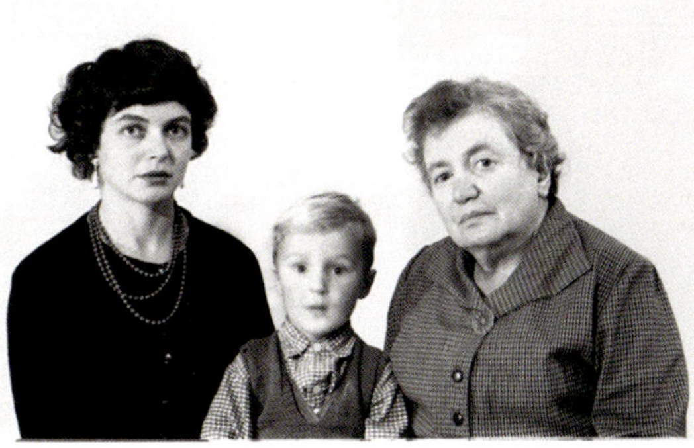

The artist with her mother and son Piotr, Christmas 1955.

titled *Droga do socjalizmu* (*Road to Socialism*).

Szapocznikow and Stanisławski decide to return to Poland, but first travel around France from mid-August to mid-October in a car bought with the help of Gaston Lerendu. They visit architectural sites and museums throughout France and visit Pablo Picasso at the villa "La Galloise" in Vallauris.

Exhibitions
"VI Exposition des Artistes Juifs," Paris

> In her first pieces—huge objects of natural size and simple sketches which she spontaneously enlarges to monumental size—Alina Szapocznikow displayed a talent for sculpture which was already very mature on the eve of her return to Poland. Busts occupy a key role among these early works, modeled with a precision that is rigorous and full of expression, and that could seem indiscreet if not for the fact that one feels in them as much love as in the psychologically cruel reality of her other works. (…) This delicate girl, whose mind, cheerfulness, liveliness and touching reasonability are so impressive, is only happy when she is working with a two ton block of stone.
>
> René Lacôte, "La jeune sculpture polonaise. Alina Szapocznikow," *Parallèle 50* (1950). Translated by Szymon Włoch.

1951

After returning to their homeland in February, Szapocznikow and Stanisławski have to face a new reality: Communist Poland. They experience housing problems and must live in the warehouses of the Central Artistic Exhibitions Office in Warsaw's Saska Kępa district. Szapocznikow begins work in the office overseeing the construction of Marszałkowska Street Residential Area (MDM) and is then assigned a flat on Marszałkowska Street.

She takes part in competitions, including one for the design of a Chopin monument, which she enters with Oskar Hansen, whom she met in Paris; they receive an honorable mention. In December, she makes her debut at the "2nd Polish Arts Exhibition" at Zachęta National Gallery of Art. Organized by the state, the exhibition awards prizes that serve as state patronage during the years of Socialist Realism. Without adequate studio space, she is forced to exhibit old works from her time in Paris, showing *Głowa Chłopca I* (*Head of a Boy*, 1949) and *Pokój* (*Peace*, 1949–50). Nonetheless, her work is warmly received by critics.

Exhibitions
"II Ogólnopolska Wystawa Plastyki" (2nd Polish Arts Exhibition), Zachęta National Gallery of Art, Warsaw, December – January (exh. cat.)

1952

She enters more competitions. For the design of a monument for Auschwitz-Birkenau she uses her Paris-era work *Kobieta w chuście* (*Woman in a Head Scarf*, 1949). For the competition connected with the Olympic Games in Helsinki, she creates *Gimnastyczka* (*Gymnast*).

Szapocznikow and Stanisławski marry on July 12. They adopt a boy, Piotr, several months after their wedding, entering his birth date as July 22, 1952, on official papers. Although Szapocznikow is unable to have children as a result of her previous illness, they do not reveal that their son is adopted, even to close friends. (Piotr finds out he is adopted only after his mother's death.)

Exhibitions
Exhibition of artworks in connection with the tenth anniversary of the Polish Workers' Party
"III Ogólnopolska Wystawa Plastyki" (3rd Polish Arts Exhibition), Zachęta National Gallery of Art, Warsaw, December – February (exh. cat.)

1953

After Stalin's death on March 5, totalitarian oppression begins to ease in the countries under Soviet control, and artistic life begins to change as well. Szapocznikow's works become more controversial in subject matter and expressive in form. The sculptural group *Getto – Walka* (*Ghetto – Fight*) at the exhibition for the tenth anniversary of the Warsaw Ghetto Uprising demonstrates her dedication to the subject. She spends spring at the seaside working on the conservation of sculptures for Gdańsk's Old Town and prepares her competition entry to design a monument commemorating the Defenders of the Coast at Westerplatte.

Exhibitions
"Dziesiąta rocznica powstania w getcie warszawskim" (10th Anniversary of the Warsaw Ghetto Uprising), Jewish Institute, Warsaw, April
"IV Wystawa OW ZPAP" (4th Exhibition of the Association of Polish Artists Warsaw Chapter), Zachęta National Gallery of Art, Warsaw, July – August (exh. cat.)

1954

A jury selects her design for a monument to Polish-Soviet friendship, and Szapocznikow receives a studio space near the Palace of Culture and Science, in the former market building (no longer extant) on Królewska Street in Warsaw, which she uses until 1959. Here she develops the model for a Stalin monument on a 1 to 1 scale in the spring and the first version of *Pomnik Przyjaźni Polsko-Radzieckiej* (*Monument to Polish-Soviet Friendship*) in the autumn.

> I usually arrive at the studio at 9 and put on a grey sweater, which I had made for myself many years ago and cannot part with. Only when I have it on do I feel like I'm ready to get to work. I finish at about 5 pm. During this time, I don't open the studio door to anyone, unless we have an appointment. Whenever I need to borrow some tools, when my pump for spraying the sculptures needs repairing, when I need a specialist to help me with shaping steel—all I need to do is step outside the gate. After all, my studio is located in the "Swamp" area, a neighbourhood of steel and craftsmen. They value their manual skills greatly and are always willing to offer professional help. One of them described my studio in a very humorous way: "that lady has a small factory for delicate things." Anything that is built, and especially from wire, steel—solid materials—gets their respect.
>
> Szapocznikow, in discussion with Barbara Henkel, "Rzeźby oddychają dopiero w przestrzeni" (Sculptures breathe only in open space), in *Sztandar Młodych*, no. 169 (1960): 1 – 2. Translated by Szymon Włoch.

Szapocznikow makes direct casts of human body parts for the first time, including a posthumous mask of friend and graphic artist Tadeusz Trepkowski.

Exhibitions
"IV Ogólnopolska Wystawa Plastyki"

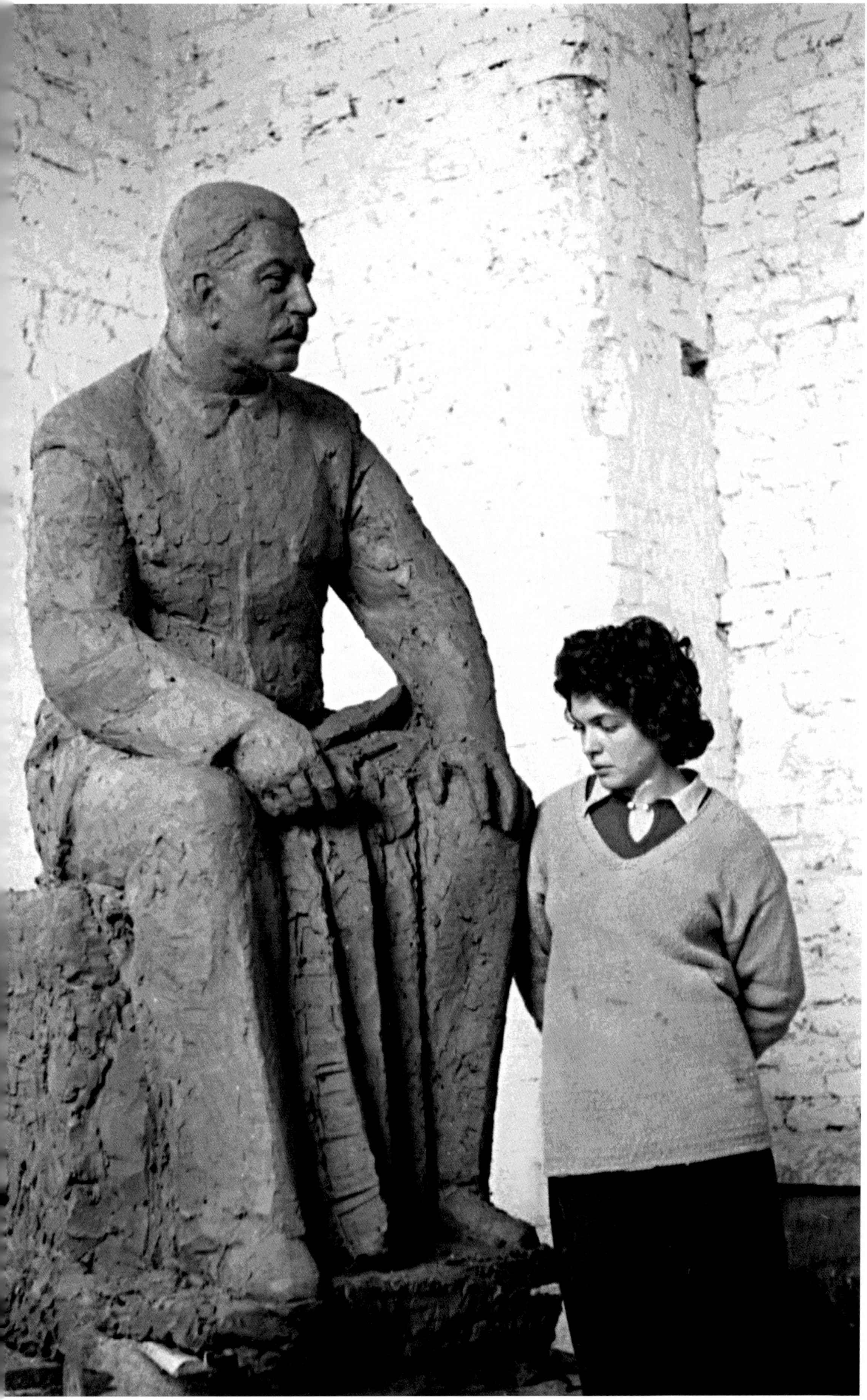

The artist next to her work *Stalin*, spring 1954.

(4th Polish Arts Exhibition), Zachęta National Gallery of Art, Warsaw, June – September (exh. cat.)

1955 Szapocznikow completes the *Monument to Polish-Soviet Friendship*, which is cast in bronze and placed in the main hall of the Palace of Culture and Science in Warsaw. Its unveiling is planned for the "5th International Festival of Youths and Students in Warsaw."

In the summer, she contributes (with Jerzy Sołtan and Zbigniew Ihnatowicz) to the Polish Pavilion in Damascus, offering *Alegoria Przemysłu* (*Allegory of Industry*) to be displayed inside the pavilion.

Szapocznikow also takes part in an exhibition during the "5th International Festival of Youths and Students." The festival exhibition, the "Polish Exhibition of Young Arts" under the banner "Against war and fascism" at Warsaw's Arsenal, and the World Youth Festival, which was characterized by a general sentiment of freedom and openness, all effect a fundamental breakthrough in Poland's cultural atmosphere. This younger generation confidently withdraws from the Socialist-Realist art propagated by the authorities. Though *Monument to Polish-Soviet Friendship* does not subscribe to this sensibility, Szapocznikow's *Pierwsza miłość* (*First Love*, 1954) [plate 147], presented at the festival exhibition, bravely turns away from the state-supported, Socialist-Realist model through a bold individuality. The year ushers in a new era, free of political pressure and open to Western art and ideas, as well as unabashed statements of personal belief.

Szapocznikow makes *Ekshumowany* (*Exhumed*) in homage to László Rajk, the Hungarian activist murdered in 1949 and vindicated during Hungary's political thaw. (She first exhibited the piece under the title *Rehabilitowany* [*Vindicated*] or *Rehabilitacja* [*Vindication*], but later gave it a more universal title.)

Exhumed, a small sculpture whose height does not exceed 60 cm, not only constitutes Alina Szapocznikow's private memento of her own experiences with the dead, but it is also a unique warning. The artist condemns Stalinism, which allows a cynical and apparent rehabilitation of its victims. The artist pays her homage to László Rajk, a Hungarian politician and victim of political purges, who was tortured to death a few years earlier and was now rehabilitated. At the same time, Szapocznikow paid homage to all the victims, including the insurgents, whose remains were often unearthed during the restoration of Warsaw; these remains were often difficult to disentangle from the burnt fragments of buildings; they stuck to the debris, likewise the figure of the Czech hermit whom she had remembered from the sculpture of Matthias Braun; the remains of the insurgents were now being unearthed, but their ideological message often continued to be derided.

Urszula Czartoryska, "Transgression. On the Message of Alina Szapocznikow's Art," in *Alina Szapocznikow. Zatrzymać życie. Rysunki i rzeźby (Capturing Life. Drawings and Sculptures)* (Kraków and Warsaw: IRSA, 2004), 69. Translated by Piotr Mizia.

Exhibitions

"V Międzynarodowy Festiwal Młodzieży i Studentów w Warszawie" (5th International Festival of Youths and Students in Warsaw), Zachęta National Gallery of Art, Warsaw, August 9 – 14 (exh. cat.)
"VI Wystawa OW ZPAP" (6th Exhibition of the Association of Polish Artists Warsaw Chapter), Zachęta National Gallery of Art, Warsaw, November – December (exh. cat.)

1956

Szapocznikow's work gains recognition among Poland's eminent critics, Andrzej Jakimowicz, Aleksander Wojciechowski, Elżbieta Grabska, and Mieczysław Porębski.

During a large retrospective of Spanish art at Zachęta National Gallery of Art, she befriends Naya Marquez-Rodilez, wife of the exhibition curator, and goes on to make *Koński ogon – Portret Meksykanki* (*A Pony Tail – Portrait of a Mexican Woman*, 1955–56) [plate 148].

She spends the summer in Paris in connection with a presentation of Polish art at Musée Rodin, organized by Mieczysław Porębski. *Pomnik dla spalonego miasta* (*Monument to a Burned-Down City*, 1954) and *First Love* are shown at the "Exposition Internationale de Sculpture Contemporaine." Thanks to a positive review of *First Love* by the French critic Jean Cassou, the piece is purchased by the Musée d'Art Moderne de la Ville de Paris.

Szapocznikow enters a contest for the design of the exhibition pavilion at "Expo '58" in Brussels. While working on the project, she meets Roman Cieślewicz, who is on the project team, with whom she would later start a relationship. She creates *Ptak* (*Bird*), a sculpture used by the team in their mock-up for the project. Though the mock-up is selected for the joint first prize, the project is ultimately awarded to the team headed by Jerzy Sołtan. Her letters to Stanisławski indicate her hopes to work on such a prestigious project.

After returning to Poland, she makes *Trudny wiek* (*Difficult Age*) [plate 149], which garners very favorable reviews. She begins to experiment with new materials, trying her hand at ceramics when invited to use the ceramics studio of Warsaw's Academy of Fine Arts. She produces *Garnki-głowy* (*Jugs-Heads*), *Czerepy* (*Shards*), and *Ludzie-drzewa* (*People Trees*, 1957). She receives several portrait commissions, including those from Krzysztof Teodor Toeplitz, Zofia Butrymowicz, and Michel Lustre.

Exhibitions

"Polish Art Exhibition in India 1956," New Delhi, Madras, Calcutta, and Bombay, India, February – June (curated by Andrzej Jakimowicz; exh. cat.)
"Exposition Internationale de Sculpture Contemporaine," Musée Rodin, Paris, June – October (curated by Mieczysław Porębski; exh. cat.)
"Junge Generation—Polnische Kunstausstellung," Berlin and Leipzig, Germany, July 21 – August 15 (curated by Elżbieta Grabska; exh. cat.)

1957

Szapocznikow meets art historian Urszula Czartoryska, who begins to follow the artist's career, and creates two sculptures based on a portrait study of her. (Years later, after Szapocznikow's death, Czartoryska would write a probing analysis of her work.) In the summer, Szapocznikow breaks up with Stanisławski (their divorce is finalized on July 21, 1958) and starts a relationship with Cieślewicz, with whom she shares her flat on Old Town Market Square in Warsaw. Stanisławski, who soon begins a relationship with Czartoryska, would remain a close friend of the artist for the rest of her life (he would later serve as director of the Muzeum Sztuki, Łódź, for many years and as custodian of her artistic legacy after her relocation to France).

The studio on Królewska Street becomes the setting for a documentary

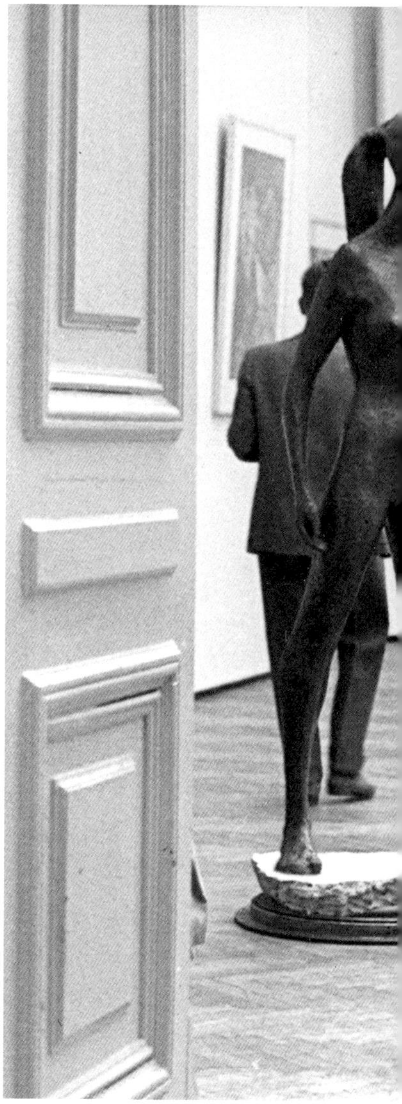

on Szapocznikow filmed by Roman Polanski on commission of Jean-Marie Drot and French television.

Szapocznikow's works continue to attract attention from Polish curators and critics. She is invited to all of the country's leading presentations of art by Jadwiga Jarnuszkiewiczowa, Toeplitz, and Wojciechowski. *Exhumed* becomes especially popular and is included in various exhibitions of Polish art abroad. Szapocznikow prepares her first large-scale monographic exhibition at Zachęta National Gallery of Art in Warsaw, curated by Porębski.

Late in the year, Szapocznikow begins casting small sculptural forms in lead without the help of a founder, making them entirely herself and shaping the material with her bare hands.

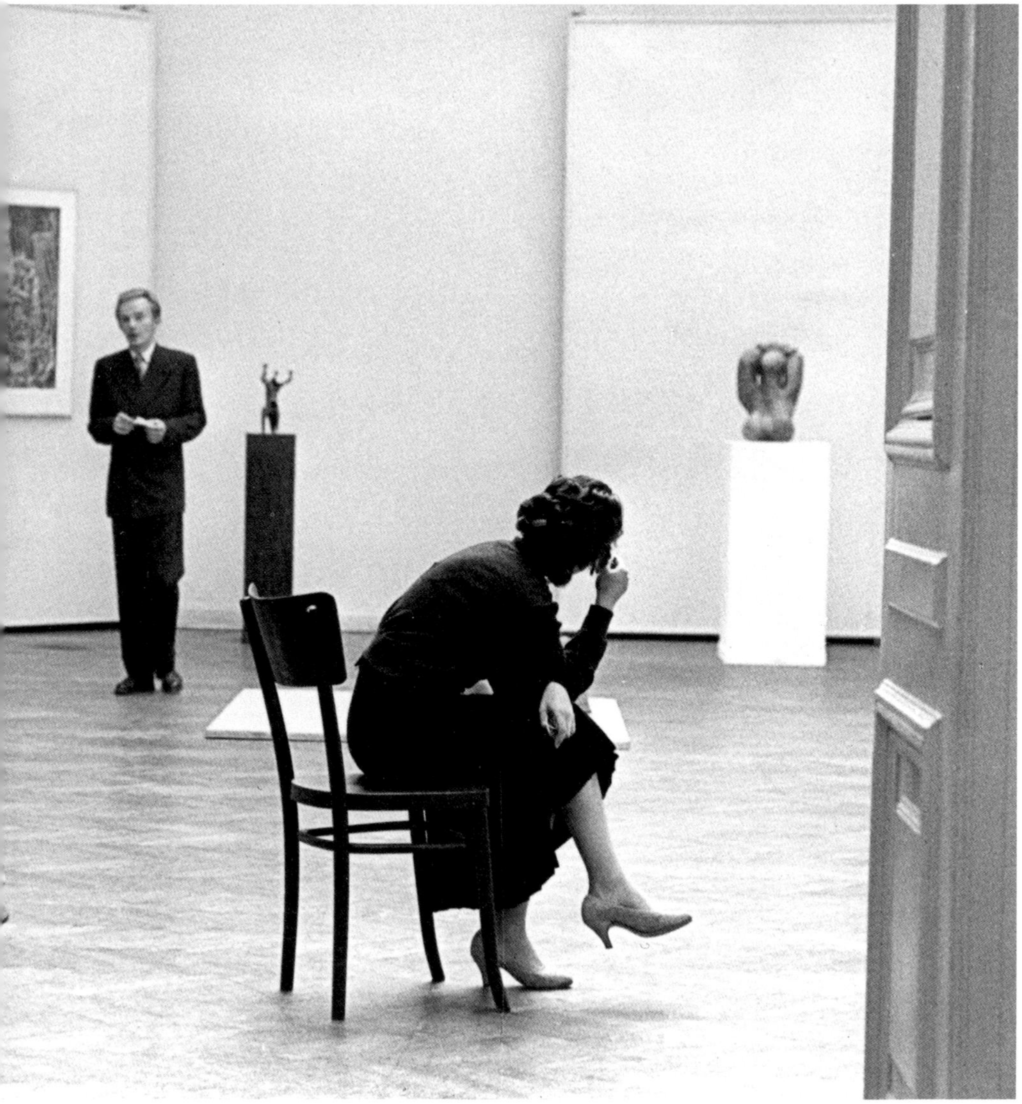

The artist sitting in her exhibition "Wystawa prac Aliny Szapocznikow i Jerzego Tchórzewskiego" at the Zachęta National Gallery of Art, Warsaw, in 1957.

Exhibitions

"Młode Malarstwo i Rzeźba. X Festiwal Sztuk Plastycznych" (Young Painting and Sculpture. 10th Festival of Fine Arts), Biuro Wystaw Artystycznych (BWA) Sopot, Poland, June 15 – July 21 (curated by Krzysztof Teodor Toeplitz; exh. cat.)
"Wystawa prac Aliny Szapocznikow i Jerzego Tchórzewskiego" (Alina Szapocznikow and Jerzy Tchórzewski), Zachęta National Gallery of Art, Warsaw, September 6 – 26 (curated by Mieczysław Porębski; exh. cat.)
"Rzeźba w ogrodzie" (Sculpture in the Garden), Stowarzyszenie Architektów Polskich (SARP) gardens on Foksal Street, Warsaw, September 12 – October 17 (curated by Jadwiga Jarnuszkiewiczowa; exh. cat.)
"II Wystawa Sztuki Nowoczesnej" (2nd Exhibition of Modern Art), Zachęta National Gallery of Art, Warsaw, October 18 – November 17 (curated by Mieczysław Porębski; exh. cat.)

1958

In January, art critic Giuseppe Marchiori visits her studio on Królewska Street, resulting in a 1960 exhibition of her work in Prato, Italy.

Szapocznikow completes the sculpture *Maria Magdalena* (*Mary Magdalene*) [plate 143], considered by critics as the most representative of her work from the late 1950s: close to organic abstraction and referencing biological forms, especially sensual/feminine ones. During this period she suspends works above the floor—heavy forms connected to tall rods, such as the huge, hanging *Macierzyństwo (Wisząca)* (*Motherhood [Hanging]*) and *Owoc* (*Fruit*, 1957–58) that seem to defy gravity. Towards the end of the year, she begins to make bronze casts without the aid of a founder, employing the lost-wax casting technique.

She enters more competitions. During the first round of a competition for a monument to the Heroes of the Warsaw Ghetto, she shows two designs developed by two independent teams. She also works on a team designing a competition submission for a monument at the Auschwitz-Birkenau concentration camp. The competition jury—including Jacob Bakema, Henry Moore, Giuseppe Perugini, and August Zamoyski—selects her team's design in the first stage of the competition.

Exhibitions

"II Ogólnopolska Wystawie Młodego Malarstwa, Rzeźby i Grafiki. XI Festiwal Sztuk Plastycznych" (2nd Polish Exhibition of Young Painting, Sculpture, and Graphic Art. 11th Festival of Fine Arts), BWA Sopot, Poland, June 14 – July 22 (exh. cat.)
"Internationale Beeldenteentoostelling in de Open Lucht," Sonsbeek Park, Arnhem, the Netherlands, June 15 – September 15 (exh. cat.)

1959

In January, the second stage of the competition for a monument to the Heroes of the Warsaw Ghetto is announced. Szapocznikow takes a new approach to the subject matter, reconstructing the original design into one of her biological/sensual forms to create *Pnąca* (*Climbing*). In spring, she and a team of fitters prepare an exposition of *Syrena III* (*Mermaid III*) at the summertime "Exhibition of Polish Industry" in Moscow's Gorky Park. The sculpture is prepared in the courtyard of the Academy of Fine Arts in Warsaw over several months.

In October, she shows *Mary Magdalene* at the "Youth Biennale" in Paris. While there, she stays at her friend César's flat, gets many professional propositions, and is generally very well received, which

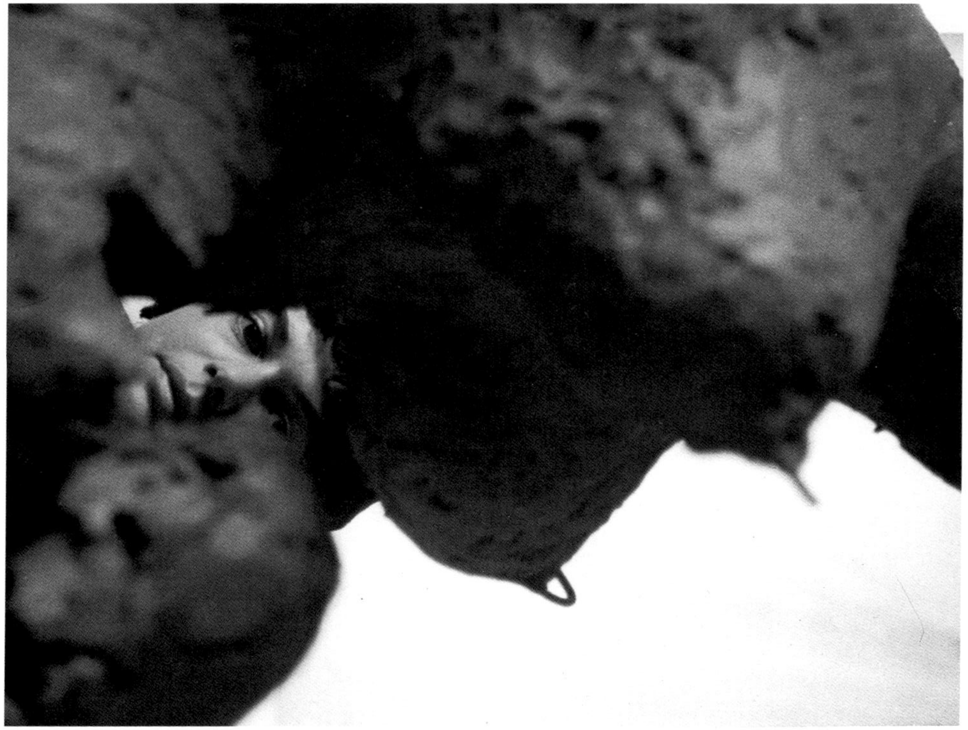

The artist in 1958.

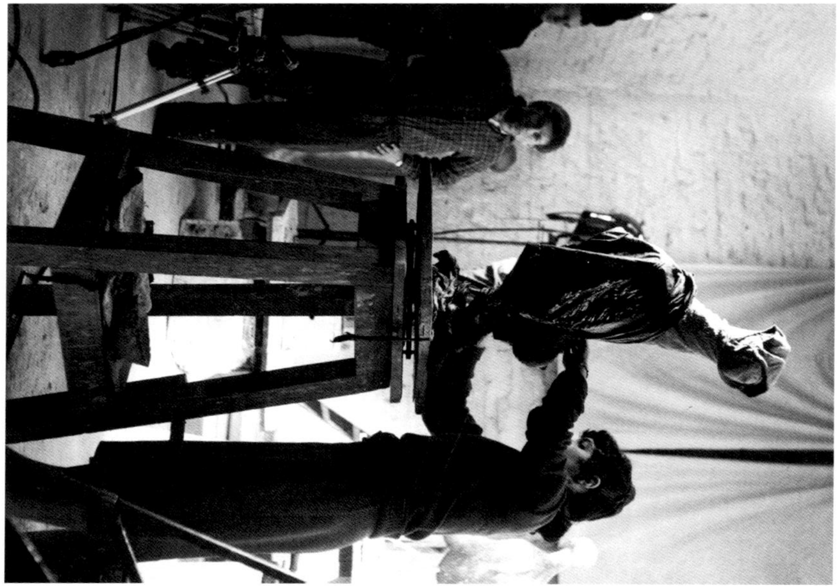

The artist in her Królewska Street studio in Warsaw during the shooting of a documentary for French television, 1957. She is working on *Kobieta (Dziewczyna z długą szyją)* (Woman [Girl with a long neck], 1957) while Roman Polański, who filmed the piece, looks on from the background.

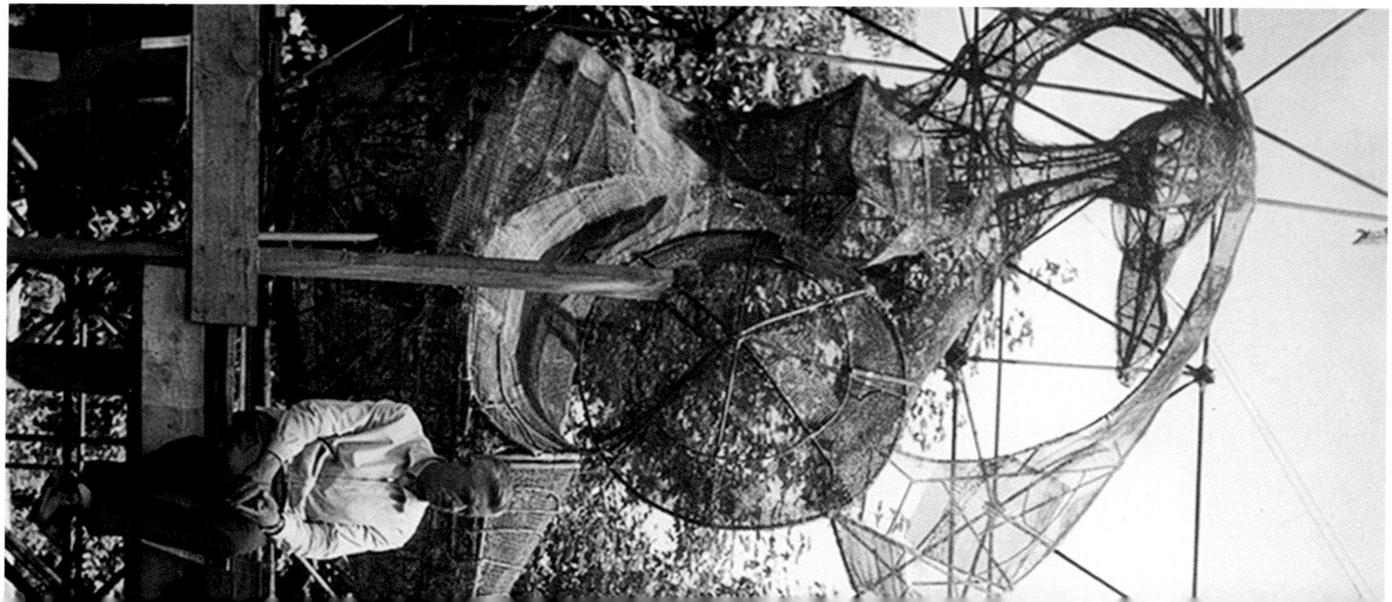

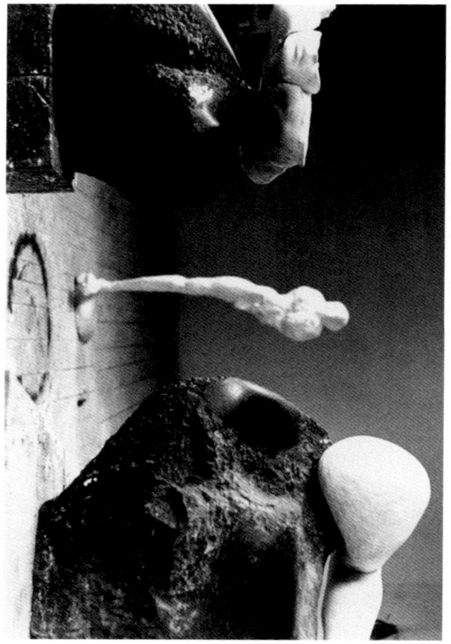

The artist's studio on Brzozowa Street in Warsaw, summer 1965. From left to right, *Portret wielokrotny (dwukrotny)* (Multiple Portrait [Double], 1965), *Filozof* (Philosopher, 1965), and *Noga* (Leg, 1965).

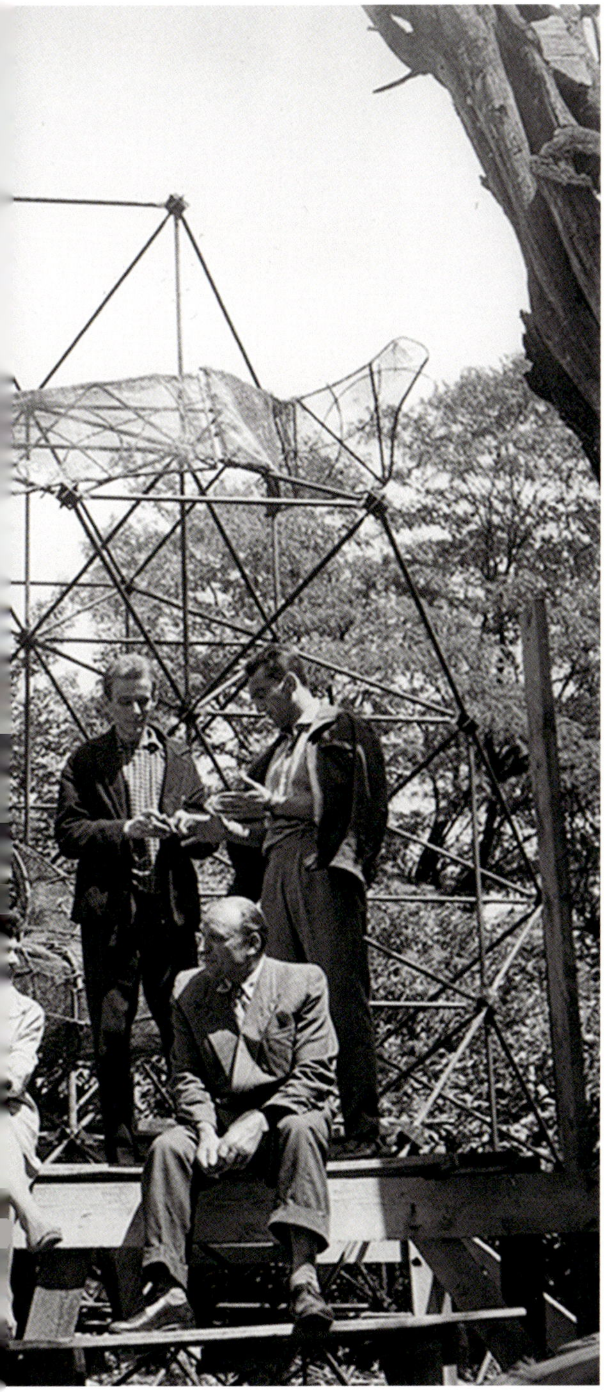

The artist in the courtyard of Warsaw's Academy of Fine Arts working on *Syrena III* (Mermaid III) for an exhibition in Moscow, summer 1959.

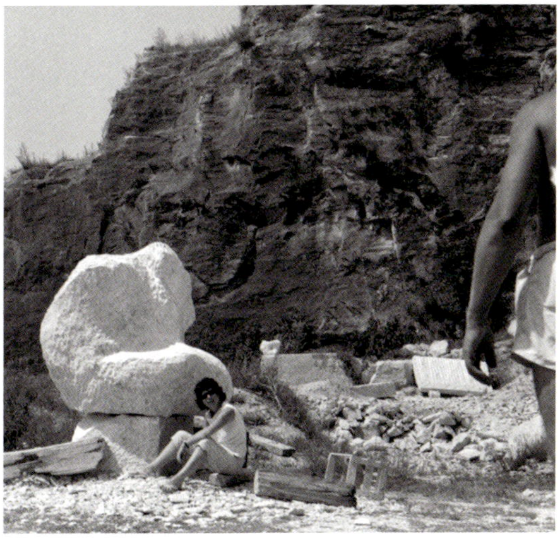

The artist at a 1961 international sculpture symposium in St. Margarethen, Austria, creating her work *Miąższ* (Pulp, 1961).

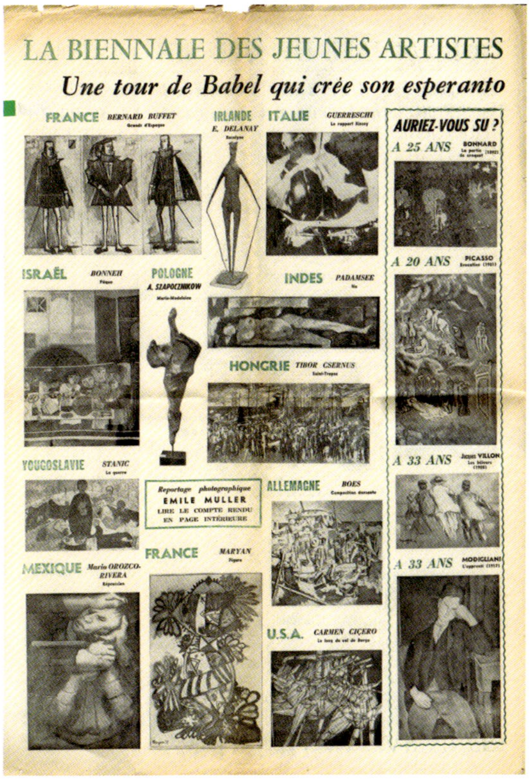

LA BIENNALE DES JEUNES ARTISTES

Une tour de Babel qui crée son esperanto

FRANCE BERNARD BUFFET

IRLANDE E. DELANAY

ITALIE GUERRESCHI

AURIEZ-VOUS SU ?

A 25 ANS BONNARD

ISRAËL BONNEH

POLOGNE A. SZAPOCZNIKOW

INDES PADAMSEE

A 20 ANS PICASSO

HONGRIE TIBOR CSERNUS

Saint-Tropez

YOUGOSLAVIE STANIC

Reportage photographique EMILE MULLER LIRE LE COMPTE RENDU EN PAGE INTÉRIEURE

ALLEMAGNE BOES

A 33 ANS Jacques VILLON

FRANCE MARYAN

MEXIQUE Mario OROZCO-RIVERA

U.S.A. CARMEN CIÇERO

A 33 ANS MODIGLIANI

An article on "La Biennale des jeunes artistes" in *Les Lettres Françaises*, no. 793 (1959).
The artist's work *Maria Magdalena* (Mary Magdalene, 1957–58) is reproduced.

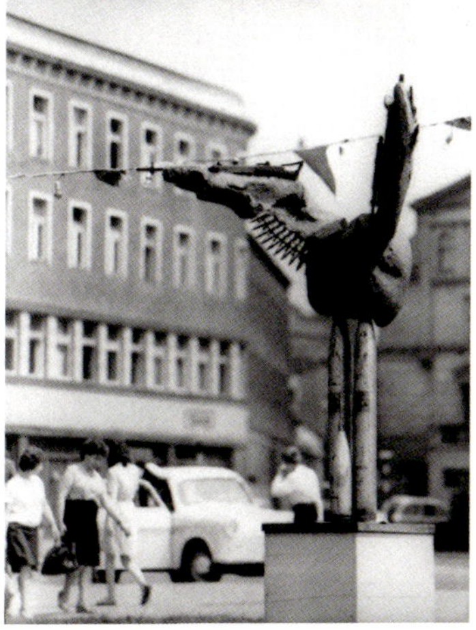

The artist's work *Nike* (1963) exhibited in "Polska rzeźba plenerowa" (Polish Plein Air Sculpture) at the Opole Silesia Museum in Opole, Poland, 1964.

awakens a desire to relocate to France again.

Exhibitions
Exhibition of designs submitted to the International Competition for a Monument at Auschwitz, Galleria d'Arte Moderna, Rome, July
"XIII Biennale d'Arte Triventa. III Concorso Internazionale del Bronzetto," Padua, Italy, September 26 – November (exh. cat.)
"III Wystawa Sztuki Nowoczesnej" (3rd Exhibition of Modern Art), Zachęta National Gallery of Art, Warsaw, September – December (curated by Roman Artymowski; exh. cat.)
"Première Biennale de Paris," Paris, October 1 – 25 (curated by Stanisław Teisseyre; exh. cat.)
"Pologne 10 ans de peinture," Musée d'Art et d'Histoire, Geneva, October 24 – November 29 (curated by Ryszard Stanisławski; exh. cat.)
"International Exhibition of Sculpture," Municipal Gallery of Modern Art, Dublin, Ireland, and Belfast, Northern Ireland, November 25 – December 20

1960

Szapocznikow further pursues technological experimentation. A series of works made of plastic cement—including *Corrida II*, *Małża* (*Mollusc*) [plate 135], and *Derwisz* (*Dervish*)—use a technique developed by the engineer Lipowski, in which the setting of molten material is delayed, allowing more time to shape the form and to encrust the cement with stone, clay, metal, or other materials. She uses a founder less often, even for larger bronze casts, which she makes herself using the lost-wax technique. Głowy (Heads) series (1960–61) and other works such as *Rozłupany* (*Shattered*) [plate 136], Gniazdo (Nests) series, *Tartuffe*, and *Diabeł* (*Devil*) exemplify this.

Szapocznikow moves to a new studio at 31/33 Brzozowa Street in Warsaw, where she lives with her son Piotr and Cieślewicz. Her work is included in numerous exhibitions both in Poland and abroad, five of which greatly solidify her position in the Polish arts scene and are widely covered in national media.

Exhibitions
"II wystawa rzeźby Aliny Szapocznikow" (2nd Exhibition of Sculpture by Alina Szapocznikow), BWA "Arsenał", Poznań, Poland, April 2 – 18 (curated by Juliusz Starzyński; exh. cat.)
"Alina Szapocznikow (Dessins)," Galleria Falsetti, Prato, Italy, May 22 – July 2 (curated by Giuseppe Marchiori; exh. cat.)
"Alina Szapocznikow. Konfrontacje 1960" (Confrontations 1960), Galeria Krzywe Koło, Warszawa zorganizowana z okazji Kongresu Krytyków Sztuki, from July 13 (curated by Aleksander Wojciechowski; exh. cat)
"Rzeźba Aliny Szapocznikow" (Alina Szapocznikow's Sculptures), part of the "13th Festival of Fine Arts," BWA Sopot, Poland, August (curated by Aleksander Wojciechowski; exh. cat.)

1961

Szapocznikow spends the summer abroad with Piotr and Cieślewicz, visiting Prague and later Rijeka, Yugoslavia (now Croatia), where a joint exhibition of her sculptures and Cieślewicz's prints takes place at Galerija Likovnih Umjetnosti. At the "Symposion Europäischer Bildhauer," an international sculpture symposium in St. Margarethen, Austria, she creates *Miąższ* (*Pulp*), which still stands on a hilltop near the Burgenland quarry. The stone mined there is not suitable for polishing, prompting her to highlight the substance of stone. The outdoor event elicits further artistic inquiry and broadens her interest in the materiality of sculpture.

Szapocznikow's mother dies of lung cancer in Warsaw.

Szapocznikow creates her first polyester work, *Pomnik kroczącej gwiazdy* (*Monument of the Moving Star*), purchased by the city of Warsaw after the exhibition "Sculpture in the 15th Year of the People's Republic" at the National Museum (the sculpture's whereabouts are currently unknown). *Naga* (*Naked*) [plate 132], which is praised at the exhibition, reveals a new motif: the head of the elongated figure is replaced by a horizontal form that dramatically contrasts with the body of the figure. Substituting a round head with an amorphous shape would become a recurring motif in Szapocznikow's work.

Another solo exhibition of her work takes place near the end of the year, this time at the Kordegarda Gallery in Warsaw.

Exhibitions
"The First Exhibition in America of Contemporary Polish Painting and Sculpture," The Gres Gallery, Washington, D.C., April 18 – May 13 (curated by Ryszard Stanisławski; exh. cat.)
"Alina Szapocznikow," Galerija Likovnih Umjetnosti, Rijeka, Yugoslavia, summer (curated by Boris Vižintin; exh. cat.)
"XIV Biennale d'Arte. IV Concorso Internazionale del Bronzetto," Padua, Italy, October – November
"Rzeźba w XV-lecie PRL" (Sculpture in the 15th Year of the People's Republic), Muzeum Narodowe w Warszawie, Warsaw, November 25 – January 9 (curated by Józef Trenarowski; exh. cat.)
"Alina Szapocznikow," "Kordegarda" Gallery, Warsaw, December 20 – January 3 (exh. cat.)

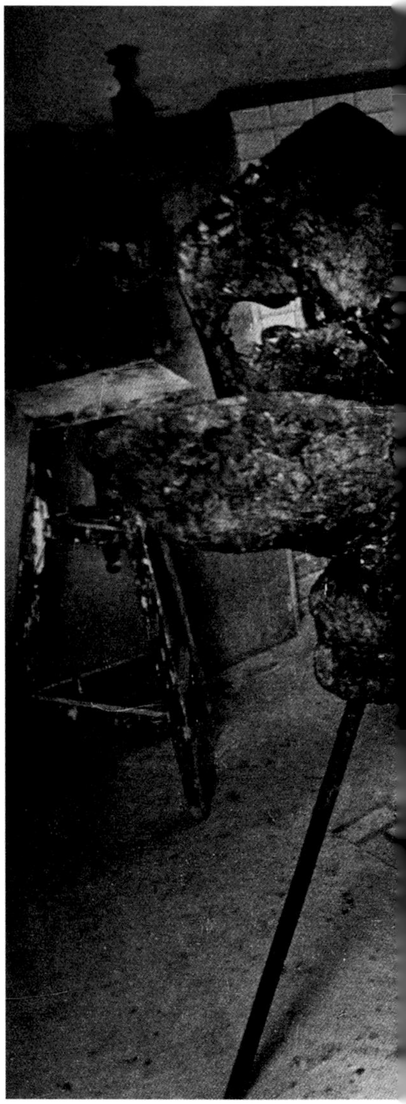

1962

Szapocznikow has a solo exhibition at the "XXXI Biennale di Venezia" in Venice, debuting the bronze versions of *Negro Spiritualis* (1961–62), *L'Incrustée* (*Encrusted*, 1961), *Przemiany* (*Transformations*), and the polyester *Monument of the Moving Star*. Further experimenting with materials, she combines sandstone and bronze for the first time. Though the exhibition is not considered a great success and mentions in the press are few, her work gets noticed by Pierre Restany, with whom Szapocznikow would remain in close contact for the rest of her life.

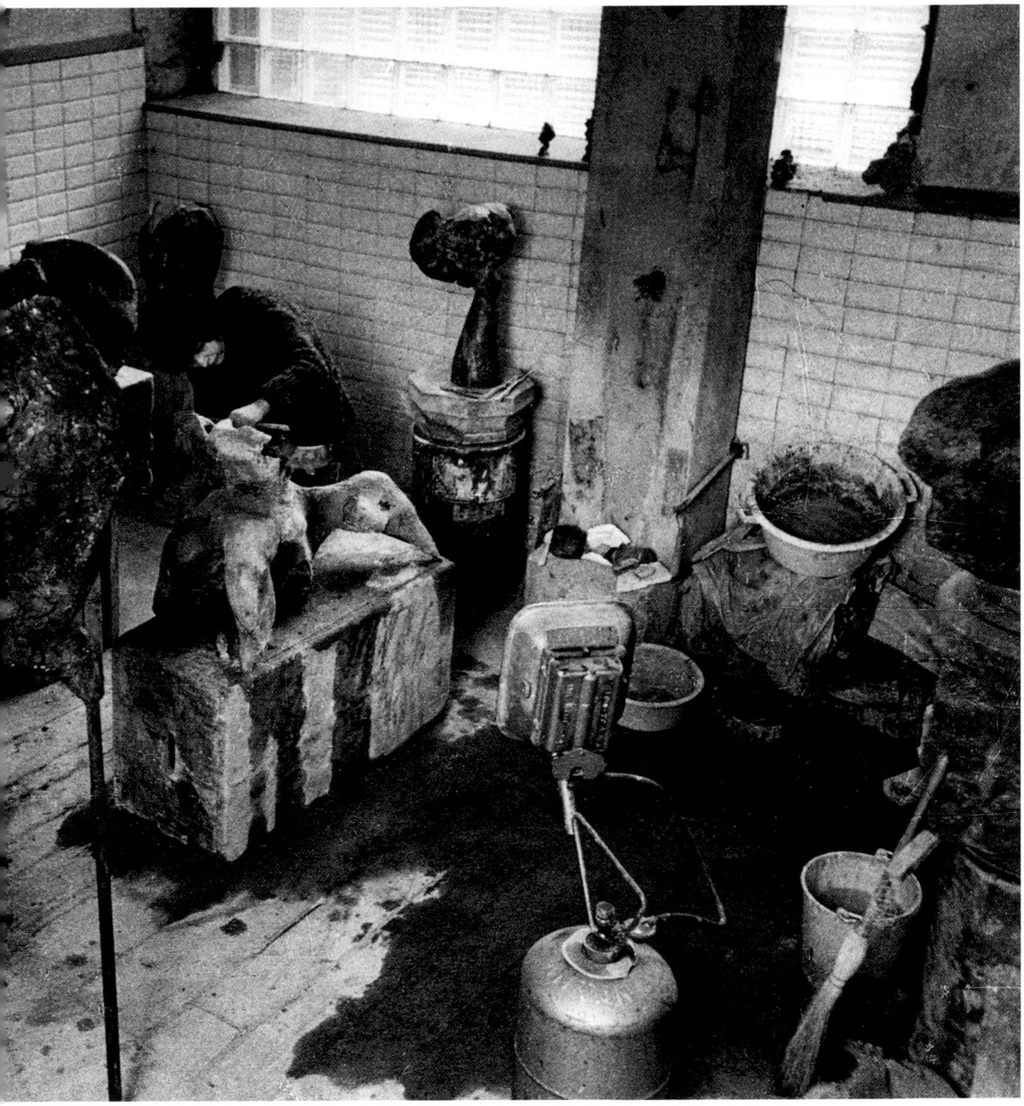

The artist working on *Crabe* (Crab, 1964) in her studio on avenue du Père-Lachaise, c. 1964. To the left is *Sculpture avec une roue tournante* (Sculpture with a Turning Wheel, 1963–64) and behind her is *Bouquet I* (1964).

She carries out commissions for public-use objects: a decorative grate for the ship Baltic of the Polish Ocean Lines and a grate for the Moda Polska (Polish Fashion) brand store on Konopnicka Street in Warsaw. (The piece was not retrieved after the store's liquidation and its whereabouts are unknown.)

Szapocznikow makes her first direct cast of her own body; the plaster cast of her leg [plate 129] becomes the starting point for her experimentation with direct casts in the mid-1960s.

> *Leg* is a genuine gesture of challenge towards human corporality, which does away with the logic of body structure, understood as a hierarchical entity. At the point where the leg has no connection with the hip, the bronze of the form is ostentatiously polished, as if it was a sovereign object, a sort of immense piece of jewellery, or a great lay relic. But one cannot resist the impression that the leg rests on a butcher's block and its ostentation is quasi-pornographic—it is not pornography in the colloquial sense of this word, but it is a cannibalistic type of pornography, which may ultimately denote the same thing. This human leg is undoubtedly another victim; it is a chopped-off member sacrificed to the gods, thus, it is a trace of the ritual transgressing the norms of the everyday. That is how I see it today—though I must admit that years ago, when I saw this sculpture for the first time, I did not think about cruelty, but about another aspect of carnality: namely, about the perfection of anatomy, about coquetry.

Urszula Czartoryska, "Transgression. On the Message of Alina Szapocznikow's Art," 71. Translated by Piotr Mizia.

Exhibitions

"Exposition internationale du petit bronze," Musée d'Art Moderne de la Ville de Paris, June 5 – 24

"Alina Szapocznikow," Polish Pavilion, Esposizione Internazionale d'Arte, XXXI Biennale di Venezia, Venice, Italy, June 16 – October 8 (Polish section curated by Stanisław Teisseyre; exh. cat.)

"III Biennale 'Città di Carrara,'" Palazzo Comunale, Carrara, Italy, July 14 – October 2 (exh. cat.)

1963

Szapocznikow begins another technological phase in her work, embedding various small elements into plastic cement. Her first assemblages include World War Two–era weapons. *Drang nach Osten* (*Drive to the East*) uses Nazi weaponry, while *Kolczasta* (*Prickly*) contains other fragments of armaments. *Nike* is studded with huge projectiles for the Russian Katyusha rocket launcher.

After making the headstone for her mother's grave in Warsaw, she gets requests for other headstones at the "communal" Powązki cemetery (otherwise known as Military Powązki).

During the summer, Szapocznikow vacations with her son and Cieślewicz in Yugoslavia and Italy. She is invited by Marjan Vidmar to the "'Forma Viva' International Sculpture Symposium" in Portorož, Yugoslavia (now Slovenia), where she creates *Rzeźba biologiczna* (*Biological Sculpture*). After the holiday, Szapocznikow and Cieślewicz decide to permanently relocate to Paris. They settle on rue Sextius-Michel in the fifteenth arrondissement. Cieślewicz joins the editorial staff of *Elle* magazine while Szapocznikow rents a studio near the Père-Lachaise cemetery (as she did in the 1940s).

Exhibitions
"Nigdy wiecej" (Never Again), Muzeum Narodowe w Warsawie, Warsaw, January
"Oświęcim. Wystawa w XVIII rocznicę wyzwolenia" (Auschwitz. Exhibition on the 18th Anniversary of the Liberation), Reduta Hall of the National Theatre, Warsaw, January 25 – February 10 (exh. cat.)
"XX rocznica powstania w getcie warszawskim" (20th Anniversary of the Warsaw Ghetto Uprising), MDM Gallery, Warsaw, April (exh. cat.: *Getto 1943*)
"XV Biennale d'Arte. V Concorso Internazionale del Bronzetto," Padua, Italy, October – November

1964

The early days in Paris are marked by difficulties. Piotr breaks his leg while skiing, resulting in financial troubles for the family. Szapocznikow is unable to work much that spring; the assemblages she does make feature used automobile parts. Despite her troubles, she manages to finish *Sculpture avec une roue tournante* (*Sculpture with a Turning Wheel*, 1963–64) for the "XVI Salon de la Jeune Sculpture" exhibition in July. On top of everything, she is forced to vacate her studio, as the building is slated for demolition.

Szapocznikow maintains contact with the art world in Poland and continues to receive interesting propositions. Stanisławski and Porębski invite her to the prestigious "Profile IV" exhibition in Bochum-Kassel, West Germany, to which she sends the largest of the works from her liquidated Paris studio, *Machine en chair*, in addition to some of the more valuable works that she had made in Poland and left behind, including *Rzeźba biologiczna II* (*Biological Sculpture II*), *Panna* (*Unmarried*, 1962–63), and *Pancerna II* (*Armored II*).

Exhibitions
"Polska rzeźba plenerowa" (Polish Plein Air Sculpture), organized by the Opole Silesia Museum on the twentieth anniversary of the Polish People's Republic, Plac Wolności, Opole, Poland, June – August (exh. cat.)
"XVI Salon de la Jeune Sculpture," Musée Rodin, Paris, July (exh. cat.)
"La boutique d'été," Galerie Lambert, Paris, July 3 – August 31
"Profile IV," Bochum-Kassel, West Germany, November 8 – January 17 (curated by Ryszard Stanisławski and Mieczysław Porębski; exh. cat.)

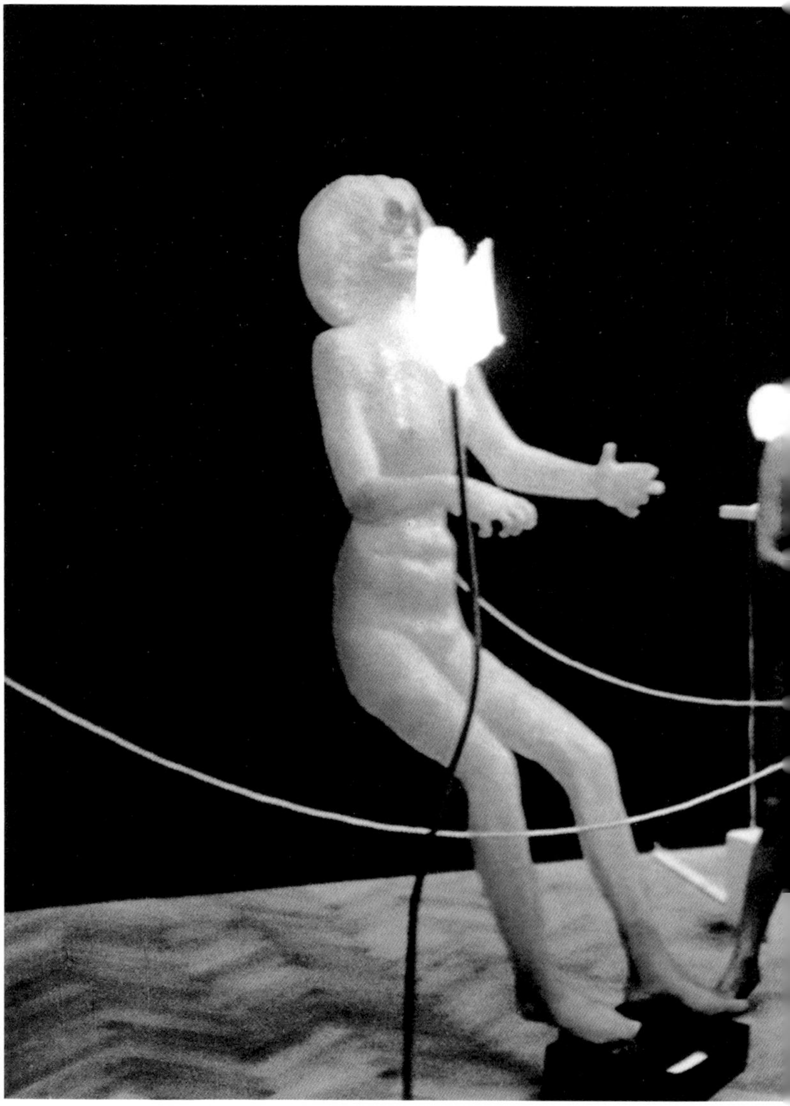

1965

In the spring, Szapocznikow and her family move to a house on rue Victor Hugo in Malakoff near Paris, where she has a private studio at her disposal. She continues to make terracotta sketches with small embedded fingerprints and casts of mouths. She begins to hone her focus on her own body while also making assemblages containing industrial objects, such as *Goldfinger* [plate 101], *Glowa X* (*Head X*), *Dwuczęściowa* (*In Two Parts*) [plate 104], *Człowiek z instrumentem* (*Man with Instrument*) [plate 99], *Femme de ménage* (*Cleaning Lady*)—occasionally embedding the works with earlier sculptures. *Goldfinger*, shown at the "XXI Salon de Mai" in May, leads to her being nominated for the Copley Foundation prize (the juror who nominated her, Marcel Duchamp, had visited her studio in the spring).

Endless financial difficulties in Paris force Szapocznikow to consider returning to Poland. In spring, she seriously contemplates taking a job at the sculpture department in Sopot (after Stanisław Horno-Popławski leaves). During the summer, she takes a long trip to Poland, where she works at the studio she still keeps on Brzozowa

Street. There, she creates a number of sculptures featuring elongated forms stretching out from the base, including *Modelka* (*Model*), *Filozof* (*Philosopher*), and *Jednonoga* (*One-Legged Woman*). She takes the plaster cast of her leg made in 1962 and places it on a pedestal. (*Noga* [*Leg*],

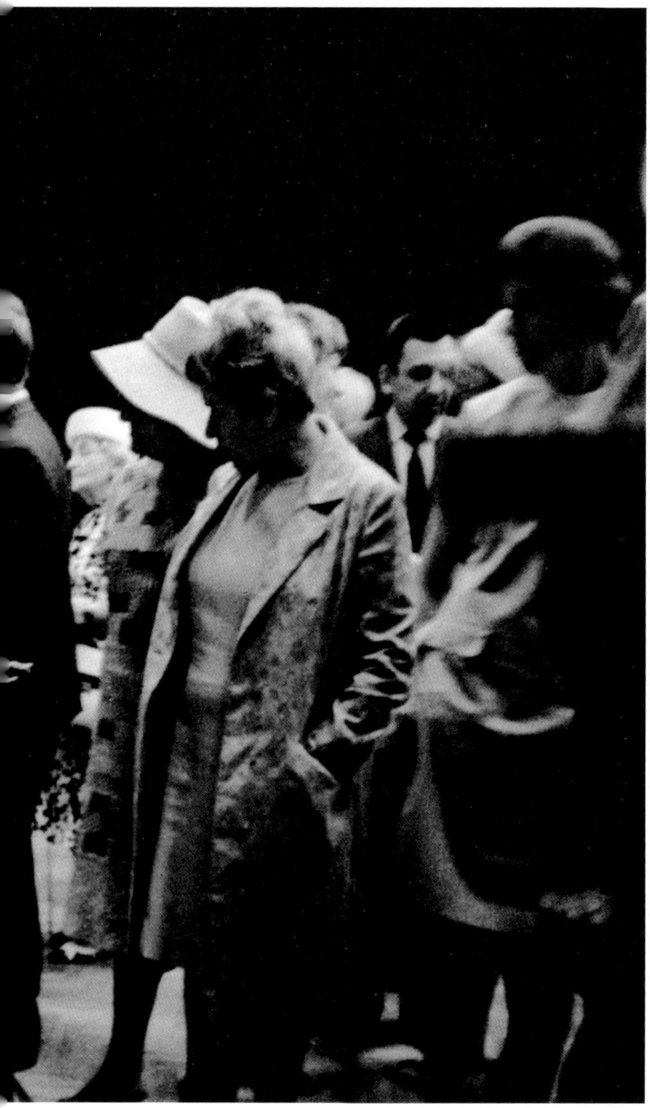

Visitors view *Le Voyage* (Journey, 1967) in the 1967 exhibition "Alina Szapocznikow, Rzeźba" (Alina Szapocznikow. Sculpture) at the Zachęta National Gallery of Art, Warsaw.

the bronze version, appears in 1967.) She also makes her first *Portret wielokrotny (dwukrotny)* (*Multiple Portrait [double]*), using casts of her own face in both plaster and bronze placed on a granite base (this version is shown at an exhibition at the Artist's House in Warsaw).

At the same time, César makes a cast of his thumb in Paris, enlarges it mechanically, and presents it at Claude Bernard's "La Main, de Rodin à Picasso" exhibition with the title *Thumb*. On this work's similarity to her own direct body casts, Szapocznikow writes:

> The exhibition was organised while I was in Warsaw. I couldn't take part in it, but... the centrepiece and main novelty at this generally dull exhibition, as is the case with most "thematic" exhibitions, was César's "thumb". (...)
>
> Dear Jerzy! You can imagine my shock and quandary, since only the photographer Marek Holzman and you, to whom I left the photographs before my departure, know that at that very time, being tormented by the fact that abstraction was becoming academic and perhaps a little out of perversity or even artistic exhibitionism, I made a cast of my own leg and a portrait montage with a cast of my face.
>
> Actually, in the Marchand jungle, the case is closed thanks to César. So, what now?! Fortunately, we know that everything in art had been done already—and therefore nothing has been done yet.
>
> Alina Szapocznikow, letter to Jerzy Stajuda, later published as "Z Paryża pisze Alina Szapocznikow [o Giacomettim]" (Alina Szapocznikow writes from Paris), *Współczesność*, no. 5 (1966). Translated by Szymon Włoch.

In November, Szapocznikow returns to Paris, a decision made possible in part by Cieślewicz's growing professional stature as he becomes artistic director at *Elle* while also beginning work at *Vogue*. Szapocznikow is denied a consular passport, which would allow her unlimited and unrestricted crossing of the border. Despite a tempting work offer in Sopot, she returns to Paris in November.

Exhibitions

"XX Salon des Réalitiés Nouvelles," Paris, April 5 – 27 (exh. cat.)
"XXI Salon de Mai," Musée d'Art Moderne de la Ville de Paris, May 3 – 23 (exh. cat.)
"IV Biennale Internazionale di Scultura," Palazzo Comunale, Carrara, Italy, summer
"8 Sculpteurs parisiennes," Botanical Gardens, Montreal, Canada
"Porównania" (Comparisons), BWA Sopot, Poland, September 25 – October 24 (curated by Ryszard Stanisławski; exh. cat.)

1966

On January 25, Szapocznikow is informed that she has won the Copley Foundation prize, whose jury consists of Jean Arp, Duchamp, Max Ernst, Roberto Matta, and Darius Milhaud.

In the winter, she finishes *Bouquet II* [plate 97], which consists of the 1962–63 plaster *Unmarried* wrapped in plastic foil, with a polyester bouquet of mouth-flowers protruding from it. Szapocznikow also makes the final version of *Table de café*, again by utilizing an old sculpture; she enters it into the "XVIII Salon de la Jeune Sculpture" at Place des Vosges in Paris.

Szapocznikow creates the Seins (Breasts) and Bouches (Mouths) series, as well as the first illuminated versions of these, lamps of polyester into which she embeds imprints of mouths—her own and those of Arianne Raoul-Auval, partner of Szapocznikow's friend Roland Topor, and actress Julie Christie [plates 15, 17]. An early lamp is shown by Michel Ragon at the "L'Objet 2" exhibition in the Lacloche Gallery in Paris.

> The plastic mass casts, constituting the artist's latest study in opening her eyes to the real world, introduce something new to Alina Szapocznikow's repertoire of technical means of expression—translucency and lighting effects. The forests of fire-red lips, the sprawling torso dunes with nipples glistening like pearls, the glowing sphere breasts heavy with electrical glare: these freshest works by Alina Szapocznikow bring to mind, among the wonder that is the new "Jugendstil," women/flowers and the splendour of bodies bulging from light flickering on the inside.
>
> Pierre Restany, "Forma między ciałem a grą" (Form between body and play), in *Alina Szapocznikow, Rzeźba (Alina Szapocznikow, sculptures)*, exh. cat. (Warsaw: Centralne Biuro Wystaw Artystycznych Zachęta, 1967). Translated by Szymon Włoch.

In summer, Szapocznikow goes to Carrara, Italy, where she chisels out part of *Autoportret I* (*Self-Portrait I*) [plate 105] at the stoneworking studio of Carlo Nicoli.

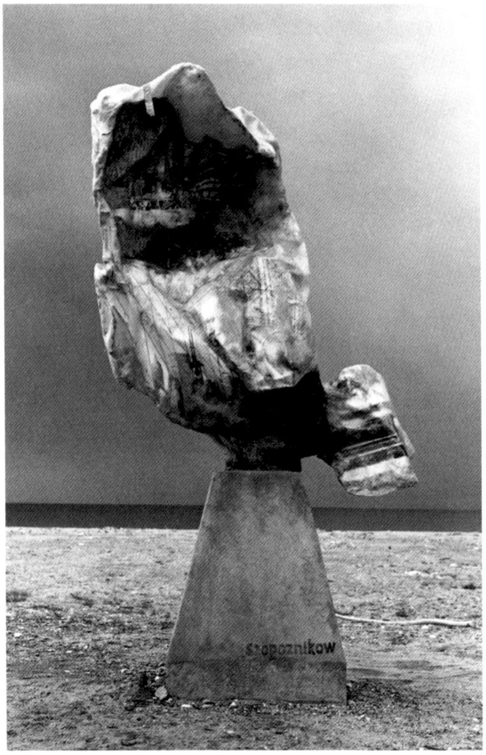

The artist's sculpture *Śmieć* (Junk, 1969) on the beach in Port-Barcarès, 1969.

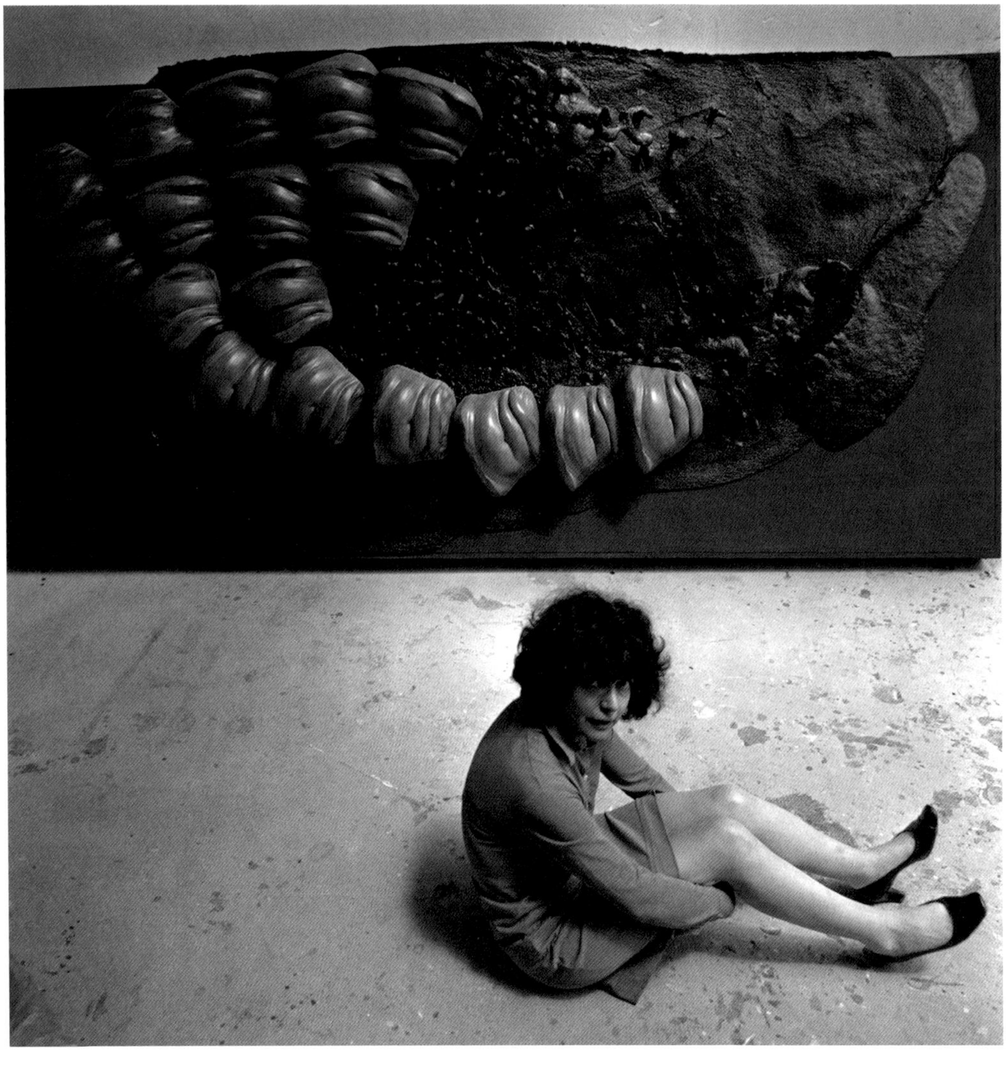

The artist and *Grande Plage* (Big Beach, 1968), 1968.

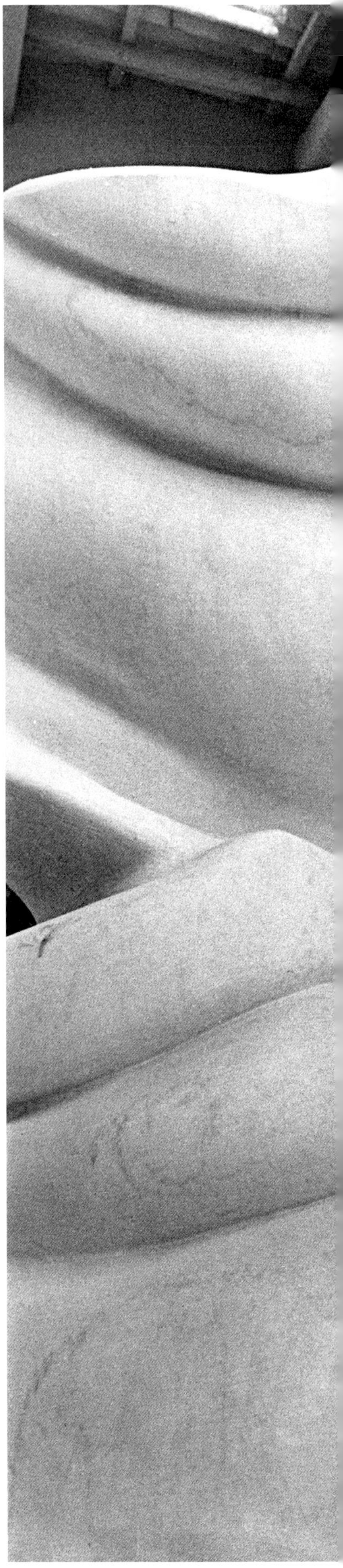

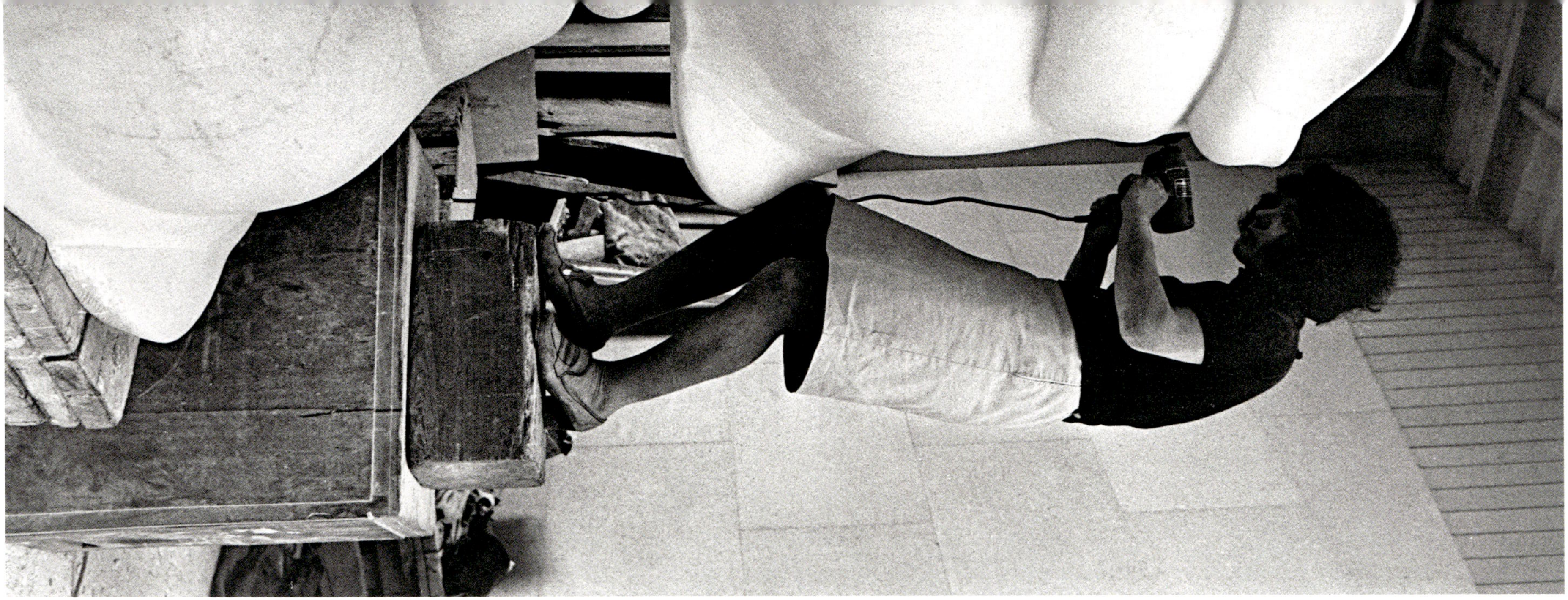

The artist working on *Grands Ventres* (Big Bellies, 1968) at the Querceta quarries, Italy, 1968.

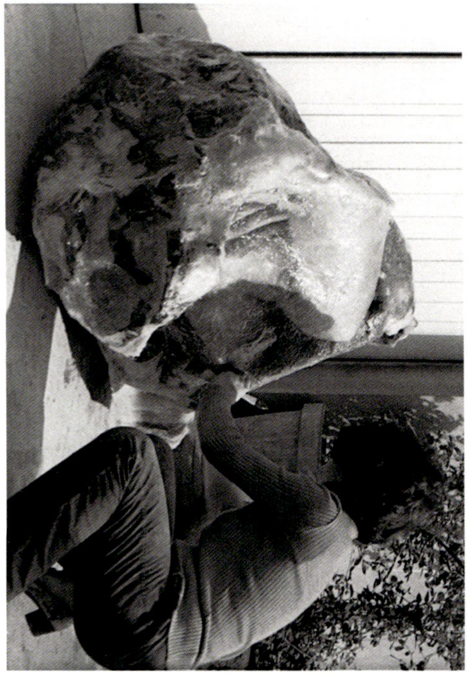

The artist with *Grande Tumeur I* (Big Tumor I, 1969), 1969.

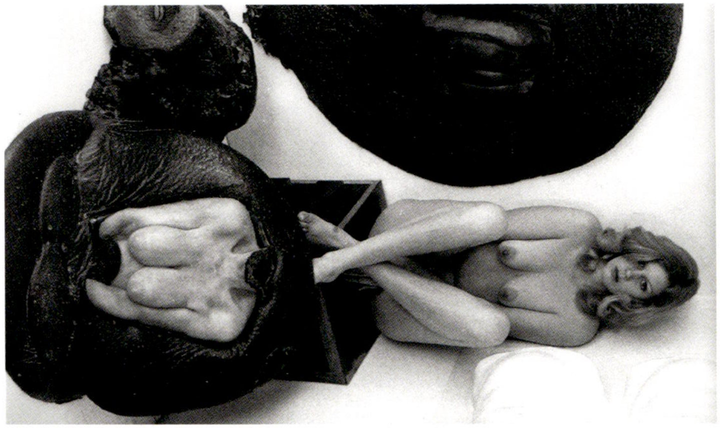

Model Anna Karin posing with various polyurethane sculptures in Szapocznikow's Malakoff studio, 1968.

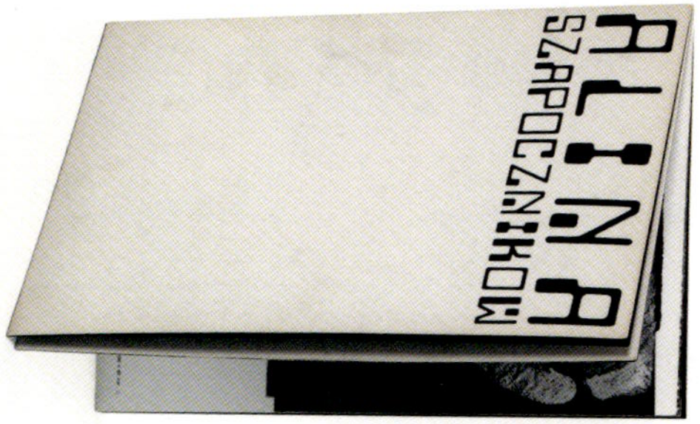

The catalogue for the exhibition "Alina Szapocznikow. 1968," Cogeime Gallery, Brussels.

In August, she spends time in Vrnjačka Banja, Yugoslavia (present-day Serbia), through a residency, for which an artist is invited annually to create a *plein air* sculpture for the spa park. Szapocznikow creates an eight-ton sculpture with the help of two stonemasons.

In September, she returns to Warsaw and makes *Człowiek w pancerzu* (*Man in Armor*). Drot's television program *Journal de Voyage en Pologne* shoots a segment at the studio on Brzozowa Street.

In late autumn, after her return to Paris, Szapocznikow makes *Femme illuminée* (*Illuminated Woman*, 1966–67) [plate 91], which uses an internal light source to illuminate a crowned figure with a winged form reminiscent of a face.

Exhibitions

"Orientacje" (Orientations), Dom Artysty Plastyka, Warsaw, February (exh. cat.: *Pierwsze wystawy*)

"XVIII Salon de la Jeune Sculpture," Place des Vosges, Paris, June 7 – July 10 (exh. cat.)

"L'Objet 2," Lacloche Gallery, Paris, autumn (curated by Michel Ragon and Jacques Lacloche; exh. cat.)

1967

In February, Szapocznikow marries Cieślewicz in Paris.

She returns to the subject matter first addressed in *Multiple Portrait*, creating a quadruple version (now in the collection of the Muzeum Sztuki, Łódź) and another double version on a large stone base, which is shown at the Palais Royal in Paris during the "XIX Salon de la Jeune Sculpture" [plate 106].

She makes *Le Voyage* (*Journey*) [plate 89], the culmination of her works that display a gradual loss of stable support and center of gravity; *L'Apesanteur (Hommage à Komarow)* (*Weightlessness [Homage to Komarov]*) [plate 90], a tall figure resembling a mummy; and *Caprice – Monstre* (*Caprice – Monster*) [plate 92], a huge illuminated form to be shown at her first solo exhibition in Paris.

On April 11, Restany opens Szapocznikow's solo exhibition at Galerie Florence Houston Brown in Paris, which in July travels to the Zachęta National Gallery of Art in Warsaw on a larger scale as the retrospective exhibition "Alina Szapocznikow. Sculpture." The Paris version of the exhibition is also shown at the Latina Gallery in Stockholm and the Marya Gallery in Copenhagen that autumn and include her latest works.

With the Paris exhibition and the support of Restany, Szapocznikow begins to be acknowledged within Parisian art circles, taking part in group exhibitions alongside artists from the Nouveau Réalisme movement: Arman, Roy Adzak, François Arnal, César, Louis Chavignier,

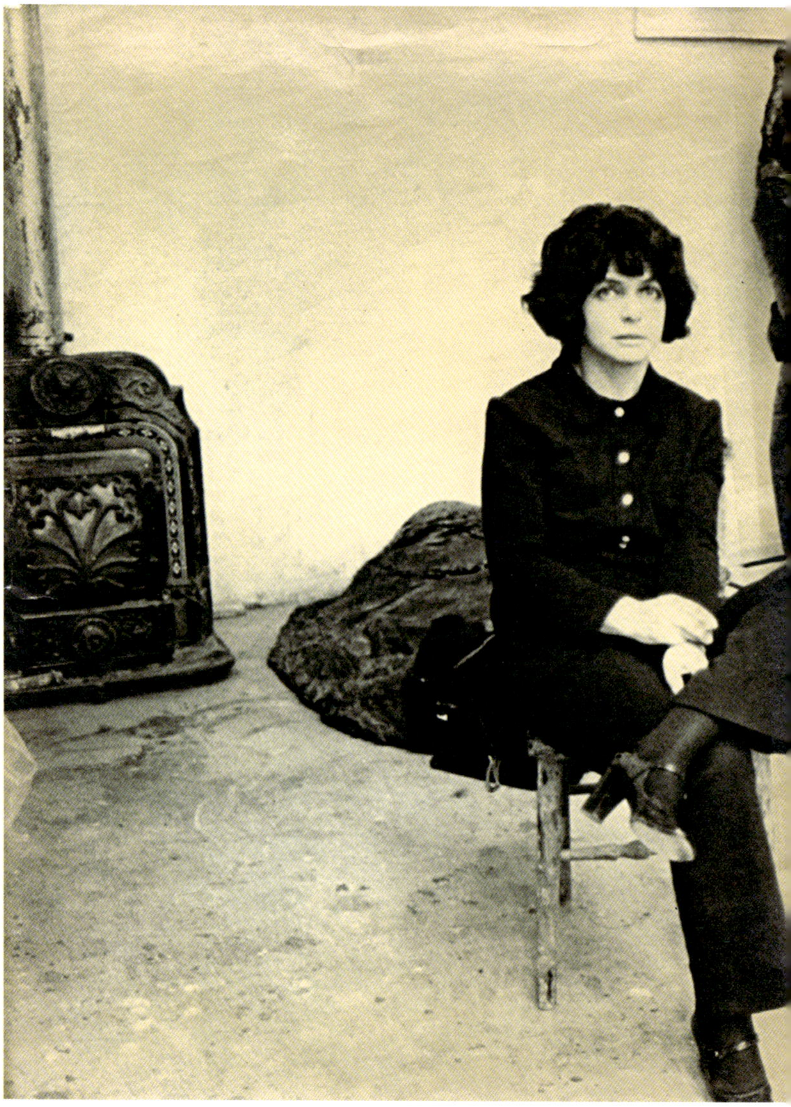

Hervé Fischer, Antoni Miralda, Mimmo Rotella, Dorothée Selz, Daniel Spoerri, and Topor.

Restany and Michel Ragon show Szapocznikow's sculpture *Le cœur de la ville* (*The Heart of the City*) in "La nature moderne" at the Palais de Glace in Paris, where she also shows *Ça coule en rouge* (*Leaking Red*), made of lingerie stuffed with cotton and stiffened with polyester. She begins a period of intense experimentation, arranging casts of bellies and other body parts in her studio, as well as making sketches using the casts and documenting the results in photo sessions with Miralda in which she "tries on" the casts.

Szapocznikow begins to experiment with using photographs, embedding them in translucent polyester. In *Souvenirs* [plate 56], she embeds photos of friends, such as Christian Boltanski and Fernando Arrabal, and of celebrities like Christie, Sophia Loren, and Monica Vitti.

That summer, she returns for the last time to her Warsaw studio and makes *Długa* (*Long*) and *O kulach* (*On Crutches*), the final works made at the studio on Brzozowa Street. In July she takes part in a sculpture symposium in Vyšné Ružbachy near Stará Ľubovňa, Czechoslovakia (present-day Slovakia), where she makes a sculpture bearing the first letter of her name.

Exhibitions

"Alina Szapocznikow," Galerie Florence Houston Brown, Paris,

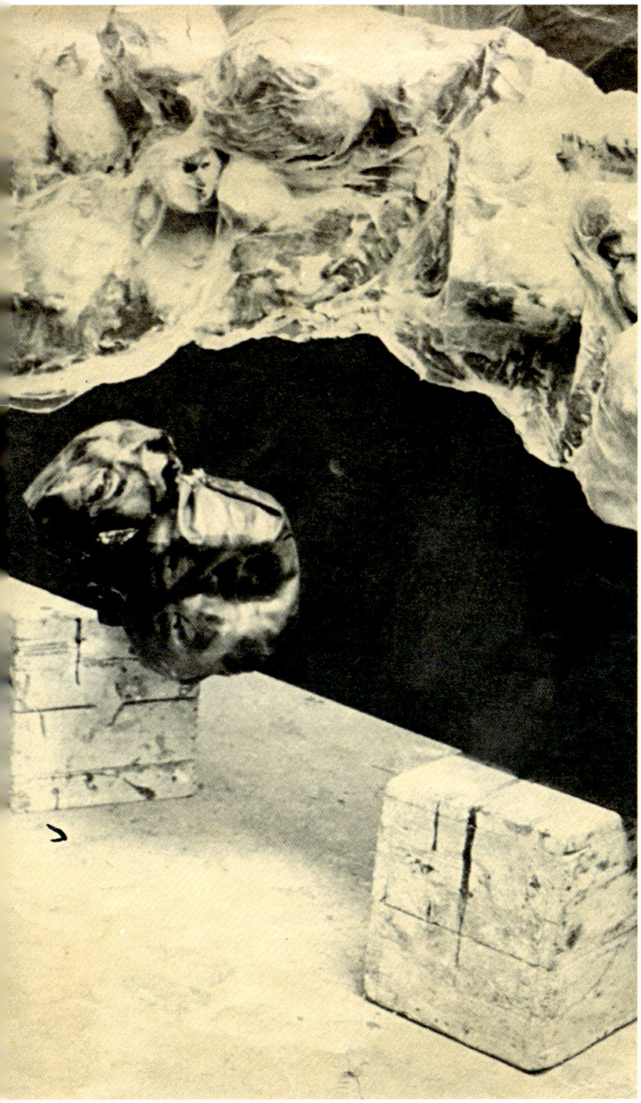

The artist in her Malakoff studio with *L'Enterrement d'Alina* (Alina's Funeral, 1970), 1970.

April 11 – May 6; traveled to Latina Gallery, Stockholm; and Marya Gallery, Copenhagen (curated by Pierre Restany; exh. cat.)
"XIX Salon de la Jeune Sculpture," Jardin du Palais Royal, Paris, June 9 – July 6 (exh. cat.)
"La nature moderne," Salles du Rond Point des Champs Elysées, Palais de Glace, Paris, June 13 – 30 (curated by Michel Ragon and Pierre Restany; exh. cat.)
"Alina Szapocznikow, Rzeźba" (Alina Szapocznikow, Sculpture), Zachęta National Gallery of Art, Warsaw, July 7 – 30 (curated by Pierre Restany; exh. cat.)
"Le Jouet," Galerie Saint-Luc, Paris, December 6 – January 6 (curated by Ceres Franco)

1968

Szapocznikow is in Warsaw just as the political upheavals in March are taking place. She witnesses a widespread anti-Semitic campaign initiated by Communist authorities and subsequently returns to Paris, where the student riots of May 1968 are taking place.

During her first visit to a hospital in Villejuif near Paris, Szapocznikow experiences a cancer scare, but no diagnosis is made.

In *Ventres* (*Bellies*), Szapocznikow uses a cast of Raoul-Auval's belly. *Modules répétés* (*Repeated Modules*) is shown at the annual "Salon de la Jeune Sculpture." During a summertime stay at the Querceta quarries, she returns to traditional materials, creating two huge belly forms from white marble. Two marble bellies also make up the hourglass-shaped *Grands Ventres* (*Big Bellies*).

In spring, Szapocznikow begins working with a new material, polyurethane, for *Ventres-coussins* (*Belly cushions*) [plate 75]. Belly forms cast in soft polyurethane foam are meant as utilitarian objects, to be used as cushions. She makes numerous casts intended for sale, showing the work in October at the inaugural exhibition of Paris's Design S.A. gallery.

For subsequent polyurethane works, such as *Grande Plage* (*Big Beach*) [plate 76] and *Janus* [plate 78], Szapocznikow is aided by her son or hired workers. The rapid spreading of polyurethane also inspires the Expansions series, while two versions of *Pollution* [plate 88], an ecologically themed piece, feature blades of grass embedded in polyurethane masses. In addition she makes a number of works called Accident [plate 87], erotic jokes in which phallic and feminine shapes collide, and a polyurethane version of the Ventres series, *Nemrod*. For *Stèle* (*Stele*) [plates 81–82] and *Torse noyé* (*Headless Torso*) [plate 83] she embeds casts of her own face or other body parts in the plastic mass. The series is shown at a solo exhibition organized by Restany and Giuseppe Marchiori at the Cogeime Gallery in Brussels, run by Ivan Lechien.

The end of the year brings another cancer scare, as Szapocznikow begins work on the series Tumeurs (Tumors) [plate 60], in which piles of newspapers, gauze, and photos are embedded in polyester and placed in various spatial arrangements.

Exhibitions

"II Salon 'L'Art pour la paix du Vietnam,'" Théâtre de la Commune d'Aubervilliers, Aubervilliers, France, April 28 – May 5
"XX Salon de la Jeune Sculpture," Jardins du Palais Royal, Paris, May 31 – June 30 (exh. cat.)
"L'Objet 3," Hilton Hotel, Orly, France, autumn (curated by Jean-Jacques Leveque)
"Design," inaugural exhibition of Design S.A., 226 Boulevard Saint-Germain, Paris, October (curated by Joe Colombo, Giorgio de Ferrari, and Gerard Saint-Fort-Paillard)
"Vision '68," Chateau de Fontainebleau, Paris, October 5 – 15 (curated by Jean-Jacques Leveque, Jean Dominique Rey, Man Ray, and Michel Troche)
"Alina Szapocznikow. 1968," Ivan Lechien's Cogeime Gallery, Brussels, November 12 – December 3 (curated by Giuseppe Marchiori and Pierre Restany; exh. cat.)

1969

On January 19, Szapocznikow is diagnosed with breast cancer at Saint-Antoine Hospital in Paris. She has surgery in the spring.

Drot's television program *Journal de Voyage en Pologne*, featuring Szapocznikow, airs on April 4.

A new installation of *Envahissement de Tumeurs* (*Invasion of Tumors*) is shown alongside *Big Bellies*, which is transported from Carrara, and *Belly Cushions* at the exhibition "Socha Peštanských Parkow '69" in Piešťany, Czechoslovakia (today Slovakia).

A summer exhibition on a French Mediterranean beach includes *Śmieć* (*Junk*), from the Invasion of Tumors series, and the latest *Big Bellies*, two huge irregularly shaped boulders consisting of large photos of the artist embedded in polyester.

Szapocznikow visits Poland for the last time in August. In addition to her illness, a sudden weakening of professional contacts within Polish sculpture circles distances her from her home country.

José Pierre includes her on his list of artists titled "Qui est surréaliste?" published in *Galerie des Arts*, where Szapocznikow appears alongside such artists as Marisol Escobar, Roberto Matta, Niki de Saint Phalle, George Segal, and Spoerri.

Exhibitions

"II Trienále Slovenského Sochárstawa: Socha Peštanských Parkow '69," Piešťany, Kúpelny Ostrow, Czechoslovakia, June 20 – September 15 (exh. cat.)
Outdoor sculpture exhibition, featuring *Junk* from the Invasion of Tumors series, Port-Barcarès, Musée de Sables, Le Barcarès, France, July 26 – October 15
"Deuxième Foire d'Art Actuelle. Kunstmark '69," Salle Arlequin, Galerie Louise, Brussels, October 3 – 13

1970

Restany invites Szapocznikow to participate in "Art Concepts from Europe" at the Bonino Gallery in New York, which she visits for the first time in March. Her text, titled "My American Dream," introduces the idea of creating a marble Rolls Royce on a 2 to 1 scale. During a summer stay in Carrara, she chisels out two miniature Rolls Royces, one of white Carrara marble, the other of pink Portuguese marble [plate 35]. She subsequently sends letters requesting funding assistance for the project to potential sponsors. Harald Szeemann, the director of Documenta 5 in Kassel, expresses interest in the marble Rolls Royce project and invites Szapocznikow if she can find funding; however, she does not appear at the exhibition. (See "My American Dream," page 58 of this volume.)

Szapocznikow's cancer goes into remission. She stops producing the Tumeurs but continues to make and sell her lamps and jewelry (featuring casts of her lips). She makes the first of the Fétiches (Fetishes) [plates 29–34], which feature casts of her own body parts and found objects, and the Desserts [plates 20–22], glass dessert bowls holding casts of breasts. This interest in fetishism is also reflected in *L'Enterrement d'Alina* (*Alina's Funeral*) [plate 66], which contains embedded photographs of herself and her friends as well as articles of her clothing.

> But we should at the same time realize that underneath the sweetness of the Dessert—a compote dish with two breasts, or a serving of pudding with the red spot of a strawberry nipple on top, the artist had concealed the provocative procedure of transgression. This mechanism operates within the bold and impudent proposition of cannibalism—the most frightening human taboo. We are truly astounded when Alina Szapocznikow asks us to help ourselves to this specific "menu" for a cannibal, who would no doubt lick all these objects, swallowing his saliva and getting ready to the most blasphemous feast under the sun. (Has anybody heard of a word "autophagia," that is, eating oneself?) The mouth on a flexible stem tempts one, promising not only an erotic game, but also tempting one to pluck them off the stem, to bite them, like an apple in paradise. It is not only an erotic game, and the experience of the warmth of an animal hide that would be the greatest act of freedom in this context, but primarily the doing away with the taboo which bids one not to touch with one's teeth, not to swallow, not to suck blood out of human flesh.
>
> Urszula Czartoryska, "Transgression. On the Message of Alina Szapocznikow's Art," 74. Translated by Piotr Mizia.

In autumn, she is invited to several events in Milan, including the "Arte Irritante" exhibition at Galleria Milano focusing on themes of cruelty, perversion, and death. Milan is bustling thanks to a festival of Nouveau Réalisme, which is set to close out the group's activity. In winter, she works on a design for the Monument to Fighters for the Freedom of Nations, for Luigi Einaudi Square in Milan. Her idea is to embed enlarged documents in polyester resin, resulting in large rocklike formations around which a paved path will run.

Exhibitions

Invasion of Tumors installation, Stedelijk Museum, Amsterdam, February
"Exposition imaginaire nr 1," installation from the Invasion of Tumors series, Szapocznikow's studio in Malakoff, France, spring
"Art Concepts from Europe," Bonino Gallery, New York, March 10 – 28 (curated by Alfredo Bonino and Pierre Restany)
"XXII Salon de la Jeune Sculpture," Orangerie and Jardin du Luxembourg, Paris, June 5 – July 5 (exh. cat.)
"L'Art dans la Ville," Salle de Jeu de

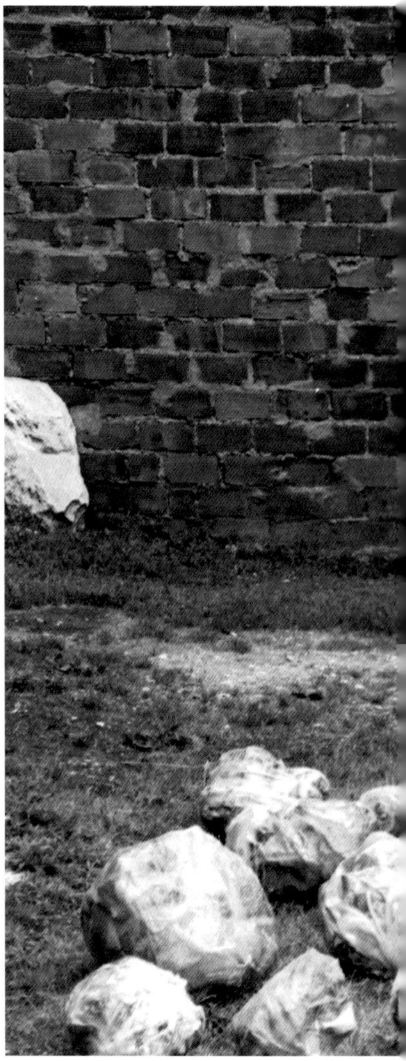

Paume, Château de Fontainebleau, Fontainebleau, France, June 6 – 28 (curated by Jean-Jacques Leveque)
"Arte Irritante," Galleria Milano, Milan, from November 18 (curated by Lea Vergine; exh. cat.)
"Contemporary Art Festival," Museum of Art, Yokohama; Kawatoku Gallery, Morioka; and Museum of Art, Sendai, Japan, November – December (curated by Pierre Restany and Shinichi Segui)

1971

Szapocznikow continues the Fetishes series, which spawns an offshoot group titled Instants that captures fleeting moments in the process of creation. *Fajrant* (*End of Day's Work*) [plate 23], for instance, features work gloves stiffened with polyester; later work features her apron as well as more intimate articles of clothing. Her increasing fascination with ephemeral art is evident in small-scale sculptures from chewing gum shaped by the artist's mouth, which would be displayed in 1978 in the form of photographs taken by Cieślewicz, titled *Fotorzeźby* (*Photosculptures*) [plates 36–55]. These relate to the casts of body parts, which she had made steadily since 1965, while also exposing her "exhibitionism," as she herself called it. This exhibitionism was based on bringing the seldom-seen aspects of human life to view. Around this time, Szapocznikow writes a text on her search for meaning in every fleeting moment, which can be read as a commentary on her own work. (See "L'autre samedi…," page 60 of this volume.)

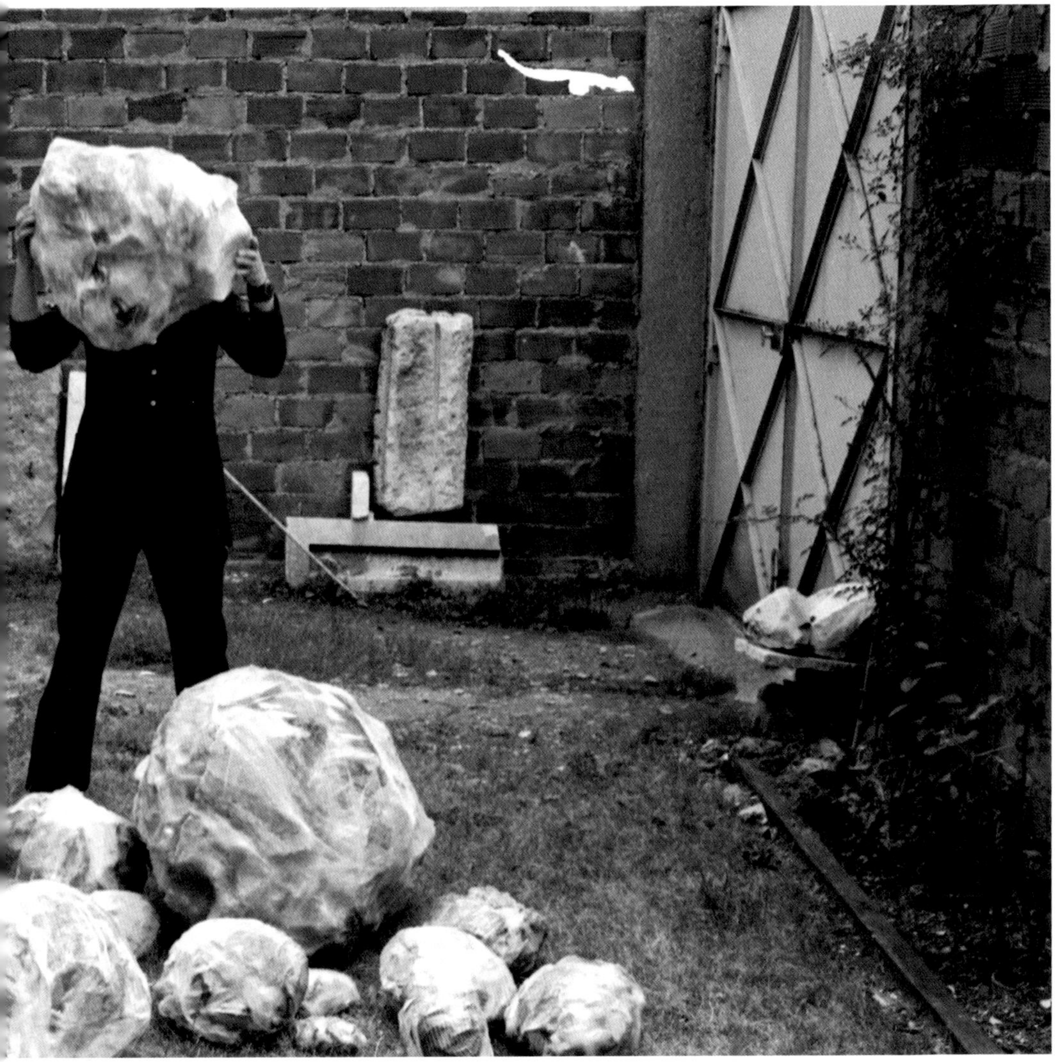

The artist posing with her work *Envahissement des Tumeurs* (Invasion of Tumors, c. 1969) in Malakoff, 1970.

Alina Szapocznikow made use of the biological, amoebic element that is characteristic of polyps; it seemed to relate to the liquid, to the element of water, which is different from the environment that is associated with man. The interior of the mouth became the artist's blind "helper," the subconscious, gustatory, and sensual executor of what the hands no longer wished to touch, the creator of forms that the hands do not wish to take responsibility for. One might say that the hands had been deprived of responsibility for form already when the series of works entitled Herbarium was created; the series consisted of fragments of thin congealed polyester emulsion which was impressed on the surface of the human body—on the face, torso, legs and hands.

Urszula Czartoryska, "Transgression. On the Message of Alina Szapocznikow's Art," 75. Translated by Piotr Mizia.

Szapocznikow makes another series of Souvenirs, this time with personal photographs. Among these is *Souvenir I* [plate 57], containing a photo of the artist with her father. Claudine Martin invites her to exhibit at the Aurora Gallery in Geneva with Boltanski, P. M. Jacote, and Annette Messager. In October, Szapocznikow opens her solo exhibition "Instants et Choses," which shows *Tumeurs personnifiées* (*Tumors Personified*) [plate 64] under the title *Désintégration de personnalité* (*Disintegration of Personality*). A series of self-portraits—irregular clumps of resin—contrast with small sharp pebbles. In later pieces in the series, the artist's facial features become increasingly obscured and blurred as she addresses her body's accelerated degradation.

Exhibitions

"XXVII Salon de Mai," Musée d'Art Moderne de la Ville de Paris and Salles, New York, April 29 – May 17 (curated by Gaston Diehl and Jacqueline Selz; exh. cat.)
"XXIII Salon de la Jeune Sculpture," Le Parc Floral, Bois de Vincennes, Paris, May 5 – June 5 (exh. cat.)
"Instants et Choses," Aurora Gallery, Geneva, Switzerland, October 7 – 30 (curated by Claudine Martin)

1972

Szapocznikow is invited to exhibit in "36 Artistes et La Laine," organized under the patronage of the Woolmark Foundation. For this occasion, she makes sculptures out of wool, *Hiver doux à Malakoff* (*Mild Winter for Malakoff*, 1971) and two versions of Wool – Tumeur. Editions of this presentation take place in Paris and Lyon.

She is invited by Restany to take part in Operazione Vesuvio, a design competition for a park at the peak of Mount Vesuvius, for which she

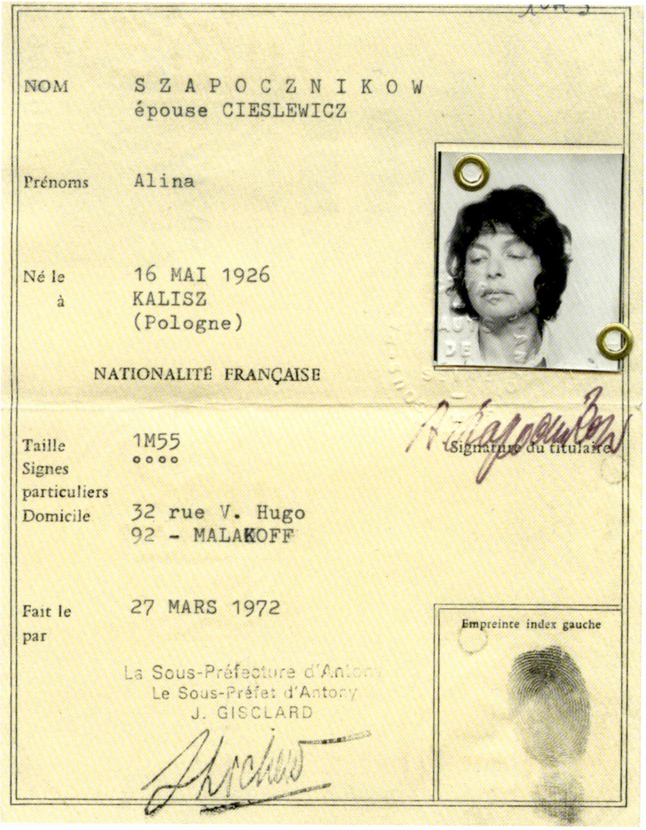
NOM SZAPOCZNIKOW
épouse CIESLEWICZ

Prénoms Alina

Né le 16 MAI 1926
à KALISZ
(Pologne)

NATIONALITÉ FRANÇAISE

Taille 1M55
Signes particuliers °°°°
Domicile 32 rue V. Hugo
92 - MALAKOFF

Signature du titulaire

Fait le 27 MARS 1972
par

La Sous-Préfecture d'Antony
Le Sous-Préfet d'Antony
J. GISCLARD

Empreinte index gauche

The artist's French identification card.

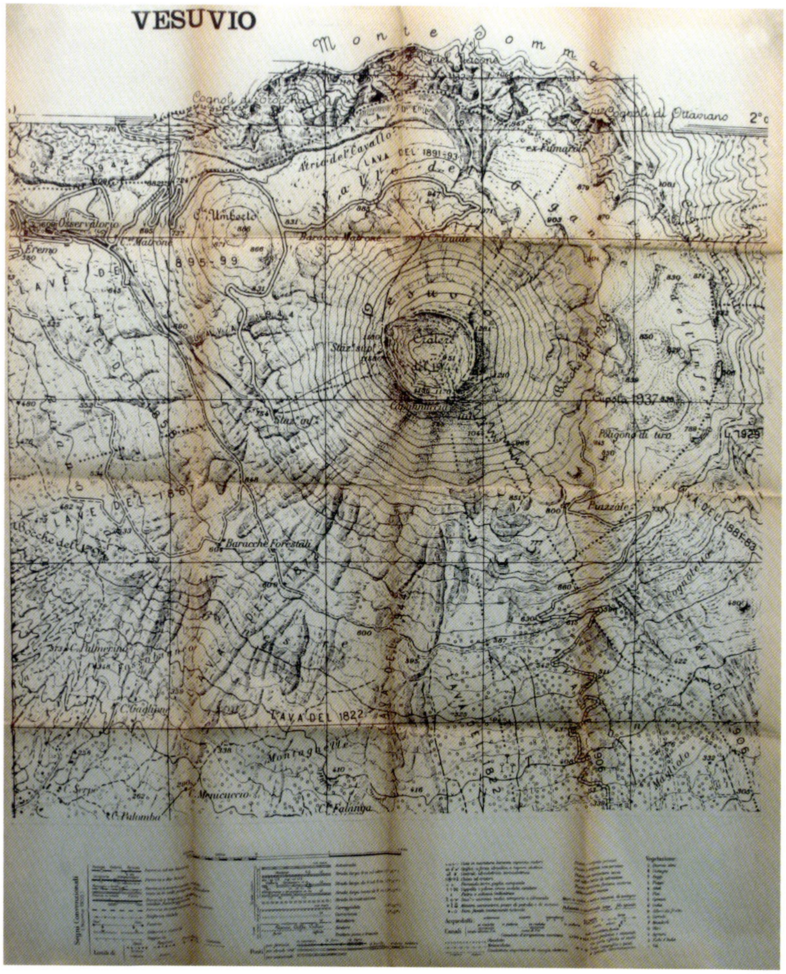

Map of Mount Vesuvius used in preparing proposal for the 1972 design competition Operazione Vesuvio.

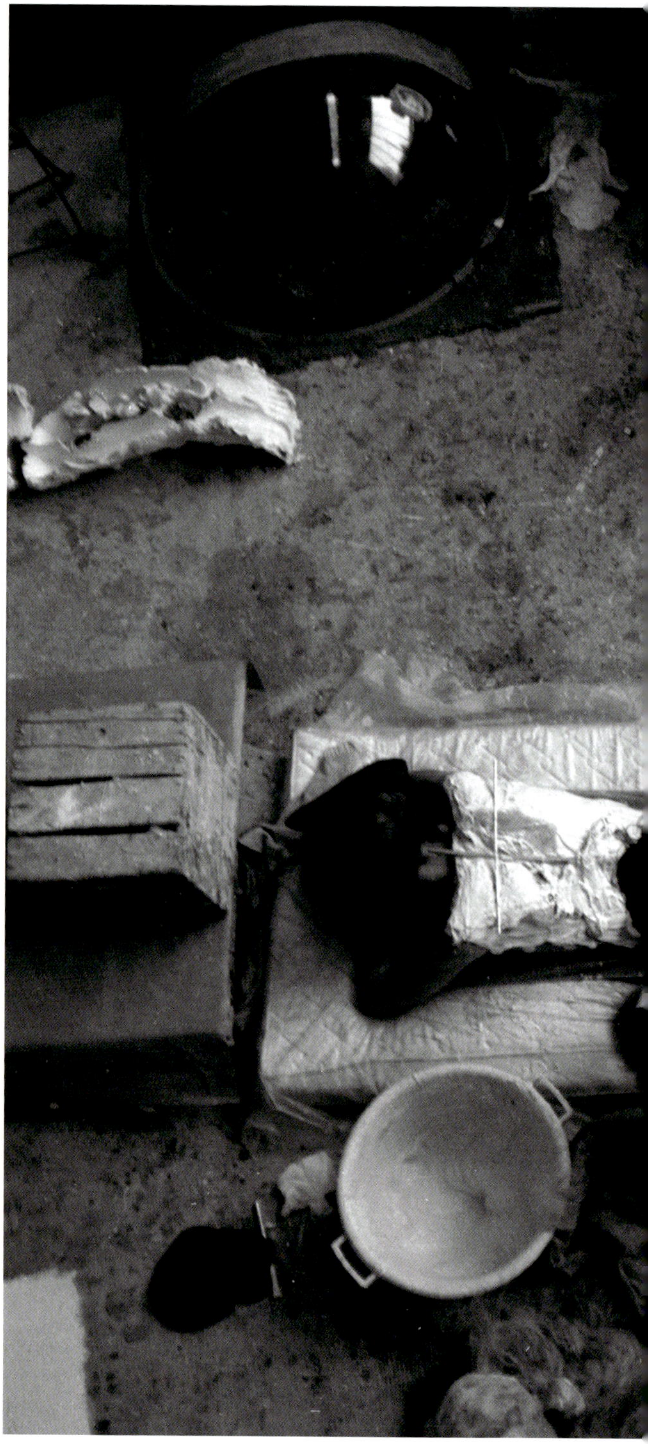

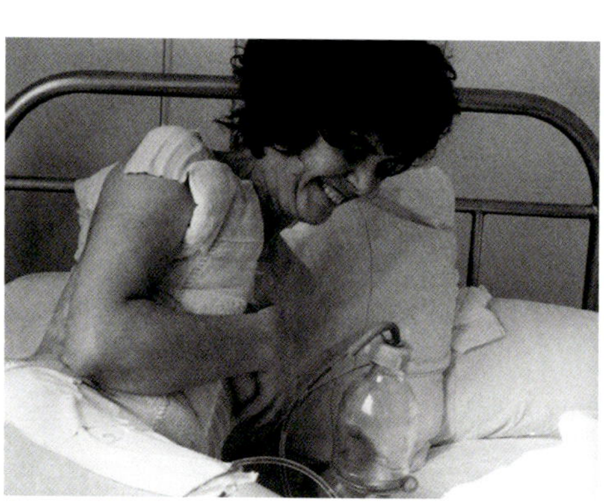

The artist at the oncology hospital in Villejuif, outside of Paris, June 1972.

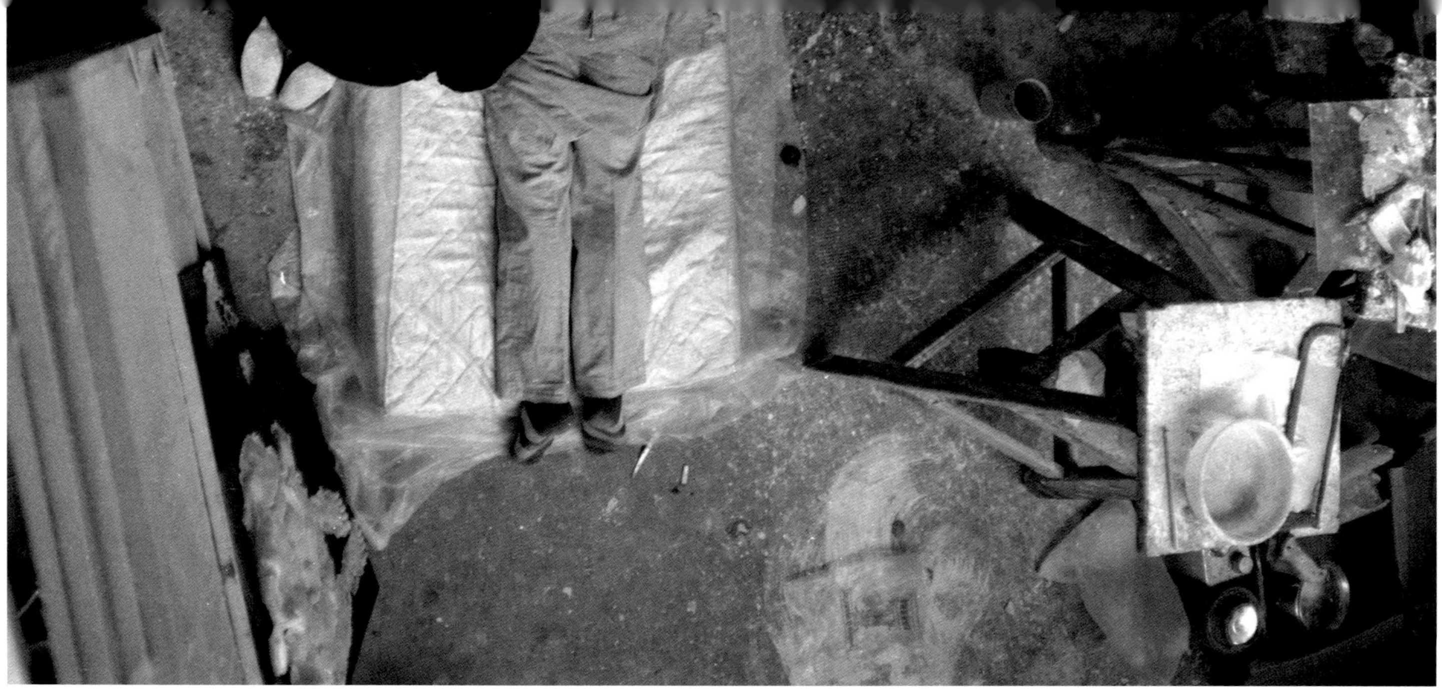

The artist preparing casts of her son Piotr in preparation for her Herbier (Herbarium) series of works, 1972.

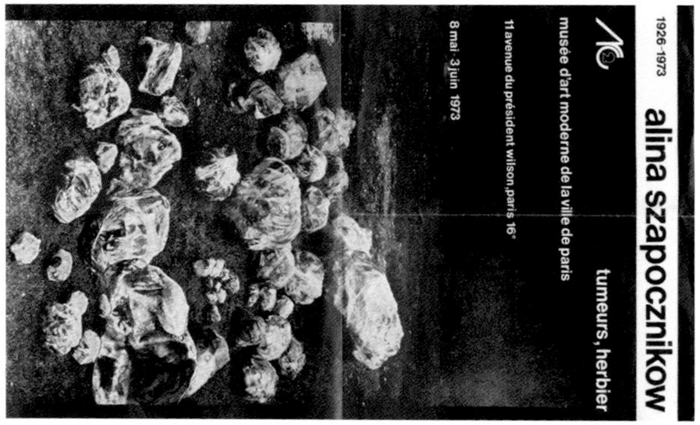

Poster for the 1973 exhibition "Alina Szapocznikow. Tumeurs, herbier," Musée d'Art Moderne de la ville de Paris.

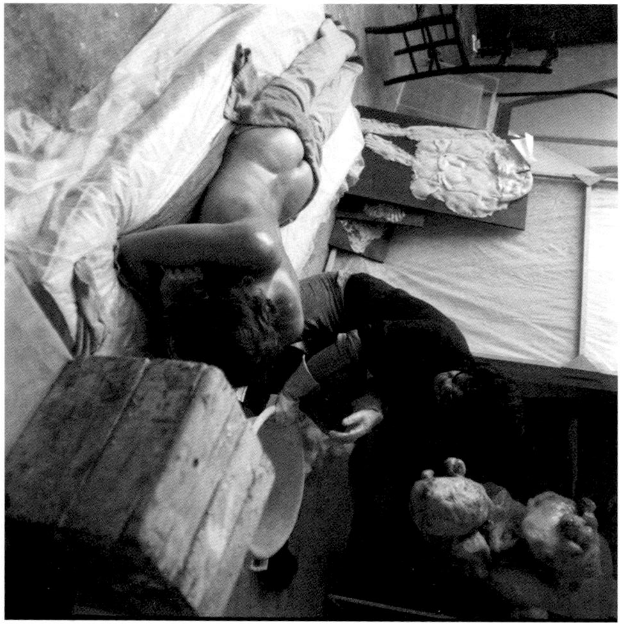

The artist preparing casts of her son Piotr in preparation for her Herbier (Herbarium) series of works, 1972.

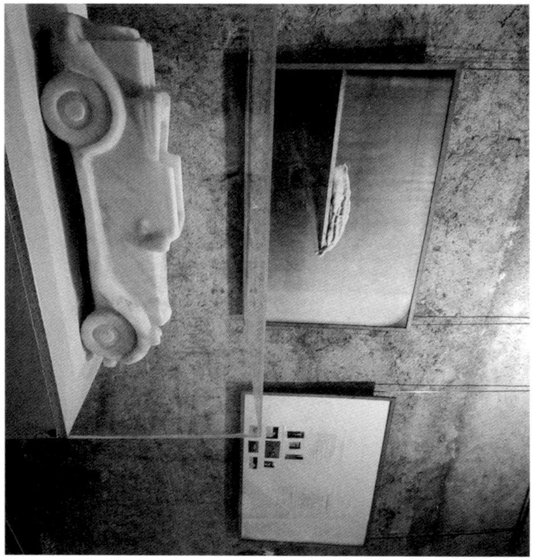

Installation view of *Rolls Royce II* (1971) and images from *Fotorzeźby* (Photosculptures, 1971) in "Instants et Choses," Aurora Gallery, Geneva, 1971.

proposes creating an ice rink in the volcano's crater with radio contact. An exhibition of competition designs takes place in the spring at Galleria Il Centro in Naples and Centro Domus in Milan.

At the pre-auction exhibition "Travaux d'aujourd'hui" at the Galerie du Palais in Paris, organized by Jean-Claude Binoche, Szapocznikow shows *Fiancée folle blanche* (*Mad White Fiancée*, 1971) [plates 9–10], which incites a controversy due to its embedded phallus form; it is eventually withdrawn from the auction.

In spring, having created the first piece of the Herbarium series *Autoportrait – Herbier* (*Self-portrait – Herbarium*) [plate 1] the previous year, she makes subsequent "layers" to the series using direct casts of her son's body parts. After plaster negatives of Piotr's body are made, polyester casts from these negatives are flattened and placed on wooden backgrounds that have been painted black. The works are designated with roman numerals I to XIII (VII and IX are missing for reasons unknown) [plates 2–4]. As part of the series, Szapocznikow also makes the sculpture *Herbier XII (Le Christ)* (*Herbarium [Head of Christ]*) for the Polish Pallottines in Paris chapel, commissioned by her friend, Father Józef Sadzik.

While making Herbarium, the most important and largest group of works from the period before her death, Szapocznikow writes her most significant text: "Mon oeuvre puise ses racines dans le métier de la sculpture." (See "Mon oeuvre puise ses racines…," page 28 of this volume.)

Her series of Cendriers de Célibataire (The Bachelor's Ashtrays) [plates 26–27], featuring cigarette butts embedded in a polyester cast of a head, is shown at François Arnal's exhibition "Cendriers et projets de cendriers." Following as part of the Ashtrays is an assemblage consisting of casts of a belly and breasts.

The Academy of Fine Arts in Nice invites Szapocznikow to supervise their sculpture department, but she is forced to decline due to her poor health; she does, however, create a first draft of a program for the sculpture studio.

In June, Szapocznikow has a mastectomy in a second operation at the oncology hospital in Villejuif. She spends that summer on vacation with Restany and his wife José Anne Decock in Plan-de-la-Tour in the south of France, at the summer house of her friend Pierre Horay. After returning from vacation, she makes her final public appearance on October 2 at the Polish Embassy in Paris. Szapocznikow shows *Stele* [plates 81–82] at her last exhibition, titled "Les Chroniques de l'Oeil de Boeuf," opening December 11 at the L'Oeil de Boeuf Gallery in Paris. She spends that Christmas at her home in Malakoff.

Exhibitions

"Travaux d'aujourd'hui," Galerie du Palais, Paris, February 29 – March 9 (curated by Jean-Claude Binoche; exh. cat.)

"36 Artistes et La Laine," Galerie Boutique-Germain, Paris, March 7 – April 7

"Operazione Vesuvio," exhibition of competition designs for Parco Culturale Internazionale, Galleria Il Centro, Naples, Italy, and Centro Domus, Milan, Italy, March – April (curated by Dina Carola and Pierre Restany)

"La Femme," Galerie Cogeime, Brussels, April 15 – May 13

"XXVIII Salon de Mai," Musée d'Art Moderne de la Ville de Paris and Salles, New York, May 4 – June 4 (curated by Jacqueline Selz; exh. cat.)

"Formes actuelles," outdoor show at Jardins des Arts, Saint-Germain-en-Laye, France, from May 26 (organized by Ghislaine Caroli)

"Raccolta Henraux," exhibition of works created at the Henraux quarry, Palazzo dei Diamanti, Ferrara, Italy, June 1 – October 30

"XXIV Salon de la jeune sculpture," Jardins de l'Unesco, Paris, and Centre Jeanne Hachette, Ivry, France, June 2 – July 2 (exh. cat.)

"Impact II," Musée d'Art Moderne, Céret, France, July 1 – September 1 (curated by Hervé Fischer)

"INTER-ETRENNES. Tombola vente du cadeau de vos rêves sous l'égide de Pierre Restany," Galerie Lara Vincy, Paris, September 8 – 16 (curated by Pierre Restany)

"Noir d'humour," Galerie Art du Monde, Paris, October 3 – 24 (curated by Michel Gayout)

"Formes pour un Espace," Jardins des Arts, Saint-Germain-en-Laye, France, from October 27

"Cendriers et projets de cendriers," Atelier A Gallery, Paris, November 28 – January 28 (curated by François Arnal)

"Les Chroniques de l'Oeil de Boeuf 62 – 72," inaugural exhibition, L'Oeil de Boeuf Gallery, Paris, December 11 – January 20 (curated by Ceres Franco)

1973

Szapocznikow's condition deteriorates, and she is admitted to a sanatorium in Praz-Coutant in Haute-Savoie, France. The cancer spreads to her bones, resulting in progressive paralysis and intense pain. Szapocznikow dies on March 2 in the sanatorium and is laid to

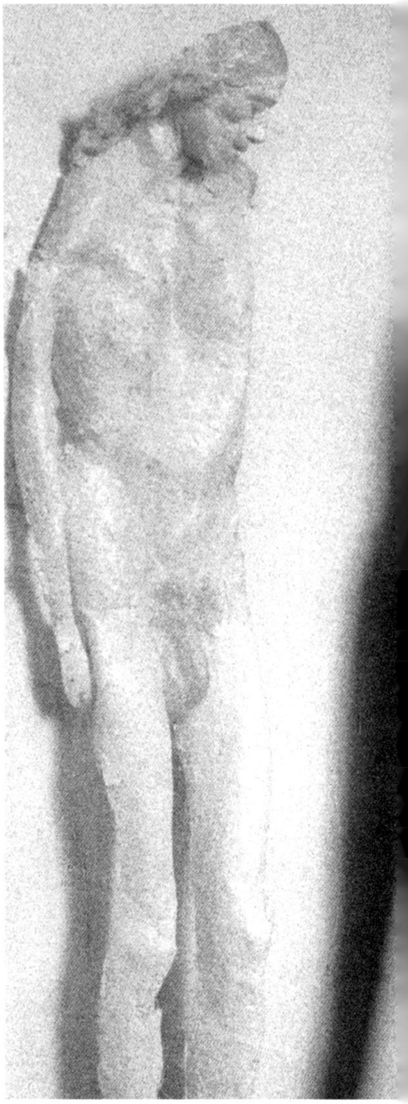

rest on March 6 at Montmartre Cemetery in Paris.

On May 8, shortly after her death, Restany organizes the exhibition "Alina Szapocznikow. Tumeurs, herbier" at the Musée d'Art Moderne de la Ville de Paris. That year's "Salon de la jeune sculpture" is dedicated to her memory ("Hommage à Alina Szapocznikow"). Additionally, the "Salon de Mai" is dedicated to artists who passed away that year: Denys Chavinger,

Pablo Picasso, and Alina Szapocznikow.

In October, during the grand opening of the Centre du Dialogue, Szapocznikow's *Herbarium* (*Head of Christ*), bearing the facial features of her son, Piotr, is blessed at the altar.

"L'Expression," Galerie Claude Bollack, Strasbourg, France, June 20 – September 20 (organized by Lara Vincy)
"WOOLART," Galerie 21, Saint-Etienne, France, December (organized by Galerie Boutique-Germain)

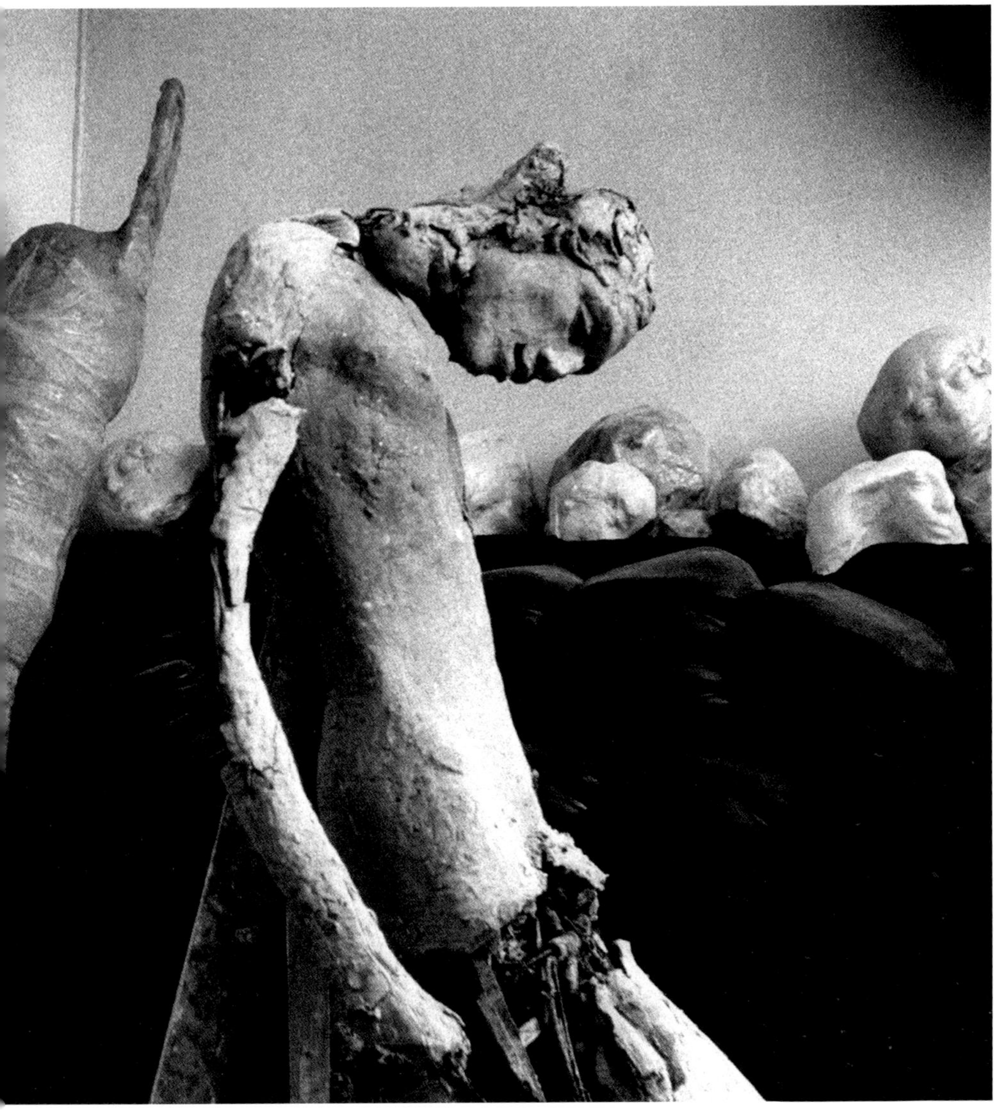

Works in the artist's studio, including studies for the sculpture *Piotr* (1972), *L'Apesanteur (Hommage à Komarow)* (Weightlessness [Homage to Komarov], 1967), *Tumeurs personnifiées* (Tumors Personified, 1971), and *Grande Plage* (Big Beach, 1968).

Exhibitions
"Alina Szapocznikow. Tumeurs, herbier," Musée d'Art Moderne de la Ville de Paris, May 8 – June 3 (curated by Pierre Restany; exh. cat.)
"XXIX Salon de Mai," Musée d'Art Moderne de la Ville de Paris and Salles, New York, May 12 – June 17 (curated by Gaston Diehl and Jacqueline Selz; exh. cat.)
"XXV Salon de la jeune sculpture. Hommage à Alina Szapocznikow," Jardin du Luxembourg, Paris, June (exh. cat.)

1974

Szapocznikow's sculptures are displayed at the much-discussed exhibition "L'Homme et son empreinte," to which she was invited before her death. The exhibition is shown in Mayenne, Bourges, and at the Musée d'Art Moderne de la Ville de Paris.

Exhibitions
"Aidez l'Espagne. En solidarité avec les prisonniers politiques espagnols. Exposition – Vente," 44 Rue de Rennes, Paris, February 11 – 16 (exh. cat.)
"Hommage à 6 flamboyants: Bandeira, Chavignier, Cherkaoui, Cheval-Bertrand, Pavlovsky, Szapocznikow," Galerie L'Oeil de Boeuf, Paris, April 16 – May 4 (curated by Ceres Franco)
"Alina Szapocznikow, 1926 – 1973. Rysunki" (Alina Szapocznikow, 1926 – 1973. Drawings), Galeria Współczesna, Warsaw, from June 6 (curated by Janusz Bogucki; exh. cat.)
"L'Homme et son empreinte," Centre d'art, Château de Saint-Susanne, Mayenne, France, June 17 – September 15; Musée d'Art Modern e de la Ville de Paris, August 20 – November 17; Maison de la Culture de Bourges, France, December (curated by Aude Fonquernie and Jean Selz; exh. cat.)
"Wool Art in Soft Art," Camden Arts Centre, London, August 16 – October 13 (organized by Woolmark Foundation and Galerie Germain; exh. cat.)
"Ni fleurs, ni couronnes," Galerie Philippe Demay, Paris, November 2 – 28

1975 — present

A large-scale retrospective exhibition, organized by the Muzeum Sztuki, Łódź, and Szapocznikow's family, is shown in eight Polish cities and in Sweden. The curator of the exhibition, Irena Kolat-Ways, is also author of the first catalogue (which remains unpublished) of the artist's works, to which Cieślewicz actively contributes. The exhibition meets with widespread media interest in Poland.

During the late 1970s, 80s, and 90s, Szapocznikow is represented in fewer and fewer exhibitions; only in Poland does her work remain consistently appreciated and relevant. Her sculptures continue to be shown in all of the serious exhibitions of Polish sculpture in Poland and abroad, including "Presences polonaises" (1983), "Europa, Europa" (1994), and "Der Riss im Raum" (1995).

A monographic exhibition and publication are initiated by Anda Rottenberg, opening in 1998 on the twenty-fifth anniversary of the artist's death. A touring solo exhibition in 1998 – 2000 allows Szapocznikow's work to be (re)discovered by many and spurred many Polish museums to add her works to their collections.

Exhibitions
1975
"Les Artistes et l'année internationale de la femme," UNESCO head-

quarters, Paris, February 22 – March 8 (exh. cat.)
"Alina Szapocznikow. Dessins," Aurora Gallery, Geneva, April 10 – May 8 (exh. cat.)
"Alina Szapocznikow. 1926 – 1973," Muzeum Sztuki, Łódź, Poland, September 6 – October 26 (exh. cat.); traveled to National Museum, Warsaw, November 17 – December 31 (exh. cat.); BWA Salon, Poznań, Poland, January 17 – February 5, 1976 (exh. cat.); Palace of Art and Pryzmat Gallery, Kraków, Poland, April 15 – May 16, 1976 (exh. cat.); BWA Salon, Bydgoszcz, Poland, June 4 – 26, 1976 (exh. cat.); National Museum, Gdańsk, Poland, July 8 – October 26, 1976; Konsthall, Lund, Sweden, April 16 – May 15, 1977 (exh. cat.); BWA Exhibition Salon, Białystok, Poland, October 1977; and Regional Museum of Kalisz Land, Kalisz, Poland, from August 30, 1978 (curated by Irena Kolat-Ways)
"Espaces intuitifs. Maison pour tous," Saint-Quentin-en-Yvelines, France, October 2 – 30
"Romantyzm i Romantyczność w sztuce polskiej XIX; XX wieku" (Romanticism and Romance in Polish Art of the 19th and 20th Centuries), Zachęta National Gallery of Art, Warsaw, October – November (exh. cat.)

1976

"Trait pour trait. 50 autoportraits," Galerie Jean Briance, Paris, March 11 – April 30 (curated by Jean Clair; exh. cat.)
"La Peur," Galerie Lacloche, Paris, May 15 – June 15 (curated by Jacques Lacloche; exh. cat.)

1977

"L'esprit romantique dans l'art polonais XIX – XX siècles," Galeries Nationales du Grand Palais, Paris, March 26 – June 27 (exh. cat.)
"Mythologies quotidiennes II," Musée d'Art Moderne de la Ville de Paris, April 27 – June 5 (curated by Gérald Gassiot-Talabot; exh. cat.)
"Regard '77," Foyers du Théâtre Municipale de Caen, France, May 7 – 28

1978

"Peinture au beurre," Galerie Jean Briance, Paris, May 18 – July 8 (exh. cat.)
"Alina Szapocznikow, Fotorzeźby, 1971" (Alina Szapocznikow, Photosculptures, 1971), Wrocławska Galeria Fotografii, Wrocław, Poland, and Critics' Salon, BWA, Lublin, Poland, June 6 – 26 (curated by Jerzy Olek; exh. cat.)
"Chemins de la création. Dessins de peintres – Dessins de sculpteurs," Château d'Ancy-le-Franc, Yonne, France, June 10 – September 17
"Escultura polaca contemporánea," Palacio de Velázquez, Parque del Retiro, Madrid, December – January; traveled to Bilbao, Lisbon, and Barcelona (curated by Aleksander Wojciechowski; exh. cat.)

1979

"Annette Messager, Alina Szapocznikow, Christian Boltanski, Jerzy Olek, Zdzisław Jurkiewicz," Wrocławska Galeria Fotografii, Wrocław, Poland, from April 20 (curated by Jerzy Olek; exh. cat.)

1980

"Figures de l'enfermement," Centre d'Échanges de Perrache, Lyon, January 12 – March 16 (curated by Jeanne Huguent; exh. cat.)
"Sculptures polonaises contemporaine," Musée d'Art Moderne de la Ville de Paris, January 23 – March 4 (curated by Aleksander Wojciechowski; exh. cat.)

1981

"Lieux de l'imaginaire," Galerie Municipale de Vitry (sculptures) and Théâtre d'Ivry (drawings), Ivry-sur-Seine, France, March 7 – April 5 (curated by Jacques Lacloche and Raoul-Jean Moulin; exh. cat.)

1983

"Presences polonaises. L'art vivant autour du musée de Łódź," Centre Georges Pompidou, Paris, June 23 – September 26 (curated by Ryszard Stanisławski and Pierre Restany; exh. cat.)

1984

"La part des femmes dans l'art contemporain," Galerie Municipale, Ville de Vitry-sur-Seine, France, March (curated by Yvette Roudy, Jean Collet, and Raoul-Jean Moulin; exh. cat.)
"Rzeźba polska 1944 – 1980" (Polish Sculpture 1944 – 1980), BWA Gallery "Arsenał," Poznań, Poland, September 20 – October 21 (curated by Krystyna Nowakowska; exh. cat.)

1989

"Alina Szapocznikow. 1926 – 73," Galeria Sztuki Sceny Plastycznej KUL, Lublin, Poland, February 26 – April 30 (curated by Urszula Czartoryska; exh. cat.)

1990

"Alina Szapocznikow. 1926 – 1973," Bibliothèque Polonaise, Paris, May 16 – June 30 (curated by Piotr Stanisławski; exh. cat.)

1994

"Europa, Europa. Das Jahrhundert der Avantgarde in Mittel und Osteuropa," Bonn, Germany, May 27 – October 16 (curated by Christopf Brockhaus and Ryszard Stanisławski; exh. cat.)

1995

"Der Riss im Raum. Positionen der Kunst seit 1945 in Deutschland, Polen, der Slowakei und Tschechien," Zachęta National Gallery of Art, Warsaw, March 13 – April 23 (Polish section curated by Anda Rottenberg; exh. cat.)

1996

"Odwilż. Sztuka ok. 1956" (Thaw. Art circa 1956), National Museum, Poznań, Poland, June – August (curated by Piotr Piotrowski; exh. cat.)
"Andrzej Wajda. To lubię" (I Like This), Palace of Art, Kraków, November 6 –

December 1 (curated by Zofia Gołubiew; exh. cat.)

1997

"Lengyelország Művészet 1945 – 1996," Műcsarnok, Szépművészeti Múzeum, Budapest, January 20 – February 23 (curated by Anda Rottenberg and Jaromir Jedliński; exh. cat.)

1998

"Alina Szapocznikow. 1926 – 1973," Zachęta National Gallery of Art, Warsaw, May 18 – July 5 (curated by Anda Rottenberg, assisted by Joanna Pużyńska; exh. cat.). Includes session

devoted to Szapocznikow's artistic legacy, May 19.
"Alina Szapocznikow. 1926 – 1973," National Museum, Kraków, October 15 – December 20 (curated by Anna Król; exh. cat.)
1999
"Alina Szapocznikow. 1926 – 1973," Muzeum Sztuki, Łódź, Poland, January 9 – February 21 (curated by Janina Ładnowska; exh. cat.)
"Alina Szapocznikow. 1926 – 1973," National Museum, Wrocław, Poland, March 12 – May 16 (curated by Mariusz Hermansdorfer)
2000
"Słońce i inne gwiazdy (The Sun and Other Stars). Abakanowicz, Kantor, Kobro, Opałka, Stażewski, Strzemiński, Szapocznikow, Witkacy, Wojtkiewicz," Zachęta National Gallery of Art, Warsaw, February 25 – March 26 (curated by Anda Rottenberg; exh. cat.)
"Alina Szapocznikow," Czech Museum of Art, Prague, April 19 – June 4 (exh. cat.)
2004
"PRYM," BWA Gallery, Zielona Góra, Poland, April 2 – 25 (organized by the Foksal Gallery Foundation; exh. cat.)
"Alina Szapocznikow. Zatrzymać życie – Capturing Life," IRSA Fine Art Gallery, Warsaw, May 14 – July 31 (curated by Barbara Falender, Dobrosława Horzela, Katarzyna Jankowska-Cieślik; exh. cat.)
"Fin des temps! L'histoire n'est plus. L'art polonais du 20e siècle," Hôtel des Arts, Tulon, Poland, July 2 – October 3 (curated by Andrzej Turowski)
"Flesh at War with Enigma," Kunsthalle, Basel, Switzerland, September 19 – November 14 (curated by Anke Kempkes; exh. cat.)
2007
"Don't cry baby – work!," Isabelle Czarnowska Gallery, Berlin, May 12 – July 28
"Alina Szapocznikow," Galerie Gisela Capitain, Cologne, Germany, June 1 – August 4
"Documenta 12," Neue Galerie, Kassel, Germany, June 16 – September 23 (curated by Roger M. Buergel and Ruth Noack)
"Alina Szapocznikow," BROADWAY 1602, New York, November 18 – January 12
2008
"Tři sochařky," Prague Castle, July 29 – October 31 (exh. cat.)
2009
"Niezgrabne przedmioty (Awkward Objects). Alina Szapocznikow, Maria Bartuszova, Pauline Boty, Louise Bourgeois, Eva Hesse and Paulina Ołowska," Museum of Modern Art, Warsaw, May 14 – July 26 (curated by Joanna Mytkowska and Agata Jakubowska; exh. cat.). Includes international conference "Alina Szapocznikow. Documents. Works. Interpretations," May 15 – 16
"Lynda Benglis, Louise Bourgeois, Alina Szapocznikow. After Awkward Objects," Hauser & Wirth, London, September 17 – December 12
"Alina Szapocznikow. Drawings and Sculptures," Galerie Isabella Czarnowska, Berlin, September 24 – November 21
2010
"Seductive Subversion: Women Pop Artists 1958 – 1968," University of the Arts, Philadelphia, January 22 – March 15; and Brooklyn Museum, New York, October 15 – January 9
"Inaugural Group Show," BROADWAY 1602, New York, February 21 – April 10
"Les Promesses du passé," Centre Pompidou, Paris, April 14 – July 19
"Alina Szapocznikow, My American Dream," BROADWAY 1602, New York, September 11 – December 11
2011
"Alina Szapocznikow (Dessins)," Galerie Loevenbruck, Paris, March 10 – April 24
"Alina Szapocznikow. Drawings," Galerie Isabella Czarnowska, Berlin, March 11 – April 9

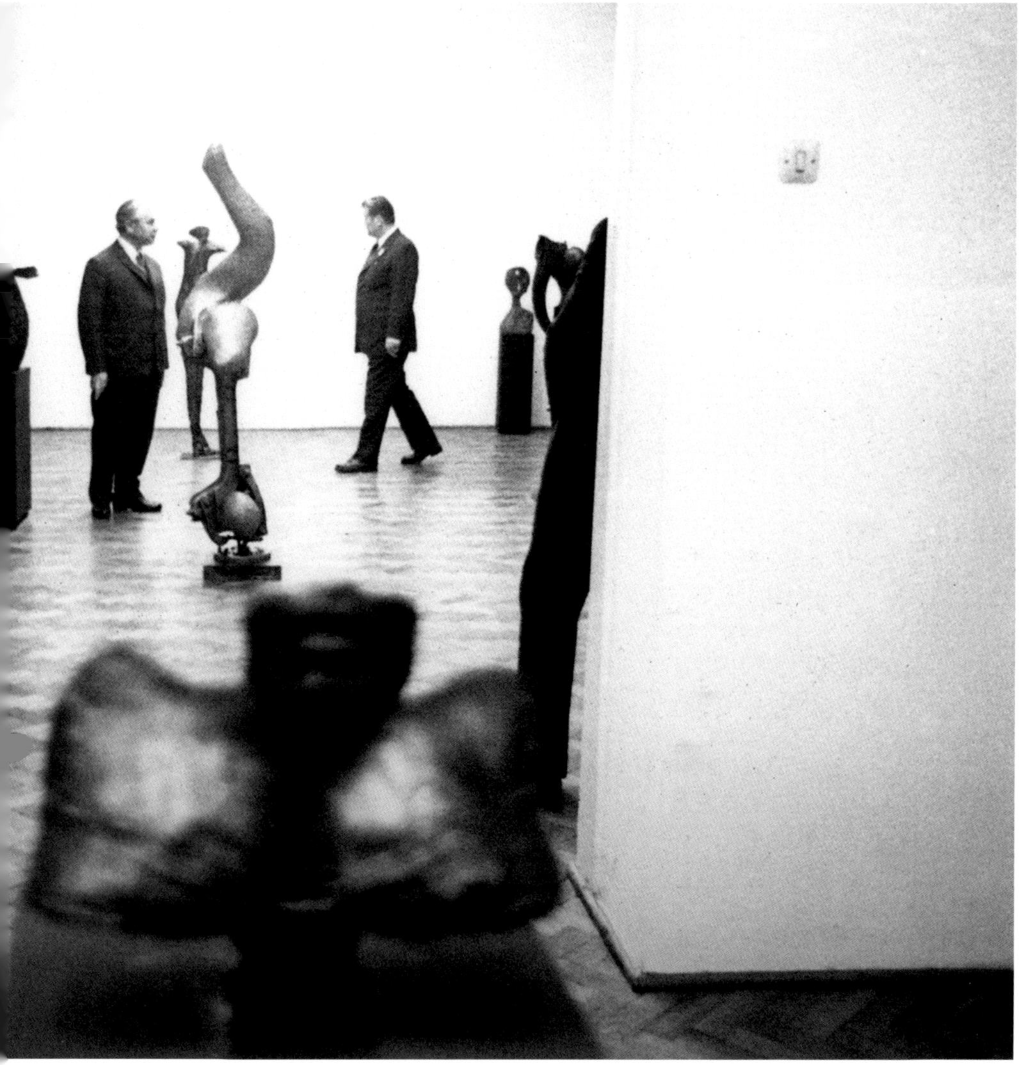

Installation view of *Goldfinger* (1965, center) in the posthumous exhibition "Alina Szapocznikow. 1926 – 1973," Muzeum Sztuki, Łódź, 1975.

Selected Bibliography

This bibliography was compiled by Jola Gola and is based on Jola Gola, "Bibliografia/Bibliography," in Józef Grabski, ed., *Alina Szapocznikow, Zatrzymać życie. Rysunki i rzeźby (Capturing Life. Drawings and Sculptures)* (Kraków and Warsaw: IRSA, 2004), 356–75.

Artist's Writings and Interviews

Henkel, Barbara. "Rzeźby oddychają dopiero w przestrzeni." *Sztandar Młodych*, no. 169 (1960): 1–2.

K., R. "Dookoła świata rozmawia dziś ze znaną artystką – rzeźbiarką Alina Szapocznikow." *Dookoła świata*, no. 73 (1959): 20.

Romanowska, Izabella. "Rzeźby Aliny Szapocznikow." *Ty i Ja*, no. 182 (1967).

Szapocznikow, Alina. Correspondence with Ryszard Stanisławski (1948–59). In the Alina Szapocznikow Archive/ Piotr Stanisławski/National Museum in Kraków. Published as "Fragments of Alina Szapocznikow's correspondence with Ryszard Stanisławski (1948–1959)." Translated by Marzena Beata Guzowska. In *Alina Szapocznikow*. Warsaw: Galeria Zachęta, 1998, 141–45.

——. "Róbmy rzeźby tak ustawione w przestrzeni, aby można było wokół nich tańczyć." *Przegląd Kulturalny*, no. 25 (1955): 5.

——. "Ankieta o nowoczesności." *Świat i Polska* 1/2, s. 14, no. 3 (1957): 20.

——. Statement, in "Plastycy o plastyce" (Visual artists on visual art). *Przegląd Kulturalny*, no. 16 (1957): 8. English translation by Maja Lavergne. In *Alina Szapocznikow*. Warsaw: Galeria Zachęta, 1998, 148.

——. "Co słychać u Aliny Szapocznikow." Interview with KUK. *Na przełaj*, no. 45 (1958): 5.

——. "Wrażenia...Uwagi...Refleksje... (Zazdrościłam zawsze Włochom...)." *Przegląd Artystyczny*, no. 2 (1958): 39.

——. "Z wizytą u Aliny Szapocznikow." *ŻycieWarszawy*, no. 521 (1959).

——. "Noworoczna ankieta 'Stolicy.' Mój Rok 1960." *Stolica*, nos. 1–2 (1960): 44.

——. "O swej wystawie mówi 'Expressowi' wybitna rzeźbiarka Alina Szapocznikow." *Express Poznański*, no. 80 (1960).

——. "Alina Szapocznikow. Twarze w 'Zwierciadle.'" *Zwierciadło* 2 (1961).

——. "Żeby za słowem kryło się pojęcie (udział w ankiecie o krytyce)." *Współczesność*, no. 3 (1962): 2–3.

——. "Z Paryża pisze Alina Szapocznikow [o Giacomettim]." *Współczesność*, no. 5 (1966): 8.

——. "Z Paryża pisze Alina Szapocznikow [o pobycie w Carrarze]." *Współczesność*, no. 11 (1966): 8.

——. "Les materiaux plastiques, que j'utilise...," March 1968. Typescript in the Alina Szapocznikow Archive/ Piotr Stanisławski/National Museum in Kraków. (Reproduced on page 108 of this publication.)

——. "Co się zdarzyło w rzeźbie naszej." *Kultura*, no. 1 (1970): 10.

——. "My American Dream," 1970. Handwritten text in the Alina Szapocznikow Archive/Piotr Stanisławski/National Museum in Kraków. (Reproduced on page 58 of this publication.)

——. "Problèmes de sensibilisation plastique dans le cadre de l'antenne pédagogique," 1970. Unpublished typescript in the Alina Szapocznikow Archive/Piotr Stanisławski/National Museum in Kraków. English translation titled "Developing artistic sensibility in sculpture students at the Academy of Fine Arts in Nice," in "Anthology of Alina Szapocznikow's texts." Translated by Wojciech Gilewski. In *Alina Szapocznikow*. Warsaw: Galeria Zachęta, 1998, 149.

——. "L'autre samedi..." (The other Saturday...), 22 June 1971. Typescript in the Alina Szapocznikow Archive/ Piotr Stanisławski/National Museum in Kraków. English translation available in the Alina Szapocznikow Archive. (Reproduced on page 60 of this publication.) Alternate English translation in "Anthology of Alina Szapocznikow's texts." Translated by Maja Lavergne. In *Alina Szapocznikow*. Warsaw: Galeria Zachęta, 1998, 149.

——. "Mon oeuvre puise ses racines..." (My work has its roots...), April 1972. Typescript in the Alina Szapocznikow Archive/Piotr Stanisławski/National Museum in Kraków. Also in "Anthology of Alina Szapocznikow's texts." Translated by Maja Lavergne. In *Alina Szapocznikow*. Warsaw: Galeria Zachęta, 1998, 148. (An earlier version of this text, dated March 1972, is reproduced on page 28 of this publication.)

——. "Patinoire dans le cratère du Vésuve," April 1972. Typescript in the Alina Szapocznikow Archive/ Piotr Stanisławski/National Museum in Kraków. (Reproduced on page 29 of this publication.)

——. "Myśli o sztuce (Przeżywamy epokę w wielkim skrócie, Co to jest talent, Tańczyć wokół rzeźby)." *Polska*, no. 9 (1973): 50–51.

Solo Exhibition Catalogues

Alina Szapocznikow. Warsaw: Centralne Biuro Wystaw Artystycznych, 1957.

Alina Szapocznikow. Prato, Italy: Galleria d'Arte Falsetti, 1960.

Alina Szapocznikow. Rijeka, Croatia: Galerija Likovnih Umjetnosti, 1961.

Alina Szapocznikow. Warsaw: Kordegarda, 1961.

Alina Szapocznikow. Venice, Italy: XXXI Biennale di Venezia, Section Polonaise, 1962.

Alina Szapocznikow. Brussels: Galerie Cogeime, 1968.

Alina Szapocznikow. Warsaw: Institute for the Promotion of Art Foundation, Galeria Zachęta, 1998.

Alina Szapocznikow. Prague: České Muzeum Výtvarných Umění, 2000.

Alina Szapocznikow, 1926–1973. Łódź, Poland: Muzeum Sztuki, 1975.

Alina Szapocznikow, 1926–1973. Kraków, Poland: Pałac Sztuki TPSP, Galeria Pryzmat – ZPAP, 1976.

Alina Szapocznikow, 1926–1973. Poznań, Poland: Biuro Wystaw Artystycznych "Arsenał," 1976.

Alina Szapocznikow, 1926–1973. Lublin, Poland: Galeria Sztuki Sceny Plastycznej KUL, 1989.

Alina Szapocznikow, 1926–1973. Paris: Musée Adam Mickiewicz – Bibliothèque Polonaise, 1990.

Alina Szapocznikow, 1926–1973. Kraków, Poland: Muzeum Narodowe w Krakowie, 1998.

Alina Szapocznikow, 1926–1973. Łódź, Poland: Muzeum Sztuki, 1999.

Alina Szapocznikow, 1926–1973. Dessins. Geneva, Switzerland: Aurora. Galerie d'Art Moderne, 1975.

Alina Szapocznikow, 1926–1973. Rysunki. Warsaw: Galeria Współczesna KMPiK, 1974.

Alina Szapocznikow, 1926–1973. Rzeźba, rysunek. Warsaw: Muzeum Narodowe w Warszawie, 1975.

Alina Szapocznikow, 1926–1973. Skulpturer. Lund, Sweden: Konsthall, 1977.

Alina Szapocznikow, 1926–1973. Tumeurs, herbier. Paris: Musée d'Art Moderne de la Ville de Paris, 1973.

Alina Szapocznikow, Fotorzeźby (1971). Lublin, Poland: Biuro Wystaw Artystycznych, 1978.

Alina Szapocznikow, Fotorzeźby (1971). Wrocław, Poland: Wrocławska Galeria Fotografii, 1978.

Alina Szapocznikow, Konfrontacje 1960. Warsaw: Galeria Krzywe Koło, 1960.

Alina Szapocznikow, Rzeźba. Warsaw: Centralne Biuro Wystaw Artystycznych Zachęta, 1967.

Alina Szapocznikow, Rzeźba. Bydgoszcz, Poland: Salon Sztuki Współczesnej BWA, 1976.

Alina Szapocznikow, Zatrzymać życie. Rysunki i rzeźby (Capturing Life. Drawings and Sculptures). Edited by Józef Grabski. Kraków and Warsaw: IRSA, 2004.

Alina Szapocznikow ze zbiorów Muzeum Sztuki w Łodzi. Kalisz, Poland: BWA, 2001.

II wystawa rzeźby Aliny Szapocznikow. Poznań, Poland: Centralne Biuro Wystaw Artystycznych, 1960.

Restany, Pierre. *Alina Szapocznikow*. Paris: Galerie Florence Houston Brown, 1967.

Rottenberg, Anda, and Zofia Golubiewowa. *Alina Szapocznikow, 1926–1973*. Warsaw: Galeria Sztuki Wspólczesnej Zachęta, 1998.

Rzeźba Aliny Szapocznikow, XIII Festiwal Sztuk Plastycznych. Sopot, Poland: Centralne Biuro Wystaw Artystycznych, 1960.

Monographs and Other Resources

Alina Szapocznikow archive. Consisting of photographs, artist's correspondence, manuscripts, unrealized projects, catalogues, invitation cards, and magazine articles, the archive is the property of Piotr Stanisławski and is housed at the National Museum in Kraków, Poland. Some documents are on the website of the Museum of Modern Art, Warsaw. Available at http://www.artmuseum.pl/archiwa.php?l=1&a=1&skrot=0.

Awkward Objects. Alina Szapocznikow and Maria Bartuszova, Pauline Boty, Louise Bourgeois, Eva Hesse, and Paulina Ołowska. Edited by Marta Dziewańska. Exh. brochure. Warsaw: Museum of Modern Art, 2009.

Chrzanowska-Pieńkos, Jolanta, Anna Cope, Benjamin Cope, and Gabriela Świtek, eds. *Zachęta 1860–2000*. Warsaw: Zachęta Narodowa Galeria Sztuki, 2003, 186–90, 214, 253, 309–311, 322, 330, 333, 342–44.

Gola, Jola. *Katalog rzeźb Aliny Szapocznikow*. Kraków, Poland: Muzeum Narodowe w Krakowie, 2001.

Gola, Jolanta. "Szapocznikow wobec władzy." In *Sztuka i władza. Materiały z konferencji zorganizowanej przez Instytut Stzuki Polskiej Akademii Nauk w dniach 30 XI – 2 XII 1998 roku, w Warszawie*. Edited by Dariusz Konstantynów, Robert Pasieczny, and Piotr Paszkiewcz. Warsaw: Polskiej Akademii Nauk, 2001, 227–31.

Hermansdorfer, Mariusz. *Między ekspresją a metaforą* (Between expression and metaphor). Wrocław, Poland: Muzeum Narodowe we Wrocławiu, 1999, 316–33.

Jakubowska, Agata. *Portret wielokrotny dzieła Aliny Szapocznikow*. Poznań, Poland: Wydawnictwo Naukowe UAM, 2008. English summary translated by Andrzej Pietrzak, 247–50.

——, ed. *Alina Szapocznikow. Awkward Objects*. Warsaw: Museum of Modern Art, 2011.

Leszkowicz, Paweł. *G.K. Collection #1: Kolekcja sztuki Grażyny Kulczyk (Art from Grażyna Kulczyk Collection)*. Poznań, Poland: Kulczyk Foundation, 2007, 68–85.

Piotrowsk, Piotr. *Awangarda w cieniu Jałty: Sztuka w Europie Środkowo-Wschodniej w latach 1945–1989*. Poznań, Poland: Dom Wydawniczy Rebis, 2005, 369–76, 385, 388–89, 422–23.

Rottenberg, Anda. "Polish Art in Search of Freedom." In *Art From Poland, 1945–1996*. Edited by Jolanta Chrzanowska-Pieńkos, Marzena Beata Guzowska, Dorota M. Karaszewska, Katarzyna Porembska, and Joanna Słodowska. Warsaw: Galeria Sztuki Współczesnej Zachęta, 1997, 11, 29–36.

——. *Sztuka w Polsce 1945–2005*. Warsaw: Wydawnictwo Piotra Marciszuka STENTOR, 2005, 9, 39–40, 43–47, 111, 213, 325, 427, 465.

Szmelter, Iwona. "The Conservation of Modern Art in Eastern Europe; A Phenomenon of Modern Art and its Conservation." In *Modern Art: Who Cares? An Interdisciplinary Research Project and an International Symposium on the Conservation of Modern and Contemporary Art*. Edited by Ijsbrand Hummelen and Dionne Sillé. Amsterdam: The Foundation for the Conservation of Modern Art and the Netherlands Institute for Cultural Heritage, 1999, 322–25.

Szymczyk, Adam, ed. *Flesh at War with Enigma*. Basel, Switzerland: Schwabe AG; and New York: Lukas & Sternberg, 2005.

Wojciechowski, Aleksander. *Polskie życie artystyczne w latach 1945–1960*. Wrocław, Poland: Zakład Narodowy im. Ossolińskich, 1992, 95–96, 152, 246–47, 304, 314, 322, 326, 341, 416, 427, 430, 441, 448, 453.

Zagrodzki, Janusz. *Alina Szapocznikow*. Warsaw: Arkady, 1979.

——. "Alina Szapocznikow." *Współczesna Sztuka Polska*. Edited by Andrzeja Ryszkiewicza. Warsaw: Arkady, 1981, 301–07.

Articles

Ahlander, Leslie Judd. "If an Art Critic Were President…" *Washington Post*, 23 April 1961, G6.

"Alina Szapocznikow." *K & C (Kunst en Cultuuragenda)*, no. 34 (1968): 7.

"Alina Szapocznikow artystka rzeźbiarka. 8 marca." *Przyjaźń*, no. 10 (1961).

"Alina Szapocznikow. 1926–1973." *CDN. Notatnik społeczno-kulturalny*, no. 3 (1998): 30.

Banaszkiewicz, Grażyna. "Rzeźby Szapocznikow." *Miesięcznik Literacki*, no. 12 (1978): 37.

Bartelik, Marek. "Alina Szapocznikow. Galeria Zachęta." *Artforum International* 37, no. 5 (1999): 128.

Basoski, C. "Alina Szapocznikow beeldhouwster uit Warschau." *De Rotterdammer*, no. 16143 (1959).

Bernntsson, A. "…bara oformliga föremål." *Sydsvenska Dagbladet*, 9 May 1977.

Bołdok, Sławomir. "Sztuka emocjonalna." *Życie i Myśl*, nos. 11–12 (1967): 207–08.

Bomanowska, Marzena. "Rzeźba ciała." *Gazeta Łódzka*, 29 December 1998.

Borowski, Wiesław. "Rzeźby Aliny Szapocznikow." *Życie Literackie*, no. 39 (1957): 5.

Boudaille, Georges. "La Biennale de Venise." *Les Lettres Françaises*, 21–27 July 1962.

Brewińska, Maria. "Strach ma moje oczy. Po wystawie Aliny Szapocznikow w Galerii Sztuki Współczesnej Zachęta." *Orońsko: Kwartalnik Rzeźby*, nos. 2–3 (1998): 28–34.

——. "Onkologia rzeźby." *Kalejdoskop*, no. 2 (1999).

De Bure, Gilles. "DESIGN s.a." *Opus International*, no. 10 (1969): 103.

Cabanne, Pierre. "Aline a corps perdu." *Le Combat*, no. 8986 (1973).

Chmielewski, Amy. "Alina Szapocznikow's Protean Body." *Artmargins*, 17 March 2008. Available at http://www.artmargins.com/index.php/3-exhibitions/106-alina-szapocznikows-protean-body.

Czartoryska, Urszula. "Rzeźba Aliny Szapocznikow." *Tygodnik Powszechny*, no. 42 (1975): 6.

——. "Alina Szapocznikow." *Poezja*, no. 2 (1976): 99–104.

——. "Wystawa Aliny Szapocznikow." *Projekt*, no. 1 (1976): 60–62.

——. "Transgresja. O przesłaniu twórczości Aliny Szapocznikow." *Twórczość*, no. 10 (1998): 73–80.

Czerni, Krystyna. "Wstyd. Wystawa Aliny Szapocznikow." *Tygodnik Powszechny*, no. 25 (1998).

Decker, Maria. "Świat kobiecej ekspresji. Retrospektywna wystawa prac Aliny Szapocznikow." *Życie Warszawy*, no. 118 (1998).

Eliasson, K. E. "Avslöjande konst i Lund." *Helsingborgs Dagblad*, 27 April 1977.

Florczak, Zbigniew. "Niezgrabne przedmioty Aliny Szapocznikow." *Polityka*, no. 25 (1974): 9.

Gain, Roger. "Alina sculpte ses ventres dans le marbre de Michel-Ange." *Elle*, no. 1191 (1968): 137, 139.

Gassiot-Talabot, Gerald. "Les Rolls d'Alina, Vela Luca." *Opus International*, no. 27 (1971): 63–64.

Gobron, Christine. "Alina Szapocznikow sculpte la chair." *Beaux Arts* (Brussels), no. 1224 (1968): 12.

Gola, Jola. "'Zielnik' Aliny Szapocznikow." *Rzeźba Polska*, 1986, 135–46.

——. "Na marginesie pewnej wystawy." *Rzeźba Polska*, 1997, 10–20.

——. "O materii rzeźbiarskiej. Wyjęte z rozważań o Alinie Szapocznikow." *Biuletyn Informacyjny Konserwatorów Dzieł Sztuki*, no. 2 (1997): 72–75.

——. "W poszukiwaniu Aliny Szapocznikow." *Art & Business*, no. 11 (1997): 7.

——. "Alina Szapocznikow. Gesty w stronę ciała." *Elle*, no. 6 (1998): 92–96.

——. "Odciski czasu." *Magazyn Gazety Wyborczej*, 12–13 June 1998, 28–29.

——. "Alina Szapocznikow." *Pro Memoriam*, no. 10 (1999): 29–34, 70.

——. "Czy Szapocznikow była potrzebna Akademia…." *Aspiracje*, Summer 2009, 44–51.

——. "Portret radosny i szokujący. Alina Szapocznikow." *Sztuka*, no. 5 (2009): 6–11.

Griffin, Jonathan. "Alina Szapocznikow." *Frieze*, 22 January 2008. Published online at http://www.frieze.com/shows/review/alina_szapocznikow/.

Grubert, Halina. "Artyści na sympozjach rzeźbiarskich." *Express Wieczomy*, no. 283 (1961): 6.

Gutowski, Maciej. "Zachować nietrwałe." *Kultura*, no. 44 (1975): 11.

——. "Intymne i ulotne." *Kultura*, no. 26 (1978).

H., G. Q. "A la recherche d'Alina…" *Journal de Genève*, no. 252 (1971).

Henkel, Barbara. "Rzeźby oddychają dopiero w przestrzeni." *Sztandar Młodych*, no. 169 (1960): 1–2.

Hermansdorfer, Mariusz. "Źródło radości, bólu, prawdy. W 25. Rocznicę śmierci Aliny Szapocznikow." *Odra*, no. 4 (1998): 94–99.

——. "Między ekspresją a metaforą." *Odra*, no. 6 (1999): 98–108.

Hniedziewicz, Magdalena. "Kształt własnych przeżyć." *Trybuna Ludu*, no. 269 (1975).

——. "Przestrzeń i linia." *Kultura*, no. 23 (1978).

——. "Przypomnienie artystki." *Pokaz. Pismo krytyki artystycznej*, no. 23 (1998): 1.
"Iwona Torbicka, Szapocznikow wychodzi z cienia. Rozmowa z Joanna Mytkowską, dyrektor Muzeum Sztuki Nowoczesnej w Warszawie." *Gazeta Wyborcza*, no. 72 (2008): 16.
Jarecka, Dorota. "'In articulo mortis' – Alina Szapocznikow." *Gazeta Wyborcza*, no. 13 (1999).
Kitowska-Łysiak, Małgorzata. "Pamięć ciała." *Kresy*, no. 26 (1996): 198–203.
Klimenšova-Judlová, Maria. "Alina Szapocznikow. 1926–1973. Retrospektiva." *Ateliér*, no. 1 (1999): 16.
Kolat-Ways, Irena. "Człowiek i jego ślad." *Sztuka*, no. 6 (1975): 24–27.
Konieczna, E. "Cień śmierci. Rozmowa z Ryszardem Stanisławskim." *Miesiąc w Krakowie*, no. 12 (1998): 62–63.
——. "Rzeźbiła śmierć. Rozmowa z Piotrem Stanisławskim, synem Aliny Szapocznikow." *Miesiąc w Krakowie*, no. 10 (1998): 40–42.
Kossakowski, Eustachy. *Polska*, no. 12 (1967): 32.
Kowalska, Bożena. "Inauguracja jesiennego sezonu w 'Zachęcie.'" *Nowe Sygnały*, no. 36 (1957): 6.
Kuc, Monika. "Ciało. Rzeźba Aliny Szapocznikow w Zachęcie." *Gazeta Wyborcza*, no. 133 (1998): 1, 18.
Kuczyńska, Teresa. "Alina Szapocznikow." *Ty i Ja*, no. 6 (1973): 2–4.
Lacôte, René. "La jeune sculpture polonaise. Alina Szapocznikow." *Parallèle 50* (Paris), no. 50 (1950).
Ładnowska, Janina. "Rzeźby-obiekty zorganizowane przestrzennie w zbiorach XX wieku w Muzeum Sztuki w Łodzi." *Rzeźba Polska*, 1987, 198, 217–18, 223.
Lameński, Lechosław. "Alina Szapocznikow 1926–1973." *Tygodnik Powszechny*, no. 14 (1989): 5.
Lévêque, Jean Jacques. "Galeries 1." *Opus International*, no. 2 (1967): 100.
——. "Une rêverie sur la matière." *Opus International*, no. 4 (1967): 69–71.
——. "Alina Szapocznikow: pour une soustraction de corps, une addition de bouches." *Opus International*, no. 6 (1968): 26–31.
——. "Les materiaux sujets." *Galerie Jardin des Arts*, no. 6 (1974): 10–11.
——. "Dictionnaire." *Galerie-Jardin des Arts*, no. 133 (1974): 67.
Libelle-Rojoux, Arnaud. "Szapocznikow la part maudite." *Beaux Arts Magazine*, June 2004: 37.
Malik, Amna. "Flesh at War with Enigma. Kunsthalle Basel, 2004." *Papers of Surrealism*, no. 3 (Spring 2005). Available at http://www.surrealismcentre.ac.uk/papersofsurrealism/journal3/index.htm.
Małkowska, Monika. "Maski miłości i śmierci." *Gazeta malarzy i poetów*, no. 3 (1998): 7.
——. "Źródło radości i bólu." *Rzeczpospolita*, no. 182 (1998).
Marchant, Sabine. "Deux talents bien divers présentés á L'ARC2." *Le Figaro*, 28 May 1973, 29.
Markowska, Anna. "Taniec życia." *Format*, nos. 31/32 (1999): 34–35.
Miliszkiewicz, Janusz. "Puls kamienia. Seans zmysłowych rzeźb Aliny Szapocznikow." *Twój Styl*, no. 6 (1998): 152.
"Młoda rzeźbiarka Alina Szapocznikow nie chce odrodzenia Wermachtu." *Gazeta Polska: Niepodleglosc. Dziennik Wychodźctwa Polskiego we Francji i Belgii* (Paris), no. 291 (1950): 1–2.
Morawińska, Agnieszka. "Szapocznikow. Buste étincelant." *Wysokie Obcasy* (supplement to *Gazeta Wyborcza*), no. 2 (2000): 32.
Moulin, Jean-Raoul. "Alina Szapocznikow. Ou la mort au défi." *L'Humanité*, no. 8882 (1973): 15.
Naggar, Carole. "Alina Szapocznikow." *Opus International*, no. 46 (1973): 39–41.
Nowak, Ewa Izabela. "Zielnik, Z Piotrem Stanisławskim, synem Aliny Szapocznikow rozmawia Ewa Izabela Nowak." *Arteon*, no. 6 (2003): 20–25.
"Nowe rzeźby Aliny Szapocznikow." *Współczesność*, no. 6 (1966): 7.
Nyman, U. "Ambassaden: Influensa Konstnärer: Inga pass." *Sydsvenska Dagbladet*, 15 April 1977.
Olek, Jerzy. "Zmiana przyzwyczajeń." *Wiadomości*, no. 30 (1978).
Osęka, Andrzej. "Nowe rzeźby Aliny Szapocznikow." *Przegląd Kulturalny*, no. 30 (1960): 8–9.
——. "Sculpture." *Polish Perspectives*, no. 1 (1961): 41.
——. "Rzeźby, które żyją." *Polska*, no. 8 (1962): 38–39.
——. "Alina Szapocznikow." *Ty i Ja*, no. 11 (1965).
——. "Biological Romanticism." *Polish Perspectives*, no. 1 (1966): 80–83.
——. "Alina Szapocznikow." *Tygodnik Kulturalny*, no. 19 (1967): 3.
——. "Alina Szapocznikow." *Polish Perspectives*, nos. 7–8 (1973): 88–93.
——. "Przemiany formy." *Miesięcznik Literacki*, no. 7 (1974): 58.
——. "Zobaczenie Aliny Szapocznikow." *Gazeta Wyborcza*, no. 301 (1998).
Pieńkos, Andrzej. "Szapocznikow. Notatnik ontologiczny." *Art & Business*, nos. 7–8 (1998): 42–46.
Pierre, José. "Qui est surréaliste." *Galerie des Arts*, no. 66 (1969): 11–13.
Piskor, Stanisław. "Taniec na kraterze." *Tak i Nie*, no. 12 (1989).
Pokaz. Pismo krytyki artystycznej, no. 23 (1998). Special issue on Alina Szapocznikow. Texts by Miloslaw Chlupàč, Urszula Czartoryska, Magdalena Hniedziewicz, Janina Ładnowska, Pierre Restany, Wojciech Skrodzki, Ryszard Stanisławski, Myśląc o Alinie Szapocznikow, Magdalena Ujma. Interview with Piotr Stanisławski by Joanna Pużyńska.
Porębski, Mieczysław. "W pracowni Aliny Szapocznikow." *Polska*, no. 8 (1958): 29–31.
——. "Wspomnienia z Biennale." *Współczesność*, no. 15 (1962): 3, 11.
Restany, Pierre. "En 10 ans les peintres polonais ont rattrapé leur retard sur l'art contemporain." *Les Galeries des Arts*, December 1962 – January 1963, 26.
——. "La tendance moderne, art total, art pour tous." *Le Nouveau Planète*, no. 3 (1968).
——. "L'art contemporaine est la langue de la révolution sexuelle." *Plexus*, no. 30 (1969): 101.
——. "Art Concept from Europe." *Domus*, no. 487 (1970): 48.
——. "Alina Szapocznikow." *Le Combat*, no. 8930 (1973).
Romanowska, Izabela. "Rzeźby Aliny Szapocznikow." *Ty i Ja*, no. 182 (1967): 14.
"Rzeźby Aliny Szapocznikow w Zachęcie." *Przegląd Artystyczny*, no. 6 (1967): 71.
Sarzyński, Piotr. "Ciało i ból. Alina Szapocznikow przypomniana w Zachęcie." *Polityka*, no. 22 (1998): 58–59.
Skrodzki, Wojciech. "Prawdy Aliny Szapocznikow." *Literatura* 58, no. 12 (1973): 13.
——. "Droga Aliny Szapocznikow." *Więź*, no. 2 (1976): 141–45.
——. "Granice ludzkiej kondycji." *Literatura* 204, no. 2 (1976): 1, 8–9.
Smith, Roberta. "Chewing Gum, Plaster Bellies and Other Sculptural Byways." *New York Times*, 28 December 2007.
Sola, Barbara. "Paryż ogląda rzeźby Szapocznikow." *Czas* (Kraków), 18 June 1990.
Sosnowski, Ryszard. "Rzeźby Aliny Szapocznikow." *Zwierciadło*, no. 19 (1957): 15–17.
Stajuda, Jerzy. "Rzeźby Aliny Szapocznikow." *Współczesność*, no. 4 (1963): 10.
Stopa, Magdalena. "Poranione rzeźby. Wystawa Aliny Szapocznikow w warszawskiej Zachęcie." *Życie*, no. 112 (1998).
Świdziński, Jan. "O rzeźbie Aliny Szapocznikow." *Tygodnik Zachodni*, no. 19 (1960): 7–9.
Szmelter, Iwona. "Fenomen Sztuki Współczesnej a Konserwacja." *Biuletyn Informacyjny Konserwatorów Dzieł Sztuki*, no. 2 (1997): 16–17.
Szubert, Piotr. "Scenariusz wystawy 'Figura.'" *Orońsko: Kwartalnik Rzeźby*, nos. 2–3 (1998): 36–40.
"Ta młoda Polka obłaskawia potężne bloki kamienia." *Świat i Polska*, no. 53 (1951): 4–5.
Taranienko, Zbigniew. "Poliester, poliuretan (Hipotezy optyczne)." *Argumenty*, no. 4 (1976): 10.
——. "Drogi Współczesnej rzeźby." *Tygodnik Kulturalny*, no. 28 (1978).
Teyssedre, B. "Un mauvais ménage. Avant-garde et musée s'accordent mal: ARC2 tente de se réconcilier." *Le Nouvel Observateur*, no. 478 (1974): 58–59.
Toeplitz, Krzysztof Teodor. "Najpiękniejszy przedmiot." *Polityka*, no. 13 (1973): 8.
——. "O Alinie Szapocznikow." *Sztuka*, no. 6 (1974): 10–11.
——. "O Alinie Szapocznikow." *Kultura i życie*, no. 3 (1976): 12–14.
Truszczyński, Olgierd. "Alina Szapocznikow (1926–1973)." *Biuletyn ZPAP*, nos. 2/3 (1974): 125–26.
Turowicz, Jerzy. "Alina Szapocznikow. W pierwszą rocznicę śmierci." *Tygodnik Powszechny*, no. 12 (1974).
"Två polska utställningar." *Skånska dagbladet*, 15 April 1977.
Verwoert, Jan. "Mouth to Mouth." *Frieze*, no. 129 (March 2010): 114–19.
Wajda, Andrzej. "Szapocznikow." *Projekt*, no. 5 (1973): 22–27.
Waltoś, Jacek. "Szapocznikow." *Odra*, no. 9 (1976): 78–83.
——. "Alina Szapocznikow." *Art & Business* 19, no. 9 (1993): 48–53.
Weimarck, T. "Bekräftelse på att ha funnits till." *Arbetet*, 10 May 1977.
Wescher, Herta. "Einige nicht preisgekronte Bildhauer der Biennale. Alina Szapocznikow." *Quadrum*, no. 13 (1962): 104–05.
Witz, Ignacy. "Szapocznikow i Tchórzewski. Warszawskie wystawy." *Życie Warszawy*, no. 229 (1957): 8.
Zbrożyna, Barbara. "Szapocznikow." *Trybuna Ludu*, no. 262 (1957): 4.

Checklist of Works in the Exhibition

Alina Szapocznikow: Sculpture Undone, 1955–1972 travels to four venues: WIELS Contemporary Art Centre, Brussels; the Hammer Museum, Los Angeles; Wexner Center for the Arts, Columbus, Ohio; and The Museum of Modern Art, New York. The checklist below indicates those works that are appearing in selected venues only. When no such notation is made, the work appears in all four venues.

Untitled (Self-Portrait), c. 1948–56
Pencil on paper
7 1/2 x 8 3/4" (19 x 22.2 cm)
Ursula Hauser Collection, Switzerland
Plate 150

Pierwsza miłość (First Love), 1954
Encrusted plastic cement
35 7/16" (90 cm) high
Muzeum Sztuki, Łódź
Plate 147

Koński ogon – Portret Meksykanki (A Pony Tail–Portrait of a Mexican Woman), 1955–56
Plaster
17 11/16 x 7 7/8 x 15" (45 x 20 x 38 cm)
Krzysztof Musial Collection
Plate 148

Trudny wiek (Difficult Age), 1956
Bronze
74 7/16 x 23 1/4 x 15"
(189 x 59 x 38 cm)
Muzeum Sztuki, Łódź
Plate 149

Dłoń. Projekt Pomnika Bohaterów Warszawy II (Hand. Monument to the Heroes of the Warsaw Ghetto), 1957
Patinated plaster, iron filings
56 7/8 x 28 3/4 x 16 9/16"
(144.5 x 73 x 42 cm)
The Estate of Alina Szapocznikow/Piotr Stanisławski
Plate 145
HAMMER/WEXNER/MOMA ONLY

Ekshumowany (Exhumed), 1957
Bronze
25 3/16 x 16 9/16 x 11 13/16"
(64 x 42 x 30 cm)
Collection Museum of Independence, Warsaw
Plate 146

Monstrum II (Monster II), 1957
Lead and metal construction
10 5/8 x 5 1/2 x 5 1/2" (27 x 14 x 14 cm)
The Estate of Alina Szapocznikow/Piotr Stanisławski
Plate 144

Maria Magdalena (Mary Magdalene), 1957–58
Plaster and iron filings
68 15/16 x 22 7/8 x 18 1/8"
(175 x 58 x 46 cm)
Muzeum Narodowe w Warszawie
Plate 143
HAMMER/WEXNER/MOMA ONLY

Balet (Ballet), 1958
Bronze
15 9/16 x 11 13/16 x 8 1/4"
(39.5 x 30 x 21 cm)
The Estate of Alina Szapocznikow/Piotr Stanisławski
Plate 109
HAMMER/WEXNER/MOMA ONLY

Untitled (Sketches of a Design for a Monument 1), c. 1958–61
Ink, crayon, and felt-tip pen on paper
11 3/4 x 7 7/8" (29.8 x 20 cm)
The Museum of Modern Art, New York. Gift of The Judith Rothschild Foundation
Plate 121
HAMMER/WEXNER/MOMA ONLY

Motyl (Butterfly), 1959
Lead
3 9/16 x 3 15/16 x 2 3/8" (9 x 10 x 6 cm)
The Estate of Alina Szapocznikow/Piotr Stanisławski
WIELS ONLY

Woltyżerka I (Horse Gymnast), 1959
Lead
5 1/2 x 5 1/8 x 2 15/16"
(14 x 13 x 7.5 cm)
The Estate of Alina Szapocznikow/Piotr Stanisławski
WIELS ONLY

Untitled (Studies of Some Organic Forms), c. 1959
Crayon and ballpoint pen on paper
16 3/8 x 11 11/16" (41.5 x 29.7 cm)
The Estate of Alina Szapocznikow/Piotr Stanisławski
Plate 142

Untitled (Study for *Kobieta-róża* [Woman-Rose]), c. 1959
Pencil on paper
10 15/16 x 8 3/16" (27.8 x 20.8 cm)
Courtesy Galerie Isabella Czarnowska, Berlin
Plate 141

Untitled (Study of a Nude), c. 1959
Pencil on paper
11 13/16 x 8 5/8" (30 x 22 cm)
Collection Dr. Werner Jerke
Plate 140

Untitled (Sketch 1), c. 1959–60
Crayon on paper
12 7/16 x 9 3/16" (31.5 x 23.3 cm)
The Estate of Alina Szapocznikow/Piotr Stanisławski
Plate 137
HAMMER/WEXNER/MOMA ONLY

Untitled (Study for *Kwiato-ptak* [Flower-Bird] 2), c. 1959–60
Ink on paper
11 3/4 x 8 1/4" (29.8 x 21 cm)
Collection Gail and Tony Ganz, Los Angeles
Plate 138

Małża (Mollusc), 1960
Plastic cement, inlaid stone, ceramic, metal
40 9/16 x 38 3/16 x 13 13/16"
(103 x 97 x 35 cm)
Muzeum Sztuki, Łódź
Plate 135
HAMMER/WEXNER/MOMA ONLY

Rozłupany (Shattered), 1960
Polyester resin and metal bars
32 11/16 x 22 7/8 x 15"
(83 x 58 x 38 cm)
Private collection, Switzerland
Plate 136

Untitled, 1960
Ink and colored ink on blotting paper
13 x 9 5/8" (33 x 24.4 cm)
Private collection
WIELS ONLY

Untitled, c. 1960
Monotype and ink on paper
8 1/4 x 8 3/16" (21 x 20.7 cm)
The Estate of Alina Szapocznikow/Piotr Stanisławski
Plate 134

Untitled, c. 1960
Monotype and ink on paper
8 3/16 x 8 3/16" (20.8 x 20.7 cm)
The Estate of Alina Szapocznikow/Piotr Stanisławski
Plate 133

Untitled, c. 1960
Ink on blotting paper
13 1/4 x 9 5/8" (33.7 x 24.4 cm)
Private collection
Plate 120

Untitled, c. 1960
Ink on paper
11 9/16 x 8 3/16" (29.4 x 20.7 cm)
The Estate of Alina Szapocznikow/Piotr Stanisławski
Plate 139
HAMMER/WEXNER/MOMA ONLY

Untitled, c. 1960–61
Ink on paper
12 x 8 1/4" (30.4 x 20.9 cm)
Hammer Museum, Los Angeles. Purchase.
Plate 115
HAMMER ONLY

Naga (Naked), 1961
Terrazzo
63 x 15 3/4 x 13 13/16"
(160 x 40 x 35 cm)
Muzeum Sztuki, Łódź
Plate 132

Untitled, c. 1961
Monotype and ink on paper
25 13/16 x 18 15/16" (64.6 x 48 cm)
The Museum of Modern Art, New York. Gift of Harvey S. Shipley Miller

Untitled, c. 1961
Monotype and ink on blue paper
25 13/16 x 18 15/16" (64.6 x 48 cm)
Collection CORREARD, Paris. Courtesy Galerie Loevenbruck, Paris
Plate 118
HAMMER/WEXNER/MOMA ONLY

Untitled (Sketch for the Sculpture *Przemiany* [Metamorphoses] 1), c. 1961
Ink and pencil on paper
11 5/8 x 16 3/8" (29.5 x 41.5 cm)
The Museum of Modern Art, New York. Gift of The Judith Rothschild Foundation
Plate 131
MOMA ONLY

Untitled (Sketch for the Sculpture *Przemiany* [Metamorphoses] 2), c. 1961
Ink and pencil on paper
11 9/16 x 16 9/16" (29.3 x 42 cm)
Collection Gail and Tony Ganz, Los Angeles
Plate 130

Noga (Leg), 1962
Plaster
7 7/8 x 19 11/16 x 19 11/16"
(20 x 50 x 50 cm)
The Estate of Alina Szapocznikow/Piotr Stanisławski
Plate 129
HAMMER/WEXNER/MOMA ONLY

Untitled, 1963
Felt-tip pen on paper
14 1/8 x 10 9/16" (35.9 x 26.8 cm)
The Museum of Modern Art. Purchased with funds provided by the Rendl Endowment for Slavic Art
Plate 126
HAMMER/WEXNER/MOMA ONLY

Untitled, 1963
Felt-tip pen and ink on paper
14 1/8 x 10 9/16" (35.9 x 26.8 cm)
Ursula Hauser Collection, Switzerland
Plate 116

Untitled, 1963
Felt-tip pen and ink on paper
12 1/16 x 9" (30.6 x 22.8 cm)
Hammer Museum, Los Angeles. Purchase.
Plate 127
HAMMER/WEXNER/MOMA ONLY

Untitled, 1963
Felt-tip pen on paper
12 1/8 x 8 3/4" (30.8 x 22.2 cm)
The Estate of Alina Szapocznikow/ Piotr Stanisławski
HAMMER/WEXNER/MOMA ONLY

Untitled, 1963
Felt-tip pen on paper
12 1/8 x 9" (30.8 x 22.9 cm)
The Estate of Alina Szapocznikow/ Piotr Stanisławski
HAMMER/WEXNER/MOMA ONLY

Untitled, c. 1963
Ballpoint pen on paper
14 9/16 x 10 9/16" (37 x 26.8 cm)
Ursula Hauser Collection, Switzerland
Plate 117
HAMMER/WEXNER/MOMA ONLY

Untitled (Study for a Sculpture 4), c. 1963
Monotype and ink on paper
16 7/16 x 15 9/16" (41.8 x 39.5 cm)
The Museum of Modern Art, New York. Gift of The Judith Rothschild Foundation
Plate 119

Untitled (Study for a Sculpture 5), c. 1963
Ink on paper
16 9/16 x 11" (42 x 27.9 cm)
Collection Stanislas Gokelaere, Brussels
Plate 114

Untitled, c. 1963–65
Monotype and ink on paper
19 11/16 x 12 3/4" (50 x 32.3 cm)
The Estate of Alina Szapocznikow/ Piotr Stanisławski
HAMMER/WEXNER/MOMA ONLY

Untitled, c. 1963–65
Monotype and ink on paper
12 5/8 x 9 7/8" (32 x 25 cm)
Collection UCLA Grunwald Center for the Graphic Arts, Hammer Museum, Los Angeles. Purchased with funds provided by the Helga K. and Walter Oppenheimer Acquisition Fund
Plate 113
HAMMER/WEXNER/MOMA ONLY

Untitled, c. 1963–65
Monotype and ink on paper
18 11/16 x 12 5/16" (47.5 x 31.2 cm)
The Museum of Modern Art, New York. Edgar Wachenheim III Fund
Plate 112
HAMMER/WEXNER/MOMA ONLY

Untitled, c. 1963–68
Ink on paper
10 5/8 x 7 3/4" (27 x 19.6 cm)
Collection Stanislas Gokelaere, Brussels
Plate 111

Untitled, c. 1963–68
Ink on paper
8 1/4 x 10 5/8" (21 x 27 cm)
Collection Loevenbruck, Paris
HAMMER/WEXNER/MOMA ONLY

Untitled, c. 1963–68
Ink on copy paper
10 9/16 x 8 3/16" (26.8 x 20.8 cm)
The Museum of Modern Art, New York. Purchased with funds provided by the Rendl Endowment for Slavic Art
Plate 110

Ołów II (Lead II), 1964
Lead
3 9/16 x 3 3/16 x 2" (9 x 8 x 5 cm)
The Estate of Alina Szapocznikow/ Piotr Stanisławski
Plate 123
WIELS ONLY

Ołów V (Lead V), 1964
Lead
5 1/8 x 2 15/16 x 3 3/16" (13 x 7.5 x 8 cm)
The Estate of Alina Szapocznikow/ Piotr Stanisławski
Plate 124
WIELS ONLY

Untitled, 1964
Ink and felt-tip pen on paper
12 3/8 x 9 1/4" (31.4 x 23.4 cm)
The Museum of Modern Art, New York. Purchased with funds provided by the Rendl Endowment for Slavic Art
Plate 108

Untitled, 1964
Ink and blue ink on paper
12 5/16 x 9 5/16" (31.3 x 23.6 cm)
The Museum of Modern Art, New York. Gift of The Judith Rothschild Foundation
Plate 107

Untitled (Study of Forms with Elements of Industrial Origin 4), 1964
Ink and felt-tip pen on paper
12 5/16 x 9 1/4" (31.2 x 23.4 cm)
Courtesy Galerie Isabella Czarnowska, Berlin
Plate 98

Forma II (Form II), 1964–65
Unfired pink terracotta
4 1/2 x 7 11/16 x 5 1/8" (11.5 x 19.5 x 13 cm)
The Estate of Alina Szapocznikow/ Piotr Stanisławski
Plate 128

Ceramika I (Ceramic I), 1965
Terracotta
5 3/4 x 3 15/16 x 6 11/16" (14.5 x 10 x 17 cm)
The Estate of Alina Szapocznikow/ Piotr Stanisławski
Plate 96 b

Ceramika II (Ceramic II), 1965
Terracotta
6 11/16 x 7 7/8 x 5 15/16" (17 x 20 x 15 cm)
The Estate of Alina Szapocznikow/ Piotr Stanisławski
Plate 96 a

Ceramika III (Ceramic III), 1965
Terracotta
5 1/2 x 9 1/16 x 6 11/16" (14 x 23 x 17 cm)
The Estate of Alina Szapocznikow/ Piotr Stanisławski
Plate 96 c

Człowiek z instrumentem (Man with Instrument), 1965
Cement, car part, black patina
58 1/4 x 15 3/4 x 13 13/16" (148 x 40 x 35 cm)
The Estate of Alina Szapocznikow/ Piotr Stanisławski
Plate 99

Dwuczęściowa (In Two Parts), 1965
Plastic cement and car part
16 15/16 x 19 11/16 x 11 1/16" (43 x 50 x 28 cm)
Wielkopolskie Towarzystwo Zachęty Sztuk Pięknych (Wielkopolska Society for the Encouragement of Arts)
Plate 104

Goldfinger, 1965
Gold patinated cement and car part
72 1/16 x 29 15/16 x 22 7/16" (183 x 76 x 57 cm)
Muzeum Sztuki, Łódź
Plate 101
WIELS/MOMA ONLY

Untitled (Sketch for *Goldfinger* 1), 1965
Ballpoint pen and felt-tip pen on paper
10 5/8 x 7 11/16" (27 x 19.5 cm)
The Estate of Alina Szapocznikow/ Piotr Stanisławski
Plate 100

Untitled (Sketch for *Goldfinger* 3), 1965
Felt-tip pen on graph paper
10 5/8 x 7 11/16" (27 x 19.5 cm)
The Estate of Alina Szapocznikow/ Piotr Stanisławski
WIELS ONLY

Untitled (Sketch of a Sculpture with Car Shock Absorber), 1965
Ballpoint pen on paper
10 5/8 x 8 3/16" (26.9 x 20.8 cm)
Courtesy Galerie Isabella Czarnowska, Berlin
Plate 102
WIELS ONLY

Untitled (Sketch of a Sculpture with Industrial Elements), 1965
Felt-tip pen on graph paper
10 5/8 x 7 11/16" (27 x 19.5 cm)
The Estate of Alina Szapocznikow/ Piotr Stanisławski
WIELS ONLY

Untitled (Studies of a Sculpture with Industrial Elements), c. 1965
Ballpoint pen on paper
10 5/8 x 8 3/16" (27 x 20.8 cm)
The Estate of Alina Szapocznikow/ Piotr Stanisławski
WIELS ONLY

Autoportret I (Self-Portrait I), 1966
Marble and polyester resin
16 1/8 x 11 13/16 x 7 7/8" (41 x 30 x 20 cm)
The Estate of Alina Szapocznikow/ Piotr Stanisławski
Plate 105

Bouquet II, 1966
Plaster, plastic foil, colored polyester resin, metal
65 x 19 11/16 x 14 3/16" (165 x 50 x 36 cm)
The Estate of Alina Szapocznikow/ Piotr Stanisławski
Plate 97

Lampe – bouche (Illuminated Lips), 1966
Colored polyester resin, metal, electrical wiring
Six lamps, ranging from 11 1/4" (28.5 cm) to 17 15/16" (45.5 cm) high
The Estate of Alina Szapocznikow/ Piotr Stanisławski
Plate 17

Sein illuminé (Illuminated Breast), 1966
Colored polyester resin and electrical wiring
22 1/16 x 6 7/8 x 6 5/16" (56 x 17.5 x 16 cm)
Museum of Modern Art, Warsaw
Plate 93

Bouches en Marche (Marching Lips), c. 1966
Polyester resin
20 7/8" (53 cm) high
Private collection. Courtesy Galerie Isabella Czarnowska, Berlin
Plate 95

Femme illuminée (Illuminated Woman), 1966–67
Plaster, colored polyester resin, electrical wiring
61 1/16 x 22 7/16 x 15 3/4"
(155 x 57 x 40 cm)
Collection Alexandre Stanisławski
Plate 91

Buste étincelant I (Glowing Bust), 1967
Colored polyester resin and electrical wiring
22 7/8 x 8 1/4 x 7 7/8" (58 x 21 x 20 cm)
Collection Loevenbruck, Paris
Plate 15

Caprice – Monstre (Caprice – Monster), 1967
Sponge, polyester resin, metal, electrical wiring
78 3/4" (200 cm) high
The Estate of Alina Szapocznikow/ Piotr Stanisławski
Plate 92

Portret wielokrotny (dwukrotny) (Multiple Portrait [Double]), 1967
Colored polyester resin and granite
29 x 19 x 17" (73.7 x 48.3 x 43.2 cm)
Collection Sandra and Gerald Fineberg
Plate 106
HAMMER/WEXNER/MOMA ONLY

Souvenirs, 1967
Polyester resin and photographs
Two works: 4 1/2 x 1 3/8 x 2 3/4"
(11.5 x 3.5 x 7 cm);
and 11 13/16 x 8 5/8 x 3 9/16"
(30 x 22 x 9 cm)
The Estate of Alina Szapocznikow/ Piotr Stanisławski
Plate 56

Accident III, 1968
Polyurethane foam and polychrome wood
39 3/8 x 28 3/16 x 18 1/8"
(100 x 71.5 x 46 cm)
The National Museum in Wrocław
Plate 87
WIELS ONLY

Centrale (Central), 1968
Polyester resin and polyurethane foam
35 7/16 x 48 1/16 x 9 7/8"
(90 x 122 x 25 cm)
The National Museum in Wrocław
Plate 79
WIELS ONLY

Grande Plage (Big Beach), 1968
Polyester resin, colored polyurethane foam, wood
22 7/16 x 133 7/8 x 65"
(57 x 340 x 165 cm)
Muzeum Sztuki, Łódź
Plate 76
WIELS ONLY

Janus, 1968
Polyurethane foam
82 11/16 x 39 3/8 x 7 1/8"
(210 x 100 x 18 cm)
The National Museum in Wrocław
Plate 78

Les capuchons, Jambes noyées (Drips, Embedded Legs), 1968
Polyester resin and polyurethane foam
37 13/16 x 54 3/4 x 5 15/16"
(96 x 139 x 15 cm)
The National Museum in Wrocław
Plate 80

La Couronne de la Mariée (Bride's Wreath), 1968
Polyurethane foam, polyester resin, grass, metal
25 5/8 x 23 5/8 x 11 13/16"
(65 x 60 x 30 cm)
The National Museum in Wrocław
Plate 86

Petits ventres (Small Bellies), 1968
Carrara marble
11 13/16 x 11 7/16 x 5 1/2"
(30 x 29 x 14 cm)
Collection Elisabeth Lechien-Cremer
Plate 77
WIELS ONLY

Pollution II, 1968
Polyurethane foam, metal, grass
15 3/4 x 18 1/2 x 2 3/4" (40 x 47 x 7 cm)
The Estate of Alina Szapocznikow/ Piotr Stanisławski
Plate 88
WIELS ONLY

Siège-Piège (Seat-Trap), 1968
Sponge and polyurethane foam
13 3/8 x 26 3/4 x 24 13/16"
(34 x 68 x 63 cm)
The Estate of Alina Szapocznikow/ Piotr Stanisławski
Plate 85
WIELS ONLY

Stèle (Stele), 1968
Polyester resin and polyurethane foam
31 1/16 x 18 1/8 x 27 3/16"
(79 x 46 x 69 cm)
Collection Sabine Labelle-Rojoux
Plates 81–82

Torse noyé (Headless Torso), 1968
Polyester resin and polyurethane foam
18 1/8 x 25 3/16 x 28 3/4"
(46 x 64 x 73 cm)
Zachęta National Gallery of Art, Warsaw
Plate 83

Untitled, 1968
Felt-tip pen on cardboard
17 1/2 x 17 1/2" (44.5 x 44.5 cm)
The Estate of Alina Szapocznikow/ Piotr Stanisławski
Plate 74

Untitled, 1968
Ink on cardboard
17 5/16 x 16 9/16" (44 x 42 cm)
BROADWAY 1602, New York
Plate 71

Ventres – coussins (Belly cushions), 1968
Polyurethane foam
Five pieces, each 5 1/8 – 7 x 11 13/16 x 13 3/8" (13 – 17.8 x 30 x 34 cm)
The Museum of Modern Art, New York. Promised gift of Marie-Josée and Henry R. Kravis
Plate 75

Lamp (Ventres) (Lamp [Bellies]), c. 1968
Polyester resin and electric wiring
9 7/16 x 19 15/16 x 16 9/16"
(24 x 49 x 42 cm)
Ursula Hauser Collection, Switzerland

Krużlowa (Macierzyństwo) (Madonna of Krużlowa [Motherhood]), 1969
Colored polyester resin, photographs, gauze
16 9/16 x 20 1/2 x 7 1/8"
(42 x 52 x 18 cm)
Société de l'Apostolat Catholique (Pères Pallottins)
Plate 63

Untitled, 1969
Felt-tip pen on paper
4 3/4 x 7 1/8" (12 x 18 cm)
The Estate of Alina Szapocznikow/ Piotr Stanisławski
Plate 72

Alex, 1970
Polyester resin, photographs, clothing
68 1/2 x 26 3/8 x 19 11/16"
(174 x 67 x 50 cm)
The Estate of Alina Szapocznikow/ Piotr Stanisławski
Plate 61
WIELS ONLY

Bouche en marche (Fétiche III) (Marching lips [Fetish III]), 1970
Polyester resin, plastic lace, Plexiglas vitrine
7 1/8 x 14 9/16 x 9 7/16"
(18 x 37 x 24 cm)
Private collection, London
Plate 29

L'Enterrement d'Alina (Alina's Funeral), 1970
Polyester resin, glass wool, photographs, wood, gauze, artist's clothing
53 3/16 x 82 11/16 x 19 11/16"
(135 x 210 x 50 cm)
From the collection of the National Museum in Kraków
Plate 66

Petit Alex (Small Alex), 1970
Colored polyester resin, photographs, gauze
9 7/8 x 11 1/16 x 9 1/16"
(25 x 28 x 23 cm)
Collection de Bruin-Heijn
Plate 62
WIELS ONLY

Sans titre (Fétiche I) (Untitled [Fetish I]), 1970
Polyester resin, glass wool, newspapers, apron, plaster
12 3/16 x 22 7/8 x 14 3/16"
(31 x 58 x 36 cm)
The Estate of Alina Szapocznikow/ Piotr Stanisławski
WIELS ONLY

Sculpture – Lampe III (Fétiche IX) (Sculpture – Lamp III [Fetish IX]), 1970
Polyester resin, plastic lace, electrical wiring
7 7/8 x 17 11/16 x 9 7/8"
(20 x 45 x 25 cm)
Museum of Modern Art, Warsaw
Plate 32

Sculpture – Lampe IV (Sculpture – Lamp IV), 1970
Colored polyester resin and electrical wiring
24 13/16 x 14 3/16 x 12 3/16"
(63 x 36 x 31 cm)
Friedrich Christian Flick Collection
Plate 16

Sculpture – Lampe VI (Sculpture – Lamp VI), 1970
Colored polyester resin and electrical wiring
22 1/16 x 12 5/8 x 13 13/16"
(56 x 32 x 35 cm)
The Estate of Alina Szapocznikow/ Piotr Stanisławski
Plate 94
WIELS ONLY

Sous la coupole (Under the Cupola), 1970
Polyurethane foam and nylon tights
14 3/16 x 28 3/4 x 39 3/8"
(36 x 73 x 100 cm)
The Estate of Alina Szapocznikow/
Piotr Stanisławski
Plate 84

Untitled (Sketch of Growths on a Leg 1), 1970
Felt-tip pen on paper
13 3/8 x 10 1/2" (33.9 x 26.7 cm)
Courtesy Galerie Isabella Czarnowska, Berlin
Plate 73

Untitled (Sketch of *Le Voyage* [Journey] with Growths 1), c. 1970
Felt-tip pen on paper
8 1/4 x 6 11/16" (21 x 17 cm)
The Estate of Alina Szapocznikow/
Piotr Stanisławski

Untitled (Sketch of *Le Voyage* [Journey] with Growths 2), c. 1970
Felt-tip pen on paper
8 1/4 x 6 11/16" (21 x 17 cm)
The Estate of Alina Szapocznikow/
Piotr Stanisławski
Plate 65

Dessert II, 1970–71
Polyester resin, glass, photographs
7 1/2 x 5 1/8 x 5 1/8" (19 x 13 x 13 cm)
Collection Sabine Labelle-Rojoux
Plate 21
WIELS ONLY

Petit Dessert I (Small Dessert I), 1970–71
Colored polyester resin and glass
3 3/16 x 4 5/16 x 5 1/8" (8 x 11 x 13 cm)
Kravis Collection
Plate 20a

Sein en chiffon vert (Fétiche II) (Breast in a Green Cloth [Fetish II]), 1970–71
Jacket, leather shoe, polyester resin, paint
14 3/16 x 19 11/16 x 12 3/16"
(36 x 50 x 31 cm)
The Estate of Alina Szapocznikow/
Piotr Stanisławski
Plate 34

Untitled, c. 1970–71
Ink on paper
28 1/4 x 22 1/4" (71.8 x 56.5 cm)
The Museum of Modern Art, New York. Purchased with funds provided by the Rendl Endowment for Slavic Art
Plate 68
MOMA ONLY

Untitled, c. 1970–71
Ink on paper
24 15/16 x 18 15/16" (63.3 x 48.1 cm)
The Museum of Modern Art, New York. Gift of The Judith Rothschild Foundation
Plate 69
MOMA ONLY

Untitled, c. 1970–71
Ink on paper
24 13/16 x 18 15/16" (63 x 48 cm)
Ursula Hauser Collection, Switzerland
Plate 70

Untitled, c. 1970–71
Ink on paper
25 5/8 x 19 11/16" (65 x 50 cm)
The Estate of Alina Szapocznikow/
Piotr Stanisławski
Plate 67

Autoportrait – Herbier (Self-portrait – Herbarium), 1971
Polyester and polychrome wood
31 7/8 x 20 1/2 x 2" (81 x 52 x 5 cm)
Collection Grazyna and Jacek Lozowski
Plate 1

Bouche sur tige (Lips on a Stem), 1971
Polyester resin, hemp, aluminum wire
13" (33 cm) high
Ursula Hauser Collection, Switzerland
Plate 28
WIELS ONLY

Dessert III, 1971
Colored polyester resin and porcelain base
7 1/8 x 9 7/16 x 9 7/8" (18 x 24 x 25 cm)
Kravis Collection
Plate 20b

Dessert V, 1971
Colored polyester resin and photographs
9 1/16 x 6 5/16 x 7 1/2"
(23 x 16 x 19 cm)
Ursula Hauser Collection, Switzerland
Plate 22

Fajrant (End of Day's Work), 1971
Polyester resin, rubber glove, brush
10 1/4 x 6 5/16 x 4 5/16"
(26 x 16 x 11 cm)
Collection Dr. Werner Jerke
Plate 23

Fiancée folle (Mad fiancée), 1971
Polyester resin
6 7/8 x 18 15/16 x 16 5/16"
(17.5 x 48 x 16 cm)
The Estate of Alina Szapocznikow/
Piotr Stanisławski
Plate 7

Fiancée folle blanche (Mad white fiancée), 1971
Polyester resin and fabric
18 1/8 x 11 13/16 x 11 13/16"
(46 x 30 x 30 cm)
The Estate of Alina Szapocznikow/
Piotr Stanisławski
Plates 9–10

Fiancée folle mariée (Mad married fiancée), 1971
Polyester resin, gauze, newspaper
8 1/4 x 18 15/16 x 7 1/8"
(21 x 48 x 18 cm)
Private collection
Plate 8

Fotorzeźby (Photosculptures), 1971/2007
Twenty gelatin silver prints
11 13/16 x 9 7/16" (30 x 24 cm)
and 9 7/16 x 11 13/16" (24 x 30 cm)
Collection de Bruin-Heijn
Plates 36–55
WIELS ONLY

Fotorzeźby (Photosculptures), 1971/2007
Twenty gelatin silver prints
11 13/16 x 9 7/16" (30 x 24 cm)
and 9 7/16 x 11 13/16" (24 x 30 cm)
Collection UCLA Grunwald Center for the Graphic Arts, Hammer Museum. Purchased with funds provided by the Helga K. and Walter Oppenheimer Acquisition Fund
Plates 36–55
HAMMER/WEXNER/MOMA ONLY

Le Monde, 1971
Polyester resin and *Le Monde* newspaper
19 7/8 x 13 3/8 x 3 9/16"
(50.5 x 34 x 9 cm)
Collection Alexandre Stanisławski
Plate 58

Le pied (Fétiche V) (Foot [Fetish V]), 1971
Colored polyester resin, newspaper, nylon stockings, glass wool, Plexiglas
9 7/8 x 21 11/16 x 14 3/16"
(25 x 55 x 36 cm)
Wielkopolskie Towarzystwo Zachęty Sztuk Pięknych (Wielkopolska Society for the Encouragement of Arts)
Plate 33
HAMMER/WEXNER/MOMA ONLY

Paysage humain III (Human Landscape III), 1971
Ink, watercolor, and felt-tip pen on paper mounted on paper
9 7/16 x 12 5/8" (24 x 32 cm)
The Estate of Alina Szapocznikow/
Piotr Stanisławski
Plate 13

Rolls Royce II, 1971
Pink Portuguese marble and hood ornament
7 7/8 x 25 3/16 x 8 1/4"
(20 x 64 x 21 cm)
Isabelle and Hervé Poulain, Paris
Plate 35

Sculpture (Fétiche IV) (Sculpture [Fetish IV]), 1971
Polyester resin, stockings, wood, lingerie
10 1/4 x 13 3/8 x 15 9/16"
(26 x 34 x 39.5 cm)
The Estate of Alina Szapocznikow/
Piotr Stanisławski
Plate 31

Souvenir I, 1971
Polyester resin, glass, wool, photographs
29 9/16 x 27 9/16 x 13"
(75 x 70 x 33 cm)
The Estate of Alina Szapocznikow/
Piotr Stanisławski
Plate 57

Souvenir II, 1971
Polyester resin and photograph
15 x 20 7/8 x 9 7/16" (38 x 53 x 24 cm)
The Estate of Alina Szapocznikow/
Piotr Stanisławski
Plate 59
WIELS ONLY

Souvenir III, 1971
Polyester resin, photograph
11 1/16 x 9 7/8 x 11 1/16"
(28 x 25 x 28 cm)
The Estate of Alina Szapocznikow/
Piotr Stanisławski. Courtesy Galerie Gisela Capitain, Cologne
WIELS ONLY

Tumeurs personnifiées (Tumors personified), 1971
Polyester resin, fiberglass, paper, gauze
Ranging from 13 x 22 1/16 x 13 3/8"
(33 x 56 x 34 cm) to 5 15/16 x 9 1/16 x 6 5/16" (15 x 23 x 16 cm)
Zachęta National Gallery of Art, Warsaw
Plate 64

Untitled (Bust-Length Figure of a Woman, Headless 1), c. 1971
Felt-tip pen on paper
13 3/8 x 10 1/2" (34 x 26.7 cm)
The Estate of Alina Szapocznikow/
Piotr Stanisławski
Plate 24

Untitled *(Fétiche VII)* (Fetish VII), 1971
Polyester resin, nylon tights, wool
13 13/16 x 19 11/16 x 15 3/4"
(35 x 50 x 40 cm)
Ursula Hauser Collection, Switzerland
Plate 30

Untitled (Male Nude with Growths), c. 1971
Felt-tip pen on paper
12 5/8 x 9 1/4" (32 x 23.5 cm)
The Estate of Alina Szapocznikow/
Piotr Stanisławski
HAMMER/WEXNER/MOMA ONLY

Untitled (Portrait of Man with Turban), c. 1971
Ballpoint pen on paper
12 3/8 x 9 5/16" (31.4 x 23.7 cm)
The Estate of Alina Szapocznikow/
Piotr Stanisławski
HAMMER/WEXNER/MOMA ONLY

Untitled, c. 1971–72
Pencil on paper
11 5/8 x 8 1/4" (29.5 x 21 cm)
The Estate of Alina Szapocznikow/
Piotr Stanisławski
Plate 19
WIELS ONLY

Untitled, c. 1971–72
Ballpoint pen on paper
11 5/8 x 8 1/4" (29.5 x 21 cm)
The Estate of Alina Szapocznikow/
Piotr Stanisławski
Plate 18
WIELS ONLY

Untitled (From the series Paysage humain [Human Landscape]), c. 1971–72
Watercolor and felt-tip pen on paper
11 9/16 x 8 1/8" (29.3 x 20.6 cm)
The Estate of Alina Szapocznikow/
Piotr Stanisławski
Plate 12

Untitled (From the series Paysage humain [Human Landscape]), c. 1971–72
Watercolor and felt-tip pen on cardboard
19 9/16 x 25 1/2" (49.7 x 64.7 cm)
The Museum of Modern Art, New York. Gift of The Judith Rothschild Foundation
Plate 14

Cendrier de Célibataire I
(The Bachelor's Ashtray I), 1972
Colored polyester resin and cigarette butts
4 9/16 x 4 15/16 x 4 5/16"
(11.5 x 12.5 x 11 cm)
The Estate of Alina Szapocznikow/
Piotr Stanisławski
Plate 27

Cendrier de Célibataire II (The Bachelor's Ashtray II), 1972
Polyester resin
5 1/8 x 10 5/8 x 7 1/8" (13 x 27 x 18 cm)
The Museum of Modern Art, New York. Promised gift of Gail and Tony Ganz
Plate 26

Cendrier de Célibataire III (The Bachelor's Ashtray III), also called *Cendrier d'Ambiance III* (Ambiance Ashtray III), 1972/2007
Gelatin silver print
12 x 15 15/16" (30.5 x 40.5 cm)
Galerie Gisela Capitain, Cologne

Cendrier de Célibataire IV (The Bachelor's Ashtray IV), also called *Cendrier d'Ambiance IV* (Ambiance Ashtray IV), 1972/2007
Gelatin silver print
12 x 15 15/16" (30.5 x 40.5 cm)
Galerie Gisela Capitain, Cologne

Herbier VIII (Herbarium VIII), 1972
Polyester resin and polychrome wood
21 1/4 x 15 3/4" (54 x 40 cm)
From the collection of the National Museum in Kraków
Plate 3

Herbier XI (Herbarium XI), 1972
Polyester resin and polychrome wood
9 7/16 x 15" (24 x 38 cm)
From the collection of the National Museum in Kraków
Plate 2

Herbier XIII (Herbarium XIII), 1972
Polyester resin and polychrome wood
43 5/16 x 31 1/2" (110 x 80 cm)
From the collection of the National Museum in Kraków
Plate 4

Piotr, 1972
Polyester resin
80 3/4 x 17 11/16 x 13"
(205 x 45 x 33 cm)
From the collection of the National Museum in Kraków
Plate 6
WIELS ONLY

Archival texts and photographic material
The Alina Szapocznikow Archive/
Piotr Stanisławski/National Museum in Kraków

Acknowledgments

"Alina Szapocznikow: Sculpture Undone, 1955–1972" has benefited from an extraordinary team of people at four institutions. We are extremely grateful for the unstinting support of our respective directors. Dirk Snauwaert, director at WIELS Contemporary Art Centre in Brussels, initially supported the idea of mounting a major Szapocznikow exhibition that would place the artist's incredible oeuvre at the center of contemporary discourse, giving impetus to this multi-institutional collaboration. The Museum of Modern Art in Warsaw has been a foundational partner since the inception of the project, as the involvement of a Polish collaborator is critical in representing the history and current reception of the artist in her country of origin. Directors Glenn Lowry, The Museum of Modern Art, New York (MoMA), and Ann Philbin, Hammer Museum, Los Angeles, were visionary in their enthusiasm for this project and its potential for the American audience. We thank them all for helping to make this ambitious project possible in Europe and the United States. We also gratefully acknowledge Director Sherri Geldin and Curator Christopher Bedford of the Wexner Center for the Arts for their enthusiasm for the artist's work and for making it possible to expand the tour of the exhibition in the United States.

We collectively thank Marta Dziewańska, curator for research at the Museum of Modern Art in Warsaw, for her dedicated efforts in helping us gather the largest ensemble of the artist's works to be shown outside of Poland and for her collaboration on every aspect of the exhibition's conception, research, and realization. We also thank Esther Adler, Assistant Curator at MoMA, for the critical and unwavering support she provided on all aspects of the exhibition and publication. Szapocznikow scholars Jola Gola and Agata Jakubowska kindly shared so much of their knowledge of the artist throughout the process, and we wish to express our profound appreciation to both of them.

It has been a privilege to produce the first major publication on the artist to be widely distributed in English. For this accomplishment, we thank the outstanding publications department at MoMA—in particular Associate Publisher Kara Kirk, Senior Editor David Frankel, and Editor Libby Hruska for expertly coordinating the project. Their colleague Lisa Gabrielle Mark heroically and intelligently edited the publication and understood the nuances of the artist's history and reception. We thank Curatorial Assistant Paulina Pobocha for her invaluable assistance on the publication's bibliography and Jane Hyun for help with proofreading. We are grateful to Griselda Pollock, a longtime expert on Szapocznikow, for her insightful comments on the book's contents. The publication's contemporary design was created by Luc Derycke; we are most appreciative of the skill and sensitivity he brought to the project. We are delighted to be publishing this book in association with Mercatorfonds, and we especially extend gratitude to Bernard Steyaert, president, and Hannelore Duflou, editor, for their enthusiasm and professionalism. Thanks to Mercatorfonds, this publication will be translated into French and Dutch, making it available to a wide audience.

On behalf of WIELS and Museum of Modern Art in Warsaw, thanks go to registrar Ari Hiroshige and curatorial assistant Benoit Lamy de La Chapelle for overseeing the loans and complex administration of the exhibition with remarkable care. Sophie Rocca managed all aspects of its financing, and Angie Vandycke handled its publicity and communication—as neither are easy tasks for such an ambitious project, they deserve special mention. The exhibition's inspired scenography is the result of collaboration with Kwinten Lavigne, Kris Kimpe, and Monika Sosnowska. We warmly thank Michèle Rollé, Martine Limberg de Stirum, and the members of the WIELS Club for their support and Maria Matuszkiewicz, Malwina Kuśmierowska, and Katarzyna Szotkowska Beylin from the Museum of Modern Art in Warsaw for their research into the archives of the artist. Finally, we gratefully acknowledge Isabella Czarnowska, Hervé Loevenbruck, Andrzej Przywara, and Adam Szymczyk for all their help along the way.

On behalf of MoMA, we thank Associate Coordinator of Exhibitions Jennifer Cohen, Coordinator of Exhibitions Maria DeMarco Beardsley, and Associate Registrar Sacha Eaton, who orchestrated the complex registration and contractual arrangements. Installations Designer Lana Hum crafted a beautiful installation for the exhibition at MoMA. We extend our gratitude to Associate Director Kathy Halbreich; Senior Deputy for Curatorial Affairs Peter Reed; and Deputy Director, Exhibitions, and Collections Ramona Bronkar Bannayan. We are also grateful to the entire Drawings Department for shepherding this project within the institution.

At the Hammer Museum, we thank Director of the Grunwald Center for the Graphic Arts and Deputy Director of Collections Cynthia Burlingham and Director of Exhibitions Management and Publications Brooke Hodge for spearheading the coordination of the exhibition in Los Angeles. Claudine Dixon, curatorial associate at the Grunwald Center, worked closely on every aspect of the organization, together with interns Caitlin Johnson and Courtney Smith. We thank Deputy Director of Exhibitions and Programs Douglas Fogle and the entire curatorial staff for their support and encouragement. Senior Associate Registrar Jennifer Garpner handled registration; we thank her and Director of Registration and Collections Management Portland McCormick for their unfailing administration of shipping and loans. Deputy Director of Advancement Jennifer Wells Green handled the development initiatives for this exhibition together with Laurie McGahey, David Morehouse, and Christine Lanoie Newman. We express our gratitude to all departmental heads and their teams, including Allison Agsten, Susan Bell Yank, Claudia Bestor, Peter Gould, Jenni Kim, Deborah Snyder, Sarah Stifler, and Vincent Valenzuela. The exhibition was expertly designed for the Hammer Museum by Silvina Niepomniszcze.

In closing, we wish to acknowledge the generous lenders who, recognizing the importance of this project, parted with cherished works. In particular, many Polish museums lent substantial bodies of work for this exhibition. Gisela Capitain offered her support throughout its development; she and Sarah Moog of Galerie Gisela Capitain, which represents the estate of the artist, demonstrated an incredible commitment to Szapocznikow's oeuvre. We extend our unending gratitude to them and to Anke Kempes at BROADWAY 1602. Special thanks are reserved for Piotr Stanisławski, the artist's son, who lent many key works from the estate and his personal collection and was unwavering in his dedication to securing both the public appreciation and scholarly attention that his mother's work so richly deserves.

Elena Filipovic
WIELS Contemporary Art Centre, Brussels

Joanna Mytkowska
Museum of Modern Art, Warsaw

Cornelia Butler
The Museum of Modern Art, New York

Allegra Pesenti
Hammer Museum, Los Angeles

Lenders to the Exhibition

BROADWAY 1602, New York
Collection de Bruin-Heijn
Collection CORREARD, Paris
The Estate of Alina Szapocznikow/Piotr Stanisławski
Sandra and Gerald Fineberg
Friedrich Christian Flick Collection
Galerie Gisela Capitain, Cologne
Galerie Isabella Czarnowska, Berlin
Gail and Tony Ganz, Los Angeles
Stanislas Gokelaere, Brussels
Hammer Museum, Los Angeles
Ursula Hauser Collection, Switzerland
Dr. Werner Jerke
Kravis Collection
Sabine Labelle-Rojoux
Elisabeth Lechien-Cremer
Collection Loevenbruck, Paris
Grazyna and Jacek Lozowski
Museum of Independence, Warsaw
The Museum of Modern Art, New York
Museum of Modern Art, Warsaw
Krzysztof Musial Collection
Muzeum Narodowe w Warszawie
Muzeum Sztuki, Łódź
National Museum in Kraków
The National Museum in Wrocław
Isabelle and Hervé Poulain, Paris
Private collections
Société de l'Apostolat Catholique (Pères Pallottins)
Alexandre Stanisławski
UCLA Grunwald Center for the Graphic Arts, Hammer Museum, Los Angeles
Wielkopolskie Towarzystwo Zachęty Sztuk Pięknych (Wielkopolska Society for the Encouragement of Arts)
Zachęta National Gallery of Art, Warsaw

Photo credits

All works by Alina Szapocznikow © The Estate of Alina Szapocznikow/Piotr Stanisławski/ADAGP, Paris. The following images, keyed to page numbers, are those for which separate or additional credits are due:

Front cover; pp 42, ill. 26; 46–47; 71, ill. 14; 109; 116–117; 127, ill. 8: Photo by Thomas Mueller, courtesy BROADWAY 1602, New York, and Galerie Gisela Capitain GmbH, Cologne. Pp 2; 8–9; 11; 12, ill. 4; 13, ill. 7; 17 (bottom); 26 (bottom); 28–29; 33; 58; 60; 61, pls. 36–38; 62, pls. 42–47; 63, pls. 49–52, 54; 65; 66, ills. 2–4; 69, ill. 7; 69, ill. 9; 74; 75, ills. 20, 21, 23; 76, ill. 24; 82–83; 86; 89 (bottom); 93; 100, ill. 16; 108; 113 (bottom); 123; 125, ill. 5; 132, ill. 21; 137; 142 (bottom); 160; 161 (bottom); 165 (bottom); 167 (bottom); 175 (bottom); 178–179; 180; 181 (middle); 184–185; 186 (top left, top right, center); 187; 192 (top, bottom); 193 (top, middle, bottom); 194–197; 198 (top, bottom left, center); 199 (middle, bottom); 200–203: The Alina Szapocznikow Archive/Piotr Stanisławski/National Museum in Kraków. Photo courtesy the Museum of Modern Art, Warsaw. Pp 12, ill. 3; 13, ill. 5; 34, ill. 5; 39, ill. 15; 39, ill. 17; 42, ill. 25; 42, ill. 28; 68, ill. 5; 97, ill. 12; 100, ill. 15; 110–111; 126, ill. 7; 136; 143; 147; 165, pl. 132; 167, pl. 135; 174, pl. 147; 175, pl. 149: Photo by Piotr Tomczyk, courtesy Muzeum Sztuki, Łódź. Pp 13, ill. 6; 22–23; 24, pl. 12; 27; 30–31; 32, ill. 1; 34, ill. 4; 35, ill. 6; 35, ill. 8; 48, pl. 21; 50, pl. 24; 52, pl. 27; 68, ill. 6; 70, ill. 11; 71, ill. 13; 71, ill. 15; 81, pl. 59; 84; 90, pl. 67; 94, ill. 4, 5; 95, ill. 7, 9; 99, ill. 14; 101, ill. 18, 20; 106, pl. 72; 119; 121, pl. 88; 124, ill. 2; 127, ill. 12; 132, ill. 20; 138; 141, pl. 94; 142, pl. 96 a, b, c; 145, pl. 99; 146; 150; 154; 158, pl. 114; 158, pls. 116–117; 159, pl. 118; 163; 166; 169, pls. 137, 139; 170, pl. 142; 172; 176, pls. 151–152: Photo © Fabrice Gousset, Paris, courtesy Piotr Stanisławski and Galerie Gisela Capitain GmbH, Cologne. Pp 13, ill. 8; 16; 17, pl. 2; 18–19; 21; 42, ill. 27; 71, ill. 16; 89, pl. 66; 102, ill. 22; 124, ill. 3: Photographic Studio of the National Museum in Kraków. Pp 14; 20; 24, pl. 11; 88; 94, ill. 3; 107, pl. 74; 148, pl. 103: Courtesy Piotr Stanisławski and Galerie Loevenbruck, Paris. Pp 24, pl. 13; 26, pl. 15; 159, pl. 120: Photo © Fabrice Gousset, Paris, courtesy Piotr Stanisławski and Galerie Loevenbruck, Paris. Pp 25; 91, pl. 69; 152; 159, pl. 121; 164, pl. 131: Courtesy The Museum of Modern Art, New York, Department of Imaging Services, photo Jonathan Muzikar. Pp 26, pl. 16; 55, pl. 31; 85: Courtesy Piotr Stanisławski and Galerie Gisela Capitain GmbH, Cologne. Pp 35, ill. 7; 141, pl. 95: Photo Stephan Höck, courtesy Galerie Isabella Czarnowska, Berlin. P 36, ill. 9: © 2011 NIKI CHARITABLE ART FOUNDATION. All rights reserved. Photo by Hans Hammarskiold, © Moderna Museet in Stockholm. P 36, ill. 10: © Estate of George Paul Thek. Photo by Lee Stalsworth, courtesy Hirshhorn Museum and Sculpture Garden, Smithsonian Institution. P 36, ill. 11: © 2011 Marsie, Emanuelle, Damon and Andrew Scharlatt – Hannah Wilke Collection and Archive, Los Angeles. Courtesy The Museum of Modern Art, New York, Department of Imaging Services. P 36, ill. 12: © Zofia Kulik. Photo by Andrzej Polakowski. P 36, ill. 13: © Katarzyna Kozyra. Courtesy Postmasters Gallery, New York. P 36, ill. 14: © 2011 Artists Rights Society (ARS), New York/ADAGP, Paris. Courtesy Galerie Michel Rein, Paris. Pp 39, ill. 16; 171, pl. 143: Photo Piotr Ligier, courtesy Muzeum Narodowe w Warszawie. Pp 40, ill. 18; 61, pls. 39–41; 63, pls. 48, 53, 55; 69, ill. 10; 75, ill. 19; 78–79; 81, pl. 58: courtesy BROADWAY 1602, New York. P 41, ill. 19: Courtesy Mrs. Ewa Sapka-Pawliczak. Photo by Piotr Tomczyk, courtesy Muzeum Sztuki, Łódź. P 41, ill. 20: © Wojciech Fangor. Photo by Piotr Tomczyk, courtesy Muzeum Sztuki, Łódź. P 41, ill. 21: © Magdalena Abakanowicz. Courtesy Marlborough Gallery, New York. P 41, ill. 22: © Filip Pagowski. Courtesy Galeria aTAK, Warsaw. P 41, ill. 23: © 2011 Artists Rights Society (ARS), New York/ADAGP, Paris. Courtesy The Museum of Modern Art, New York, Department of Imaging Services, photo by John Wronn. P 41, ill. 24: © 2011 Yayoi Kusama. Photo by John D. Schiff, courtesy Gagosian Gallery, New York. Pp 43; 69, ill. 8; 72; back cover: Photo by Antoni Miralda, © 2011 Artists Rights Society (ARS), New York/VEGAP, Madrid. The Alina Szapocznikow Archive/Piotr Stanisławski/National Museum in Kraków. Photo courtesy the Museum of Modern Art, Warsaw. P 48, pl. 22: Stefan Altenburger Photography, Zürich. Pp 49; 170, pl. 140: Photo by Eric Jobs/Sandra Schunke. Pp 50, pl. 25; 52, pl. 28; 106, pl. 71; 155, pl. 111: Photo © Bernhard Schaub, Cologne, courtesy Piotr Stanisławski and Galerie Gisela Capitain GmbH, Cologne. P 51: Courtesy The Museum of Modern Art, New York, Department of Imaging Services, photo by Thomas Griesel. Pp 53, pl. 29; 57; 127, ill. 11; 162: Photo by Adam Reich, courtesy BROADWAY 1602, New York, and Galerie Gisela Capitain GmbH, Cologne. Pp 53 (bottom); 120 (bottom); 125, ill. 4; 131, ill. 18–19; 199 (top): The Alina Szapocznikow Archive/Piotr Stanisławski/National Museum in Kraków. Photo by Jacques Verroust, courtesy the Museum of Modern Art, Warsaw. Pp 55 (bottom); 115 (bottom); 139 (bottom); 145 (bottom); 173 (bottom); 177 (bottom): The Alina Szapocznikow Archive/Piotr Stanisławski/National Museum in Kraków. Photo by Zdzisław Sowiński, courtesy the Museum of Modern Art, Warsaw. Pp 56, pl. 32; 140: Photo courtesy the Museum of Modern Art, Warsaw. Pp 56, pl. 33; 75, ill. 22; 127, ill. 9; 149: Photo by Bartek Buśko. Pp 70, ill. 12; 151: Photo by Thomas Mueller, courtesy BROADWAY 1602, New York. P 80: Photo Lothar Schnepf, Cologne, courtesy Piotr Stanisławski and Galerie Gisela Capitain GmbH, Cologne. Pp 87, pl. 64; 102, ill. 21; 118; 128, ill. 13: Courtesy Zachęta National Gallery of Art, Warsaw, and Agencja Medium Sp. z o.o. Pp 90, pl. 68; 103; 153; 155, pl. 110; 159, pl. 119; 161, pl. 126: Courtesy The Museum of Modern Art, New York, Department of Imaging Services, photo by John Wronn. Pp 91, pl. 70; 176, pl. 150: Photo Bernhard Schaub, Cologne. P 94, ill. 2: © INA, L'art et les hommes, 09/04/1969, Jean-Marie Drot. P 95, ill. 8: © Louise Bourgeois Trust/ Licensed by VAGA, New York. P 95, ill. 10: © 2011 Reproduced with the permission of the Estate of Eva Hesse, Galerie Hauser & Wirth, Zurich. Courtesy The Museum of Modern Art, New York, Department of Imaging Services, photo by John Wronn. Pp 101, ill. 17; 125, ill. 6; 133; 186 (bottom): The Alina Szapocznikow Archive/Piotr Stanisławski/National Museum in Kraków. Photo by Marek Holzman, courtesy the Museum of Modern Art, Warsaw. P 101, ill. 19: © 2011 Marsie, Emanuelle, Damon and Andrew Scharlatt – Hannah Wilke Collection and Archive, Los Angeles. Courtesy The Museum of Modern Art, New York, Department of Imaging Services, photo by David Allison. Pp 107, pl. 73; 144; 148, pl. 102; 170, pl. 141: Photo by Bernd Borchardt, courtesy Galerie Isabella Czarnowska, Berlin. P 112: Photo © 2011 Marc Wathieu. Pp 113, pl. 78; 114; 115 pl. 80; 120, pl. 86; 121, pl. 87: courtesy The National Museum in Wrocław. P 139, pl. 92: Photo John Berens, courtesy BROADWAY 1602, New York. P 156: Courtesy The Museum of Modern Art, New York, Department of Imaging Services, photo Robert Gerhardt. Pp 157; 158, pl. 115; 161, pl. 127; 164, pl. 130; 169, pl. 138: Photo by Robert Wedemeyer. P 171 (bottom): The Alina Szapocznikow Archive/Piotr Stanisławski/National Museum in Kraków. Photo by Jósef Myszkowski, courtesy the Museum of Modern Art, Warsaw. P 174, pl. 148: Photo Andrea Stappert, courtesy: Galerie Isabella Czarnowska, Berlin. P 177, pl. 153: Photo Stephan Höck. Pp 181 (top, bottom); 183: The Alina Szapocznikow Archive/Piotr Stanisławski/National Museum in Kraków. Photo by Ryszard Stanisławski, courtesy the Museum of Modern Art, Warsaw. Pp 188–189: The Alina Szapocznikow Archive/Piotr Stanisławski/National Museum in Kraków. Photo by Władysław Sławny, courtesy the Museum of Modern Art, Warsaw. Pp 190–191: The Alina Szapocznikow Archive/Piotr Stanisławski/National Museum in Kraków. Photo by Eustachy Kossakowski, courtesy the Museum of Modern Art, Warsaw. Pp 192–193: The Alina Szapocznikow Archive/Piotr Stanisławski/National Museum in Kraków. Photo by Roger Gain for *Elle*, courtesy the Museum of Modern Art, Warsaw. P 198 (bottom right): The Alina Szapocznikow Archive/Piotr Stanisławski/National Museum in Kraków. Photo by Roman Cieślewicz, courtesy the Museum of Modern Art, Warsaw.